The Macintosh iLife '08 in the Classroom

by Jim Heid

Teacher supplement by
Ted Lai

The Macintosh iLife '08 in the Classroom

Jim Heid

Teacher supplement by Ted Lai

Peachpit Press
1249 Eighth Street
Berkeley, CA 94710
510/524-2178
510/524-2221 (fax)
Find us on the Web at: www.peachpit.com
To report errors, please send a note to errata@peachpit.com

Peachpit Press is a division of Pearson Education

Editor: Barbara Assadi, BayCreative
Book Design and Illustration: Arne Hurty, BayCreative
Compositors and Layout Design: Jonathan Woolson, thinkplaydesign, and David Van Ness
Production Coordinator: Myrna Vladic
Indexer: Emily Glossbrenner, FireCrystal Communications
Cover Design: Arne Hurty, BayCreative

Portions originally appeared in *Macworld* magazine, ©Mac Publishing LLC.
Macintosh and iPod product photography courtesy Apple, Inc.

ISBN 13: 978-0-321-54926-6
ISBN 10: 0-321-54926-0
9 8 7 6 5 4 3 2 1
Printed and bound in the United States of America.

The Macintosh iLife in the Classroom

Change Your (i)Life Now!

"With great power comes great responsibility."
—Uncle Ben (of *Spider-Man* fame, not the rice products)

Teachers have a great deal of influence and power. With 20 to 30 kids hanging on their every word, teachers impact students by being role models. For example, as a proud violist, I always had an unusually large number of students in my classroom who played viola in the orchestra. A friend of mine teaches history and coaches track, and he always has a large following of runners. So, it's with care that most teachers use their opinions to influence the lives of students and their parents. However, it can be difficult with all the questions that face educators:

- "What after-school program should my child be in?"
- "Where should we buy books for our child?"
- "Which sport or after-school activities will be the best to help my child get into college?"

In the classroom, we're cautious when non-curricular topics such as politics, religion, or even dietary choices come up. After all, whatever thoughts we have on topics like those are just our opinion, and we don't necessarily want to offend anyone if they have a differing viewpoint. Our job is to educate the minds of the kids in our care, and if a topic comes up that isn't really about the curriculum, then we shouldn't focus on it. Ask us a question about strategies for struggling readers, and we're all over it. Want to know how to improve memorization of math facts? Teachers have at least a dozen ideas. But ask us whom we're voting for in the next presidential election, and we hem and haw until we sound like we're anarchists who don't believe in publicly appointed government representatives. For good reason, most teachers stick to educational decisions and opinions.

Like most teachers, I toed the line. I made sure I stuck to those "safe" academic topics when I spoke to my students or their parents. In fact, for a long time, I even tried to be diplomatic about technology choices. Even though my students were creating inspiring videos with iMovie, despite the fact that they were composing authentic music with GarageBand, regardless of their thought-provoking digital photography essays and other real-life projects ... when faced with the question of "Mac or PC?" I went with the safe, diplomatic answer, "It depends on what you'll be doing with the computer."

I'd continue by telling the parents and students, "If you're mainly using productivity applications like the Microsoft Office suite or surfing the Internet, then a PC is fine. If you're looking to do those things plus live a digital lifestyle with the power to create and organize images, audio, and video, then a Mac is your best choice."

I continued with this lie for many years. I gave noncommittal technology advice to parents about what I originally thought was a personal opinion—that is, until my own children became elementary students. This made me think more about what I wanted my own children to get out of their home and school experience, and I finally concluded that deciding on a computer platform isn't merely a personal opinion; it's an educational choice and, therefore, fair game for me to speak my thoughts.

In teacher preparation classes, we're taught that students should construct their own knowledge by synthesizing information and creating new meaning. One of the best ways to do this is to integrate project-based learning into the classroom with meaningful and creative digital projects using the iLife suite. With iLife, students easily create projects that demonstrate mastery of the curriculum and personal involvement in their learning.

As educators, we want the best for our students. We want them to be inspired, engaged, educated, and empowered. Is that too much to ask? I don't think so... at least not with the integrated, easy-to-use iLife suite. With the latest rendition of iLife, the tools are even easier to use, and some handy new features improve productivity and ease.

Any educator who has seen how excited and engaged students become when they're using technology in the classroom knows that it's a worthwhile endeavor. The education of students is not just about test scores and standards. It's about inspiring and motivating students to be lifelong learners through digital tools. It's about challenging students through the use of 21st-century life skills such as time management, communication, media literacy, and team collaboration. What educator wouldn't want digital tools that could act as the cornerstone for promoting all those things?

"Mac or PC?" The answer is simple. If you want to truly educate students using digital tools, if you want to concentrate on meaningful projects that emphasize 21st-century skills, if you want to engage and reach all learners, and if you want to focus on the project and not on learning how to use the technology, then the Mac is the only choice, and iLife '08 is the ultimate suite of tools for the lifelong learner in all of us.

In your hands, you have the ultimate guide to help you get started with the iLife suite and begin integrating it into curricular lessons and your digital lifestyle. The opening section of this book focuses on three main ideas:

- Why should you integrate technology into education?
- How will the technology be most effectively integrated?
- What are some appropriate tools to form the basis of a technology vision?

New to this edition of *The Macintosh iLife in the Classroom* are mini-lessons to help teachers get started quickly with meaningful curricular lessons. I hope these activities will motivate teachers to begin designing digital projects. Thanks for continuing the journey with us.

—Ted Lai
ted@podpiperproductions.com
http://podpiperproductions.com
http://web.mac.com/tntnzing

Meaningful Technology Integration

Why should schools make an effort to utilize technology in classroom projects? In fact, what does *technology integration* really mean? Should typing an essay in a word-processing application be considered technology integration? How about taking a weekly computer-based reading test, learning a typing program, or playing an arcade-style video game to drill in math facts? In a sense, these are examples of different levels of technology integration, but they merely replace traditional pencil-and-paper learning. They don't transform the activities into 21st-century learning. The goal of technology integration should be to *enhance* teaching and learning with digital tools, instead of merely replacing analog choices. The crux of the matter lies in a phrase that's been gaining momentum in educational circles: *21st-century skills*.

Several organizations have been espousing these ideas. From the Partnership for 21st Century Skills (P21) to the North Central Regional Educational Laboratory (NCREL) to the International Society for Technology in Education's (ISTE) new National Educational Technology Standards for Students (NETS•S), the idea that we need to teach students more than just curricular standards is attracting attention. Our students need to learn life and literacy skills that will help them thrive in the global economy of the 21st century. Or, as ISTE writes, these skills are "What students should know and be able to do to learn effectively and live productively in an increasingly digital world...." According to ISTE, the following skills are essential for students to master for 21st-century learning:

- Creativity and innovation
- Communication and collaboration
- Research and information fluency
- Critical thinking, problem solving, and decision making
- Digital citizenship
- Technology operations and concepts

So, what is *meaningful* technology integration? It can't begin and end with using a word processor or searching for information on the Internet. If multiple technology standards are to be addressed, then students need to be creating projects that utilize problem-solving skills and collaborating to create an end product that demonstrates understanding of the curriculum as well as the technology used.

Writing a report is 20th-century homework. If you are able to transform that report into a digital project with a video or enhanced podcast, it makes the curriculum relevant to the learner both now and into the future. Take it further and publish it on the Internet where peers, parents, and the community can view the work, and you have created an opportunity to develop an interested audience. The curricular standards are taught, but so are essential workforce skills such as time management, collaboration, problem solving, and communication. In a similar way, researching the Web for information is an essential skill, but having a purpose for that research transforms the task into something much more meaningful. It ceases to become an exercise in merely knowing how to use a search engine but refashions it into the skill of evaluating information on the Internet and being able to make meaning from the text.

However, good teaching has to be at the root of a technology-based project. After all, in any well-planned educational unit, there needs to be an authentic purpose. Before having students do any lesson, teachers must ask themselves questions like these: Why are we doing this assignment? What is the purpose of this project? Does the use of technology provide students with an opportunity to think more deeply about the curriculum and develop 21st-century skills, or is the lesson mainly an exercise in using technology solely to claim that the students have learned those digital tools? Thus, it is imperative to explore these questions when infusing technology meaningfully into the curriculum. Flashy technology should never be a replacement for the content that students should be learning.

After all, the use of technology doesn't inherently make a teacher better or a student smarter. It doesn't automatically transform a poorly developed lesson into a brilliant one. What it can do, though, is transform a well-thought-out assignment into a product that is both meaningful and relevant. If we, as educators, are dedicated to helping students master the curricular standards, then we should be jumping at the opportunity to create assignments that will be more memorable for our students, because that means they will *remember* the information more readily and retain it over a longer period of time.

My former students still instant message me and talk about some of the different projects they created like the Ancient Egyptian Raps or the Gold Rush Commercials. They remember it years later because they were engaged in the learning process and found meaning and enjoyment in the projects. We marvel that they still are able to sing their fact-filled rap, proving yet again, that they developed mastery of the information.

Creativity and innovation are essential to meaningful projects because those qualities challenge students to work at a higher level of thinking. The recent publication *Tough Choices or Tough Times: The Report of the New Commission on the Skills of the American Workforce* states, "Creativity, innovation, and flexibility will not be the special province of an elite. It will be demanded of virtually everyone who is making a decent living." Apple believes in that. With the iLife suite, anybody can create a video, compose music, or compile a picture book. Through iLife, all teachers can support our students by giving them relevant assignments that empower them to use multimedia to creatively extend their learning.

However, the most important reason for integrating technology into education is engagement. Students these days are digital learners, and many prefer to learn through technology. After all, they're using these digital tools on a daily basis for work, hobbies, and communication. To come to school and be restricted on the use of technology is both confining and "demotivating." When you tell a student you're going to do a project with digital tools, their eyes light up, they sit up straighter in their chair, and their attention is focused on the teacher. In other words, they're engaged; and when they're engaged and attentive, they're more likely to listen, learn, and master the information.

Why should we use technology? When it's meaningful, it helps make the curriculum more relevant, memorable, and enjoyable.

iLife = iEasy

What tools should you use to promote 21st-century skills? In schools, and life, that decision is simple...the iLife suite. This integrated suite of applications is included on every new Mac, and the newest upgrades are always inexpensive. One of the keys to the iLife suite is that it empowers users to organize and create digital audio, image, and video projects. *Most important, the iLife suite is easy.* People often comment on how painless it is to import images into iPhoto, compose music in GarageBand, edit video in iMovie, upload content into iWeb, or burn a professional-looking DVD in iDVD. The fact that the applications are so simple to use doesn't mean they lack features. In fact, there have been several iMovie-created entries in prestigious film festivals across the world. My Two Friends, a former "Best of Berkeley" band, cut all its early tracks in GarageBand.

Unless it's easy, technology will not get utilized in the classroom. Especially for nervous digital-immigrant teachers, as soon as an application gets a little confusing, it gets put away in favor of more familiar analog tools. The more *transparent* technology is, the more likely it will be integrated into the curriculum. Although digital kids usually have no problem sitting down and learning through experimentation, having easy, user-friendly interfaces and powerful tools still benefits them as well. With straightforward tools, our students are able to access the power at a younger age. My younger daughter began creating her own podcasts by the age of 5. By the age of 6, she could record, edit, and enhance them on her own. Although I know she's a genius (yes, I'm biased), I truly believe that all kids are capable of achieving at this level given the right tools and parameters for creating content.

In fact, iLife '08 is even more effortless than before. Composing music in GarageBand was already easy with the included loops and software instruments. Apple has gone one step further by creating the Magic GarageBand option. All users, but especially younger students, will benefit from being able to audition the different instrument sounds in the Magic GarageBand samples, changing them to match the style of music in which they're interested.

Once a user begins organizing and creating content in iLife, the brilliance of the integration becomes apparent. Need an image for your iMovie creation or GarageBand podcast project? Just open the Media Browser, and drag one from your iPhoto library. Need to add content to iWeb or iDVD? Open the Media Browser, and drag any audio from iTunes, image from iPhoto, or video in the Movies folder. In fact, when saved as an iLife preview, even GarageBand projects can be dragged into any of the other iLife applications. If you've purchased the iWork suite, you'll notice that the Media Browser integration is included for Keynote, Numbers, and Pages as well. Notice a pattern? The Media Browser is the key to all the integration. It's present in every application that deals with combining multimedia for projects, and it's all drag and drop. People might be amazed at how professional the iLife and iWork projects look, but you can always answer, "It was easy."

Hearing All Voices: Being a Content Producer

One of the newest technology trends today is Web 2.0. Blogs, wikis, podcasts, and other collaborative Web services that are considered to be Web 2.0 technologies have one significant commonality: they give everyone a chance to have their voice heard. They empower all people to take charge and be a *producer* of content instead of just a *consumer.* These different technologies invite all people, including students and teachers, to participate in creating and sharing content.

Apple empowers users to actively participate in this exciting new technical world. From creating to publishing to distributing, Apple has a solution for every user. Take the example of podcasting. Users can create a podcast in GarageBand and post it to iWeb for easy publishing. With a single click, iWeb creates the RSS feed and can upload audio, video, and images to a .Mac account or other server. iWeb isn't just for podcasting, either. Users can create traditional Web sites, photo galleries, movie pages, and blogs as well. Whatever students create can be published with iLife.

iPhoto also features one-click creation of easily shared Web galleries, and iMovie now has an option to publish directly to a YouTube account. Not considered a fad anymore, YouTube has become a viable alternative media source. Before its acquisition by Google, YouTube was averaging more than 20 million unique visitors each month and had more than 100 million videos available (CNET News, *www.news.com/Google-makes-video-play-with-YouTube-buy/2100-1030_3-6124094.html*).

Despite questions surrounding YouTube's educational merits, California State Superintendent of Schools Jack O'Connell posted an informative and entertaining Back-to-School video on the site. In this video, posted at the beginning of the 2007–2008 school year, O'Connell gives advice on how to succeed in school and make the most of the academic year. O'Connell isn't the only one taking YouTube seriously as a means of distributing media. Film studios, television stations, and news outlets are all submitting YouTube videos to promote their work. However, the vast majority of YouTube content still comes from individual users who want to have their voices heard. Now with iMovie '08, everyone can publish video content with a single click to one of the most watched video sites on the Internet.

Although the trend is toward more immediate publishing directly to the Internet, Apple hasn't abandoned fans of more "traditional" media like CDs and DVDs. They can still use iTunes and iDVD to create their own musical mixes and video compilations. With more themes and features to choose from, iDVD projects are even simpler and more professional-looking. Commemorative CDs and DVDs of student work can still be created for fundraisers and educational memories.

Most important for education, when students publish their work to a CD, DVD, Web site, or RSS feed, they realize they're sharing their work with their immediate family, distant relatives, friends, and, possibly, strangers. Every student will want to excel when they know that anyone and everyone has access to their creations. Students have been known to rehearse a rap during recess, lunch, and before and after school just so they sound good. Kids will read their podcast script multiple times to sound more natural. As educators, we know that when students repeat things over and over, they master the information and retain it for a longer amount of time. Students are empowered to have their voices heard, and they are motivated to improve their communication when they are encouraged to publish their work.

Tips for Hesitant Integrators

As an educational technology advocate, my "mission" is to help educators feel comfortable enough to integrate technology into the curriculum. Although "digital-native" students are ready and willing to use any technology, a common obstacle is convincing the "digital-immigrant" teachers to design the curriculum for those projects. The main problem is that many teachers won't integrate a new idea or technology unless they feel personal proficiency. They are hesitant to integrate anything that might not work seamlessly, and they fear not knowing what to do when something goes wrong. The following are some of the basic tips for those hesitant integrators (HIs):

- Start small.
- Carpe technologia.
- Focus on the content.
- The process is the product.

Start Small

All people are afraid of change. For teachers, this is especially true if there is a perception that the change includes learning something new and teaching that additional material. With educational technology, there is still the prevailing view that it's just another thing to teach. When it is an extra, then the time to teach technology battles with the time to teach the rest of the standards. So, technology is often pushed aside because state testing is about the curriculum. Despite that technology can enrich the lives of the students, help teachers be more efficient, and enhance teaching and learning, just starting out can be intimidating.

To begin integrating technology into the curriculum, keep in mind the philosophy that you should just *start small.*

You don't have to drastically change your teaching methods or prepared units of instruction. Think about the lessons you've already created, and consider how you could enhance one by adding digital photos, music, or videos. Find that one technology-based project, such as recording a podcast, you can integrate into a lesson or unit to give students a deeper understanding of the subject matter. The first assignment might seem awkward, but it gets easier and easier with each project. Here are a few ideas for beginning to integrate the iLife suite into your classroom curriculum:

- In mathematics, students take digital photos of mathematical concepts around the classroom and school. For example, they can take photos of plane or solid shapes, fractions, or patterns. These images can be used to create a simple book or slide show in iPhoto, a podcast in GarageBand, or a presentation in Keynote.
- In a science lab, students take photos or record video of the experiment, import the footage into iMovie, and narrate their findings.
- While studying a historical period, students study the music of the time and compose a song in that style with similar-sounding loops and instruments. For example, if the topic were western expansion or the Gold Rush, students could use loops or instruments of that time such as banjos, violins, guitars, or harmonicas.
- During or after a field trip, students create a digital field journal by recording their thoughts or feelings aloud using GarageBand or an iPod and recorder.
- In literature groups, students select important moments or turning points in the story and reenact them through audio, video, or both.
- While studying planets, students download images from NASA and create slide shows, podcasts, books, or Web sites showcasing their knowledge.
- In readers' theater projects, students record their voices, add mood music and sound effects, and produce a radio show for podcasts or CDs.
- When studying persuasive writing techniques and propaganda, students create commercials or public service announcements through podcasts, videos, or Pages documents.
- In history, students use photos to assemble a video to compare and contrast their lives with their parents' lives.
- In any subject, the students conduct an "interview" of a famous individual important to that topic. This interview, recorded with an iPod or through GarageBand, can then be used for a podcast or video.
- With students who are younger, who are English-language learners, or who have reading disabilities, running records and reading samples are collected, and the audio files are utilized as part of a digital portfolio demonstrating students' progress toward fluency and comprehension.
- Instructions for science labs and projects can be recorded for student reference as children complete the experiment or activity. Instead of asking, "What's next?" the students need only to listen to the audio file for the directions.
- In any content area, students write and record their work orally so that they learn the concepts of voice and audience. The recording can be distributed as a podcast.
- Students take traditional writing assignments such as essays and use Pages to design a more effective layout for communicating the information (such as a newsletter or brochure). Another alternative is to utilize iWeb to create a multimedia site to enhance their writing.

Carpe Technologia

Carpe technologia might not be a real phrase (especially since it combines Latin and Greek), but the philosophy behind it is very genuine. Classrooms need to "seize the technology," so to speak. In a time where school budgets are getting tighter and tighter, it's essential that we adopt a "use it or lose it" mentality when dealing with technology. We need to make the most of whatever tools we've been given to justify further expenditures. So, teachers need to be willing to take a few risks by incorporating technology into their projects. That might sound intimidating, but the good news is that teachers are not alone.

It would be great if every classroom in every school had a dedicated technology expert to help support the teachers working with digital tools. The reality is that we actually do have that support. Every single child can be a technology expert when given the opportunity to work with the tools. That's not to say that all our kids enter the classroom ready to teach every hardware or software tool in the school. However, this does mean the teacher doesn't have to know everything. As long as a teacher knows how to navigate an application's menus and understands the basics of what that software can do, then technology projects can be assigned. As students use the technology, they will explore more and learn the hardware and software much more quickly than the teacher would. After that, it's a simple matter of just allowing students to communicate and share what they know; essentially, the students become the technical experts and support staff in the class.

To make this work successfully, the teacher needs to be willing to allow for a true partnership in learning, creating a supportive environment where it's OK for the students to feel empowered to learn these tools and share what they know. For teachers who are hesitant, they need only take a moment to consider the students they're dealing with on a day-to-day basis. Our students are digital natives. They're used to using technology for communication, entertainment, and information. In a lot of ways, they're not just *using* technology. They're *living* technology in that their daily lives are often infused with digital tools. They're born and raised in an age where the Internet, video games, instant messaging, and megapixels are the norm. It's not a stretch to think that there are probably children in our world who learn to type their name before they can write it. As the saying goes, when it comes to technology, they "take to it like fish to water." Naturally curious, children begin exploring and creating without the petrifying fear of doing something wrong. That isn't to say that they have no fear whatsoever, but they don't let it stop them from exploring and experiencing.

Unless you're already leading the digital life—creating, organizing, and enjoying your multimedia—then it's a sure bet that your students will learn the technology faster than you. Kids don't read manuals for digital video recorders, video games, or handheld devices because they learn the functions through hands-on experience with these tools.

In the end, teachers really don't need to completely master every option, pull-down menu, and button of the iLife tools because the kids will do that for you. Of course, the teacher must understand the interface and basic essentials of each application, but it's OK for teachers to learn along with the students. In fact, if the students are the experts, then it should be fine to allow them to teach their peers (and the teacher) what they've discovered in a new application, and that's a real-life skill. Don't be afraid to say to a student, "I'm not sure, but I know that you can figure it out and get back to me."

As effective educators, we need to take our students' strengths and use them. We want to make sure we promote learning in ways that attract our students, and we need to maximize our time for planning projects to teach the curriculum. To be effective and efficient, we need to rely on students to help us. In doing so, we'll seize the technology and make it a relevant part of the learning.

Focus on the Content

With students empowered to master the technology to complete projects, teachers are left to do what they do best: design lessons and focus on content. It might not sound much different from what teachers are already doing all across the world, and the truth is that it's not. Regardless of whether technology is utilized in a lesson, teachers need to focus on the standards. They need to design activities and projects around the curriculum. iLife and other technology tools don't change that focus. What those things do is give teachers and students more tools to creatively express what they know about those standards. iLife helps teachers design lessons that push students to synthesize what they learn through multimedia.

The iLife suite, with photo books, podcasts, Web pages, and videos, can be thought of as the final stage of publishing. Students still need to research, brainstorm, plan, write, revise, and edit their work, but the final step will be to publish a multimedia-rich project. The teacher's main goal, then, is to design the lesson and think about the parameters and guidelines that the students will use to plan projects and master the standards. The multimedia tools in the iLife suite are just a means to an end. It comes down to solid, effective teaching and lesson planning. Good teachers know to keep the end goal in mind when dealing with project-based learning, and the integration of technology doesn't change that. Know which standards need to be taught, and design lessons where students will creatively show mastery of what they've learned. It's all about focusing on the content.

The Process Is the Product

During a recent conference I attended, keynote speaker Marco Torres remarked, "The process is the product." That simple phrase had a huge impact on my thinking. It succinctly states what many educators believe. When students are collaboratively creating a project, they will be using real-life skills that go beyond the standards. Throughout the process, students demonstrate 21st-century skills such as digital-age literacy, inventive thinking, effective communication, and high productivity. They're gaining valuable experience in teaming, collaboration, self-direction, prioritizing, planning, managing for results, and the effective use of real-world tools. Those are the same skills that will help any person succeed in any position.

It doesn't matter whether the end result is perfect. The reality is that the end product isn't always going to be professional-looking, but that's understandable because our students aren't professional videographers, audio engineers, or photographers. However, instead of focusing on the things to improve the end-product, students and teachers can create rubrics that deal with the different parts of the project leading up to the final creation. Assessments on the organization, teamwork, rough draft, and storyboard, as well as the final product, ensures that students will build on successes and improve subsequent projects because they are reflecting effectively on the process. It's the constant striving for improvement in future work that helps drive students to exceed expectations.

Additionally, even if assessments aren't developed for all the parts of the process, the experience of actually creating and publishing content, working with their peers toward a common goal, and learning in a technology-rich environment makes the learning more meaningful and relevant to the students. The skills and experience that our students gain from the process will be something that they can take with them into "real" life when they join the global workforce.

Tools for the Digital Classroom

A hammer isn't always the best tool for fixing things around a house. That's why you can find wrenches, screwdrivers, saws, and a plethora of other tools at the local hardware store. Sometimes, two tools can be used to do a similar task, but we choose the one that we're more familiar with. In the same way, a five-paragraph essay isn't always the best way to convey information, and that's why students also create dioramas, posters, pop-up books, and other projects that help them communicate their ideas; and, for our digital learners, technology projects are often the preferred tool. So, what do you need to accomplish a successful digital project? Well, as with most technology, digital media tools are moving targets. Manufacturers are constantly releasing new models and adding and removing features; the improvements are never-ending. However, some pieces of hardware and software are essential to help facilitate digital projects.

Hardware Tools		
Essential Equipment	**Good to Have**	**Nice-to-Have Extras**
• A laptop or desktop computer with a built-in microphone	• Digital camera • Digital video camera • External USB microphone • Headphones	• External microphones for video cameras • Tripods • Audio interfaces with XLR microphones • Probes and digital microscopes • iPods with recorders

Hardware Tools

Hardware describes any physical piece of equipment that can be utilized for assignments. The following are some of the essential tools for creating digital projects. The most essential tool, of course, is a Mac with the iLife suite, but other tools help facilitate digital image, video, and audio projects.

The following are some basic tips for selecting specific hardware for the classroom:

- Macs are definitely the most important element for completing iLife projects in the classroom because iLife isn't sold for any other platform. Laptops are a mobile, flexible solution. Desktop machines are often faster and more powerful, but they are stationary. One of the greatest things Apple has done is make every Mac a multimedia center for creativity. All Intel iMacs, MacBooks, and MacBook Pros have built-in microphones and iSight cameras. Mac minis and Mac Pro towers require an external microphone. Double-check the iLife '08 system requirements to determine whether your computer can run all the applications. In general, all the applications in the iLife '08 suite can run on a Mac with a G4, G5, or Intel processor. iMovie '08 is the lone exception that will not work on a G4 computer, but iMovie HD remains an effective, easy-to-use video editor. When purchasing a computer, the minimum random access memory (RAM) should be 1 GB, but systems with more memory will run faster.
- Digital still cameras come in all shapes and sizes. Because of developments in technology, even the most basic digital camera is capable of taking very good images. Many still cameras can record full-motion video, but it is usually recorded in a compressed MPEG-4 format, and that's lower quality than digital-video footage taken with a video camera. If you really want high-quality video, purchase a video camera. Here are a few features to keep in mind when selecting a digital still camera:
  - *Megapixels*: What are the megapixels per image that this camera can take? In general, more megapixels mean more detailed but larger file sizes. For classroom use, a camera with a minimum 4- or 5-megapixel sensor is recommended. However, it's not unusual to find 6-megapixel and higher cameras for approximately $200 or less. For the most part, any brand will do, but Canon and Nikon have some of the highest-rated cameras at the best prices. With more megapixels, you can crop smaller areas of an image and still print a clear photo. Keep in mind that more megapixels will result in a larger file size.
  - *Zoom*: Optical zooms enlarge images by manipulating lens elements. In other words, the optical zoom truly brings the subject closer in higher quality. However, digital zooms enlarge the pixels instead of actually zooming in. Using a digital zoom often causes images to look blotchy or out of focus. Most digital cameras will have an optical setting and a digital zoom setting, but there will usually be a menu option to disable the digital zoom and ensure better-quality images.

  - *Flash memory*: Schools need to maximize their technology money, so it's recommended to purchase cameras that utilize the same flash memory (for example, compact flash, smart media, or memory sticks) as any previously purchased cameras. The price of flash memory has dropped in the past few years, so it's possible to buy several extra flash memory cards. Prices vary, but it's common to find flash memory that's approximately $10 per gigabyte. One general rule is to purchase larger-capacity cards for cameras with a higher megapixel rating.
  - *Batteries*: What types of batteries does this camera accept? Are they rechargeable? What is the price of extra or replacement batteries? Rechargeable batteries are best for the classroom because extra costs are not incurred every time the teacher has to replace the batteries. Some camera makers have proprietary batteries that are more expensive to replace. Try to find cameras that use standard AA batteries so the school can just purchase extra rechargeable AA batteries and have them on hand. As a classroom norm, one or two students can be responsible for recharging batteries after the project time is finished.
- Digital video cameras (sometimes called camcorders) also come in a variety of makes and models. Prices have dropped dramatically, and it is possible to get a quality video camera for less than $300. The first, and most important, thing to consider in a digital video camera is whether it will connect to your computer. To do so, it needs to have a FireWire port. It is often also referred to as an iLink, DV, or IEEE 1394 port. If the camera can connect to the computer via FireWire, then it can import video into iMovie. If a video camera only connects with USB, the files can still be used on a Mac, but it often doesn't import as seamlessly into iMovie. Some digital video cameras can also take still images on a memory card, but they rarely have more than a 2 megapixel camera, so the resolution of the images will not be as good as a dedicated still camera. Consumer high-definition video cameras have also dropped in price to the point of making them a legitimate option for schools. The following are a few other qualities to keep in mind when selecting a digital video camera for the classroom:
  - *Microphone port*: A classroom video project is often only as good as the audio quality. Many of the less-expensive video cameras are incapable of accepting an external microphone. Look for one that allows any microphone with a ⅛-inch input like the Canon ZR800 series. Several of the other consumer video cameras will accept a proprietary (more expensive) external microphone.
  - *Media type*: What does the camera record to? For years, the most common media video cameras recorded to was mini-DV tapes, but that has changed in the past two years. Although mini-DV tapes are relatively inexpensive and can be recorded on multiple times, more and more cameras record to other media like mini-DVD, flash memory, or hard drives. In general, mini-DV cameras are less expensive and more universal for computers. Footage easily imports from and exports to these camcorders for editing and viewing. Beware of the DVD camcorders. The miniature size is not compatible with slot-loading optical drives. Camcorders that record to hard drives aren't always compatible with Macs. To ensure full compatibility, be sure to read the system requirements before you purchase a new camcorder.
  - *Size*: Compact video cameras are convenient, but they usually have smaller lens elements. That affects their ability to capture light, so they will have poor performance in darker conditions and might not have the same color quality as larger lenses. At the same time, less-compact video cameras have clearer footage but are heavier. Larger video cameras often include more features and easier-to-use

buttons. Look at your classroom situation to determine the size camera you need.

- *CCD*: Also known as a *charge-coupled device*, these are sensors for recording images. In the past few years, 3-CCD cameras (ones that have separate elements for recording red, green, and blue) have become much less expensive. They provide sharper images with more realistic colors. A few sub-$1,000 3-CCD camcorders are available. The Panasonic PV-GS320 can usually be found for less than $500. For most regular classroom situations, this is probably overboard, but there will be classrooms where this is important. If your classroom is considering two models of cameras that are the same price but one is a 3-CCD, then you should purchase the three-chip camera.
- *HD*: High-definition video cameras are generally more expensive than standard-definition ones. However, prices have dropped dramatically in the past year. The Canon HV20 can even be found for less than $1,000, and there are several flip-style HD video cameras that record to flash memory and are less than $200. With iMovie '08, support for the popular ACVHD formats has been added, so more HD video cameras are compatible with the Apple video editor.

- External microphones provide better audio input into the video camera. The built-in microphone on the camcorder is less effective when the subject is farther away. In fact, most video cameras with built-in microphones cannot record effectively farther than ten feet away. Unlike with images, the zoom does not make the subject sound closer. In fact, because video cameras have gotten so much smaller, manufacturers can't make the built-in microphone too sensitive, or else it would record the sound of the motor running. Having an external microphone that connects to the camera helps record clear dialogue. Make sure that the microphone has a ⅛-inch connector. If it does not, then it is possible to purchase an adapter that allows it to plug into the camera. The following are a few items to keep in mind when purchasing a microphone for use with video cameras:
  - *Lavalier microphones*: Also known as *lapel microphones*, these are generally compact mics that clip onto clothing and are less obtrusive than handheld. They can be wired or wireless. If you purchase a wired lavalier microphone, it might be necessary to purchase ⅛-inch extension cables. With wireless lavalier microphones, distance isn't as much of a concern, but battery life will be an added issue.
  - *Shotgun microphones*: These are highly directional microphones that can be mounted on the top of the camera or attached to a boom pole. Because of their sensitivity, it is unnecessary to place them on the body of the speaker. When attached to a pole, they can be hung above the actors to record their dialogue.
  - *Handheld microphones*: These provide a tool that students can use for interviews. They're often directional and lightweight.
  - *Windscreens*: Often constructed of lightweight foam, windscreens are created for all three types of microphones listed previously. They can help cut down on wind and other external noises. For example, if you have an older building or a constantly running HVAC system in your room, you might consider purchasing windscreens to reduce the background noise.
- External computer microphones allow students to record straight into the computer. As stated earlier, if the classroom has a laptop, an iMac, or an eMac, there is a built-in microphone. However, built-in microphones can also pick up noise from the computer fans, keyboard typing, and taps to the display because they are omnidirectional; in other words, they gather sound from everywhere. External microphones provide better quality because they move the recording elements away from

the computer and often have higher-quality components. Some professional microphones require audio interfaces to connect to the computer. The following are some options when purchasing microphones for computer-based recording:

- *Studio-quality USB microphones*: A more recent addition to the computer-based recording options, these are large diaphragm microphones that provide much higher-quality recording. Instead of an XLR connection, they require only a USB port to maintain the power. With only three manufacturers a few years ago, 2007 saw several new models announced. Samson, Blue, M-Audio, MXL, Alesis, RODE, and SE Electronics all offer at least one model of a studio-quality USB microphone, and RODE's Podcaster microphone was the first broadcast-quality USB microphone. These high-quality USB microphones range in price from approximately $50 to $400, and the best value of these microphones is the Samson Q1U. At $49, it provides very good quality at an extremely affordable price. Some of the microphones, such as the Samson C03U and the Blue Snowball, have a switch that allows the user to record in a normal cardioid pattern for solo recording (it mainly records in a single direction), in a figure-eight pattern for interviews (it will record equally from two sides), or in a circular omnidirectional pattern for group discussions (it records sound from all sides).

- *Other USB desktop microphones*: There are also several USB desktop microphones that are not studio-quality, but they are still better options than the built-in microphone on a computer. Logitech, Labtec, and Plantronics all offer models that range in price from approximately $20 to $50. They are more directional than the built-in microphones, so they will have better audio quality, but they are nowhere near the quality of the studio-quality microphones.
- *USB headset microphones*: Integrated headphones and microphones are often popular for kids who are very active. Students don't have to worry about microphone placement and are able to look at notes in their hands without as much concern over accidentally recording paper-shuffling noises. One problem with the USB headset microphone is that the mic is often too sensitive and picks up plosives easily (puffs of air when you say words that begin with *p* or *b*).
- *Audio interfaces*: If recording multiple speakers or instruments on separate tracks is the number-one concern, then using an audio interface with XLR microphones will provide the learners with the best recording tools available. By recording to separate tracks, each voice can be adjusted to compensate for louder or quieter students. Audio interfaces can connect to the computer via USB or FireWire ports. USB audio interfaces are less expensive but also have more latency (delays in recording). If students are working on spoken-word projects such as poetry or podcasting, then this isn't a huge problem, but if they are singing, then the latency can be confusing. With an audio interface, professional microphones with XLR connections can be used. These dynamic and condenser microphones provide much better recording because they are capable of capturing a wider range of sounds. Most of these audio interfaces require the computer to be shut down before plugging them in. However, the Edirol FA-66 FireWire audio interface has two microphone inputs, and it requires no audio drivers on the Mac because it works with Apple's Mac OS X standard driver and CoreAudio. It's truly plug-and-play without shutting off the computer. Audio interfaces range in price from approximately $150 to more than $1,000.

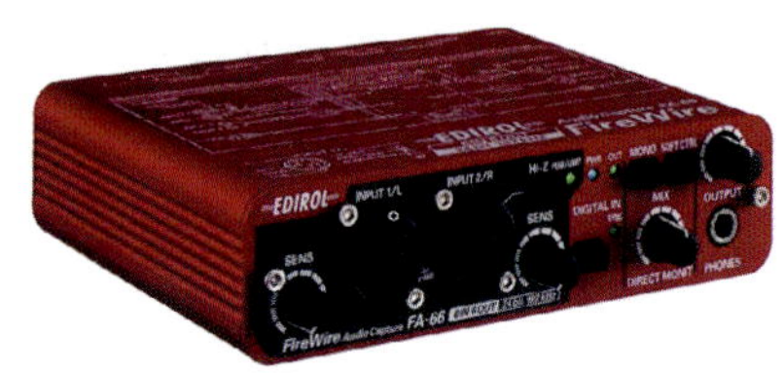

- *Audio interface/mixing boards*: There are several varieties of audio interfaces. Some audio interfaces, such as the Alesis MultiMix FireWire 8 and the M-Audio NRV-10, combine the interface with a mixing board so that multiple microphones can be plugged in at the same time. GarageBand can record up to eight tracks simultaneously.

- *Compact microphone pre-amps*: New to the audio recording mix are the compact microphone pre-amps. These devices that include the SoundTech LightSnake, MXL Mic Mate, and the CEntrance Inc. Mic Port Pro range in price from approximately $40 to $125. They connect a single XLR microphone to a computer via USB. They're a great option if the school already has XLR microphones and wants to use them for classroom projects.
- *Mobile audio recorders*: The iPod is a great tool for recording field journals and anecdotal observations. However, it does need a third-party add-on. Several options are available through Griffin, Belkin, and XtremeMac. Starting with the fifth-generation iPod and second-generation iPod nano, iPods record CD-quality sound. Other than the iPod, there are a variety of other recording devices with built-in microphones and higher-quality recording capabilities. Some of the convenient mobile recorders include the M-Audio MicroTrack, the Edirol R-09, and the Samson H2. These devices record better-than-CD-quality audio and have inputs for external microphones, instruments, and mixing boards. These mobile recorders require external media cards.

- Pasco and Vernier both produce convenient probeware and other tools for use in science labs. They connect to the computer and can graph temperature, acidity, motion, heart rate, and more. The best aspect of probeware is that it's able to record temperature more accurately over time than people can with nondigital means. Additionally, probeware can graph the data.

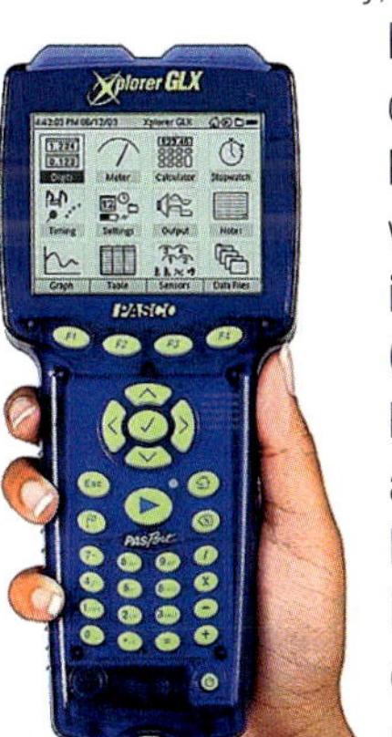

Bodelin manufactures a versatile digital USB microscope called the ProScope that records images and video. The captured media can be imported into iPhoto, iMovie, GarageBand, iWeb, iWork, and Keynote for use in presentations and projects. The beauty of the ProScope is that it can be used as is for 3D objects or hooked up to even archaic microscopes to look at wet or dry mount slides.

- When filming footage for video projects, a tripod lends stability. It is not necessary, but when used properly, a tripod eliminates the distraction of shaky videography. Many types of tripods are available. The lower-priced ones are often lightweight. Heavier ones are more stable.

Software

Software describes the applications that communicate with the hardware. Although the iLife suite comes with every Mac, some other very innovative applications are free or low-priced. The following are useful software suggestions for classroom educational technology projects:

- iWork: Although iWork is an additional cost, it is a dynamic, media-rich productivity suite. With iWork '08 (and iLife '08), educational institutions can now purchase a 500-seat license for each suite for $249. The iWork suite includes Pages, Keynote, and Numbers. All three applications have very similar controls including the Inspector, the Media Browser, and the new formatting bar for easier adjustments to the text and graphics. Because of iWork's integration with the iLife suite, projects created in each application come alive with images, video, and audio. The drag-and-drop interface makes each application more transparent so learners can focus on the content they are adding to their project instead of how to use them.

  - Pages is a word-processing application with easy-to-use page layout themes. It comes with dozens of templates that can be used educationally, including brochures, lab reports, letters, invitations, fliers, and newsletters.
  - Keynote is a presentation application. Students can create media-rich presentations quickly with one of the dozens of templates. Transitions and builds are cinema-quality and easy to use. New to Keynote '08 is the ability to record audio so that a presentation can be exported as a podcast with narration. Another option is to use Keynote to create titles, graphs, and graphics for enhanced podcasts.
  - Numbers is the newest application in the iWork suite. It's a spreadsheet application with templates for beautifully laying out and presenting data. The canvas can include multiple tables, graphs, and media. The templates give users the ability to create stunning spreadsheets that bring data to life.

- Comic Life: This easy-to-use comic book creation application links to the iPhoto library. It helps students create visual stories and present findings with digital images and text. Although it isn't part of the iLife suite, it was included on all Macs with an Intel chip for a few years. Regardless of whether it continues to be a part of the manufacturer's image on the Mac, it's a low-cost, amazing application that is a great addition to any classroom. The integration with iPhoto makes it a simple and dynamic way to express ideas with images.

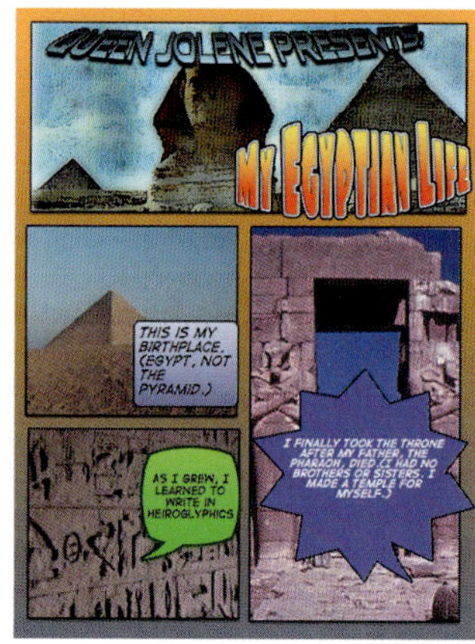

Creating educational comic books is an engaging activity that results in content-rich collectibles. The final product can then be exported to iPhoto, .Mac, or the desktop for easy sharing. For tutorials or more information on Comic Life, please visit www.plasq.com.

- Mind-mapping software: Inspiration, NovaMind, Kidspiration, and other similar software help students organize their thoughts. They aid in the brainstorming process. Mind-mapping software can be used to connect ideas and assemble concepts. These applications are effective additions to the planning/preproduction stage of a project. Ultimately, more complete prewriting results in well-thought-out projects, and these tools truly help students organize.

Lessons

At the end of this book are two types of lessons. People who are familiar with previous versions of this book will recall the in-depth lesson format that provides model iLife curricular projects with detailed information. Teachers who are interested in providing in-depth lessons from beginning to end will find that type of scaffolding present in the full lessons. New to this edition of the book are mini-lessons for quickly getting started with the iLife suite. The mini-lessons emphasize how easy it is to begin using iLife and multimedia in the classroom.

Each of the accompanying in-depth lessons follows a similar format of seven steps to set up, complete, and share the project. Each of the lessons is specific to a curricular area or grade level, but teachers can adapt any of the lessons to their specific grade level or curriculum. In essence, the in-depth lessons and mini-lessons can be utilized as a template for developing multimedia projects with iLife, iWork, and other tools. The following are descriptions of what you'll find in each section of the in-depth lessons.

I. Getting Started

This section is an overview of the project with the lesson goals and objectives, material needed, and suggestions for preparation. The goals of each lesson will answer the following questions: What will be learned? What product will be created? What is expected of students in terms of the length of the project and included elements? By conveying clear goals, students will understand what is expected and be able to successfully complete the tasks in the project. It often helps if a rubric or checklist is created so that students can stay organized, budget their time, and understand the steps they need to take to demonstrate mastery of concepts.

II. Making Connections

The main components of this step are an introduction of the project and a connection of the information to the lives of students. This is a good time to discuss prior knowledge, brainstorm ideas, and extend their ideas to new learning. Some of the activities that are typical in this section include the following:

- KWL (what I Know, what I Want to know, what I Learned) charts are used to begin setting goals according to what students already know and want to find out. Students can differentiate their learning by deciding on what they want to know.
- Students in small groups discuss the project and brainstorm ideas.
- The whole class discusses how to gather and compile ideas and resources.
- Students create checklists of important benchmarks they need to achieve.
- Rubrics are presented. If a rubric has not been prepared, students can work with the teacher to create one as a whole class. Student-created rubrics promote ownership and responsibility. Goals are clearer to students if they help create a rubric.

III. Planning the Project (Preproduction)

The key to any project, to ensure that it will proceed as smoothly as possible, is planning. Often known as *preproduction*, this is a time for students to research information, gather images, create storyboards, write scripts, and rehearse what they will say. It helps to have a central location, such as a project folder, for all the planning materials. The following are some of the items that can go in a project folder:

- Observation journals: Whether they're called observation, thinking, QuickWrite, or reflection journals, they're all the same; they are a central place where students can write down their thoughts. Even at an early age, keeping a journal of goals, planning, procedures, and reflections helps students improve with each project. The observation journal is for on-the-spot reflections and well-thought-out plans. It is an effective place to put all brainstorming, KWL work, production notes, and reflections on the project. It's an aid for keeping students on task and process-oriented. The teacher should consider the work in the observation journal while assessing the project. If the classroom is integrating blogs or wikis, then students can also use their online writing as observation journals. Students are motivated to write more if they are using 21st-century tools for their journal writing.
- Project checklists: These are used to help segment the project into manageable tasks. Having a checklist allows students to see what else needs to be done to complete their project. Checklists can also be used to help assign tasks to the students in each collaborative learning group.
- Rubrics: The teacher- and student-created rubric should be in the project folder. Students are able to refer to the rubric throughout the project to assess the quality

of their work and consider how to improve it. If they see that they aren't showing mastery on an area of the rubric, they are more likely to know what needs to be done to excel.

- Storyboards and scripts: One of the most important elements in the preproduction process, a storyboard is used to organize a variety of projects and can help students visualize the final product they will assemble. In projects with less visual elements, a script might be the main planning piece used. Pages includes storyboard and script templates. The following are some examples of how storyboards and scripts can be integrated into the planning of projects:
  - Visualizing the composition and action in shots that make up a scene in a video project. Special attention should be paid to what each shot communicates prior to filming it. Transitions and effects can also be indicated on a storyboard.
  - Diagramming the information on each slide that will be created in a Keynote presentation. The details can include colors, fonts, data, and multimedia elements.
  - Presenting the images that will be used in a slide show or podcast. Storyboards might include the duration that each slide will be visible and the timing of the words with the pictures.
  - Planning the individual pages that will make up a Web site. Storyboards help students see the "big picture" when used to plan each Web page on a site.
- Distribution of roles: Collaborative learning groups promote communication and individual responsibility. By having individual roles, students are in charge of one section of the project and can help support the other elements that need to be completed.
- Research notes: The project folder should also contain any notes, research, and outlines that the students have gathered and created during the planning of their project.
- The writing process: This is the time for students to write a rough draft of the script and then revise and edit it. Whether students are writing a script for a podcast or video, creating the text for a photo book, or planning the content for a Web site, the writing process is essential for clear communication.
- Equipment and planning sheets: Students should know what equipment they will need for their project so they can gather the pieces prior to the production time.

IV. Creating the Project (Production)

Once planning has been completed, and preparation material (such as a storyboard or script) has been checked off, students will begin creating the project, also known as the *production phase*. This stage includes videotaping footage, taking digital pictures, recording narration and thoughts, composing music, creating presentations, or compiling information in a Pages document or a Web site. Although each project is slightly different, a few similarities will help students and teachers achieve success on any project. The following are some components to completing a successful assignment:

- Follow the storyboard or script: Although changes can be made during filming, writing, or audio recording, the group should follow the storyboard and script that were created as much as possible. Just as writers base their rough draft on the brainstorming and planning, videographers, presenters, and podcasters base their project on the storyboard and script.
- Focus on the checklist and goals: Students should be aware of which tasks have been completed and what goals remain to complete the project. When referring to a checklist, students are more likely to stay on task and take ownership of their project.
- Assign a timekeeper: Someone is usually chosen during the project planning, but it's important for one person to have the task of keeping track of the time that has elapsed and knowing how much is left to complete each part of their project. This student is also in charge of

communicating with the teacher about the status of the project each day.

- Modify as needed: Although the team will follow the storyboard and script, if something isn't working right and a different word, sentence, shot, or photo will work better, then it's OK to modify the plan. The important issue to keep in mind is to make changes only for a reason that ultimately helps the project. Why is the plan being modified? Does the change clarify information?
- Communicate with the group: During a project, learners should communicate throughout all stages of the project. This will help them complete the tasks in a timely fashion, clarify any confusion, and improve mastery of the information. Additionally, students will be practicing the 21st-century skills of collaboration and communication.

V. Refining the Project (Postproduction)

No matter what the students are creating, whether it's a podcast, video, Web site, DVD, comic book, presentation, or something else entirely, there will come a time in the project that they complete the production process and need to begin editing it. Just like with the writing process, further refinement is necessary to ensure that communication is clear and main ideas are presented in a cohesive manner. The following are some of the issues to keep in mind with specific genres of projects:

- Video: Students should always view their final movie. If this is not required, many students will assume they are done when all editing is complete and never watch the video from start to finish. This is true of almost any digital project. Did the editing of the clips help communicate the ideas presented? Are the shots clear? Do any clips need to be edited to eliminate empty space? Are all words spelled correctly in the title and credits? If effects and transitions are used, do they contribute to the communication of the story or concepts? How is the audio? Is there a balance in volume levels for the music, sound effects, and video track?
- Photo: Make sure all images represent what the students meant to highlight. If any cropping is done, check that nothing important was eliminated. In slide shows, look over the transitions and timing of each slide. Did the students select the correct music or audio to accompany the pictures? In photo books, calendars, or greeting cards, check the spelling and content of captions and entries.
- Music: Do all music compositions convey the emotions and energy of the work that it will be integrated with (if it's used with another project). Do audio levels bring out intended sounds and instruments? Are all lyrics clear and louder than background music?
- Podcasts: After listening for content, the most important consideration is the audio levels of each track. Do any of the audio tracks light up the red clipping indicators? If underlying music is used (known as a music bed), can the vocals still be heard clearly? Are all images placed in the correct spot for enhanced podcasts? Are there any gaps between images? Are all chapters, URL titles, and links spelled correctly?
- DVDs: All DVD projects should be played in the iDVD simulator prior to burning the final copy. Students can check navigation and playback of slide shows and videos. Does the navigation work correctly? Are all menu and chapter titles spelled correctly? Are all themes and music appropriate to the project? Prior to burning multiple copies, a single DVD should be created and tested in a variety of DVD players.
- Web sites: In iWeb projects, learners should look at the general design of the page. Are the colors appealing? Do all video and audio files function as intended? Is the spelling and grammar correct on all blogs entries, Web pages, and blog notes? Students should examine all links to Web sites and files to make sure that they work correctly.
- Presentations: Students should rehearse the presentation so that they are comfortable with the timing of slides and builds. Partners and groups should also

discuss what they should say with each slide. Spelling should be checked on titles and bulleted information. Are all images and video clear? Are any transitions or builds distracting?

- Pages: The students should pay special attention to the colors and fonts used to convey their information. Do their choices help communicate the subject matter? Do all video and audio files play correctly? Have all the facts been verified? Spelling and grammar should be checked.
- Tables and Spreadsheets: Whether in Numbers, Pages, or Keynote, students should make sure that all tables have formulas that calculate the correct numbers. Data should be double checked for accuracy. Spelling on charts should be verified as well.

VI. Publishing the Project

When students create multimedia projects, their engagement and enthusiasm will often be motivating enough for them to excel. However, when projects are published, and students are aware that all their relatives, friends, community members, and even people from the rest of the world might be listening or watching, they tend to push themselves to improve even more because suddenly they have a real audience. Everybody wants to create a project that they're proud of. Through the act of printing hard copies or publishing to a Web site, the students have a real purpose and are able to share their work and review or enjoy it for years. The following are some options for showcasing student work throughout the year:

- When kids present their project to other classes, it gives them a chance to share their work with peers outside of their classroom. By presenting multiple times in a variety of situations, students develop confidence and understand how to speak formally with inflection. Most important, students begin to understand the concepts of voice and audience.
- Student multimedia festivals are an enjoyable tradition to begin at the site or district level. By highlighting student work at a fair or festival, technology is brought to the forefront. Support for integrating technology often grows after a big event. Multimedia projects created in iLife are the perfect centerpiece for festivals and viewings.
- School Night at the Apple Store is a wonderful program for exhibiting student multimedia projects. Held at local Apple Stores, student success is showcased as learners present their work. Invitations are sent out to parents and community members.
- CD and DVD compilations are another way to publish and distribute the projects for sharing with others. Labels and covers can be designed to follow the project themes. Creating a concrete record of their work also generates a sense of accomplishment.
- iWeb and .Mac work seamlessly to create stunning Web sites. Classrooms can utilize the templates to post dynamic Web pages with PDFs, podcasts, videos, and photos from the classroom. With the posted projects, parents, grandparents, and students can enjoy an easily maintained home/school connection. With iWeb 08, classrooms can upload their Web sites to any server without a .Mac account.
- Assignments in iPhoto and Pages can be printed on high-quality paper and bound as a keepsake book. The project can be sent home or included in a portfolio for assessment. iPhoto includes a printing service where students and teachers can purchase any of the work they create in the program.
- Podcasts can be posted with iWeb, but they can also be posted on any number of podcast hosts. School servers can also be used. Once a classroom or school has a podcast, the RSS feed can be added to the iTunes Podcast Directory (and other directories as well) so that people can easily find the projects.
- Student projects can be posted to YouTube. With one-click sharing to YouTube built into iMovie '08, any user can contribute to the Web 2.0 video site easily.

VII. Reflection, Assessment, and Differentiation

Teachers should always assess the process and final product of any multimedia project. It is often through assessing the process that the teacher will find out how well students collaborate, communicate, and learn from experiences. It's through the final product that teachers will see how well students have synthesized information and constructed new knowledge.

It is equally important for all students to self-assess their work. When students have time for reflection, they can begin to celebrate their successes as well as consider how they would improve their work for the next project. The following are a few activities that students can perform while reflecting and assessing their own work:

- Students can use the class-created rubric to determine how well they performed each task in addition to the final product. When students practice assessing themselves and compare the results with how the teacher has scored them, the "norming" process begins. The more this is done, the more accurately students will be able to judge the score they deserve.
- Students can view the other students' projects and reflect on what aspects of that project "worked" for them.
- Students can compose additional reflective entries in their journal. The topics can include the following:
  - An explanation of how they assessed themselves with the rubric
  - A reflection of their final product, describing the successes and areas for improvement on the current project
  - Goals for future projects
  - Written reactions after viewing other completed projects
  - A description of the information they learned during the completion of this assignment
- Within collaborative learning groups or whole-group discussions, students can reflect on some of the skills they learned throughout the process of creation. The students should also take time to reflect on how they will be able to use this experience to help themselves in other subject areas and future assignments.
- The teacher can take time to also reflect on how this lesson can be customized and modified to reach all learners. By differentiating projects, students can all succeed and learn.

Mini-lessons

Although it's beneficial to think about all the aspects of a lesson, like the in-depth lesson format, the simplicity of creating quick projects with the iLife suite means that it's even easier for teachers and students to get started right away. The mini-lessons in this book have been included to help encourage teachers to jump in and begin creating with their students. Educators will also see that they can do a mini-lesson with very little additional preparation.

The two main areas the mini-lessons will focus on are a specific function in an application (for example, creating a calendar in iPhoto) and how it can be utilized in the curriculum. So, time will be spent explaining what the application feature is and how it would look in the classroom. Once the teacher feels more comfortable integrating technology into the curriculum, then any of the mini-lessons can also be transformed into a more in-depth lesson. Although the mini-lessons will concentrate on specific topics, they can be modified and adapted for any grade level and standard.

Additional Thoughts

It would be wonderful if every classroom project were created without any problems at all. However, the reality is that sometimes things do go wrong (regardless of whether technology was utilized). Batteries die. Software crashes. Students get sick. The following sections are intended to provide some ideas for managing the integration of technology into the classroom as well as to provide some general troubleshooting tips. The most important thing is to just try it! The more technology projects you and your students do, the more comfortable everyone will feel, and that, of course, will lead to using even more digital tools. If you stay relaxed as problems occur, you will be a wonderful role model for how students should act when things go wrong. Take a deep breath, and work together with your students to develop solutions. What a wonderful 21st-century learning skill to give your students!

Flexibility

All projects can be modified to include whatever technology is available to the classroom. For example, if video cameras are unavailable, then the students can create movies with still images. If iPods are not on hand, then anecdotal thoughts can be written down and recorded with GarageBand. Video projects can be created with or without extra microphones. It's all a matter of utilizing the equipment that is available in the classroom and understanding how to adapt to change.

The majority of classrooms will not have a video camera for every group. However, that shouldn't stop the class from creating digital video projects. Students will naturally be in different parts of the production process, so they will probably be able to share the limited number of video cameras. Additionally, the teacher can create a rotation schedule that will limit the amount of time each camera can be checked out. This often results in more productive and efficient collaborative groups because they have limited time with equipment.

Also, there is no reason that every single group needs to create the same project. After all, many applications are interchangeable to a certain extent. For example, a project intended as a Pages document can be published as an iWeb site instead. Video projects can be adapted so that they utilize still images and end up as an enhanced podcast. The beauty of the iLife technology is that you can modify any idea to fit your precise needs. This works very well in the classroom with limited technology because each group can create a different project to represent their findings. One group could be working with the digital video camera while another records their project as a podcast. This flexibility works much better after a few projects have been completed, but if the teacher feels comfortable allowing students to learn the technology on their own, then this modification can be done earlier in the year.

Classroom Management of Technology

Planning a digital project isn't much different from planning a student-centered project with analog tools such as construction paper, markers, and glue. The most important step is to lay down the parameters for the project. What are the expected norms when entering into a multimedia project? How should students handle equipment after it has been checked out? What is the time limit for each project? How much time does each group have with the equipment? What are the courtesies that learners should provide to each other when recording audio and video in the classroom? The following are a few tips for managing projects in the classroom:

- Emphasize responsibility: Technology projects should not be considered an extra or a reward; they are a privilege. Teachers need to make it clear that students are being entrusted with equipment and tools that they are fortunate to be able to use in the classroom. Students need to be careful with the tools, or there may not be working equipment for the next project. Students with a vested interest in the classroom technology will make an effort to keep everything in working condition.
- Initiate a training procedure: Students get access to technology tools when they have proven they know how to use the equipment responsibly. A quick check-off sheet can be used to prove students understand how to use the tools properly. Periodic retraining sessions can be scheduled if students are becoming careless or complacent. One day with analog tools like a magic marker and paper has also been known to retrain a group quickly.

- Train specialists: It is beneficial to have several students act as specialists on certain pieces of equipment or software applications. This promotes empowerment and collaboration on assignments. It also provides scaffolding at the beginning of the year so that by the end every child knows how to work the equipment. The specialists can also be assigned to train other students on the equipment throughout the year. This sets up an environment where students are more willing to help each other out and the teacher will feel less pressure to train all the students at once because that responsibility will be assumed by the specialists.
- Establish checkout policies: In any multimedia assignment, before students gain access to equipment, they need to prove that they have completed the prerequisite work leading up to the production stage. For example, students might have to provide their teacher with a copy of their storyboard or other planning that they've completed; this might include a script and any visual elements that will be incorporated into the project. By establishing a set procedure, students will understand the amount of planning that needs to be done prior to receiving equipment to complete the project. Additionally, they will be more likely to work hard throughout the entire process because they want to use the equipment.
- Have a silent signal: Whether a hand signal, verbal cue, or flicking the lights on and off, the kids need to know when they are expected to be silent. This is especially helpful if students are recording narration or dialogue for a video. Ultimately, it helps students show courtesy by developing an awareness of other groups and learning to work quietly when others need to record.
- Recruit volunteers: This isn't as essential in older grade levels, but it's always helpful to have parent volunteers who can help watch the groups. This is especially true if you have students working in more than one location throughout the school. One of the best things about having volunteers is that they will learn the technology as well and be more useful with the technology as time goes by. Former students who understand the classroom routines and know how to use the equipment can also be invited to help.
- Work with a teaching partner: If there are no volunteers, one way to ensure safety is to work with another teacher. The students who are planning or already editing their project can work in the other classroom. The teacher who assigned the project supervises the learners who are actively recording or finding footage.
- Create "tech buddies": It's not uncommon to have upper-grade classrooms work with primary students in an elementary school. Usually, this takes the form of "reading buddies." However, it's worthwhile to have "tech buddies" who can help less experienced teachers and students create technology projects.
- Time limits: If a classroom or school is lucky enough to have multiple copies of all the hardware and software used, then there are no issues. However, for schools that have limited supplies, make sure each group understands how much time they will be allowed to create before handing the equipment to the next group. Time pressures are not optimal, but they often result in better organizational skills and more time spent on task. Twenty to thirty minutes with a camera is adequate if there aren't enough for everyone. Creating a technology pass or public timer helps students keep track of their remaining time.

Purchasing Equipment

Time and money always stand in the way of adopting technology tools in education. These two issues affect equipment purchases, teacher training, and software acquisition. Although an ideal world would present educators and students with all the hardware and software they need for creative projects, there are several ways of obtaining technology:

- Create a vision: If teachers, administrators, and parents come together with a shared vision of enhancing the curriculum through technology integration, the school is more likely to have an annual line item in its budget for hardware and software expenditures. A vision also means that the teachers and administrators will seek out professional development opportunities for further learning. When creating a shared vision, it is essential to answer these key questions: What kinds of projects would the school like to see students creating? How will we get there? How will we maintain the program for the future?

- Pool resources: Buying a new desktop computer for each classroom is not as cost-effective as purchasing wireless, portable laptop carts. Most classroom computers are not used throughout the day. By having laptops for checkout, more students in greater numbers of classrooms will have access to the technology. Teachers can reserve multiple laptops for an hour, decreasing the student-to-computer ratio during any given project. Sometimes called computers on wheels (COWs), laptop carts also solve the problem of lack of space for multiple desktop computers.
- Work with the parent-teacher organization: Through a partnership with the PTA or PTO, a technology budget can be created so that specific fundraisers go toward the purchase of new equipment. Depending on the rules of the district, the money can be gifted to the school, or the PTA can purchase the technology and donate it. Sometimes by developing a technology partnership with PTA, parents will begin volunteering to help because they want to see how the technology is being utilized.
- Create commemorative DVDs: DVD yearbooks, collectible discs of events, and portfolios of student work can be used as fundraisers with the PTA. This model can also be used for student-created CDs of music, spoken-word projects, and even podcasts. All the money raised can go directly into the technology fund. When a tradition of selling commemorative discs is developed, the technology program can truly get an ongoing boost.
- Partner with parents: Sometimes parents have older equipment at home that isn't being used but is still functional. Many parents are more than willing to donate it to the class or allow it to be used for projects. Also, when parents know that you need help, they are more likely to volunteer and even look out for product donations from their friends and business associates.
- Request donations: Local businesses, community-service organizations, and public broadcasting stations are often interested in educational donations. Especially with DVD productions, local businesses are sometimes willing to donate money if their organization is recognized. This is especially true if there is a specific project that is being displayed or viewed to a wide audience. Public broadcasting stations will even donate studio time in their professional stages. It's important to acknowledge these donating organizations on your Web site or place a plaque on the equipment to recognize their contribution.
- Actively search and secure grants: Local organizations, county offices, large companies, statewide entities, and the federal government often have grants and fellowships for educational organizations. Many of these grants are specifically for technology, but even the ones that are focused on a curricular area can include a technology component.
- Enter contests, festivals, and competitions. Several awards are available to classrooms for their multimedia projects. When a classroom or school wins a local, state, or federal competition, the positive press facilitates acquiring more equipment. Many of these festivals also include prizes. One issue to keep in mind is that student projects should never use commercial music or images. This is especially true if you are entering competitions that award prizes.

Final Tips

As always, my most important bit of advice is to have fun and enjoy the process! Education should be informative, exciting, and empowering. By integrating multimedia, learners will find the curriculum engaging and enjoyable. Students will develop a love of learning as they complete projects, discover responsibility, master the curriculum, and gain confidence in their own abilities. That's the true meaning of "making the curriculum more relevant." Students will make connections to the curriculum, enjoy coming to school more, and take charge of their learning. With that said, here are a few final suggestions for continuing happily on the road to transforming your classroom into the digital utopia of 21st-century skills with the iLife suite:

- Practice makes perfect. As with any project, things might go wrong, and at first, nervous teachers will think that something always goes wrong; however, it gets easier. Tasks might not be trouble-free, but the more the technology is used, the smoother the process will be. Using technology ensures that you will continue to model the lifelong learning skill.
- Begin with the end in mind. Often called backwards planning, this is a skill that will truly keep the teacher and students clear on the project goals. When planning an assignment, it's important to address what standards or curricular area will be assessed. The goal is to have technology be a tool leading toward mastery. It's easy to mistake flashy, multimedia-rich projects for rigorously educational projects, but try not to fall into the trap of "style over substance."
- The process is the product. Any one of our students could be the next Spielberg, Lucas, or Mozart and what they learn in our classrooms will help them achieve these goals eventually, but for now their skills won't be there quite yet. By assessing all the tasks and reflections that students create, it ensures that the teacher will be clear on what was truly learned. Who knows? If one of your students ends up being the best new, up-and-coming filmmaker, they just might mention you on the red carpet as the teacher who helped empower them to embrace creativity at a young age.
- Become a lifelong learner with other teachers, and create a support system amongst each other. Magazines, organizations, and conferences are dedicated to educational technology. Learning with other educators and developing a professional learning community will make technology integration easier because everyone will feel supported and encouraged. With ongoing professional development, educators are sure to learn, take risks, and stay on the cutting edge.

Resources

Several Internet resources can help teachers find tips, tutorials, and lessons for multimedia projects. Some Web sites also provide royalty-free, legal media for use in classroom assignments. These resources are not necessary but facilitate planning, creation, and assessment:

- Apple iLife tutorials provide tips, keyboard shortcuts, and tutorials for using iPhoto, iTunes, GarageBand, iMovie, iDVD, and iWeb. This is a good place to begin when learning the iLife suite. There are some very informative video tutorials. (www.apple.com/support/ilife)
- Apple iWork tutorials provide tips, keyboard shortcuts, and tutorials for using Keynote, Numbers, and Pages. This is an excellent place to begin when learning the iWork suite. There are video tutorials here as well. (www.apple.com/support/iwork)
- Apple iPod 101 is a section dedicated to helping users learn what an iPod is capable of doing. It's especially effective for people who are just getting started using an iPod. (www.apple.com/support/ipod101)
- iLife in Education contains information, lessons, and links for utilizing each part of the iLife suite. There are links for each part of the iLife suite, so teachers can easily find out how GarageBand or iWeb can be used effectively in the classroom. There are also links with success stories of schools that are integrating the iLife suite in education. (www.apple.com/education/digitalauthoring/ilife.html)

- iPod in Education incorporates lessons and examples of using the iPod to enhance content creation and delivery in education. There is also information on the all-new iPod Learning Lab. (www.apple.com/education/products/ipod)
- iWork in Education contains information on Pages, Keynote, and Numbers. There are links to lesson plans and tutorials. (www.apple.com/education/digitalauthoring/iwork.html)
- 4teachers is a Web site for teachers who are interested in integrating technology into learning. There is a very easy-to-use online rubric maker called RubiStar. There are more than a dozen tools for students and teachers to use to help create quizzes, plan projects, and take notes. (http://4teachers.org)
- kitZu is a collection of free educational, copyright-friendly media resources for classroom use created by the Orange County Department of Education in California. Kits are categorized by subject and grade level, and they contain images, text documents, video, and audio. (http://kitzu.com)
- Pics4Learning is a collection of copyright-friendly images for teachers and students created by Tech4Learning. Thousands of images have been donated for free, educational use. Each image also has a bibliography that can be copied for citation purposes. (www.pics4learning.com)
- NASA has an area for searching for multimedia that the organization has collected throughout the years. The images, audio, and video are free for educational and informational purposes. (www.nasa.gov/multimedia/highlights/index.html and http://nix.nasa.gov)
- Wikimedia Commons contains more than 500,000 media files for free use. The images, videos, and audio are either donated or in the public domain. Because it is not an educational project, some of the images might be inappropriate for younger students. (http://commons.wikimedia.org/wiki/Main_Page). There is also a free multimedia search engine that finds items on the Wikimedia Commons. It's called Mayflower. (http://tools.wikimedia.de/~tangotango/mayflower/)
- Incompetech is a collection of royalty-free music that can be used for educational projects. Although there is a requested donation of $5.00 per song, that can be waved if the site and Kevn MacLeod are acknowledged in the credits of a project. (http://incompetech.com/)
- George Lucas Educational Foundation is a site for educators, students, and community leaders who are interested in integrating technology in the curriculum. There are good examples of best practices and articles on emerging technologies in education. Edutopia also has a free magazine and e-newsletter for educators. (www.edutopia.org)
- International Society of Technology in Education is a nonprofit, worldwide organization for educational technology professionals. It's the parent organization that plans the National Educational Computing Conference each year. Educators can find research, resources, and other news and events. (www.iste.org)
- Dashboard Widgets are tiny applications that usually serve a single purpose. There are several widgets that can be used in education. Some educational widgets include The Periodic Table, 3-2-1 Countdown, Dictionary, and Unit Converter. There are several widgets that come with every new Mac (including the Dictionary and Unit Converter), but the rest can be easily downloaded and installed on any computer. Most widgets are free and can be found on the Apple Dashboard downloads page. (www.apple.com/downloads/dashboard)

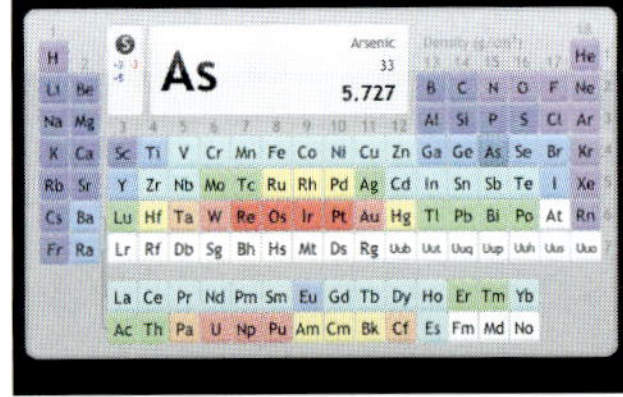

- The Apple Learning Interchange is quite simply the best source of educational lessons created with iLife and iWork. (http://edcommunity.apple.com/ali)

The Macintosh
iLife '08

by Jim Heid

For Maryellen,

for my mother,

and in loving memory

of George Heid, my dad.

A master of the analog

hub, he would have

loved this stuff.

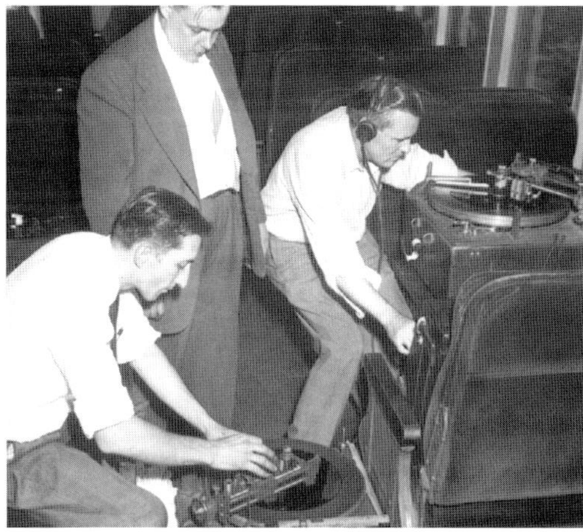

George Heid (right), recording direct to disc on a moving train, in the early 1950s.

About the Author

Jim Heid describes himself as a poster child for iLife: he has been taking photos, making movies, and playing music since he was a kid.

He began writing about personal computers in 1980, when he computerized his home-built ham radio station with a Radio Shack TRS-80 Model I. As Senior Technical Editor of one of the first computer magazines, *Kilobaud Microcomputing,* he began working with Mac prototypes in 1983. He began writing for *Macworld* magazine in 1984, joined the masthead as Contributing Editor, and is now a Senior Contributor. He has also written for *PC World, Internet World,* and *Newsweek* magazines, and wrote a weekly, nationally syndicated technology column for the *Los Angeles Times.*

In 2007, Apple approached Jim to help develop the iLife '08 video tutorials that are available at Apple's Web site.

Jim is a frequent speaker at user groups, conferences, and other events. He has taught at the Kodak Center for Creative Imaging in Camden, Maine, at the University of Hawaii, and at dozens of technology conferences in between. He also co-hosts "Point & Click Radio," a biweekly computer radio show, which you can listen to at www.kzyx.org/pc.

Jim and his standard poodle and mascot, Sophie, divide their time between San Francisco and the rugged coast of Mendocino, California.

Acknowledgements

This book wouldn't exist if it weren't for Arne Hurty and Barbara Assadi of San Francisco's BayCreative. You two are a constant inspiration, and I am so happy to be working together.

Jonathan Woolson, principal of thinkplaydesign, crafted the layouts in Adobe InDesign. I'm hugely grateful for the aesthetics, precision, and attention to detail that you bring to the table. You wield a mean waxer, my friend.

My thanks also go to Jeff Carlson, for expertly revising the iMovie and iDVD chapters; and to Glenn Fleishman, for making the first-pass revisions to the iWeb chapter.

My thanks and respect also go to the Apple engineers and product managers behind iLife '08, and to everyone at Peachpit Press. The best computer platform and the best publisher: what more could a geek author want?

Another group of friends provides support and immeasurable amounts of inspiration. Cate, Deborah, Elin, Karmen, Mona, Rita, Sharon, Cynthia, Kayla, Anita, Lisa, Mark, John, Johny, Laurie, Amy, Karen, Karin, Caitlin, Bruno, Laura, Shawn, Ken, David, George, Jeanné, Luke, Chris, Christy, Gina, Jen, Jan, Jinx, and Von, among many more. You mean the world to me.

Thanks also to Mitch and everyone at MCN; to Judy, Terry, Mimi, Pierre, Laura, Chuck, Rennie, Hope, Bob, Doug, Stephanie, and Marley; and to Sophie, my sweet iPoodle.

My thanks and love also to Toby, for being there and for being you. Like the man said, you are special.

And finally, to Marjorie Baer and Maryellen Kelly: For completely different reasons, this book wouldn't exist without you. I wish you were here to see it.

Jim Heid

Table of

Contents

Read Me First

How the Book Works

This book devotes a separate section to each of the iLife '08 programs: iTunes and iPod for enjoying music, videos, and podcasts; iPhoto for photography; iMovie for video editing; iDVD for creating DVD-Video discs, GarageBand for making music and podcasts, and iWeb for creating Web sites. Each section is a series of two-page spreads, and each spread is a self-contained reference that covers one topic.

Most spreads begin with an introduction that sets the stage with an overview of the topic.

Many spreads refer to this book's companion Web site, where you can get updates and more information.

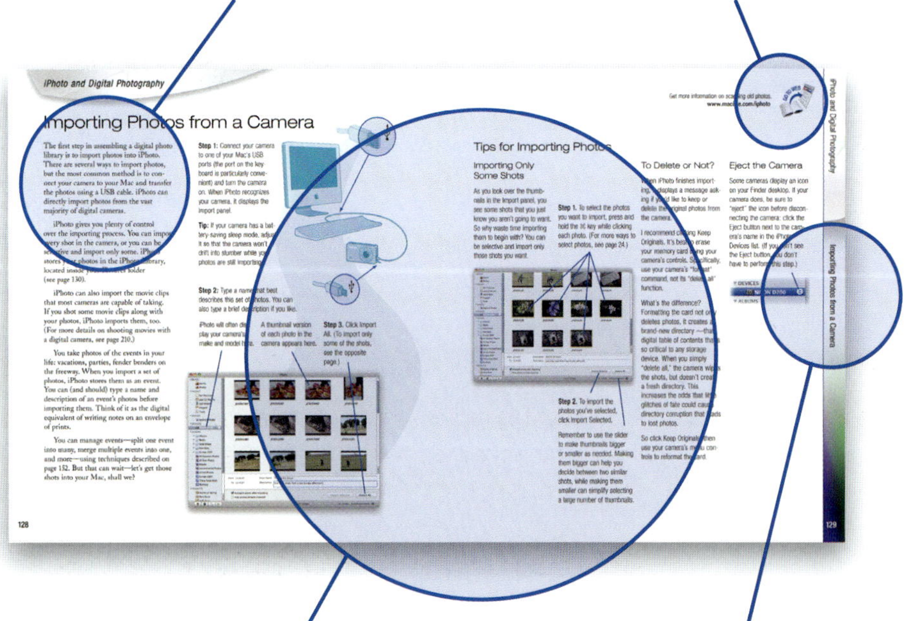

Here's the main course of each spread, where you'll find instructions, background information, and tips.

The section and spread names appear on the edges of the pages to allow you to quickly flip to specific topics.

The Book, the Web Site

There's just one thing this book doesn't cover: tomorrow. The iLife scene is always evolving as new programs and new developments change the way we work with digital media.

That's why this book also has a companion Web site: www.macilife.com. At this site, you'll find links to the products discussed in the book as well as tips and news items, updates, and reviews of iLife-related products.

You'll also find convenient links to the video tutorials that I discuss on the opposite page.

Read the Book, Watch the Movies

You can't beat the printed page for delivering depth and detail, but some people learn best by watching. If you're in this second group, head to Apple's iLife Web site, www.apple.com/ilife.

There, you'll find a collection of video tutorials that I helped to develop. For the big picture, watch the iLife '08 Guided Tour movie. Each of the iLife programs also has its own overview movie.

To drill into specific topics, click the Video Tutorials button or head directly to www.apple.com/ilife/tutorials, where over 100 video tutorials await. They'll help you get up to speed with iLife and set the stage for the details that you'll read in these pages.

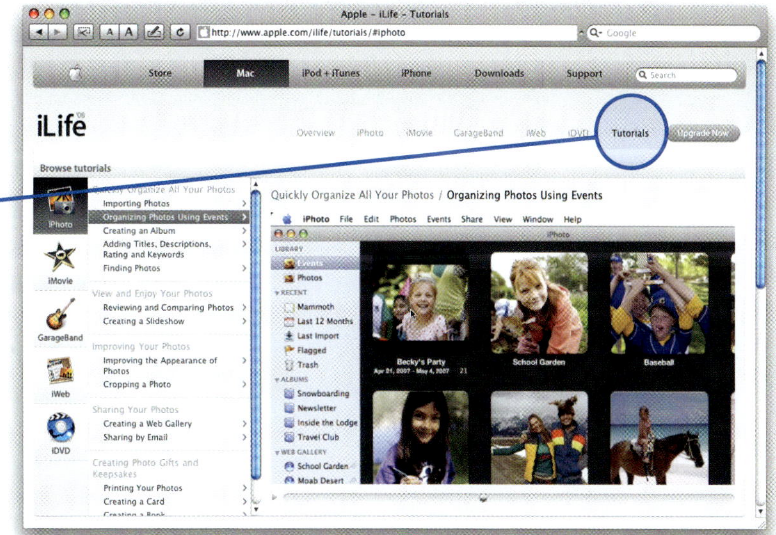

Tip: You can also get to the video tutorials using each iLife program. Just head up to the Help menu and choose the Video Tutorials command. If you're working in one of the iLife programs and want to see a feature in action, that command is your fastest path to the movie theater.

A Short History Lesson

The Macintosh iLife '08 is the sixth edition of a book that was originally called *The Macintosh Digital Hub.* The first edition contained about 120 pages and debuted in 2002—before Apple brought iTunes, iPhoto, iMovie, and iDVD under the iLife umbrella. When that happened, in January 2003, the second edition, renamed *The Macintosh iLife*, appeared.

Since then, a new version of iLife—and a new edition of this book—have become an almost-annual adventure. The book has grown to over 400 pages and become the best-selling book on iLife.

And I couldn't be happier. Apple and the Mac are on a roll, thanks in part to the iLife programs. And I get to spend a healthy (okay, sometimes unhealthy) part of each day listening to music, playing music, taking photos, and making movies: things I've loved since I was a kid.

If you've bought previous editions of this book, thank you and welcome back. If you're new to iLife, you're in for a treat. Watch the video tutorials, dig into the book, check out my Web site, and have *fun.*

Welcome to *The Macintosh iLife '08.*

Introducing
iLife
The Macintosh
iLife '08

Personal Computers Get Personal

Music, photographs, and movies can inspire, amuse, persuade, and entertain. They're time machines that recall people and places. They're vehicles that carry messages into the future. They're ingrained in infancy and become intensely personal parts of our lives. And they've all gone digital.

It's now possible to carry a music library in your pocket, to take photos without film, and to edit video in your den—or on a cross-country flight. It's easier than ever to combine music, images, and video. And it's easy to share your finished product, whether with loved ones in the living room, clients in a conference room, or a global audience on the Internet.

Behind this digital age are breakthroughs in storage technologies, processor speed, chip design, and even in the types of connectors and interfaces used to attach external gear. In the past, personal computers weren't powerful enough to manage the billions of bits that make up digital media. Today, they are.

You might say that personal computers have finally become powerful enough to become truly personal.

Audio

1972
Nippon Columbia Company begins digitally recording master tapes.

1979
Sony's Walkman is the first portable music player.

1982
Billy Joel's *52nd Street* is the first album released on CD.

1988
CDs outsell vinyl albums for the first time.

1989
MP3 audio compression scheme is patented.

Imaging

1969
Bell Labs researchers invent the charge-coupled device (CCD).

1991
Kodak adapts Nikon F-3 camera with 1.3-megapixel CCD.

1994
Apple's QuickTake 100 camera debuts at $699.

1997
The Associated Press switches to digital photography.

1998
1-megapixel cameras proliferate. Online photo sites offer prints and other services.

Video

1956
First videotaped TV program is broadcast.

1967
Sony delivers first portable videotape recorder.

1975
Bell Labs demonstrates CCD TV camera. Sony Betamax debuts.

1983
Sony's Betamovie is the first one-piece camcorder.

1991
Apple's QuickTime 1.0 brings digital video to the Macintosh.

Storage

1956
IBM disk system holds 5 megabytes and uses disks two feet wide.

1973
First hard disk: 30MB on an 8-inch disk platter.

1980
Philips and Sony develop the compact disc standard.

1984
First Mac hard disks store 5MB and cost over $2500.

1992
Apple includes CD-ROM drives with Macs.

Truly Personal Computing

1996
Fraunhofer releases MP3 encoder and player for Windows PCs.

1999
Napster and other Internet services enable swapping of MP3 files.

2001
Apple introduces iPod. First copy-protected audio CDs appear amid controversy.

2003
iTunes Store debuts for Macs and Windows.

2004
Internet radio shows called podcasts begin to proliferate.

2005
iTunes Store ranks among the top ten music retailers for the first time.

2007
Apple, now the third-largest music retailer, introduces the iTunes Wi-Fi Music Store.

1999
2-megapixel cameras, led by Nikon's $999 Coolpix 950, are the rage.

2000
3-megapixel cameras add movie modes. Digital cameras represent 18 percent of camera sales.

2001
Consumer cameras hit 4 megapixels. Digital cameras comprise 21 percent of camera market.

2002
Apple introduces iPhoto. Consumer cameras reach 5 megapixels.

2004
8-megapixel cameras appear as digital cameras outsell film cameras for the first time.

2006
Consumer cameras reach 10 megapixels. Nikon discontinues most of its film cameras.

2007
Apple's iPhone contains a 2-megapixel camera—and so much more—and costs less than 1994's QuickTake 100.

1994
miniDV format debuts: digital audio and video on 6.3 mm wide tape.

1995
FireWire, invented by Apple in the early 90s, is adopted as industry standard.

1999
Apple builds FireWire into Macs and releases iMovie 1.0.

2003
Sony, Canon, and others announce HDV high-definition standard.

2005
iPod gains video playback. Apple sells videos through iTunes.

2006
Google buys online video site YouTube for $1.65 billion.

2007
Tapeless camcorders proliferate; iMovie '08 provides YouTube sharing.

1993
A 1.4GB hard drive costs $4559.

1995
DVD standard is announced.

1999
IBM MicroDrive puts 340MB on a coin-sized platter.

2001
5GB Toshiba hard drive uses 1.8-inch platter; Apple builds it into the new iPod.

2001
Apple begins building SuperDrive DVD burners into Macs.

2005
Some Macs include dual-layer SuperDrives capable of burning over 8GB.

2007
Apple introduces 160GB iPod classic.

A Sampling of the Possibilities

This technological march of progress is exciting because it enables us to do new things with age-old media. I've already hinted at some of them: carrying a music library with you on a portable player, shooting photographs with a digital camera, and editing digital movies.

But the digital age isn't about simply replacing vinyl records, Instamatic cameras, and Super 8 movies. What makes digital technology significant is that it lets you combine various media into messages that are uniquely yours. You can tell stories, sell products, educate, or entertain.

And when you combine these various elements, the whole becomes greater than the sum of its parts.

Go Digital

Pictures That Move

The latest digital video formats have transformed video for amateurs and professionals alike. Shoot sparkling video with stereo sound using a camcorder that fits in the palm of your hand. Transfer your footage to the Mac, then edit to tell your story.

Forget Film

Use a digital camera just once, and you'll never want to go back to film. Review your shots instantly. Delete the ones you don't want. Transfer the keepers to your Mac, and then share them—through the Internet, through CDs and DVDs, and much more.

Bring It All Together

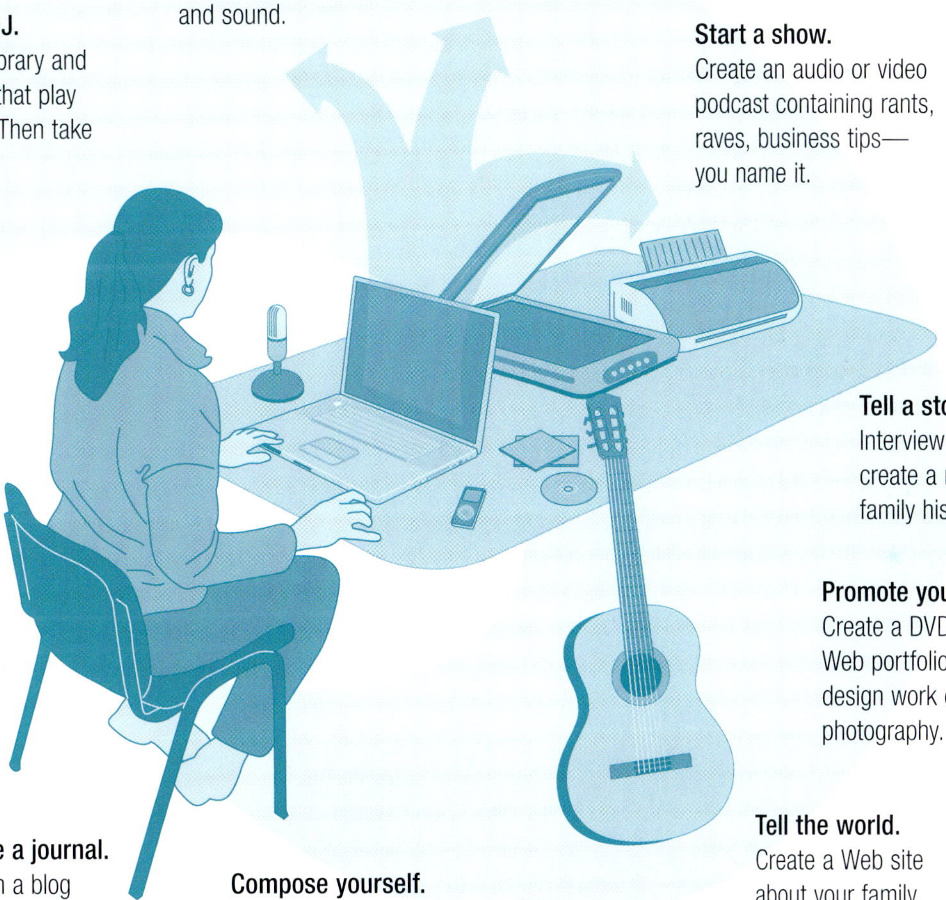

Become a digital DJ.
Assemble a music library and create music mixes that play back your favorites. Then take it all on the road.

Preserve the past.
Relive a vacation with pictures, video, and sound.

Create for the future.
Produce a book that commemorates a baby's first year.

Start a show.
Create an audio or video podcast containing rants, raves, business tips—you name it.

Tell a story.
Interview relatives and create a multimedia family history.

Promote yourself.
Create a DVD or Web portfolio of your design work or photography.

Tell the world.
Create a Web site about your family, company, vacation, or favorite cause.

Gather 'round.
Share photos, videos, and ideas on social networking Web sites, such as YouTube and Flickr.

Compose yourself.
Record your own original music, then use it in your video and DVD productions.

Create a journal.
Publish a blog containing ongoing opinions, tips, or vacation dispatches.

Educate.
Create a training video that teaches a new skill or lets people see your product in action.

Where the Mac Fits In

All of today's personal computers have fast processors, fat hard drives, and the other trappings of power. But powerful hardware is only a foundation. Software is what turns that box of chips into a jukebox, a digital darkroom, a movie studio, a recording studio, and a soapbox with a global audience.

Software is what really makes the Macintosh digital hub go around. Each of Apple's iLife programs—iTunes for music, iPhoto for photography, iMovie for video editing, iDVD for creating DVDs, GarageBand for recording music, iWeb for creating Web sites—greatly simplifies working with, creating, and combining digital media.

Similar programs are available for PCs running Microsoft Windows. But they aren't included with every PC, and they lack the design elegance and simplicity of Apple's offerings. It's simple: Apple's iLife has made the Mac the best personal computer for digital media.

iWeb

- Create Web sites and publish them on Apple's .Mac service
- Publish photo albums from iPhoto
- Publish movies from iMovie
- Create and maintain Web journals (blogs)
- Publish podcasts from GarageBand

iMovie

- Capture video from camcorders
- Edit video and create titles
- Add music soundtracks from iTunes
- Add photographs from iPhoto
- Share video through tapes, DVDs, or the Web

iDVD

- Create slide shows from iPhoto images
- Add music soundtracks from iTunes
- Present video created in iMovie
- Distribute files in DVD-ROM format

GarageBand

- Create songs by assembling loops
- Connect a keyboard to play and record software instruments
- Record vocals, acoustic instruments, and electric guitars
- Create podcasts and add soundtracks to movies
- Transfer your productions to iTunes or iWeb

iTunes

- Convert music CDs into digital music files
- Organize songs into playlists, and burn CDs
- Shop for music, videos, and audiobooks at the iTunes Store
- Transfer music to portable players
- Listen to Internet radio, podcasts, and audiobooks

iPhone and iPod Family

- Carry your favorite songs with you
- Synchronize with your iTunes library
- Connect to stereo system or car audio adapter
- Store contacts, calendars, photos, video, and more
- Use your iPhone or iPod touch to shop at the iTunes Wi-Fi Music Store

iPhoto

- Import photos from digital cameras
- Organize photos into albums
- Crop, modify, and print photos
- Share photos via Web galleries
- Order prints, calendars, cards, and books

No Medium is an Island

Combining multiple media is a key part of audio-visual storytelling—even silent films had soundtracks played on mighty Wurlitzer theater organs.

Combining media is easy with the iLife programs. There's no need to plod through export and import chores to move, say, a photograph from iPhoto into iMovie. That's because the iLife programs have *media browsers* that make it easy to access your music, photos, and movies. The media browsers also have Search boxes to help you find the music track, photo, or movie you want.

You can also move items between programs by simply dragging them. Drag a photo from iPhoto into iMovie, iWeb, GarageBand, or iDVD. Drag a music track from iTunes into iPhoto, iMovie, or iDVD. And when you've finished a hot tune in GarageBand, add it to your iTunes music library with a click of the mouse.

These lines of communication extend beyond iLife, too. For example, Apple's iWork programs also provide media browsers that make it easy to add photos, music, and movies to documents and presentations.

The iLife programs work together in other ways, which I'll describe as we go. In the meantime, think about ways to marry your media and tell a stronger story.

Feel free to browse. With the media browser (iWeb's is shown here), it's easy to access—and combine—audio, photos, and movies.

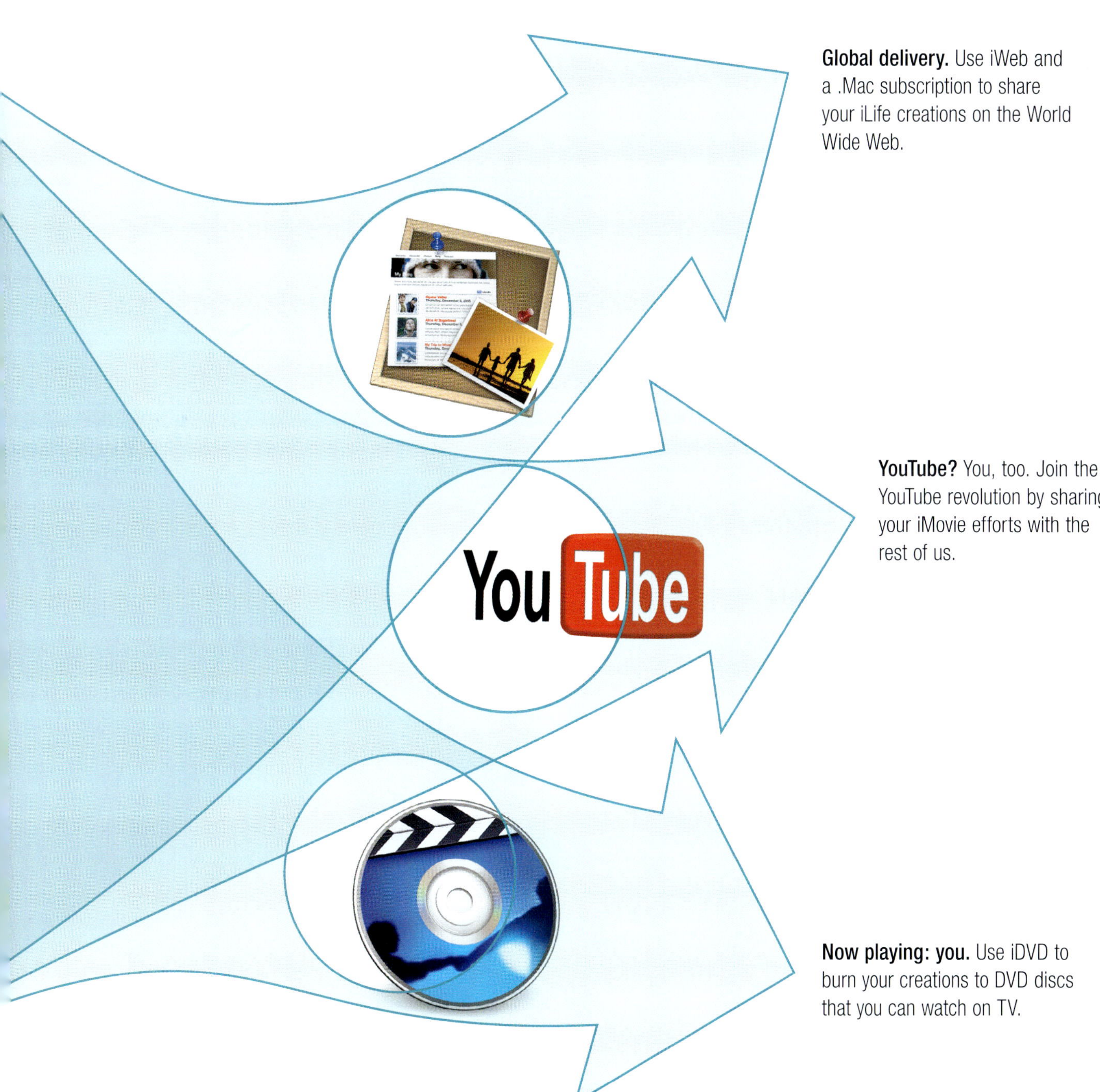

Global delivery. Use iWeb and a .Mac subscription to share your iLife creations on the World Wide Web.

YouTube? You, too. Join the YouTube revolution by sharing your iMovie efforts with the rest of us.

Now playing: you. Use iDVD to burn your creations to DVD discs that you can watch on TV.

iLife Keeps You Connected

It's no secret that the Internet is a great way to stay current—with news, family, and anything else you find interesting.

A relatively new Internet technology makes it even easier to stay current with subjects of interest. It's called *RSS*, and it allows you to *subscribe* to information, called *feeds*, from Web sites and other Internet sources.

Say your hometown newspaper is called *The Banner*, and you're interested in keeping tabs on it. If the newspaper provides an RSS feed, you can subscribe to the feed using the latest versions of Apple's Safari browser or a separate *newsreader* program, such as NetNewsWire (www.ranchero.com).

After you've subscribed to a feed, it's updated at regular intervals—for example, every 30 minutes in Safari. Want to see what's new in the hometown? There's no need to go *The Banner*'s home page. Simply check your RSS feed in Safari. RSS brings the news to you.

What does all this have to do with iLife? Apple has built RSS into several of the iLife programs. As a result, you can subscribe to audio content, you can publish and subscribe to photos, and you can create Web journals (called *blogs*) to which others can subscribe.

I'll cover the details behind RSS and how it relates to iLife '08 throughout this book. Here's an overview of how iLife '08 and RSS work together to keep you current.

Subscribe to Podcasts

A new kind of Internet radio program, the *podcast*, is all the rage. iTunes is your gateway to thousands of podcasts. When you subscribe to a favorite podcast, iTunes downloads new episodes for you whenever they become available.

Use Safari RSS or a newsreader program? Don't forget to subscribe to the feed for this book's companion site at **www.macilife.com**

Publish and Subscribe to Web Galleries

Keep friends and family current with your favorite photos and movies by publishing Web galleries and photo albums. Use an optional password to keep your photos private if you like. You can even allow other people to add their own photos, turning your gallery into a collaborative adventure.

Know someone who's published a Web gallery? Use iPhoto to subscribe to it. The remote photos appear in your iPhoto library, and when the gallery is updated, the latest photos appear in your iPhoto. It can be a lot more fun than emailing photos back and forth.

Publish Audio and Video Podcasts

Use GarageBand and iMovie to create audio or video podcasts, then use iWeb to publish them via Apple's .Mac service so that others can subscribe to them.

Share Video on YouTube

Use iMovie to edit video, then share the final product on YouTube. Your biggest fans can subscribe to your movies.

Create Your Own Blog

Create an online journal: a vacation travelogue, a diary, or daily tips for your business clients. Create it in iWeb, then publish it via Apple's .Mac Internet service. iWeb automatically creates an RSS feed for you, enabling others to subscribe to your blog.

What Does RSS Stand For?

RSS is YACA: yet another computer acronym. Some say it stands for *really simple syndication* while others maintain it stands for *rich site summary.* It doesn't matter. Just as you don't need to know what DVD stands for in order to create or play one, you don't need to know what RSS stands for to enjoy its benefits.

Putting the Pieces Together

Software is important, but so is hardware. Several aspects of the Mac's hardware make it ideally suited to digital media work. All Macs contain fast processors and copious hard drives—essential ingredients for storing and manipulating digital media.

Another factor in the hardware equation is ports: the connection schemes used to attach external devices, such as portable music players, digital cameras, camcorders, printers, and speakers. Every Mac contains all the ports necessary for connecting these and other add-ons.

And finally, the Mac's hardware and software work together smoothly and reliably. This lets you concentrate on your creations, not on your connections.

Here's a quick reference to the ports and connectors you'll use in your journey through iLife.

Audio Line Out

Standard 3.5 mm stereo minijack connects to headphones, amplifiers, and other audio equipment.

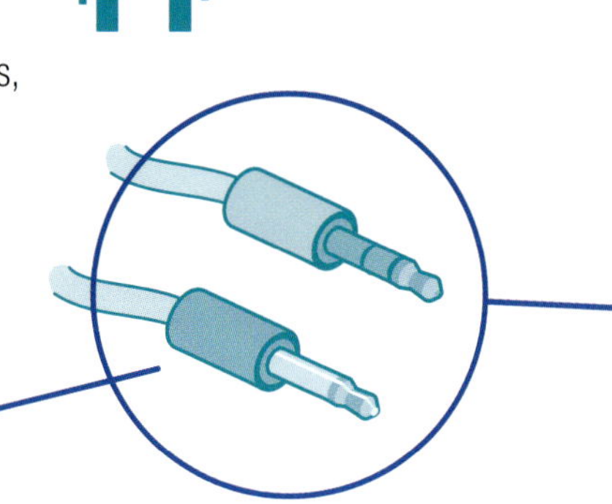

On the iMac shown here, this connector also provides optical digital audio output for connection to home theater and stereo systems (see page 74).

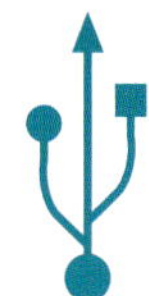

Universal Serial Bus (USB)

Connects to iPods and iPhones, digital cameras, some camcorders, some hard drives, microphones, printers, some music keyboards and interfaces, and other add-ons.

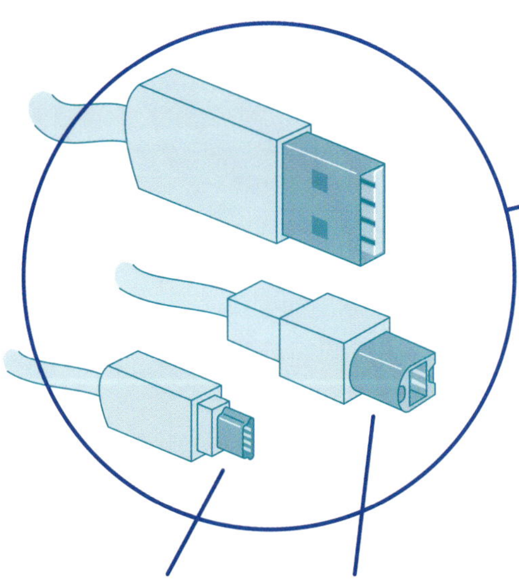

Many digital cameras use this miniature USB connector.

Many printers, scanners, and USB hard drives use this type of connector.

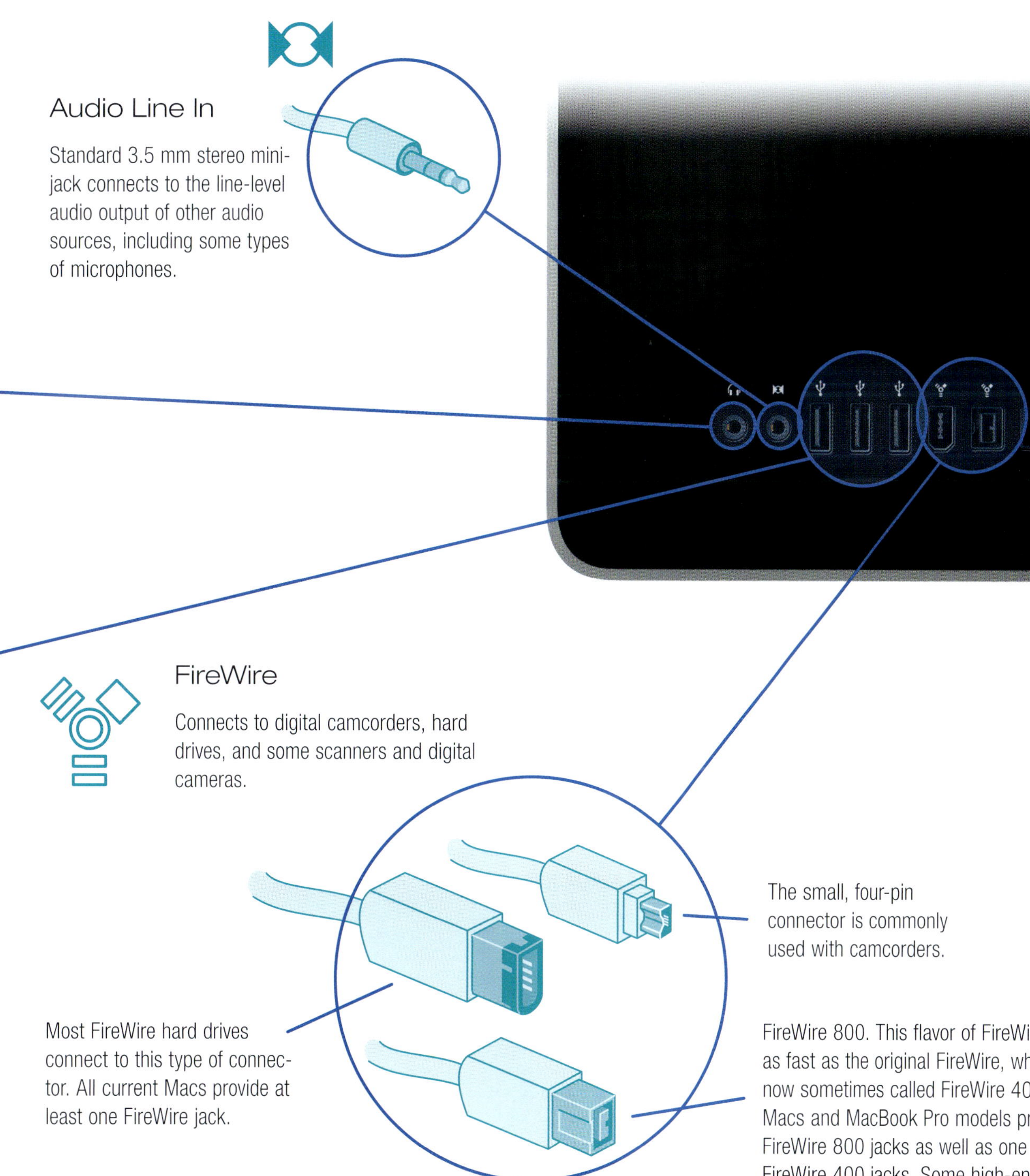

Audio Line In

Standard 3.5 mm stereo mini-jack connects to the line-level audio output of other audio sources, including some types of microphones.

FireWire

Connects to digital camcorders, hard drives, and some scanners and digital cameras.

The small, four-pin connector is commonly used with camcorders.

Most FireWire hard drives connect to this type of connector. All current Macs provide at least one FireWire jack.

FireWire 800. This flavor of FireWire is twice as fast as the original FireWire, which is now sometimes called FireWire 400. Some Macs and MacBook Pro models provide FireWire 800 jacks as well as one or more FireWire 400 jacks. Some high-end external hard drives use FireWire 800.

Outfitting Your Mac for Digital Media

The digital lifestyle is many things, but inexpensive is not one of them. iPods, cameras, camcorders, music keyboards, microphones, accessories of all kinds—spending opportunities abound. Just ask my credit cards.

I explore many of these buying opportunities throughout this book. But first, it's important to ensure that your Mac is well equipped for your iLife endeavors.

With their built-in USB and FireWire ports, today's Macs are able to connect to cameras, portable music players, camcorders, and other digital devices.

But there's always room to grow, especially where digital media are concerned. To get the most out of iLife, consider upgrading several key components of your Mac. At right is a shopping list.

And if you're outfitting an older Mac for iLife '08, consider throwing in a copy of the latest version of Mac OS X. The iLife '08 programs run on Mac OS X 10.4.9 or a later version, but as we'll see in later pages, Mac OS X 10.5 (Leopard) enhances iLife in some significant ways.

To learn more about the latest version of Mac OS X, see www.apple.com/macosx.

Storage in Two Flavors

Digital media takes up space—lots of it. Upgrading your Mac's storage capacity is an essential first step in outfitting it for digital media.

Memory Upgrade. Adding memory is a great way to boost any Mac's overall performance. On a Mac with insufficient memory, programs run slowly, particularly if you're trying to run several at once. Each of the iLife programs can benefit from plenty of memory, but GarageBand in particular will appreciate it.

With all current Mac models, you can install a memory upgrade yourself. If you have a Mac mini, Apple recommends having memory installed by a qualified technician. But if you have dexterous hands and a modicum of bravery, you can do the job yourself.

How much memory should you add? As much as you can afford. A gigabyte (1GB) or more is ideal. Memory is relatively inexpensive, especially compared to the performance benefits it provides—not just in iLife, but in other programs, too.

Hard Drive. All digital media eat up disk space—except for video, which utterly devours it. If you're serious about digital media, you'll want to expand your Mac's storage.

It's easy to do. If you have a tower-style Mac, you can install a second hard drive inside the Mac's case. For iMacs, Mac minis, and laptops, you can connect an external FireWire hard drive—or several of them, if you like.

External FireWire hard drives are available in a wide range of capacities and case sizes. Portable drives are particularly convenient: they fit in a shirt pocket and can draw power from a Mac's FireWire jack—no separate power supply needed. On the downside, though, portable drives cost more than conventional external drives, and they tend to be slower—a big drawback for GarageBand, which greatly benefits from a fast hard drive.

Digital Hubs

The Mac's FireWire connectors are durable, but they aren't indestructible. All that plugging and unplugging of camcorders, hard drives, and other doodads can take its toll. What's more, some Macs have just one FireWire connector, limiting the number of devices you can connect directly to the Mac.

A FireWire hub is an inexpensive add-on that addresses both issues. A hub is to FireWire what a power strip is to a wall outlet: it provides more jacks for your devices. After connecting the hub to your Mac, you can connect several devices to the hub.

You can also buy USB hubs that provide the same expansion benefits for USB devices. Belkin (www.belkin.com) is a major supplier of hubs and accessories of all kinds.

The Right Accounts

In order to buy music from the iTunes Store and order prints and more with iPhoto, you'll want an Apple Account. It's easy to set up; see page 30.

If you're serious about living the iLife, take the next step and subscribe to Apple's .Mac service. Currently $99 per year, .Mac enables you to publish Web galleries with iPhoto as well as Web sites with iWeb. You'll also be able to access Apple's iDisk remote storage service, where you'll find lots of software downloads.

To sign up for .Mac, go to www.mac.com. Unsure whether .Mac is for you? Sign up for a free trial membership.

Sounding Better: Speaker Options

Alfred Hitchcock once said, "In radio, sound is a rather important element." That understatement also applies to iLife. Whether listening to music or creating a narration for a movie, you'll want to hear more sound than your Mac's built-in speaker can reproduce.

You have options aplenty. If your Mac and stereo system are close to each other, you can connect them with a cable and listen through your speakers. You can also use Apple's AirPort Express Base Station or AppleTV to wirelessly beam audio to your stereo. For details on these options, see page 74.

When working at your Mac, you'll want speakers that are directly adjacent to your display. This delivers the most realistic stereo field—and that's essential whether you're mixing a song in GarageBand or just wanting to enjoy your favorite tunes while you type.

Several companies sell speaker systems designed for use with computers. Harman Multimedia (www.harman-multimedia.com) sells a large selection under the venerable Harman/Kardon and JBL names. Another highly regarded audio brand, Bose (www.bose.com), also sells speaker systems designed for computers and portable music players. Most systems include a *subwoofer* that sits under your desk and provides a deep, gut-punching bass.

If you're a GarageBand musician, you might prefer a set of *monitor* speakers, whose frequency response is superior to that of typical computer speakers. For my GarageBand setup, I use a pair of Yamaha MSP5 monitors. At about $500 a pair, they're pricey by computer speaker standards, but inexpensive by studio monitor standards. And they sound great—beefier and truer than a pair of inexpensive computer speakers and a subwoofer. For reviews of numerous monitor speakers, see www.emusician.com/speakers.

iTunes and iPod: Music and More

The Macintosh
iLife '08

iTunes at a Glance

iTunes is your gateway to music, audiobooks, Internet radio programs, TV shows, movies, music videos, and much more.

With iTunes, you can create digital music files from your favorite audio CDs. You can buy and download music, videos, and more from the iTunes Store. You can create your own music mixes by creating playlists. And you can listen to your playlists on your Mac, burn them onto CDs, or transfer them to an iPod portable music player.

When iTunes debuted in 2001, it was a relatively simple digital music jukebox. Since then, iTunes has evolved into the computer industry's leading gateway to digital media. In 2005, the iTunes Store was the seventh-ranked music retailer in the United States—ahead of giants, such as Tower Records and Sam Goody—and it was the first time an online music service ever appeared among the top ten. By 2007, the iTunes Store had pulled ahead of Amazon and Target to become the third-largest music retailer in the US.

iTunes is also the control center for the Apple iPhone: you use iTunes to activate a new iPhone and to manage the contents of an iPhone. With the runaway success of the iPod family and with Apple continuing to add new forms of media to the iTunes Store, iTunes seems poised to remain the dominant digital jukebox.

Anybody have a quarter?

The arrow buttons skip to the previous or next song in a playlist.

Play/Pause (keyboard shortcut: spacebar).

Adjusts the volume (keyboard shortcut: ⌘-up arrow and ⌘-down arrow).

The library holds your music, videos (page 32), podcasts (page 34), audiobooks (page 92), and ringtones (page 44).

Listen to Internet radio stations (page 70).

Shop at the iTunes Store (page 28).

Use the Party Shuffle playlist to have iTunes quickly create a mix for you (page 83).

Add songs to playlists to control their playback order and create your own music mixes (page 46). Use smart playlists (⚙) to have iTunes create playlists for you (page 52).

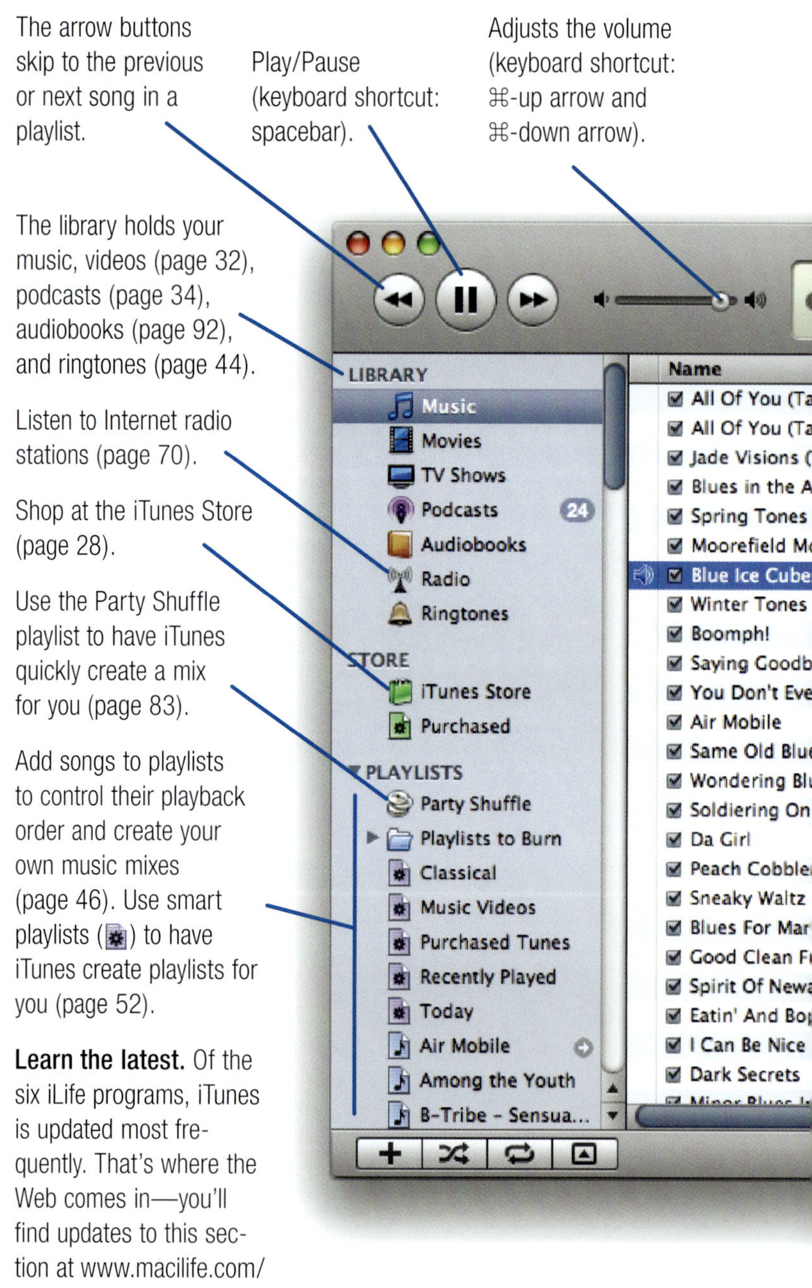

Learn the latest. Of the six iLife programs, iTunes is updated most frequently. That's where the Web comes in—you'll find updates to this section at www.macilife.com/itunes.

Click this tiny button to switch between song information and a flashy animation.

Share your playlists with iMix playlist publishing (page 50).

To view the song's album, click the artist name.

Drag the diamond left or right to skim through whatever is playing.

Display related songs in the iTunes Store (page 30) or your library (page 57).

To quickly locate the currently playing song, click the SnapBack button (page 81).

View your iTunes library in several ways (page 66).

Use the Search box to quickly locate items in your library (page 56) or the iTunes Store (page 29).

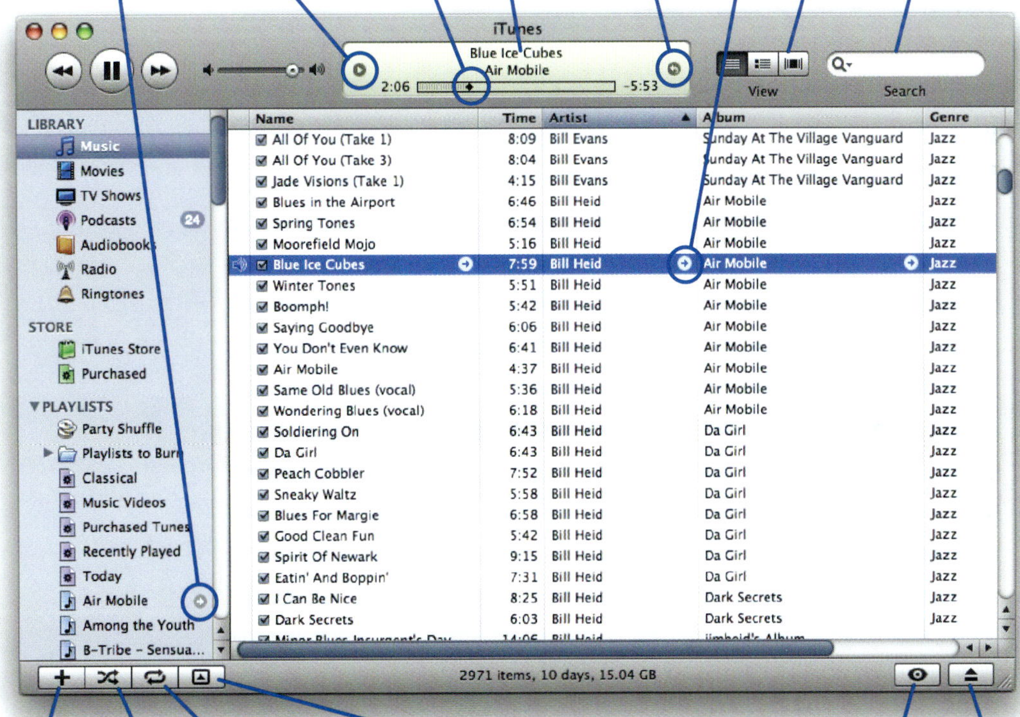

Click to add a new playlist (page 46). Option-click to create a smart playlist (page 52).

To have iTunes play songs in random order, click this shuffle button (page 82).

Click once to have iTunes repeat a set of songs over and over. Click twice to repeat the currently playing song over and over.

You can store album artwork along with each song and display it by clicking this button (page 65). Videos can also play in this area (page 32).

Opens your Mac's CD tray.

Use the Browse button to view your music by artist and album (page 57).

When you've selected a playlist, the Burn Disc button appears (page 60).

Importing Music from CDs

The first step in stocking your digital jukebox might be a sprint to the iTunes Store to start buying and downloading (page 28). But if you have a library of music CDs, you'll want to invite them to the party, too.

It's easy to add CDs to your iTunes library—a process often called *ripping*. Insert a compact disc into your Mac's CD drive, and iTunes launches, connects to the Internet, and retrieves the name of the CD and its tracks. Click the Import CD button, and iTunes converts the CD's contents into digital music files that are stored on your Mac's hard drive.

That's the big picture. You can create a vast digital music library with iTunes without having to know any more than that. But iTunes has several features that give you more control over the ripping process. You can, for example, specify that iTunes import only certain songs—no need to waste disk space by storing songs you don't like.

And as I describe on the following pages, you can choose to store the tracks that you import in a variety of formats, each with its own advantages and drawbacks. But don't feel obligated to delve into those details if you don't want to. Feel free to skip on to page 28 after you've mastered the ripping three-step: insert, import, eject.

Importing a CD

Step 1. Insert the CD into your Mac's optical drive. iTunes asks if you'd like to import it. Click Yes or press the Return key.

Step 2. To import all the tracks on the CD, click Yes or press Return. (To control which tracks iTunes imports, click No, then see the notes below.) As iTunes imports, it displays a status message. To cancel the import, click the X.

When iTunes finishes, it plays a little beep.

Step 3. Eject the CD: press your keyboard's Eject key or click the Eject button (⏏) in the corner of the iTunes window or next to the CD's name.

Notes and Tips

Being selective. Don't want to import every track? Uncheck tracks you don't want. **Tip:** To uncheck all tracks, press ⌘ while clicking any track's check box.

10	☐ Things We Said Today	2:39	The Beatles
11	☑ When I Get Home	2:18	The Beatles
12	☐ You Can't Do That	2:38	The Beatles
13	☑ I'll Be Back	2:21	The Beatles

To import the remaining songs, click the Import CD button.

Dragging tracks. You can also import tracks by dragging them to the Library area in the left side of the iTunes window.

Joining tracks to eliminate gaps. In some cases, you might not want a gap of silence between songs. For example, the songs on a CD might be composed so that one flows seamlessly into the next.

You can prevent gaps between two or more songs by importing the songs as joined tracks. Select the tracks, then choose Join CD Tracks from the Advanced menu. iTunes will import the tracks as one file. If you decide to not join the tracks after all, choose Unjoin CD Tracks from the Advanced menu.

Note that you can't join tracks that you've already imported.

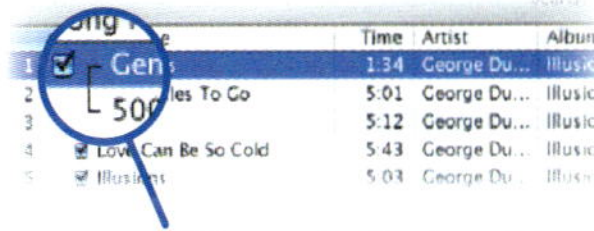

iTunes indicates joined tracks with a bracket.

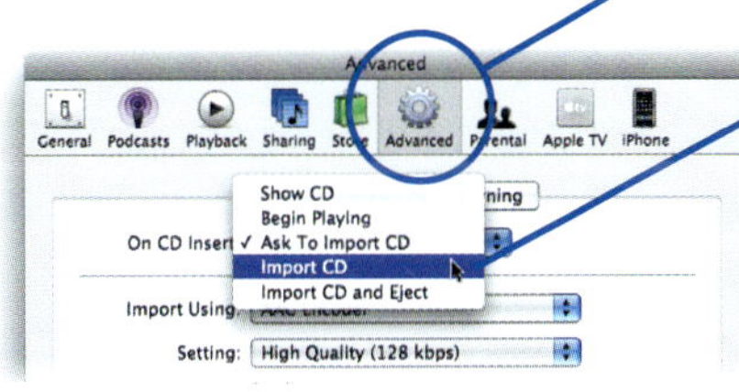

Power ripping. Doing some binge ripping?

Save yourself time and set up iTunes to automatically begin importing as soon as you insert a CD. Choose Preferences from the iTunes menu, then click the Advanced button.

Next, click the Importing button. Finally, choose Import Songs or, better yet, Import Songs and Eject.

Where iTunes Stores Your Tunes

iTunes stores your library in your Music folder. The fastest way to locate the Music folder is to choose Home from the Finder's Go menu. The Music folder also appears in the sidebar of Finder windows.

You don't have to venture inside the Music folder—indeed, you should always add and remove songs and other items to and from your library by using iTunes itself, not by dragging files into and out of the Music folder.

iTunes Library

If you're curious, here's how the Music folder is organized. The Music folder contains another folder named iTunes, and inside *this* folder is a file named iTunes Library. This file contains a database of all the songs you've added to iTunes, as well as all the playlists you've created. But it doesn't contain the song files themselves; those files live in the folder named iTunes Music.

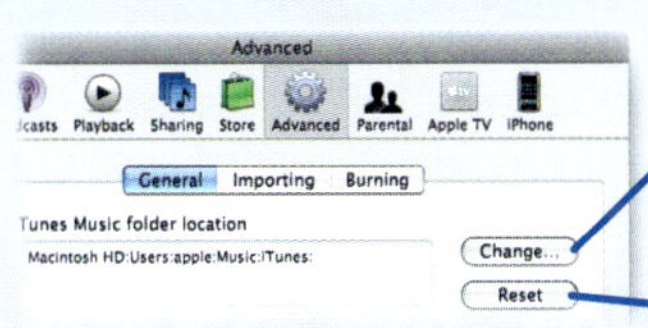

To tell iTunes where to store your music, click Change.

To restore the default location, click Reset.

Note that you don't have to store your music in the Music folder. You might want to store it elsewhere—on a portable hard drive, for example. To specify a different location for your music library, choose Preferences from the iTunes menu, click the Advanced button, and then specify the desired location. (For more iTunes library tips, see page 86.)

Note: If you've been using iTunes for a while, you may find older music library files in your iTunes folder. These files will be stashed in a folder named Previous iTunes Libraries. It's safe to delete these older library files.

Choosing an Audio Format

The factory settings that iTunes uses for importing music from CDs are perfectly fine for most music lovers and listening scenarios. So if you'd rather explore some of the more musical and less technical aspects of iTunes, feel free to skip to page 28. But if you're an audiophile or are just curious, read on for a look at how audio compression works—and at how you can adjust the way iTunes applies it.

CD-quality stereo sound requires about 10MB of disk space per minute. By using *compression*, iTunes can lower audio's appetite for storage by a factor of 10 or more. Most audio-compression schemes use something called *perceptual encoding*, which eliminates those portions of an audio signal that our ears don't hear well anyway. Because some information is lost in the process, this form of compression is called *lossy*.

iTunes supports two lossy compression schemes: MP3, the format that helped fuel the Internet music revolution; and a newer method called AAC (short for *Advanced Audio Coding*). Each scheme has advantages and drawbacks.

iTunes also offers a lossless compression scheme called *Apple Lossless* encoding. It doesn't provide nearly as much compression as MP3 or AAC—files are only about half the size of the original. But true to its name, Apple Lossless imposes no quality loss. If you're a golden-eared audiophile with plenty of hard-drive space, you might prefer to rip your CDs using the Apple Lossless encoder.

Changing Importing Settings

From the factory, iTunes is set up to encode in AAC format. By adjusting the Importing options in the Preferences dialog box, you can change the encoding settings to arrive at your own ideal balance between sound quality, storage requirements, and listening plans.

Step 1. Choose Preferences from the iTunes menu.

Step 2. Click the Advanced button.

Step 3. In the Advanced preferences area, click the Importing button.

Encoder Options at a Glance

Encoder	Comments
AAC	Best balance between sound quality and small file size.
MP3	Not as efficient as AAC, but broadly compatible with non-Apple portable players and computer systems.
Apple Lossless	Creates much larger files than the MP3 or AAC encoders, but with no audio quality loss. Files won't play on iPod shuffle or older iPods.
WAV and AIFF	Create uncompressed files that use 10MB of disk space per minute. (AIFF, which stands for Audio Interchange File Format, is a standard audio format on the Mac; WAV is its equivalent on Windows. Both formats are broadly supported on Macs and Windows computers.)

Step 4. Adjust importing settings as shown here.

Fine-tune compression settings (page 24).

Want to listen while you rip? Check this box.

Check this box, and iTunes adds a number to each digital music file—for example, *01 Blues on the Road.* This can help when burning MP3-format CDs (page 62), and it lets you see tracks in their correct sequence when viewing files in the Finder.

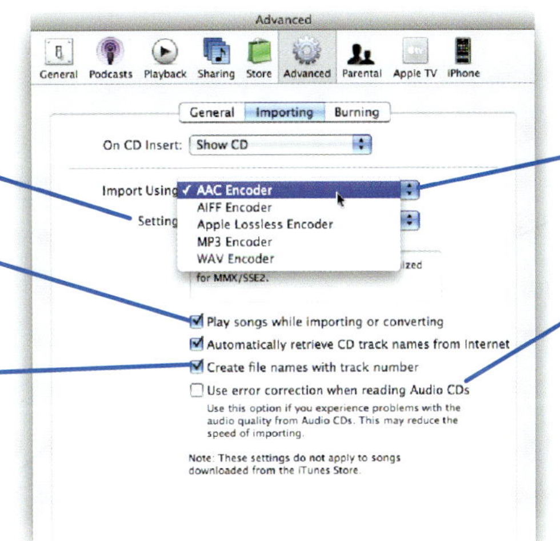

Specify the format you'd like iTunes to use when importing.

If a song that you've imported has audible pops or clicks, consider checking this box and then importing the song again.

AAC: More Bang for the Byte

You want the storage efficiency that a lossy encoder provides. Should you rip your CDs using the AAC encoder or the MP3 encoder? If you'll always use iTunes, an iPod, and the other iLife programs to play music, by all means use AAC—I do.

Here's why. Audio compression is measured in terms of *bit rate*, the average number of bits required for one second of sound. To obtain near CD-quality audio, MP3 requires a bit rate in the range of 128 to 192 kilobits per second (kbps). Higher bit rates mean less compression and better sound quality.

AAC is more efficient than MP3—it does a smarter job of encoding music, which means you can use lower bit rates and still get great sound quality. Audiophiles love to argue the fine points, but to most ears, a 128 kbps AAC file sounds at least as good as an MP3 file encoded at 160 kbps.

What does this mean to you? If you use AAC when importing CDs, you'll use disk space more efficiently. This can help you shoehorn a mammoth music library onto an iPod.

The downside to AAC? Your music files might not play on non-Apple portable players. (Yes, there are some out there.)

There's one more reason you might consider using MP3 instead of AAC. If you plan to burn CDs in MP3 format, as described on page 62, you should rip your music in MP3 format.

One more thing. As page 28 describes, the iTunes Store delivers its tracks in AAC format. The AAC music you buy usually contains some copying restrictions. But AAC files that you rip from your own CDs contain no such restrictions.

Mix and match. The beauty of the digital music world is that you don't have to choose just one format for your music library. This isn't a replay of the VHS-versus-Betamax wars. Use whichever formats best suit your ears, disk space, and listening goals.

Fine-Tuning Compression Settings

Adjusting MP3 Settings

iTunes is set up to encode MP3 at a bit rate of 160 kbps. To change the bit rate and other MP3 settings, choose Custom from the Setting pop-up menu.

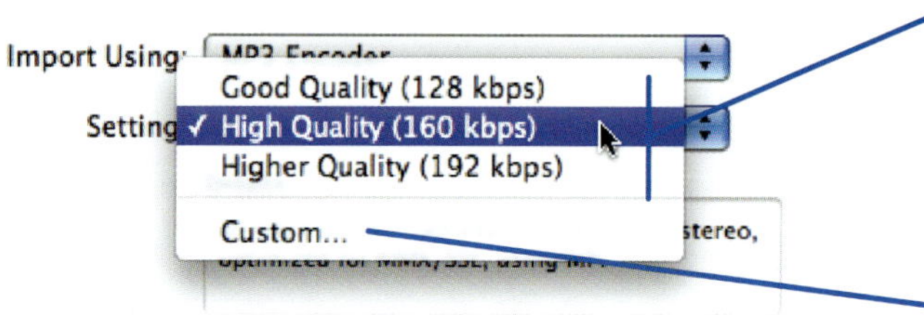

128 kbps is closer to FM-radio quality than to CD quality—you may notice a swirling quality to instruments that produce high frequencies, such as strings and cymbals. 192 kbps delivers better quality than 160 kbps, although my ears have trouble detecting the difference.

To explore the kinds of adjustments MP3 allows for, choose Custom to display the dialog box shown below. See below for custom setting choices.

Variable bit rate (VBR) encoding varies a song's bit rate according to the complexity of the sound. For example, a quiet passage with a narrow range of frequencies is less "demanding" than a loud passage with a broad range of frequencies. VBR uses disk space more efficiently and, according to many MP3 fans, sounds better, too. Many MP3 users turn on VBR and then lower the bit rate—for example, encoding at 128 kbps with VBR instead of at 160 kbps without VBR.

Specify the bit rate here.

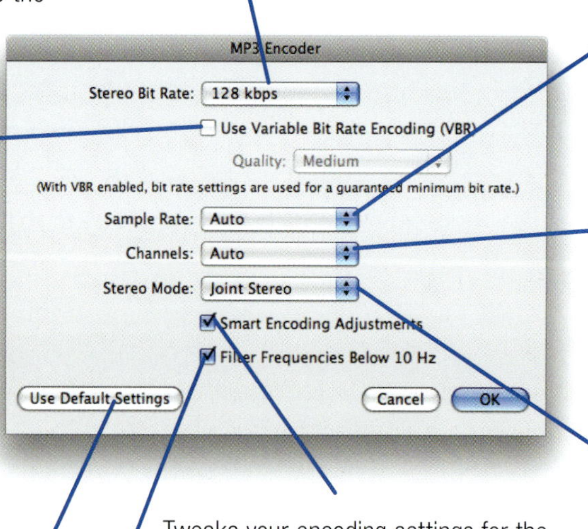

For most uses, leave this menu set to Auto. If you're encoding a voice recording, however, you can save disk space by lowering the sample rate to 22.050 KHz or even 11.025 KHz.

In the Auto setting, iTunes detects whether the original recording is in stereo or mono. To force iTunes to encode in mono—for example, to save disk space—choose Mono.

Our ears have trouble discerning where high frequencies are coming from. Joint Stereo encoding exploits this phenomenon by combining high frequencies into a single channel, saving disk space. Careful listeners say they can sometimes hear a difference in the spatial qualities of a recording.

Tweaks your encoding settings for the best quality given the bit rate settings you've specified. You can usually leave this box checked, but if you're a control freak who doesn't want iTunes making adjustments for you, uncheck it.

Restores iTunes' original settings.

iTunes will filter out inaudible, low frequencies. Leave this one checked.

Adjusting AAC Settings

iTunes is set up to encode AAC at a bit rate of 128 kbps. To change the bit rate, choose Custom from the Setting pop-up menu, then choose the desired bit rate.

Some audiophiles say VBR improves audio quality. Let your ears be the judge. (For an overview of VBR, see the opposite page.)

Filters the audio to enhance voice recordings. Avoid this option for music.

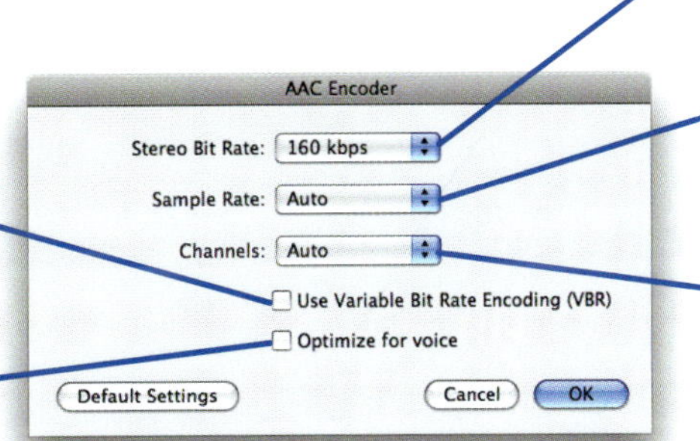

Choose the desired bit rate. Lower bit rates yield smaller files and poorer sound quality.

You can choose a 44.1 KHz or 48 KHz sample rate. Use the Auto setting: iTunes encodes to match the original recording.

You can choose to encode in mono or stereo. Use the Auto setting: iTunes detects whether the original recording is monophonic or stereophonic, and encodes to match.

Converting from MP3 to AAC and Apple Lossless

iTunes can convert existing MP3s to AAC, but you'll lose quality in the process. That's because both AAC and MP3 are lossy formats: each discards audio information in order to save disk space. Thus, when an MP3 file is compressed with AAC, the lossiness is compounded.

Bottom line: to take advantage of AAC's space savings, re-rip your original CDs instead of recompressing existing MP3s.

This re-ripping requirement also applies if you want to take advantage of the Apple Lossless encoder. You can't convert an MP3 (or an AAC) file into Apple Lossless and gain the quality benefits of the latter—the sonic damage has already been done.

iTunes has some smarts that make re-ripping less laborious: if you re-rip a CD that iTunes already has in its library, iTunes tells you that the songs have already been imported and asks if you want to import them again. Thus, you're spared from having to rebuild your playlists, retype any song information, or manually delete your old MP3s.

Note: If you've edited a song's information—changed its name or that of the artist or album as described on page 26—iTunes won't recognize that you're importing it again, and you'll end up with two copies of the same song.

To avoid this, make the same edits before you import the CD, or edit the song information of the existing MP3s to match that of the audio CD. Or just make a mental note to delete the old MP3 files after re-ripping.

To replace the existing MP3 version, click Replace Existing.

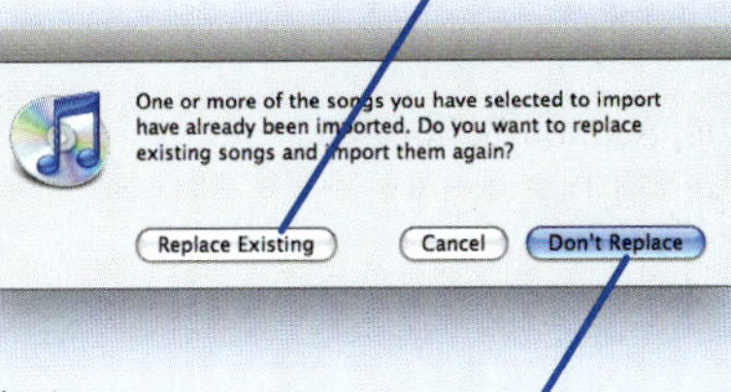

To import the CD without replacing the MP3 versions, click Don't Replace. You'll end up with two versions of each song.

Editing Song Information

A digital music file holds more than just music. It also holds information about the music: the song's name, the name of the artist who recorded it, the year it was recorded, and more. These tidbits of information are sometimes referred to as *tags*.

There may be times when you'll want to edit this information. Maybe the song is from an obscure CD that iTunes can't identify, and iTunes has given its tracks generic names like *Track 5*. (This also happens if you rip a CD when not connected to the Internet.)

Or maybe a particular artist is listed in slightly different ways on different CDs—for example *Bill Evans* and *Bill Evans Trio*. When you transfer those songs to your iPod, you'll have two separate listings in the Artist view—even though both listings refer to the same artist.

For situations like these, you can use iTunes' Get Info command to edit the information of one or more songs. First, select the song whose attributes you want to edit, and then choose Get Info from the File menu, or press ⌘-I.

You can also edit song information directly within the iTunes window: simply select the song and then click on the item you want to edit.

To edit a song's information, click Info (see opposite page).

Customize how iTunes sorts the song (page 87).

Change equalization, volume, and other playback settings here (see pages 58 and 81).

Add and remove album artwork here (see page 65).

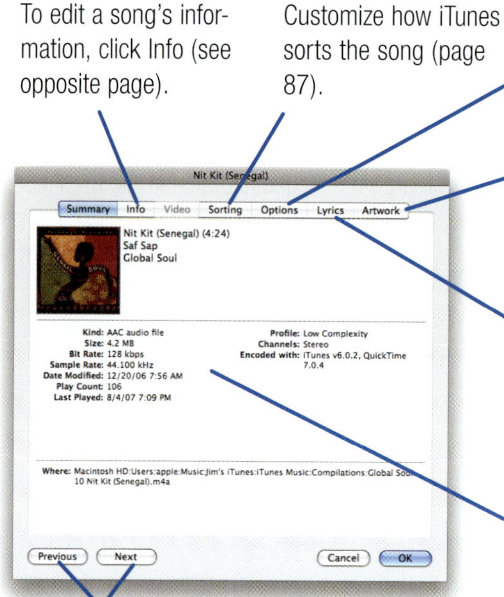

The latest iPods can store and display lyrics (see page 113). Store those words here.

Information about how the song is encoded appears here.

Need to edit information for multiple songs? Rather than repeatedly choosing Get Info, just click Previous to display information for the previous song (the one above the current song in iTunes' window) or Next to get info for the next song.

Keyboard control. Editing a lot of information? Don't reach for the mouse. Press ⌘-P and ⌘-N to "click" the Previous and Next buttons, and ⌘-[and ⌘-] to move between each pane of the dialog box.

Fixing "Anonymous" Music Tracks

You've ripped a few audio CDs while on a cross-country flight. Since you didn't have Internet access, iTunes wasn't able to retrieve album and song information, and now you have songs named Track 01, Track 02, and so on.

Must you venture into the Song Information dialog box to manually enter album, song, and artist information? Of course not. Simply connect to the Internet, select those "anonymous" tracks, and then choose Get CD Track Names from the Advanced menu. iTunes connects to the Internet and retrieves the information you crave.

Tips for Editing Song Information

To edit information for a song, click the Info button in the song information dialog box. While many of the items in the Info area are self-explanatory, some aren't. Let's take a look.

As you delve into this dialog box, keep in mind that you don't have to play by the rules. For example, you can store *any* piece of text in the Composer field—iTunes won't complain. Feel free to use the more obscure items in this dialog box to describe and categorize your music library as you see fit. Your efforts will pay off when you start creating smart playlists (described on page 52).

Edit the most important song information here.

On many CDs, some tracks are related to each other. For example, a classical CD may contain two Mozart symphonies, with tracks 1 through 4 representing one work and tracks 5 through 8 representing the second work. You can use the Grouping box to store this kind of information: in the Mozart example, you might select tracks 1 through 4, choose Get Info, and then type the name of the work here. But the fact is, you can store whatever information you like here—the names of soloists who play on a given track, or even a subgenre, such as *smooth jazz* or *Euro techno*.

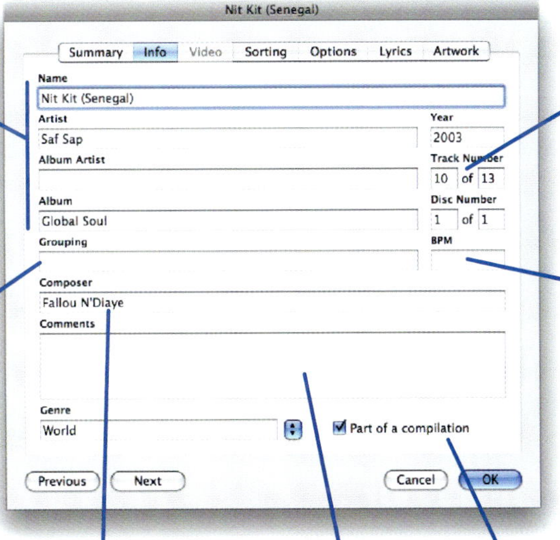

With some genres—particularly classical—a work's composer is at least as important as the name of the artist who performed it. You can use the Composer field to hold any information, but it's intended for storing the name of the person who composed a given piece. On the iPod, you can browse by composer.

Use the Comments box to hold anything you like: a list of musicians, the record label's name, the city where it was recorded, the name of its recording engineer—or just comments such as *This song rocks!* When creating smart playlists, you can search for part or all of a comment.

To force tracks to play in a different order, edit the track numbers. (Playlists are generally better for customizing playback order, though; see page 46.)

BPM stands for *beats per minute*—this field is designed to hold a numeric value that corresponds to how many beats per minute are in a song. DJs can use this information when compiling smart playlists. Don't know the exact tempo of a song? Some iTunes users create codes that represent a song's tempo: 1 for a ballad, 2 for a medium-tempo song, 3 for an up-tempo song, and so on. If you use a scheme like this, you can use smart playlists to gather and play songs in a similar tempo range.

Indicates that the song is part of a compilation; when browsing, you can have iTunes display a Compilations category to make it easy to find albums featuring multiple artists (see page 86).

Shopping at the iTunes Store

At the iTunes Store, you can search for, browse, audition, and buy music, music videos, TV shows, and more. Wander the store's virtual aisles or search for specific items. Check out 30-second clips of your finds. Buy entire albums, or just the songs you want. iTunes downloads your purchases into your music library, from which you can add them to playlists, burn them to CDs, and transfer them to an iPod or iPhone.

You can use the store with any kind of Internet connection, but a high-speed connection—for example, a cable modem or DSL line—works best. Music takes a long time to download over a slow modem connection—and videos take forever.

Have an iPhone or iPod touch? Get yourself in range of a Wi-Fi wireless network. With the iTunes Wi-Fi Music Store, you can browse and buy even when you're away from your Mac. iTunes transfers your purchases to your Mac the next time you connect your iPhone or iPod touch (see page 102).

Before you can buy, you must set up an account by providing billing information and creating a password. Once that's done, you can buy with a couple of mouse clicks.

The music you buy is stored in AAC format and is tied to your account in ways that guard against the piracy that pervades the MP3 scene. And yet you still have plenty of freedom to burn CDs and move your music between computers.

Let's go shopping.

Getting Set Up: Signing In

Step 1: Step into the Store

Be sure you're connected to the Internet, then click the iTunes Store item. iTunes connects to the store. You can browse and search at this point, but you can't buy until you sign in.

Step 2: Sign In

To sign in, click the Sign In button in the upper-right corner of the store, then complete the dialog box below.

If you don't have an Apple account, click Create New Account and then supply your billing information.

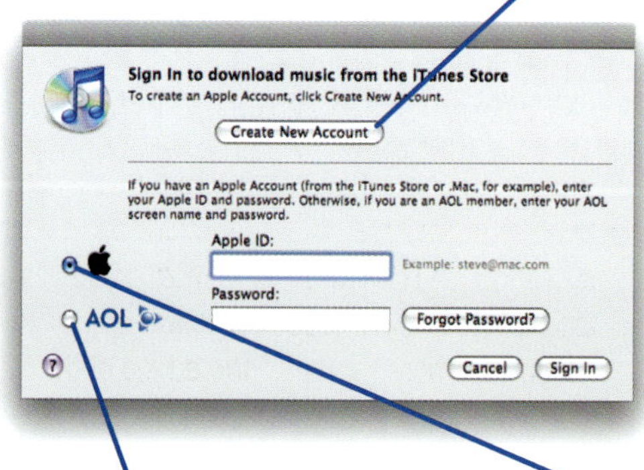

If you're an America Online subscriber, you can charge your purchases to your AOL account. Click AOL, specify your screen name and password, then click Sign In.

If you're a .Mac member, have purchased from the Apple online store in the past, or have ordered prints or books through iPhoto, you already have an Apple account. Specify your ID and password here, then click Sign In.

The iTunes Store at a Glance

Search the store. For example, type the name of a song, artist, or album, then press the Return key. (For more searching tips, see page 31.)

The Quick Links box is a fast way to get where you (often) want to go.

What's everyone else buying? Top downloads appear along the sides of the store.

Each department's home page lists new releases, usually in several categories. To see all recent new releases, click See All.

Browse by genre, artist, and album (page 31).

Navigate within the store (see below).

Each department has its own home page sporting new releases, top downloads, featured items, and more.

Featured items appear in these virtual aisles. To move within an aisle, click the blue arrows at the edges of the aisle.

Getting Around in the Store

The navigation bar changes as you move within the store; click the buttons to jump to areas that relate to what's on your screen.

Go back or forward one screen (keyboard shortcuts: ⌘-[and ⌘-]).

Go to the store's home screen.

The current genre; click it to go to that genre's main screen.

To go to the current artist's discography, click the artist's name.

The album you're currently viewing. (I highly recommend this one, by my brother!)

From Browsing to Buying

Once you've created an account and signed in, you're ready to shop at the iTunes Store. You might start by browsing the store's virtual aisles, clicking on the little album thumbnail images or the text links around them. (The links are underlined when you point to them.)

You might jump to a different music genre by clicking its link, or head to a different department to browse TV shows or music videos. You might use the Browse button to quickly see what's available. Or you might use the Power Search option to home in on exactly what you're looking for.

The end result of any searching or browsing session is a list of items—songs, TV show episodes, music videos, and so on. Here's where you can play previews, locate related items, and most important, buy and download your finds so you can start enjoying them.

Working with an Item List

You've searched or browsed your way to a list of songs, TV shows, or other items. What happens next is up to you.

If you arrived at this list by doing a search, you can narrow down the search results—for example, to see just music—by clicking these options.

Go elsewhere: Click an album name or photo to display its songs. Click an artist name for a discography. Click the genre name to go to that genre.

Play a preview: Double-click an item to hear (or watch) a sample.

See more: In the Artist column, click the arrow for the artist's main page.

Drill down: In the Album column, click the arrow to show the entire album.

Buying an Item

Find something? Here's how to make it yours.

Step 1. Click the Buy button.

Step 2. If iTunes asks for your ID and password, supply them.

Step 3. iTunes asks if you really want to buy the item; click Buy. (To avoid this query in the future, click the check box in the message.)

The item begins to download. For tips on managing downloads, see page 41.

To Shop Faster, Browse

If you're the type who heads for a mall directory instead of wandering around, try the store's browse mode, where you can quickly home in on genres, sub-genres, artists, and albums. Browsing is efficient, and because it discards graphics in favor of all-text displays, it's fast. Browsing is also the only way to see a complete list of all artists, genres, and so on.

Step 1. With the store displayed, click the Browse button ( ).

Step 2. Choose a genre, then a sub-genre (if appropriate), then an artist.

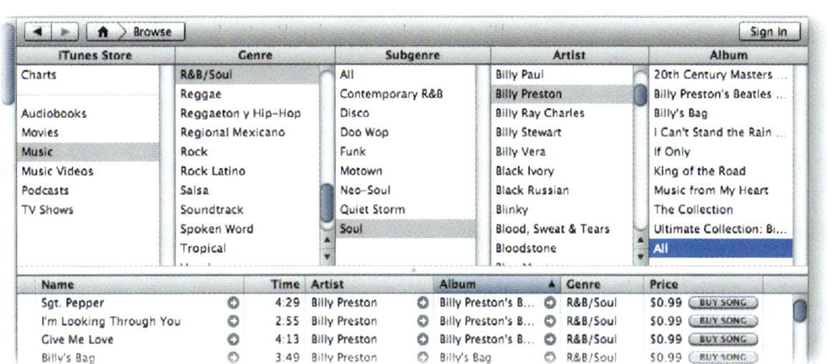

Power Searching

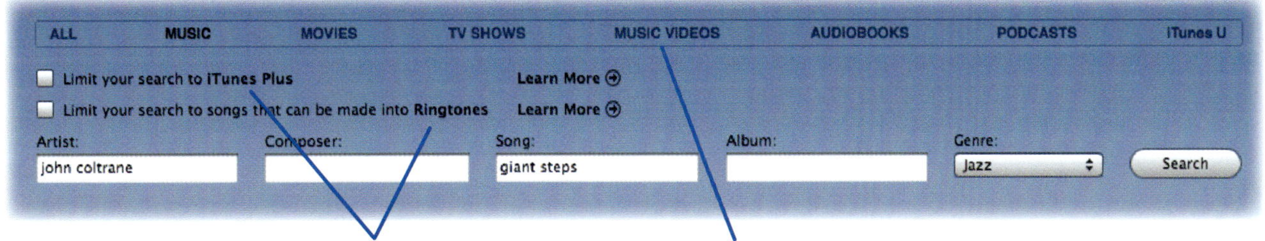

With the store's Power Search feature, you can specify multiple search criteria at once—for example, to search for only those versions of *Giant Steps* performed by John Coltrane.

You can choose to search only those songs that are available in the higher-quality iTunes Plus format (page 40) and that are available as iPhone ringtones (page 44).

You can also focus your search on specific media (for example, just music or just TV shows).

Step 1. Click the Power Search link (Power Search), or choose Search from the Store menu.

Step 2. Specify your search criteria and click Search.

Buying and Watching Videos

The iTunes Store is about more than music. You can also buy video: music videos, TV shows, short films, comedy performances, and more.

Buying videos is a lot like buying music. Browse your way to a video or do a search for a specific video. Watch a preview if you like; it appears right within the iTunes window. Like what you see? Click the Buy button, and iTunes downloads your video and adds it to your library. At this writing, most videos cost $1.99 each. Some TV shows are available on a $9.99 per month subscription basis called a *multi-pass*.

You can use iTunes to watch your videos at your desk—or at 30,000 feet. You can also copy videos to an iPhone or any iPod with video capabilities. Or add an Apple TV (page 78) and watch them on your TV set.

Let's go channel surfing.

Finding Videos

You can locate videos in a few ways.

Wander. Click the links on the music store's home screen.

Browse. You can also use the Browse mode described on the previous pages. As with music, browsing is a fast, efficient way to quickly get a glimpse of everything that's available.

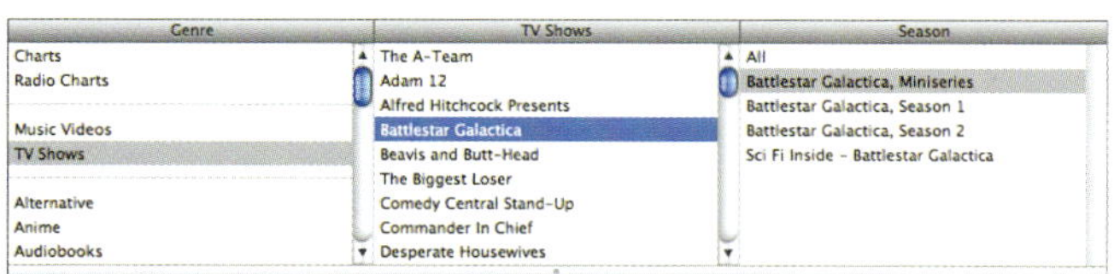

Search. You can use the Search box to search for a specific show or video. If your search results contain too many songs and other non-video items, click one of the video-related buttons to narrow down the list of results.

You can also use the Power Search feature to home in on video content. In the Power Search window, click one of the video-related options—for example, Music Videos or TV Shows.

Previewing What You Find

As with music, you can check out a short preview of a video by double-clicking the video's name.

Tips for Watching Videos

Where to watch. Normally, iTunes plays videos within its window. If you resize the iTunes window by dragging its lower-right corner, the video grows or shrinks accordingly.

To start and stop playback, press the spacebar or click the play/pause button. To skip around in the video, drag the little diamond-shaped playhead marker. To return the iTunes window to its normal display, press the Esc key.

If you move the mouse pointer into the video area during playback, controls appear that let you expand to a full-screen view or cancel playback.

You can customize how iTunes plays video. Choose iTunes > Preferences, then click the Playback button in the Preferences dialog box.

You can specify different playback options for music videos and for movies and TV shows.

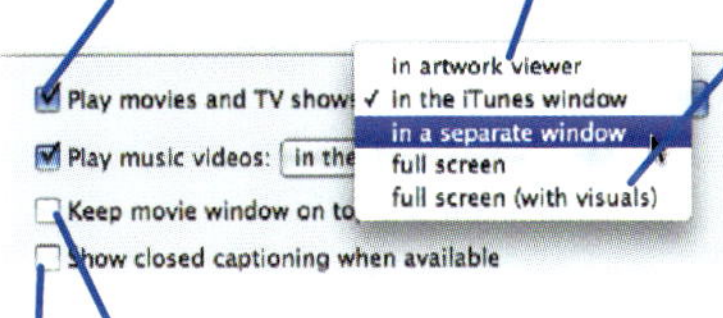

Prefer the separate video window? Check this box, and the window remains above other windows, even when you use other programs—perfect for watching while working.

If the video has caption text, the text appears during playback.

Plays video in the little box in the lower-left corner of the iTunes window: handy for previewing from the iTunes Store, but not exactly Panavision.

Like to mix videos and songs in playlists? Choose this option, and iTunes displays its flashy visualizer (page 90) when songs are playing. It's great for parties.

Resizing the video window. To adjust the size of the separate video window, drag its lower-right corner or use the commands in the View menu.

Controlling playback. When viewing video full-screen or in a separate window, you can access playback controls by moving your mouse into the video area. The controls let you play and pause playback, switch between full-screen and small-window modes, and step forward or backward one frame at a time (keyboard shortcut: the left and right arrow keys).

More iTunes Video Tips

Viewing your video library. The Library area of the iTunes window lets you quickly view just the movies or just the TV shows in your library: click the Movies item or the TV Shows item.

Adding your own movies. iTunes can also store your own QuickTime movies, such as ones you've downloaded from the Internet or have created in iMovie or iPhoto. (For details on preparing your iMovie efforts for iTunes, see page 276.) With add-on products, such as Elgato's EyeTV, you can record TV shows and save them in a format compatible with iTunes and the iPod (page 85).

To add a movie to your iTunes library, simply drag the movie file into the iTunes window.

Next, consider using the Get Info command to add information about the video, such as the year it was created (see page 26). With the Video portion of the Get Info dialog box, you can specify whether the video is a movie, TV show, or music video. iTunes uses this information to categorize the video; you can use it when creating smart playlists (page 52).

The iPod angle. iTunes can store and play just about any kind of QuickTime-compatible video, but that doesn't mean the video will play back on a video iPod or iPhone. The iPod and iPhone require video to be in a specific format; for details on converting video for iPod playback, see page 106.

Tuning In to Podcasts

Podcasts bring you radio and more whenever you want it. A *podcast* is typically an audio recording of a radio program—either an actual radio show that has been archived for Internet distribution, or an Internet-only program. Thousands of free podcasts await your ears, and they range from mainstream programs from the likes of National Public Radio to amateur productions that only a mother's ears could love.

Internet radio isn't new, but podcasts sweeten the pot with a couple of innovations. Foremost among them is that you don't have to remember to download podcasts. Instead, you use iTunes to *subscribe* to your favorite podcasts. When you subscribe to a podcast, iTunes automatically checks for new episodes at regular intervals. If iTunes finds a new episode, it downloads it.

At the iTunes Store, you'll find thousands of podcasts in over 20 categories, from technology to politics to talk radio and public radio.

Podcasts also come in several flavors. Video podcasts add the dimension of video, while *enhanced* podcasts provide extra goodies, such as photos, Web links, and chapter markers for convenient navigation (see page 36).

And if you're curious, the term *podcast* was coined by former MTV veejay Adam Curry. A major force behind the development and popularization of podcasting, he's referred to by many in the podcasting community as the "podfather."

Radio (and more) in every imaginable category, retrieved for you automatically: now that's an offer you can't refuse.

Finding Podcasts

As with music and videos, you can find podcasts in a few ways. To wander the podcast aisles of the iTunes Store, click the Podcasts link on the store's home screen. The podcasts page appears.

iTunes STORE
Music
Movies
TV Shows
Music Videos
Audiobooks
Podcasts
iPod Games
iTunes Latino
iTunes U NEW

To quickly scan what's available in each podcast category, click Browse.

To search for podcasts, use the Power Search feature (page 31). You can refine your search to specific categories, titles, authors, and languages.

Previewing and Subscribing

Once you've made your way to a specific podcast, you can preview episodes, download them, and subscribe to the podcast.

To subscribe to the podcast, click Subscribe. iTunes subscribes to the podcast and begins downloading the most recent episode.

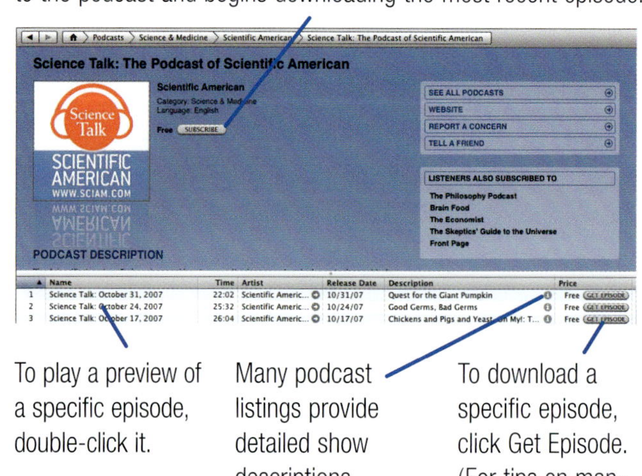

To play a preview of a specific episode, double-click it.

Many podcast listings provide detailed show descriptions. To see the full description, click ⓘ.

To download a specific episode, click Get Episode. (For tips on managing downloads, see page 41.)

Tune in to my podcast, "The Digital Hub," and get links to more podcast tips.
www.macilife.com/podcast

Managing Your Podcasts

The Podcasts Playlist

Podcasts to which you've subscribed appear in the Podcasts playlist. To display this playlist, click Podcasts in the Library area.

Episodes that you haven't downloaded appear dimmed; to download an episode, click its Get button.

Specify various podcast preferences (below).

To show or hide the episodes for a particular podcast, click the triangle.

This episode is currently downloading. To cancel a download, click the X.

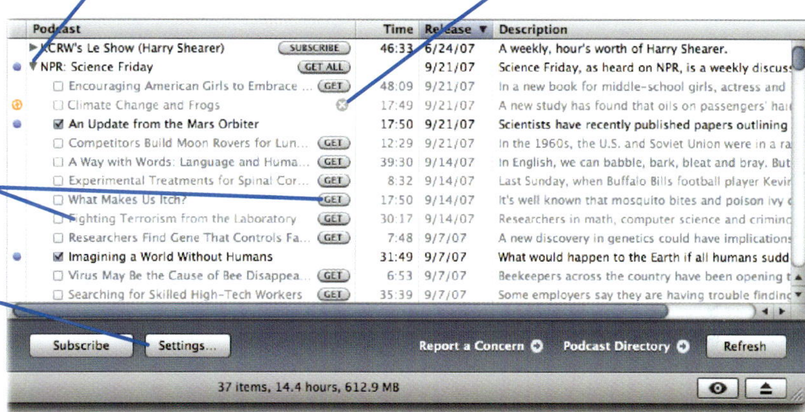

Setting Podcast Preferences

You can control how often iTunes checks your podcast subscriptions, what happens to podcasts you've played, and more. Click the Settings button in the Podcasts playlist, or choose Preferences from the iTunes menu, then click the Podcasts button.

How often should iTunes check for new episodes? If you've subscribed to podcasts that update often (such as National Public Radio's hourly news), you might choose Every hour.

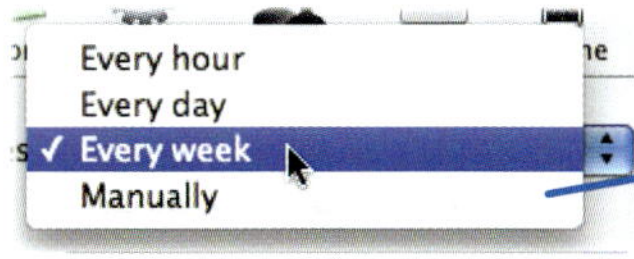

Then what? Specify what you'd like iTunes to do when it finds a new episode. If you prefer to read each episode's description and then download only those episodes that sound interesting, choose Do nothing. Then download the episodes you want by clicking their Get buttons.

And when you're done? Specify how many episodes iTunes should keep. To save disk space, you might want to keep two or three previous episodes—or only those episodes you haven't yet played.

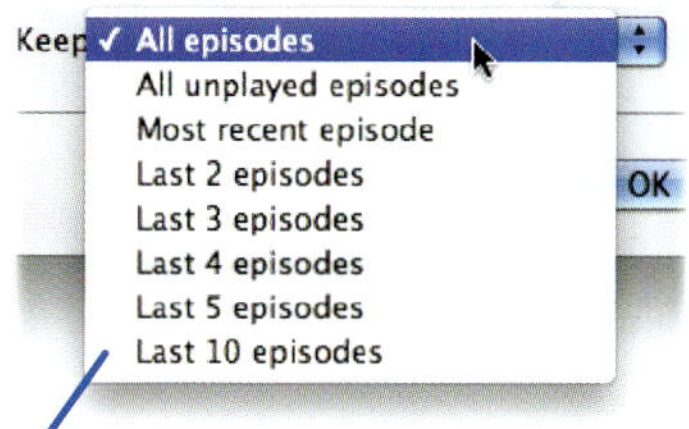

Tip: You can override this preference setting on a per-podcast basis. For example, to keep iTunes from deleting a particular episode of a podcast, locate the episode in the Podcast playlist, then Control-click on it and choose Do Not Auto Delete from the shortcut menu.

Podcast Tips

Tuning Out

If you decide you no longer want to subscribe to a podcast, you have a couple of options for tuning out. Begin by displaying your podcasts: click the Podcasts list in the Library area.

To unsubscribe to a podcast without deleting episodes you've already downloaded, select the podcast and click the Unsubscribe button at the bottom of the iTunes window. iTunes won't check that podcast for updates any more, but you can still do so manually: select the podcast and click the Refresh button. And you can subscribe again by clicking the Subscribe button next to the podcast's name.

If you want to unsubscribe *and* delete all episodes, select the podcast and press the Delete key on your keyboard. iTunes asks if you want to delete the episodes, and then if you want to move their files to the Trash.

Subscribing Manually

The iTunes Store has a vast podcast directory, but you may sometimes encounter a podcast on the Web that isn't listed in the music store. You can still use iTunes to subscribe to such a podcast.

On the Web site hosting the podcast, locate the link for the podcast's feed. Then, if you're using Apple's Safari browser, simply drag the link into the iTunes window.

If that doesn't work—or if you're using a different browser—try this more-laborious method. First, copy the podcast feed's link to the Clipboard: Control-click on the link and choose Copy Link from the shortcut menu. Next, switch back to iTunes and choose Subscribe to Podcast from the Advanced menu. Paste the link you copied, and click OK or press Return.

Adding Downloaded Podcasts

If you have podcasts that you've already downloaded with a Web browser, you can add them to your iTunes library by simply dragging their icons to the Library area of the iTunes window. Note that such podcasts will not appear in the Podcasts list in the Library area, however. That list shows only podcasts that you've subscribed to with iTunes.

Send to a Friend

You've subscribed to a great podcast and want to let a friend know about it. It's easy. In the Podcasts list, choose the title of the podcast, then drag it to the desktop. iTunes creates an address file with a file extension of .pcast.

You can email this file to your friends, who can drag it into their copies of iTunes to subscribe to the podcast.

Want to share *all* of your podcast subscriptions? In the Library area, Control-click on the Podcasts list, then choose Export Song List from the shortcut menu. In the Save dialog box that appears, choose OPML from the Format pop-up menu. Type a name for the list, then save it somewhere convenient—on your desktop, for example.

Now email that file to your friends. They can subscribe to those podcasts by dragging the file into the iTunes window.

This is also a handy way of moving a set of podcast subscriptions from one computer to another: export the Podcast list, email the file to yourself, retrieve the email on the other computer, then drag it into that computer's copy of iTunes.

The Blue Dot

You've probably noticed that podcast subscriptions and individual episodes often have a blue dot (●) next to them. A blue dot next to a podcast episode indicates that you haven't started listening to that episode. A blue dot next to a podcast subscription indicates that there's at least one episode of that podcast you haven't started listening to yet.

If you listen to even just part of a podcast, the blue dot disappears. More to the point, iTunes figures you've listened to the entire podcast. If you have your preferences set up to delete a podcast after you've listened to it, you'll lose the podcast—and the chance to hear the rest of it.

The solution? Tell iTunes to treat a particular podcast as if you had never played it. Control-click on the podcast, and from the shortcut menu, choose Mark as New. iTunes restores the blue dot next to the podcast's name—as if you'd never played it.

Enhanced Podcasts

Enhanced podcasts can contain artwork, such as photos, that plays back along with the audio.

Enhanced podcasts can also contain Web links that appear in the iTunes video viewer. You can click on the link to go to a Web site.

And enhanced podcasts can contain chapter markers that make it easy for the listener (or viewer) to jump from one part of the podcast to another. iTunes displays a Chapters menu that lets you jump to specific spots.

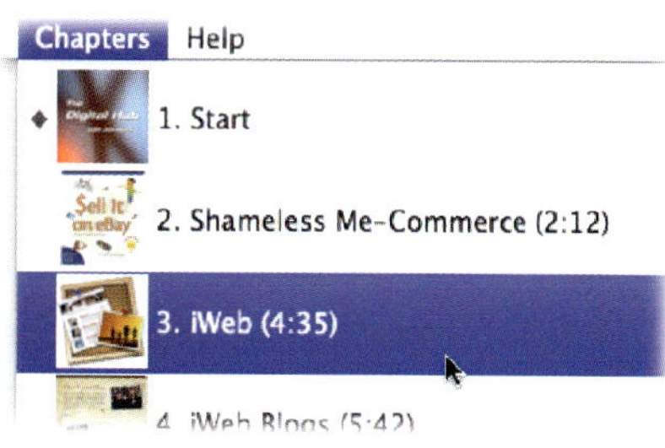

You can also navigate from one chapter to the next by pressing the Next and Previous buttons on an iPod.

Finding enhanced podcasts. So where can you find these podcasts with punch? Alas, the iTunes Store doesn't devote a category to enhanced podcasts, nor does it provide a way to search specifically for them. Try using the store's Power Search screen to search for podcasts with the word *enhanced* in their descriptions.

A Google search for the phrase *enhanced podcast* will also turn up lots of interesting results.

Managing Downloads from the iTunes Store

iTunes is able to download three items (podcasts, songs, TV shows, movies, and so on) at a time. If you're on a shopping spree and you try to download more, iTunes stashes the additional items in its download queue and gets to them as soon as it finishes downloading other items.

You can control how iTunes downloads items. For example, you can pause a lengthy movie download to free up your Internet connection for some song downloads.

When iTunes is downloading, a Downloads item appears in the Store area.

To manage your downloads, click Downloads.

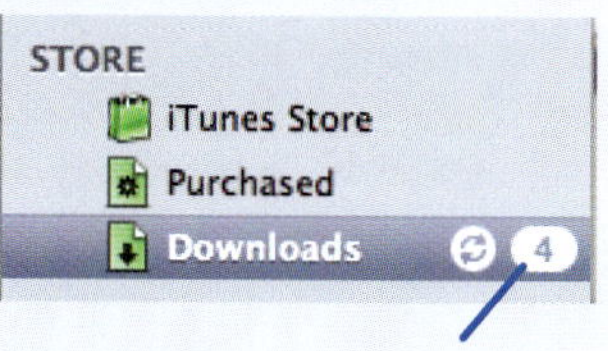

Here, four items are being downloaded.

To prioritize downloads, drag items up or down. In a hurry for a song? Drag it to the top of the list. This can be handy when you don't want to wait for an entire movie to download before a song download begins.

To cancel a download, click the X symbol. If you don't want to download an item after all, select it and press the Delete key.

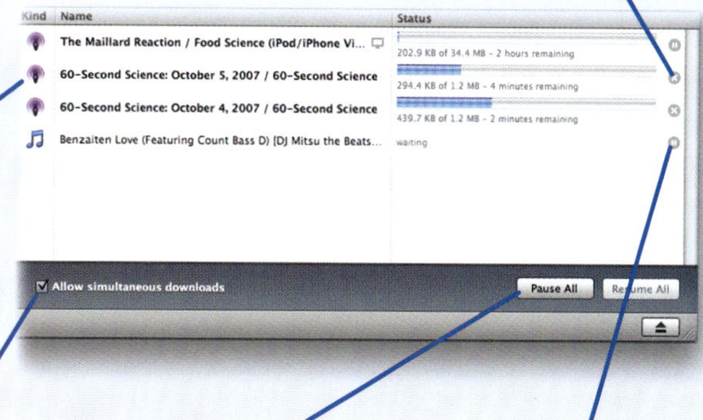

Have a slower Internet connection? Uncheck this box, and iTunes will download just one item at a time.

Need all your Internet bandwidth for a critical visit to eBay? Click Pause All to put iTunes on hold.

To pause downloading for an individual item, click the pause symbol.

Tips for the iTunes Store

More Shopping Avenues

Looking for more ways to discover new music? Here are a few shopping avenues to explore. To access most of the following options, click the Music link on the store's home screen.

iTunes Essentials. In the iTunes Essentials area of the store, you'll find meticulously categorized lists of tunes selected by the staff of the store. Categories run the gamut from "Motorcycle Music" to "Romantic Moods," and each category is divided into several subcategories that let you drill ever deeper into the groove at hand.

Celebrity Playlists. If you're interested in what your favorite musicians listen to, check out Celebrity Playlists, where top artists share their favorites.

iMixes. As page 50 describes, you can publish your own playlists for other music store customers to check out and rate. To check out and rate other shoppers' iMixes, click the iMix link.

iTunes Originals. In the iTunes Originals area of the store, you'll find exclusive tracks, song compilations, and artist interviews.

Just for You. This area of the store's home screen lists songs that Apple thinks you'll like, based on previous purchases you've made.

Starbucks Entertainment. In late 2007, Apple and Starbucks joined forces to offer the iTunes Wi-Fi Music Store in Starbucks outlets (see page 102), and to offer Starbucks' growing music library at the iTunes Store.

The Starbucks Entertainment section of the iTunes Store has a great selection of compilations from Starbucks-owned Hear Music. You'll also find Artist's Choice compilations, which are similar to the iTunes Store's Celebrity Playlists.

Billboard Charts. The Charts category lists the top tunes from *Billboard* magazine. You can get lists of top tunes going back to the 1940s, as well as current country and R&B favorites.

Click the Browse button at the bottom of the iTunes window, then click the Charts entry. Choose the chart you want to view, then drill down to specific years.

Free Downloads. Look for the Free On iTunes heading on the store's home screen for links to free songs and videos.

Parental Controls

Concerned about your kids buying music and sapping your credit card? Or about them buying music or downloading podcasts that contain explicit content?

By using the Parental option of the Preferences dialog box, you can control what the munchkins can access. Choose Preferences from the iTunes menu, then click the Parental button.

Next, choose the options you want. For example, to prevent access to music store content labeled as explicit, click Restrict Explicit Content. Finally, click the lock icon and enter your password.

To remove restrictions, click the lock icon again, enter your password, and then uncheck options as desired.

Stopping Stutters

Saddled with a slow connection? Improve previewing by tweaking iTunes' preferences.

Choose Preferences from the iTunes menu, click the Store button, and then check the box labeled Load Complete Preview Before Playing. From now on, iTunes will load the entire preview before playing it. You'll wait longer for the preview, but at least it won't be interrupted.

Authorizing and Deauthorizing

Unlike the music files that iTunes creates when you rip a CD, the music tracks you buy contain some playback and copying restrictions designed to prevent music thieves from sharing the songs through Internet file-swapping services.

When you buy a song, the iTunes Store embeds your Apple ID in the music file that downloads to your hard drive. To play the song, you must authorize your Mac, a one-time process that simply involves typing your Apple ID and password. You can authorize up to five Macs (or Windows PCs) per Apple ID.

If you've already authorized five computers to play your purchases and you want to play them on a sixth computer, you'll have to deauthorize one of the other five. Choose Deauthorize Computer from the Store menu, choose Apple Account in the subsequent dialog box, and then type your Apple ID and password. You must be connected to the Internet to deauthorize a computer.

Parting with your computer? If you're parting with your Mac for any reason—selling it, giving it away, or even just sending it off for repairs—be sure to deauthorize it first.

Deauthorizing everything. You forgot to deauthorize a computer that you no longer have—and you've reached your five-computer limit and thus can't authorize your newest Mac. What do to? Wipe the slate clean.

You can deauthorize all the computers that are tied to your account. To do so, go to your account information screen by signing into the store and clicking the account button in the upper-right corner. On the Account Information screen, click the Deauthorize All button.

Important: You can deauthorize all your computers only once a year, so don't use this option unless you really need to.

Burning What You Buy

You can burn purchased songs to audio CDs, but iTunes imposes a minor restriction on your burning endeavors. If a playlist contains purchased music, you can burn a maximum of seven CDs containing that playlist.

Chris Breen, editor-in-chief of *Playlist* magazine, has done some interesting research on how iTunes tracks the number of times you've burned a playlist—and on steps you can take to work around the seven-CD limit. I've linked to the articles at www.macilife.com/itunes.

And incidentally, you can't burn DVDs containing videos that you've purchased from the iTunes store. You can burn backups of the video files themselves (and you should), but you can't, for example, use iDVD to create a DVD that contains some episodes of *Lost* that you've bought.

iTunes Plus

In 2007, Apple and some other online music retailers began selling music that wasn't shackled by the surveillance bracelet of copy protection. It was a major step for a recording industry terrified of music piracy.

Apple calls its offerings iTunes Plus, and they do indeed have some pluses. An iTunes Plus song has no copy protection, or *digital rights management (DRM)*, attached to it. You can play the song on a computer that hasn't been authorized for your iTunes account, and you can burn it to a CD as many times as you like. It's unshackled—just like a music file that you rip from a CD.

Sweeter still, it sounds better than a standard iTunes Store purchase. iTunes Plus songs are encoded at twice the bit rate as DRM-shackled songs you buy: 256 kilobits per second, instead of 128kbps.

In the iTunes Store, an iTunes Plus song is indicated by a plus sign symbol (⊞). To browse iTunes Plus offerings, click the iTunes Plus link in the Quick Links box that appears on most store pages.

One more thing: although iTunes Plus songs lack copy protection, they are still "stamped" with your Apple ID: you (and anyone else) can see it in the Get Info dialog box. Keep that in mind should you be tempted to pass along some iTunes Plus purchases to a friend.

Upgrading to Plus. If you've purchased songs that are now available in iTunes Plus form, you can upgrade to the higher-quality, DRM-free versions. On the iTunes Plus page of the store, look for the Upgrade My Library box. Click the See Details button to view a list of previous purchases available in Plus form.

More Tips for the iTunes Store

Creating Playlists from Collections

A huge number of song compilations are available at the iTunes Store—just a few examples include the iMixes that your fellow music lovers create; the iTunes Essentials mixes that Apple creates; the celebrity playlists that, well, celebrities create; and the iTunes Originals compilations described on page 38.

When you buy a song compilation, you'll probably want to create a playlist containing its tunes. That way, you'll be able to easily listen to (and burn) the entire compilation instead of simply having its songs scattered throughout your music library.

iTunes has a feature that automatically creates playlists for you when you buy a compilation. Choose Preferences from the iTunes menu, click the Store button, and verify that the box labeled Automatically Create Playlists When Buying Song Collections is checked.

For details on playlists, see page 46.

When Downloads Go Awry

If your Internet connection is interrupted during a download, you haven't lost your money. Simply reconnect and choose Check for Purchases from the Store menu. iTunes will resume any incomplete downloads.

Complete My Album

You buy a couple of songs from an album, then, as you grow ever fonder of them, decide to buy the rest of the album. The iTunes Store makes it easy with a feature called Complete My Album.

With Complete My Album, you have 180 days after you buy a track to buy the rest of the album at a discount. (Well, not really a discount: the iTunes Store simply sells you the rest of the songs, omitting the ones you've already bought.) The feature is also available for some music videos.

To access Complete My Album, click the Complete My Album link in the Quick Links box that appears on most store pages. A screen appears listing the albums eligible for completion.

Apple has published a list of frequently asked questions about Complete My Album. You'll find a link to it by going to macilife.com/itunes.

Keep Informed

Want to be informed when a favorite artist releases a new album? Click the Alert Me link that appears in the artist's screen. From there, you can sign up to be notified when that artist—and other artists whose work you've purchased—releases something new.

That isn't the only way to stay informed. If you use iCal (page 118), you can subscribe to daily calendar updates of top songs, albums, and new releases by going to Apple's iCal site, www.apple.com/ical.

And if you use a newsreader program, such as NetNewsWire or the latest versions of Apple's Safari Web browser, you can create RSS newsfeeds that contain this information by going to www.apple.com/rss.

PDF Liner Notes

One of the drawbacks of the digital music era is that you don't get a booklet of lyrics and other liner notes with your purchases. That's slowly changing: Apple now offers liner notes in PDF form for some albums. Many iTunes Originals collections also include PDF booklets.

The PDFs are downloaded automatically with your purchase, and appear in your iTunes library. Double-click the PDF, and your Mac launches Preview (or Adobe

Acrobat Reader, if installed) and opens the PDF.

To learn more about working with PDFs in iTunes, see page 84.

Get that Song's Address

Every item—song, album, video, podcast—in the iTunes Store has its own Internet address. You can copy this address and include it in an email, or link to it from your personal Web site. Using this address is a fun way to let other people know about the stuff you've found.

To copy an item's Web address, point to the item, press the Control key (that's Control, not ⌘), and choose Copy iTunes Store URL from the shortcut menu that appears.

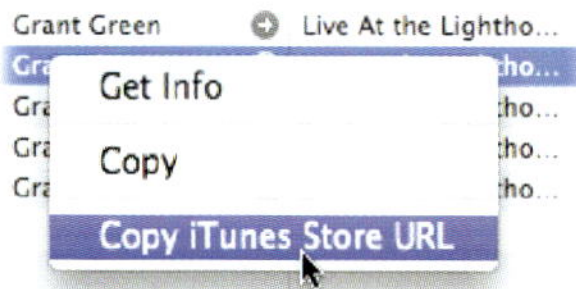

Next, switch to your email program, create a blank email, then paste the address into the body of the email.

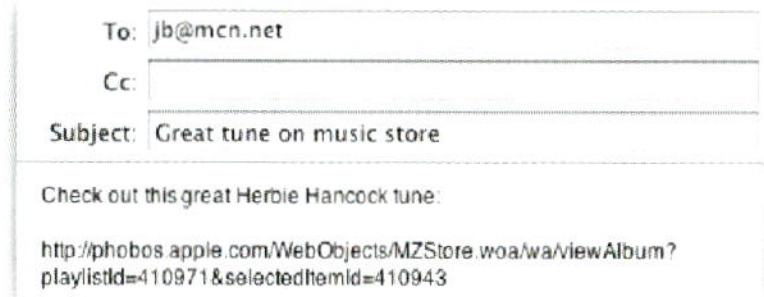

Bookmarking Items

You can also drag any item in the iTunes Store to the desktop; this creates an icon that, when double-clicked, takes iTunes to the appropriate item. If you've stumbled onto an interesting-sounding album but you want to wait and explore it later, use this technique to put a temporary "bookmark" on your desktop.

In a similar vein, you can also bookmark a favorite artist or genre. Navigate to the artist's home screen, then drag the artist's name to the desktop. To bookmark a genre, click the Music link on the store's home page, then drag the desired genre out onto the desktop. You can also create these "bookmark icons" by dragging the buttons in the store's navigation bar (shown on page 29).

Hiding the Link Buttons

The music store provides link arrows (➔) that let you jump to a page for an artist, album, or song. These buttons also appear when you're viewing your music library or a playlist. The buttons are Apple's way of letting you search for (and buy) songs related to ones that you already have.

If you'd rather not see these buttons—maybe so you don't accidentally click one and beam yourself into the music store—you can disable them. Choose Preferences, click the General button, then uncheck the box labeled Show Links to the Music Store.

Shopping via Wi-Fi

The iTunes Store is addictive enough when you're sitting at your desk; now it's possible to carry that addiction with you. If you have an iPhone or iPod touch, you can use its Wi-Fi capabilities to shop at the iTunes Wi-Fi Music Store. Browse for and preview songs, then buy them with a tap. When you sync your Mac and iPhone or iPod touch, iTunes copies your purchases to your iTunes Library. You'll find details and tips on page 103.

Giving the Gift of iTunes

Thinking of buying a music CD for someone? That's *so* twentieth century. If the music lovers in your life use iTunes, treat them to some music at the iTunes Store. Or buy them music videos, movies, or TV shows.

The iTunes Store offers a few gift-giving options. If you want to give a specific album, song, or video to someone, you can. Don't have anything specific in mind? You can also buy prepaid cards and gift certificates that let your lucky recipients pick and choose exactly what they want. You can even set up a monthly allowance that keeps on giving.

To access most of these options, click the Buy iTunes Gifts link located in the Quick Links box that appears on most store pages.

Allowance: Music Monthly

Want to give all year long? Set up an allowance to give a monthly iTunes stipend. You can give as little as $10 per month—about one album's worth—or as much as, gulp, $200.

You aren't giving cash, of course, but rather the ability to buy a given amount of music each month. And if your recipient ends up being a bad boy or girl, you can cancel the allowance at any time during the subsequent year. Try *that* with a music CD.

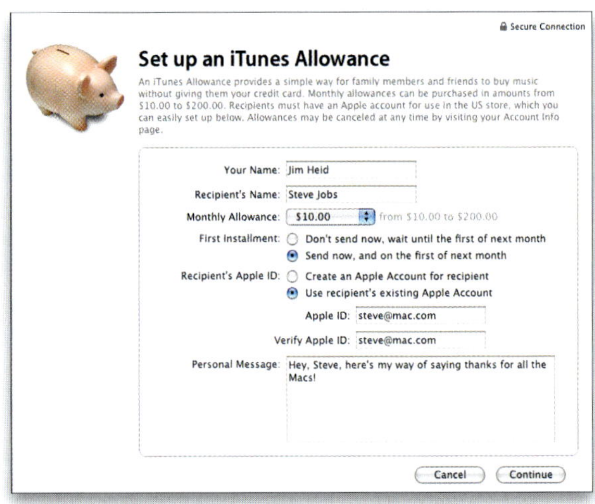

Your recipient must have an Apple account. If he or she doesn't have one, you can set up an account when creating an allowance.

Note: If you know your recipient has an Apple account but you don't know what the account name is, *don't* set up a separate account for the allowance. That would complicate your recipient's life, since music store purchases are locked to a specific account. Instead, either find out what the recipient's Apple account is, or, if you want to maintain the element of surprise, buy a gift certificate or prepaid card instead.

Gift Certificate

If you don't know your recipient's Apple account name—or you aren't feeling generous enough for a monthly allowance—consider a gift certificate. You can give between $10 and $200. Apple emails the gift certificate to the recipient, who can redeem it by simply clicking a link.

For an analog touch, you can also have the gift certificate printed and mailed to the recipient. Or print it yourself and tuck it into a card.

Prepaid Cards

Prepaid iTunes Gift Cards are available in various denominations from many retail stores as well as the Apple online and retail stores.

To redeem the card, your recipient clicks the Redeem link on the store's home screen, then types the card's serial number (it's printed on the back of the card, beneath a scratch-off coating). After the card is redeemed, the recipient's copy of iTunes will show that he or she has an additional credit.

Giving Specific Items

You can give any item that's sold at the iTunes Store. Make your way to the main page for an album or TV series, then click the Gift link. (For albums, the link reads Gift This Album; for shows, it reads Gift This TV Show.)

A new screen appears that enables you to give the entire album (or season, for TV shows) or only certain songs or episodes.

You can also give something that you already have in your music library; see page 50.

Note: The recipient of your gift must have an Apple account registered in the same country as yours.

More Musical Gift Ideas

Don't want to give music? Consider a gift that enhances a music collection.

An iPod. If your music lover doesn't have an iPod, he or she is missing out on one of the best parts of the digital music era.

Headphones. My favorite earwear is a pair of Bose QuietComfort 3 headphones, with noise-cancelling circuitry that does an amazing job of removing annoying background noise. They're ideal for long plane flights, not to mention vacuuming sessions.

Portable speakers. Does your music lover travel? A pair of portable speakers makes listening in a hotel room a lot more fun. Bose, JBL, Altec Lansing, and other companies sell portable speakers designed for the iPod; check out iLounge (www.ilounge.com) and Playlist magazine (www.playlistmag.com) for reviews.

I frequently travel with Sony's SRS-T88 speakers, which, unlike iPod-specific speakers, also connect to the headphone jack on my MacBook Pro.

iPod accessories. Carrying cases, radio adapters, microphones, and car chargers are among the accessories competing for your dollars. Check out iLounge and Playlist for some ideas.

Before you buy, remember that many accessories are designed for specific iPod models. Be sure that the item you're considering works with your recipient's specific iPod model.

Creating iPhone Ringtones

Want your iPhone to play a certain tune when a certain someone calls? Create a custom *ringtone*.

Like any mobile phone, the iPhone lets you store contact information: names, addresses, and phone numbers (see page 116). And like most mobile phones, the iPhone lets you associate specific ringtones with specific people. By adding musical ringtones to your iPhone, you can match the music to the caller.

Ringtones are fun—you can probably imagine many songs that would pair up with the people in your life. But ringtones are practical, too. They let you know who's calling without your having to extract the phone from your pocket to look at its screen. That makes for safer driving.

At the iTunes Store, you can buy a ringtone for 99 cents. Use iTunes to choose which portion of a song you want to be the ringtone, then transfer the ringtone to your iPhone.

That's the Apple Way, and it works just fine, but with limitations. You must buy an entire song for 99 cents before you can turn it into a ringtone—for another 99 cents. And because of the mysteries of record-label licensing, a relatively small selection of the songs on the iTunes Store can be turned into ringtones.

Fortunately, there's another way: an inexpensive little program that lets you turn *any* song in your music library—or any sound on your Mac—into a ringtone.

Here's how to make your iPhone sing when it rings.

Creating a Ringtone

Here's how to create a ringtone from a song you've already purchased. **Note:** Before performing these steps, display the Ringtone column in iTunes: choose View > View Options, then check the Ringtone box.

Step 1. Click the bell (🔔) next to the song's name, or select the song and choose Store > Create Ringtone.

(No bell? The song isn't licensed for ringtone fun. Choose a song that is, or consider Plan B: see the sidebar on the opposite page.)

Step 2. Use the ringtone editor to create and buy the ringtone.

A ringtone can be up to 30 seconds long; the highlighted region represents the ringtone. To reposition the region elsewhere in the song, drag it left and right. To change its start and end points, drag its edges.

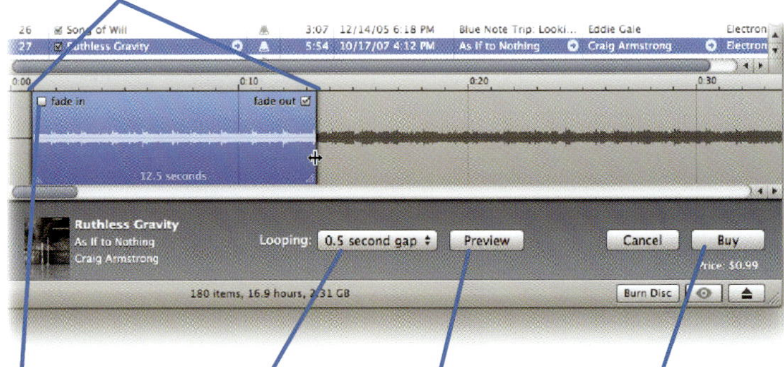

Tip: If you want the ringtone to start at the very beginning of the song, consider unchecking the Fade In box.

Specify a gap of silence between each ring. The half-second preset is ideal.

Listen to the ringtone. To preview a specific point, double-click directly in the song waveform.

All done? Click Buy to pay up and download.

Step 3. Sync your iPhone with iTunes (see page 108).

Step 4. On your iPhone, assign the ringtone to one or more contacts.

Learn more about iPhone ringtones and tools.
www.macilife.com/itunes

Notes and Tips

Your ringtone library. To view ringtones that you've created in iTunes, click the Ringtones item in the Library area. (And if you don't have an iPhone, feel free to remove this item using the General portion of the iTunes preferences dialog box.)

Ringtone candidates at a glance. Want to quickly view a list of your purchases that are licensed for ringtones? Click the Music item in the Library area, then click the bell at the top of the ringtone column; this sorts your library by the ringtone column. To re-sort the library display, click a different column heading, such as Artist.

Just one chance. Once you buy a ringtone, you can't change it without buying it again, so make that session with the ringtone editor count.

Making Ringtones with iToner

With Ambrosia Software's $15 iToner, you can copy any AAC- or MP3-format audio file to your iPhone and use it as a ringtone.

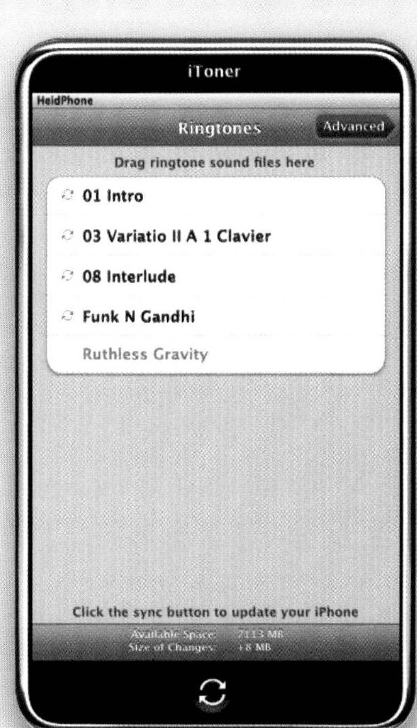

Simply connect your iPhone, then drag AAC or MP3 files into the iToner window. You can drag songs, including ones you've purchased, directly from the iTunes window. Then, click iToner's Sync button to copy the songs to the phone.

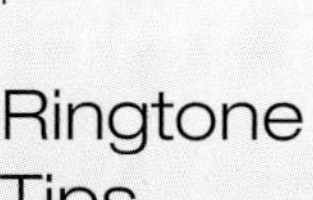

Ringtone Tips

Editing songs. iToner copies entire songs to your iPhone. If you'd rather save space on the phone—and have ringtones that are a reasonable length—you'll need to edit AAC or MP3 files before copying them. The best tool for the job is Rogue Amoeba Software's Fission.

Recording your own. Many Macs contain built-in microphones. If yours does (or if you have a separate mike), you can also use GarageBand to record your own ringtones: record your friend saying, "Hey, it's me. Answer the phone!"

After recording the audio in GarageBand, use its Export Song to Disk command to create an AAC or MP3 version of the recording (page 357). Then fire up iToner and drag the recording into its window.

More sound sources. Speaking of GarageBand, its sound effects, loops, and podcast jingles are great ringtone fodder. Create a new GarageBand project, add a sound, customize it with effects if you like, then use the Export Song to Disk command to create a version for iToner.

Cat and mouse. New updates to iTunes have been known to cause iToner to stop working. Ambrosia Software says it will keep iToner updated as long as it's able to, but before downloading iToner, check Ambrosia's Web site to verify that it's compatible with the latest version of iTunes.

Sequencing Songs with Playlists

After you've created a digital music library, you'll want to create *playlists*: collections of songs sequenced in whatever order you like.

You might create playlists whose songs set a mood: Workout Tunes, Road Trip Songs, Romantic Getaway Music.

You might create playlists that play all your favorite tunes from specific artists: The Best of U2, John Coltrane Favorites, The Artistry of Britney Spears. (That last one is pretty small.)

With playlists, you can mix and match songs in any way you see fit. You can add a song to as many playlists as you like, or even create a playlist that plays one song five times in a row.

Once you've created playlists, you can, of course, play them. And you can also transfer them to an iPod, iPhone, or Apple TV (page 108) and burn them to create your own compilation CDs (page 60).

This section describes how to create playlists "by hand." You can also use the smart playlists feature to have iTunes create playlists for you. For details on smart playlists, see page 52.

After you've created some playlists, share them with the rest of us. As page 50 describes, you can publish your playlists on the iTunes Store for everyone to see and rate. And if you're feeling generous, you can buy the songs in a playlist as a gift for someone.

Hint, hint.

Creating a Playlist

Step 1. Create a new playlist.

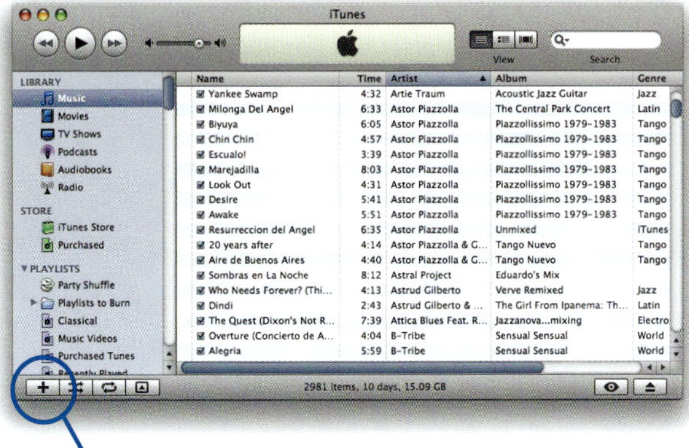

To create a new playlist, click the plus sign, or choose New Playlist from the File menu.

Step 2. Rename the new playlist.

Type a name for the new playlist.

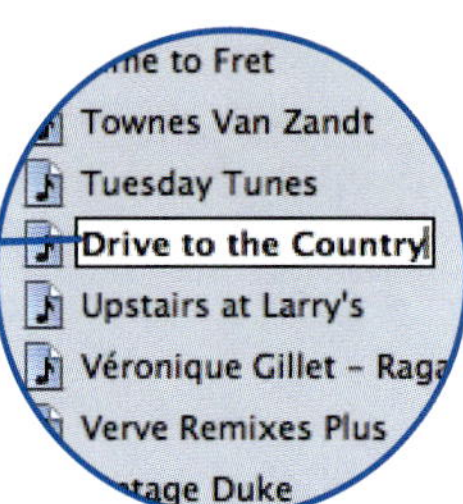

Step 3. Drag songs to the playlist.

You can drag songs into the playlist one at a time, or select a series of songs and drag them all at once.

Selecting multiple songs. You'll often want to select multiple songs—to drag them into playlists, copy them to an iPod, and more. To select a range of songs that are adjacent to each other, use the Shift key: click on the first song, then Shift-click on the last one. To select songs that aren't adjacent to one another, press ⌘ while clicking on each song.

Viewing and Fine-Tuning a Playlist

To view a playlist's contents, simply click on its name. To change the playlist's name, click again and then edit the name. To delete a playlist, select it and press Delete. (Deleting a playlist *doesn't* delete its songs from your library.)

To omit a song from a playlist, select the song and press the Delete key. To omit the song without deleting it—for example, if you want to keep it in the playlist but not burn it or play it back this time—uncheck the box next to the song's name.

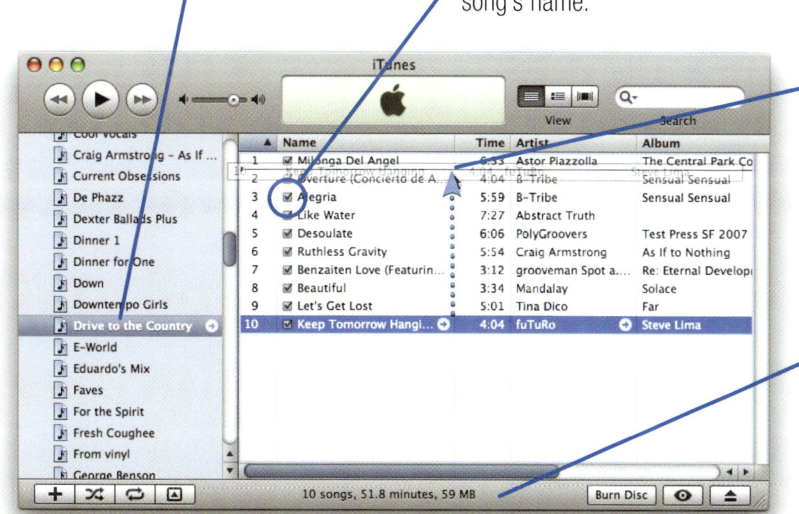

To change the playback order of the songs in the playlist, drag songs up or down. Here, the last song in the playlist is being moved to between songs 1 and 2.

iTunes displays the playlist's statistics, including its duration, here.

Important: If you plan to burn this playlist to an audio CD, keep the playlist's duration under 74 minutes.

Organizing Playlists with Folders

As your collection of playlists grows, consider organizing them by stashing related playlists in folders. To create a new folder, choose File > New Folder. Then, drag playlists into that folder.

To open or close a folder, click the triangle.

How you use folders is up to you. You might create one for all your jazz playlists and another for your classical playlists. If you have a lot of playlists for various artists, consider stashing each artist's playlists in a folder. If a few members of your household use iTunes, create a folder for each person's playlists. You get the idea.

Tip: Folders are also a great way to assemble "playlists of playlists." If you select a folder in your library, iTunes displays (and will play) all the tracks in each of the playlists contained in the folder.

You can also use folders as criteria in smart playlists, described on page 52.

Playlist Tips

Designing Playlists

A well-crafted playlist is more than a slew of songs slung into one place.

Consider the setting. A good playlist complements an event. For example, say you're creating a playlist for a dinner party, and you expect that guests will be mingling for an hour or so before sitting down to dinner. Start your playlist with about 15 minutes of fairly mellow tunes, then build up to some more energetic ones for the next 30 minutes or so. Then start to wind down again, and lead into a solid block of fairly unobtrusive music that won't overwhelm the dinner conversation.

Similarly, for a workout playlist, you might start and end with slower songs to accommodate warm-up and cool-down times, and put the pulse-pounding tunes in the middle. You get the idea: if your playlist will be accompanying an event, assemble tunes that complement the event's "story arc."

Mix artists. To make a playlist that's more interesting to the ears, mix and match artists.

Consider the transitions. Think about how the songs in your playlist flow from one to the next. You might follow a barn-burner with a slower ballad, for example, or put an instrumental after a vocal. To assess the transitions between songs, start playing one song and then fast-forward by dragging the little playback diamond to near the end of the song (see page 19). Then listen as the songs change. If the transition sounds jarring, consider reorganizing the songs to create a more pleasing segue.

Opening a Playlist in a Separate Window

To open a playlist in its own window, double-click the playlist's name. iTunes opens the playlist in a new window, and switches its main window to the Library view.

You can open as many playlist windows as you like and drag songs between them, as shown here. It's a handy way to work, since it lets you see the contents of your library and your playlist at the same time.

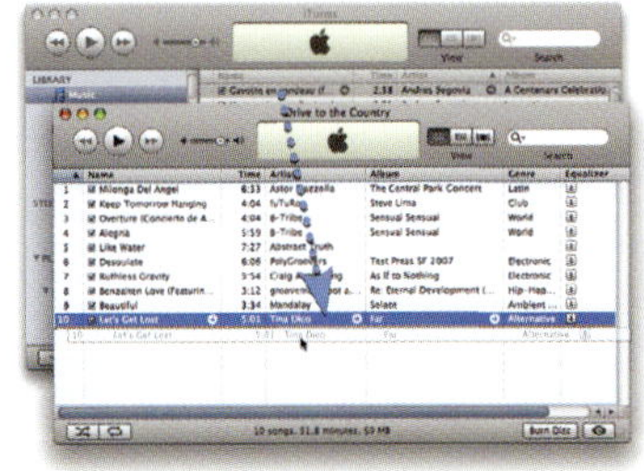

Previews in Playlists

You can drag a song preview from the music store into a playlist. This can be a handy way to put together a temporary shopping list—drag previews into a playlist, then go back and review them again before deciding what to buy.

You can also publish a wish list of tunes: drag previews into a playlist, then publish the playlist as described on page 50. Who knows? Maybe someone will buy the tunes for you.

To help you tell a preview from a full-length song, iTunes displays a little badge (30) adjacent to a preview song's name.

Creating a Playlist From a Selection

Here's a shortcut for creating a playlist: in the Library view, select the songs you want to include in a playlist, and then choose New Playlist From Selection from the File menu. iTunes adds the songs to a new playlist, which you can then rename.

Naming Playlists with iPod in Mind

If you plan to transfer your playlists to an iPod, there's a trick you can use to ensure that a given playlist will appear at the top of the iPod's Playlists menu. This cuts down on the time and scrolling required to find a specific playlist.

To have a playlist appear at the top of the iPod's Playlists menu, precede the playlist's name with a hyphen (-) character, as in - *Mac's Greatest Hits*.

A few other punctuation characters, including period (.), will also send a playlist to the top of the heap.

Adding One Playlist to Another

You can add the entire contents of one playlist to other playlists. Simply drag one playlist to another.

Playlist Shortcuts

Curious about which playlists contain a particular song? Hold down the Control key, click on the song, and a shortcut menu appears. Open the Show in Playlist submenu to see which playlists contain the song. To jump to a specific playlist, choose its name.

You can also add a song to an existing playlist using this shortcut menu: choose the playlist's name from the Add to Playlist submenu.

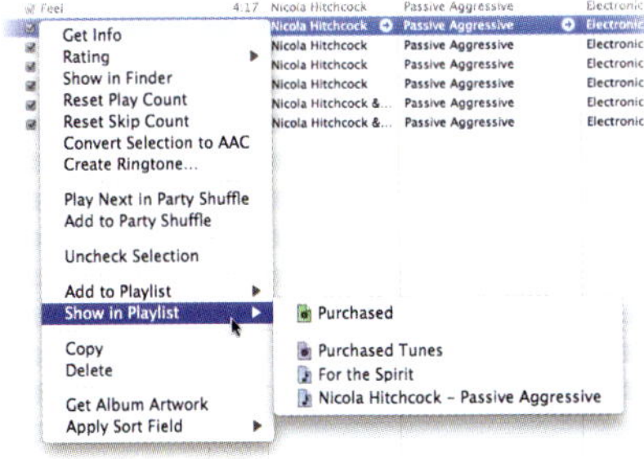

From CD to Playlist in One Drag

You're about to rip an audio CD and you're planning to add some of its tracks to a playlist. Here's a shortcut: simply drag the tracks from the CD list to the playlist. iTunes will import the tracks and add them to the playlist for you.

Exporting and Importing Playlists

You've crafted the perfect playlist and now want to move it over to a different Mac, or email it to a friend. Here's how: select the playlist, then choose Export from the File menu. In the Save dialog box, choose XML from the Format pop-up menu, choose a location for the exported playlist (the desktop is convenient), then click Save.

Next, move the playlist over to a different computer. On that computer, choose Import from the File menu. Locate the playlist and double-click its name. You're done.

Note that iTunes exports and imports only *information* about the songs in a playlist—it doesn't copy the songs' music files themselves. If any of the songs are missing on the importing computer, iTunes displays a warning and removes those songs from the imported playlist.

To export all of your playlists (an ideal prelude to backing them up), choose Export Library from the File menu.

Export Playlists as Plain Text

By choosing the Plain Text format in the Export Playlist dialog box, you can export a playlist in text format—perhaps to bring it into a database manager or spreadsheet program. (Hey, some iTunes users are very obsessive audio librarians.)

When you export a playlist in this way, iTunes creates a text file containing all the information about each song, from its name to its bit rate. You can open this text file using a word processor, or you can import it into a spreadsheet or database program. The items—artist, song name, album name, and so on—in an exported playlist are separated by tab characters. (In geek speak, this command creates a *tab-delimited* text file.) Most spreadsheet and database programs can read these tabs and use them to put each piece of information in its own spreadsheet cell or database field.

Some programmers have created free AppleScripts that provide more control over playlist exporting. (To learn about expanding iTunes with AppleScript, see page 90.)

Printing to PDF

Another way to publish a song list is to use the Print command in iTunes. With Mac OS X's ability to "print" to a PDF file, you can create a PDF listing of songs, then email it or post it on a Web site.

In the Print dialog box, click the Song Listing or Album Listing option, pick a theme, then click Print. Click Save As PDF in the next dialog box, and give the PDF a name. Now share the PDF as you see fit. You can even drag the PDF into the iTunes window and store it as part of your iTunes library. (For more details on working with PDFs in iTunes, see page 86.)

Tip: Looking for yet another way to get information from iTunes into another program? Print to a PDF, then open the PDF, copy its text, and paste it elsewhere.

iMix: Publishing Your Playlists

You've crafted the perfect playlist? Share it with the rest of us by publishing it at the iTunes Store. (You must have an account at the store or with America Online before you can publish a playlist.)

A published playlist is called an *iMix*, and it appears in its own screen, much like an artist or album page. Each iMix is available for one year. After you create one, you can tell your friends by sending them e-cards or by publishing your iMix's address on a Web site. If you have a Web site of your own (including one you've created with iWeb), you can also publish snazzy-looking boxes that list the tunes in your iMix and allow visitors to buy them.

Giving a Playlist

Want to buy the songs in a playlist for a friend? In the dialog box that appears after you click the arrow to the right of the playlist's name, click the Give Playlist button.

iTunes displays a list of the songs that are available in the music store, along with options that let you notify the recipient via email or print a note that you can tuck into a card.

For more music-giving options, see page 42.

Creating an iMix

Step 1. Select the playlist you want to publish, and click the arrow next to its name.

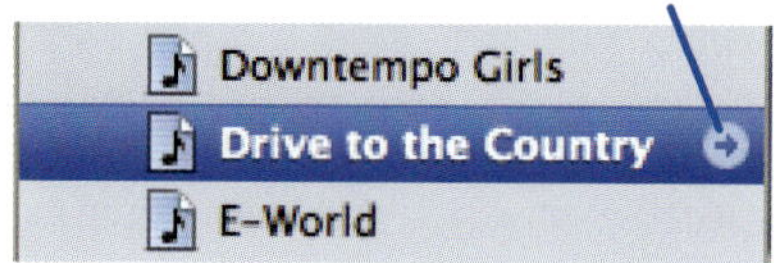

iTunes asks if you'd like to give the playlist as a gift or publish it as an iMix. For details on giving the playlist as a gift, see the tip at lower left. Otherwise, click Create iMix.

If iTunes displays its sign-in screen, supply your account name and password.

Step 2. Describe your iMix.

Just do it: you can have workout-themed mixes appear in a special area.

Type a description of your iMix and change its name, if you like.

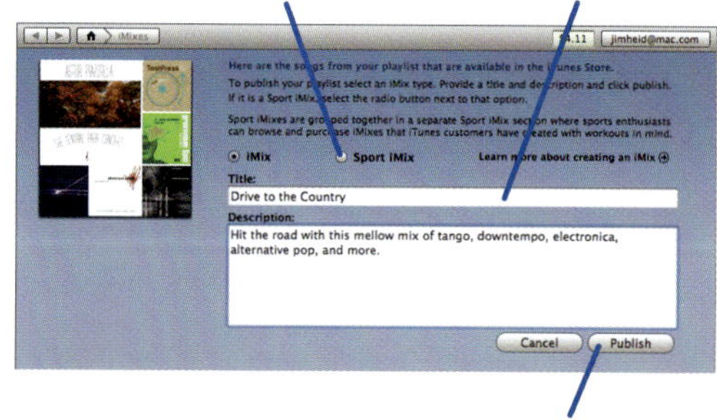

To publish the iMix, click Publish. If your playlist includes songs that are *not* available at the iTunes Store, those songs don't appear in your iMix.

Step 3 (optional). Tell the world, or at least a friend.

After your iMix is published, you'll receive an email containing a summary of its tunes and a link that you can include in an email or on a Web page.

iMix Tips

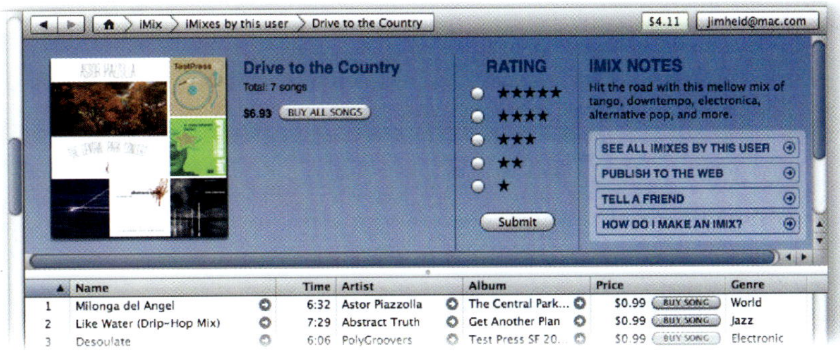

Exploring iMixes. To explore the iMixes that other people have created, click the Music link on the store's home screen, then click the iMix link.

You can view mixes chronologically or in order of their rating. On the iMix page, you can also search for songs, artists, and albums that others have included in their iMixes. Highly rated iMixes also appear in relevant artist and album pages.

What else? If you like someone's iMix, you might want to explore other iMixes that he or she has created. In an iMix window, click the link labeled *See all iMixes by this user.*

Linking to an iMix. Want to grab the Internet address for an iMix? Control-click on the iMix's name or artwork, and choose Copy iTunes Store URL from the shortcut menu. Paste the resulting link into an email or the Web tool of your choice.

As with other items in the store, you can also create a desktop icon for an iMix—just drag its title or artwork icon to the desktop.

Publishing an iMix to the Web. Have a Web site? Click the *Publish to the Web* link, and your browser will display a snippet of code that you can paste into a Web page. The code creates a box listing the tunes, with links to the store. It works nicely with iWeb; see page 404.

Updating an iMix. To make changes to an iMix, edit the original playlist, then publish it again. When you've published a playlist, a link arrow appears next to it, even when the playlist isn't selected.

A Piece of the Action: iTunes Affiliates

Now that you're recommending songs to people, you might as well get a piece of the action. It's easy: if you have a Web site of your own, you can join the iTunes Affiliate Program and receive commissions when you send customers to the iTunes Store.

Start by signing up for the iTunes Affiliate Program at Apple's Web site (www.apple.com/itunes/affiliates). Be prepared to provide some information, such as the Web address, a brief description of your site, and a Social Security number. Then wait a few days for your acceptance email to arrive.

Once you're enrolled in the program, you can build links to specific songs, albums, artists, iMixes, or audiobooks. You can also embellish your site with banner ads and other graphics that shuttle visitors off to the music store.

What's in it for you? A commission (at this writing, five percent) of any purchases made through your links. If you have an obscure, infrequently visited blog, don't expect any instant riches. But if you have a heavily visited site—maybe one that deals with music—the commissions can add up.

Smart Playlists: iTunes as DJ

iTunes can create playlists for you based on criteria that you specify. When you're in a hurry—or if you're just curious to see what iTunes comes up with—use iTunes' *smart playlists* feature to quickly assemble playlists. Smart playlists take advantage of all that information that's stored along with your music—its genre, artist, year, and more—to enable you to enjoy and present your music library in some fun ways.

Creating a smart playlist involves specifying the criteria for the songs you want included in the playlist—for example, songs whose genre is jazz and whose year is in the range of 1960 to 1969. You can choose to limit the size of the playlist using various criteria, including playing time (don't create a playlist longer than 74 minutes); disk space (don't create a playlist larger than 2 GB); number of songs (limit this playlist to 20 songs); and much more. You'll find some smart playlist ideas on page 54.

You can also use smart playlists to corral videos and podcasts. For example, you might create a smart playlist that collects all unplayed podcasts or all unwatched episodes of a TV show.

The smart playlists feature is really just a sophisticated search command. But remember, a good playlist is more than a series of songs that meet certain rules—it also presents those songs in a musically and emotionally pleasing way. For tips on building good playlists, see page 48.

Creating a Smart Playlist

To create a smart playlist, choose New Smart Playlist from the File menu or press the Option key while clicking the playlist button (⚙) in the lower-left corner of the iTunes window.

What are you interested in? Choose options from the pop-up menus and type text in the box. Here, I'm building a smart playlist of all my Herbie Hancock tunes.

iTunes normally organizes the songs in a smart playlist in random order, but you can choose to organize them by artist name, song name, and other criteria.

Want to be more specific? Click ⊕ to add another criterion (see opposite page).

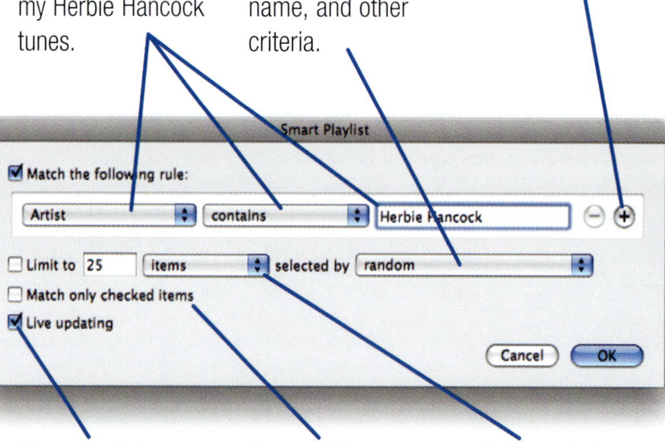

iTunes updates a smart playlist's contents as you add items to (or remove them from) your music library.

To turn a smart playlist into a static one, uncheck Live Updating.

To have iTunes search only those items that have a checkmark next to them in your library, check this box.

You can limit the size of the smart playlist to a maximum number of items, minutes, hours, megabytes (MB), or gigabytes (GB).

Be More Specific: Adding Criteria

When you want to be more specific, use more than one rule in your smart playlist. In this example, my smart playlist will contain all George Duke songs from the 1970s that are under five minutes long.

To add another rule, click the plus button (⊕). To remove a rule, click the minus button (⊖) .

To have iTunes apply all of your criteria as it searches and compiles the playlist, choose All. If you choose Any, iTunes adds an item if it matches any of your criteria.

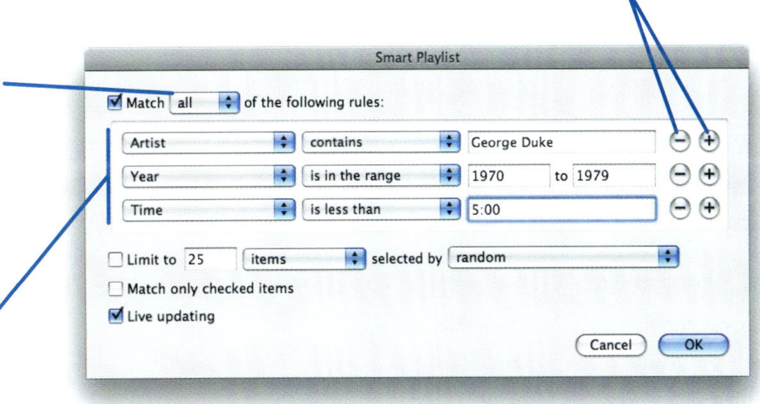

You can choose from and combine rules in more than twenty categories. For some inspiration, see the following pages.

Smart Playlist Tips

Changing a Smart Playlist

To modify a smart playlist's criteria or update settings, select the smart playlist and choose Edit Smart Playlist from the File menu (or press ⌘-I).

Create a Purchased Items Playlist

iTunes lists items you've purchased from the iTunes Store in a special playlist named Purchased. However, the Purchased playlist lists only songs you've purchased using that particular computer. If you move those purchased songs to a different computer, they won't show up in its Purchased playlist. And that can complicate backup sessions.

The solution? Create a smart playlist containing only items you've purchased. Set up the Smart Playlist window to contain two criteria: Kind contains *protected* and Kind contains *purchased*. Then, from the Match pop-up menu, choose Any. These criteria cover protected (that is, DRM-shackled) songs and videos as well as DRM-free iTunes Plus songs. Keep the Live Updating box checked, and you'll always have a full list of your purchases, no matter which Mac you use to do your buying.

A Cookbook of Smart Playlists

Some smart playlist ideas are obvious: a playlist containing songs from your favorite artist, a playlist of dance tunes, and so on.

But smart playlists aren't just a quick way to create playlists; they're also a great way to rediscover your music and explore your library in ways you might not think of otherwise. In short, don't restrict yourself to the obvious.

As you can see, the Smart Playlist dialog box lets you search on more than 30 criteria. Here are some smart playlist ideas to get your creative juices flowing.

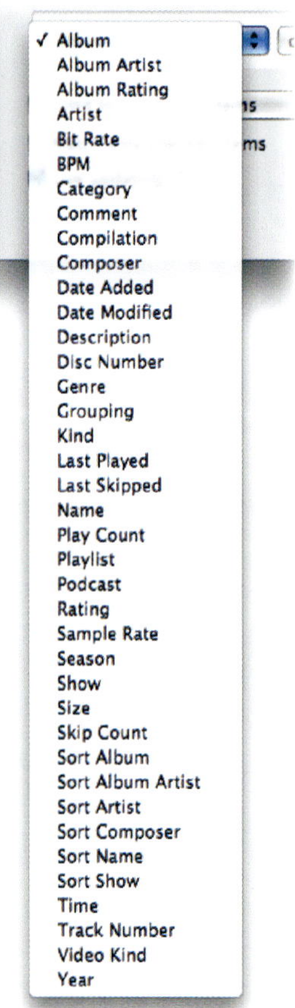

Smart Playlist Suggestions

For a Compilation of	Specify These Criteria
Short dance tunes	Genre is *Dance* and Time is less than 5:00 minutes
The same song performed by various artists	Song Name is equal to *name*
Songs added to your library recently	Date Added is in the last 1 week (adjust date value as desired)
Songs from a particular artist and era	Artist is *name* and Year is in the range *years here*
Songs you haven't listened to recently	Last Played is not in the last *x* days (adjust date value as desired)
Items with missing info—for example, no album name	Album is (leave the third field blank)
Audio files that are not in MP3 format	Kind is not *MPEG audio file*
Songs you've added but never listened to	Play Count is 0 (zero)
Songs you've created in GarageBand and exported to iTunes	Kind contains *AIFF audio file* (assuming that you haven't compressed them)
Audiobooks from Audible.com	Kind contains *audible*
PDF documents in your music library	Kind contains *PDF*
Songs that ask a question	Song Name contains *?*
Songs from your high-school days (assuming that you've reached them)	Year is in the range 1975 to 1978 (for example)
TV shows you've purchased	Video Kind is *TV Show*
Videos you've purchased	Kind contains *protected MPEG-4 video*
Podcasts you haven't listened to	Podcast is true and Play Count is 0 (zero)

More Smart Playlist Tips

A Smart Playlist for Small iPods

Do you have an iPod with a relatively limited capacity—an iPod shuffle or nano, for example? Instead of letting iTunes decide what to copy to the iPod as described on page 111, you might want to set up a smart playlist that selects only songs you like and omits ones in space-consuming audio formats.

The smart playlist below, based on one originally developed by *Playlist* magazine's Chris Breen, does exactly that.

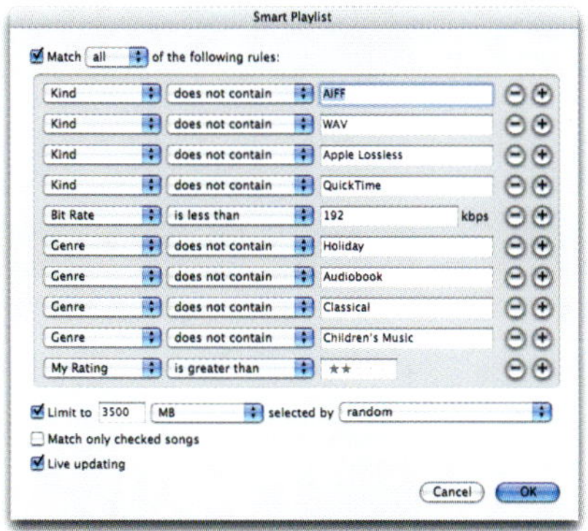

You might want to fine-tune the *Limit to* value to accommodate your specific iPod. The 3500MB value (roughly 3.5GB) is ideal for a 4GB iPod nano.

After creating this playlist, set up your iPod preferences to update only that playlist (see page 108).

Including or Excluding Existing Playlists

You can have iTunes include or exclude specific playlists when putting together a smart playlist. Choose the Playlist item from the leftmost pop-up menu, choose "is" or "is not" from the middle pop-up menu, then choose a playlist name from the rightmost pop-up menu.

This gives you more control over which songs iTunes selects. For example, to put together a playlist of all the jazz you've bought from the iTunes Store, create two criteria: Genre is jazz, and Playlist is Purchased Music.

Or, assemble a playlist of the highest rated songs in a favorite playlist: My Rating is greater than three stars, and Playlist is My Favorites (for example).

You can also use this feature to create more sophisticated search rules. For example, say you want to assemble a smart playlist of your R&B and jazz tunes from the 1960s. First, create a smart playlist that locates all your R&B and jazz. Create two criteria: Genre is R&B *and* Genre is Jazz, then choose Any from the Match pop-up menu. Name this playlist something like "R&B and Jazz."

Next, create another smart playlist with the following two criteria: Playlist is R&B and Jazz, and Year is in the range 1960 to 1969.

Don't Forget Comments

As described on page 26, you can assign comments and other tidbits of information to your songs. These tidbits pair up beautifully with smart playlists. For example, if you're a jazz buff, you might use the Comments field to store the sidemen who appear on a given song—Ron Carter on bass, Freddie Hubbard on trumpet. You could then create a smart playlist containing songs in which Freddie Hubbard appears: Comment contains *Freddie Hubbard.*

Something Completely Different

Want to explore your music library in a completely different way? Try making a smart playlist built around the Track Number field. For example, to create a smart playlist containing the first song in all of your albums, specify Track Number is 1. If one of your favorite artists always starts his or her albums with a particularly cool track, add the artist's name: Artist is George Duke and Track Number is 1.

Want More?

Looking for even more smart playlists? Believe it or not, there's a Web site devoted to them: www.smartplaylists.com. Check it out for smart playlist ideas and iTunes tips of all kinds.

Find that Tune: Searching and Browsing

As your iTunes library grows, you'll want to take advantage of the features iTunes provides for locating songs, artists, videos, podcasts, and albums.

With the Search box, you can quickly narrow down the list of items displayed to only those items that match the criterion you typed.

With the Browse button, you can quickly scan your library by artist, album name, or genre. You can also browse your library of ringtones, podcasts, and audiobooks.

And with the Show in Finder command in the File menu, you can quickly display the actual disk file that corresponds to a given item in your library or in a playlist. That can be handy in a variety of circumstances.

Searching

Step 1. Select the part of your library that you want to search.

For example, to search music, click the Music item in the Library list. To search movies, click Movies. To search a specific playlist, click the playlist's name.

Step 2. Click within the Search box and begin typing.

As you type in the Search box, iTunes narrows down the list of items displayed. To see everything in the selected area of your library, select the text in the Search box and press Delete, or simply click the ⊗ in the Search box.

Notes and Tips

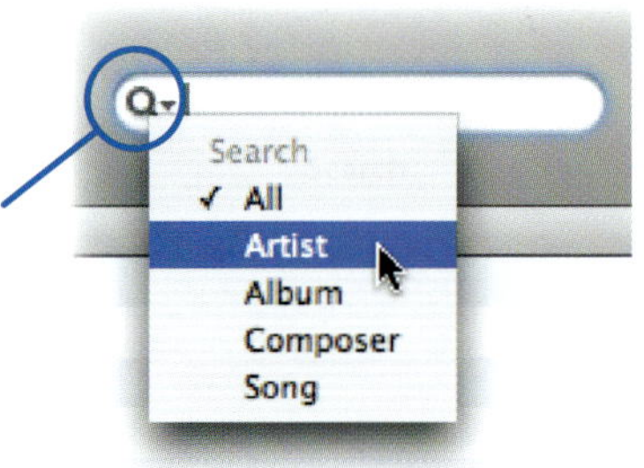

Narrow your searches. To search with more precision, choose an option from the pop-up menu. For example, to find songs from Jennifer Love Hewitt without also displaying songs with "love" in their names, choose Artist.

Searching comments, too. When you search for music, iTunes searches the album title, artist, genre, composer, and song title items. If you make use of the Comments field in the Get Info dialog box, you can have iTunes search it, too. Just display the Comments column: choose View > View Options and check the Comments box.

Finding an Item's Disk File

There may be times when you want to locate an item's disk file on your hard drive—to back it up, for example, to move it to another drive, or to simply determine where it's stored.

To locate an item's disk file, select the song and choose Show in Finder from the File menu (or press ⌘-R). iTunes switches you to the Finder, opens the folder containing the song, and highlights the song file.

Browsing

To browse your music library by artist and album name, click the Browse button (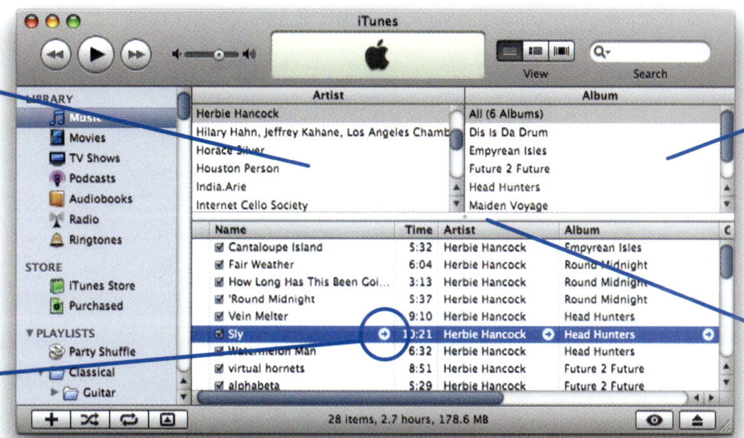).

The Artist pane lists all the artists in your library. Select an artist name, and iTunes displays that artist's albums in the Album pane.

Use the link arrows to quickly browse your library: press the Option key while clicking on the link arrow for an artist, song, or album. (To customize this feature, see page 86.)

The Album pane lists all the albums in your library or those from a selected artist. Select an album name, and iTunes displays the songs from that album.

Drag the separator up or down to resize the window panes.

Browsing by Genre

Have a lot of CDs that feature multiple artists? Check this box, and iTunes adds a Compilations item to the Artist list.

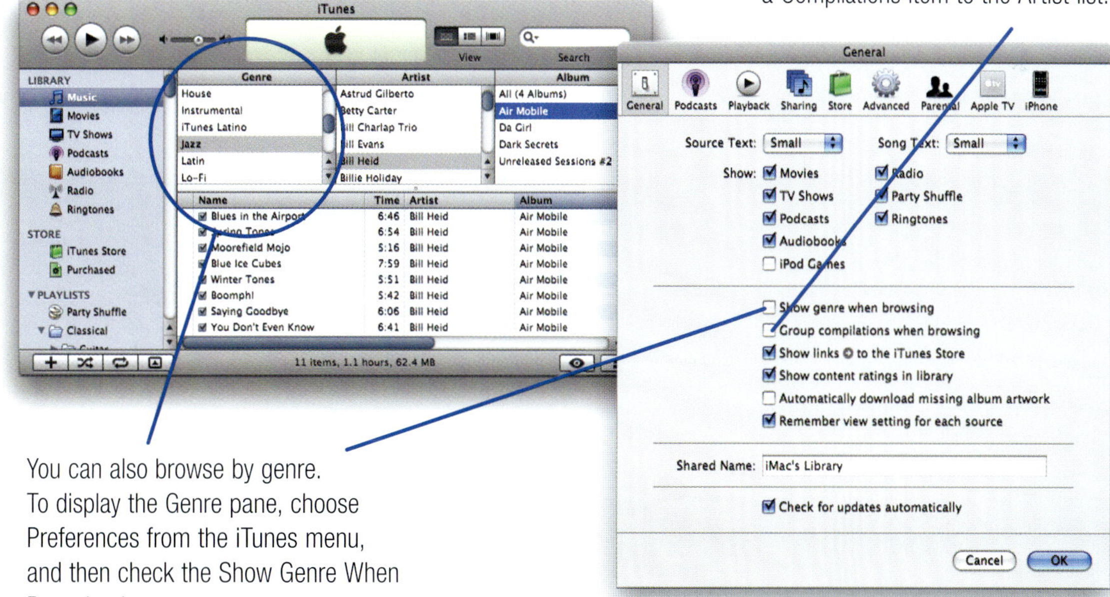

You can also browse by genre. To display the Genre pane, choose Preferences from the iTunes menu, and then check the Show Genre When Browsing box.

Improving Sound Quality with the Equalizer

The iTunes *equalizer* lets you boost and attenuate various frequency ranges; think of it as a very sophisticated set of bass and treble controls. You might pump up the bass to make up for small speakers. You might boost the high frequencies to make up for aging ears. Or you might just prefer a little extra sonic seasoning on your music.

The iTunes equalizer (EQ) divides the audio spectrum into ten *bands*, and provides a slider that lets you boost or attenuate frequencies in each band. The bands start at 32 hertz (Hz), a deeper bass than most of us can hear, and go all the way up to 16 kilohertz (KHz), which, while short of dog-whistle territory, approaches the upper limits of human hearing. (If you've been around for more than several decades or have listened to a lot of loud music, 16 KHz is probably out of your hearing range.)

iTunes provides more than 20 equalization presets from which to choose. You can listen to all your music with one setting applied, or you can assign separate settings to individual songs. You can also adjust EQ settings by hand and create your own presets.

Your iPod will also grant your EQ wishes. If you assign an EQ setting to a song and then copy the song to an iPod, the iPod plays the song with that setting.

Note: Although iTunes allows you to assign EQ settings to videos, it ignores them; iTunes applies EQ to music only.

Using the Equalizer

To display the equalizer, click the Equalizer button (▥) near the lower-right corner of the iTunes window, or choose Equalizer from the Window menu (Option-⌘-2).

Check this box to turn on the equalizer.

Drag a slider up to boost the frequencies in that range; drag it down to attenuate them.

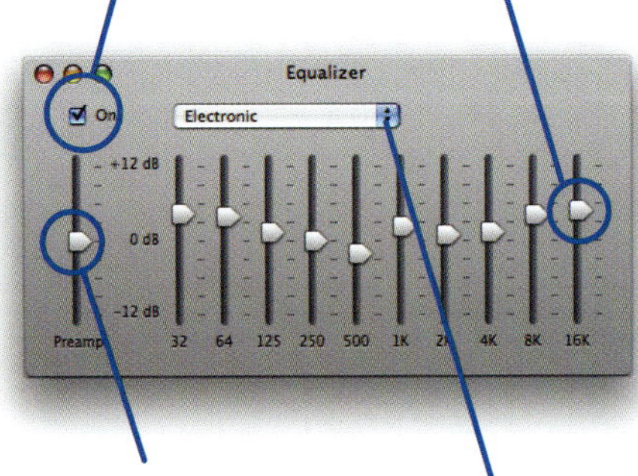

The preamp boosts or attenuates the volume for all frequencies equally. For example, if you create a custom EQ setting for your quiet classical guitar recordings, you might boost the preamp volume as well.

Manual
Presets
✓ Acoustic
Bass Booster
Bass Reducer
Classical
Dance
Deep
Electronic
Flat
Hip-Hop
Jazz
Latin
Loudness
Lounge
Piano
Pop
R&B
Rock
Small Speakers
Spoken Word
test treb boost
Treble Booster
Treble Reducer
Vocal Booster

Choose a preset, create a new preset, or manage your list of presets.

Creating Your Own Preset

Step 1. To save a customized preset, choose Make Preset from the preset pop-up menu.

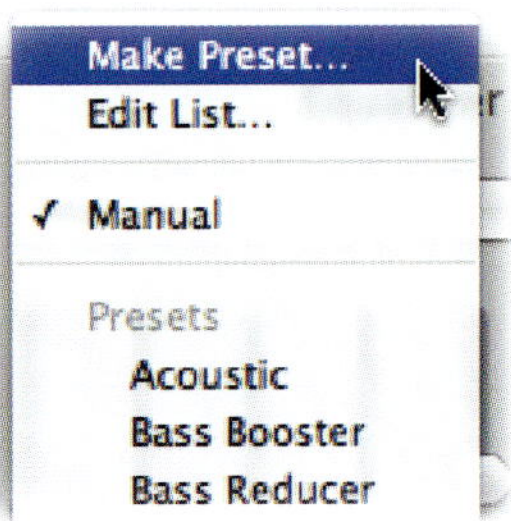

Step 2. Name the preset and click OK.

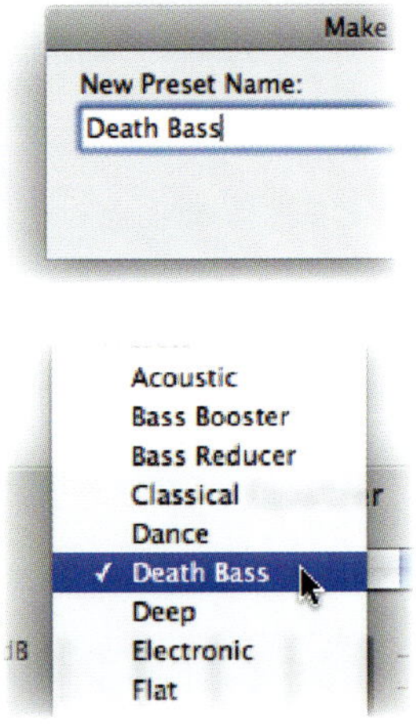

The new preset appears in the pop-up menu.

Assigning Presets to Individual Songs

If you've turned on the equalizer, iTunes applies the current EQ setting to any song you play back. However, you can also assign EQ settings on a song-by-song basis.

Step 1. Choose Edit > View Options and verify that the Equalizer box is checked.

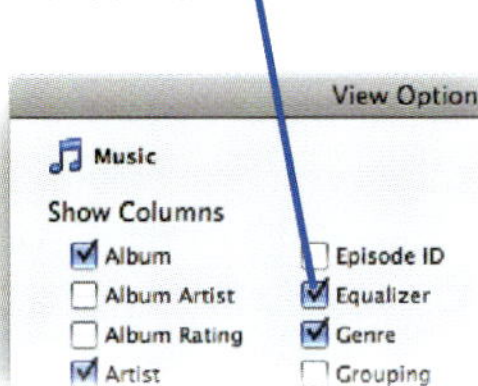

Step 2. Choose the desired preset from the pop-up menu in the Equalizer column.

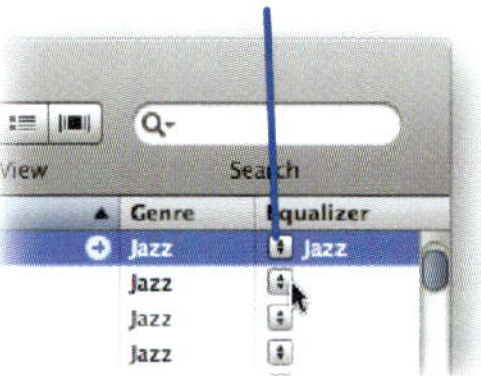

Tip: To change the EQ settings for several songs at once, select the songs and choose Get Info from the File menu. Then choose the desired EQ setting.

Presets that Make You Smile

You may have noticed that many of iTunes' presets have a smile-like appearance: the low- and high-frequency ranges are boosted to a greater degree than the mid-range frequencies.

Audio gurus call this shape the *Fletcher-Munson curve*. It reflects the fact that, at most listening levels, our ears are less sensitive to low and high frequencies than they are to mid-range frequencies.

Chances are your stereo system has a Loudness button. When you turn it on, the stereo applies a similar curve to make the music sound more natural at lower volume levels.

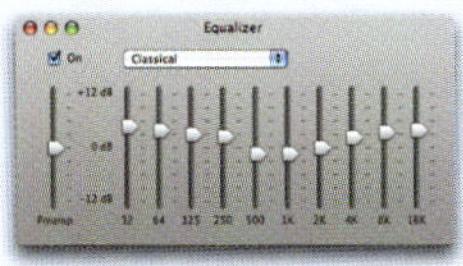

Classical

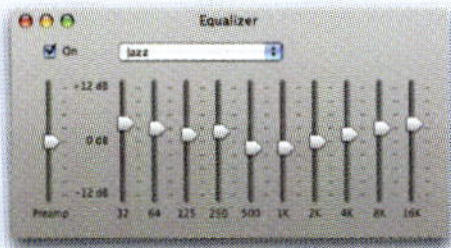

Jazz

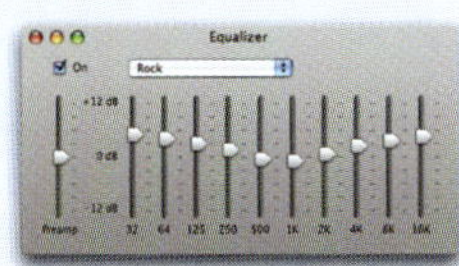

Rock

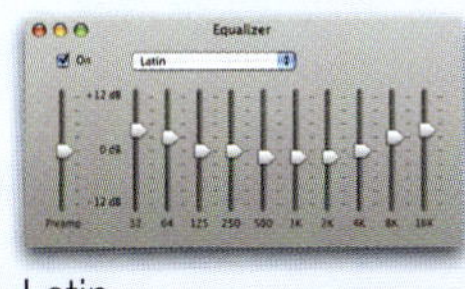

Latin

"That Song Needs a Bit More 250"

Being able to control the volume of 10 different frequency ranges is great, but how do you know which ranges to adjust? Here's a guide to how frequency ranges correlate with those of some common musical instruments and the human voice. Note that these ranges don't take into account harmonics, which are the tonal complexities that help us discern between instruments. Harmonics can easily exceed 20 KHz.

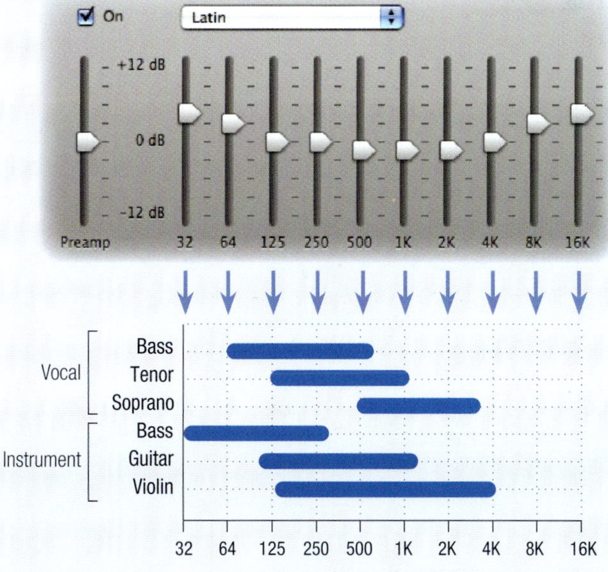

Burning Audio CDs

It may be on life support, but the compact disc player isn't dead yet. Using the CD or DVD burner in your Mac, you can create your own audio CDs—to play in the car, in the living room, on a boombox, or at a friend's house.

To burn some songs onto a CD, you must first add them to a playlist. Once you've done that, burning a CD is a two-click proposition.

iTunes also has some advanced burning features that enable you to burn other types of discs; for details on them and for tips for all your burning endeavors, see page 62.

Chances are you'll be burning using the CD or DVD burner built into your Mac. But iTunes also works with many external burners sold by La Cie, Formac, EZQuest, and others. These drives typically connect to the Mac's USB or FireWire connector.

Step 1.
Select the Playlist You Want to Burn

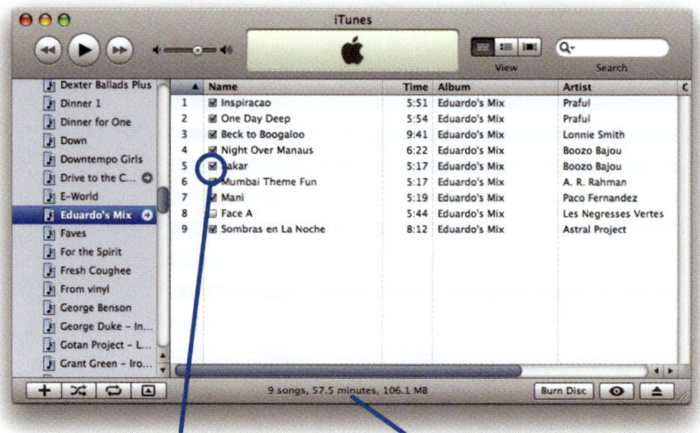

If the playlist contains a song that you don't want to burn, uncheck the box next to the song's name.

iTunes displays the playlist's total duration here.

Notes and Tips

Duration matters. If you're burning an audio CD, keep the playlist's duration under 74 minutes. If your entire playlist won't fit on one audio CD, iTunes will prompt you to burn additional discs.

Your burning desires. By using the Preferences dialog box, you can customize how iTunes burns audio CDs. For example, the Sound Check option ensures that songs on the CD have a consistent volume level, while the audio-gap options let you control how much silence separates each track. For details on these options, see the following pages.

Step 2.
Click the Burn Disc Button

When you click Burn Disc, iTunes opens your Mac's CD tray and instructs you to insert a blank CD.

Note: As an alternative to clicking the Burn Disc button, you can choose Burn Playlist to Disc from the File menu.

To cancel the burn, click here.

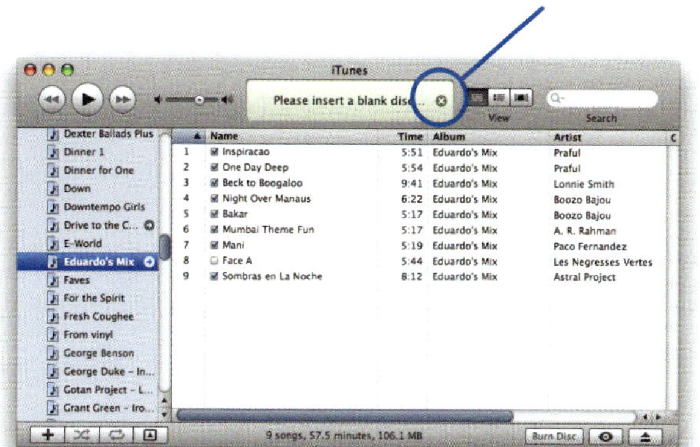

Step 3.
Insert a Blank Disc

As the CD burns, iTunes displays a status message. You can cancel a burn in progress by clicking the ⊗ button, but you'll end up with a *coaster*—a damaged CD blank whose only useful purpose is to sit beneath a cold drink.

What You Can't Burn

iTunes lets you burn audio CDs containing just about anything—just about.

Here are some items that are *not* flammable.

Purchased videos. You can't burn audio CDs or DVD-Video discs containing videos purchased from the iTunes Store. You can, however, burn backups of the videos by burning a data CD as described on the following pages.

Unauthorized protected music. You can't burn a DRM-protected song purchased from the iTunes Store unless your Mac is authorized for the same account as the one used to buy the tune. If you try, a dialog box appears asking for the account and password for the account used to buy the song. This restriction and the following one don't apply to iTunes Plus songs (see page 41).

The pesky eighth copy. As noted on page 39, you can't burn more than seven copies of a playlist that contains protected music.

Tips for Your Burning Endeavors

By adjusting burning preferences, you can control the pause between songs, volume levels, and even the format of your final CD. Choose Preferences from the iTunes menu, click the Advanced button, then click Burning.

Gap Control

When iTunes burns an audio CD, it uses a two-second gap to separate songs. Depending on what you're burning, you may want to omit, or at least change, that gap. On many albums, one song flows seamlessly into the next. When burning these kinds of tracks, close the gap: choose None from the Gap Between Songs pop-up menu.

Unfortunately, because of the nature of audio compression, you may still hear a tiny gap between songs. If you can't bear even the smallest pause, rip the songs from an audio CD using the Join Tracks option (page 20).

Volume Control

Not all albums are mastered at the same volume level, and if you mix and match tracks from a few CDs, some songs may sound much quieter than others. Don't reach for the volume knob—click the Sound Check box before burning, and iTunes adjusts each track to make the final CD's levels consistent.

You can also apply Sound Check when playing music in iTunes; see page 80 for details.

Burning MP3 CDs

Normally, iTunes burns CDs in standard audio CD format. But you can also burn tracks as MP3 files; this lets you take advantage of MP3's compression so you can squeeze more music onto a CD—roughly ten times the number of songs that an audio CD will hold.

But there are a couple of catches. Catch Number One: Most audio CD players can't play MP3-format CDs. If you're shopping for a CD or DVD player, you may want to look for one that supports MP3 playback.

Catch Number Two: When you burn a playlist in MP3 format, iTunes skips over any songs that are stored in AAC format. If you've built a library of purchases from the iTunes Store—or if you use AAC when ripping your audio CDs—MP3 CD format won't be of much use to you.

To have iTunes burn in MP3 format, click the MP3 CD button in the Burning preferences dialog box.

When ripping CDs that you'll subsequently be burning in MP3 format, you might find it useful to activate the iTunes track numbering option: in the Preferences dialog box, click Importing and then check the box labeled Create file names with track number.

Track numbering is useful because many players play the songs on MP3 CDs in alphanumeric order—activating track numbering will enable the tracks to play back in the correct order.

Using CD Text

Many CD and DVD players are able to display track information—song and artist name, for example—when that information is present on the disc. This capability comes from a part of the audio CD standard called *CD Text.*

If you have a player that supports CD Text, you can have iTunes record the track information on the CD: just check the Include CD Text box in the Burning portion of the preferences dialog box.

Players that don't support CD Text simply ignore the information on the disc, so it can't hurt to choose this option when burning audio CDs.

To learn more about CD Text—and how iTunes retrieves track information from your audio CDs—see macilife.com/itunes.

Backing Up Your Library

You've bought some music—and then your hard drive dies. The songs and videos you bought are gone, and the only way to download them again is to buy them again.

Clearly, backing up is good to do. iTunes can help.

Choose File > Back Up to Disc, and iTunes offers to back up your entire library and all playlists or only iTunes Store purchases.

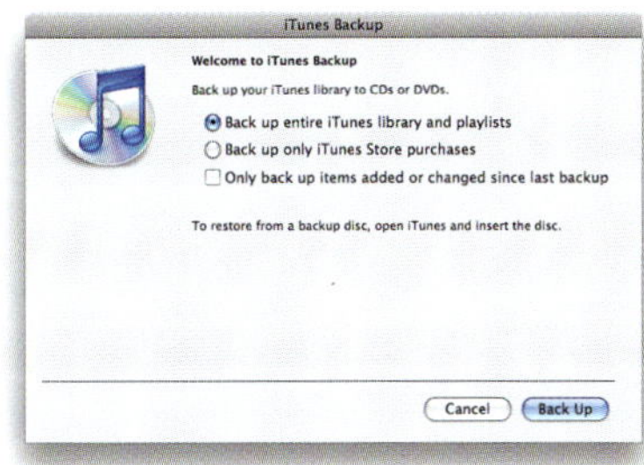

If you've backed up once before, you can also choose to back up only those items that you've added since the last backup session.

Which option should you choose? If you have a modest-sized iTunes library—or a generous supply of blank discs—back up everything. Or just back up your purchases. If the worst happens, you'll have to re-rip your CDs and recreate your playlists—but at least you won't have to buy your purchases again.

Tip: Most current Macs provide dual-layer SuperDrives. Buy dual-layer DVD blanks, and you can burn 8.5GB on each disc—enabling you to fit even a large iTunes library on a relatively small number of discs.

If the worst does happen and your iTunes library is lost or damaged, start iTunes and insert the first disc in your backup set. iTunes asks if you'd like to restore from the disc.

The built-in backup feature in iTunes works well, but the easiest way to back up a large iTunes library is to drag it to a second hard drive. An external FireWire or USB hard drive is inexpensive and makes great backup media for music and photos alike. Go to your Home directory (choose Home from the Finder's Go menu), then locate and double-click your Music folder. Locate the folder named iTunes and drag it to the other hard drive. Unlike the burning approach, this technique also backs up all of your playlists.

Tip: If you've copied your entire music library to an iPod, you can recover your library from your iPod; see page 110.

Blank Advice

Many brands of CD-R media are available, and some people swear by a given brand. Some users even claim that certain colors of CD-R blanks are better than others.

My advice: don't sweat it—just buy name-brand CD-R blanks. And don't fret about their colors. Color varies depending on the organic dyes used by the CD-R's manufacturer, and different manufacturers use different dye formulations. Color isn't a useful indicator of CD-R quality anyway.

How long will your burned CDs last? Manufacturers toss out figures ranging from 75 to 200 years, but these are only estimates based on accelerated aging tests that attempt to simulate the effects of time.

One thing is certain: a CD-R will last longer when kept away from heat and bright light. Avoid scratching either side of a CD-R—use a felt-tipped pen to label it, and don't write any more than you need to. (The solvents in the ink can damage the CD over time.)

Also, think twice about applying a peel-and-stick label to the CD. The label's adhesive can damage the CD over time, and if you don't center the label perfectly, the CD will be out of balance as it spins, which could cause playback problems.

To learn more about CD-R media, visit the CD-Recordable FAQ at www.cdrfaq.org.

Burning to RW Media

For broadest compatibility with CD players, you'll want to burn using CD-R blanks, which can't be erased and reused. But the CD burners in all current Macs can also use RW media—rewritable media, which costs more but can be erased and reused again and again.

A growing number of CD players can play back rewritable media, and if yours is among them, you might consider using rewritable media for some burning jobs—such as burning some podcasts for car listening or to back up your iTunes library.

Note that iTunes can't erase an CD-RW disc. To do that, use Mac OS X's Disk Utility program; it's located in the Utilities folder, inside the Applications folder.

Finishing Touches: Printing Case Inserts and More

After you've burned a CD, you might want to print an insert that you can slide into the disc's jewel case. With the printing features in iTunes, you can do this and more.

When printing a case insert, you can choose from a variety of insert designs, called *themes*. Some themes take advantage of the album artwork feature described on the opposite page. If your playlist's songs have corresponding album art, iTunes uses the art for the front and back of the case insert. With a few mouse clicks, you can even put your own artwork on a jewel case insert.

You can also print several types of song and album lists. They're a great way to produce a hard-copy reference of your music library and favorite playlists.

If your playlist contains songs from multiple albums, you can use the Mosaic themes to produce a collage of album art.

Want to use just one album's art for the cover? Before you choose Print, select the song containing that art.

To Print a Jewel Case Insert

Step 1. Select the playlist for which you want a case insert.

Step 2. Choose Print from the File menu and choose a theme.

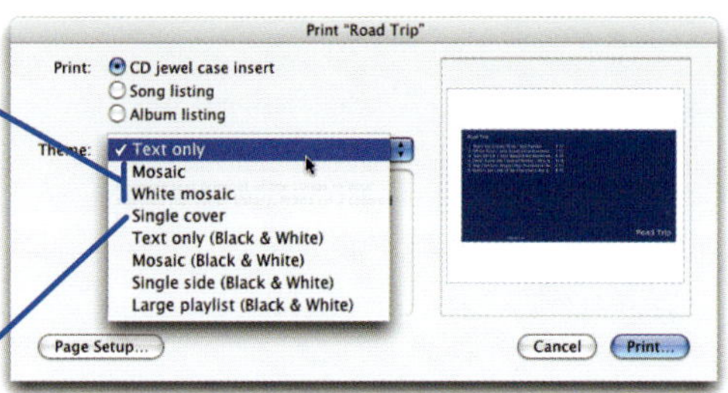

Step 3. Adjust Page Setup options as needed, then click Print or press Return.

Step 4. Trim the case insert, using the crop marks as a guide.

More About Artwork

iTunes can store album artwork—for example, an image of a CD cover—along with your music. The artwork also displays elsewhere, as the following pages describe.

Items you buy from the iTunes Store include artwork. To display it, click the Show/Hide Artwork button.

To switch between the currently playing song and the currently selected song, click here. A song can contain multiple images; click the little arrows to display other images.

To hide (or show) the artwork, click this button.

To display the artwork in a larger window, click here. To add an image to the currently selected song, drag an image here. To copy the art into another program, drag it from here to the program.

To rearrange the images, drag them left and right. To use a specific image in a jewel case insert, drag it so that it's the first image in the list.

To add another image, click Add or simply drag the image into the artwork area. To delete an image, select it and then click Delete.

More Artwork Tips

You can also view and modify a song's artwork by using the Song Information dialog box. Select a song, choose Get Info from File menu, and click the Artwork button. In the example below, the song contains four images. You can store even more, but keep in mind that each image increases the size of your music file, thus leaving less free space on your hard drive and iPod.

To make the thumbnail images smaller or larger, drag the slider.

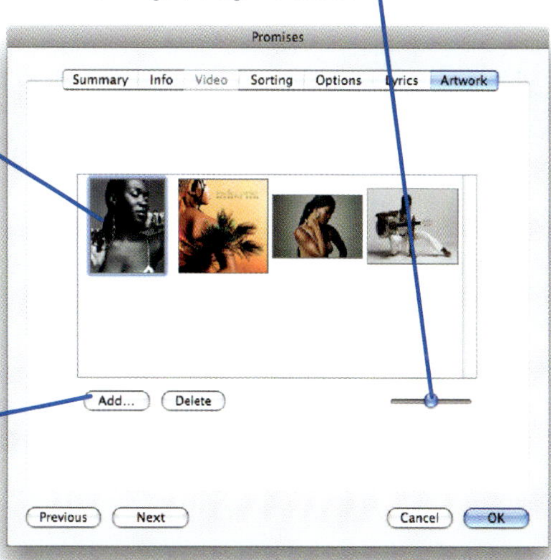

Print your own artwork. You can print your own artwork—including a photo from your iPhoto library—on a jewel case insert. First, add the image to a song. (For a photo, simply drag it from the iPhoto window to the artwork area.) Drag the image so it's the first image in the list, then print. To reduce the size of the song file, delete the image after printing.

Cover Flow and Other Art Matters

Compact discs, DVDs, and vinyl albums have an advantage that digital files don't: you can touch them. There's a tactile pleasure to handling cases and jackets and discs that the digital world doesn't provide (though fondling an iPod is rather fun in its own way).

Artwork plays a large role in the world of spinning discs. Over time, you associate an album's cover with the music. Every music lover has experienced it: you see an album cover with your eyes, and hear the songs in your head.

Apple's Cover Flow feature puts your senses of sight and touch back to work. Found in iTunes, the iPod family, and elsewhere, Cover Flow shows the artwork for your albums in a carousel-like display.

Other items from the iTunes Store, including videos and audiobooks, also include artwork, making Cover Flow a great way to visually explore your library. Click to "paw" through your collection. You can even have the artwork fill your screen while your music plays. That's bigger than a vinyl album cover.

Full Screen. Use the controls at the bottom of the screen to pause, skip songs, adjust volume, and more.

Using Cover Flow View

Step 1. In the Library area of the iTunes window, select the item you want to view in Cover Flow view.

You can view your entire library or a specific item, such as your TV Shows list or a playlist.

Step 2. Click the Cover Flow button to the left of the Search box (▣) or choose View > Cover Flow View.

Artwork for the currently selected song appears front and center. To paw through your library, click the album covers to the left and right of the current one.

To resize the Cover Flow area, drag this separator up and down.

You can also browse by clicking the scroll bar, or tapping the left and right arrow keys on your keyboard.

Switch to full-screen view. Keyboard shortcut: ⌘-F.

Learn how iTunes works with artwork under the hood.
www.macilife.com/itunes

Artwork Tips

Songs with No Art

If you've ripped songs from obscure CDs or downloaded them from the Internet, there's a good chance your library contains artless music.

You have several options for completing your art collection.

Use iTunes. Select one or more artless songs, then choose Advanced > Get Album Artwork. iTunes retrieves the artwork—provided the songs are available in the iTunes Store. Start with this option: iTunes retrieves nice, large images that look great.

Use a utility. Artwork utilities, such as Fetch Art by Yoel Inbar, retrieve artwork from other sources, such as Amazon.com. For links to artwork utilities, see macilife.com/itunes.

Do it yourself. By going to Google's Image Search page (www.google.com/images), you can search for artwork or artist photos. Look for the largest image size available (300 by 300 pixels, which is much smaller than iTunes Store artwork, is often the best you'll find). When you find one, drag the image from your browser window into the song information window, as described on page 67.

Other Art Openings

Artwork and Cover Flow figure prominently in Apple's world. Here are some more places where your art might pop up.

In your hand. The latest iPod models provide a Cover Flow display. Choose Music > Cover Flow, then use the click wheel to flip through your library. To see a list of songs on the album, press the Center button.

Have an iPod touch or iPhone? Navigate to your songs, then turn it sideways to activate Cover Flow view. Sweep your finger through your library. To see the songs on an album, tap the cover.

In the Front Row. Artwork appears when you browse your iTunes library using the Front Row software that is included with many Macs.

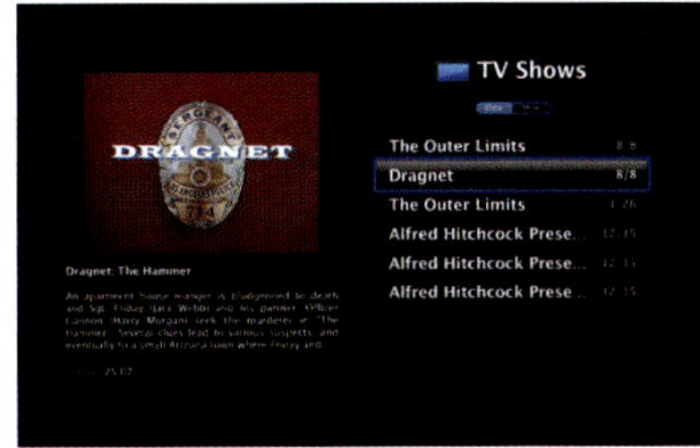

On your TV. If you have an AppleTV (pages 76–79), artwork appears on your TV screen while you browse and listen.

On your newest cat. In Mac OS X 10.5 Leopard, you can use the Desktop & Screen Saver system preference to display an animated artwork screen saver. In the Screen Savers list, choose the iTunes Artwork visualizer.

Tip: For a particularly mesmerizing display, click the Desktop & Screen Saver window's Options button and increase the number of rows while decreasing the delay.

In other utilities. Many iTunes add-ons, such as the magnificent CoverSutra (page 91), make use of album artwork in the course of enhancing iTunes.

Sharing Libraries on a Network

If you have multiple Macs or Windows PCs on a network, you can use iTunes' sharing feature to turn them into media jukeboxes. Share a computer's iTunes library, and other computers on the network can connect to it and play its music, podcasts, and videos. (You'll need to install iTunes for Windows on the PCs.)

Sharing enables all manner of media networking options. You might keep all of your music and videos on one Mac—no wasting disk space by storing an iTunes library on each Mac or PC on your network. Conversely, you might prefer to segregate your library—put your kids' music on their iMac and your music on yours—while still giving each Mac access to every song. You might want to set up a jukebox Mac to dish out tunes to the office. Or use AirPort wireless networking to listen at poolside using your MacBook.

If you use a Mac that supports Apple's Front Row software, you can also access shared music libraries using Front Row's Music mode. In Front Row, choose Sources, then select an iTunes library from the list. You can also access shared libraries with an Apple TV (page 78). And if you're connected to a hotel's high-speed network, try looking for shared iTunes libraries. You may be surprised by how many you find.

The sharing feature relies on streaming: when you play something from another computer's library, the files are streamed across your network. The files are never actually copied from one computer to another.

Activating Sharing

To share your iTunes library with other computers on your network, choose iTunes > Preferences, then click the Sharing button.

To have your Mac look for shared libraries on your network, check this box.

To share your library, check this box.

You can share your entire library or only selected playlists. To share a specific playlist, click its check box.

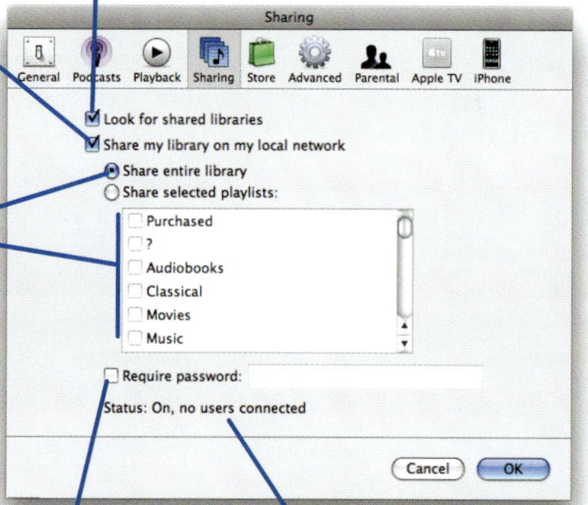

Don't want your kids (or parents) to access your shared library? Check this box, then specify a password.

When sharing is on, the Status area also shows how many users are connected.

Note: Be sure you're using the same version of iTunes on each computer on the network. Apple changes the format of the iTunes library now and then, and as a result, different versions of iTunes aren't always able to share libraries. If a shared library appears grey and an error message appears when you select it, it's probably because the shared library is coming from an incompatible version of iTunes.

Accessing Shared Libraries

If you've checked the Look for Shared Libraries box in the Sharing portion of the Preferences dialog box, iTunes scans your network and lists the shared libraries it finds.

SHARED
iMac's Library
Jim Heid's Music
Sophie's Library

To connect to a shared library, click its name. If the library requires a password, a dialog box appears.

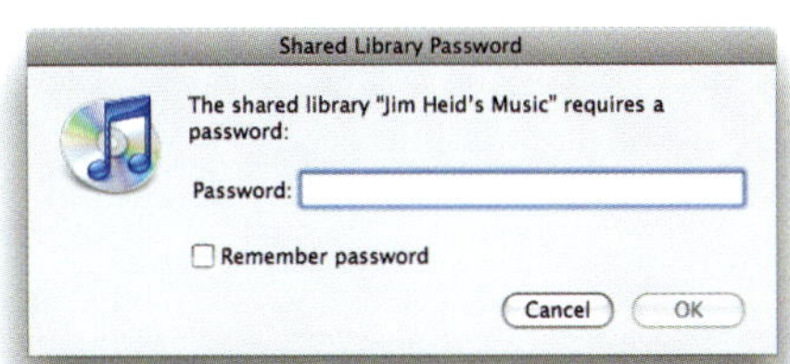

To view playlists in a shared library, click the little triangle next to the library's name.

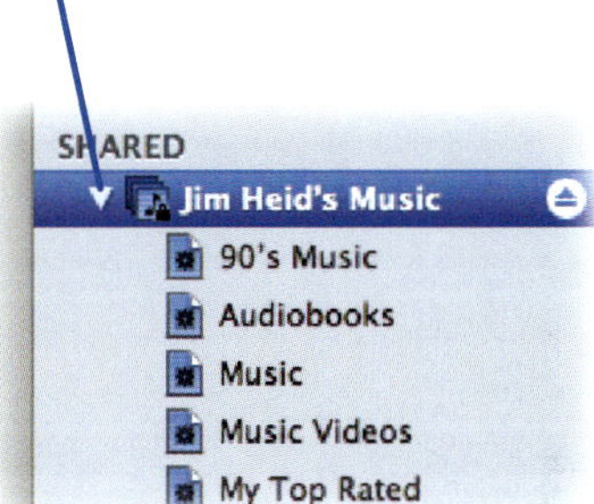

Tips for Sharing

Shared Items Are Play Only

Because shared songs and other items don't reside on your hard drive, you can't add them to playlists, delete them, burn them to a CD, or modify their names or other information.

Up to Five a Day

Up to five computers can connect to a shared library on a given day. If a sixth user tries to connect, he or she sees an error message along these lines: *The shared music library "Jim's Music" accepts only five different users each day. Please try again later.*

There is but one solution to this restriction: wait until tomorrow.

Disconnecting

To disconnect from a shared library, click the Disconnect button ( ) in the lower-right corner of the iTunes window, or Control-click on the library's name and choose Disconnect from the pop-up shortcut menu. Or, click on the eject button that appears next to the library's name.

Authorization

If you want to play a purchased item from a shared library, you'll have to authorize your Mac by supplying your account name and password. (This doesn't apply to iTunes Plus purchases.) As noted on page 38, you can authorize up to five computers per account.

Tuning In to Internet Radio

The Internet is transforming a lot of things, and broadcasting is one of them. You can tune in to thousands of streaming Internet radio stations using iTunes and other programs.

Many of these stations are commercial or public broadcasters that are also making their audio available on the 'net. But most stations are Internet-only affairs, often set up by music lovers who simply want to share their tastes with the rest of us. You can join them—create your own radio station using a service such as Live365 (www.live365.com) or a streaming server program such as Rogue Amoeba's NiceCast (www.rogueamoeba.com).

If part of streaming audio's appeal is its diversity, the other part is its immediacy. Streaming playback begins just a few seconds after you click on a link—there's no waiting for huge sound files to download before you hear a single note.

Several formats for streaming audio exist, and MP3 is one of them. Using the iTunes Radio tuner, you can listen to Internet radio stations that stream in MP3 format.

To Listen to Internet Radio

Step 1. To display the radio tuner, click the Radio item.
Tip: To display the tuner in its own window, double-click.

Step 2. To display the stations in a genre, double-click the genre name or click the triangle to its left.

Note: If you don't see the Radio item, choose iTunes > Preferences, click General, and be sure the Radio check box is selected.

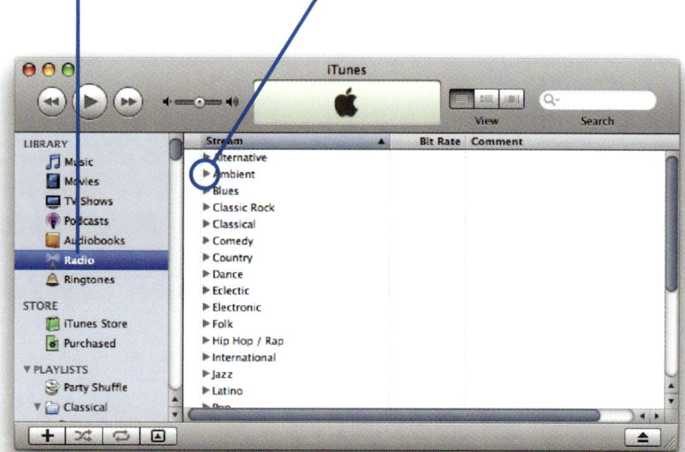

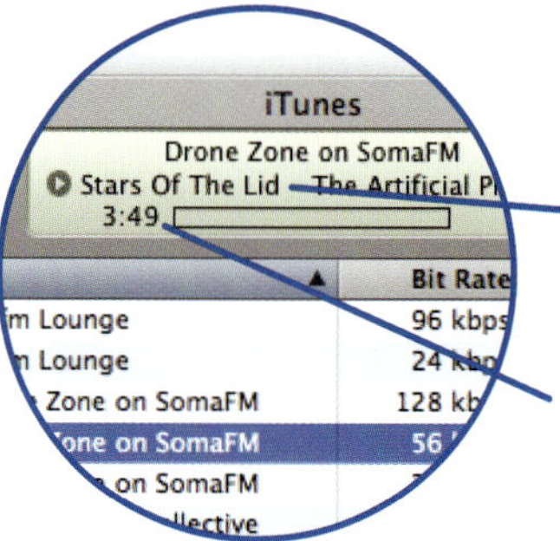

Step 3. To listen to a station, double-click its name.

Some stations show the name of the currently playing song.

iTunes shows how long you've been listening to a stream. Notice that when you're listening to a live stream, there is no control for skipping forward and backward within a song.

Bandwidth: Internet Radio's Antenna

The quality of your Internet radio "reception" depends in part on the speed of your Internet connection.

With Internet radio, information listed in the Bit Rate column is particularly important. It reflects not only how much the audio has been compressed, but also how fast a connection you'll need in order to listen without interruption. For example, if you have a 56 kbps modem connection, you won't be able to listen to a stream whose bit rate is higher than 56 kbps. (Indeed, even a 56 kbps stream may hiccup occasionally.)

▲	Bit Rate	Comment
	96 kbps	Sit back and en
	24 kbps	Sit back and en
›maFM	128 kbps	Served best chi
›maFM	56 kbps	Served best chi
›maFM	24 kbps	Served best chi
llective	128 kbps	Live ambient, d
SomaFM	128 kbps	A nicely chilled

The best-sounding stations use a bit rate of 128 kbps. Many stations provide multiple bit rates—for example, a 24 kbps version for modem users, and a 128 kbps version for broadband users.

If your broadband connection is relatively slow—for example, 128 kbps or 256 kbps—and you want to listen to Internet radio while also surfing Web sites, you might consider tuning in to a lower bit rate version of a station. That way, you free up some bandwidth for your other Internet activities.

How Streaming Works

When you begin playing back an Internet radio stream, iTunes connects to a streaming server, which downloads several seconds' worth of audio into an area of memory called a *buffer*. When the buffer is full, playback begins. The player then continues downloading audio into the buffer while simultaneously playing back the audio that it has already buffered. It's this just-in-time downloading that gives streaming its near-immediate gratification—most of the time, anyway.

If Internet congestion or connection problems interrupt the incoming stream, the buffer may empty completely, stalling playback while the buffer refills.

Recording Internet Radio and More

Internet radio is a fleeting affair—just as your radio doesn't store programs, iTunes and other streaming players don't store Internet audio on your hard drive. That means you can't add your favorite streaming radio programming to your iTunes library or listen to it on your iPod.

At least not without a little help. Several inexpensive programs can record streaming audio on your hard drive. In fact, they can record any sound your Mac can play. Thus, you can also record audio from DVDs: record some tunes from a favorite concert movie—or some dialog from your favorite Cheech and Chong romp—and burn an audio CD to play in the car.

You can also use one of these programs to record real-time performance effects in GarageBand. You can even record the soundtrack and explosions of a favorite video game, if that's your idea of easy listening.

Incidentally, if you have favorite AM or FM radio broadcasts that you'd like to record and add to your iTunes library (and iPod), check out Griffin Technology's RadioShark. It turns your Mac into a TiVo for radio, enabling you to schedule and record radio broadcasts.

Hijacking in Three Easy Steps

The top tool for recording the unrecordable is Rogue Amoeba Software's Audio Hijack (see opposite page for a look at other tools). Here's how to use it.

Step 1. Hijack.

Create a preset for the program with the audio you want to record. If you like, set a timer to start or stop recording at specific times. You can also specify that Audio Hijack run an AppleScript after recording (see page 90 for an introduction to AppleScripts). Audio Hijack includes scripts that use iTunes to encode a recording into AAC or MP3 format.

Step 2. Click the Record button and start playback.

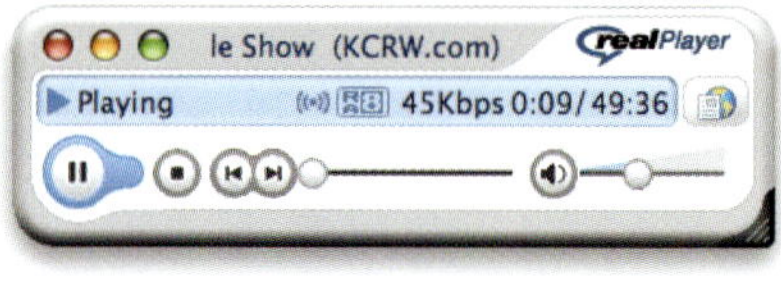

Click Audio Hijack's Record button and then begin playing back the audio. Audio Hijack starts recording when playback begins.

Step 3. Add to iTunes and tweak track info.

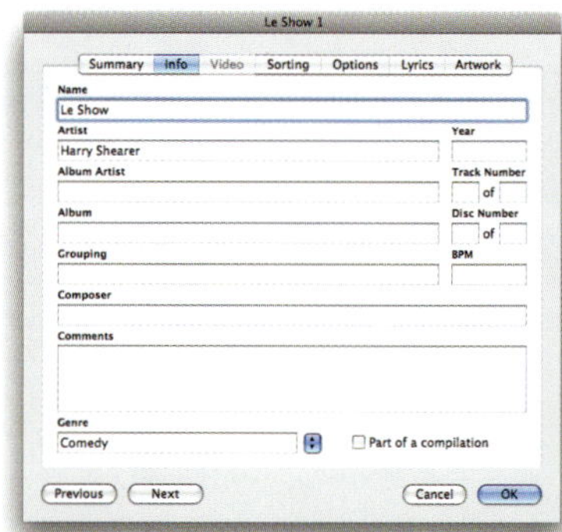

Add the recording to iTunes if necessary (if you run either of the encoding scripts after recording, this happens automatically). Then, locate the track in your iTunes library, choose Get Info from the File menu, and edit the song information.

For more information about adding audio files to iTunes "by hand," see page 86.

Link to audio-recording programs and more.
www.macilife.com/itunes

Getting the Best Sound

When recording Internet audio, you'll often have to make audio-quality decisions.

The right rate. Internet audio is often heavily compressed to allow streaming over slow modem connections. To avoid degrading the sound quality even more, encode at a relatively high bit rate, such as 96 kbps for spoken-word programming, and 128 or 160 kbps for music.

If you're recording talk radio, record in mono rather than stereo.

As for format decisions, as I've mentioned elsewhere, AAC provides better sound quality at a given bit rate than does MP3.

Before or after? With some programs, including Audio Hijack Pro, you can choose these settings before you record. With most of the other tools, you must use iTunes to encode after you record.

Being able to encode as you record is a timesaving convenience that uses disk space more efficiently. On the downside, you don't have the opportunity to experiment with different encoding settings. If you're recording music and want to get the best sound quality, record in uncompressed AIFF format first, then use iTunes to encode, experimenting with different bit rates and formats until you arrive at the combination that sounds best to your ears.

Which Program to Use?

Several stream recorders are available, and each fills a useful niche.

Serious sound. The premiere programs for recording the unrecordable are Rogue Amoeba Software's Audio Hijack and Audio Hijack Pro. And if you don't want to hear the audio as you're recording it, one click of the Mute button silences the stream even as it's being recorded.

Both Audio Hijack programs have VCR-like timers that let you start and stop recording at specific times. Both programs also allow you to make bass and treble adjustments as you record, and both provide a feature that removes some of the muddiness associated with Internet audio. Audio Hijack Pro goes much further, providing a broad selection of audio-processing effects: apply the reverberation effect, and you can make Howard Stern sound like he's in a cathedral—at least from an acoustical standpoint.

Ambrosia Software's WireTap Studio provides similar features, and adds a waveform editor that lets you splice and edit your recordings.

For the radio lover. Bitcartel's RadioLover specializes in recording MP3 stations, such as those that iTunes can tune in. Many MP3-based stations send artist and song information along with their streams, and RadioLover can use this information to create separate song files as it records. Set up RadioLover to record for a few hours, and you'll return to find dozens of separate MP3 tracks, already named and ready to add to your iTunes library.

Rogue Amoeba's Radioshift takes a different approach: it's a portal to not only many Internet radio stations, but also thousands of AM and FM radio stations from around the world. Find that station in your distant hometown, then use Radioshift to record it.

For YouTube, too. With the right software, you can snag YouTube videos and add them to your iTunes library. Then, copy them to your iPod or burn them to DVDs using iDVD. I'm fond of Chimoosoft's TubeTV, but many YouTubers also like Stinkbot's TubeSock—and not just because it's fun to say "Stinkbot's TubeSock."

Converting Old Tapes and Albums

If you're like me, you're desperate to recapture the past: you want to create digital audio files from audio cassettes and vinyl albums.

Bridging the gap between the analog and digital worlds requires some software and hardware. The process involves connecting your Mac to an audio source, such as a cassette deck or stereo system, and then using recording software to save the audio on your hard drive as it plays back. You can encode the resulting files into AAC or MP3 format and add them to your iTunes library.

All current Mac models contain audio-input jacks to that you can connect to a sound source, such as a cassette deck or stereo system. Older Macs need an adapter such as Griffin Technology's iMic (below), which is inexpensive and includes Final Vinyl, a cutely named recording program. Griffin, M-Audio, and other companies also sell more sophisticated (and better-sounding) audio hardware that you might prefer if you're an audiophile or you plan to record acoustic instruments using GarageBand.

Step 1. Make the Connections

Recording analog sources is easiest when you connect the Mac to the audio output of a stereo system. This will enable you to record anything your stereo can play, from vinyl albums to cassettes to FM radio.

Most stereo receivers have auxiliary output jacks on their back panels. To make the connection, use a cable with two RCA phono plugs on one end and a ⅛-inch stereo miniplug on the other. Connect the phono plugs to the receiver's output jacks, and the miniplug to the input jack on your Mac or audio adapter.

Step 2. Prepare to Record

Before you record, set your audio levels properly: you want the audio signal to be as loud as possible without distorting the sound.

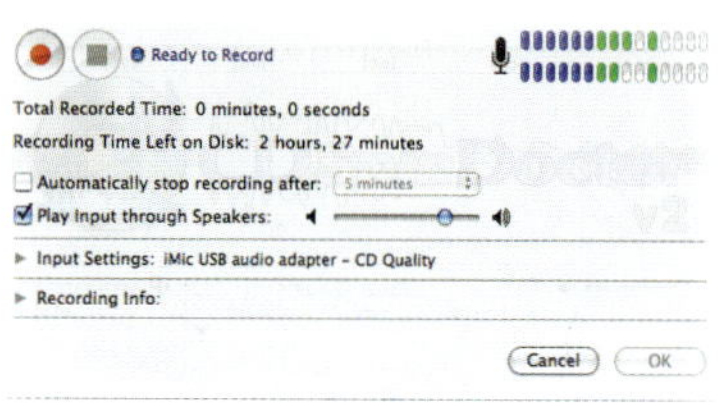

Fire up your audio recording software (Roxio's CD Spin Doctor is shown here), and adjust its recording levels so that the loudest passages of music fully illuminate the volume meters.

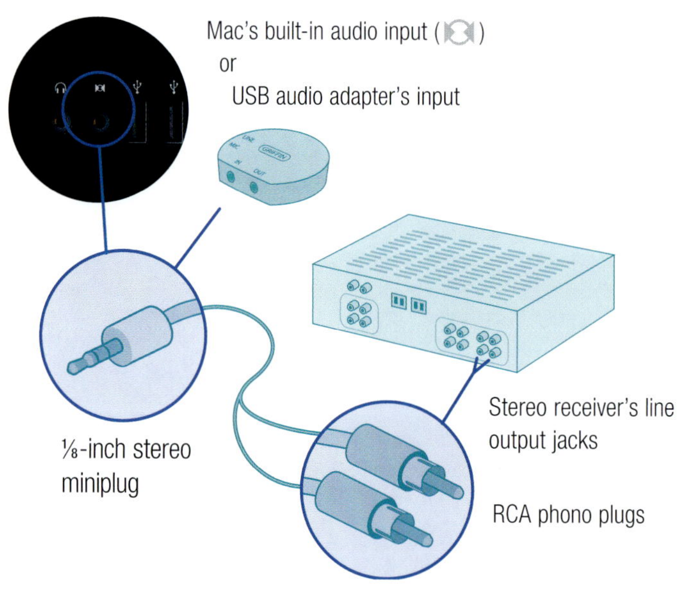

Learn more about recording old tapes and CDs.
www.macilife.com/itunes

Step 3. Record

First, do a test recording. Activate your software's Record mode and begin playing back the original audio, preferably a loud passage. After a minute or two, stop and play back the recorded audio to verify that the recording levels you set are correct. Listen for distortion in loud passages; if you hear any, decrease the levels slightly.

Once you've arrived at the correct setting for recording levels, record the original audio in its entirety.

Step 4. Encode and Edit Song Information

Your completed recording will almost certainly be stored in uncompressed AIFF format—the format used by Mac recording programs.

To save disk space, you'll probably want to encode the recording into AAC or MP3 format. Naturally, you can use iTunes to do this.

Before encoding your recordings, use the Preferences command to choose your preferred encoding settings as described on page 22. Next, hold down the Option key and check out the Advanced menu—you'll see a command that reads Convert to AAC. (If you specified the MP3 encoder in the Preferences dialog box, the command reads Convert to MP3.)

Choose the Convert to AAC (or Convert to MP3) command, and then locate and double-click on the recording you just made. iTunes will encode the track and will store the resulting digital audio file in your iTunes library.

iTunes can also encode multiple recordings in one operation. After choosing Convert to AAC (or Convert to MP3), simply ⌘-click on each file you want to import.

After you've encoded your recordings, edit their song information to add artist, song, and album names (see page 26). And consider adding artwork so the songs look their best in Cover Flow view (page 66).

Choosing a Recording Program

The spectrum of audio-recording software ranges from free (Audacity) to inexpensive (SoundStudio and Amadeus II) to pricey (Bias Peak) and beyond.

One of my favorites is CD Spin Doctor, included with Roxio's Toast Titanium CD burning software. CD Spin Doctor creates AIFF files, which you can encode into AAC or MP3 format using iTunes, as described above.

A few features make CD Spin Doctor ideal for converting analog recordings into digital form. One is the Auto-Define Tracks command: choose it, and CD Spin Doctor scans a recording, detects the silence between each song, and then divides the recording into multiple tracks. This makes it easy to record one side of an album and then divvy it up into separate tracks.

CD Spin Doctor also has noise and pop filters that can clean up abused records, as well as an "exciter" filter that enhances old recordings by beefing up bass and improving the sense of stereo separation. (Bias' SoundSoap provides even more noise-cleanup features.)

For detailed audio editing, try Amadeus II or SoundStudio. Get links to these and other audio programs at the iTunes page of my Web site.

iTunes and Your Stereo

Once you've assembled a digital music library, you're going to want to listen to it using your stereo system. One option is, of course, an iPod: copy your music library to one, then connect the iPod to your stereo (or anyone else's) as shown on page 120.

But you can also connect your Mac to an audio system, and there are some good reasons to do so. You can play music with DJ-like crossfades: one song fades out even as the next song fades in (see page 80). You can play Internet radio—another trick no iPod can perform. You can play audio from other sources, from games to DVDs, and from streaming players to GarageBand. And if your Mac supports Apple's Front Row software and includes a remote control, you can control your music playback without having to leave your recliner.

The journey from Mac to stereo system has several possible paths; the best one for you depends on the distance between your computer and your audio system, the specific Mac model you have, and your listening goals. Here's a roadmap of some popular routes. And if you want to also view iTunes videos on your TV, detour to page 78 to learn about AppleTV.

Three Ways to Connect

iMac

optical out

⅛-inch stereo miniplug

or

optical digital miniplug

optical digital miniplug

or

⅛-inch stereo miniplug

The audio-output jack on the AirPort Express base station accepts either a ⅛-inch stereo miniplug or an optical digital miniplug (it's the same type of jack provided by all current Macs).

AirPort Express

Connect an AirPort Express base station to your stereo, and you can transmit music from any AirPort-equipped Mac within range. In iTunes, simply select the base station from the pop-up menu.

Works with: Any AirPort-equipped Mac.

Best when: Mac and stereo aren't close enough for convenient cabling.

Downside: Works with iTunes only, unless you use Airfoil software (see page 91).

Analog Direct Connection

You can connect any Mac to a stereo system by plugging a cable into the Mac's headphone jack.

Works with: Any Mac.

Best when: Mac and audio system are relatively close together.

Downside: Audio is less pristine than with digital connections, although most ears will never notice.

RCA phono plugs: connect to a free pair of audio inputs.

Optical Digital Connection

All current Macs models have optical digital outputs that use fiber optic cables to provide pristine, hum-free signals, even with cable lengths of over 30 feet. (Add an inexpensive repeater for even longer cable runs.)

Works with: Any Mac with digital audio output.

Best when: You demand top audio quality and have an audio system with optical digital inputs.

Downside: Not an option for if your Mac and stereo lack digital outputs and inputs.

TOSLINK plug: connect to your audio system's digital input.

Apple TV: iTunes and Your TV

An iPod puts your iTunes library in your pocket. Apple TV puts your iTunes library in your living room.

Apple TV is a bridge between iTunes and your TV set and stereo system. Synchronize part or all of your iTunes library with Apple TV: iTunes copies items to the Apple TV's hard drive via AirPort wireless networking or an Ethernet cable.

Once that's done, use the Apple TV's remote control to navigate your library, watch videos, listen to music and podcasts, and view photos. If you've used Apple's Front Row software on your Mac, you'll feel right at home: Apple TV's menus work identically.

Once you marry Apple TV and your iTunes library, the two remain in sync. Buy some tunes or TV shows, and iTunes copies them to your Apple TV. You can also take control yourself and, for example, copy only certain playlists and videos.

It gets better. Apple TV also lets you search for and view videos from YouTube. You can even sign in to YouTube to access your favorites. You can also preview top songs and videos from the iTunes Store. And if you have additional Macs or Windows PCs in your house, they can stream music and videos to the Apple TV—much as you can share iTunes libraries between computers (page 68).

If you use iTunes for music only, consider one of the stereo-connection schemes on the previous pages. But if you're into iTunes video or you want to view photos or YouTube on your TV, tune in to Apple TV.

Tuning In to Apple TV

Step 1. Set up.

Connect your Apple TV to your TV and stereo. You have several options, depending on the kind of video- and audio-input jacks your TV and stereo provide. (For some advice, see the following pages.)

You'll also need to provide a way for your Mac and the Apple TV to communicate. An AirPort wireless network is ideal—no need to string more wires into your TV cabinet. You can also run an Ethernet cable from your Mac to the Apple TV.

Next, configure the Apple TV. This involves connecting to your wireless (or wired) network and specifying some video options. Finally, a five-digit passcode appears on your TV screen.

Tip: On the latest Macs, Ethernet transfers data much faster than AirPort. If you're syncing a large library, consider connecting your Mac directly to the Apple TV using an Ethernet cable. After the first sync, you can switch to AirPort wireless syncing for subsequent updates.

Step 2. Connect to iTunes and sync.

Sit down at your Mac and launch iTunes. Your Apple TV appears in the Devices list. Select it, and then type the passcode that appeared on your TV.

This step pairs your Mac's copy of iTunes with your Apple TV. iTunes then begins syncing: copying your iTunes library to the Apple TV's hard drive. A status message appears in iTunes.

If you don't want to sync everything in your library, take the reins yourself: click the Apple TV item in the Devices list, then use the tabs to specify what you'd like to sync. For details on syncing options, see page 108.

Step 3. Enjoy and repeat.

Crack open a Dr. Pepper and start watching or listening. Use the Apple TV's remote control to navigate and choose options from the menus on your TV. Explore your iTunes library, or detour to YouTube if you'd like.

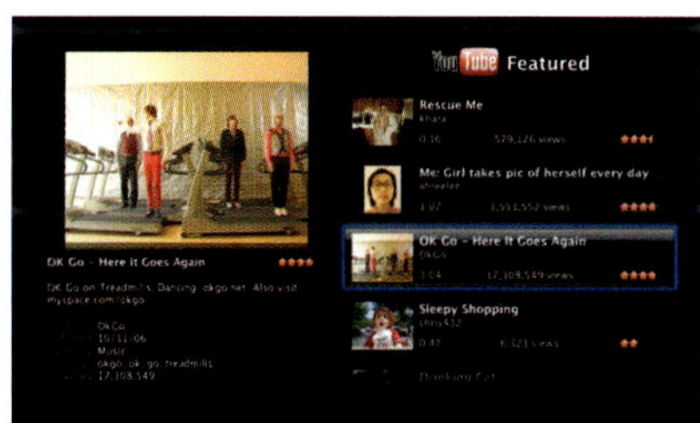

Sync or Stream? Or Both?

The Apple TV works best when you've copied your iTunes library to the Apple TV's hard drive, as described here. Syncing enables you to use the Apple TV without your Mac having to be up and running.

But as I mentioned on the opposite page, you can also stream music and videos to the Apple TV. Streaming has the advantage of not using up disk space on the Apple TV. If your iTunes library is larger than will fit on the Apple TV's hard drive, streaming is an excellent option.

Up to five Macs or Windows PCs can stream to a single Apple TV. If everyone in the house has his or her own computer, each person can tap into his or her copy of iTunes and watch videos and listen to music.

You can also combine syncing and streaming with a single library. Maybe you have a slower AirPort network—you have a base station that uses the original, 801.11b standard—and video playback is choppy when streaming. Solution: Sync your videos to the Apple TV, but stream the music. (To set up this kind of selective syncing, use the options described on page 108.)

Streaming downsides. Streaming has some limitations. You can't stream photos to the Apple TV—they must be stored on its hard drive. And to state the obvious, the computer from which you're streaming must be up and running; put it to sleep, and the stream dries up.

To set up streaming on the Apple TV, select Sources > Connect to New iTunes. A passcode appears; peck it into iTunes, just as you did when setting up for syncing. Your Apple TV connects to the remote iTunes library, and you're off and running—just add Pringles.

Tips for Playing Music

Crossfading Songs

You hear it on the radio all the time: as one song nears its end, it begins to fade as the next song starts to play. You can recreate this effect in iTunes. First, choose Preferences from the iTunes menu, click the Playback button, and then check the Crossfade Playback box.

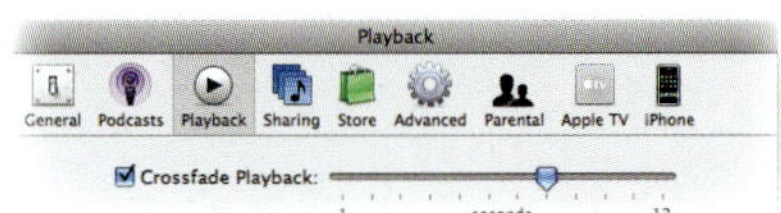

With crossfading, one song fades out...

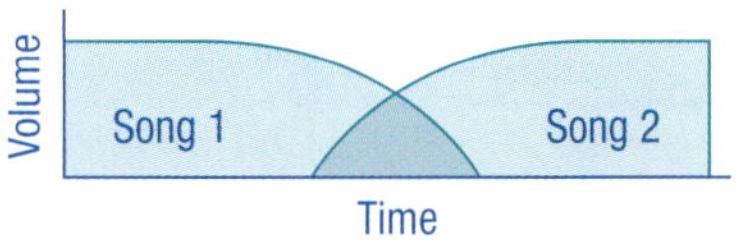

...as the next song fades in.

With albums whose songs flow seamlessly into one another, you don't want crossfading: that would ruin those seamless segues. To prevent iTunes from crossfading a particular song, select it and choose File > Get Info. In the dialog box, click Options, then click the Part of a Gapless Album check box. To set this option for an entire album, select all its tracks (⌘-click on each), then choose File > Get Info.

Dock Control

When iTunes is running, you can start and stop playback and perform other tasks using the iTunes icon in your dock. Point to the icon and hold down the mouse button (or simply Control-click on the icon), then choose the desired command from the shortcut menu. For even more control over iTunes, check out Synergy and CoverSutra, described on page 90.

Making iTunes Tiny

To instantly miniaturize the iTunes window, click the green button in its upper-left corner.

To make the window even smaller, drag the size control in the lower-right corner.

Stash this micro-iTunes window in a corner of your screen for convenient access. And if you always want it to be visible, even when you're working in other programs, choose Preferences from the iTunes menu, click Advanced, click General, and then check the box labeled *Keep Mini Player on top of all other windows.*

To restore the full iTunes window, click the green button again.

Optimizing Levels

When you create a playlist containing songs from numerous albums, you may notice that some songs are louder than others. To compensate for this, use the Sound Check option, which optimizes playback volumes so that all songs play back with similar volume levels. To turn Sound Check on, choose Preferences from the iTunes menu, click the Playback button, then check the Sound Check box.

The Sound Enhancer

You can add aural punch by improving what audio gurus call *presence*, the perception that the instruments are right in the room with you. To do this, use the Sound Enhancer option in the Playback tab of the Preferences dialog box. Drag the slider toward the High setting, and you may notice brighter-sounding high frequencies and an enhanced sense of stereo separation. Experiment with the setting that sounds best for your ears—and your audio equipment.

Skipping to the Next or Previous Album

As I noted on page 19, you can skip to the next song by clicking ⏩ and to the previous song by clicking ⏪. To skip to the next or previous album, press the Option key while clicking these buttons.

You can also skip to the next and previous album using the keyboard: press Option along with the right-arrow or left-arrow key.

Adjusting Volume with a Scroll Wheel Mouse

Apple's Mighty Mouse and many third-party mice have a scroll wheel. If your rodent is so equipped, you can use the scroll wheel to adjust the volume when iTunes is in its tiny-window mode—just point to the volume slider and roll the wheel.

Showing the Current Song

Here's a common scenario: As you listen to a tune, you begin browsing your music library or maybe even shopping at the iTunes Store. Then you decide to add the currently playing song to a playlist.

How can you quickly find it? Easy: choose File > Show Current Song (⌘-L), and iTunes displays and highlights the song that's currently playing.

You can also click the SnapBack button, which appears near the right-hand side of the iTunes LCD—that wide area at the top of the iTunes window.

How to "Crop" Songs

Scenario #1: You have an album that was recorded live, and each song starts with a long, rambling introduction by the recording artist. You'd like to cut out that intro and just start with the music.

Scenario #2: There's a song you really want to like but, two thirds of the way through, it degenerates into an ear-bleeding cacophony of noise.

iTunes has a little-used feature that beautifully addresses both of these scenarios: you can "crop" a song—lop off part of the beginning, part of the end, or both—to hear only the part you want to hear. This cropping is even retained when you transfer the song to an iPod. And best of all, it's easy.

First, listen to the song you want to crop, and use the iTunes time display to note where the offensive portion ends or begins. Now select the song, choose Get Info from the File menu, and click the Options button.

Next, configure the Start Time and/or Stop Time boxes as needed. In the example below, I'm skipping over the first 34 seconds of the song.

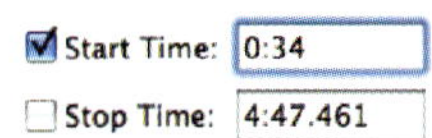

Click OK when you've finished, and you're done.

And if you ever do want to hear that cropped-out portion, you can do so by simply dragging the little playback diamond that appears near the top of the iTunes window. Or, return to the Get Info dialog box and uncheck the Start Time and/or Stop Time boxes.

Note: Your adjustments apply to iTunes and iPod playback only; if you add a "cropped" song to iMovie, for example, you'll still hear the entire song. But there is a workaround: in iTunes, select the cropped song, then choose Advanced > Convert Selection to AAC (or whatever your preferred import format is). iTunes makes a new file containing just the cropped portion.

Marking Your Place

iTunes has the ability to remember the point where you stopped listening to or watching an item, and then resume at that point the next time you play it back. Audiobooks and videos work this way automatically, but you can add the "bookmarking" capability to any item. Select the item, choose Get Info from the File menu, click the Options button, then check the Remember Playback Position box.

Bookmarking extends to the iPod, too: when you play an item that you've already started, the iPod resumes where you left off.

Surprise Me: Shuffle Playback Options

When long-playing albums appeared in the 1940s, recording artists gained the ability to present more than one song at a time. LPs enabled artists to present songs in a sequence of their choosing. And for the next forty years or so, music lovers would be locked into their choices.

Then compact discs appeared. Unlike phonographs, CD players could instantly access any part of an album. To take advantage of this, player manufacturers added *shuffle* features: press a button, and the player skipped around within a CD, playing tracks at random. One comedian even worked the concept into his routine: "I ran into a famous musician on the street and I told him, 'I'm familiar with your latest CD—but not in the order you want me to be.'"

iTunes takes the shuffle concept to the next level. Sure, you can play tracks or albums at random, but with the Party Shuffle playlist, you can combine the serendipity of shuffle mode with the forethought of a well-crafted playlist.

Some music lovers want full control over playback; others love the game of chance that shuffle modes provide. One thing is certain: random-playback features are a great way to rediscover songs you haven't listened to in a while.

Here's how turn your music jukebox into a slot machine.

Using Shuffle Mode

The simplest form of random playback is shuffle mode. To play random songs from your library, select the Library item, then click the shuffle button ( ).

Shuffling a playlist. To simply hear a playlist in random order, select the playlist, then click the shuffle button. If you'd like to *see* what kind of random order iTunes comes up with, click the playlist's leftmost column heading to sort it in numeric order, *then* click the shuffle button.

Keeping a shuffle. Sometimes a random pick is perfect—just ask any lottery winner. If you like the way iTunes has shuffled a playlist, you can tell iTunes to reorder the songs so that they always play back in that order. Simply Control-click on the playlist's name and then choose Copy to Play Order from the shortcut menu.

Album and grouping shuffle. Normally, shuffle mode plays back songs in random order. You can, however, also choose to shuffle by album or by grouping. In album-shuffle mode, iTunes plays back an entire album in its original song order, then randomly chooses another album and plays all of it. Grouping is similar, but applies to grouped tracks within an album—for example, the four movements of a symphony.

To use these modes, use the Playback pane of the iTunes Preferences dialog box. While you're there, you can also drag the Smart Shuffle slider to fine-tune how likely you are to hear multiple songs in a row by the same artist or from the same album.

Tip: To ensure that a particular item—for example, a podcast—never plays in shuffle mode, select that item and choose File > Get Info. Next, click Options and check the Skip When Shuffling box.

Read some articles about the joys of shuffle.
www.macilife.com/itunes

Mix it Up: Party Shuffle

The Party Shuffle playlist is a hybrid of random shuffle mode, smart playlists, and conventional playlists.

To use Party Shuffle, click it in the Playlists area of the iTunes window. iTunes instantly assembles a list of songs.

Another good reason to rate your music (page 86): you can have iTunes weight its selection toward higher-rated songs.

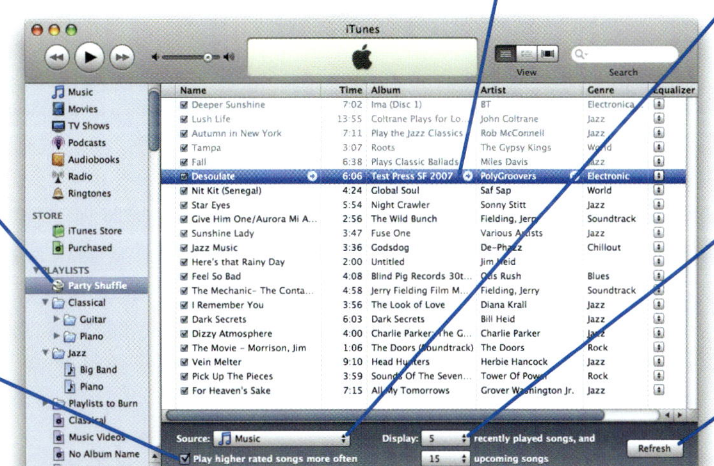

The blue bar separates songs that have been played from upcoming songs.

You can tell iTunes to narrow its pool of eligible songs to specific playlists. **Tip:** To create a party shuffle mix based on a specific genre, create a smart playlist for that genre (for example, genre is Rock), then specify that smart playlist here.

You can have iTunes display the last songs it played from the shuffle, and up to 100 upcoming songs.

Don't like what iTunes has come up with? Click Refresh, and iTunes rolls the dice and chooses another batch of songs.

Party Shuffle Tips

Customizing the mix. As with other types of playlists, you can change the Party Shuffle playlist on a song-by-song basis: drag songs up or down to change their playback order, delete songs you don't want to hear, and manually add songs from your iTunes library by dragging them into the playlist.

Adding a song. You can add a song to the Party Shuffle playlist by simply dragging it, but there's a shortcut. Control-click on a song, then, from the shortcut menu, choose either Play Next in Party Shuffle (to hear the song next) or Add to Party Shuffle (to add the song to the end of the Party Shuffle playlist).

Selecting from multiple playlists. To base a party shuffle mix on more than one playlist, create a smart playlist that selects those playlists (for example, Playlist is *My Favorites* and Playlist is *Jazz Hits*), then specify that smart playlist.

Freeze the mix. If you like what Party Shuffle comes up with, you can save the mix as a conventional playlist: choose Select All (⌘-A), then choose New Playlist from Selection (Option-⌘-N).

Adding to a playlist. You can also add the results of a Party Shuffle refresh to an existing playlist: select the songs you want to add, then Control-click on one of them. From the shortcut menu, choose Add to Playlist, then choose the playlist.

Rating Items, Customizing, and More

Rating Songs, Albums, and More

iTunes lets you express your inner music critic by assigning a rating of between one and five stars to songs, albums, videos, and other items in your library. You don't have to assign ratings, but if you do, you can use the Rating and Album Rating categories as criteria when creating smart playlists. You can also have iTunes take ratings into account when compiling Party Shuffle playlists (page 83).

Rating items. The fastest way to rate an item is to Control-click on it and then choose the desired rating from the Rating pop-up menu.

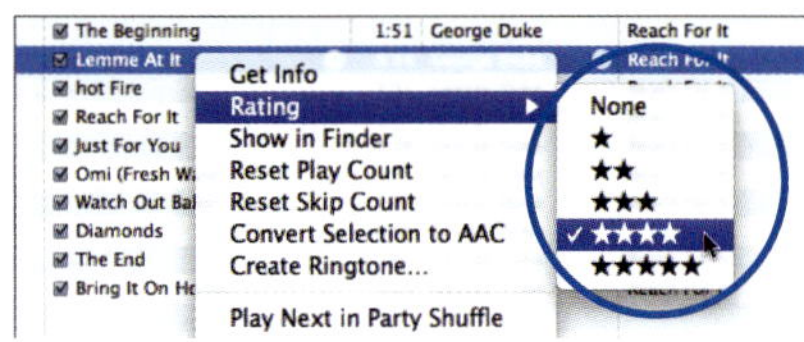

You can also rate items by clicking within the Ratings column in the iTunes window or by opening the Options portion of the Get Info dialog box. And finally, you can rate the item that is currently playing by using the iTunes icon in your dock. Control-click on the iTunes icon, and a pop-up menu appears. Use the Ratings submenu to assign a rating.

You can also assign ratings to multiple items at once: Shift-click or ⌘-click to select them, then use any of the above techniques.

Rating albums. You can also rate an entire album; when you do, iTunes gives all its songs the same rating.

To rate an album, begin by displaying the Album Rating column (see the following tip to customize columns). Then, select any song in the album and click its rating stars.

Incidentally, if you rate individual songs in an album but not the entire album, iTunes still gives the album a rating: the average of the songs you rated.

Customizing Columns

You can specify which columns of information iTunes displays in its windows—to remove columns you never use, or to add ones that iTunes normally doesn't display.

One way to customize columns is to use the Edit menu's View Options command. Here's an easier way: Control-click on any column heading, and uncheck or check columns in the shortcut menu.

You can also use the shortcut menu to automatically resize columns to fit the longest item in each one. And you can change the order of the columns themselves, moving them left and right to suit your tastes. To move a column, click on its heading and then drag left or right.

It's worth mentioning that you can customize columns on a playlist-by-playlist basis. For example, if you want to see the Composer column when viewing a favorite classical music playlist, click on the playlist's name in the Playlists list, then display the Composer column using the techniques described here.

Customizing the Library List

I've mentioned it elsewhere, but it's worth repeating: you can customize the Library list by using the Preferences dialog box. Most of your customizing opportunities lurk within the General pane: that's where you can change the font size iTunes displays; show or hide Party Shuffle and more; and show link arrows.

To control whether the iTunes Store appears, use the Parental portion of the Preferences dialog box.

Tip: When the Preferences dialog box is open, you can use keyboard shortcuts to access specific panes. Press ⌘-1 for General, ⌘-2 for Podcasts, ⌘-3 for Playback, and so on.

Watch Me Listen

While you're listening, iTunes is watching: the program keeps track of how many times you listen to a song and when you last listened to it.

iTunes displays this audio odometer in its Play Count and Last Played columns. This means you can sort your music library or a playlist according to how many times you listened to a song (click the Play Count column heading) or when you last listened to it (click the Last Played column heading). Note that you'll probably have to scroll the iTunes window to the right to see these columns.

You can also use these data as criteria when creating a smart playlist (see

Get links for even more sources of free music, radio, and video.
www.macilife.com/itunes

pages 52–55)—have iTunes create a playlist of your favorite songs or of those you haven't listened to lately.

iTunes uses its play-count records for other tasks. Play count can factor into whether a song is included in the Party Shuffle playlist (page 83). Play count also comes into play if you've told iTunes to create an iPod Selection playlist (page 111).

iTunes also keeps track of how many times you skip over a song or other item. If, within about 20 seconds of beginning playback, you click the next track button (⏩) or choose Next from the iTunes dock shortcut menu, iTunes consider that a skip. This extends to the iPod, too: jump to the next track within about 20 seconds, and the iPod records a skip that is transferred back to iTunes the next time you sync.

Want to weed out songs you tend to skip over? Create a smart playlist whose criteria include the Skip Count item—for example, Skip Count is greater than 10. You might also use Skip Count when crafting smart playlists that select tunes for a small-capacity iPod, such a shuffle or nano.

Your Own PDFs

On page 39, I mentioned that some songs on the iTunes Store include liner notes in PDF form. You can add your own PDFs to your iTunes library. Scan a CD booklet, and then save it as a PDF. Find an online article about a favorite artist? Save it as a PDF. (Mac OS X makes it easy to create a PDF: just choose a program's Print command and then use the PDF options in the Print dialog box.) Then, drag the PDF into your iTunes window to add it to your library.

Doug Adams has created an AppleScript that associates a PDF with a specific artist or album. The script is called PDF Adder, and you can get it at Doug's site (www.dougscripts.com).

More iTunes Food: Free Music and More

I've already mentioned that Apple offers a free weekly song download. Many Web sites also publish links to freebies; see iLounge (www.ilounge.com) and Playlist magazine (www.playlistmag.com/downloads).

Peer-to-peer networks. Although record industry executives wouldn't want me to say so, you can also download music using utilities such as Acquisition (www.acquisitionx.com) and LimeWire (www.limewire.com), both of which access peer-to-peer file-sharing networks. Put on your eye patch first—most of the songs available through file-swapping networks have been shared without the permission of their copyright holders.

The Internet Archive. Another bottomless repository of free music—and video—is the Internet Archive (www.archive.org). Here you'll find tens of thousands of public-domain or otherwise free recordings, live concert and club recordings, cartoons, films, and more.

Most the audio files are available in MP3 format, and the video files are often provided in multiple formats. (As described on page 107, you can use iTunes and other tools to convert video into formats playable on an iPod.)

Podiobooks. Check out www.podiobooks.com, where you can download free audiobooks in podcast form.

RadioLovers. Like old-time radio? At www.radiolovers.com, you can download thousands of old shows, from Gunsmoke to Buck Rodgers and beyond.

Miro. This innovative "software tuner" software brings Internet TV to your desktop and makes finding interesting video easier than ever. You can learn more and download the free software at www.getmiro.com.

You. With products such as El Gato's EyeTV, you can record favorite TV shows and then add them to your iTunes library—and your iPod. And, of course, you can create your own music and movies in GarageBand and iMovie and add your efforts to your iTunes library.

Regardless of where your other items come from, you can add them to your iTunes library by simply dragging them into the iTunes window or by using the File menu's Add to Library command.

For details on adding items to your iTunes library, see the following pages.

Tips for the iTunes Library

Adding Items to iTunes

When you import music from a CD or buy items from the iTunes Store, iTunes stashes the audio or video files in your iTunes library for you. And as described in the following tip, iTunes is set up to manage the items in your library for you.

But what about items that you get from other sources—for example, audio files downloaded from Web sites or from file-sharing networks, or video files created with a product such as El Gato's EyeTV? How do you get those items to show up in your iTunes library?

Easy: simply drag their icons into the iTunes window. When you do, iTunes copies the item to your iTunes folder and adds it to your library. To add the item and put it in a specific playlist, simply drag its icon to the playlist in the Playlists list.

As an alternative to dragging icons into the iTunes window, you can also use the Add to Library command in the File menu. Choose the command, then locate and double-click the item you want to add.

Keeping Your Music Library Organized

iTunes normally stores your music in the Music folder, as described on page 21. If you download an MP3 file from the Internet and drag it into the iTunes window, you'll actually have two copies of the MP3 file on your hard drive.

If you don't want iTunes to copy files to the iTunes Music folder—if you'd prefer to have your music files scattered throughout your hard drive—choose Preferences from the iTunes menu, click the Advanced button, and then uncheck the box labeled Copy Files to iTunes Music Folder When Adding to Library. You can also temporarily override the copying feature: press Option while dragging a file into the iTunes window. Note, though, that having music scattered across your hard drive makes backing up your music library much more cumbersome. I don't recommend it.

Tip: If you already have files scattered across your hard drive and you want to move them all to the Music folder, choose Consolidate Library from the Advanced menu.

About Compilations

Chances are you have some compilation CDs in your music collection: *Solid Gold 70s, The Best of Bartok, Tuvanese Throat Singing Mania*, and so on. You can have iTunes store the music files for compilations in a separate folder within your iTunes Music folder. This helps reduce folder clutter and makes it easier to locate and manage your music files.

For example, say you have a compilation CD that contains tracks from a dozen different artists. Normally, iTunes would create a separate folder for each artist—even though that folder might contain just one music file. But when those songs are designated as being part of a compilation, iTunes will store all of those tracks together in their own folder.

Compilation albums that you buy from the iTunes Store are all set up this way. And chances are that when you rip a compilation CD, its tracks will be, too. Here's how to make sure. Select all the tracks on the album, then choose File > Get Info. Then, be sure that Yes is chosen in the Compilation pop-up menu at the lower-left corner of the Get Info dialog box.

iTunes stores compilations within a folder whose name is, you guessed it, Compilations. Within this folder, iTunes creates a separate folder for each compilation you've specified.

One User, Multiple Libraries

If you're like the vast majority of people who use iTunes, one library is quite enough. But one library does not fit all. Some people like to create multiple iTunes libraries, and designate each for certain types of media. For example, maybe you have a MacBook containing your music library, but you don't want to store gigantic video files on your laptop's hard drive. Solution: Create a second library on an external hard drive, and store your iTunes Store video purchases there.

To create a new iTunes library, quit iTunes. Then, start iTunes and immediately hold down the Option key on your keyboard. A dialog box appears that lets you choose a library or create a new one.

Get more tips for managing iTunes libraries.
www.macilife.com/itunes

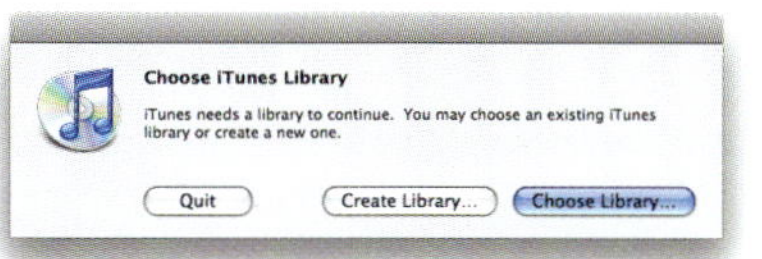

Click the Create Library button, then give the new library a name. If you want to store it somewhere other than your Music folder, specify the location. It's that easy.

Switching from one library to another is a similar process: Quit iTunes, then start it while pressing the Option key. This time, though, click the Choose Library button and aim iTunes at the library you want to use.

Advanced Sorting

You already know that iTunes sorts the contents of its window according to which column heading you've selected. And you also know that you can reverse the sorting order (for example, z to a) by clicking a column heading a second time.

But there's more to sorting.

Album-sorting options. If you click the Album column heading, it changes to read Album by Artist. Click it again, and it changes to Album by Year.

When Album by Artist is active, iTunes sorts the window by album name, then artist name. For example, all albums by Al Green are grouped together, sorted by their album name (*I Can't Stop* appears above *Still In Love With You*).

When Album by Year is active, iTunes sorts the window by album, then year. In this case, Al Green's 1972 *Still In Love With You* appears ahead of 2003's *I Can't Stop*.

Both views give you more ways to look at your library. And incidentally, to reverse the sort order of the Album column, click the little triangle in the column heading.

Customizing sorting. You might have some items that don't sort the way you want them to. For example, maybe you'd like *The Beatles* to appear in the Ts instead of in the Bs. Or perhaps you want artists to be sorted by last name (*Brown, James* instead of *James Brown*). Or maybe you'd like your songs by rapper 50 Cent to appear in the Fs rather than in, well, the fives.

To change how iTunes sorts items, head for the Get Info dialog box. Select an item, such as a song, then choose File > Get Info. Click the Sorting button, and you'll find half a dozen fields where you can specify how *you* want iTunes to sort the item.

For example, to have a 50 Cent tune sorted in the Fs, type *Fifty Cent* in the Sort Artist field. Or to have James Brown's tracks sorted by his last name, type *Brown, James* in the Sort Artist field.

There's just one catch: iTunes lets you change sort information for just one track at a time. You've changed one James Brown tune—what about the rest?

Easy. (Not obvious, but easy.) Control-click on the one James Brown tune that you customized, then, from the shortcut menu, choose Apply Sort Field > All Matching Fields. A confusingly worded dialog box appears; click Yes.

That may be more than you ever wanted to know about iTunes sorting. But as I've said before, some iTunes users are obsessive librarians. And tricks like these become useful when you deal with libraries containing tens of thousands of items.

More Tips for the iTunes Library

Multiple Users, One Library

When you use Mac OS X to set up separate accounts for different people, each person gets his or her own iTunes library. But what if you want to have just one library that can be accessed by everyone who uses your Mac?

It isn't difficult, and my colleague Chris Breen has explained how to do it. I've linked to his able explanation at www.macilife.com/itunes.

Keep Your Music Library Healthy

I've already mentioned the importance of backing up your iTunes playlists and your music (page 62). This message bears repeating. Make a habit of backing up your playlists by using the Export Library command in the File menu, and of backing up your music files by burning them to CDs or DVDs. Or simply drag your entire iTunes folder to an external hard drive every now and then.

Dealing with Duplicates

As your library grows, you may end up with more than one copy of some songs. This can happen if you frequently buy compilation CDs or iTunes Essentials mixes: you might have John Coltrane's *Giant Steps* from the CD of the same name, and the identical recording from the compilation *Heavyweight Champion: The Complete Atlantic Recordings*. It's a great tune, but why waste space storing two copies of it?

iTunes can help you find those duplicates. First, tell iTunes what kind of duplicates you want to find: in the Library area, click one of the categories (Music, Movies, TV Shows, and so on).

Next, choose View > Show Duplicates. The iTunes window changes to show just duplicate items. Study those duplicates to verify that they really are duplicates.

iTunes simply matches item names, so it will consider Norah Jones' *Don't Know Why* from her *Come Away with Me* album to be a duplicate of the same tune from her *Live in NYC* album. A glance at the Time column is usually all it takes to identify genuine duplicates: their times will be identical or extremely close to it. In the example below, iTunes thinks it has found duplicates, but a look at the Time column (and, in this case, the album name) shows that the songs aren't duplicates at all.

If you do indeed find a duplicate that you'd like to get rid of, select it and press the Delete key. When iTunes asks if you'd like to move the file to the trash, click Move to Trash.

To restore the iTunes window to its normal view, click the Show All button at the bottom of the window.

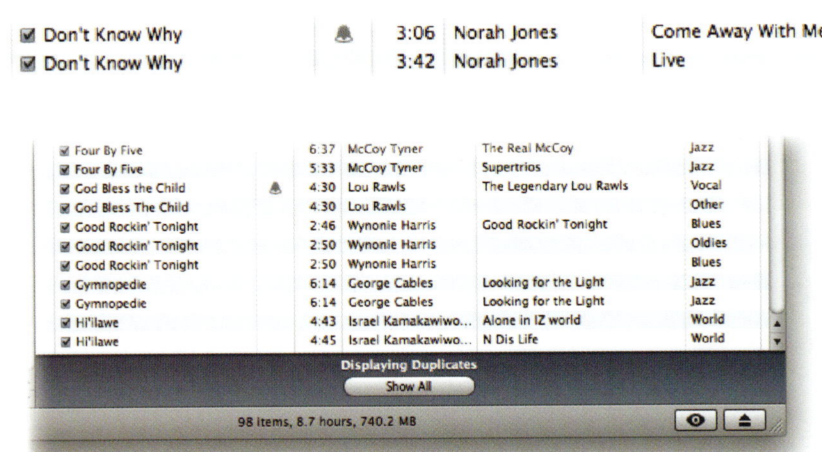

Merging Libraries

It's a frequently asked question: how do you merge two iTunes libraries into one? Maybe you've been maintaining separate libraries on your MacBook and your iMac, and you'd like to unite them into a single, unified library.

To synchronize two libraries or merge one library's contents into another, turn to an iTunes library utility. Several are available; SuperSync and TuneRanger are the most capable ones I've tested. Both will open two iTunes libraries, compare the two, and the let you know which items are present in one library but not the other. From there, you can have the program synchronize the two libraries (making them identical) or just copy items from one library to another.

Both programs also enable you to access the contents of an iPod and copy items from it into your library. (For more programs that do this, see page 110.)

Using library-synchronization utilities can be tricky. Unless you're trying to sync up two very large, very different libraries, you might consider synchronizing libraries by hand. Consider simply copying items from one library to another yourself: use Mac OS X's file-sharing features, copy the items to a USB Flash drive or external hard drive, or burn them on a CD or DVD. It's a bit more work, but it will give you a chance to examine both libraries and remove unwanted or duplicate items.

Recreating a Damaged Music Library

Sometimes the worst happens: a power failure or other glitch may damage your iTunes Library file, that all-important music database that I described on page 21. If this file becomes corrupted, you may see an error message when you start iTunes—something along the lines of "The iTunes Library file cannot be read because it does not appear to be a valid library file."

Don't despair. Okay, go ahead and despair, but don't lose hope. Your entire iTunes library is almost certainly still intact; it's just that the librarian has lost its mind. Here's how to restore some sanity to the situation.

Got backup? If you've used iTunes Backup as described on page 63, you'll be up and listening within minutes. Insert your backup disc (or, for multiple-disc backups, the first disc in the set). iTunes asks if you'd like to restore your library. Click Restore, and iTunes does the rest.

If you backed up by dragging your entire iTunes folder to an external hard drive, simply drag the backup iTunes folder to the Music folder in your home directory.

No backup? If you don't have current backups of the files named iTunes Library and iTunes Music Library.xml, you have more work to do. First, locate the corrupted versions of these files and drag them to the Trash. If you also find older Music Library files there (for example, one named iTunes 4 Music Library), drag them to the Trash—these files are left over from older versions of iTunes that you had installed on your computer, and you don't need them anymore. Do not delete anything inside the iTunes Music folder.

Next, start up iTunes. When you do, you'll notice its library window is completely empty. Let's fix that. Choose Add to Library from the File menu, navigate to your iTunes Music folder, and click Choose. iTunes will read all your music files and recreate your library.

Alas, performing these steps will cause you to lose the playlists you've created. To avoid this heartache, back up your iTunes Music Library.xml file now and then—by dragging it to another drive, by burning it to a CD, or by using the File menu's Export Library command.

Adding On: Scripts and Beyond

I've already mentioned that you can enhance the capabilities of iTunes through AppleScripts that automate iTunes in various ways.

You can also enhance the iTunes visualizer—the feature that displays those psychedelic patterns as your music plays back—by adding plug-ins. Visualizer plug-ins may not be as practical as AppleScripts, but on-screen psychedelics can often be more fun than practicalities.

Here's how to download and install iTunes AppleScripts and visualizer plug-ins, as well as information on some other programs that can round out the audio spoke of your digital hub.

Visualize Cool Graphics

If you're a fan of the iTunes visualizer, try out some of the free or inexpensive visualizer plug-ins available on the Web. One favorite is Andy O'Meara's free G-Force, which goes well beyond the built-in iTunes visualizer. For example, you can "play" G-Force—controlling its patterns and colors—by pressing keys on your keyboard as a song plays back.

You can find G-Force and other visualizer plug-ins by going to www.macilife.com/itunes. Or do a Google search for *iTunes visualizer.*

Most visualizers include installation programs that tuck the plug-ins into the appropriate spot. But, just for the record, visualizers and other plug-ins are stored in a folder within your Library folder—specifically, in Library > iTunes > iTunes Plug-ins.

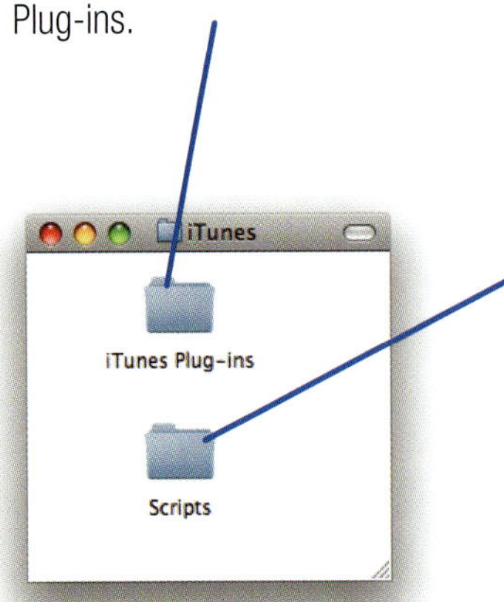

Automating with AppleScript

AppleScript is a powerful automation technology that is part of the Mac OS and many Mac programs, including iTunes. AppleScript puts your Mac on autopilot: when you run a script, its commands can control one or more programs and make them perform a series of steps.

Dozens of useful scripts are available for iTunes. The hands-down best source for them is Doug's AppleScripts for iTunes (www.dougscripts.com). When it comes to automating iTunes, no one has done more than Doug Adams.

Installing scripts. After you've acquired an iTunes AppleScript, you need to move it to a specific place in order for iTunes to recognize it. First, quit iTunes. Then, click the Home button or choose Home from the Finder's Go menu. Next, locate and open the Library folder, and then locate and open the iTunes folder within that Library folder. Create a folder named Scripts inside this iTunes folder and stash your scripts here.

Find iTunes add-ons aplenty.
www.macilife.com/itunes

Completing Your Audio Arsenal

Dozens of programs are available that enhance or complement iTunes. Here's a quick look at a few of my favorite audio things. For links to these and many more iTunes companions, see the Web address above.

Synergy This inexpensive program lets you control iTunes without having to switch into iTunes. Synergy provides keyboard shortcuts that let you play, pause, change volume, and even assign ratings to songs—no matter which program you're using at the moment. Synergy also adds a menu to your Mac's menu bar that lets you start and stop playback, skip to a particular playlist, and much more. When a song begins playing, Synergy displays a cool-looking "floater" that lists the song and artist name, album cover art, and other information.

CoverSutra. Cute name, cool program. CoverSutra also enhances iTunes playback with features similar to those of Synergy. But CoverSutra goes further. It supports the Apple Remote Control that is included with many Macs, enabling you to control playback and volume using the remote control but without switching into Apple's Front Row. CoverSutra can also tap into the last.fm social networking site, sending songs you play to your last.fm profile.

Toast Titanium Roxio's Toast Titanium is a burning program for serious CD arsonists. Toast can burn DVDs as well as audio and data CDs, and provides more control over the burning process. Just one example: while iTunes puts the same amount of time between each song on a CD, Toast Titanium lets you specify a different interval for each song. You can also have DJ-like crossfades between the tracks on your CDs. Toast Titanium also includes the CD Spin Doctor audio-recording program discussed on page 74.

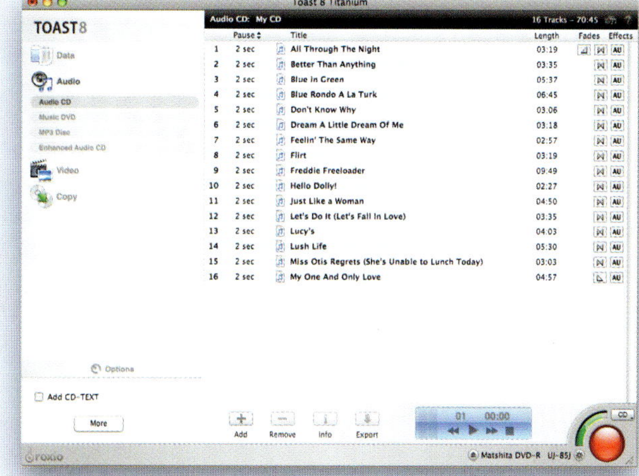

iWOW. Strange capitalization, cool program. iWOW, from SRS Labs, installs within iTunes and essentially remasters your music as it's playing back. iWOW lets you increase the stereo "presence" of a recording as well as add punch to bass and treble. Download a trial version from the company's Web site and hear for yourself.

Airfoil On page 76, I lamented that the AirPort Express base station supports wireless streaming from iTunes only. With Rogue Amoeba's Airfoil, you can work around this limitation. Airfoil hijacks any program's audio output and routes it through AirPort Express, making it possible to pump RealAudio and Windows Media sound to your AirPort Express.

Salling Clicker If you have a Bluetooth-equipped Mac and a Bluetooth-equipped phone or other handheld device, you can turn the handheld into a powerful remote control for iTunes (and many other Mac programs, including iPhoto). Combine Salling Clicker with an AirPort Express base station, and you've got a wireless audio system with a remote control.

Books on Bytes: Listening to Audiobooks

iTunes isn't just about tunes. You can also use it to listen to recorded *audiobooks* that you can buy and download from the iTunes Store or from Audible.com (www.audible.com). Listen to a novel on your next flight, burn it to a CD so you can listen to it in the car, or transfer it to your iPod and listen while you jog. You can buy audio versions of novels, magazines, newspapers, comedy shows, and much more. With the latest iPods, you can even speed up or slow down the reading speed (see page 111).

The easiest way to shop for audiobooks is to use the iTunes Store. Simply click the Audiobooks link on the store's home page.

If you want a much larger selection, shop at Audible.com's Web site. Buying audiobooks through Audible.com is a bit trickier than buying them through the iTunes Store. You'll also have to perform an extra couple of steps to add your purchased audiobooks to your iTunes library. These steps are outlined at right.

And to ensure that your Mac handles audiobooks correctly, be that sure iTunes is set up to handle Internet playback. Quit your Web browser and email program, then choose Preferences from the iTunes menu. Click the Advanced button at the top of the Preferences window, then click the General button. Finally, click the Set button that appears next to the label Use iTunes for Internet Music Playback.

Now your Mac is ready to read aloud.

Working with Audiobooks

If you already have an Apple account, you're ready to buy audiobooks from the iTunes Store. If you're interested in the broader selection available from Audible.com's site, visit www.audible.com and create an account. Then read on for details on working with Audible.com files.

Step 1. Purchase and Download

When buying an audiobook from Audible.com's Web site, you typically have a choice of formats, which are numbered 1 through 4. The iPod supports formats 2, 3, and 4. Which should you use? If you're in a hurry or using a modem connection, you might choose format 2—its files are smaller and thus download faster. If you have a fast connection, you might lean toward formats 3 or 4. They sound better, but they'll take longer to download and use more disk space on your Mac and iPod. (Audiobooks that you buy from the iTunes Store are available in AAC format only.)

Step 2. Add the Audiobook to Your iTunes Library

When you download an audiobook from Audible.com's site, the audiobook should be added to your iTunes library automatically. If it if isn't, you'll need to do the job yourself. Locate the audiobook on your desktop or Downloads folder (its name ends with the file extension .aa), then drag its icon into the iTunes window.

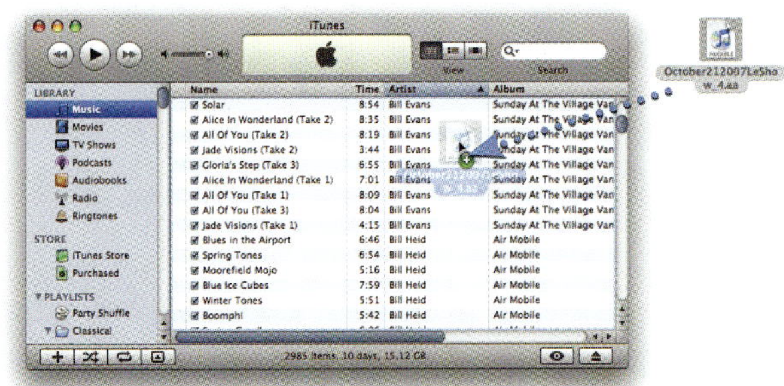

Step 3. Specify Account Information

The first time you add an audiobook to iTunes, you must specify the user name and password you created when signing up at Audible.com. iTunes contacts Audible.com to verify your account information.

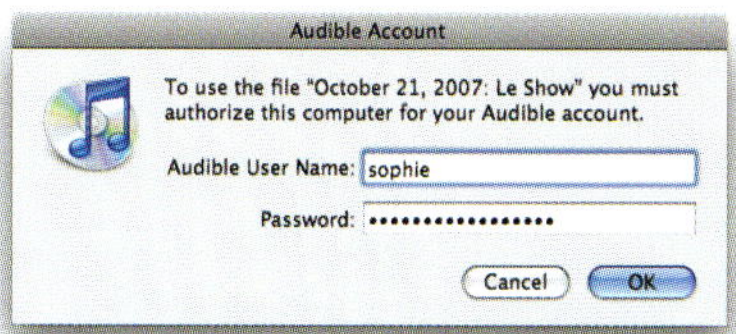

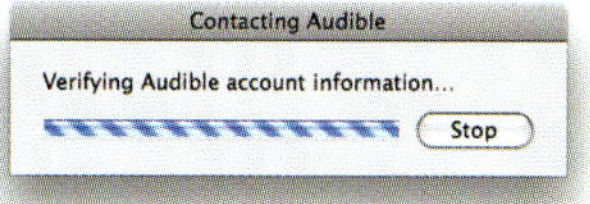

Step 4. Listen

An audiobook appears in the Audiobooks area of your library. You can listen to it, apply equalization to it, and burn it to a CD.

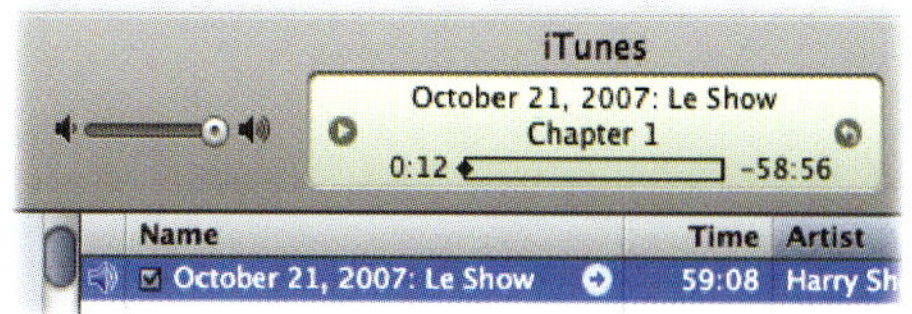

Audiobooks Tips

One Account

You can use one Audible.com account with up to three computers. If you try to add an account to a fourth computer, an error message appears. If you want to add the account to that computer, you must deauthorize one of the other three. Choose Deauthorize Computer from the Advanced menu, choose the Audible account button, and click OK.

To remove an account, choose Deauthorize Computer from the Advanced menu.

Audiobookmarks

The audiobook format provides bookmarks: when you pause or stop an audiobook, iTunes creates a bookmark at the point where you stopped. When you resume playing the audiobook, playback resumes at the bookmark's position.

It gets better. The iPod also supports audiobookmarks, and it synchronizes them with iTunes when you synchronize your music library. This synchronization process works in both directions: if you pause an audiobook on your iPod, the bookmark is transferred to your Mac when you sync. Thus, you can use your iPod to start listening to an audiobook on your evening commute, then use your iMac to pick up where you left off when you get home.

Chapter Markers

On the latest iPods and the iPod mini family, audiobooks can have chapter markers that allow for convenient navigation between chapters or other sections. To jump from one chapter to the next, press the iPod's Center button while the audiobook is playing. If the audiobook has section markers, they appear as vertical bars in the iPod's on-screen navigation bar. Use the Rewind and Fast Forward buttons to jump between chapters.

On an iPhone or iPod touch, you have even faster chapter access. While a book is playing, tap the tracks button in the upper-right corner of the screen. A list of chapters appears; to play one, tap it.

Burning a Book

To burn an audiobook to a CD, create a playlist and drag the audiobook to the playlist. Next, select the playlist and click the Burn Disc button.

If your audiobook is longer than roughly one hour, it won't fit on a standard audio CD. No problem. iTunes will burn as much as will fit on one CD, and will then prompt you to insert additional blank discs until you've burned the entire book.

iPod: Portable Music and More

It's hard to appreciate the significance of the iPod until you load it up with hundreds of songs and begin carrying it around with you.

Then it hits you: all of your favorite songs are right there with you, ready to play—in the car, on a walk, in the living room, on a plane. There's no finding and fumbling with CDs, and every song is only a couple of button presses away.

Several factors work together to make the iPod the best portable music player, starting with its integration with the iTunes Store: no other portable music player can tap into the store's vast selection of music, videos, podcasts, and more.

Another factor is the iPod's integration with iTunes: connect the iPod to your Mac, and iTunes automatically synchronizes your music library and playlists.

And finally, there's the iPod's versatility. Its ability to store videos, photos, contact information, your calendar, appointment schedule, and other files make the iPod more than a portable music player.

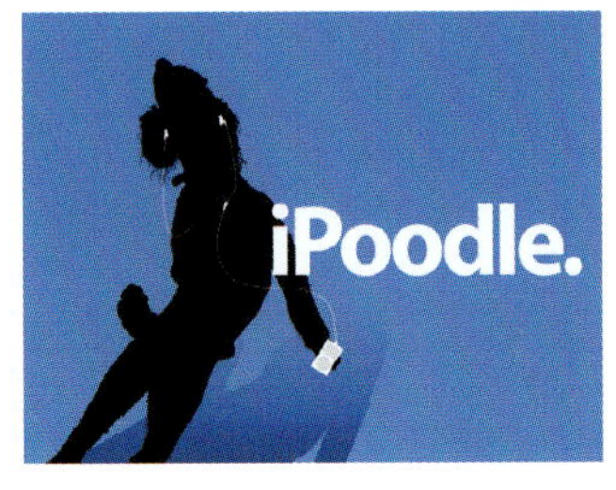

The iPod is more than a music player—it's a cultural phenomenon. There's even a service, podapic.com, that will turn a photo you supply into a mock iPod ad. Here's Sophie modeling the latest earwear.

Life with an iPod

Step 1. Build an iTunes Library

Use the techniques described earlier in this section to import songs from audio CDs, buy music and videos from the iTunes Store, subscribe to podcasts, assign equalization settings (optional), edit song information (if necessary), and create playlists.

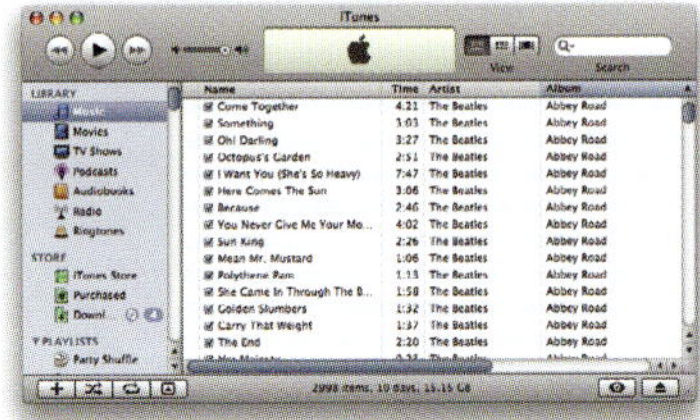

Step 2. Transfer to the iPod

Connect the iPod to your Mac's USB port (older iPods connect to the FireWire port instead). You can also buy a dock that makes connecting to the Mac even faster and more convenient (see page 120). Whether you use the dock or just a cable, when you connect the iPod to a Mac, iTunes copies your library and playlists to the iPod.

You can adjust settings for updating the contents of your iPod. For example, you can have iTunes copy only certain playlists, or copy songs but not videos. For details on syncing options, see page 108.

While the iPod is connected, its battery charges. The battery charges to 80 percent of its capacity in an hour or two, and charges fully in about three to four hours.

The iPod's battery gauge is located in the top right corner of its screen.

Step 3. Enjoy and Repeat

Disconnect the iPod and start listening and watching. When you modify your iTunes library or playlists, you can update the iPod's contents to match by simply connecting the iPod again.

Opposite the iPod's audio-output jack is the Hold switch. Slide it to disable the iPod's buttons. This is useful when you're transporting the iPod in a briefcase or purse, where its buttons could get pressed, causing the battery to drain.

If you don't have a dock, you can use the headphones jack to connect the iPod to a stereo system or other audio hardware, such as an FM transmitter. To connect to a stereo system, use a cable with a ⅛-inch miniplug on one end and two RCA phono plugs on the other. Connect the cable as described on page 76.

The battery gauge shows how much power remains.

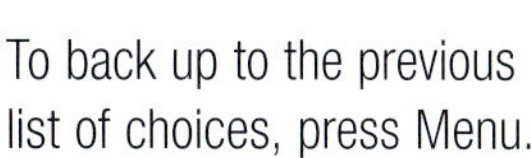

To back up to the previous list of choices, press Menu.

To choose an item in a menu, press the Center button.

To pause and resume playback, press Play/Pause. To turn off the iPod, press and hold this button for a few seconds.

The iPod's menu system uses a "drill-down" scheme: select an option and press the Center button to drill down one level to another menu or list of choices.

To skip to the previous or next item, press Previous or Next.

Use the click wheel to move the menu highlight up and down, adjust the playback volume, and browse when in Cover Flow view.

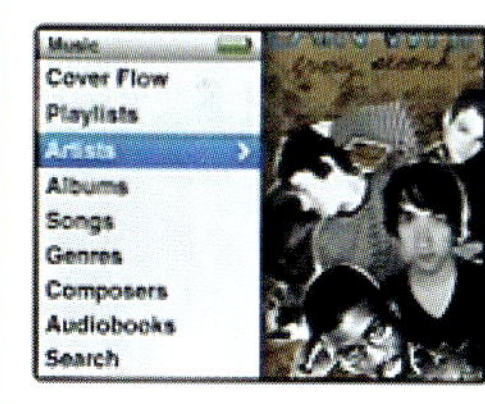

The Full-Sized iPods

The iPod has changed since its debut in 2001, and it continues to evolve. Sometimes the changes are simple: bigger hard drives to store even more songs. Sometimes the changes bring significant new capabilities, such as the ability to store photographs and play video. And sometimes, the changes are downright revolutionary, such as the touch-screen iPod touch and its telephonic cousin, the iPhone.

Each new generation brings improvements and enhancements to the software inside the iPod. Apple often makes these enhancements available as software updates for older iPods, although the oldest models have been left behind by some upgrades. For example, older iPods (specifically, ones that do not have dock connectors) can't play back songs compressed using the Apple Lossless encoder, nor do they provide as many menu-customizing options.

The features change, but the iPod's name remains the same. Because of this, the iPod family is often categorized according to "generations"—at least until 2007, when Apple gave the full-sized iPod its own name: classic. Here's a look at each generation of full-sized iPod and the features and capabilities that are common across the iPod line. On later pages, we'll take a closer look at the littlest iPods—the mini, the nano, and the shuffle—as well as at the iPhone and iPod touch.

iPod Common Ground

All current iPods that have display screens (as opposed to the tiny, screenless iPod shuffle) provide a common set of features and capabilities—starting with the obvious ability to play audio files. All iPods support iTunes playlists and provide shuffle modes for random-listening fun. And they all provide sound-enhancing equalizer settings similar to those provided by iTunes itself (page 58).

Beyond these basics, all current iPods also have some non-musical talents, which are covered in the following pages.

Video Playback

All current full-sized iPods (and the latest iPod nano) can store and play videos that you buy from the iTunes Store (page 32) or convert for iPod playback

An iPod Timeline

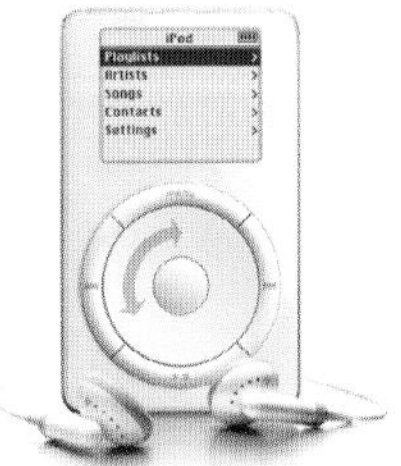

First Generation
2001–2002

5GB and 10GB capacities; mechanical scroll wheel.

Second Generation
2002

10GB and 20GB capacities; non-moving *touch* wheel.

yourself (page 106). You can watch the videos on the iPod's screen or connect the iPod to a TV set.

Photo Display

Use iTunes to transfer photos from your iPhoto library, then view them on the iPod's screen or on a connected TV set (page 104).

Address Book

If you store addresses in the Mac OS X Address Book, Microsoft's Entourage, or other programs, you can transfer that information to your iPod and carry your contacts with you (page 116).

Voice Recording

The fifth-generation iPod and the iPod classic support optional microphones that let you record voice memos and similar snippets.

Games

All iPods have some built-in games, but the fifth-generation iPod and the iPod classic support sophisticated games that you can buy from the iTunes Store.

Calendar

Similarly, you can stash calendar events in the Mac OS X iCal software and transfer them to your Mac. You can even have the iPod sound an audible alarm when a calendar event arrives.

Extras

All current iPods also provide some fun and practical (and sometimes both) extras: a stopwatch function, an alarm clock mode, and the ability to display text notes copied from your computer.

Dock Connector

An iPod's dock connector is the gateway to a world of accessories and expansion opportunities, from radio receivers to radio transmitters to external speaker systems (page 120).

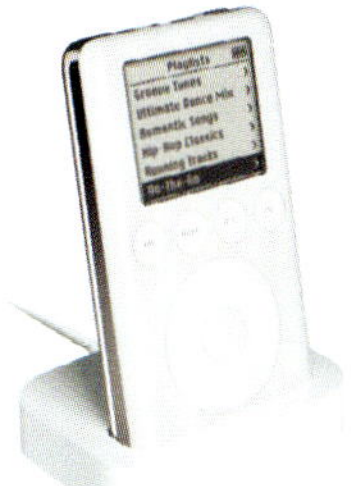

Third Generation
2003

10GB–40GB capacities; backlit buttons; dock support.

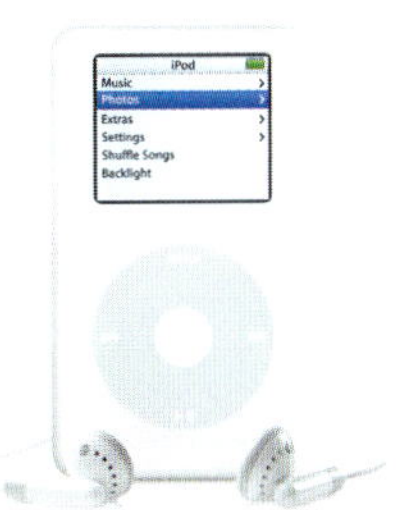

Fourth Generation
2004

20GB–40GB capacities; color screen and photo-display capabilities (iPod photo only); elegant *click wheel* controller.

Fifth Generation
2005

30GB–80GB capacities; large color screen; video display capabilities; enhanced game features; voice recording features

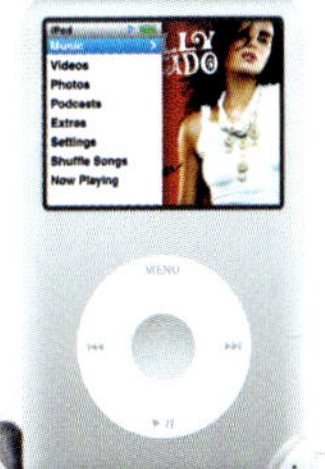

iPod classic
2007

80GB and 160GB capacities; new, all-metal enclosure; enhanced interface, including Cover Flow browsing.

The Compact iPods: mini and nano

Honey, I shrunk the iPod—that about sums up the iPod mini and iPod nano. Both have most of the talents of their bigger brethren, but are much more compact—or, in the case of the nano, much, much more compact.

The iPod mini was the first of Apple's petite iPods. It's no longer made, but if you crave a pink iPod, a visit to eBay will probably turn up plenty. Like full-sized iPods, the mini contained a hard drive. Functionally, its features match those of the 4G iPods. The mini can't store photos or videos.

As for the iPod nano, it makes the mini look maxi. Its compact size is due in part to its use of flash memory—the same type of memory used by your digital camera—instead of a hard drive. And while the nano may be a fraction of the size and half the weight of the mini, it does more—you can store photos and video on it, and watch them on its screen or on a connected TV set.

All of the general iPod techniques described in this section apply to the mini and the nano. Here's a look at what's different about these compact iPods.

iPod Model	Weight (ounces)
80GB iPod classic	4.90
iPod touch	4.20
iPod mini	3.60
iPod nano	1.74

iPod mini

About the height and width of a business card, the iPod mini debuted in January 2004 with a 4GB capacity. In February 2005, Apple added a 6GB model and changed the available colors.

On top are a hold switch and jacks for earphones and an optional remote control.

Made of anodized aluminum, the mini's case was available in several colors.

The click wheel, now standard across the full-sized iPod line, debuted on the mini.

iPod nano

The original iPod nano debuted in September 2005. Available in 1GB, 2GB, and 4GB capacities, it stored photos as well as music, but did not provide video playback or the ability to display photos on a TV set. Its color screen was bright and readable, but at 1.5 inches, it wasn't the best place to view photos.

In September 2006, Apple introduced a second-generation nano. It was available in several colors and in capacities of 2GB, 4GB, and 8GB.

The Hold switch is the only occupant of the nano's top floor.

The nano's audio-output jack is on the bottom, next to the dock connector.

iPod nano

Introduced in September 2007, the latest iPod nano is a bit larger than the original nano, but it does so much more: the nano, like the iPod classic, plays video and connects to a TV set.

Initially available in 4GB and 8GB capacities, the third-generation nano also matches the other enhancements of the iPod classic, including Cover Flow browsing, a search function, and advanced game support. The nano's energy-efficient flash memory and improved battery provide roughly 24 hours of continuous music playback, and about five hours of video playback. Caffeine not included.

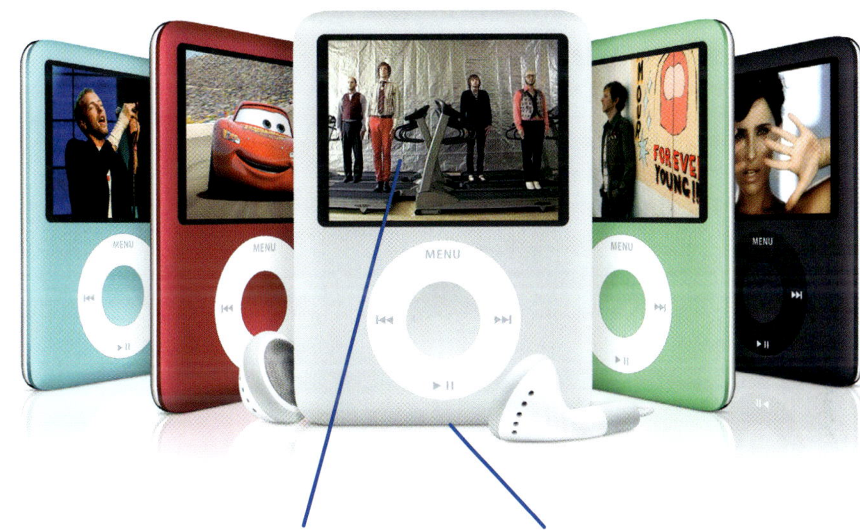

The two-inch screen isn't Panavision, but it's bright and crisp—and completely adequate for in-flight (or on-bus) viewing.

The Hold switch and audio-output jack are on the bottom.

The One-Size-Fits-All Dock

Remember that chorus of primal screams you heard a couple of years ago? It came from the many companies that build iPod docking accessories, and the reason for it was that Apple kept rendering their products obsolete. The problem was that companies were basing their dock dimensions around one specific iPod model, but new models would often be slightly thicker or thinner.

To quiet the screams, Apple standardized on one size of docking socket, and most iPod docking accessories now use this size. (Look for products that say "Made for iPod.") Each iPod now includes a dock adapter, a small piece of plastic that sits inside a dock and accommodates a specific iPod model.

As a result, you can buy an Apple Universal Dock—or an accessory from another company—and know that it will work with all iPods that include a dock adapter. (It's still smart to verify that your iPod is compatible with a specific accessory, though.)

For more on iPod dock and accessory options, see page 120.

The Littlest iPod: shuffle

iPod shuffle is something completely different. It lacks a display and click wheel. You can navigate to the next and previous song, but you can't skip around within songs or jump to a specific song in a playlist or album. And forget about storing photos, contacts, and calendar information.

But where iPod shuffle shines is in your pocket—and pocketbook. This is a truly tiny music player—you've carried bigger clothespins. It's also the least expensive iPod, costing just $79.

And true to its name and marketing campaign, iPod shuffle embraces the random world of shuffle discussed on page 82. iTunes has a special Autofill feature that will pack your iPod shuffle with a random selection of tunes. You can, of course, also take the reins yourself and manually copy specific songs, albums, and playlists.

First generation iPod shuffle

iPod shuffle at a Glance

iPod shuffle debuted in January 2005 in two capacities: 512MB (about 120 songs) and 1GB (about 240 songs). The original shuffle had a white plastic case (lower left). In September 2006, the second-generation shuffle debuted, sporting an even more compact aluminum case and a 1GB capacity. In September 2007, the third-generation shuffle added new color schemes.

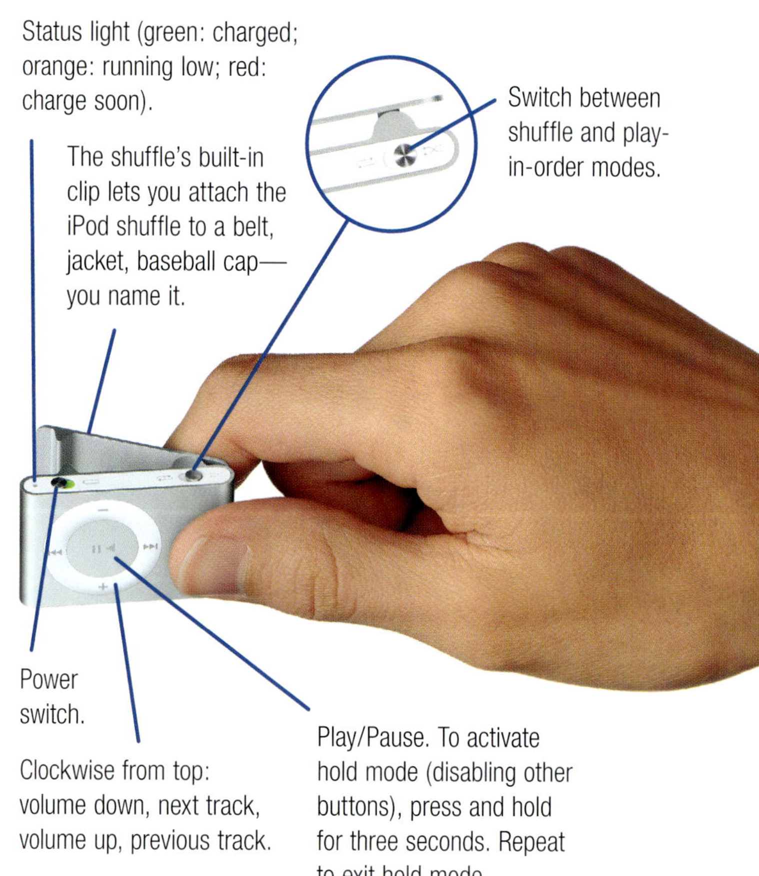
Status light (green: charged; orange: running low; red: charge soon).
The shuffle's built-in clip lets you attach the iPod shuffle to a belt, jacket, baseball cap—you name it.
Switch between shuffle and play-in-order modes.
Power switch.
Clockwise from top: volume down, next track, volume up, previous track.
Play/Pause. To activate hold mode (disabling other buttons), press and hold for three seconds. Repeat to exit hold mode.

Filling your iPod shuffle

Unless you have a ridiculously small iTunes library, you won't be able to fit all your music into an iPod shuffle. That's where the Autofill feature comes in: it lets you easily corral a collection of songs into your shuffle.

Normally, the Autofill feature chooses songs from your entire music library. To have Autofill choose songs from a specific playlist, choose its name.

If you uncheck this box, iTunes transfers songs in the order they appear in the library or selected playlist.

Click Autofill to have iTunes roll the dice, choose some songs, and then transfer them.

To add to iPod shuffle's contents instead of replacing them, uncheck this box.

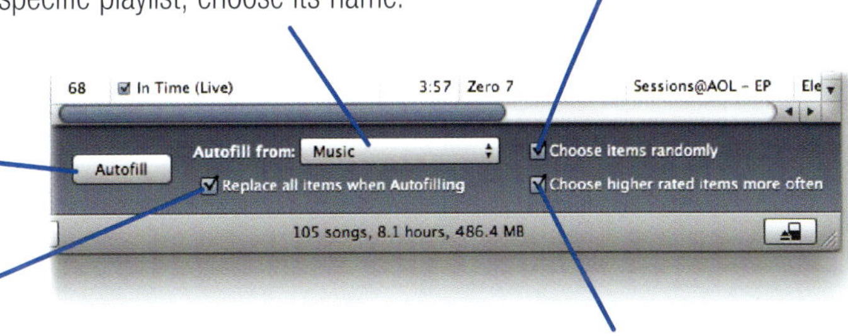

If you've rated your songs, you can increase the chances of their being chosen for Autofill transfer by checking this box.

iPod shuffle Tips

Keeping the fill. Like what Autofill has come up with? You can save it as a standard playlist: select any song in the Autofill list, and then choose Select All from the Edit menu (⌘-A). Finally, choose New Playlist from Selection from the File menu.

Autofill based on playlists. When you simply Autofill your shuffle from your main library, you're likely to end up with a lot of songs you might not have chosen otherwise. When you want more control over Autofill, choose a specific playlist from the Autofill From pop-up menu.

Indeed, you might want to create some smart playlists that allow you to Autofill based on genre—classical, jazz, rock, and so on—or on other key criteria, such as an artist's or composer's name. (For details on smart playlists, see pages 52–55.)

Self-serve fill-up. Autofill is an easy way to sling some songs onto a shuffle, but you might prefer more control over what gets copied. No problem—fill your shuffle yourself. You can copy songs directly to the shuffle by simply dragging them from your iTunes library to the iPod shuffle in the Devices list. Drag songs one at a time, or use the selection techniques described on page 46. You can also copy an entire playlist by simply dragging it to the shuffle.

Middle ground. You can combine the convenience of Autofill with the control of manual management. If you like most of what Autofill has come up with, just delete the tunes you don't want on your shuffle: be sure that your shuffle is selected in the Devices list, then select tunes you don't want on the shuffle and press the Delete key on your keyboard. Then, add some additional tunes if you like.

Or take the opposite approach: start off by manually adding the songs and playlists that you want, and then click Autofill to finish the job.

Take it from the top. When your iPod shuffle is in play-in-order mode, you can jump to the first song in the shuffle's playlist by pressing the Play/Pause button three times.

For more iPod shuffle tips, see page 112.

iPhone, iPod touch, and Wi-Fi Music

With the iPhone and iPod touch, your iTunes library is at your fingertips. Flick your way through lists of songs and artists. Rotate the screen, then sweep your finger across it to browse in Cover Flow view. Tap album artwork to flip it over and view its tracks. It's the most tactile way to explore music without becoming a tour-bus groupie.

With only a few exceptions, the iPhone and iPod touch have the same talents as their untouchable cousins: playlists, shuffle modes, equalizer settings, and the ability to browse by song, artist, album, composer, and genre. And like other iPods, they also display photos and videos—and on a screen whose size and vividness no click wheel iPod can match.

But these touchy-feely iPods provide a luxury no other iPod does: the ability to browse and buy songs using the iTunes Wi-Fi Music Store. Wander into Wi-Fi range, and you've got a music store in your hand. Search for songs. Listen to previews. Buy and download. When you return to your Mac, sync up to copy your purchases to your iTunes Library.

Throughout this book, I discuss the unique capabilities of the iPhone and iPod touch as they relate to iLife. Here's an audition of iTunes Wi-Fi Music Store.

Shopping the iTunes Wi-Fi Music Store

The iTunes Wi-Fi Music Store provides a streamlined slice of the full iTunes Store. You can browse new and featured releases and "top ten" lists in all major genres, and you can preview, search for, and buy songs.

To shop the Wi-Fi Store, be sure that Wi-Fi is active on your iPhone or iPod touch, and then tap the iTunes button.

The store's Featured screen appears.

To explore new releases and featured items in a specific genre, tap Genre, then take your pick.

To see the tracks on an album, tap the album.

Manage downloads here (opposite page).

Search for songs, albums, and artists (opposite page).

View top ten songs or albums in the genre of your choice.

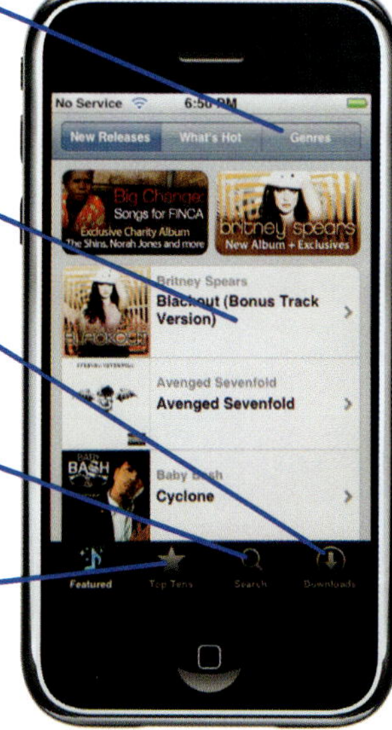

What isn't on hand. You can't buy or download videos, audiobooks, or podcasts from the Wi-Fi Store. Also, the Wi-Fi Store doesn't offer access to Apple's compilations (for example, iTunes Essentials and celebrity playlists), iMixes, and more-esoteric browsing features, such as Billboard charts. You can't redeem gift certificates here (though you can use store credits if you've already redeemed them on your Mac), nor can you read reviews and artist biographies. But every song and album in the iTunes Store is available, including the higher-quality, DRM-free iTunes Plus offerings (page 39).

Step 1. Shop

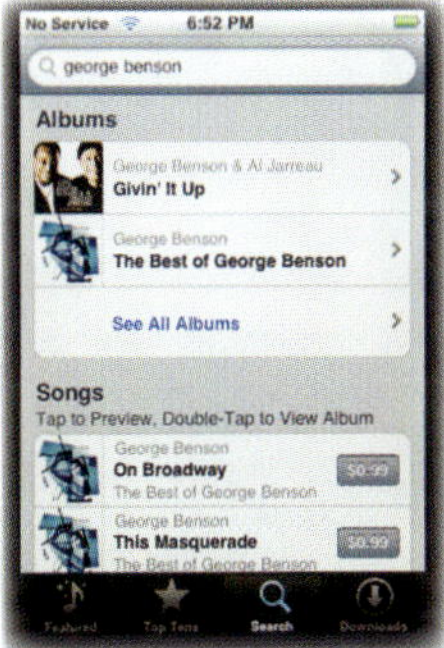

Browse. Explore featured and top ten albums and songs in your favorite genres. To view a song's album, double-tap the song.

Search. Tap Search, then tap the text box near the top of the screen. Type an artist, album, or song name, then tap the blue Search button for a list of matching songs and albums.

Step 2. Preview

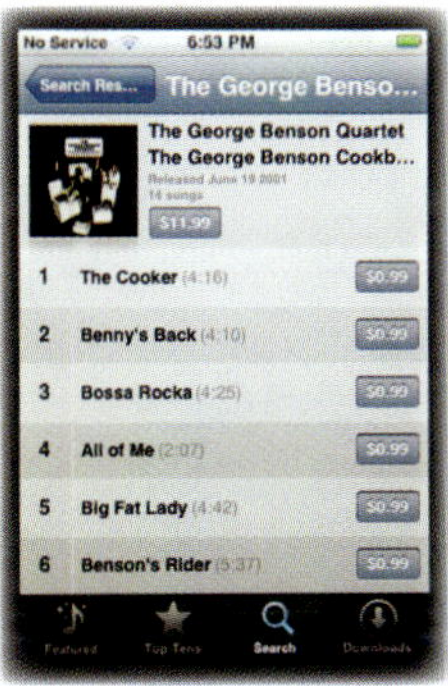

To hear a 30-second preview of a song, tap it. To stop the preview before it finishes playing, tap the song again or tap any other item on the screen.

Step 3. Buy

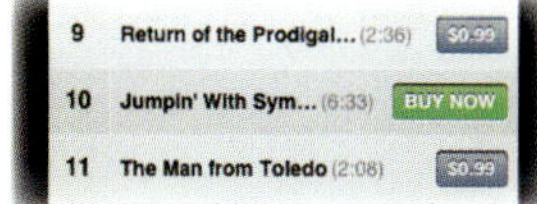

To buy a song or an entire album, tap the price, then tap Buy Now. Tap out your password, tap OK, and the download begins. If you wait more than 15 minutes to buy another item, you must enter your password again.

Tips for the iTunes Wi-Fi Music Store

Managing downloads. Unlike iTunes, the Wi-Fi Store doesn't provide a shopping cart option that lets you stash tunes, *then* download them. You can, however pause downloads until you're finished shopping, thus simulating the cart and not slowing browsing. Tap Downloads, then tap the pause button next to the downloading song.

Download, interrupted. Can't hang around the coffee house while the entire album you just bought downloads? Leave—the download resumes when you get to another a Wi-Fi network. Or, when you return to your Mac, start iTunes and choose Store > Check for Purchases. Anything that hasn't downloaded will.

Back to the Mac. While at your Mac, connect your iPhone or iPod touch and sync up—this copies your mobile purchases to your iTunes library.

In the Store area of the iTunes window, you'll find a playlist named Purchased on *your iPod's name*. iTunes lists hand-held purchases here, but of course, you can add them to any other playlist.

Goodies. Some albums include extras: PDF booklets or videos, for example. These won't download from the Wi-Fi Store. They will download to your Mac when you next use iTunes, though.

Starbucks. When it launched the Wi-Fi Store, Apple also linked up with Starbucks. At relatively few (at this writing) Starbucks outlets, you can shop the Wi-Fi Store and also buy music from the growing Starbucks catalog—including whatever is playing while you sip your 680-calorie Frappuccino. Learn more at apple.com/itunes/starbucks.

Viewing Photos on Your iPod

Talented musicians often branch out into other arts after a while. Except for the tiny shuffle, all current iPods can store and display photos. (Some older models can, too.) Stash some favorite shots on your iPod, then show them to friends, family, or the person sitting next to you on the plane. Or connect your iPod to a TV set and view your shots on its screen.

Scroll through photos one at a time at your own pace, or have your iPod display a slide show, complete with music from your iTunes library. You can even play the game of chance and view a slide show in shuffle mode—which photo will appear next?

Just as iTunes is the conduit between your music library and your iPod, it's also the bridge between your iPhoto library and your iPod. Using iTunes, you can copy all photos and albums, or only the ones you want to carry with you.

Because large photos devour space, iTunes creates a small, iPod-friendly version of each shot before transferring it to the iPod. You can also choose to transfer the full-resolution photos. This can be a handy way to back up photos or take them to a friend's house for sharing.

Here's how to turn your iPod into a pocket slide projector. Unless otherwise noted, everything on these pages also applies to the iPhone and iPod touch.

Step 1. Create Albums

There are several ways to transfer photos to an iPod. For example, you can transfer your entire photo library or just the albums you want to carry along with you.

For the latter approach, use iPhoto to create an album containing the photos you want to show. If you want to create iPod slide shows for several different events—your summer vacation, the Halloween party, your family reunion—create a separate album for each event. (For tips on creating albums, see pages 146–151.)

Don't forget music. The iPod can play music while displaying a slide show. If you want a particular song or playlist to play during a slide show, assign that song or playlist to the album, as described on page 182.

Viewing Photos on an iPod

When you use the iPod's menus to select an album or folder, the iPod displays thumbnail versions of your photos. To scroll the thumbnails, use the click wheel.

To see a full-screen version of the highlighted photo, press the Center button.

To display the next and previous screen of thumbnails, press Next or Previous.

To begin a slide show, press the Play/Pause button.

Step 2. Sync Your iPod

Connect your iPod to your Mac. In the Devices list at the left side of the iTunes window, select the iPod.

To access photo-updating options, click Photos.

To transfer photos stored in a folder that isn't part of your iPhoto library, use the pop-up menu.

To transfer only some albums, choose this option and then check the albums you want to transfer.

Check this box to include full-resolution photos, which are stored on the iPod in a folder named Photos. To access the originals, activate the iPod's disk mode as described on page 109. (Note: this option isn't available for the iPhone or iPod touch.)

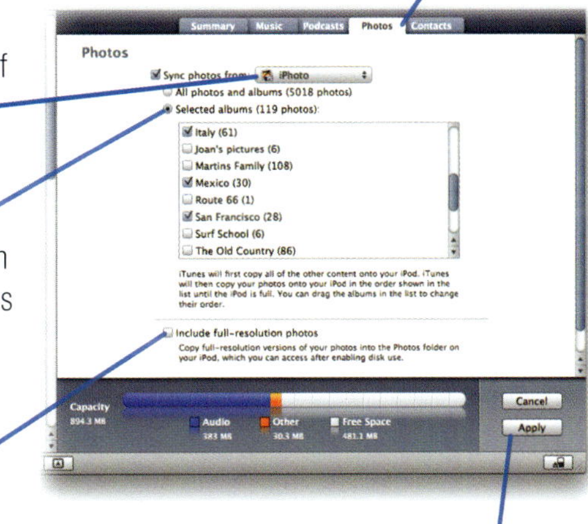

Click Apply to have iTunes prepare and transfer the photos.

Step 3. Start the Show

Navigate to the album that holds the photos you want to display, and press (or tap) the Play/Pause button. If your iPod is connected to a TV (see page 120), you have the option of viewing the slide show on the big screen.

To jump to the previous or next photo, during the slide show press the Previous or Next buttons. To pause the slide show, press Play/Pause. To end the show, press Menu (clickwheel iPods) or the Home button (iPhone and iPod touch).

Tip: Use the iPod's menus to adjust slide show settings, such as the duration for each photo and whether a transition appears between each one.

Touching Your Photos

To view photos on an iPhone or iPod touch, tap the Photos button on the home screen, then tap the album you want to view. A screen of photo thumbnails appears. To view a photo, tap it.

Return to the album thumbnails.

To hide photo controls, tap the photo. To restore the controls, tap again. To view the previous or next photo, flick across the screen. To zoom in, double-tap the photo. You can also use the standard pinch and drag maneuvers to zoom and pan.

Don't forget to rotate your hand-held projector 90 degrees to view horizontally oriented photos.

Left to right: display photo options, such as emailing; view previous photo; start slide show; view next photo.

Video and Your iPod

The latest iPods can play videos that you purchase from the iTunes Store (page 32) or that you prepare for the iPod yourself.

Watching video on an iPod isn't all that different from listening to music. Use the iPod's menus to locate the video, start playback, and watch, hopefully not while also driving.

Video that you buy from the iTunes Store is in a format that's ready for iPod playback. But what about movies you find on the Web? Or that friends or family email to you? Or that you create yourself? Although iTunes can store nearly any type of movie, the iPod is a more finicky eater. To play on an iPod, a movie must be compressed in a specific way.

And as with audio compression (page 22), video compression comes in various formats. I delve into this glamorous topic in further detail on page 240 and elsewhere in the iMovie chapter but, for now, the names to drop when you're talking iPod compression are *MPEG-4* and *H.264*. And the virtue to practice is called *patience*—compressing video can take a long time.

iTunes can compress video for the iPod, as can other programs, some of which are free. Here's an overview of the options you have for preparing movies for their small-screen debut, as well as a collection of video-related iPod tips.

A Handful of Video Tips

The TV connection. All video-capable iPods can connect to TV sets, the vast majority of which provide larger screens than an iPod's. Better still, a growing number of TVs, including many in hotels, provide front-panel input jacks that allow you to make connections without groping around the back of the cabinet.

To connect your iPod to a TV, use one of the cable accessories described on page 120.

Once you connect the cable, you need to tell your iPod to display video on the TV set. On the iPod, go to Videos > Settings > TV Out, then choose On. (If you'd rather switch this setting each time you play a video, choose Ask. On an iPhone or iPod touch, simply tap Yes in response to the Display on TV? prompt.)

Other video devices. You can also connect the iPod to video-recording devices, such as a VCR, camcorder, or set-top DVD recorder. This lets you record videos you've purchased from the iTunes store, not to mention slide shows displayed with the iPod's photo display features.

Got juice? When playing video, an iPod's battery charge will drain much more quickly—partly because the hard drive will spin more often, but largely because the screen's backlight is on the entire time.

Video playlists. You can add videos to playlists and smart playlists. You can even mix and match videos and music in the same playlist. If you frequently buy music videos from the iTunes Store, you may want to listen to their soundtracks along with tunes from your music library.

Bookmarks and chapters. As with audiobooks, videos that you buy from the iTunes Store provide bookmarking: if you stop playback partway through, playback continues at that point when you resume. When watching a movie that provides chapters, you can also skip to the next and previous chapter using the iPod's Next and Previous buttons.

Get more tips and tools for playing video on your iPod.
www.macilife.com/itunes

Converting Movies for iPod Playback

Converting with iTunes. First, add the movie to your iTunes library (page 86). Then, select the movie in iTunes and choose Convert Selection for iPod from the Advanced menu.

Converting with QuickTime Pro. Apple's $29 QuickTime Pro adds the ability to export movies using the QuickTime Player that you already have. QuickTime Pro provides a Movie to iPod setting that delivers fine results, albeit with long encoding times. You can also take the reins yourself and specify encoding settings.

Converting with other tools. Splasm Software's ViddyUp! is an inexpensive conversion program. Techspansion's iSquint is free, and its inexpensive VisualHub is my favorite—it's able to convert between just about every major video format. ViddyUp! and VisualHub are also handy for preparing movies for Apple TV playback.

Handbrake and Instant Handbrake. Video on a DVD-Video disc is compressed in MPEG-2 format (page 313). Video on a commercial DVD, such as a Hollywood movie, is also shackled by encryption to thwart copying.

Neither of these issues bothers either of these programs. HandBrake is a power tool that gives you precise control over the conversion process, including the ability to tweak compression settings and even choose which chapters you want to extract.

Video Conversion at a Glance

Source	Best Option(s)
A DVD	Use Handbrake or Instant Handbrake.
A QuickTime movie that a friend emailed to you	Use iTunes, QuickTime Pro, ViddyUp!, iSquint, or VisualHub.
A movie in Windows Media format	Use VisualHub.
An MPEG-format movie taken by a digital camera or camcorder	Use ViddyUp! or VisualHub, or add the movie to iMovie and then share (page 276).
A movie you've created in iMovie	Use iMovie Share menu (page 276).
A Final Cut Express or Final Cut Pro project	Choose File > Export > Using QuickTime Conversion, then choose iPod from the Format pop-up menu.

Instant Handbrake can also suck video from a DVD, but doesn't let you tweak settings or choose specific chapters.

El Gato's EyeTV. Got a TiVo's worth of shows you'd like to pod? Connect El Gato's EyeTV box to your TiVo, then record the shows on your Mac's hard drive. Then, use the EyeTV software to export a version encoded for the iPod.

What quality settings? Conversion programs provide several encoding settings that let you balance compression time, image quality, and file size. I recommend sticking with the default settings. iPod video is all about portability, not high-definition quality.

But if you want to sweat the details, here are a few guidelines: the H.264 setting often gives better quality and smaller file sizes, though encoding can take much longer than MPEG-4. For maximum quality, specify two-pass H.264.

If you'll be connecting your iPod to a TV and viewing on the big screen, consider choosing the 640- by 480-pixel frame size. This larger frame size appears more crisp on a TV than the standard iPod video size of 320 by 240 pixels.

What kind of video? After preparing some video for the iPod and adding it to your iTunes library, consider using the Get Info command to specify a category for the movie. This allows the video to appear in the right category on the iPod's Videos menu (and on an Apple TV). In iTunes, select the video, choose File > Get Info, click Options, then choose an option from the Video Kind pop-up menu.

Syncing Options

Normally, iTunes will synchronize all your playlists and your entire iTunes library, or at least as much of it as will fit on the iPod.

But there may be times when you want to manually control which items iTunes copies to the iPod. Maybe your iTunes library is larger than will fit on the iPod, and you'd like to specify what you want to copy. Or maybe you listen to some podcasts on your Mac but not on your iPod, and you don't want to waste iPod capacity by copying those podcasts.

Whatever the reason, you can use iTunes to specify syncing options. You can also use iTunes to activate *disk mode*, in which the iPod appears on your desktop just like a hard drive (which, for a full-sized iPod, it is). In disk mode, you can use the Mac's Finder to copy files to and from the iPod. This is a handy way to shuttle documents to and from work, to back up your iPhoto library, or to carry backups of important programs or files with you on the road. (Disk mode isn't available on the iPhone or iPod touch.)

Here's the lowdown on syncing. Although the focus is on the iPod and iPhone, the basic techniques described here also apply to the Apple TV (page 78).

The Summary Panel

Whether you've connected an iPod, an iPhone, or an Apple TV, the Summary panel provides quick access to key information and basic preferences.

Manage media. Each tab leads to options that let you control what is synced (opposite page).

Information. Your device's name, rank, and serial number, plus a lovely portrait.

Update and restore. If a software update is available, get it here. Having big problems? Try restoring factory settings (see page 110).

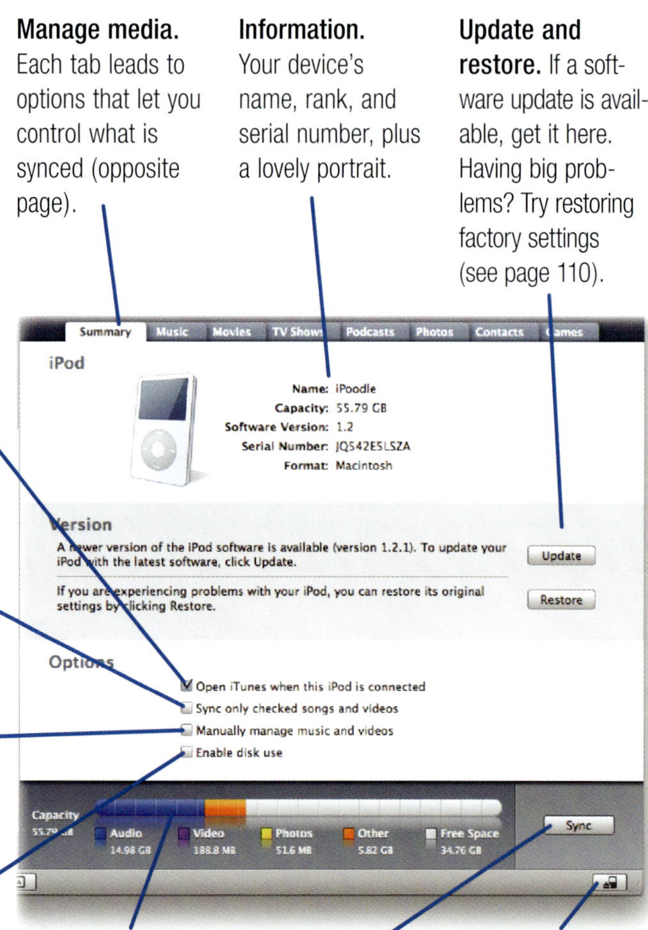

Don't want iTunes to launch when you connect this iPod or iPhone? Uncheck this box.

Selective syncing: iTunes copies only items with check marks next to their names (☑).

Very selective syncing: iTunes copies nothing automatically; you drag items by hand (see page 110).

To enable the iPod to appear on the desktop as described at left, check this box.

Thermometer. No, it isn't—it's a graph depicting the space used by each type of media.

Make it so. Update the content on your device.

Eject. Before unplugging your iPod or iPhone, click here. Or click the similar button in the Devices area (⏏).

Syncing Specifics

Each tab leads to options specific to certain media. The Music pane appears here, but each pane provides three basic ways to control syncing. (For photo-syncing details, see page 105. For details on syncing contacts and calendar information, see pages 116–119.)

Sync everything. Copy every item (song, TV show, podcast, ringtone, and so on) in that category. This is the preset option.

Sync nothing. Don't copy anything in that category—for example, you might not want to copy to your iPod movies that you watch only on your Apple TV.

Sync just some things. Use check boxes to specify which items you want to sync. In the Podcasts and TV Shows panes, you have even more control—the ability to specify that only the most recent episodes are copied, for example, or that only unplayed ones are. (This last option pairs up well with the ability to mark items as new or not new, as described on page 36.)

Don't want to store music on your iPod (maybe you use it for movies and TV shows only)? Uncheck this box.

Normally, iTunes copies all songs and playlists. To copy only some playlists, choose this option, then check the box next to each playlist you want to copy.

Maybe you watch music videos on your Apple TV, but not on your iPod. Uncheck this box to keep music videos off your iPod.

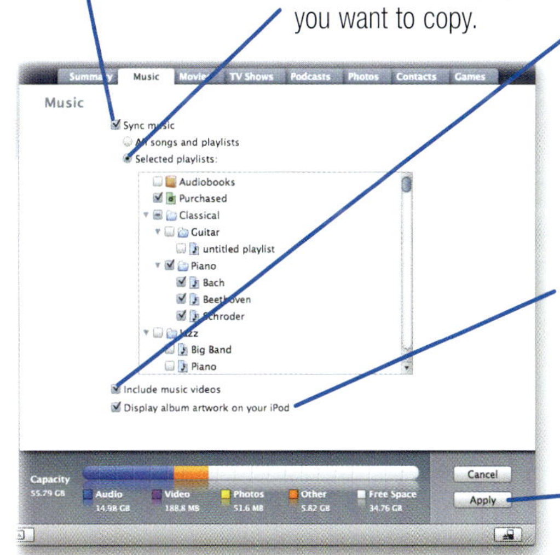

You can save a small amount of iPod space by unchecking this box, but you lose the eye candy that artwork and the iPod's Cover Flow view provide.

To apply your changes and begin the sync, click Apply. If you need to tweak options in other tabs, wait to click Apply until you've done so.

Setting iPod shuffle Preferences

The iPod shuffle has its own preferences and syncing options.

Digital dieting: this option lets you play Apple Lossless and AIFF files, formats that the iPod shuffle doesn't otherwise support (page 112).

Activate the sound-check feature, which optimizes volume levels from one song to the next (page 110).

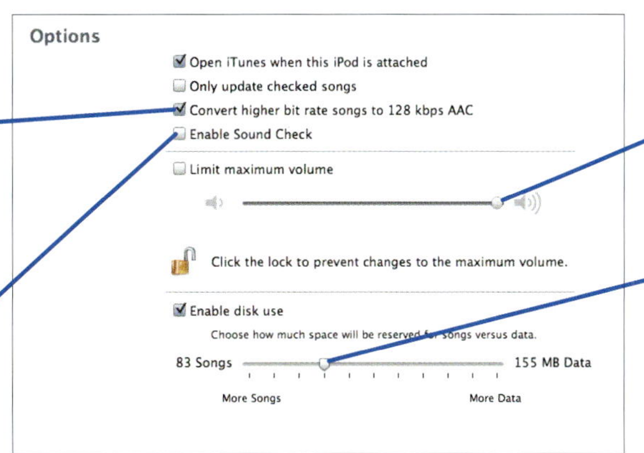

Regulate the maximum volume (see page 110).

When using disk mode, you can specify how much space to reserve for songs and data.

iPod Playback Tips

Not So Loud!

Do you love music? Then turn it down. At the risk of sounding like a nagging parent, I'm telling you that you shouldn't listen to music at high volume levels, especially when you're wearing headphones or earbuds. Your brain can acclimate to loud volume levels, but your ears can't—they'll be damaged.

When you're wearing headphones or earbuds, set the iPod's volume so that it's *just* loud enough. When you start playing back a tune, you should be thinking to yourself, "I wish that was a just a little bit louder."

Pay attention, kids. In a couple of decades, a lot of iPod users are going to be cupping their ears and saying, "Pardon me?" Don't be one of them. Just remember: your hearing is the only sense you can damage with too much of a good thing.

With the latest iPods (as well as the fifth-generation iPod and the original iPod nano), you can set a maximum volume limit. If you're a parent concerned about your kids' hearing, you can dial down the iPod. You can also create a password that prevents anyone from changing the limit you set.

Click wheel iPods. Go to Settings > Volume Limit. Use the click wheel to specify a maximum, then press the Center button. To prevent changes to the setting, choose Set Combination, then dial in a code.

iPhone and iPod touch. Go to Settings > iPod > Volume Limit. Drag the volume control. To lock the setting, tap Lock Volume Limit, then type a code.

iPod shuffle. Use the Summary panel, as shown on page 109.

For details and more background on the importance of safe listening, see www.apple.com/sound.

Sound Check

Speaking of volume control, if you use the Sound Check feature in iTunes (page 80), you might want its volume-adjustment talents to extend to iPod playback, too.

Easy: navigate to your iPod's Settings menu, then activate Sound Check. With the iPod shuffle, use the Summary pane shown on page 108.

Moving Around within an Item

You can quickly move around, or scrub, within an item while it plays. Go back and listen to a favorite song verse again, or skip that movie's boring love scene and get to the fiery car chase.

Click wheel iPods. Press the Center button, and the elapsed-time gauge on the iPod's screen is replaced with a little diamond—just like the one iTunes displays during playback. Using the click wheel, move the diamond left and right to scrub within the item.

iPhone and iPod touch. You can move forward or backward by holding your finger on the Next or Previous buttons at the bottom of the screen. For faster navigation, tap the screen to display the playback controls at the top of the screen. Then, drag the playhead left or right. (When viewing video, tap the screen to make these controls appear.)

All iPods. When listening to an enhanced podcast or audiobook, or when viewing a movie containing chapter markers, you can skip between chapters by pressing the Next or Previous buttons.

Audiobook Speed Control

You love listening to audiobooks, but sometimes you wish the narrator spoke a bit faster or slower. You can get your wish.

Click wheel iPods. Go to Settings > Audiobooks, and then choose Slower or Faster.

The iPod adjusts its playback speed without changing the pitch (a trick it may have learned from GarageBand). To restore the normal playback speed, go to Settings > Audiobooks and choose Normal.

iPhone and iPod touch. To adjust playback speed, go to Settings > iPod > Audiobook Speed. Alas, choosing Faster will not help with long, droning phone calls.

Rating on the Road

You can use the iPod to assign star ratings (page 86) to an item while it's playing. When you sync your iPod, iTunes retrieves the rating and assigns it to the item in your library.

Click wheel iPods. Navigate to the Now Playing screen, then press the Center button until the rating screen appears. Use the click wheel to assign a rating.

iPhone and iPod touch. Double-tap the Now Playing screen to display a list of tracks on the album. Tap the dots near the top of the screen to assign stars.

The On-The-Go Playlist

You have a sudden hankering to hear some songs from six different albums, but you're on the road and thus can't build a new playlist using iTunes. Solution: the On-The-Go playlist, a special, temporary playlist that lives within the iPod. Create the playlist on the iPod, and it's copied back to the Mac the next time you sync.

Click wheel iPods. To add a song to the On-The-Go playlist, scroll to the song and then press and hold the Center button until the song flashes a few times. Repeat for the next song.

You can even add entire albums, artists, genres, and playlists to the On-The-Go playlist. Simply scroll to the item you want and hold down the Center button.

To delete a song that you've added to the playlist, go to the On-The-Go playlist, highlight the song, and hold down the Center button until the highlight flashes.

To clear the On-The-Go playlist, navigate to it, scroll to the bottom of the song list, and choose Clear Playlist. The playlist is also cleared when you connect the iPod to your Mac, but if you've set up iTunes to automatically update the iPod when you connect it, the On-The-Go playlist will be copied to iTunes so you can use it again.

To save the On-The-Go playlist, scroll to the bottom of its song list, then choose Save Playlist. The saved playlist will have the name *New Playlist* followed by a numeral. When you sync up your iPod, the saved playlist is transferred to iTunes, where you can rename it. Now you can create another On-The-Go playlist, if you like.

Note: The On-The-Go playlist is not available on the 1G and 2G iPod models.

iPhone and iPod touch. Go to Playlists > On-The-Go, then tap songs to add them. (You can't add entire albums or artists in one fell swoop, as on click wheel iPods.) When you're finished, tap Done.

To edit the On-The-Go playlist, tap its name, then tap Edit. To add more songs, tap the plus sign at the top of the screen. To remove a song, tap the minus sign in front of it. To change song order, drag the horizontal bars to the right of a song's name. To clear the playlist, tap Clear Playlist.

iPod Management Tips

Chances are the syncing features in iTunes are all you need to manage the contents of your iPod. But when you want to go beyond automatic syncing—or if you need to recover items from your iPod because of a Mac hard-drive crash or other calamity—here are some options.

Manual Management

As pages 108–109 show, the syncing panes in iTunes give you a lot of control over what iTunes copies to the iPod, especially if you use the "sync only checked songs and videos" option. But for real control freaks, there's another path: manual updating. In this mode, you can manage the iPod's music and videos by hand using iTunes—copying and deleting individual songs and videos to and from the iPod to control exactly how its storage space is used.

Manual updating is great when you have a huge iTunes library and a lower-capacity iPod, such as the nano. Assemble playlists containing just the songs and videos you want to enjoy on your next workout (or cross-country flight), then sling them into the iPod.

Note that manual updating is available for click wheel iPods only; the iPhone and iPod touch don't allow it. And the iPod shuffle is always in manual-update mode.

To activate manual updating, connect your iPod and, in the Summary pane, click the Manually Manage Music and Videos box. iTunes asks you to confirm your choice; click OK.

Now a world of opportunities awaits.

Copying items. To copy songs or videos to the iPod, drag them from the iTunes window to the iPod's name in the Devices list. To copy an entire playlist to the iPod, drag it from the Playlists area to the iPod.

You can even copy an item and add it to an existing playlist on the iPod. Click the triangle next to the iPod's name in the Devices list, and you see a list of the playlists on the iPod. Now drag items to the existing playlist.

Deleting items. To remove songs or videos from the iPod, click the triangle next to the iPod's name. Next, select one of the items below the iPod's name—for example, Music. Now select the doomed items and press the Delete key.

Playing items. You can play items on the iPod without having to copy them to the iTunes library. This is a big deal—it lets you connect your iPod to a friend's Mac and then play tunes or watch videos that are on the iPod. (Alas, to play a protected item purchased from the iTunes Store, you'll have to authorize that Mac with your Apple ID and password.)

iPod-only playlists and content. When you have the iPod set up for manual updating, you can use iTunes to create playlists that exist only on the iPod. In the Devices area of the iTunes window, select the iPod and then create the new playlist.

You can also copy audio and video files directly to the iPod without storing them in your iTunes library. Just drag items from the Finder to the iPod in the Devices area.

Notes and Tips. You might find it easier to sling items into your iPod if you open a second window in iTunes. In the Devices list, click the triangle next to the iPod's name. Now double-click a library category on the iPod—for example, if you'll be copying music, double-click Music. A second window opens that you can position next to the main iTunes window.

When manual updating is active, you must manually unmount the iPod when you're done with it. Select the iPod in the Devices list and then click the Eject button next to the iPod's name or in the lower-right corner of the iTunes window.

If you ever decide to switch back to iTunes' automatic updating mode, iTunes will replace the iPod's contents with the current iTunes library and playlists, according to the syncing options you specify (page 108).

Library Too Big?

When you have more media than you have iPod capacity, manual management is the best solution. But there's also an automatic alternative. iTunes can create a playlist containing only songs that will fit on your iPod. This playlist is called the iPod Selection playlist, and iTunes will offer to create it for you if it determines that your library won't fit on your iPod.

The iPod Selection playlist uses a five-step process to determine which songs to copy to your iPod.

1. iTunes groups all tracks into albums.

2. iTunes calculates an average play count and average rating for each album.

3. iTunes begins filling the iPod with albums that have non-zero average play counts and non-zero ratings, in descending order. In other words, albums with higher play counts and higher ratings get higher priority.

4. If Step 3 completes and there's still some free space, iTunes starts copying albums that were recently played or recently added to your library.

5. If there's still some free space after Step 4 completes, iTunes adds random albums until the iPod is filled to the gills and loosening its belt.

If there's a lesson here, it's this: rate your music. Ratings clearly play an important role in the iPod Selection playlist, so if you rate your songs, you'll stand a better chance of shoehorning your favorites into your iPod.

Of course, in the end, there's no substitute for your own smarts: you can probably do a better job of budgeting iPod capacity by manually managing your iPod's library.

Transferring Purchases via iPod

You have more than one Mac and you want to move items purchased from the iTunes Store from one Mac to another. You could burn data CDs or copy the items over a network, but you can also use your iPod.

Be sure that the purchased items are on your iPod, then connect it to the Mac to which you want to copy the items. If the iPod is set up for automatic updating, iTunes asks if you want to transfer the purchases to the Mac's iTunes Library. Click Transfer Purchases.

If the iPod is set up for manual updating, you need to start the transfer yourself. In the Devices area of the iTunes window, Control-click on the iPod's name, then choose Transfer Purchases from the pop-up shortcut menu.

Accessing Your Music Directly

The music and video files on an iPod are stored in invisible folders. Thus, you can't use the Finder to copy items from the iPod to your hard drive, even if you put the iPod into disk mode. Except for the ability to transfer iTunes Store purchases as noted in the previous tip, transfer is a one-way street: from the Mac to the iPod.

However, several free or inexpensive utilities let you directly access the files on an iPod. This can be a great way to recover your iTunes library should something happen to the copy on your Mac.

I'm fond of Findley Designs' iPod Access, which lets you access and play items on an iPod as well as copy them to your Mac's hard drive. iPod Access also works with the iPhone and iPod touch.

Extracting Photos from an iPod

You copied some photos to your iPod, but didn't include the original, high-resolution versions. Now you're at a friend's house and she'd like a copy of the photos. You connect your iPod to her Mac, put it in disk mode, and open up the Photos folder. But instead of seeing individual image files, you see only a couple of files with cryptic names, such as F1023_1.ithmb.

When iTunes prepares photos for iPod storage, it stashes them in a format that isn't readable by imaging programs, such as iPhoto or Photoshop. But that doesn't mean there isn't a way to get to those photos.

Click wheel iPods. A free utility, Keith's iPod Photo Reader, lets you copy some or all of the images. Consider stashing it on your iPod for those times when you want to copy photos. And if you want a more fully featured photo-access program, check out Findley Designs' inexpensive iPod Access Photo.

iPhone and iPod touch. To access your photos directly, use Ecamm Network's iPhoneDrive, described on page 112.

iPod Tips

Having Trouble? Try the Five Rs

iPod acting up? Apple has developed a nicely alliterative troubleshooting plan of attack that it calls "The Five Rs."

Reset. Reboot the iPod using the key sequences shown in the table at right. This will often clear its head.

Retry. Connect the iPod to a different port on your computer, not on a USB hub. Then try syncing again.

Restart. Reboot your Mac. Open the Software Update system preference and see if you have the latest Mac OS X software updates.

Reinstall. Download and install the latest version of iTunes, then launch it. If iTunes recognizes the iPod, check the Summary pane to see if an update to the iPod software is available (page 108).

Restore. Wipe the iPod clean and restore its factory settings by clicking the Restore button in the Summary pane.

Apple has created a special Web page that walks you through each of the five steps after you specify which iPod model you have. It's called The Five Rs Assistant, and I've linked to it at macilife.com/itunes.

iPod Key Sequences

To Do This	Do This
Turn off the iPod	Hold down Play/Pause.
Restart the iPod	**3G and older iPods:** Hold down Menu and Play/Pause until the Apple logo appears on the screen (five to 10 seconds). **4G and later:** Toggle the Hold switch, then hold down Menu and the Center button until the Apple logo appears (about six seconds).
Access the iPod's diagnostic mode	**3G and older iPods:** Restart, then immediately hold down Previous, Next, and the Center button. **4G and later:** Restart, then immediately hold down Previous and the Center button.

When the Music Dies

The iPod's battery doesn't last forever. For $59 plus shipping, Apple will replace any iPod whose only problem is a dead battery. For details on the iPod Out-of-Warranty Battery Replacement Program, see the link to Apple's page on macilife.com/itunes.

Some companies also sell replacement batteries that you can install yourself—if you dare to crack open the iPod's case and venture inside. One source is www.ipodbattery.com. For details on replacement batteries and information on iPod batteries in general, see www.ipodbatteryfaq.com.

Extending battery life. There are a few things you can do to get more playback time out of each iPod charge. Avoid frequently jumping between songs, especially on hard-drive iPods. Use the Settings menu to turn off the Equalizer. Put the iPod to sleep when you aren't playing it. Turn off screen backlighting on click wheel iPods (Settings > Backlight Timer > Off). And don't watch video—the screen backlight is one of the iPod's biggest power consumers. For more tips, see macilife.com/itunes.

Menu Customizing

You can add items to, and remove them from, the iPod's main menu. For example, if you frequently browse your library by artist, add an Artist menu to the main menu.

Click wheel iPods. Choose Settings > Main Menu. Scroll to the desired option (for example, Artist), then press the Center button—the word On appears next to that option to indicate it will be in the menu. You can add as many items to the main menu as you like.

(Note: Menu customizing isn't available on the now-elderly 1G and 2G iPod models.)

iPhone and iPod touch. Menu customizing is limited: you can replace the four browse buttons at the bottom of the screen with ones you might use more. For example, if you like podcasts but you rarely browse by artist, replace the Artist button with Podcasts.

Tap the More button, then tap the Edit button. Drag one of the buttons (for example, Podcasts) to the bottom of the screen so that it's over the button you want to replace. (The doomed button glows when you're at the right spot.)

You can also rearrange the browse buttons: drag them left or right. When you're finished, tap the Done button.

iPod shuffle: Converting to AAC

The iPod shuffle can play all audio formats supported by larger iPods, with two exceptions: Apple Lossless and AIFF. What if you've been ripping your CDs in Apple Lossless format and want to play those tunes with your shuffle? Or what if you've exported some GarageBand songs and want to shuffle around with your music clipped to your belt?

As page 109 showed, the iPod shuffle has a preference setting that lets you accomplish both tasks: it's the check box labeled *Convert higher bit rate songs to 128 kbps AAC*. That's a mouthful, but it's a useful option.

When this box is checked, iTunes creates 128 kbps AAC versions of any Apple Lossless or AIFF songs that you try to copy to your iPod shuffle. The song files remain in their original format in your iTunes library; iTunes simply encodes an AAC version on the fly before transferring it to the iPod shuffle.

Getting Lyrical

Starting with the 5G and nano models, the iPod has the ability to display song lyrics. (At this writing, the iPhone and iPod touch can't display lyrics.)

If you use the Song Info window to add lyrics to a song (page 26), you can display the lyrics on the iPod as the song plays. Navigate to the Now Playing screen if necessary, then press the Center button until the lyrics appear.

To retrieve song lyrics, try Eternal Storm's GimmeSomeTune, available from download sites. You can also find lyrics on innumerable Web sites; search for *song lyrics* using your favorite search engine. Once you've found lyrics for a tune, copy them, then open the Get Info window for the song and paste them into the Lyrics panel.

Notes and Museum Mode

The Notes feature, provided by 3G and later click wheel iPods, supports hyperlinks not unlike those on Web sites. A text note can contain a link to another note or even to a song: navigating to the link and then clicking the iPod's Center button is the equivalent of clicking on a hyperlink.

If you're interested in learning more about creating hyperlinked text notes, check out the article that my *Macworld* colleague Chris Breen wrote in the September 2004 issue. The article is called "Hack the iPod's Notes," and is online at macworld.com.

Notes are also the key to the iPod's *museum mode*, so named because some museums have used it to create interactive tours of their displays. Apple has created some Web pages that discuss how museums can use the iPod—and how some already are. Go to macilife.com/itunes and click the link named "iPod as Tour Guide."

iPod Scripts

Numerous programmers have created useful AppleScripts for the iPod that enable you to manage playlists, copy songs, and more. The best source for these scripts is Doug Adams' excellent Doug's AppleScripts for iTunes site (www.dougscripts.com).

iPod as Address Book and More

Your iPod can hold more than just audio-visual treats. It can also store names and addresses and short text notes.

Every Mac includes Address Book, a straightforward but powerful digital Rolodex program. Besides being able to store contact information, Address Book can tap into other Apple programs. When using iPhoto to create a calendar, for example, you can have birthdays from Address Book automatically added to calendar dates. Address Book can also sync your contact information to Apple's .Mac service. It's a great way to back up your address book and synchronize it across multiple Macs.

Address Book is also on speaking terms with iTunes: you can use iTunes to sync your collection of contacts to your iPod or iPhone. If you use Address Book to categorize your contacts into groups—friends, business associates, bookies—you can even selectively sync only certain groups.

Once you sync, you can view your contacts on the iPod. With click wheel iPods, choose Extras > Contacts. (And if you do so frequently, add a Contacts item to the main menu; see page 114.)

On the iPhone and iPod touch, you can also edit and delete contacts and create new ones. When you sync, iTunes copies your changes into Address Book.

Click wheel iPods can also store text notes that are accessible through the Notes menu item: simply peck your notes into a text-only file and then copy the file to the iPod's Notes folder.

Syncing Address Book Contacts

Step 1. Connect your iPod.

Step 2. In the Devices area of the iTunes window, click your iPod's name. The Summary panel appears (page 108).

Step 3. Click the Contacts tab. The Contacts pane appears.

Step 4. Specify sync options.

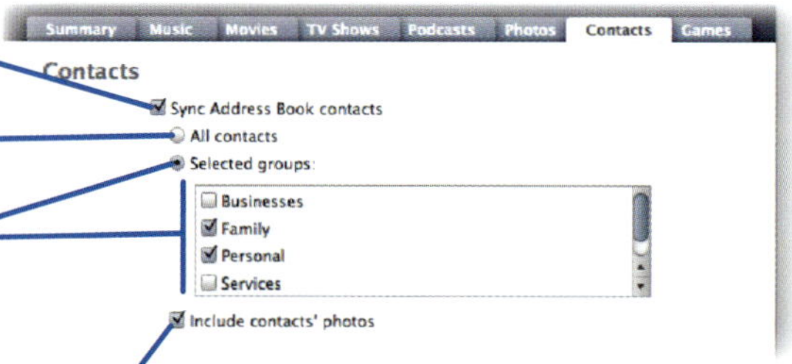

Be sure this is checked.

Everyone goes along for the ride.

Exclusive club: Address Book lets you organize contacts into groups. To sync only some groups, choose this option, then check the groups you want.

Address Book can store a photo of each contact. To copy contact photos to the iPod, check this box. To save a bit of iPod space, uncheck it.

Step 5. Click the Apply button near the lower-right corner of the iTunes window. (**Tip:** You can tweak settings in other tabs if you like, then click Apply when you're done.)

Find these and other iPod utilities.
www.macilife.com/itunes

Adding Contacts from Elsewhere

Don't use Address Book? You should try it. Because of its tight integration with Mac OS X, the iPod, and other Apple tools, it's the best place to stash your friends and colleagues. But if you do store contacts elsewhere, you can still sync them with your iPod. It may not work as smoothly and you may need additional tools, but you can do it.

If you use Microsoft Entourage, you can sync by enabling Sync Services in Entourage's Preferences dialog box.

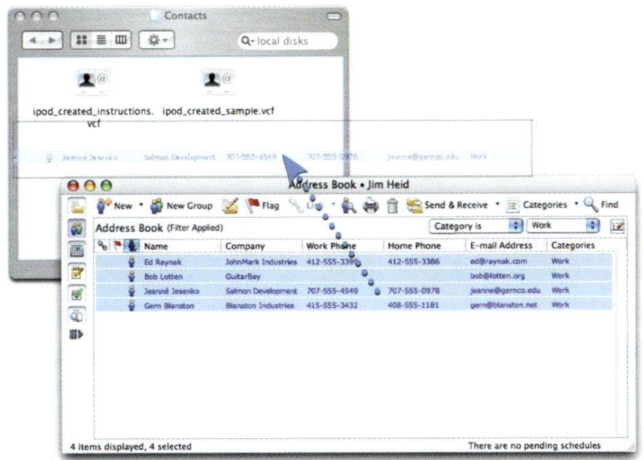

For click wheel iPods, you can also copy Entourage contacts by hand. Activate your iPod's disk mode (see page 108), then drag contacts from Entourage into the iPod's Contacts folder.

If you've used this manual-copying technique, you can remove contacts from the iPod by dragging them from the Contacts folder to the Trash. If you frequently shuttle contacts from Entourage to your iPod, consider Zapptek's iPDA software, described below.

In general, any contact-management program that supports the industry-standard vCard format can provide contacts to the iPod, although if the program doesn't support Mac OS X's Sync Services, you may have to copy them by hand as described at left.

A Sampling of iPod Utilities

Dozens of free or inexpensive utilities are available that let you store all manner of information on an iPod. Here's a sampling of a few noteworthy offerings.

iSpeak It. With Michael Zapp's iSpeak It (www.zapptek.com), you can create your own audiobooks—kind of. iSpeak It turns any text file or Microsoft Word document into an MP3 or AAC audio file. Add the resulting file to your iTunes library, and listen.

iSpeak It uses the Mac's text-to-speech technology to create its files, so your homemade audiobooks will have a decidedly robotic quality to them.

iPresent It. Also from Michael Zapp, iPresent It converts presentations created in PowerPoint or Apple's Keynote into iPod slide shows. (It also works with any PDF file.) Create a presentation and run it through iPresent It. Then connect your iPod to a projection system and pontificate—no laptop required.

iPDA. Yet another Michael Zapp creation, iPDA can export calendar events, email, notes, and contacts from Microsoft Entourage X, iCal, and the Mac OS X Mail program. It can also download news headlines and weather forecasts.

PocketMac iPod. This inexpensive utility specializes in syncing contacts, email, and notes from Microsoft Office. Try it at www.pocketmac.net.

Text2iPod. This freeware utility by Beniot Terradillos will convert any text-only file into a note file that you can read on the iPod.

iPod as Calendar: Using iCal

With Apple's iCal software, you can keep track of appointments, schedules, and events of all kinds. You can create multiple calendars—for example, one for personal events such as birthdays and another for work appointments.

Use iCal to display multiple calendars at once to quickly identify schedule conflicts. You can also share calendars—with friends, coworkers, or complete strangers—by *publishing* them through your .Mac account.

You can even download and use calendars that other people have created. Hundreds of free calendars are available in categories ranging from TV schedules to holidays to the phases of the moon.

You can also use appointment information from iCal calendars when creating wall calendars in iPhoto. Check a box, and iPhoto adds iCal events to your calendar. For details, see page 216.

What does iCal have to do with the iPod? Simply this: You can copy your calendars to the iPod and view them on the road. On the iPhone and iPod touch, you can create and update calendar events. When you sync, iTunes copies changes back to iCal. You can also set up alarms in iCal and have your iPod notify you of important appointments.

Or TV shows.

Updating Calendars

To set up iTunes to update your Calendars, connect your iPod to your Mac, then select the iPod in the Device list and click the Contacts tab (for an iPhone or iPod touch, click Info). Calendar-syncing options lurk here.

Begin by checking this box.

To copy all of your calendars to the iPod, select this option.

To copy only certain calendars to your iPod, select this button and then check the calendars you want to copy.

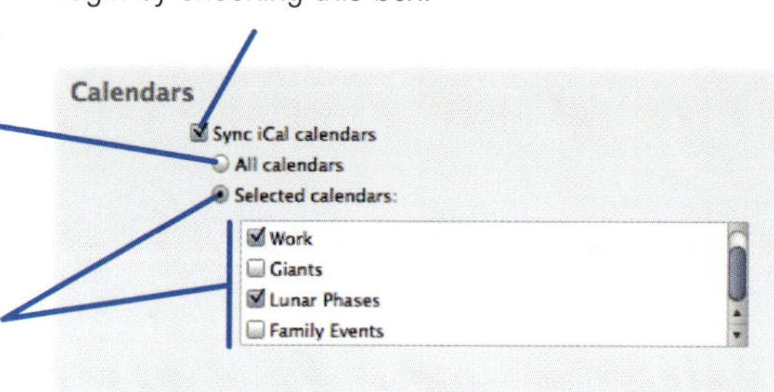

Syncing calendars from elsewhere. You may also have calendar files that originated somewhere other than in your copy of iCal—perhaps you downloaded a calendar from a Web site, or someone emailed it to you as an attachment, or you simply copied it from a different Mac. To add a calendar file to the iPod, activate the iPod's disk mode (page 108), then drag its icon into the Calendars folder.

The iPod can also store calendars in the industry-standard vCal format. Files in vCal format end with the extension .vcs.

Navigating Calendars and Events

Here's how to explore your calendars on a click wheel iPod. The process is similar on the iPhone and iPod touch, but involves your fingertip.

To display calendars, go to Extras > Calendar.

Each calendar appears as a separate menu item. To display a specific calendar, use the click wheel to highlight it, then press the iPod's Center button.

Days that have events associated with them are indicated with a small dot. To see a day's events, highlight the day, then press the iPod's Center button.

The iPod displays a summary of the event. To see event details, select the event and press the Center button again.

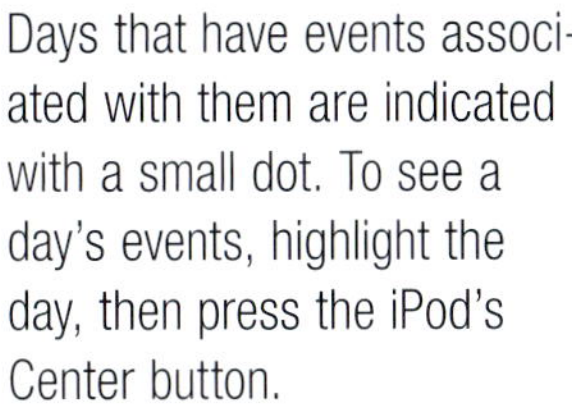

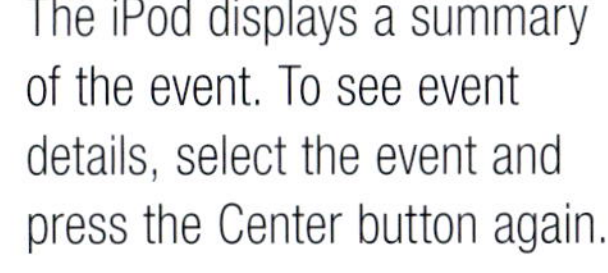

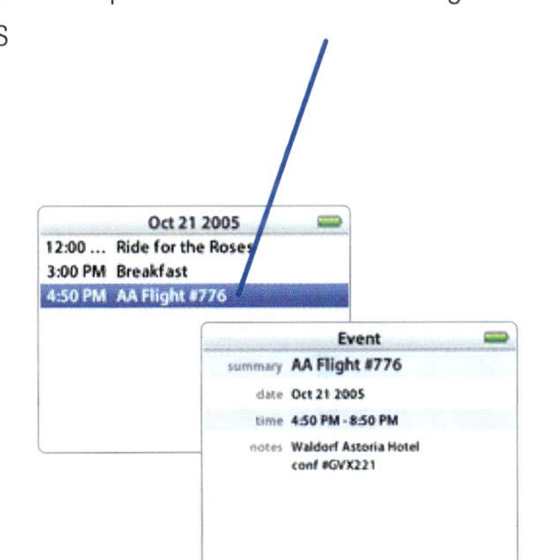

Calendar Tips

iCal Calling iTunes

Doug Adams' iCal Calling iTunes is a slick AppleScript that turns iCal and iTunes into a musical alarm clock: it enables iTunes to play a specific playlist at a time you specify.

iCal Calling iTunes is a cinch to use. Simply create an iCal event whose name is the same as one of your iTunes playlists. When the event time arrives, iTunes begins playing the playlist.

Silencing Alarms

If you've used iCal to specify that some events have alarms, your click wheel iPod will beep at the specified times. But there may be times when you don't want the iPod to beep.

To silence the iPod's alarms, go to Extras > Calendar > Alarms where you'll find three options: On (the iPod beeps and the alarm text appears on the iPod's screen); Silent (no beep but the alarm text still appears); and Off (no beep or alarm text).

Dates of All Kinds

You don't use iCal to manage your schedule? Don't let that stop you from sampling the world of calendars that other people have published on the Web. You can download hundreds of calendars in dozens of categories: sports schedules, TV schedules, lunar phases, celebrity personal appearances, holidays of all kinds, and more.

One place to find calendars is Apple's iCal Web site, but the ultimate collection of calendars lives at an independent site called iCalShare (www.icalshare.com). I downloaded the Moon Phases calendar, and now my iPod knows the phases of the moon through the year 2015.

So even if you don't use iCal to manage your appointments, you might find it a useful tool for keeping track of events that take place elsewhere in the solar system.

Accessories for the Fully Powered iPod

The iPod line has spawned an industry of accessories—speaker systems, cases, docks, TV and car interfaces, and more. Apple calls it the "iPod ecosystem," and it's a thriving one. You'll even find iPod interfaces in toilet paper dispensers and in a $14,000 dining-room table, though you won't find them in my house.

Here's a sampling of some accessories. For reviews of iPod add-ons, checkout Playlist magazine (www.playlistmag.com) and iLounge (www.ilounge.com). And because iPod models change now and then, be sure whatever accessory you're considering is compatible with your specific iPod or iPhone model.

TV Connections

The iPhone and all current iPods, except for the shuffle, can connect to a TV set: view movies and TV shows on the big screen, or display slide shows from photos that you've synced (page 104).

Apple sells a couple of cable accessories that let you connect your video-capable iPod to a TV and stereo system.

Apple Composite AV Cable. If you're going to buy just one cable to connect your iPod to a TV and stereo, make it this one. Compatible with all video-capable iPods as well as the iPhone, it connects to the composite video jack that virtually every TV provides. (Look for a yellow, female RCA jack.)

To use this cable, plug the flat connector into your iPod or iPhone, then connect the yellow plug to the yellow video-input jack of your TV (or VCR or other device). Connect the red and white plugs to the red and white audio-input jacks of your TV or stereo. The red cable is for the right channel, and the white cable is for the left channel. (To remember that, just remember that *red* and *right* both start with R. It works for me.)

Apple Component AV Cable. This is a more-specialized beast. Not all TV sets provide component video inputs, though most high-definition sets do. Component video provides a better picture than does composite—the red, green, and blue portions of the video signal travel on their own lines instead of being merged into a composite signal.

If your TV has red, green, and blue video-input jacks, use this cable. Connect each plug to its matching input jack, then connect the audio leads as described above.

Note that the Apple Component AV Cable does not work with the fifth-generation iPod (the original "video iPod") or the iPod photo.

Incidentally, both cables also include AC power adapters and USB jacks, so you can charge your iPod while you watch.

On the Dock

A dock makes it convenient to update your iPod and charge its battery. Some iPod (and especially iPhone) owners buy multiple docks—one for home, one for the office, for example.

Apple Universal Dock. This dock works with all click wheel iPods as well as the iPhone and iPod touch. It pairs up nicely with the cables described on this page: set the dock next to your TV and connect the flat end of your AV cable to the dock. When you're ready to view, slide the iPod or iPhone into the dock.

The Apple Universal Dock also includes a remote control, enabling you to start and stop playback and adjust the volume from across the room.

Apple iPod shuffle dock. This diminutive dock is for charging second-generation iPod shuffle models and connecting them to a stereo. It won't work with the original shuffle—the one shaped like a pack of gum.

Speak up, dock. Several companies, including Apple, sell self-contained amplifier and speaker systems containing iPod docks. Apple's offering is called iPod Hi-Fi. Similar products are available from Bose, Altec Lansing, Griffin Technology, and JBL, among others.

Get links to iPod accessories aplenty.
www.macilife.com/itunes

Tune In

An FM transmitter plugs into the iPod and then transmits its signal so that you can tune it in on a radio. Griffin's iTrip connects to the top of the iPod, while Sonnet's highly regarded Podfreq packs an FM transmitter into a rugged carrying case.

I use an FM transmitter from C. Crane (www.ccradio.com). It doesn't have a fancy dock connector—it simply plugs into the iPod's headphone jack. But on the plus side, it works with every iPod made. I also plug it into the headphone jack of one of my Macs, enabling me to listen to its audio throughout my house.

Want to *receive* radio instead of transmit it? Apple's iPod Radio Remote adds FM radio tuning to the fifth-generation iPod model as well as to first- and second-generation nanos (but not the newest, video-capable nanos). Use the click wheel to tune in stations, viewing a virtual dial on the iPod's screen.

Sound and Pictures

Recording. Most recent iPods accept microphone attachments that let you record voice memos, lectures, family fights—you name it.

Photo storage. In the field with your iPod and digital camera—and not enough camera memory cards? Many iPod models accept add-ons that let you transfer photos and store them on the iPod. Apple's iPod Camera Connector is one example; Belkin sells similar models. In general, though, these devices have proven to be less useful for photographers than "digital wallets" from Epson, Archos, and Nikon.

Play Longer

Griffin, Belkin, and others sell battery packs that let you power an iPod using standard batteries. And if you listen in the car using an FM transmitter or cassette adapter, consider a cigarette-lighter adapter that lets you charge on the road. Shown here: Griffin's PowerJolt.

The iPod and Your Car

Thousands of songs in your pocket? Outstanding. Thousands of songs in your car? Road trip! There are several ways to get from hear to there.

Cassette adaptor. These are inexpensive, easy to use, and reasonably good sounding. Plug the adaptor's cable into the iPod's headphone jack, then insert the adaptor into your car's cassette deck.

FM transmitters. Described on this page, they transmit the iPod's signal on the FM radio band. In a car, reception can be a problem, as can interference from strong stations.

Direct connections. The best way to listen to the iPod in your car is to use a cabling system that lets the iPod's audio output go directly into your car stereo. Many car manufacturers provide iPod-ready stereo systems that let you stash the iPod in the glove compartment and control it using the buttons on the car's steering wheel or dashboard.

Several companies sell cabling kits that let an iPod tap into the audio inputs that would otherwise be used for a trunk-mounted CD changer. Check out the Ice-Link Plus from Dension (www.dension.com), as well as the cabling offerings from peripheralelectronics.com, logjamelectronics.com, and soundgate.com.

And if you're shopping for a new car stereo system, you might consider one of the iPod-ready systems from Alpine and Pioneer, among others. I have Pioneer's amazing AVIC-Z1 in my car—it lets you control the iPod from a touch-screen display. For a detailed write-up, see the link named "iPod Your Car" on www.macilife.com/itunes.

iPhoto:
Organizing and
Sharing Images
The Macintosh
iLife'08

iPhoto at a Glance

Millions of photographs lead lives of loneliness, trapped in unorganized boxes where they're never seen. Their digital brethren often share the same fate, exiled to cluttered folders on a hard drive and rarely opened.

With iPhoto, you can free your photos—and organize, print, and share them, too. iPhoto simplifies the entire process. You begin by *importing* images from a digital camera, your hard drive, a CD from a photofinisher, or another source. Then you can create *albums*, organizing the images in whatever order you want. You can even have iPhoto create the albums for you.

Along the way, you might also use iPhoto's editing features to make your photos look better. And you might use iPhoto's organization and searching features to help you file and locate images.

When you've finished organizing and editing photos, share them. Order prints or make your own. Design gorgeous photo books, arranging photos on each page and adding captions. Design calendars and greeting cards. Create slide shows, complete with music from iTunes, and then watch them on the Mac's screen, burn them to DVDs, or transfer them to an iPod or Apple TV.

Prefer to share over the Internet? Email photos to friends and family. Have an Apple .Mac account? Create Web photo galleries with iPhoto (page 188), or Web albums with iWeb (page 394).

Welcome to the Photo Liberation Society.

Beyond the Shoebox

You can't enjoy photos if you can't find them. Use iPhoto's tools to organize and find your shots.

Organize
Name photos, add captions, and assign descriptive keywords.

Information pane (page 140)

Keywords window (page 142)

Find
Use the Search field to locate photos based on names, dates, keywords, and more.

Search for text (page 136)

Search by date (page 136)

Search for keywords (page 144)

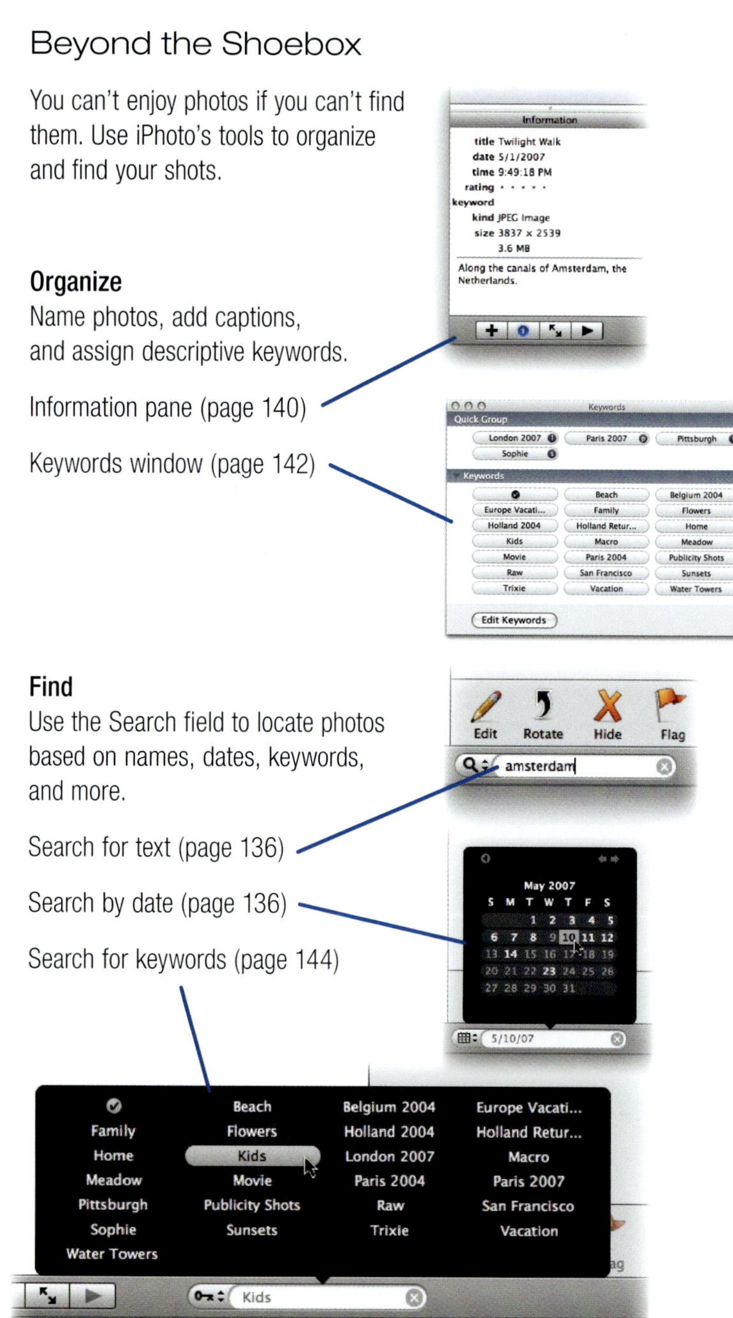

Your eventful life: iPhoto stores each set of photos you import as an *event*. You can create new events, combine events, and much more (page 138).

Skim and browse: To preview the photos in an event, skim the mouse pointer over the event (page 136). There isn't a faster way to browse.

To view photos from multiple events at once, click Photos (page 136).

To see the most recent photos you imported, click Last Import.

You can share photos with other Macs on your network (page 194).

Use albums to organize related photos—before creating a book or slide show, for example (pages 146–149).

iPhoto can create albums for you, based on criteria you specify (page 150).

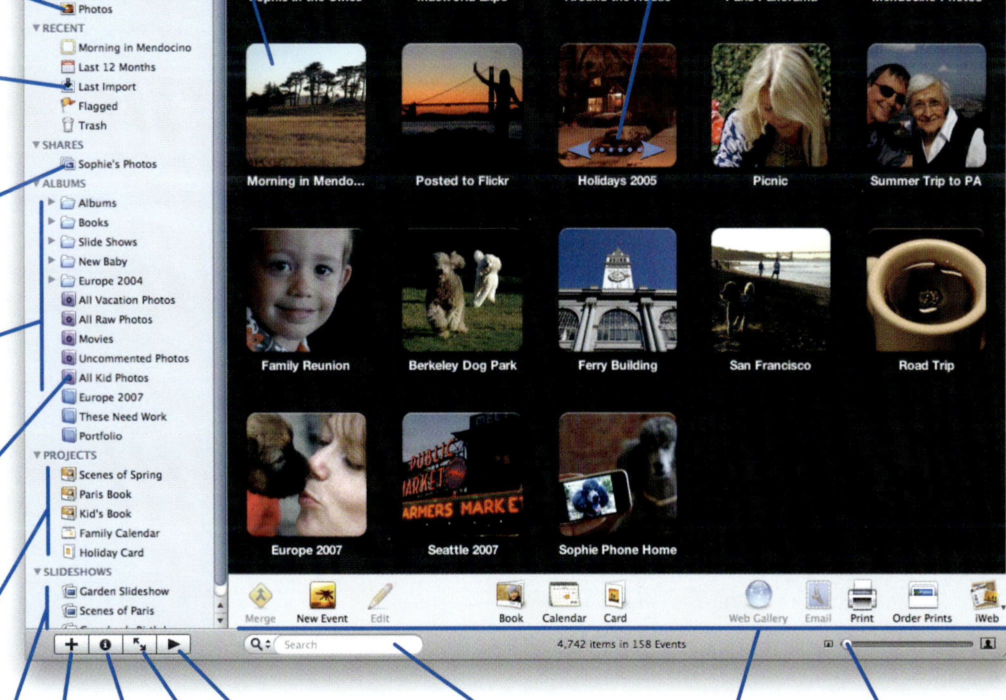

The Projects area holds books, greeting cards, and calendars (pages 204–219).

Create and display slide shows (pages 180–189).

Create a new album, Web gallery, or print project.

View and edit photo names and captions (opposite page).

Play a basic slide show (pages 130 and 178).

View a photo in full-screen view (page 130).

Search for photos (opposite page).

Use these buttons to manage events, create print projects, and share photos.

To change the size of photo thumbnails, drag the slider.

The Essentials of Digital Imaging

Like the digital audio world and other specialized fields, digital imaging has its own jargon and technical concepts to understand. You can accomplish a lot in iPhoto without having to know these things, but a solid foundation in imaging essentials will help you get more out of iPhoto, your digital camera, and other imaging hardware.

There are two key points to take away from this little lesson. First, although iPhoto works beautifully with digital cameras, it can also accept images that you've scanned or received from a photofinisher.

Second, the concept of resolution will arise again and again in your digital imaging endeavors. You'll want big, high-resolution images for good-quality prints, and small, low-resolution images for convenient emailing to friends and family. As described on page 187, you can use iPhoto to create low-resolution versions of your images.

Where Digital Images Come From

iPhoto can work with digital images from a variety of sources.

Digital camera

Digital cameras are more plentiful and capable than ever. One key factor that differentiates cameras is *resolution*: how many *pixels* of information they store in each image. Even inexpensive digital cameras now provide resolutions of between 6 and 10 megapixels—more than enough to make large prints.

Most digital cameras connect to the Mac's USB port. Images are usually stored on removable-media cards; you can also transfer images into iPhoto by connecting a *media reader* to the Mac and inserting the memory card into the reader (page 134).

Scanner

With a scanner, you can create digital images from photographs and other hard-copy originals.

Scanners also connect via USB, although some high-end models connect via FireWire. Film scanners are a bit pricier, but can scan negatives and slides and deliver great image quality (page 226). Save your scanned images in JPEG format, and then add them to iPhoto by dragging their icons into the iPhoto window (page 135).

For tips on getting high-quality scans, visit www.scantips.com.

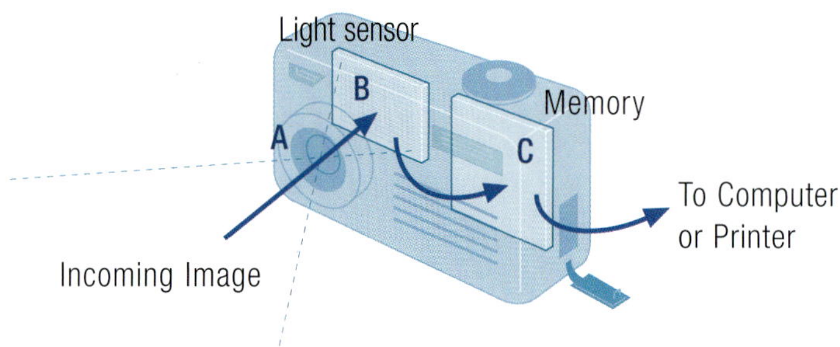

In a digital camera, the image is focused by the lens (**A**) onto a sensor (**B**), where tiny, light-sensitive diodes called photosites convert photons into electrons. Those electrical values are converted into digital data and stored by a memory card or other medium (**C**), from which they can be transferred to a computer or printer.

Compact Disc

So *you're* the person who's still shooting film? Good news: for an extra charge, most photofinishers will burn your images on a compact disc in Kodak Picture CD format. You get not only prints and negatives, but also a CD that you can use with the Mac.

To learn more about Picture CD, google the phrase *picture cd*.

Internet

Many photofinishers also provide extra-cost Internet delivery options. After processing and scanning your film, they send you an email containing a Web address where you can view and download images. After downloading images, you can drag their icons into iPhoto's window.

A Short Glossary of Imaging Terms

artifacts Visible flaws in an image, often as a result of excessive *compression* or when you try to create a large print from a low-resolution image.

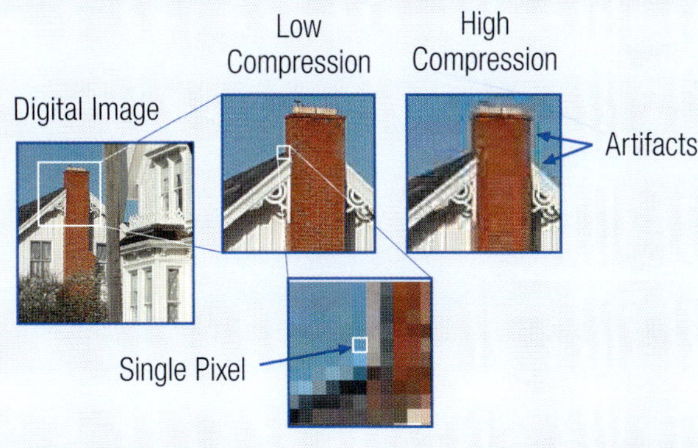

CompactFlash A removable-memory storage medium commonly used by digital cameras. A CompactFlash card measures 43 by 36 by 3.3 mm. The thicker *Type 2* cards are 5.5 mm wide.

compression The process of making image files use less storage space, usually by removing information that our eyes don't detect anyway. The most common form of image compression is *JPEG*.

EXIF Pronounced *ex-if*, a standard file format used by virtually all of today's digital cameras. EXIF files use JPEG compression but also contain details about each image: the date and time it was taken, its resolution, the type of camera used, the exposure settings, and more. iPhoto retrieves and stores EXIF information when you import images. EXIF stands for *Exchangeable Image File.*

JPEG Pronounced *jay-peg*, the most common format for storing digital camera images. Like MP3, JPEG is a *lossy* compression format: it shrinks files by discarding information that we can't perceive anyway. And as with MP3, there are varying degrees of JPEG compression; many imaging programs enable you to specify how heavily JPEG images are compressed. Note that a heavily compressed JPEG image can contain *artifacts.* JPEG stands for *Joint Photographic Experts Group.*

megapixel One million pixels.

pixel Short for *picture element*, the smallest building block of an image. The number of pixels that a camera or scanner captures determines the *resolution* of the image.

raw An image containing the data captured by the camera's light sensor, with no additional in-camera image processing applied (see page 172).

resolution **1.** The size of an image, expressed in pixels. For example, an image whose resolution is 640 by 480 contains 480 vertical rows of pixels, each containing 640 pixels from left to right. **2.** A measure of the capabilities of a digital camera or scanner.

SmartMedia A commonly used design for removable-memory storage cards.

Importing Photos from a Camera

The first step in assembling a digital photo library is to import photos into iPhoto. There are several ways to import photos, but the most common method is to connect your camera to your Mac and transfer the photos using a USB cable. iPhoto can directly import photos from the vast majority of digital cameras.

iPhoto gives you plenty of control over the importing process. You can import every shot in the camera, or you can be selective and import only some. iPhoto stores your photos in the iPhoto Library, located inside your Pictures folder (see page 135).

iPhoto can also import the movie clips that most cameras are capable of taking. If you shot some movie clips along with your photos, iPhoto imports them, too. (For more details on shooting movies with a digital camera, see page 282.)

You take photos of the events in your life: vacations, parties, fender benders on the freeway. When you import a set of photos, iPhoto stores them as an event. You can (and should) type a name and description of an event's photos before importing them. Think of it as the digital equivalent of writing notes on an envelope of prints.

You can manage events—split one event into many, merge multiple events into one, and more—using techniques described on page 138. But that can wait—let's get those shots into your Mac, shall we?

Step 1: Connect your camera to one of your Mac's USB ports (the port on the keyboard is particularly convenient) and turn the camera on. When iPhoto recognizes your camera, it displays the Import panel.

Tip: If your camera has a battery-saving sleep mode, adjust it so that the camera won't drift into slumber while your photos are still importing.

Step 2: Type a name that best describes this set of photos. You can also type a brief description if you like.

iPhoto will often display your camera's make and model here.

A thumbnail version of each photo in the camera appears here.

Step 3. Click Import All. (To import only some of the shots, see the opposite page.)

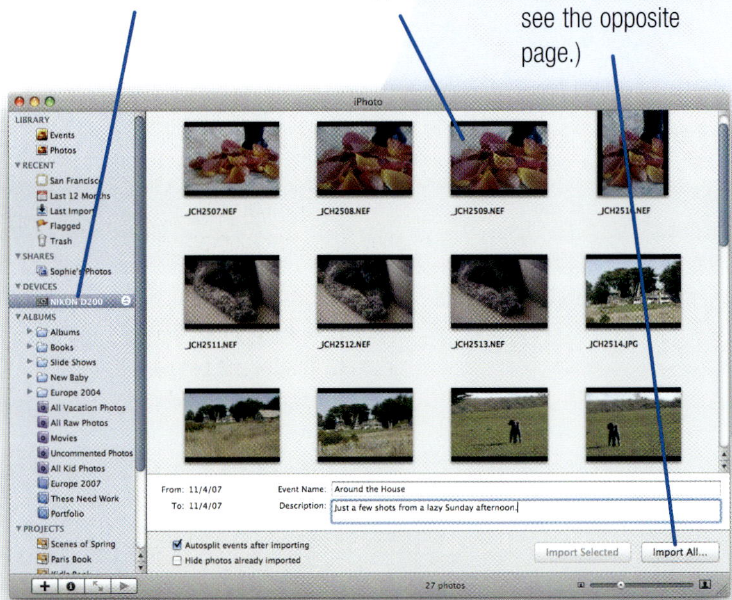

Tips for Importing Photos

Importing Only Some Shots

As you look over the thumbnails in the Import panel, you see some shots that you just know you aren't going to want. So why waste time importing them to begin with? You can be selective and import only those shots you want.

Step 1. To select the photos you want to import, press and hold the ⌘ key while clicking each photo. (For more ways to select photos, see page 147.)

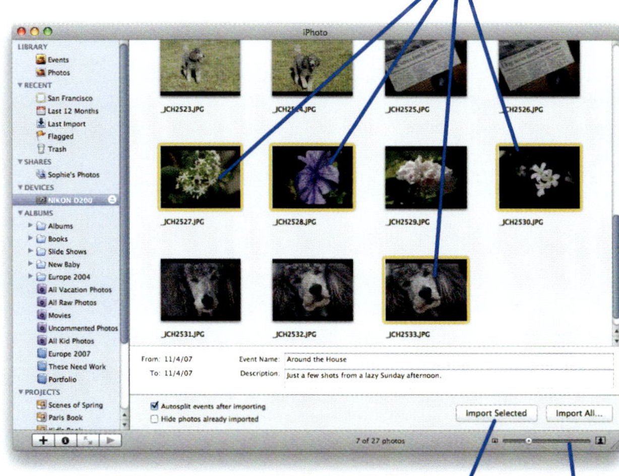

Step 2. To import the photos you've selected, click Import Selected.

Remember to use the slider to make thumbnails bigger or smaller, as needed. Making them bigger can help you decide between two similar shots, while making them smaller can simplify selecting a large number of thumbnails.

To Delete or Not?

When iPhoto finishes importing, it displays a message asking if you'd like to keep or delete the original photos from the camera.

I recommend clicking Keep Originals. It's best to erase your memory card using your camera's controls. Specifically, use your camera's "format" command, not its "delete all" function.

What's the difference? Formatting the card not only deletes photos, it creates a brand-new directory—that digital table of contents that's so critical to any storage device. When you simply "delete all," the camera wipes the shots, but doesn't create a fresh directory. This increases the odds that little glitches of fate could cause directory corruption that leads to lost photos.

So click Keep Originals, then use your camera's menu controls to reformat the card.

Eject the Camera

Some cameras display an icon on your Finder desktop. If your camera does, be sure to "eject" the icon before disconnecting the camera: click the Eject button next to the camera's name in the iPhoto Devices list. (If you don't see the Eject button, you don't have to perform this step.)

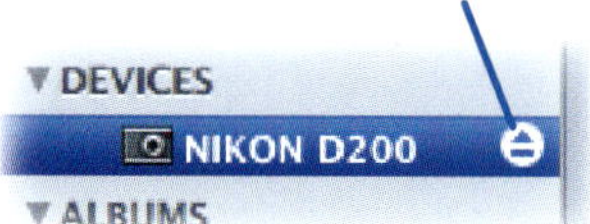

After the Import

What happens after iPhoto imports a set of photos? That's up to you. Admire your shots. Start filing and organizing them. Email a few favorites to a friend.

If you're like me, you'll want to check out your shots right away. A couple of clicks gives you a full-screen slide show, complete with music—perfect when you have a circle of eager friends and family watching over your shoulder. Or be selective: display thumbnails of your new photos, then take a close-up look at the best of the bunch.

Some housekeeping may await, too. Delete the shots you don't want. Rotate vertically oriented shots, if necessary. As you tidy up, you'll probably start getting ideas for sharing the photos. Email, prints, books, calendars, cards, Web galleries, DVDs, YouTube: if you like to share images, this is a great time to be alive.

And along the way, you'll want to celebrate your inner librarian. Organize your photo library with events, titles, captions, keywords, and albums. Trust me: you'll accumulate thousands of photos in no time. A few simple steps will make them easier to find.

But filing can wait. We have some fresh photos to explore.

Viewing Your Shots

Start by clicking the Last Import item in the Library area. This is the fastest way to access the most recent set of shots.

Selective viewing. Adjust the size of the photo thumbnails to your liking: jump down to the lower-right corner and use the size slider.

To magnify a photo so that it fills the iPhoto window, double-click its thumbnail, or select the photo and press the spacebar. **Tip:** Maximize your viewing area: choose Window > Zoom or click the green zoom button in the upper-left corner.

To return to thumbnails, click the mouse or press the Esc key.

Full-screen variation. To fill the entire screen with a photo, click . To return to the thumbnails, double-click the mouse or press Esc. (For more about full-screen view, see page 168.)

Tip: To move to the next or previous photo in either magnified view, press your keyboard's right- or left-arrow key.

Instant slide show. To screen your photos with more style, display a slide show. Hold down the Option key on your keyboard and click . To stop the slide show, click the mouse or press Esc.

(Pressing the Option key bypasses a step: choosing a soundtrack song. When you want to take time for that extra step, don't press Option. See page 179 for soundtrack details, and pages 178–183 to learn all about slide shows.)

Notes and Tips

Rotate Verticals

Some cameras automatically rotate photos taken in vertical orientation. If yours doesn't, the job is yours. Select the photo or photos and then click the Rotate button or press ⌘-R (to rotate counterclockwise). To rotate clockwise, Option-click the Rotate button or press ⌘-Option-R. You can also rotate photos while viewing a slide show; see page 179.

Tip: If you find yourself doing a lot of clockwise rotation, you can tweak iPhoto preferences to eliminate having to press Option while clicking Rotate. Choose iPhoto > Preferences, click the General button, then click the leftmost Rotate option:

Rotate:  

Now you can rotate clockwise by simply clicking the Rotate button.

Delete the Dregs

See a photo that you know you don't want to keep? Trash it. To delete a photo, select it (click it once), then press the Delete key. You can also delete a photo by dragging it to the Trash on the left side of the iPhoto window.

When you put a photo in the Trash, iPhoto doesn't actually erase the photo from your hard drive; that doesn't happen until you choose Empty Trash from the iPhoto menu. If you change your mind about deleting a photo, click the Trash item in the library list, select the photo you want to keep, and choose Photos > Restore to Photo Library (keyboard shortcut: ⌘-Delete.)

Playing Movies

If your last import included a movie clip, you can play it by double-clicking its thumbnail. iPhoto starts the QuickTime Player program, which loads the movie. To play the movie, press the spacebar or click the Play button.

Customizing iPhoto's Appearance

As the tip above described, the Preferences dialog box is the key to customizing how iPhoto's Rotate button works.

The Preferences dialog box is also the gateway to many other iPhoto settings, which we'll explore as we go along. But you might want to begin by exploring the options in the Appearance pane—they let you tweak how iPhoto looks.

Choose iPhoto > Preferences, then click Appearance.

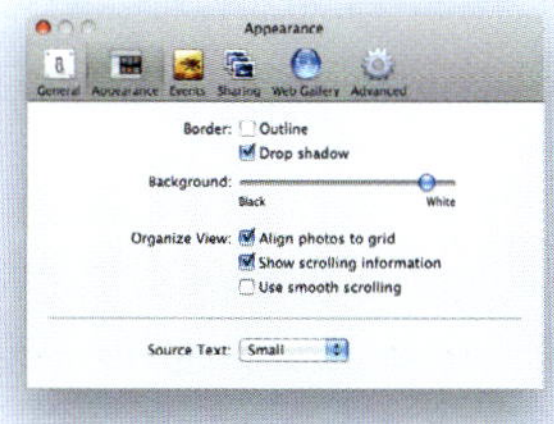

Want to see your thumbnail photos against a dark gray background? Drag the Background slider to the left.

With the Border options, you can turn off the shadow effect that iPhoto puts behind each photo, and display a thin border around each photo.

If you'd prefer larger text in the Library area of the iPhoto window, choose Large from the Source Text pop-up menu.

Event customizing. With the Events pane of the Preferences dialog box, you can fine-tune how iPhoto displays events. For more details, see page 138.

Window customizing. You can adjust the width of the Library area of the iPhoto window. Position the mouse pointer over the vertical line that separates the Library area from the rest of the window. It changes into a double-headed arrow: ✛. Drag left and right to adjust the width. A thinner Library area gives you more room for photo thumbnails, as well as a larger canvas for magnified views.

More Ways to Import Photos

Most people import photos directly from a camera using the technique I described on the previous pages. But you have more than one way to get photos into iPhoto.

A media reader is a great way to import photos from a camera's memory card. Plug the reader into your Mac, then insert the memory card into the reader. Because you aren't using your camera to transfer photos, its battery charge will last longer.

Be sure to get a reader that supports the type of memory cards your camera uses. Or get a multi-format reader that supports several types of memory cards. And look for a reader that connects to the Mac's FireWire jack or to its USB 2.0 jack. FireWire and USB 2.0 readers transfer images much faster than the older, USB 1.0 interface.

You can also import images by dragging their icons into the iPhoto window. If you've scanned a batch of images, you can use this technique to bring them into iPhoto. You can also use this technique to save photos that people email to you or that you find on Web sites.

Using a Media Reader

Here's the photo-importing technique I use most often.

Step 1. Connect the media reader to your Mac.

Step 2. Be sure your camera's power is off, then remove the memory card from the camera and insert it into the reader. iPhoto recognizes the card and displays the Import panel shown on page 130.

Step 3. Type a name and description for the photos you're about to import, then import all or some of the photos, as described on the previous pages.

Step 4. After iPhoto has imported the photos, click the Eject button next to the memory card's name in the Devices list. Finally, remove the memory card from the reader, return the card to your camera, and then erase the card.

Laptop Media Readers. You can buy a media reader that plugs into the PC Card slot of a PowerBook. If you're traveling with a PowerBook, a PC Card-based reader is a compact alternative to a FireWire or USB reader.

Media readers are also available for the ExpressCard/34 slot provided by the MacBook Pro laptops, too. Unfortunately, the ExpressCard/34 slot is too small to accommodate a Compact Flash card, requiring you to use an awkward adaptor. If you use Compact Flash cards and own a MacBook Pro, you're probably better off with an external FireWire or USB 2.0 reader. Look at it this way: at least your external modem will have company in your briefcase.

Importing from the Finder

To import an entire folder full of images, drag the folder to the Photos item or into the photo area.

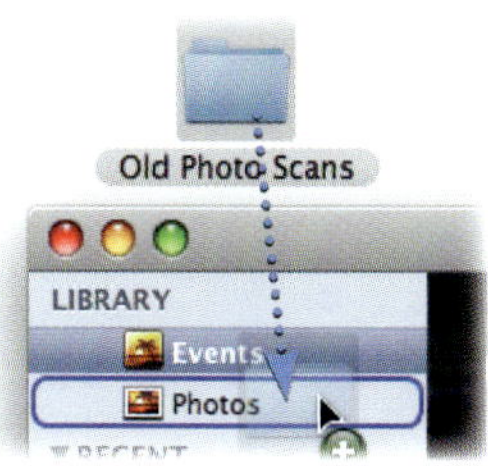

iPhoto gives the new event the same name as the folder from which its images came. You can rename the event using the techniques described on page 138.

To import only some images, select their icons and then drag them to the Photos item or into the iPhoto window.

Note: When you import images that are already stored on your hard drive, iPhoto makes duplicate copies of them in your iPhoto library. You can change this using the Preferences command; see the following pages.

Importing from Email and Web Pages

A friend has emailed some photos to you, and you want to add them to your iPhoto library. If you're using Mail, the email program included with Mac OS X, simply drag the photos from the email message into the iPhoto window. If the email message contains several photos, Shift-click on each one to select them all before dragging.

If you use Microsoft Entourage, your job is a bit more difficult. First, save the photos on your Mac's desktop. Next, drag them into the iPhoto window as shown at left. Finally, delete the photos from your desktop.

To save a photo that's on a Web page, just drag the photo from your Web browser into the iPhoto window. In Apple's Safari browser, you can also Control-click on a photo and choose Add Image to iPhoto Library from the shortcut menu.

Importing from Picture CDs and PhotoCDs

iPhoto can also import images saved on a Kodak PhotoCD or Picture CD. (PhotoCD is an older format that you aren't likely to see too often. Picture CD is a newer format that most photo finishers use.)

Picture CD. Choose Import to Library from iPhoto's File menu, locate the Picture CD, and then locate and double-click the folder named Pictures. Finally, click the Import button. Or, use the Finder to open the Pictures folder on the CD and then drag images into iPhoto's window.

PhotoCD. Simply insert the PhotoCD in your Mac's optical drive. iPhoto launches and displays its Import panel. Type a name and description for the photos, then import some or all of the photos, as described on the previous pages.

Where iPhoto Stores Your Photos

When you import photos, iPhoto stores them in the iPhoto Library, located inside the Pictures folder. (If you like, you can store your iPhoto Library elsewhere, such as on an external hard drive. For details, see page 225.)

Get in the habit of frequently backing up your iPhoto Library to avoid losing your images to a hardware or software problem.

You can use iPhoto's disc-burning features to back up photos (page 222), or you can copy your iPhoto Library to a different hard drive—or even to your iPod. For advice on backing up your photos, see page 225.

For more details on the iPhoto Library, see page 228.

Importing Tips

iPhoto gives you plenty of control over the importing process. Do you want iPhoto to automatically split up the photos into numerous events? If so, what time interval do you want to use?

If you're adding photos by dragging them from folders on your hard drive, where do you want iPhoto to store the photos?

If questions like these burn in your brain, your fire extinguisher has just arrived. Otherwise, feel free to skip on. You can always return here when the embers begin to glow.

Hiding Already-Imported Shots

You wisely took my page 129 advice and told iPhoto to not delete photos from your camera after an import (see page 129). But you forgot to erase the card before shooting another two-dozen shots.

No problem. When you connect your camera and switch to iPhoto's Import panel, check the box labeled Hide Photos Already Imported. Photos you've already imported will disappear from the Import panel, making it easy to import some or all of the new shots.

Dealing with Duplicates

Even if you forget to check the aforementioned box, iPhoto has you covered. If you try to import a photo that already exists in your library, iPhoto asks if you really want to import the duplicate.

To cancel the import session, click Cancel.

To have iPhoto apply your choice to all duplicates it finds during this import session, click Apply to all duplicates.

To not import the duplicate, click Don't Import.

To import the duplicate displayed, click Import.

Adjusting Event Settings

As I mentioned on page 128, iPhoto stores imported shots as events. When you import photos from a camera, iPhoto automatically splits them into events (unless you uncheck the Autosplit Events After Importing box in the Import pane).

Normally, iPhoto considers one day's worth of photos to represent an event. For example, if you import some shots taken over a weekend, you'll have two events: Saturday's photos and Sunday's.

Using the Preferences command, you can change the interval of time iPhoto uses when splitting photos into events. Choose iPhoto > Preferences, then click Events. You have three additional choices.

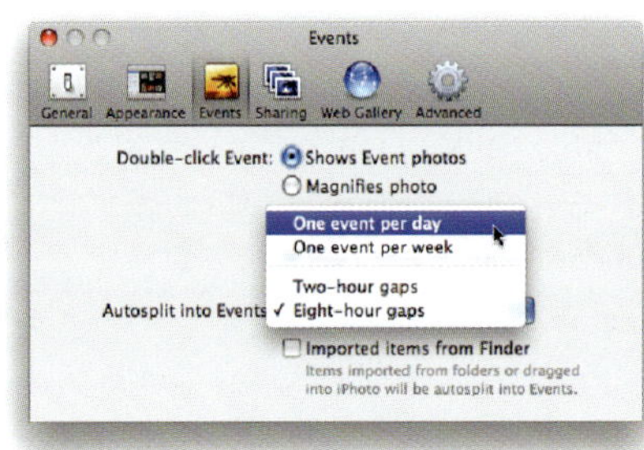

One event per day. iPhoto creates a new event for each 24-hour period. Take a week's vacation, import all your shots, and you'll have seven events.

This is an ideal option for vacations and similar getaways.

Two-hour gaps. iPhoto creates a new event every two hours. Say you do a day's worth of shooting: a sunrise hike at 6:00 a.m., a brunch with friends at 10:00 a.m., and a party at night. Import the shots, and iPhoto will create three events.

When you shoot a lot of shots throughout a day, this option can help corral them into manageable (and related) chunks. Surviving the busy day is your problem.

Eight-hour gaps. iPhoto creates a new event every eight hours. In the busy-day example above, you'd end up with two events: the first containing the hike and brunch photos, and the second containing the party pix.

Before you import a set of photos, think about what kind of time intervals the photos represent, then consider tweaking the interval preference to match.

Or don't bother. You're never locked into the way iPhoto divvies up your life. You can move photos between events in whatever way you like, and you can have iPhoto autosplit events for you *after* you've imported photos. Pages 138–139 have all the details.

Events and Imports from the Finder

When you import photos from the Finder—by dragging their icons into iPhoto, as described on the previous page—iPhoto does not split the photos into events. That makes sense when you think about it: if you're importing a dozen scanned images of photos that are decades old, how would iPhoto know how to divvy them up?

But in some circumstances, you might want iPhoto to automatically split photos imported from the Finder. For example, maybe you're about to import a CD's worth of digital photos that a friend burned for you.

For times like these, return to the Events portion of the Preferences dialog box, and check the box labeled Imported Items From Finder.

File it Your Way

Since the dawn of time—well, since the dawn of version 1.0—iPhoto has always stored images in the iPhoto Library. Generally, that's exactly what you want: when you copy photos from a camera or memory card, you want them stashed safely in your iPhoto Library.

But under some circumstances, iPhoto's "do things my way" approach to organization can work against you. When you add photos that are already stored on your hard drive—for example, images that you've scanned and saved—iPhoto makes additional copies in the iPhoto Library.

After adding photos to your Library that are already on your hard drive, you need to delete the originals. That isn't exactly a sweat-breaking chore, but it does take time. And you might prefer to stick with your existing filing system.

You have the option to not copy image files to the iPhoto Library. If you have a large library of meticulously filed scanned images on your hard drive, you might want to take advantage of this option. You won't have duplicate photos to delete, and you won't have to change the filing system you've developed for your scanned images.

To activate this option, choose iPhoto > Preferences, click the Advanced button, and then uncheck the box labeled Copy Items to the iPhoto Library.

From now on, when you add items from your hard drive to your iPhoto library, iPhoto simply creates aliases for each item. (In Mac OS parlance, an alias is a small file that simply points to an existing file.) If you edit an image, iPhoto stores the edited version in your iPhoto Library.

And by the way, unchecking this option does not change how iPhoto stores photos that you're importing from a camera or media reader. Photos that you import from a location other than a hard drive are always stored in your iPhoto Library.

Browsing Your Photo Library

Unlike any shoebox, iPhoto gives you several ways to browse and explore your photo library. Use Events view to get an at-a-glance look at your library. Forget which photos are in an event? Move your mouse pointer across the event thumbnail, and its photos flash before your eyes.

Events view is the most convenient way to work with your photo library, and chances are it's the view you'll use most of the time. But there's another way to see your shots. Click the Photos item in the Library list, and iPhoto displays your events in a different format—one that you may find useful for some browsing and photo-management tasks.

(If you're an iPhoto veteran, you'll recognize the Photos view—it's similar to the "film rolls" view provided by earlier versions of iPhoto.)

In both views, iPhoto provides little conveniences that help you home in on the photos you seek. For example, as you scroll the iPhoto window, semi-transparent *scroll guides* appear that show the date and title of each event.

Knowing the basics of photo browsing is important—the faster you can get around in your photo library, the greater the chances that you'll explore and enjoy your photos.

Here's an overview of the ways iPhoto lets you browse.

Basic Event Techniques

Here are the basic techniques you'll use when working with events.

Skimming thumbnails. Pass your mouse pointer over the event without clicking. **Tip:** You can also skim by combining the mouse and keyboard: point to an event, then press the left- or right-arrow keys. I like to use this technique when an event has a lot of photos in it, or when I've used the size slider to make the event thumbnails small.

Changing an event's name. Click the event's name, then type a new name and press Return.

Accessing an event's photos. Double-click the event thumbnail. Or select the event (click it once) and press the Return key. To return to Events view, click the All Events button (All Events) above the thumbnails, or press the Esc key.

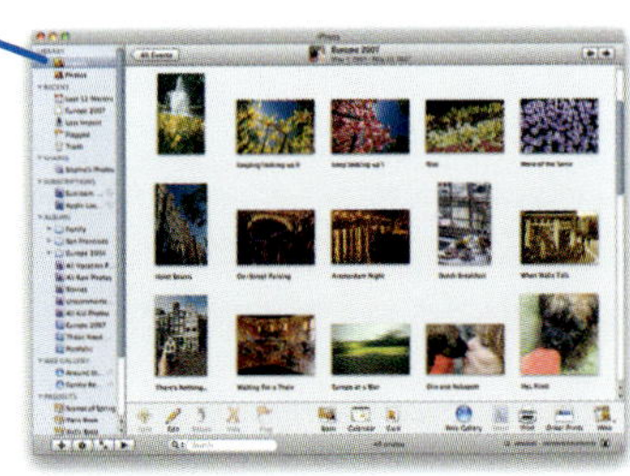

Tips: Want to browse using just the keyboard? First, be sure the mouse pointer isn't over an event. Then, use the arrow keys to select an event. Press Return to see its thumbnails. Press Esc to return to Events view, then arrow-key your way to a different event and repeat.

When you're viewing an event's photos, you can jump to the previous or next event by clicking the arrows in the upper-right corner of the iPhoto window.

Setting the key photo. Each event is represented by one photo, called the key photo or the poster photo. You can change the key photo to one that best represents the event. Skim across the event, and when you see the photo that you want to be the new key photo, press the spacebar. You can also Control-click on the photo and choose Make Key Photo from the shortcut menu. (This latter technique also works in Photos view.)

More Ways to Display Events

Detail view. Sometimes, you need to view the photos of more than one event at once. Maybe you're organizing some recent imports and you want to work on multiple events at the same time—to move some photos from one event to another, for example.

To open more than one event, select each event (click it once), then double-click one of the selected events or press Return. iPhoto opens each selected event.

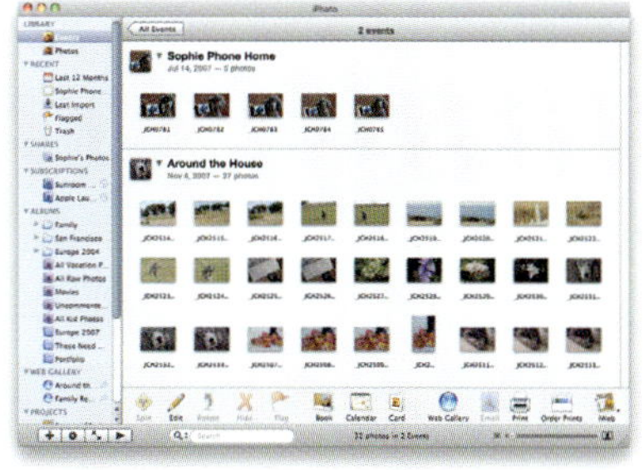

To return to Events view, click All Events or press Esc.

Separate event window. You can also open an event in its own window: select the event, then choose Events > Open Event in Separate Window. A new window opens containing the event's photos.

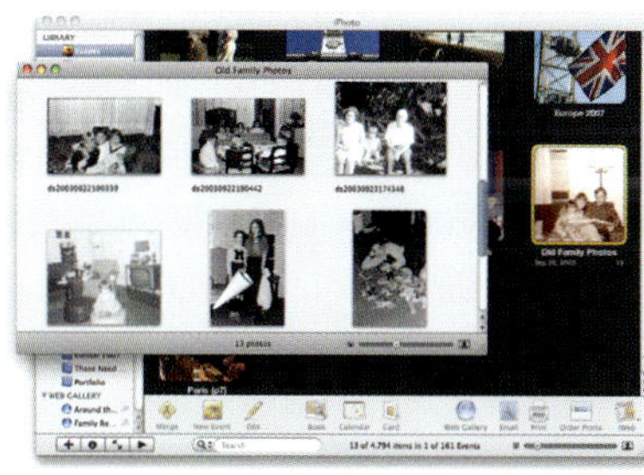

The separate window is a great way to focus in on the shots in one event while retaining quick access to the rest of your library. The window provides its own size slider for adjusting the size of photo thumbnails. You can even zoom the separate window to fill your screen or a second display, if your Mac has one: choose Window > Zoom.

The following pages describe more uses for the separate event window.

Note: The separate event window debuted in iPhoto 7.1. If you don't see its command in the Events menu, use the Software Update system preference to update to the latest iPhoto version.

Another Way to Look: Photos View

The Events view is so efficient and versatile that you'll probably spend most of your time there. But there's another option: Photos view. To use it, click the Photos item in the Library area.

The Photos view can be handy for moving photos between events and for combining and splitting events, though as the following pages describe, you can do all of these tasks in Events view, too.

To open an event, click its triangle. **Tip:** To expand every event in your library, press the Option key while clicking any closed event's triangle. Conversely, to close every event, press Option while clicking any open event's triangle.

To rename an event in this view, click the title, then type the new name.

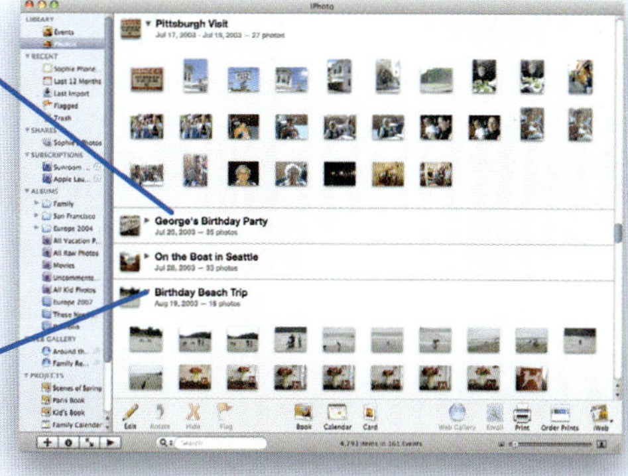

Tips for Working with Events

Anxious to start having fun with your photos? Go ahead and skip to page 146, where you can learn about creating photo albums and much more.

Eventually, you'll want to learn about the power tools that iPhoto provides for managing photos and events. These maneuvers can help you organize your iPhoto Library and make it easier to corral photos prior to sharing them.

Hiding Photos

A lot of photos fall into that middle ground between bad and beautiful: not awful enough to trash, not good enough to look at all the time. iPhoto lets you hide those mediocre shots to tidy up an event, but bring them back whenever you like.

Hiding photos is also a good strategy when you've taken several nearly identical shots—some portraits, each with a different smile. Pick the best, hide the rest.

To hide a photo, select it and click the Hide button (or press ⌘-L). The photo vanishes, and adjacent photos snuggle in to fill the void.

Bringing them back. When you're viewing an event, iPhoto lets you know if any of its photos are hidden.

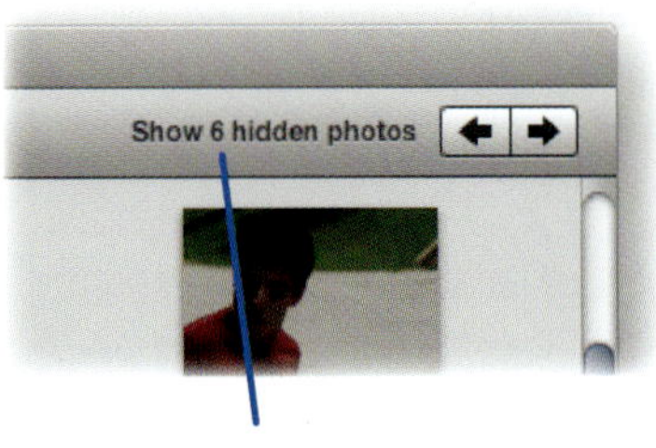

To see hidden photos, click the message. A photo marked as hidden has an X on its corner.

To hide the photos again, click the message again. To unhide a photo, select it and click Unhide or press ⌘-L.

Splitting and Merging

You can split one event into two. Say you have an event containing a hundred shots from an afternoon bike ride and an evening dinner. You may prefer to split the event into two separate, more manageable ones.

To split an event, open it to display its thumbnails. Then, select the photos you want to split off (the dinner shots, for example), and click the Split button. Finally, name the new event.

Merging events. You can also combine two or more events into one. Maybe you fired off some shots at a party, imported them so everyone could see, then took some more. You want all the party shots to be in one event. Easy: drag one event to the other.

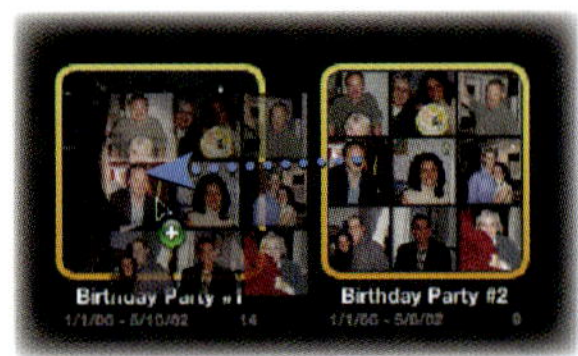

You can also merge more than two events: Shift-click or ⌘-click on each event, then drag them to another event. Or select all the events, then click the Merge button.

Moving Photos Between Events

Sometimes, your life as an event planner requires you to move individual photos between events. Maybe you want to fine-tune the way iPhoto autosplit an event. Or maybe a travel companion emailed you some shots that she took, and you want to add a few of them to your vacation event.

There are moving plans aplenty.

Dragging. Open the events in detail view: select them and double-click one of them (page 137). Now drag thumbnails from one event to another. To give yourself more dragging room, zoom the iPhoto window (Window > Zoom) and make the thumbnails smaller (drag the size slider).

The separate event window, described on page 137, can be handy when dragging photos between events, especially if the events aren't near each other in your library.

Cut and paste. Select the photos you want to move, and choose Edit > Cut. Select the event where you want them, then choose Edit > Paste. When dragging seems like too much work—too many photos, too many events—this is an efficient alternative.

Flagging. This can be the most powerful way to move photos, and it's described at right.

A New Event

You can create a new, empty event and then add photos to it. Be sure no events are selected, then choose Events > Create Event.

(You can also use Create Event to merge events or split photos off into their own event: Select the events or individual photos, then choose Create Event.)

Flagging Photos

Flagging is like attaching a sticky note to a photo. Trying to decide which shots to add to a book? Flag the best candidates, and you can return to them in a flash.

To flag a photo, select it and click the Flag button or press ⌘-period. A flag badge appears on the photo's thumbnail.

You can flag multiple photos at once–select them first, then click Flag–and you can flag as many shots as you like. To quickly see the shots you've flagged, click the flagged item in the Recent area of the Library list.

You've flagged some shots. Then what?

Move them to an existing event. After flagging the shots, return to Events view. Select the event where you want to move the photos, then choose Events > Add Flagged Photos to Selected Event. If you need to move some shots that are scattered throughout your library, this is the best way to do it.

Move them to a new event. To move flagged photos into a new event of their own, choose Events > Create Event From Flagged Photos. Keep in mind, though, that iPhoto will move those photos from their original events.

Work with them. Select the Flagged item in the Library area. The flagged shots lurk there, ready to be edited, shared—whatever you like.

Lower the flags. Done working with some flagged photos? Here's the easiest way to unflag them all: click the little number next to the Flagged item in the Library area.

What's in a Double-Click?

Normally, when you double-click an event thumbnail, you see the event's photos. With this trick, you can double-click to magnify whichever photo is visible under the mouse pointer. Skim across an event, see a photo you want to magnify, and double click.

Choose Preferences > iPhoto, click Events, then choose the Magnifies Photo option.

You can also tweak iPhoto so that a double click opens a photo in edit view (page 152)—the way earlier iPhoto versions worked. Choose iPhoto > Preferences, click General, and choose the Edits Photo option.

Creating Titles and Captions

iPhoto forces some organization on you by storing each set of imported images as a separate event. Even if you never use iPhoto's other organizational features, you're still ahead of the old shoebox photo-filing system: you will always be able to view your photos in chronological order.

But don't stop there. Take the time to assign *titles* and *descriptions* to your favorite shots. By performing these and other housekeeping tasks, you can make photos easier to find and keep your library well organized.

Titles are names or brief descriptions that you assign to photos and events: Party Photos, Mary at the Beach, and so on. iPhoto can use these titles as captions for its Web photo albums and books. Using the View menu, you can have iPhoto display titles below each thumbnail image. You can also search for photos by typing title or description text in the Search box (page 142a).

There's one more benefit to assigning titles to photos: when you're working in other iLife programs, you can search for a photo by typing part of its title in the photo media browser's Search box.

Of course, you don't have to type titles and descriptions for every photo in your library. But for the ones you plan to share in some way—or that you'll want to search for later—it's time well spent.

Using the Information Pane

When you want to give photos titles and descriptions, turn to the Information pane. To display the Information pane, click the button.

Step 1. Select the photo to which you want to assign a title and/or description.

Step 2. Click in the Title or Description area of the Information pane, then type the title or description.

Keep your titles fairly short.

Think of a description as the text you'd normally write on the back of a photo.

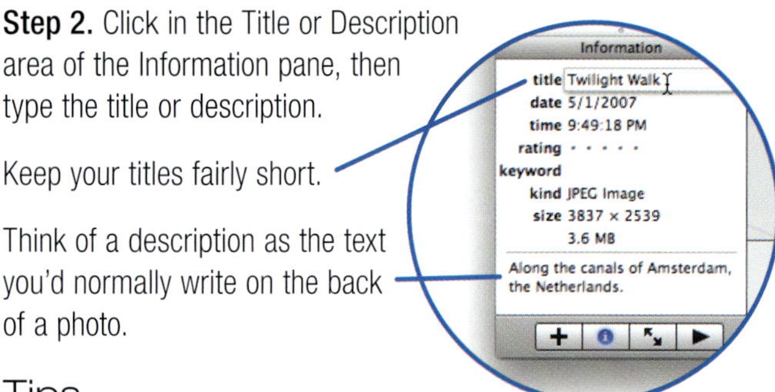

Tips

On a roll. Want to quickly title (or describe) one photo after another? Press ⌘-] after typing a title or description, and iPhoto selects the next photo and highlights its title or description field so you can immediately begin typing. To move to the previous photo, press ⌘-[. And to keep your hands on the keyboard, press Tab and Shift-Tab to jump from one field to the next in the Information pane.

Check your spelling. Want to check the spelling of your titles and descriptions? Select the text you want to proofread, then choose Edit > Spelling > Check Spelling. Or select the text you want to proofread and press ⌘-;.

Many at once. To change information for many photos at once, select them and choose Photos > Batch Change (see the opposite page). If you're like me and are often too lazy to assign titles and descriptions to individual photos, this can be a good compromise: assign a phrase to a set of related photos, and you can search for that phrase later.

Editing Photo Information Directly

The Information pane is a great place to view and change all kinds of details: a photo's title, its description, the date and time it was taken, and more.

But there's another way to edit photo information, and it's often more convenient than opening the Information pane. Simply click the title beneath a photo's thumbnail, and start typing:

(If you don't see titles beneath your photo thumbnails, choose View > Titles.)

The keyboard-shortcut tips described at lower left work here, too: type a title, and press ⌘-] to jump directly to the title field of the next photo. Or move the next and previous photo by pressing Tab and Shift-Tab.

As the following pages describe, you can also assign keywords and ratings by working directly beneath photo thumbnails. You can't, however, type a description or change a photo's date or time. For those tasks, turn to the Information pane.

Changing the Date

Time is important. The date stored along with a photo determines how iPhoto sorts the photo. Accurate dates also simplify searching and organizing your library.

All digital cameras store date and time information along with the image (see the sidebar on page 145). But what if your camera's clock is off? Maybe you forgot to adjust its time zone when you flew to Hawaii.

Or maybe you've scanned some old family photos and you want their dates to reflect when they were *taken*, not scanned. That Aunt Mary photo is from 1960, not 2008.

Time travel is easy in iPhoto. You can edit the date of an event, a selection of images, or just one photo. The steps differ depending on what you want to change.

An event. Select the event, choose Photos > Adjust Date & Time.

More than one photo. Select the photos, and choose Photos > Batch Change.

Just one photo. Select the photo, open the Information panel, and type new dates and times.

Tip: Of all these techniques, only one has a keyboard shortcut: Batch Change (⌘-Shift-B). If you're a keyboard jockey, you might find it's actually the *fastest* way to change the date of just one photo—a batch of one.

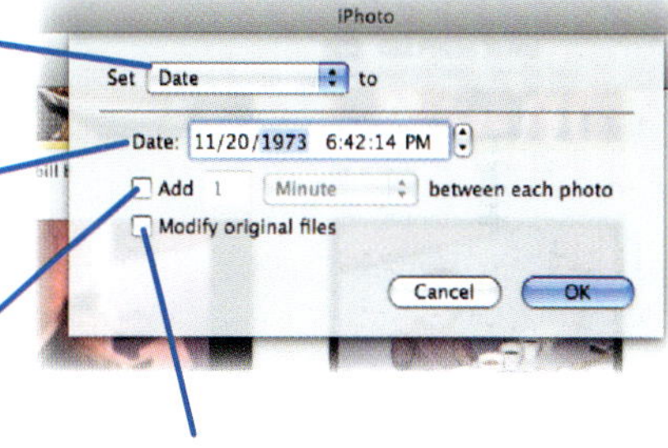

Choose Date from the pop-up menu.

Type the date and time, pressing Tab to move from one value to the next.

To aid sorting, you can have iPhoto add a time increment between each photo.

If you check this box, iPhoto records the modified date in the image file itself. (Otherwise, iPhoto simply notes the changed time in its internal database, leaving the original image unchanged.) You might choose this option if you plan to export the image for use in another image-management program, such as Apple's Aperture or Adobe Bridge or Lightroom.

Assigning Keywords and Ratings

Chances are that many of your photos fall into specific categories: baby photos, scenic shots, and so on. By creating and assigning *keywords*, you make related images easier to find.

Keywords are labels useful for categorizing and locating all the photos of a given kind: vacation shots, baby pictures, mug shots, you name it.

iPhoto has several predefined keywords that cover common categories. But you can replace the existing ones to cover the kinds of photos you take, and you can add as many new keywords as you like.

You can assign multiple keywords to a single image. For example, if you have a Beach keyword, a Dog keyword, and a Summer keyword, you assign all three to a photo of your dog taken at the beach in July.

Keywords are one way to categorize your photos; ratings are another. You can assign a rating of from one to five stars to a photo—rank your favorites for quick searching, or mark the stinkers for future deletion.

As with many iPhoto housekeeping tasks, assigning keywords and ratings is entirely optional. But if you take the time, you can use iPhoto's search and Smart Albums features to quickly locate and collect photos that meet specific criteria.

Creating and Editing Keywords

Step 1. Choose Window > Show Keywords (⌘-K).

Step 2. Click the Edit Keywords button.

Step 3. Edit keywords as shown below, then click OK.

Use the checkmark keyword (or not) however you like—to mark some photos for future use, for example.

Editing a keyword. Select the keyword, click Rename, then type the new name. Or simply double-click directly on the keyword.

Creating a new keyword. Click the plus sign, then type the keyword and press Return.

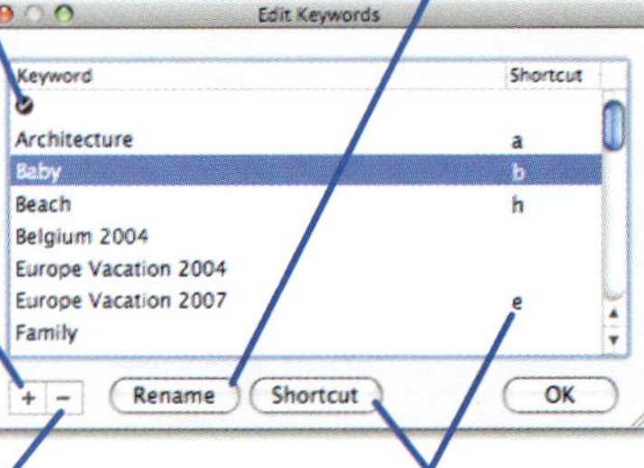

Don't want to use a certain keyword any more? Select it, then click the minus sign. **Note:** The keyword is removed from any photos to which you'd assigned it.

Use certain keywords often? Give them one-key shortcuts (see the opposite page). To create or edit a shortcut, select the keyword and click Shortcut, or simply double-click on that keyword's shortcut area.

Tips

Displaying keywords. To have iPhoto display keywords beneath photo thumbnails, choose View > Keywords.

Creating a keyword directly. When viewing keywords beneath thumbnails, you can create a new keyword by simply typing it beneath a photo thumbnail. Point beneath the thumbnail until the text *add keywords* appears.

Click this text, then type a keyword and press Return. This both creates the keyword and assigns it to the photo.

Sophie's on the Phone
add keywords

Assigning Keywords

You have a few ways to assign keywords.

The keywords window. Choose Window > Show Keywords. Select the photo(s), then click one or more keywords.

The keyboard. If you assigned a keyboard shortcut to the keyword, reap your reward now. Select the photo(s), and tap the shortcut key.

If you have to assign various keywords to a set of photos, combine shortcut keys with the arrow keys. Select a photo, tap a key, tap an arrow key to move to a new photo, tap a key. There's never been a faster way to assign keywords in iPhoto.

Directly beneath the thumbnail. See the tip on the opposite page, at lower left.

Keyword Tips

Removing a keyword. To remove a keyword from a photo, select the photo and click the keyword in the Keywords window, or tap the keyword's keyboard shortcut, if you created one.

Keywords window tips. Here are a few tips for the Keywords window.

Want to add a shortcut to an existing keyword? No need to click Edit Keywords: simply drag the keyword into the Quick Group area. Similarly, to remove a shortcut from a keyword, drag the keyword down to the Keywords area.

Keywords for which you've created keyboard shortcuts appear in this area, along with their shortcuts.

Just working with keyboard-shortcut keywords at the moment? Hide the rest of your keywords by clicking the triangle.

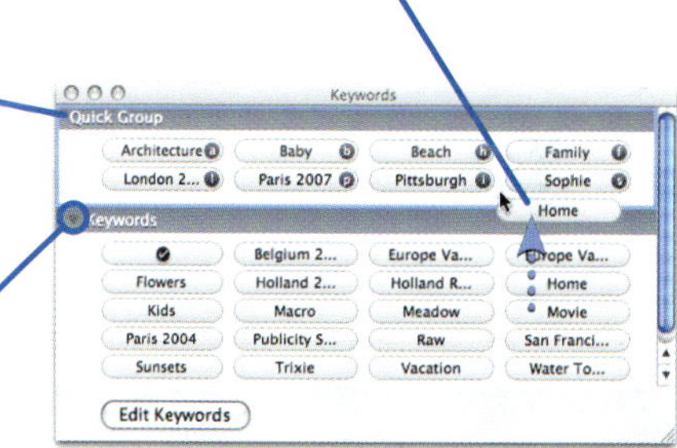

Art Critic: Rating Your Photos

You can assign a rating of from one to five stars to a photo, and there are a few ways to do it.

The Photos menu. Choose a rating from the My Rating submenu.

The keyboard. Press ⌘ along with 0 (zero) through 5. This shortcut pairs up nicely with the arrow keys: rate a photo, press an arrow key to move to the next photo, and repeat.

The Encounter
★★★★★

Veiled
★★★

The shortcut menu. Control-click on a photo and choose a rating from the My Rating submenu.

In one fell swoop. Want to give a bunch of photos the same rating? Select them, then use one of the previous techniques.

With the Information pane. Select a photo and then click the stars in the Information pane.

During a slide show. Move the mouse, then click the desired rating. Or just press 0 (zero) through 5 to rate the currently displayed photo.

Ratings Tips

To see ratings beneath your photo thumbnails, choose View > Rating (Shift-⌘-R). When ratings are visible, you can change them by clicking the stars and dots.

Searching for Photos

Browsing is fun, but not when you're looking for something specific. When you're on the hunt, you want help: directions from your car's navigation system, a directory in a shopping mall, or a search feature in your digital photography program.

iPhoto lets you search in several ways. For quick searches, jump down to the Search box and start typing. As you type, iPhoto narrows down the photos it displays—much as iTunes does during song searches. The more time you spend giving titles and descriptions to your best shots (page 140), the better the search feature works.

Next to the Search box, a pop-up menu lets you search in more specific ways. Look for photos taken on certain dates. Or photos with a four-star rating, or with certain keywords.

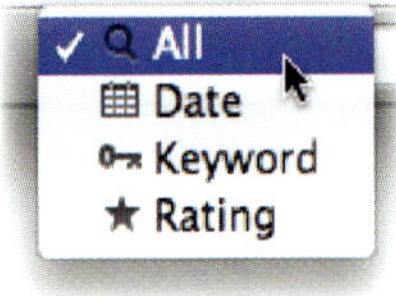

And when your searching needs are *very* specific—show me the four-star photos of the dog taken before noon at the beach with my Nikon camera during the month of July—iPhoto can accommodate. Just create a smart album (page 150).

So go ahead and browse when you want to relive random memories. But when you're on a mission? Search.

Search Box Basics

No matter what kind of search you perform, keep this in mind: iPhoto searches whatever item you've selected in the Library list. If you want to search your entire library, be sure to click Events or Photos. To search the last year's worth of photos, click Last 12 Months. To search a specific album, click the album. You get it.

Step 1. Click in the Search box or press ⌘-F.

Step 2. Type something. iPhoto searches photo filenames, event names, titles, descriptions, and keywords.

Step 3. To clear a search (displaying everything again), click ⊗ in the Search box.

Variations

Searching by rating. From the Search box pop-up menu, choose Rating. Click the dots to specify a minimum number of stars a photo must have.

Note: Higher-rated photos also appear: if you click three stars, four- and five-star photos also appear. To find *just* three-star photos, for example, create a smart album.

Searching by keyword. From the Search box pop-up menu, choose Keyword, then click one or more keywords. (For tips on keyword searching, see the opposite page.)

Searching by date. From the Search box pop-up menu, choose Date, then specify a date or range of dates (see the opposite page).

Searching By Date

Even if you never give a photo a title, description, or keywords, you can always search by date, since your camera records the date and time when you take a photo.

And remember, you can use iPhoto to adjust the dates of your photos to make date searches as accurate as possible (page 141).

The Big Picture

When you display the Calendar panel, it shows the current year.

Display the previous or following year.

Switch between viewing by year or by a specific month.

Months in which you've taken photos appear in bold. To see photos from a specific month, click that month. To select more than one month, drag across months, Shift-click, or ⌘-click.

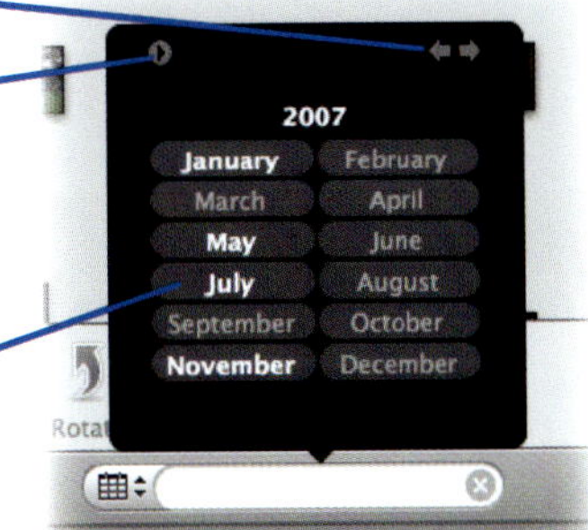

Narrow Your View

To explore a specific month, double-click its name.

Display the previous or following month.

Return to year view.

Days on which you've taken photos appear in bold. To see photos from a specific day, click the day. To see photos from a range of days, drag across the days. To see photos from discontinuous days (for example, every Saturday), ⌘-click the days.

Tip: If you point to a month or date without clicking, iPhoto tells you how many photos you took during that month or on that date, as shown here.

Advanced Keyword Searches

When you click multiple keywords, iPhoto puts an *and* between each one: "find all photos with the keywords Sophie *and* Beach."

Sometimes, *and* isn't what you want.

Excluding a keyword. To exclude a keyword, press Option while clicking it. Say you want to find all Sophie photos that *weren't* taken at the beach. Click the Beach keyword, then Option-click the Beach keyword. Notice the Search box: it reads *not Beach and Sophie.*

Either/or. To search for photos with one keyword or another, press Shift while clicking keywords. For example, to find all photos of the baby *or* the dog, Shift-click the Baby and Dog keywords.

Combinations thereof. By combining the Shift-click and Option-click variations, you can conduct some fairly complex searches, though it can be confusing to figure out which key sequences to use. For very specific searches, smart albums are easier.

Creating Albums

Getting photos back from a lab is always exciting, but what's really fun is creating a photo album that turns a collection of photos into a story.

An iPhoto album contains a series of photographs sequenced in an order that helps tell a story or document an event. Creating an album is often the first step in sharing a set of photos. For example, before creating a slide show or book, you'll usually want to create an album containing the photos you want to use.

Creating albums in iPhoto is a simple matter of dragging thumbnail images. You can add and remove photos to and from albums at any time, and you can sequence the photos in whatever order you like. You can even include the same photo in many different albums.

The photos in an album might be from one event, or from a dozen different events. Just as an iTunes playlist lets you create your own music compilations, an iPhoto album lets you create your own image compilations.

You don't have to create albums for every set of photos you import. But when you want to combine photos from different events, particularly when you're planning to share the photos in some way, albums are the answer.

Step 1. Choose File > New Album

You can also use the ⌘-N keyboard shortcut, or click the + button and then choose Album in the subsequent dialog box.

Step 2. Type a name, then click Create or press Return.

Tip: To create an album and add photos to it in one step, select the photos *before* choosing New Album (page 148).

Step 3. Add photos.

After you've created the album, begin dragging photos into it. You can drag photos one at a time, or select multiple photos and drag them in all at once.

As you drag, iPhoto indicates how many photos you've selected.

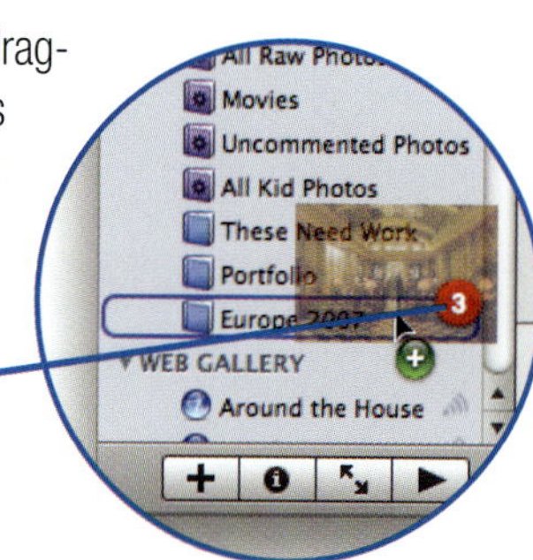

Organizing an Album

The order of the photos in an album is important: when you create slide shows, books, or Web photo galleries, iPhoto presents the photos in the order in which they appear in the album.

Once you've created an album, you may want to fine-tune the order of its photos.

To edit an album's name, double-click it or use the Information pane.

To move an album to a different location in the Albums area, drag it up or down. As the following pages describe, you can also create folders to organize related albums.

To change the order of the photos, drag them. Here, the flower close-up is being moved so it will appear after the other flower shots.

Removing a photo. Don't want a photo in an album after all? Select it and press the Delete key. This removes the photo from the album, but not from your hard drive or photo library.

Tips for Selecting Photos

Selecting photos is a common activity in iPhoto: you select photos in order to delete them, add them to an album, move them around within an album, and more.

When working with multiple photos, remember the standard Mac selection shortcuts: To select a range of photos, click on the first one and Shift-click on the last one. To select multiple photos that aren't adjacent to each other, press ⌘ while clicking on each photo.

As the screen below shows, you can also select a series of pictures by dragging a selection rectangle around them.

Tips for Working with Albums

Albums are Optional

You don't *have* to create an album in order to share photos: you can create slide shows, books, calendars, and Web pages by simply selecting photos in your library, and then using the appropriate button or command.

This has always been true in iPhoto, but it's more applicable than ever in iPhoto '08. By hiding less-than-perfect photos (page 138), you can "edit" an event to contain only those photos you want to use in a project.

Still, when you're about to create a photo project of some kind, it's better to create an album first. Albums give you the ability to change the sequence of photos. You can resequence photos while creating slide shows, books, and the like, but creating these items is easier when you start with the photos that are in roughly the final order that you plan to use.

Album Shortcuts

You can create an album and add images to it in one step. Select one or more images and choose File > New Album. In the dialog box that appears, check the box labeled Use Selected Items in New Album. Or select some photos, then choose File > New Album from Selection (Shift-⌘-N).

You can also drag the images into a blank spot of the Library area. When you use this technique, iPhoto gives the new album a generic name, such as *untitled album*. To rename the album, double-click its name and type a new name.

If you have photos on a storage device—your hard drive, a Picture CD, or a digital camera's memory card—you can import them into iPhoto *and* create an album in one fell swoop.

Simply drag the photos from the Finder into a blank area of the Library list. iPhoto imports the photos, storing them in their own event. iPhoto also creates an album and adds the photos to it.

Tip: As your collection of albums and other items grows, you may find that you no longer have a "blank area" at the bottom of the iPhoto window. To create one, close some of the items in the Library list—for example, close the Albums list by clicking its triangle.

Albums and flagging. iPhoto's flagging feature (page 138) teams up nicely with albums. Want to create an album of shots that are scattered throughout your library? Flag the shots, then select the Flagged item in your Library list. Next, choose Edit > Select All, then choose File > New Album from Selection.

From Album to Event

You've created an album containing the best photos of a friend's wedding. The photos are from various events; indeed, some were emailed to you from other attendees.

You'd prefer that the photos were in an event of their own. Easy. Select the album, choose Edit > Select All, then choose Events > Create Event. iPhoto creates a new event, and moves the photos in the album into the event. Note, however, that the photos are removed from the events where they originated.

Photo Count

You can have iPhoto display the number of photos in each album next to each album's name. In the Preferences dialog box, click General, then check the Show Item Counts box.

To Experiment, Duplicate

You have a photo that appears in multiple albums, but you want to edit its appearance in just one album, leaving the original version unchanged in other albums. Time for the Duplicate command: select the photo and choose Duplicate from the Photos menu (⌘-D). Now edit the duplicate.

Duplicating an album. There may be times when you'll want several versions of an album. For example, you might have one version with photos sequenced for a slide show and another version with photos organized for a book. Or you might simply want to experiment with several different photo arrangements until you find the one you like best.

iPhoto makes this kind of experimentation easy. Simply duplicate an album by selecting the album and choosing Duplicate from the Photos menu. iPhoto makes a duplicate of the album, which you can rename and experiment with.

You can make as many duplicates of an album as you like. You can even duplicate a smart album—perhaps as a prelude to experimenting with different search criteria. Don't worry about devouring disk space. Albums don't include your actual photos; they simply contain "pointers" to the photos in your library.

Albums and iLife

Another good reason to create albums surfaces elsewhere in iLife: iMovie, iDVD, GarageBand, and iWeb all display iPhoto albums in their photo media browsers.

Have a batch of photos you want to use in another iLife program? Rather than searching through your library using those programs' media browsers, first stash the photos in an album. Then, choose that album in the other iLife program.

iPhoto album support is also built into other programs, including Mac OS X's screen saver and Apple's iWork programs. And you can choose to sync only certain albums to a photo-capable iPod (page 210) or Apple TV (page 214).

Organize Your Library with Folders

As you create albums, slide shows, and books, your Library list may become cluttered. iPhoto helps a bit by providing separate areas for albums, slide shows, projects, and other items. But you can do your part, too. Take advantage of the ability to create folders in the Albums area of the Library list.

Folders in iPhoto have the same benefit that they have on your hard drive: they let you store related items. And as with the documents on your hard drive, the definition of "related items" is up to you.

Filing strategies. You can use folders in any way you like. You might want to set up a project-based filing system: create a folder for a project, then stash albums, books, and slide shows in that folder.

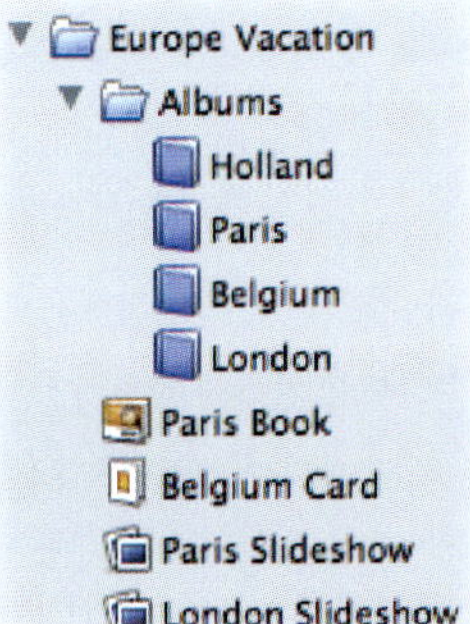

Or you might prefer an object-oriented filing system: stash all your albums in one folder, all your slide shows in another, and all your books in yet another.

You might want to mix and match these approaches or come up with something completely different. What's important is that you create a filing scheme that helps you quickly locate items.

Creating a folder. To create a folder, choose New Folder from the File menu. Or, Control-click on a blank area of the Library list and choose New Folder from the shortcut menu. iPhoto names a new folder *untitled folder*, and selects its name. To rename the folder, just start typing.

Working with folders. To move an item into a folder, simply drag it to the folder until you see a black border around the folder.

To close or open a folder, click the little triangle to the left of its name.

Like folders in the Mac's Finder, iPhoto folders are "spring loaded"—if you drag something to a closed folder and pause briefly, the folder opens.

Folders within folders. You can create folders inside of folders. You might use this scheme to store all the albums, books, and slide shows that relate to a specific event or theme.

To open a folder and all the nested folders within it, press Option while clicking on the folder's triangle.

Creating Smart Albums

iPhoto can assemble albums for you based on criteria that you specify. The *smart album* feature works much like the smart playlist feature in iTunes: spell out what you want, and your Mac does the work for you.

A few possibilities: Create an album containing every shot you took in the last week. Or of every photo you took in November 2002. Or of every November 2002 photo that has *Sophie* in its title. Or of every photo from 2007 that has *Paris* as a keyword, *croissant* in its title, and a rating of at least four stars.

If you've taken the time to assign titles, comments, and keywords to your photos, here's where your investment pays off. You can still use smart albums if you haven't assigned titles and other information to photos; you just won't be able to search on as broad a range of things.

You can also create smart albums that have criteria based on information that your camera stores with each photo (see page 229). Create one smart album that corrals all the shots you took with your Sony camera, and another that collects all your Canon shots. Or create a smart album of all your photos shot at a high ISO speed (page 232), or at a fast shutter speed, or with a telephoto lens.

Smart albums are a great way to quickly gather up related photos for printing, backing up, browsing, emailing—you name it.

Creating a Smart Album

Step 1. Choose New Smart Album from the File menu (Option-⌘-N).

You can also create a new smart album by pressing the Option key and clicking on the [+] button in the lower-left corner of the iPhoto window.

Step 2. Specify what to look for.

Type a name for the smart album.

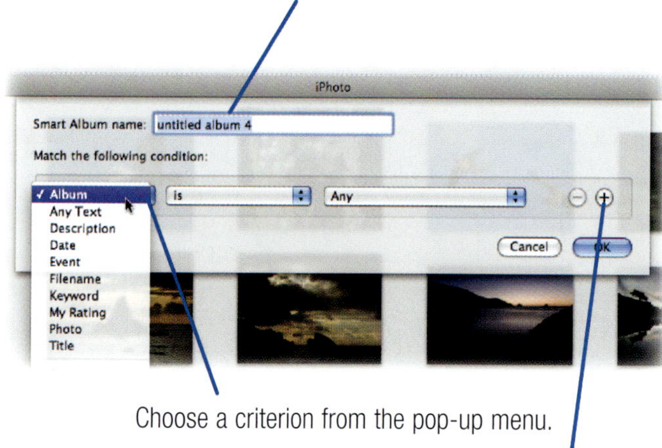

Choose a criterion from the pop-up menu.

To add another criterion, click the ⊕ button (see opposite page).

Step 3. Click OK or press Return.

In the Albums area, iPhoto indicates smart albums with a special icon: [icon].

Changing a Smart Album

To modify a smart album, select it in the Albums area and choose File > Edit Smart Album or Photos > Smart Album Info (⌘-I).

Get more smart album ideas.
www.macilife.com/iphoto

Be More Specific: Specifying Multiple Criteria

By adding additional criteria, you can be very specific about what you want to find.

Normally, iPhoto locates photos that meet all the criteria you specify. To have iPhoto locate a photo that meets any of the criteria, choose any.

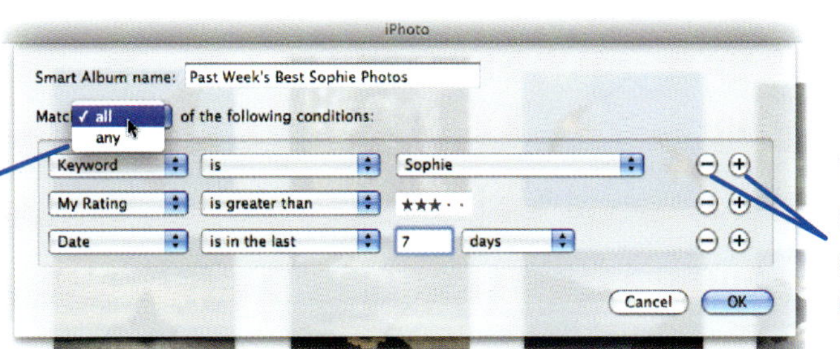

To delete a criterion, click the ⊖ button. To add a criterion, click the ⊕ button.

Tips for Smart Albums

They're alive. iPhoto is always watching. If you import photos that meet a smart album's criteria, iPhoto adds those photos to the album. iPhoto may also add to a smart album when you edit photo information. For example, if you change a photo's title to *Beach picnic*, iPhoto adds the photo to any smart album set up to search for *beach* in the title.

From smart to dumb. You can't turn a smart album into a static one—unlike iTunes, iPhoto doesn't provide a Live Updating check box. Here's a workaround. Click the smart album in the Album list, then select all the photos in the album. (Click one photo, then press ⌘-A.) Next, choose New Album from Selection from the File menu. This creates an album containing the photos currently in the smart album.

Deleting photos. To delete a photo from a smart album, select it and press ⌘-Option-Delete. Note that this also deletes the photo from your library and moves it to the iPhoto Trash.

Smart Album Suggestions

For a Compilation of	Specify These Criteria
All your movies	Photo is Movie
All your raw-format photos	Photo is Raw
All flagged or hidden photos	Photo is Flagged or Photo is Hidden
Recent favorites	Date is in the last 1 month (for example) and My Rating is greater than three stars
All your Winter photos	Date is in the range 12/21/2006 to 3/20/2007
All photos that aren't in any album	Album is not Any
Photos from a specific camera	Camera Model is *model*
Photos from the second-to-last event you imported	Event is not in the last 1 event and Event is in the last 2 events
Photos from two weeks ago	Date is not in the last 1 week and Date is in the last 2 weeks
Photos taken with a telephoto lens	Focal Length is greater than 150 (for example)

Basic Photo Editing

Many photos can benefit from some tweaking. Maybe you'd like to crop out that huge telephone pole that distracts from your subject. Maybe the exposure is too light, too dark, or lacks contrast. Or maybe the camera's flash gave your subject's eyes the dreaded red-eye flaw.

iPhoto's edit view can fix these problems and others. And it does so in a clever way that doesn't replace your original image.

Better still, a significant improvement in iPhoto '08 gives you more editing flexibility. In earlier iPhoto versions, making changes to an already-edited image wasn't the best idea—because of JPEG compression (there's that word again), you'd lose a bit of image quality with each editing session.

iPhoto '08 works differently. When you edit a photo, iPhoto keeps a list of the changes you made. If you reopen an edited image and make more changes, iPhoto applies your entire list of changes to the *original* version of the photo. It's called *non-destructive* editing, and the result is fewer passes through the JPEG-compression meat grinder—and better photo quality. (For more about iPhoto non-destructive editing, including an important caveat, see page 229.)

As you get accustomed to iPhoto editing, you might want to experiment with full-screen editing (page 168), the separate editing window (page 170), and the ability to tweak some editing preferences (pages 24 and 175).

Editing Essentials

To work on a photo, open it in iPhoto's edit view.

Step 1. Select the photo you want to edit.

Step 2. Click the Edit button.

The photo opens in edit view, and new tools and buttons appear (opposite page).

Step 3. Now what? Here are some the ways iPhoto can help an ailing photo.

Photo First-Aid

Symptom	Cure (and Page)
Red-eye from flash	Red-Eye tool (154)
Poor contrast and "punch"	Enhance button (156); for more control, the Adjust panel (162)
Crooked and/or badly framed	Straighten and/or Crop tools (155)
Scratches or blemishes	Retouch tool (157)
Color balance is incorrect	Adjust panel (164)
Photo is "grainy" from low light	Adjust panel (167)

Notes and Tips

Change your mind? To exit edit view without saving any changes, press the Esc key.

Global or local? When you edit a photo, you change the photo everywhere you've used it—in slide shows, books, and calendars, for example. There's another way to fine-tune an image. When printing a photo or using it in a book, greeting card, or calendar, you can modify the photo's appearance in just that place—without changing its appearance elsewhere.

I'll remind you of these local editing opportunities as we go.

Edit View at a Glance

A row of thumbnails shows adjacent photos in the library or selected event or album. To edit a different photo, click its thumbnail. To hide the thumbnails and get more working room, choose View > Thumbnails > Hide (Option-⌘-T).

To resize the thumbnail browser, drag this bar up or down. Shrink it to get more working room; enlarge it to see the differences between similar shots.

Switch to full-screen edit view (page 168).

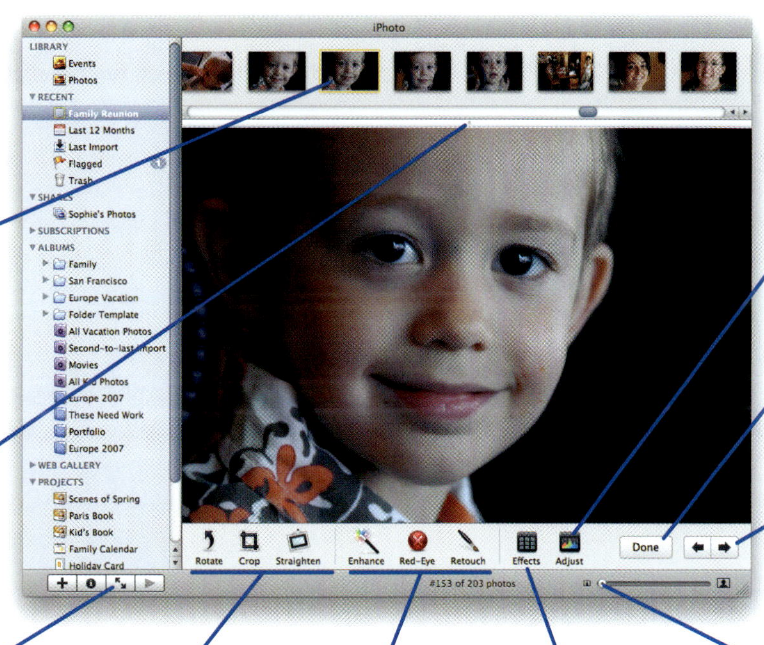

Fix the geometry: rotate a photo (page 131) or crop or straighten it (page 155).

Fix the pixels: use One-Click Enhance (page 156), fix red-eye (page 154), or retouch flaws (157).

Apply a variety of effects (page 158).

Finely control exposure, color balance, sharpness, and more (pages 160–167).

Save any changes and return to Events or Photos view.

Save any changes and open the previous or next photo for editing (keyboard shortcut: left or right arrow).

Zoom in and out.
Tip: When zoomed in, you can quickly scroll by pressing the space-bar and dragging within the photo.

Two Things to Remember When Editing

Here are two tips to keep in mind as you edit photos.

Before-and-after view. To see how your photo looked before you made the latest round of changes, hold down the Shift key. By pressing and releasing Shift, you can see a before-and-after view of your latest edits.

Safety nets: undo and revert. Not happy with your very latest change? Choose Edit > Undo.

Not happy with the changes you made since you opened the photo? Choose Photos > Revert to Previous, and iPhoto discards your edits and restores the photo to its previous state.

Fixing Composition Problems and Red-Eye

Some photos can benefit from...less. Maybe you weren't able to get close enough to your subject, and you'd like to get rid of some visual clutter. Or maybe a scenic vista is marred by a dumpster that you didn't notice when you took the shot. Or maybe you want to order a print, and you want your photo's proportions to match the size you want.

iPhoto's Crop tool is the answer for jobs like these. By cropping a photo, you can often improve its composition and better highlight its subject matter.

Similarly, some photos need a bit of straightening. It's easy to tilt the camera when you're shooting, making the whole world look just a little crooked.

To put your world on the level, use the Straighten tool. A drag of the mouse is all it takes.

Then there's red-eye. Biologically, it's caused by the bright light of an electronic flash reflecting off a subject's retinas and the blood vessels around them. Aesthetically, it makes people look like demons.

iPhoto can help here, too. The Red-Eye tool gives you a couple of ways to get the red out.

Removing Red-Eye

Step 1. Open the photo in edit view.

Step 2. Drag the size slider to zoom in on the subject's eyes.

Step 3. Click the Red-Eye tool.

Step 4. Click the red eyes.

If you aren't happy with the results—maybe there's some red left over—choose Edit > Undo, then customize the Red-Eye tool and try again.

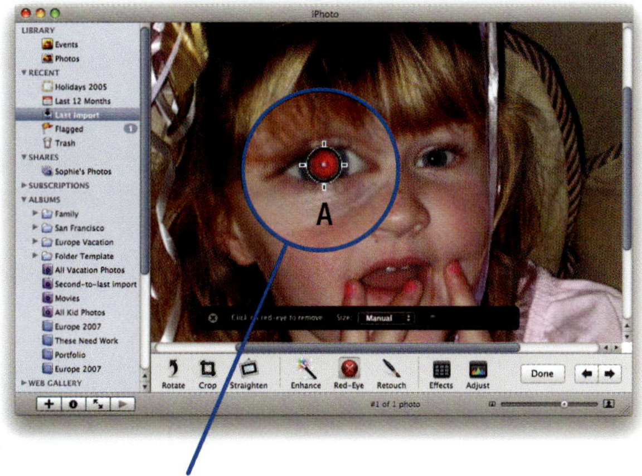

As described at right, you may get better results by controlling the size of the Red-Eye tool. Choose Manual, then drag the slider until the tool (A) is slightly larger than the red area of the eye. Then, click the red area of each eye.

Step 5. To turn off the Red-Eye tool, click it again or choose a different tool.

Cropping a Photo

Step 1. Open the photo in edit view.

Step 2. Click the Crop button.

Step 3. Adjust the size and position of the crop rectangle to enclose the portion of the image you want to keep, then click Apply.

When you move or resize the crop area, you see a grid that divides the crop area into thirds. You can often improve the composition of a photo by placing its main subject along this grid (see page 233).

To move the crop area, drag inside it.

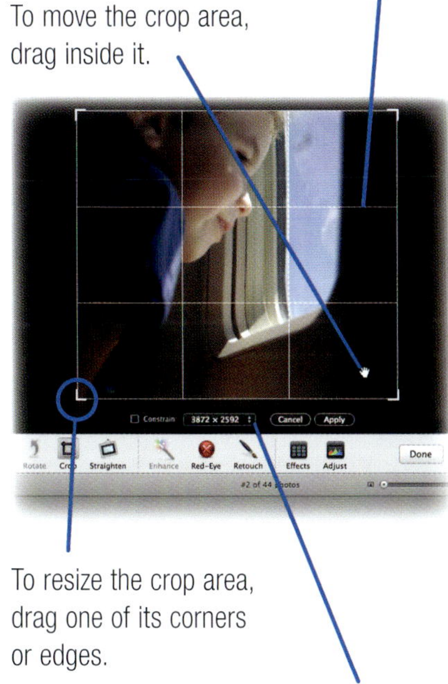

To resize the crop area, drag one of its corners or edges.

You can control the proportions of the crop area so that your photo fits a certain print size or display dimension.

Notes and Tips

Constraining the crop. You can make the crop area any size you like. But sometimes, you may want to control the proportions of the crop area—to ensure that your photo's proportions match a certain print size, for example.

Click the Constrain box, then choose an option.

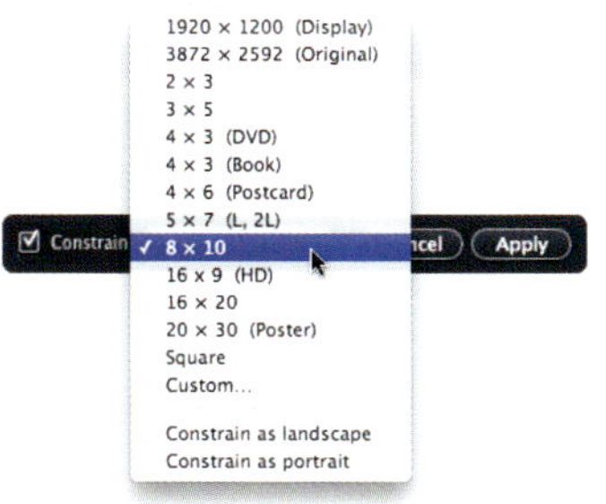

For example, if you plan to order an eight- by ten-inch print of the photo, choose 8 x 10.

To switch between a horizontal and vertical crop area, choose Constrain as Landscape or Constrain as Portrait. To override the constrain setting, press Shift while resizing the crop area.

Resetting the crop. To start over, press Option—the Cancel button changes to Reset. Click Reset, and iPhoto restores the original crop rectangle.

Cropping and resolution. When you crop a photo, you throw away pixels, lowering the photo's resolution. If you print a heavily cropped photo, you may notice ugly digital artifacts. Always shoot at the highest resolution your camera provides; this gives you more flexibility to crop later (see page 232).

The local option. If you're printing a photo on your own printer, or using the photo in a slide show or print project, you might prefer to use iPhoto's zoom tools to crop—that way, you won't change the photo everywhere you've used it. See pages 181 (for slide shows), 198 (for printing), and 211 (for print projects).

Straightening a Photo

Step 1. Open the photo in edit view.

Step 2. Click the Straighten tool.

Step 3. Drag the slider left or right, using the on-screen grid as a guide.

Tip: To straighten in very small increments, click the icons to the left or right of the slider.

Enhancing and Retouching Photos

Old photos can appear faded, their color washed out by Father Time. They might also have scratches and creases brought on by decades of shoebox imprisonment.

New photos can often benefit from some enhancement, too. That shot you took in a dark room with the flash turned off—its color could use some punching up. That family photo you want to use as a holiday card—the clan might look better with fewer wrinkles and blemishes.

iPhoto's enhance and retouch tools are ideal for tasks like these. With the enhance tool, you can improve a photo's colors and exposure, and rescue a photo you might otherwise delete. With the retouch tool, you can remove minor scratches and blemishes, not to mention that chocolate smudge on your kid's face.

iPhoto's editing features make it easy to fix many common image problems, but iPhoto isn't a full-fledged digital darkroom. You can't, for example, remove power lines that snake across an otherwise scenic vista, nor can you darken only a portion of an image. For tasks like these, you'll want to use Adobe Photoshop or Photoshop Elements—both of which pair up beautifully with iPhoto (see page 176).

Using One-Click Enhance

To apply one-click enhance, open a photo in edit view, and then click the Enhance button at the bottom of the iPhoto window.

Before

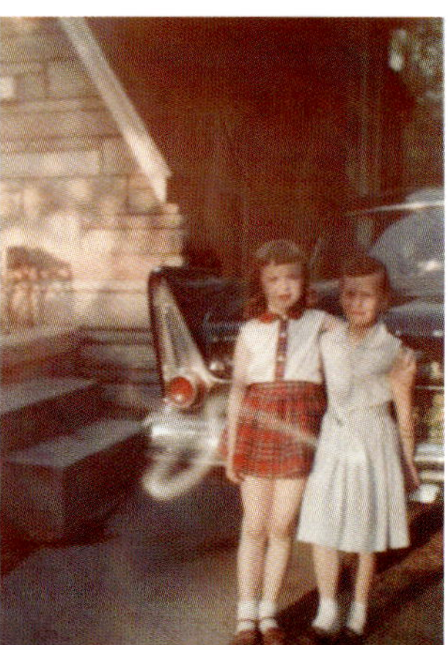

After

Tips

If at first you don't succeed, click, click again. Each time you click Enhance, iPhoto processes the image again. But too much enhancement can make an image appear grainy and artificial. If that happens, choose Undo Enhance Photo from the Edit menu as many times as needed to backtrack.

If the Enhance tool isn't doing the job—maybe its results are too harsh—undo your enhancements and turn to the tools in the Adjust panel (see page 160).

Retouching a Photo

Step 1. Open the photo in edit view.

Step 2. Click the Retouch tool.

Step 3. Click on or drag across on the flaw you want to remove.

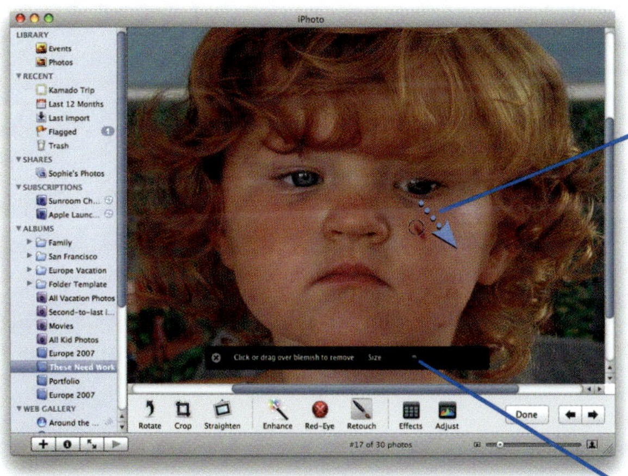

For larger scratches and flaws, try dragging in short strokes. This helps iPhoto blend your retouching into the surrounding area. For small blemishes, a single click is often all you need. Experiment and undo as needed.

You can enlarge or reduce the size of the retouch brush. A larger brush makes short work of large flaws, but you may find it picks up extraneous colors or patterns from surrounding areas. When that happens, undo your work, reduce the size of the brush, and try again.

Notes and Tips

Zoom for precision. To retouch with more precision, use the size slider to zoom in on the area of the image that you're working on. You can also zoom by pressing the 0 (zero), 1, or 2 keys.

Undo and revert. You can undo each mouse click or drag by choosing Edit > Undo Retouch from the Edit menu.

To undo all of your retouching, choose Photos > Revert to Previous. Note that you'll also lose any other edits, such as cropping, that you performed since switching into edit view. Because of this, you might want to retouch first—that way, you won't lose work if you decide to revert. Or take a different approach: Do your cropping and other adjustments, then click Done to exit edit view. Reopen the photo, and retouch.

Brush keyboard shortcuts. To make the retouch brush smaller, press the left-bracket ([) key. To make the brush larger, press the right-bracket key.

Applying Effects to Photos

With the Effects panel, you can alter a photo to give it a unique look. Evoke the colors of an old, faded tintype. Turn a color photo into a black-and-white one. Blur the edges of a scene to create a gauzy, romantic look. Juice up the colors in a photo or tone them down.

As the tips at right describe, you can apply more than one effect to a photo, and you can apply an effect more than once.

Keep in mind that applying an effect to a photo changes that photo everywhere it appears—in albums, books, slide shows, and so on. If you want to retain the previous version of a photo, be sure to duplicate it before applying an effect: select the photo and choose Duplicate from the Photos menu or use the ⌘-D keyboard shortcut.

And there's a local editing angle, too: You can apply black-and-white or sepia effects locally in a slide show. In print projects, you can apply these effects as well as an antique effect.

Applying Effects

Step 1. Open a photo in edit view.

Step 2. Click the Effects button to display the Effects panel (opposite page).

Step 3. Click the desired effect(s).

Effective Tips

Combining effects. Some effects pair up particularly well. For a dream-like look, try combining Edge Blur with the B&W effect. For an old-fashioned look, pair the Sepia or Antique effects with the Vignette effect. To create an oval border around a photo, combine the Matte and Vignette effects.

Don't be afraid to try offbeat combinations, either. It might seem contradictory to follow the Boost Color effect with the Fade Color effect, but you can get some interesting results when you do.

If you effect yourself into a corner, just click the Original button in the center of the Effects panel to return to safety.

When once isn't enough. You can apply most effects up to nine times: simply click the desired effect's button over and over again. (The two exceptions are the B&W and Sepia effects; clicking their buttons repeatedly will only wear out your mouse.)

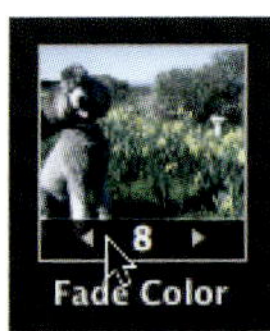

iPhoto lets you know how many times you've applied an effect. To backtrack one time, click the left-pointing arrow.

Refining an effect. You can refine the appearance of an effect by using the controls in the Adjust panel (discussed on the following pages). In particular, you can improve the contrast and tonal range of a black-and-white conversion by adjusting the Saturation, Tint, and Temperature sliders. For details, see page 165.

A Gallery of Effects

No single photo is ideally suited to every effect, but that didn't stop me from working my dog into this example.

To remove the effects you've applied, click the Original thumbnail in the center of the Effects panel.

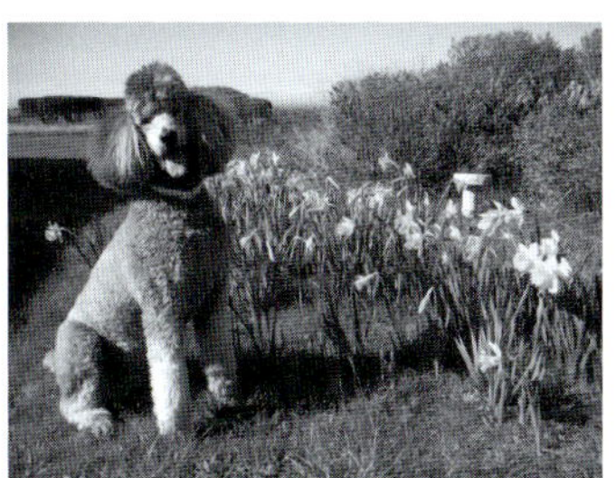

B&W. Convert to black and white.

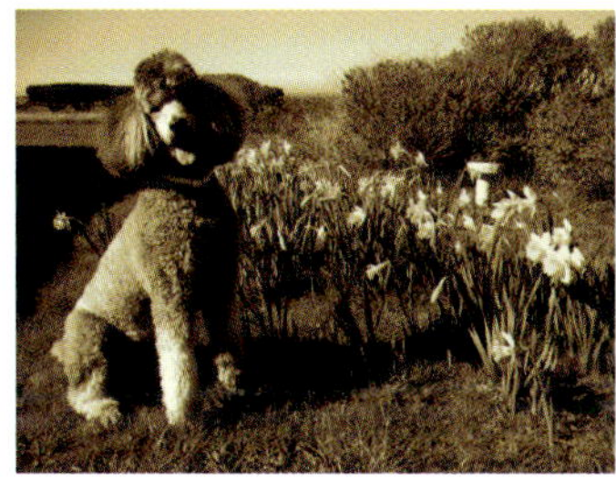

Sepia. Add a warm brown cast.

Antique. Simulate the faded colors of an old photo.

Fade Color. Decrease a photo's color saturation (for more control, use the Adjust panel; page 164).

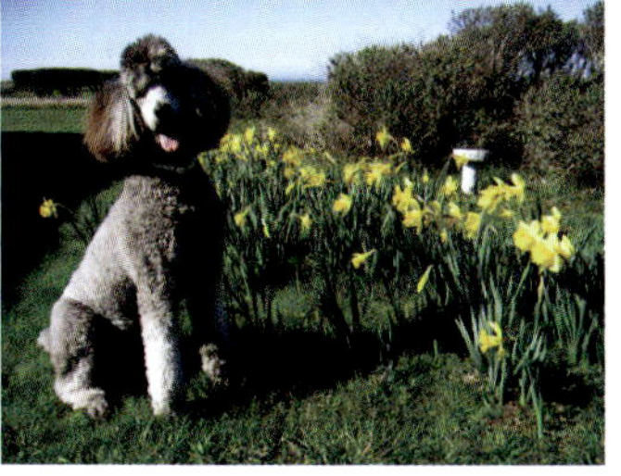

Boost Color. Increase a photo's color saturation (for more control, use the Adjust panel; page 164).

Matte. Add a soft-edged white border.

Vignette. Add a soft black border.

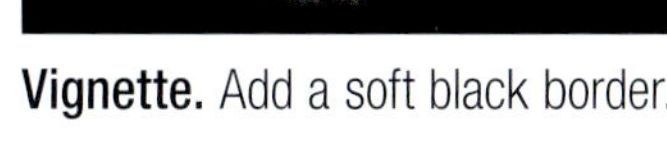

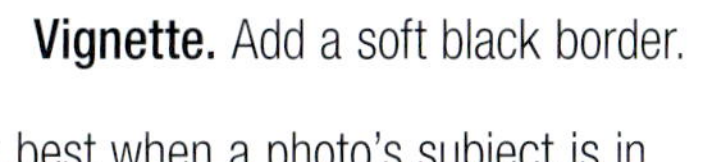

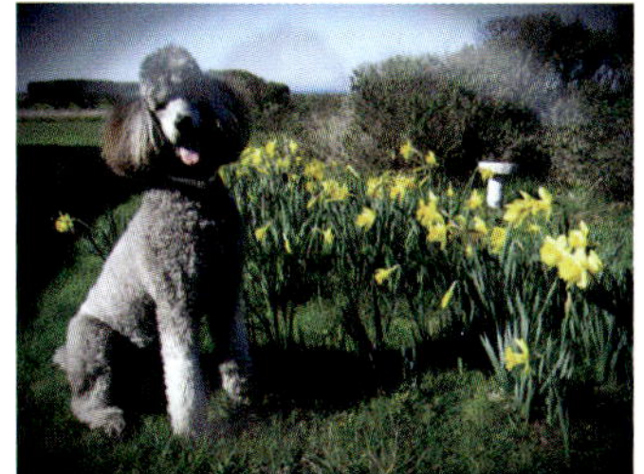

Edge Blur. Blur the edges of a photo. **Tip:** Try clicking this one a few times and combining it with the B&W effect.

Tip: The Matte and Vignette effects work best when a photo's subject is in the center of the image. For these examples, I cropped the photo before applying the effect, and I clicked the effect's button several times.

Advanced Editing and the Adjust Panel

Some photos need more help than others. That portrait captures the essence of your subject—but it's just a bit dark. That shot of a beautiful white gardenia would be prettier if the flower didn't have a jaundiced yellow color cast. And that shot of the dog playing in the park would be cuter if you could actually see the dog.

To fix problems like these, use the Adjust panel—its controls let you fine-tune exposure, tweak color balance, sharpen details and more.

The basics of the Adjust panel are a cinch: after opening a photo for editing, summon the Adjust panel by clicking the Adjust button in the edit view toolbar. Then, drag the appropriate sliders left or right until you get the desired results.

Adjust

That last part—getting the desired results—isn't always a cinch. Adjusting exposure, color balance, and sharpness can be tricky, and knowing a few digital imaging concepts can help you reach your goals. You'll find a detailed look at these concepts in the following pages. Here's the big picture.

A Sampling of Adjustments

Adjust Exposure

Use the Exposure and Levels sliders to brighten or darken photos and improve contrast (page 162).

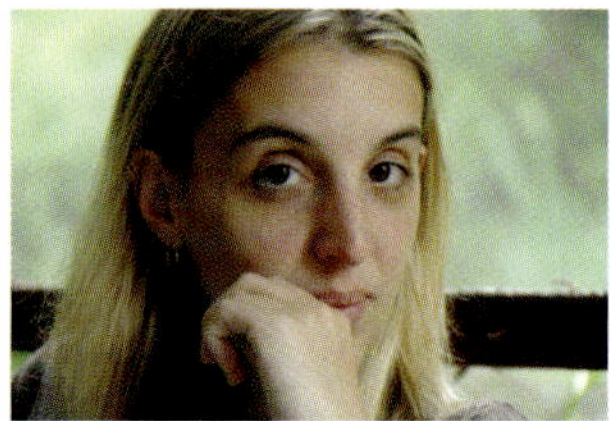

Fix Color Problems

Use the Saturation, Temperature, and Tint sliders to remove unwanted color casts, increase or decrease color vividness, and more (page 164).

Recover Shadow and Highlight Detail

Use the Shadow and Highlight sliders to bring detail out of dark shadows and overly bright areas (page 163).

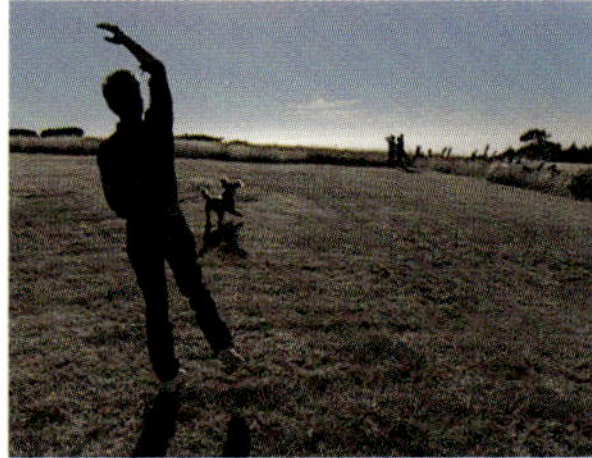

The Adjust Panel at a Glance

The histogram is a bar graph that shows a photo's distribution of tonal values—blacks, whites, and everything in between. Knowing how to read the histogram can help you improve brightness and contrast (see the following page).

The Exposure slider adjusts overall brightness; use it and the Levels sliders to fix exposure and contrast problems (page 162).

The Contrast slider increases or decreases the contrast range.

The Highlights and Shadows sliders restore details hidden in dark shadows and bright areas (page 163).

The Saturation slider makes colors less vivid or more vivid (page 164).

The white-point tool corrects color casts by adjusting the color of white or gray areas (page 164).

The Sharpness slider increases clarity and crispness; sharpening before printing can improve your output (page 166).

Low-light or high-ISO shots often have digital noise that the Reduce Noise slider can help to minimize (page 167).

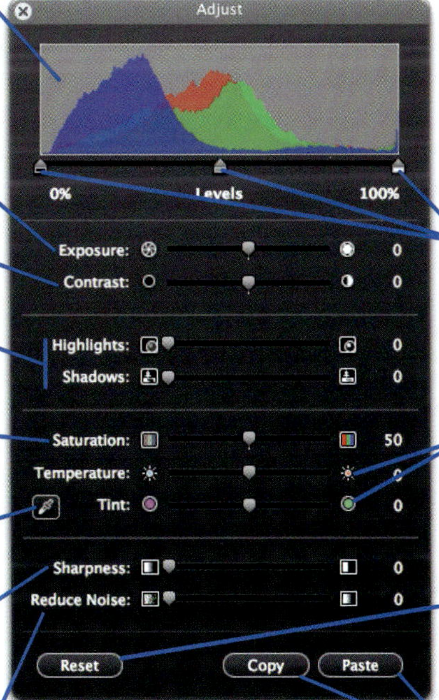

The local angle. You'll find an Adjust panel elsewhere in iPhoto: there's one in the custom print view (page 198) and in the calendar, greeting card, and book views (page 211). These Adjust panels aren't identical to the one in edit view, but they're very similar—and they're great places to adjust a photo without changing it everywhere you may have used it.

The Levels sliders are often the best tools for improving brightness and contrast (page 162).

The Temperature and Tint sliders adjust color balance; use them to fix unwanted color casts and create special effects (page 164).

Never mind! If you've adjusted yourself into a corner, click Reset to restore all the sliders to their factory settings.

Use the Copy and Paste buttons to apply adjustments made in one image to another image (page 170).

Adjusting Exposure and Levels

iPhoto's Enhance button often does a good job of punching up a photo, but it's a "my way or the highway" feature: you either like its results or you undo.

The Adjust panel is a more accommodating place to fix brightness and contrast problems. For improving a photo's exposure and contrast, use the Levels sliders and the Exposure slider. By adjusting them—while keeping a close eye on the photo's histogram—you can often make dramatic improvements in a photo's appearance.

Which tools should you use? It depends on the photo. Some photos respond better to the Exposure slider, while others benefit from levels adjustments. Still other photos benefit from both approaches: do some initial tweaks with the Exposure slider, then fine-tune the levels.

When you drag the these sliders, you tell iPhoto to stretch the photo's existing tonal values to cover a broader tonal range. Oversimplified, when you change the black point, you tell iPhoto, "See this grayish black? I want you to treat it as a darker black and adjust everything else accordingly."

The Levels sliders can often work wonders, but they can't work miracles. If a photo has an extremely narrow contrast range, you may see visible *banding*—jarring color shifts instead of smooth gradations—after adjusting levels. You're telling iPhoto to stretch a molehill into a mountain, and there may not be enough data to allow for smooth gradations in shading and color.

Reading a Histogram

A *histogram* is a bar graph that shows how much black, white, and mid-tone data a photograph has. Pure black is on the left, pure white is on the right, and the mid-tones are in between. iPhoto displays a color histogram that breaks this information down into an image's three primary-color channels: red, green, and blue.

Beneath the histogram is a set of sliders that let you change what iPhoto considers to be pure black, pure white, or mid-tone values.

A Sampling of Histograms

This properly exposed shot has a good distribution of dark, bright, and mid-tone areas. Notice that the histogram shows a lot of bright blue data: the ocean and sky.

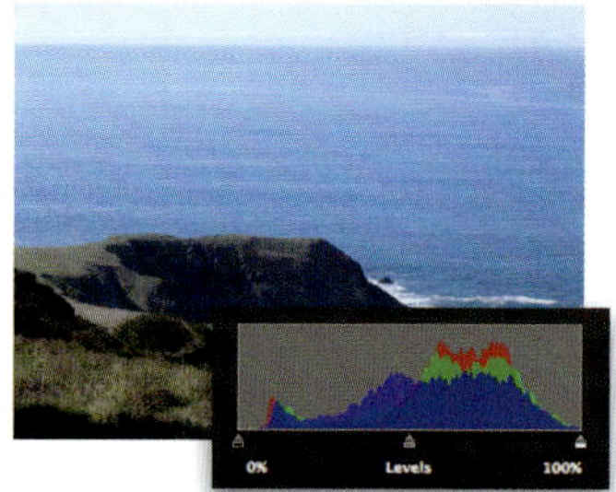

This overexposed shot has very little data in the blacks; everything is bunched up toward the right side—the white side—of the histogram.

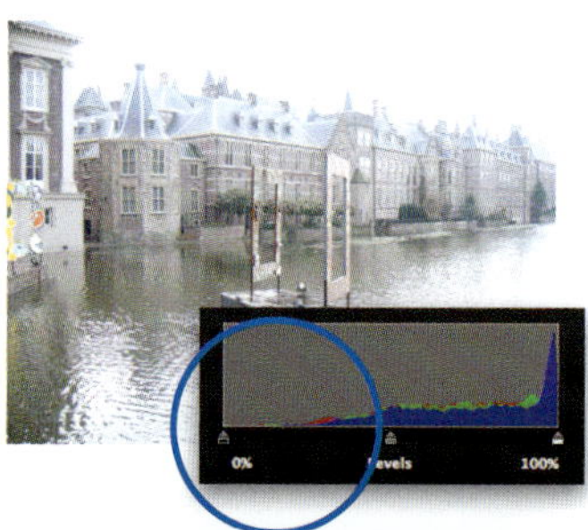

Nice close-up, but the whites could be a bit whiter; notice the absence of data at the right end of the histogram.

Using the Levels Sliders

Before

Cute kid, flat photo. The histogram tells the tale: there's little data in the brightest whites.

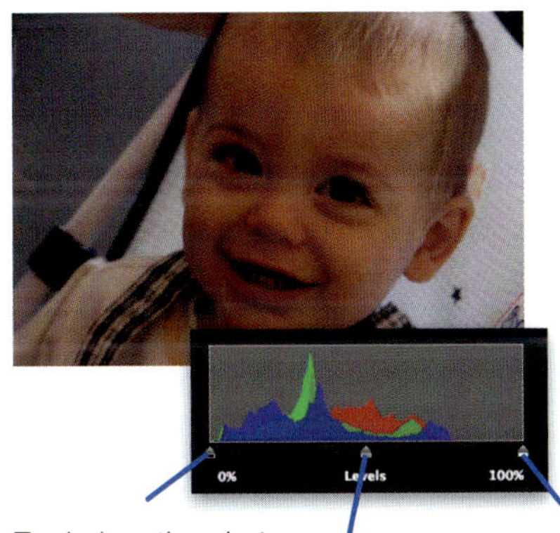

After

The photo's brightness and contrast are improved, and its histogram shows a broader tonal range.

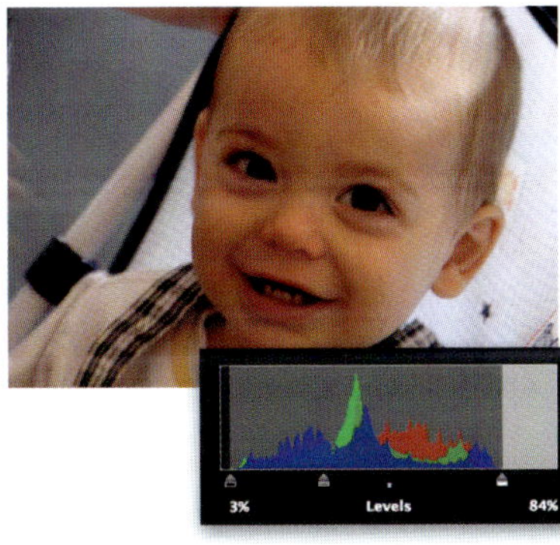

To darken the photo, drag the *black-point* slider to the right.

To adjust the overall brightness of the photo, drag the mid-tone slider.

To brighten the photo, drag the *white-point* slider to the left.

Drag until the sliders almost reach the point where the image data begins. These sloped areas are often called the *shoulders* of the histogram.

Using the Exposure Slider

The Adjust panel's Exposure slider makes a photo brighter or darker.

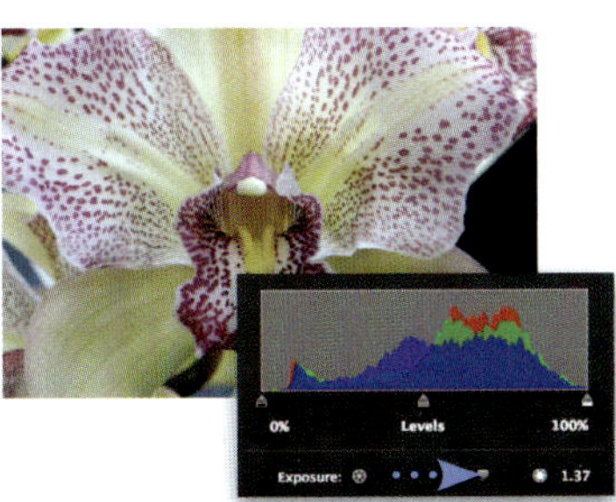

I enhanced this underexposed photo by dragging the Exposure slider to the right. Notice that its histogram is broader than the original (see opposite page).

Note: The Exposure slider works best with raw-format images. For JPEG-format images, the Levels sliders tend to provide more precision. For more details, see page 175.

Shadow and Highlight Recovery

Cameras don't perceive high-contrast scenes as well as our eyes do. As a result, high-contrast photos are often missing something. Shadows are dark and devoid of detail, or bright areas are washed out to nearly pure white. Take a photo of a friend under a beach umbrella, and you'll probably see a silhouette, not a smile.

The Shadow and Highlight sliders in the Adjust panel can help. To bring out details hidden in dark areas of a photo, use the Shadow slider. It might just bring a smile to your silhouetted friend's face. And to recover details in the brilliantly lit beach sand, drag the Highlights slider.

But a little goes a long way. It's easy to end up with an artificial-looking photo that has strange halos where bright and dark areas meet. To recover shadow details, try brightening the photo with the mid-tone or white-point Levels slider, then drag the Shadow slider a bit. You might even try brightening the photo until highlights appear too bright, then darken them a bit by using the Highlights slider.

And that's a good guideline for all your Adjust panel endeavors: the best results often come from combinations of several adjustments, not just one.

Changing a Photo's Colors

The Adjust panel lets you perform several types of color-related adjustments. With the Saturation slider, you can adjust the vividness of a photo's colors. Turn down the saturation to create a muted look or to compensate for a camera's overly enthusiastic built-in color settings. Or turn up the saturation to make a photo's colors more intense.

With the Temperature and Tint sliders, you can change a photo's color balance. Fix a color cast introduced by artificial light or caused by fading film. Or create a special effect to make a photo feel warmer or colder.

How can you tell if the colors you see on your screen will accurately translate to an inkjet or photographic print? Advanced Photoshop users rely on display-calibration hardware and other tools to calibrate their systems so that displayed colors match printed colors as closely as possible.

You can apply this strategy to iPhoto. Or you can take a simpler approach. First, calibrate your screen using the Displays system preference. Second, if you'll be creating your own inkjet prints, make test prints as you work on a photo, duplicating the photo as necessary to get different versions.

Finally, as with many aspects of the Adjust panel, there's a local angle to color adjustments. When you're printing a photo or using it in a print project, you can use the Adjust panel in those views to change colors without changing the photo everywhere you've used it.

Adjusting Color Saturation

To make a photo's colors more vivid, drag the Saturation slider to the right. To make colors more muted, drag the slider to the left.

Original

Increased Saturation

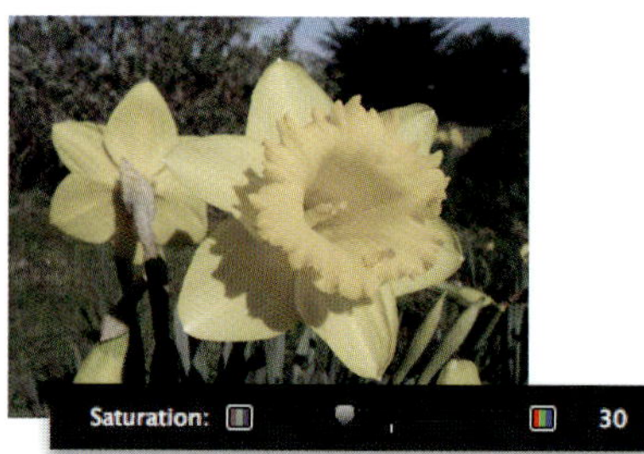

Decreased Saturation

Tips

Pale and pastel. To give a pastel-like quality to a photo's colors, decrease the saturation.

Going gray. If you drag the Saturation slider all the way to the left, you create a *grayscale* version of the photo. Generally, the B&W button does a better job, but experiment and see which version you like best.

Watch your gamut. If you significantly increase a photo's saturation, you probably won't be able to print a version that matches what you see on screen. Printers have a much narrower color range, or *gamut*, than does the Mac's screen.

Adjusting Color Balance

To adjust a photo's color balance, use the Temperature slider, the Tint slider, or both.

Temperature. The Temperature slider adjusts a photo's color temperature. To make a photo appear *cooler* (more bluish tones), drag the slider to the left. To make a photo appear warmer (more yellow/orange tones), drag the slider to the right.

Original

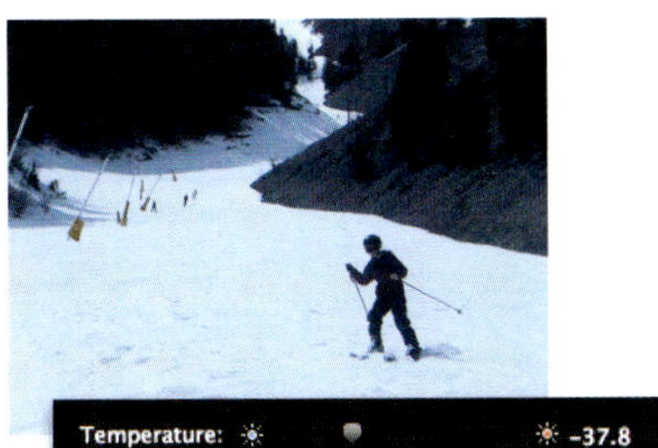

Cooler

Warmer

Tint. The Tint slider adjusts red/green color balance. If you drag the slider to the left, iPhoto adds red, making a photo appear less green. If you drag the slider to the right, you add green and lessen the amount of red. The Tint slider can help remove the greenish color cast that you may find in photos taken under fluorescent lighting.

Colorful Tips

Temperature Tips. Photos taken under incandescent light with your camera's flash turned off tend to have a yellowish cast to them. I like this warm look, but if you don't, try dragging the Temperature slider to the left to cool things off. If the corrected image looks dark, bump up the Exposure or mid-tone Levels slider.

You can often simulate different lighting conditions by shifting a photo's color temperature slightly. Warm up a photo to simulate late afternoon sun, or cool it down to simulate shade or twilight.

Old color photos often take on a reddish-yellow appearance as their color dyes fade. To fix this, drag the Temperature slider to the left a bit.

Gray Balancing. If you have an off-color photo containing an object that you know should be gray or white, click the eyedropper tool ( ), then click on part of the photo that should be gray or white. iPhoto adjusts the Temperature and Tint sliders as best it can to make the object a neutral gray.

Better Black and White

iPhoto's B&W effect does a good job of converting a color photo to black and white, but you can often improve on its efforts: after clicking B&W, adjust the Saturation, Temperature, and Tint sliders.

When you drag the color sliders after converting a photo to black and white, iPhoto blends the photo's red, green, and blue color channels in different ways. To make a black-and-white photo appear richer, bump up the saturation after clicking the B&W button. While you're experimenting, drag the Temperature and Tint sliders to see how they alter the photo's tonal values. (For you film fogies, this is the digital equivalent of exposing black-and-white film through color filters.)

After Clicking B&W Button

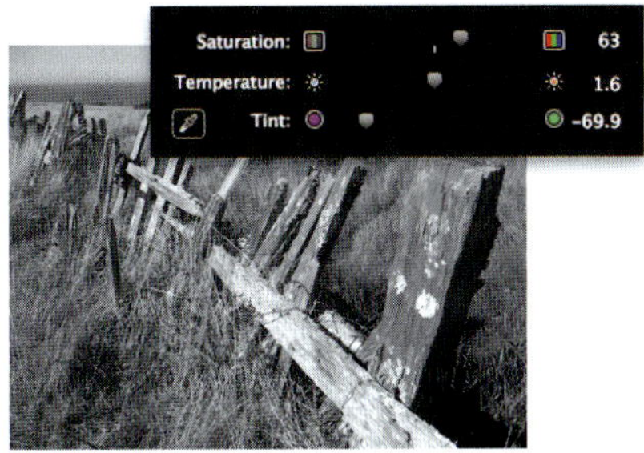

After Adjustments

Sharpening and Reducing Noise

All digital images—whether captured by a scanner or a camera—have an inherent softness. Some softness is introduced by inexpensive lenses. Still more is introduced by imaging sensors and their fixed grid of pixels.

Digital cameras compensate for this inherent softness by applying some sharpening immediately after you take a photo. You can often adjust the amount of sharpness they apply; I like to turn down the sharpness settings on my cameras, preferring to sharpen later, if necessary. (If you shoot in raw mode, your camera applies little or no sharpening to the image; see page 172.)

Inkjet printers and offset printing presses (including the kind used to print iPhoto books, greeting cards, and calendars) also introduce some softness. The bottom line: several factors are working against your image to obscure fine details.

And *that's* where sharpening can help. By sharpening a photo just before printing it, you can often get a much better print.

Sharpening Basics

To sharpen a photo, drag the Adjust panel's Sharpness slider to the right.

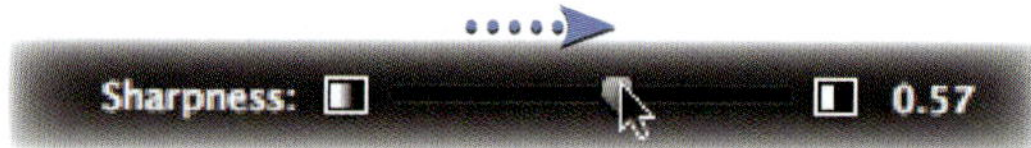

After Sharpening

Before Sharpening

Sharpening Tips

Should You Sharpen?

Just because digital images have an inherent softness doesn't mean that you should apply sharpening to every photo you take. First, consider the photo itself. A photo that lacks fine details—say, a close-up of a baby's face—won't gain much from sharpening, and may even be hurt by it. Conversely, a photo containing fine details—such as the one on the opposite page—may benefit greatly from sharpening.

Also consider how you'll be using the photo. A photo destined for an iDVD slide show or iMovie project probably doesn't need sharpening. A photo that you plan to print—either yourself or by ordering prints or a book—is a better candidate for sharpening, especially if the photo contains fine details.

Printing? Sharpen heavily. Don't be afraid to heavily sharpen a photo that you're going to print. Even if the photo looks a bit too sharp on screen, chances are it will print nicely.

View Right

iPhoto's edit view introduces some softness of its own when it scales a photo to whatever zoom setting you've made. To get the most accurate on-screen view possible, view your photo at 100 or 200 percent when making sharpness adjustments: press the 1 key to view at 100 percent, and the 2 key to view at 200 percent.

Also consider the paper you're using. Premium glossy photo paper shows fine details best, so photos destined for it can benefit from sharpening. On the other hand, matte- and luster-finish photo papers have a fine texture that obscures detail a bit.

The local angle. Just want to sharpen a photo for printing on your inkjet printer? Don't forget the option of sharpening using the Adjust panel in the custom print view—see page 199.

How it Works

Regardless of what you see on TV, no digital imaging program can turn a blurry photo into a sharp one. Instead, iPhoto detects boundaries of light and dark, and it makes light edges a bit lighter and dark edges a bit darker. When it's done right—that is, not to excess—our eyes perceive this as increased sharpness.

Reducing Noise in Photos

Photos taken in low light—indoors, with the flash turned off, for example—often have a grainy appearance, especially if you've used your camera's menus to turn up the ISO setting (page 232).

With a digital camera, high ISO settings basically amplify the signal from the camera's sensor. It's a bit like turning up the volume on a radio: it doesn't make the radio more sensitive to weak signals, but it does boost whatever signal is there.

But when you crank up the volume of a weak signal, the static gets louder, too. In a digital photo, this "static" is called *noise*, and it's especially noticeable in areas of little detail—a blue sky or a smooth-cheeked baby.

At moderate ISO settings, such as 200, noise tends to be subtle and may not even show up in prints. But at high ISO speeds, noise can be deafening, creating a speckled, snowy appearance like that of a weak TV signal.

To quiet down noisy shots, use the Adjust panel's Reduce Noise slider. The further you drag the slider, the stronger the noise reduction. Applied too heavily, noise reduction can give detailed areas a mottled, plastic look. Experiment with your noisy shots, remembering to zoom in for a closer look.

The Big Picture: Full-Screen Editing

When you're editing and enhancing a photo, it's often helpful to see the big picture—that is, to display your photo at as large a size as possible. When you go big, it's easier to perform color and exposure adjustments and to find flaws that need retouching.

iPhoto's full-screen editing view gives you a picture window into your pictures. Click the Full Screen button, and your Library list and iPhoto's buttons and controls step aside to make room for your photos. Move the mouse pointer to the top or bottom of the screen, and the menu bar or toolbar glide into view.

If you prefer to use full-screen view for all your editing tasks, use iPhoto's Preferences command to always have photos open in full-screen view; see page 170.

Full-screen view teams up nicely with another iPhoto feature: the ability to compare two or more photos in order to find the best shot in a series. You can display two or more photos side-by-side and even edit them.

It's worth noting that you can also compare photos in iPhoto's standard edit view and in the editing window (see page 232). But, because full-screen view maximizes your screen space, it's the best place for your photo-comparison sessions.

Switching to Full-Screen View

To edit a photo in full-screen view, select the photo and then click the Full Screen button ( ).

If you're already in the standard edit view, you can switch to full-screen view by clicking the same button.

To display a different photo, click its thumbnail.

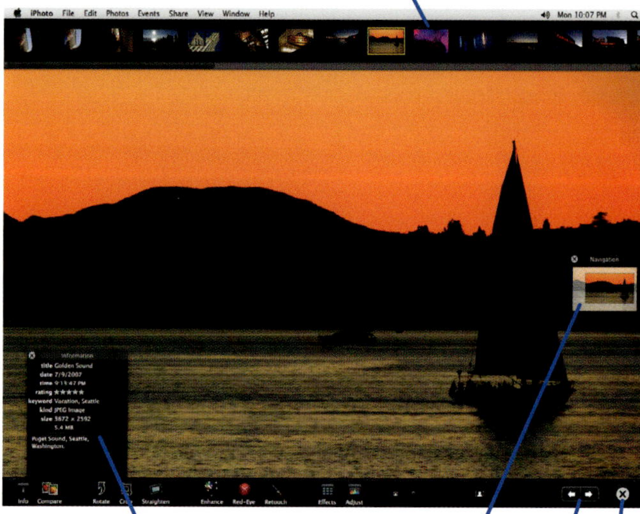

You can view and edit photo information in full-screen view; click the Info button to display the Information panel shown here.

If you've zoomed in on a photo, the Navigation panel appears. Drag the rectangle to quickly pan around the zoomed photo.

You can also move to the next or previous photo by clicking the arrow buttons or by using the arrow keys on your keyboard.

To exit full-screen view, click the ⊗ button. **Note:** You can also exit full-screen view by pressing your keyboard's Esc key, although this discards any edits you made.

Comparing Photos

It's always smart to take more than one version of an important shot—to experiment with different exposure settings or to simply increase your chances of capturing that perfect smile.

After you've imported those multiple variations into iPhoto, compare the photos to find the best one. (And if you don't want to see the rest, consider hiding them; see page 138.)

To compare photos

Comparing in edit view. If you're already working in full-screen edit view (opposite page), click the Compare button (). iPhoto loads the next photo and displays both side-by-side.

To remove a photo from the comparison, click the ⊗.

When you click a different thumbnail, its photo replaces the selected photo (in this example, the one on the left). To compare more than two photos, ⌘-click on their thumbnails. (You can compare up to eight photos.)

From browsing to comparing. You can also set up a comparison *before* entering edit view. Select the photos first, then click the Full Screen button (). For a review of ways to select photos, see page 147.

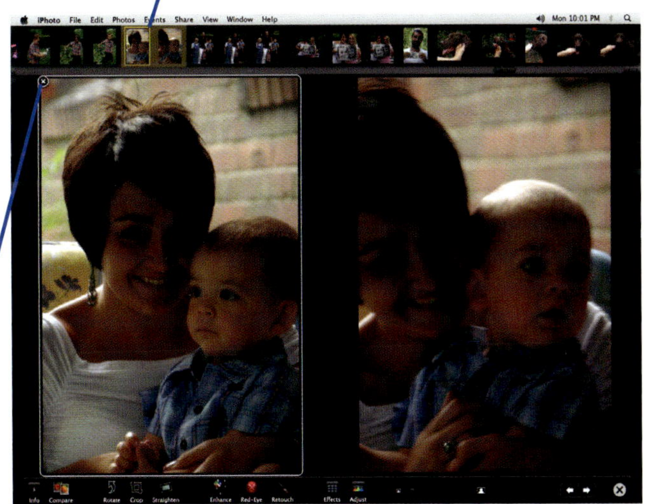

Tips for Full-Screen View

Show your stuff. Normally, iPhoto hides the thumbnails and toolbar unless you mouse to the top or bottom of the screen. But you can choose to display either or both all the time. To always see the toolbar, choose View > Show Toolbar; for thumbnails, choose View > Thumbnails > Always Show.

Move your thumbs. Thumbnails can appear along the left or right edge of the screen instead of along the top. Choose View > Thumbnails > Position on Left (or Position on Right). Since your screen is wider than it is tall, moving thumbnails to the side uses space more efficiently, especially when you are working with vertically oriented photos.

Grow more thumbs. You can see more than one row of thumbnails—handy when you want to edit a lot of photos. Choose View > Thumbnails, then choose how many rows or columns you want.

The shortcut menu. In full-screen view, you can still access some editing functions with the shortcut menu: just Control-click within the photo, and choose a command.

Editing Tips

The Edit Window

Normally, iPhoto displays the image you're editing within the iPhoto window itself. But you can also open and edit a photo in a separate window that has its own editing toolbar.

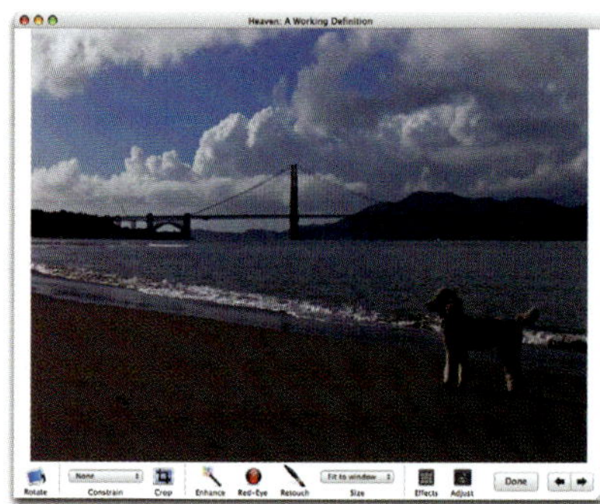

You can have multiple edit windows open simultaneously, which makes it easy to compare images. For example, if you've duplicated a photo a few times and are trying out different sharpening or exposure-correction approaches, you can open each version in its own window and compare them—and work on them at once.

To open an image in a separate window, Control-click on it and choose Edit in Separate Window from the shortcut menu.

Specifying Edit Preferences

Prefer editing in full-screen view? Or in the separate editing window? Use the Preferences command to control where iPhoto opens your photos for editing.

Choose iPhoto > Preferences, click General, then choose an option from the Edit Photo pop-up menu. To always edit in full-screen view, choose Using Full Screen. For the separate edit window, choose In Separate Window.

Tips for the Edit Window

Here are a few tips for taking advantage of the edit window.

Showing thumbnails. Normally, the edit window doesn't display a photo browser containing thumbnails of adjacent images. If you'd like to see them, choose View > Thumbnails > Show.

Switching between windows. When you have multiple edit windows open simultaneously, use the Window menu to switch between them and the main iPhoto window. Or use the keyboard: press ⌘-~ (that's the tilde, located above the Tab key) to cycle through open windows. That key sequence works in many Mac programs.

Zooming differently. Unlike iPhoto's standard edit view, the edit window has a Size pop-up menu that lets you choose a specific zoom percentage for your photo. As I mentioned on the previous page, if you're sharpening, you'll get the most accurate preview of your work by viewing at 100 or 200 percent.

Resizing the window. Remember that you can quickly resize the edit window to fill your screen by clicking the green button in the upper-left corner of the window or choosing Window > Zoom.

Copying and Pasting Adjustments

Sometimes, you might have a series of photos that can benefit from the same adjustments—maybe they're all similarly dark, for example, or all have the same color cast.

With the Copy and Paste buttons in the Adjust panel, you can apply one photo's adjustments to other photos. After tweaking a photo to perfection, click the Copy button in the Adjust panel. Next, open a different photo in edit view, display the Adjust panel, and click Paste.

The Keys to Editing

You can activate various editing tools by pressing a single key on your keyboard (see the table below).

Keyboard Editing

For this tool	Press
Crop	C
Straighten	S
Red-eye	R
Retouch	T
Adjust panel	A
Effects panel	E
White-point tool	W

While you're pawing your keyboard, remember that you can open a photo for editing by selecting the photo and pressing the Return key—you don't have to click the Edit button. To save changes and return to thumbnail browsing, press Return. To save changes and edit an adjacent photo, press an arrow key. To discard changes and exit edit view, press Esc. And to switch to full-screen edit view, press Option-⌘-F.

From Browsing to Editing

Want to go straight from browsing photos to editing one? Press Option while double-clicking a photo's thumbnail, and it opens in edit view. (And remember, if you always want iPhoto to work this way, use the Preferences command to set it up.)

From Publisher to Editor

Most of the time, you probably enter edit view while browsing your library or an album. But you can also enter edit view while working on a book, calendar, or greeting card: just Control-click on the photo and choose Edit Photo from the shortcut menu.

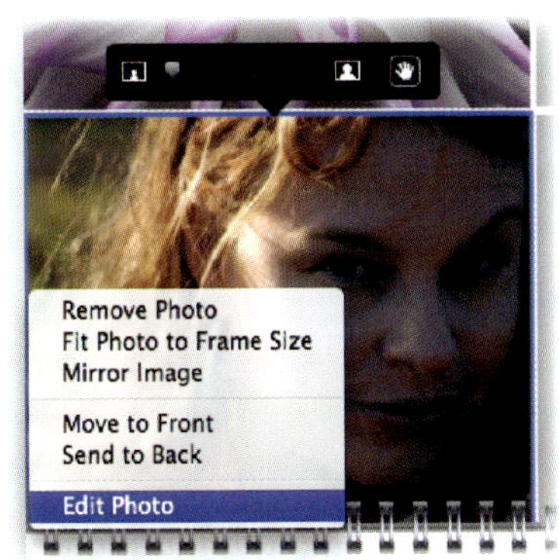

From Edit Thumbnails to Elsewhere

The thumbnail browser—that row of images at the top of the edit view—is a handy tool for quickly accessing another photo in the same event or album.

But it has another use, too: you can drag a thumbnail from the photo browser directly into an album, book, or slide show. If you're on an editing binge and suddenly realize that a certain photo would go nicely in a specific album, slide show, or book, there's no need to exit edit view. Just drag the photo from the photo browser to the album, slide show, or book.

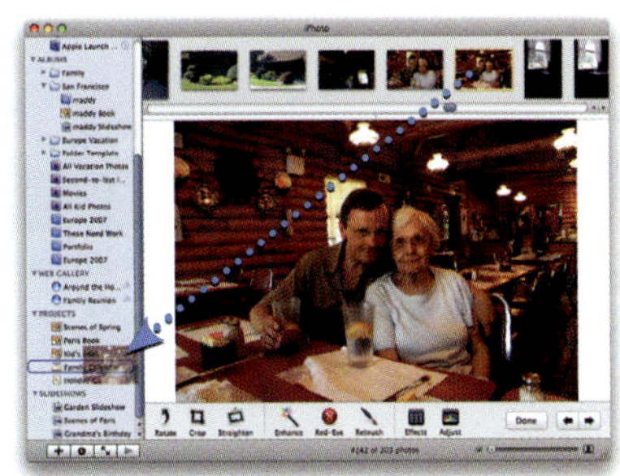

Shooting in Raw Mode

If you're an advanced photographer, a control freak, or both, there's an image format that may change the way you shoot. The image format is called *raw*, and it's supported by many mid-range and virtually all high-end cameras.

Here's why raw matters. When you shoot in JPEG format, your camera permanently alters the photo: tweaking color balance and saturation, adjusting sharpness, and compressing the image to use less space.

Today's cameras do these jobs well, but you pay a price: you lose some control. You can still adjust the color balance, exposure, and sharpness of a JPEG image, but within a relatively narrow range. Exceed those limits, and you risk visible flaws.

When you shoot in raw mode, your camera saves the exact data recorded by its light sensors. Instead of being locked into the camera's alterations, you get the original, unprocessed image data: the raw data. Transfer this raw image to the Mac, and you can use iPhoto or other imaging software to fine-tune the image to a degree that the JPEG format doesn't permit.

Shooting raw has drawbacks, and many photographers prefer the convenience and efficiency of JPEG. But for pixel perfectionists who want maximum control—especially over shots taken in tricky lighting conditions, such as candlelight—raw is the best way to shoot.

Choosing Raw

To shoot in raw mode, venture into your camera's menus—specifically, to the menu that controls image format. In some cameras, you'll find this option in the Mode menu. With others, such as the Canon EOS-10D shown here, this option is in the Quality menu.

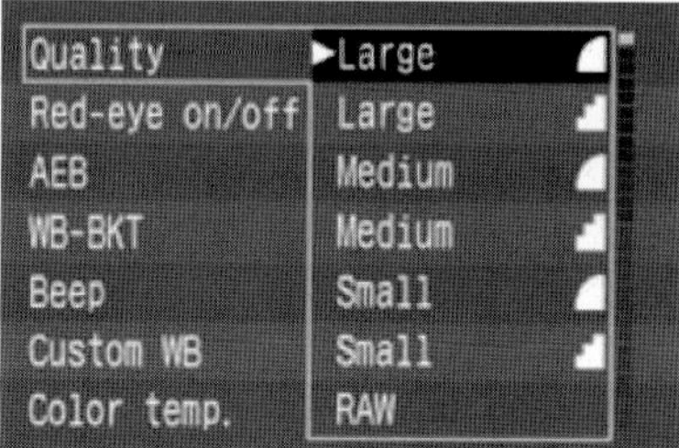

Make sure. It's a sad fact of life: each camera company has created its own raw format. Even if iPhoto supports your camera, it may not recognize its raw-format images. Before shooting raw, verify that iPhoto supports your camera's raw format. You may find that you need to update to a newer Mac OS X version—Apple often adds support for new cameras when it releases a Mac OS update. For a current list of supported cameras, go to www.macilife.com/iphoto.

Make room. Raw files are often several times larger than their JPEG equivalents. For example, an eight-megapixel JPEG might use 4MB while its raw version uses 16MB. Because you'll get fewer raw images on a memory card, you might want to buy a few extra cards.

Make time. With some cameras, raw images can take longer to save after you snap the shutter. If you're shooting a fast-changing scene, verify that your camera's raw mode is fast enough to keep up with your subject.

Those large raw files also take longer to transfer to the Mac. If your camera and Mac don't provide USB 2.0 interfaces, get a FireWire media reader and use it to transfer your shots (see page 133).

Learn more about raw-format photography.
www.macilife.com/iphoto

The Basics of Working with Raw Photos

In some ways, working with raw photos in iPhoto is no different than working with JPEG photos. You can import raw photos into your library, edit them using all of the edit-view features I've described previously, and share them using all of iPhoto's sharing features.

Importing raw photos. Aside from making sure you have plenty of free disk space, you don't have to do anything special to import raw photos into iPhoto. If iPhoto supports your camera's raw format, it imports the raw photos and stores them in your photo library.

JPEG companions. When you import raw photos, iPhoto creates JPEG versions of them. You don't see thumbnails for these JPEG companions in your photo library, but they're there.

iPhoto creates these JPEG versions for use by programs that don't understand the raw format. For example, when you access your iPhoto library from a different program, such as iDVD, that program uses these JPEG versions.

However, when you open a raw photo in edit view, iPhoto does indeed use the original raw-format image. For details on how iPhoto handles raw images during and after the editing process, see the following pages.

Raw plus JPEG. Some cameras save a JPEG version of a photo at the same time that you shoot a raw version. This is a handy convenience that gives you the best of both worlds: a compact JPEG and a *digital negative*—a phrase often used to describe raw-format images.

When you import photos from such a camera, iPhoto imports both the JPEG and the raw versions of each shot. It also *displays* both versions, and if you're planning to do some editing, you'll want to make sure you open the raw version—you want iPhoto to base your changes on the highest-quality version available.

To see which photo is the JPEG version and which is the raw version, open the Information pane and select one of the photos. iPhoto displays its format in the Kind area of the Information pane.

Raw and Leopard. Mac OS X 10.5 (Leopard) provides improved image quality for raw-format images. For more details, see the following pages.

Max Headroom: The 16-Bit Advantage

I've already mentioned one big benefit of shooting in raw format: you aren't locked into the color, sharpness, and exposure settings made by your camera.

Another advantage deals with something called *latitude* or *headroom*: the ability to make dramatic adjustments without risking visible flaws. Simply put, a raw image is more malleable than a JPEG.

Raw photos have more latitude because they store more image data to begin with. JPEG images are eight-bit images; each of the three primary-color channels—red, green, and blue—are represented by eight bits of data. That means that each channel can have up to 256 different tonal values, from 0 (black) through 255 (white). (Yes, things are getting a bit technical here, but such is life in the raw.)

Most cameras, however, are capable of capturing at least 12 bits of data for each color channel, for a possible 4,096 different levels. When a camera creates a JPEG, it essentially throws away at least one-third of the data it originally captured.

Most of the time, that loss of data isn't a problem. But if you need to make significant changes to an image's exposure and color balance, the more data you have to start with, the better. Where this extra latitude really pays off is with photos that were poorly exposed or taken under tricky lighting conditions.

Think of the extra data as money in the bank: when times get tough, you'll be glad it's there.

Working with Raw Images

How iPhoto Manages Raw Photos

iPhoto works hard to insulate you from the technicalities of working with raw photos. Here's a summary of how iPhoto works with raw captures.

When you import a raw photo, iPhoto stores it in your photo library.

iPhoto also creates a JPEG "stand-in" for printing and for use by other programs.

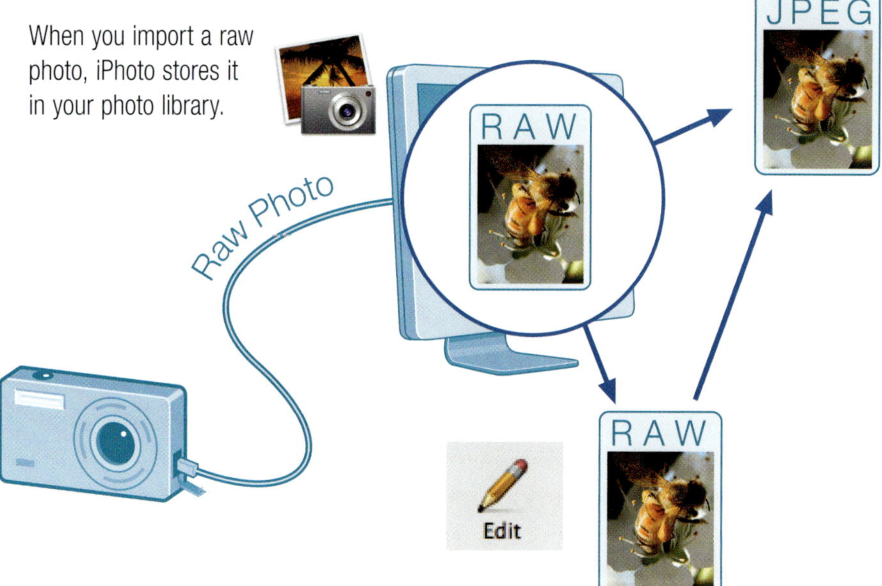

When you open a raw photo in edit view, iPhoto uses the original raw data that you imported. The RAW badge shown below appears near the bottom of the iPhoto window. RAW

When you leave edit view, iPhoto applies your edits to the raw data, then creates a JPEG photo that reflects the edits. The original raw file always remains unchanged, and you can access it in a couple of ways (see next page).

Editing an Already-Edited Raw Photo

If you edit a raw photo that you've already edited, iPhoto returns to the original raw version of the photo, and applies all the changes you've made—today's as well as yesterday's. This is a big step forward—as I mentioned on page 124, iPhoto '08's non-destructive editing gives you far more flexibility than earlier iPhoto versions provided. You can edit an image as many times as you like without worrying about introducing quality loss each time.

The exception to the rule. Ah, but there's an exception. If you edited a raw photo using an earlier iPhoto version, iPhoto '08 applies your latest edits to the edited JPEG that the older version of iPhoto created. Open that edited raw photo in edit view, and you won't see the RAW badge at the bottom of the iPhoto window—and any new edits you make are applied to the JPEG version.

So what do you do if you've been using iPhoto for a while and you want the full power of non-destructive editing? Select the edited version of the raw photo and choose Photos > Revert to Original. iPhoto discards the JPEG version (and any edits you made). Now you can bring iPhoto '08's non-destructive editing power to bear.

Exporting the Original Raw File

There's another way to get to your original raw data after making edits: export the original raw file from iPhoto.

First, select the JPEG version of the photo that iPhoto created after you edited the raw file. Next, choose Export from the File menu. Finally, in the Export Photos dialog box, choose Original from the Kind pop-up menu. Save the file somewhere convenient, such as on your desktop.

When might you use this approach? Here's one scenario. You've edited a raw photo in iPhoto, but then you decide to try editing the original raw file in Adobe Photoshop Elements. You want to keep the version you edited in iPhoto, so instead of reverting the photo or duplicating the edited version, you export a raw version for use in Photoshop.

Raw Photos and Photoshop

As I describe on the following pages, iPhoto pairs up beautifully with the Adobe Photoshop family. This marriage is particularly happy where raw images are concerned: in my experience, Adobe's Camera Raw software does a better job than iPhoto when it comes to decoding and processing raw files. Camera Raw, even the version included with Photoshop Elements, provides more control than iPhoto's edit view—and control is what raw is all about.

I use iPhoto to import and store raw photos, but when I'm after maximum quality, I bring those photos into Photoshop. I fine-tune the photos in Photoshop, export them as JPEGs, then import those JPEGs back into iPhoto for sharing. It's more work, but the results are better.

To ensure that iPhoto supplies Photoshop with the original raw file and not the JPEG stand-in, choose Preferences from the iPhoto menu, click Advanced, and then check the box labeled Use RAW Files with External Editor. If you don't, iPhoto will hand Photoshop a JPEG when you double-click the raw file—exactly what you *don't* want.

Saving as TIFF

Given that you're obsessed enough with image quality to be shooting in raw mode to begin with, you might lament the fact that iPhoto saves your edited images in the lossy JPEG format. You have a higher-quality alternative: tell iPhoto to use the TIFF format when saving edits to raw images.

To do so, choose Preferences from the iPhoto menu, click Advanced, and check the box labeled Save Edited RAW Files as 16-bit TIFFs. The resulting file will be much larger than a JPEG, but it will have that 16-bit headroom described on page 173, and it won't have any lossy compression.

Is it worth the extra storage space? Possibly, particularly for images whose brightness or levels you've altered dramatically. JPEG versions of these images might show that undesirable banding I mentioned on page 162. Consider doing some tests—let your eyes be your guide.

Raw Differences in the Exposure Slider

The Adjust panel's Exposure slider works differently when you're editing a raw photo. When you're editing a raw image, the Exposure slider works hard to avoid clipping blacks or whites: as data approaches the black or white limits of the histogram, it tends to bunch up before it finally spills over the brink into the abyss of clipping.

With JPEG photos, the Exposure slider shifts tonality in a different way, one that is more analogous to decreasing or increasing the camera's shutter speed.

One side effect of this approach is that it's much easier to introduce clipping by dragging the slider too far in either direction. A little bit goes a long way. For this reason, it's best to use the Levels sliders, particularly the mid-tone slider, to brighten or darken JPEG images.

Using iPhoto with Photoshop

The editing features in iPhoto can handle many image-tuning tasks, but at the end of the day, Adobe Photoshop is a better-equipped digital darkroom. Photoshop and Photoshop Elements, its lighter-weight, less-expensive cousin, provide far more sophisticated retouching tools and more ways to improve a photo's lighting and exposure. And as I mention on the previous page, Photoshop is also a better tool for serious raw-format work.

Photoshop (and Elements—everything on these pages applies to both) has slick features that have no counterparts in iPhoto. A library of exotic visual effects lets you simulate pastels, watercolors, brush strokes, and more. You can cut out the subject of a photo and superimpose it over a different background. You can stitch photos together into dramatic panoramas.

Using Photoshop for retouching doesn't mean abandoning iPhoto. The two programs work well together: you can use iPhoto to import, organize, and share photos, and Photoshop to enhance and retouch them.

Here's an introduction to some ways to turn iPhoto and Photoshop into collaborators.

From iPhoto to Photoshop

A photo in your iPhoto library needs some help. How do you open it in Photoshop? You have a few options.

Drag and drop. If you've already started Photoshop, its icon appears in your dock. To open a photo, simply click on the photo in your iPhoto library and drag it to the Photoshop icon in the dock. When the icon highlights, release the mouse button, and Photoshop opens the photo directly from your iPhoto library. This drag-and-drop technique is handy if you use Photoshop only occasionally.

Direct connection. If you end up using Photoshop for all your image editing, you can set up iPhoto to directly hand off photos to Photoshop.

Choose Preferences from the iPhoto menu and click the General button. From the Edit Photo pop-up menu, choose In Application. In the dialog box that appears, navigate to your Applications folder, then locate and double-click the icon for your version of Photoshop.

From now on, when you double-click a photo in your library, iPhoto will hand that photo off to Photoshop.

Note: If you plan to send raw images from iPhoto to Photoshop, be sure to follow the instructions on the previous page.

Middle ground. Maybe you use Photoshop frequently, but you also use iPhoto's edit view for cropping and other simple tasks. Head for the middle ground: specify Photoshop as your external image editor as described above, then return to the Preferences dialog box and choose one of the other Edit Photo options, such as In Main Window or Using Full Screen.

This restores iPhoto's factory setting: double-clicking a photo opens it in Edit view. But iPhoto doesn't forget that you're also a Photoshop user. To open a photo in Photoshop, Control-click on the photo and choose Edit in External Editor from the pop-up shortcut menu.

A Sampling of Elements Editing Ideas

Recovering Shadow and Highlight Details

iPhoto does shadow and highlight recovery (page 163); Photoshop does it better, providing finer control and better quality—especially if you shoot raw.

The Power of Layers

One of the best reasons to use Photoshop is a feature called *layers*. In Photoshop, an image can have multiple layers, and each layer can contain imagery or image-correction information. By using layers, you can make dramatic modifications to an image without ever altering the original data. This not only gives you more editing flexibility, it helps preserve image quality.

One particularly powerful use of layers involves selective lightening and darkening: changing the brightness of part of a photo without affecting other areas. It's a common technique in darkrooms, it's easy in Photoshop—and impossible in iPhoto.

There is more to layers than I can describe here. To learn about them, open Photoshop's online help and search for *layers* and *adjustment layers*.

Retouch the Flaws Away

iPhoto's Retouch tool does a good job of removing blemishes, dust specks, and other minor flaws. But it's no plastic surgeon.

In this photo, a pair of utility wires slice across a scenic vista. I used two retouching tools to improve the view.

Spot healing brush. Photoshop's *spot healing brush* works much like iPhoto's Retouch tool, only better. Click the spot healing brush tool in the tool palette, then specify a brush size that's slightly larger than the flaw you want to remove.

You can choose a brush size in the Tool Options toolbar, but it's more efficient to use the keyboard: press the right bracket key (]) for a larger brush, and the left bracket key ([) for a smaller one.

Next, simply click on the flaw you want to remove. To remove a larger flaw, such as a scratch or utility wire, click and drag to paint over it.

Clone stamp tool. The spot healing brush works best when the area surrounding the flaw is similar to the area containing the flaw. For this example, the spot healing brush did a great job of removing the wires from the areas surrounded by open sky or water, but it had trouble with areas that were surrounded by fine details, such as the offshore rocks and distant shoreline.

To fix those areas, I used Photoshop's clone stamp tool, which copies pixels from one area of an image to a different area.

After activating the clone stamp tool, point to an area adjacent to the flaw you want to fix. Then, hold down the Option key and click. Option-clicking tells Photoshop what area to use as a guide when healing the flaw, a process Photoshop gurus refer to as "defining the *source point*." After you've done that, paint across the flaw to copy pixels from the source point.

Slide Shows: iPhoto as Projector

With iPhoto's slide show features, you can display on-screen slide shows, complete with background music from your iTunes music library. iPhoto even displays a gorgeous transition between images. With the dissolve effect, for example, one photo fades out as the next one fades in.

And with the automatic Ken Burns effect, you can have iPhoto pan and zoom across each photo.

You can create two different types of slide shows: a *basic* slide show that provides quick results, and a *saved* slide show that allows for much more control, including the ability to specify different durations and transitions for every photo, and to design your own Ken Burns panning and zooming moves (see page 180). Apple calls this kind of slide show a *cinematic* slide show.

Most of the time, you'll want to add photos to an album before viewing them as a basic slide show. That way, you can arrange the photos in a sequence that best tells your story. If you're in a hurry, though, just select some photos in your library and then display the slide show as described at right. Or fine-tune an event, hiding photos you don't want to show, then select the event thumbnail.

Somebody get the lights.

Viewing a Basic Slide Show

In a hurry? Select the album or photos you want to screen, press the Option key, click the ▶ button near the bottom of the iPhoto window, and sit back and watch.

Want more control? Follow these instructions to customize your slide show's music, transitions, and more.

Step 1.

Select the photos you want to show.
To show an entire album or event, select the album or event.

Step 2.

Click the ▶ button.
The Slideshow dialog box appears.

Choose a transition style.

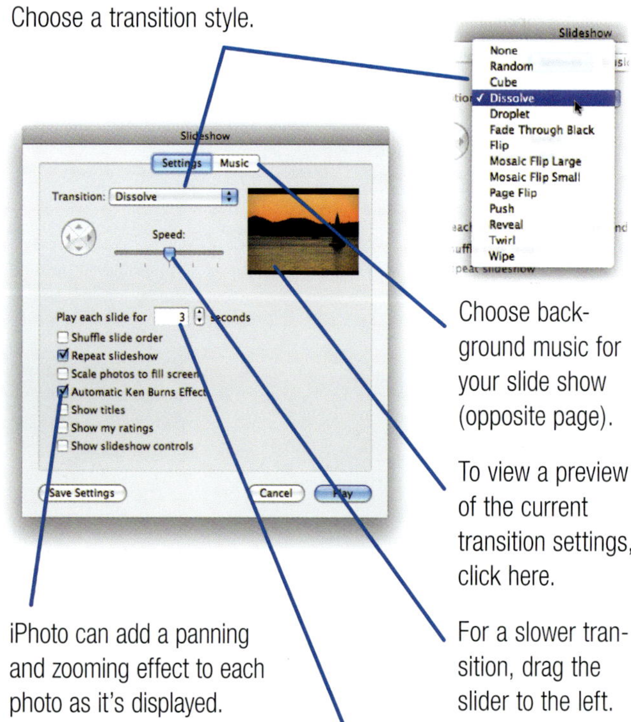

Choose background music for your slide show (opposite page).

To view a preview of the current transition settings, click here.

For a slower transition, drag the slider to the left.

iPhoto can add a panning and zooming effect to each photo as it's displayed.

Type a duration for each image, or click the up and down arrows to set a duration.

Step 2 (continued).

When this box is checked, iPhoto repeats the slide show until time itself comes to an end or until you press the Esc key or the mouse button, whichever comes first.

iPhoto can adjust the way it projects each picture to ensure that the screen is always completely filled, with no black borders. Note that vertically oriented shots and photos you've cropped may display strangely.

Display information and do some housekeeping while the slide show plays (below).

Displays the photos in random order instead of in the order they appear in the iPhoto window.

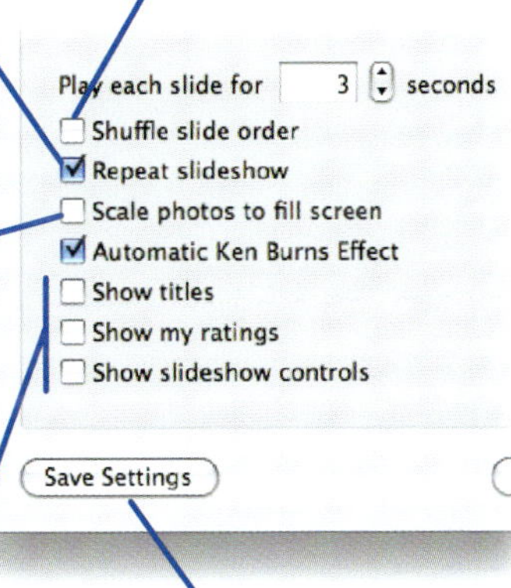

To save your slide show settings but not actually view the slide show, click Save Settings.

For a silent slide show, uncheck the box.

To assign an entire playlist to the slide show, choose the playlist's name.

Note: If you plan to export a slide show as a QuickTime movie, avoid using songs from the iTunes Store; see page 228.

To hear a song, double-click it or select it and click the ▶ button.

To sort the song list, click a column heading. You can also move the columns (drag their headings) and resize them (drag their boundaries).

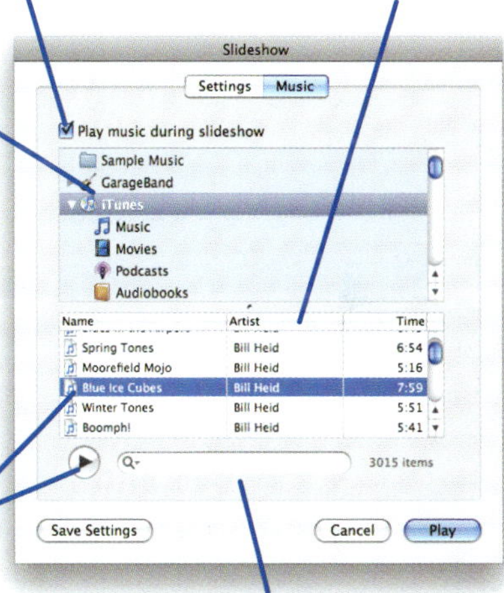

To narrow down the list of songs displayed, type part or all of a song or artist name.

Step 3.

Click Play to begin.

Screen Test: Reviewing Photos

If you move the mouse while a slide show plays back, a set of controls appears that lets you rotate, rate, and delete the currently displayed photo. This is a handy way to perform common housekeeping chores on a freshly imported set of photos: click Last Import, start the slide show, and get to work.

Note: The workings of the Trash button depend on what you're viewing. If you're viewing a slide show of an album, clicking the Trash button removes a photo from the album. If you're viewing photos directly from the Photo Library (for example, you clicked the Last Import item), clicking the Trash button moves the photo to the iPhoto Trash.

Beyond the Basic Slide Show

iPhoto's basic slide shows are easy to create, but they have design limitations. Every photo appears on the screen for the same amount of time. All photos have the same transition between them. And you can't design your own Ken Burns pan-and-zoom moves.

iPhoto provides a second type of slide show that shatters these limitations. Depending on whom you ask, it's called a saved slide show or a *cinematic* slide show. You'll call it cool.

With a saved slide show, you can specify different durations for each shot. That opening view of the Parisian skyline? Five seconds. That montage of mouth-watering bakery shots? Just a couple of seconds apiece.

A saved slide show also lets you mix and match transitions. For example, you might want a dissolve between most shots, but when you change major themes, spice things up with a page peel.

With a saved slide show, you can also tell Ken Burns exactly what to do. Set up your own pans and zooms to highlight a photo's subject. Or simply zoom in to crop a photo—no need to change the original photo in your library.

Similarly, you can apply black-and-white and sepia effects to the photos in a saved slide show without having to edit the original photos.

When you've finished designing your slide show, you can view it on screen, export it as a QuickTime movie (page 220), or send it to iDVD (page 298).

Creating a Saved Slide Show

Step 1.

Select the photos you want to include in the slide show. To include an entire album, select its name in the Albums list.

Step 2.

Choose File > New Album, select the Slideshow item, then click Create.

iPhoto creates a saved slide show, adds it to your Slideshows list, and displays the slide show editor.

Use the photo browser to jump to a specific photo. To change the sequence of photos, drag photos left or right. To delete a photo from the slide show, select it and press the Delete key. You can also select multiple photos by Shift-clicking and ⌘-clicking.

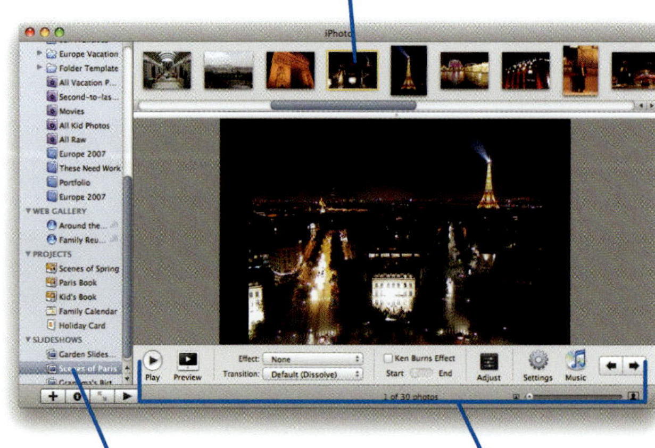

A saved slide show is a separate item in your library. If you based the slide show on an album, you can change the album without affecting the slide show. To rename a saved slide show, double-click its name.

Change slide show and music settings (see opposite page).

Step 3.

Use the tools in the slide show editor to design your slide show.

Most of these tools operate on the currently selected photo—the one that appears above the tools and is selected in the photo browser. But you can also apply some settings, such as transition, to several photos at once: select the photos' thumbnails in the photo browser, then make your settings.

Preview the selected photo's Ken Burns, duration, and transition settings.

Choose an effect and transition for the selected photo or photos.

Create a custom Ken Burns move for the selected photo (see "Tips for Ken Burns," below).

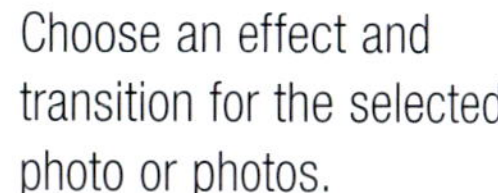

Play the slide show full-screen.

Choose music for your slide show; see page 179.

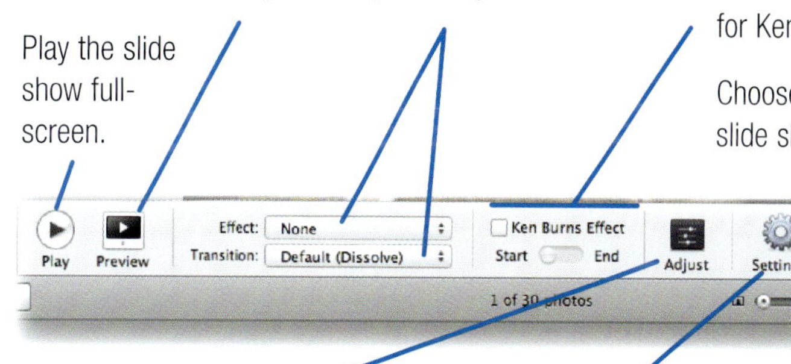

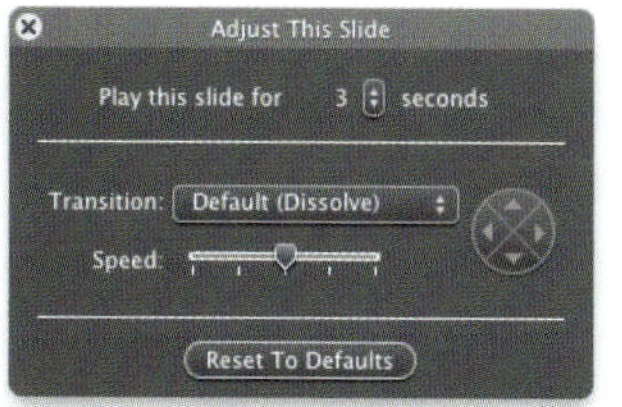

Display the Adjust panel, which lets you set a duration and transition for the selected photo or photos.

Most of these settings are identical to their counterparts on the previous page; for details on the differences, see the next page.

Display the previous or next photo (keyboard shortcut: left- or right-arrow key).

Tips for Ken Burns

By creating your own Ken Burns moves, you can better showcase and crop your photos, and more.

Creating a custom move. To create a Ken Burns move, check the Ken Burns Effect box. Then, use the size slider in the lower-right corner to specify the starting and ending zoom positions for the move. When you've zoomed in, you can specify which part of the photo you want to see by dragging within the photo.

Zooming without moving. You want to show only part of a photo, but you don't want to crop it because that would change its appearance throughout your library. Solution: Check the Ken Burns Effect box, click the Start position, then zoom in. Now press the Option key and click the End position.

Pressing Option tells iPhoto to copy the starting position to the ending position. I call this technique *soft cropping*—it's a great way to improve a photo's composition in a slide show without having to actually crop the photo.

Panning without zooming. This Option-key trick also lets you set up moves that pan across an image but don't zoom in or out. Set up the starting position, and drag within the photo to indicate which portion you want to see. Next, Option-click the End position and drag within the photo again.

Slide Show Tips

More Settings Options

When you're creating a saved slide show, you have some additional settings options. Use the Transition pop-up menu to specify a default transition for the slide show—that is, a transition that iPhoto will use unless you specify a different transition for a specific photo or photos.

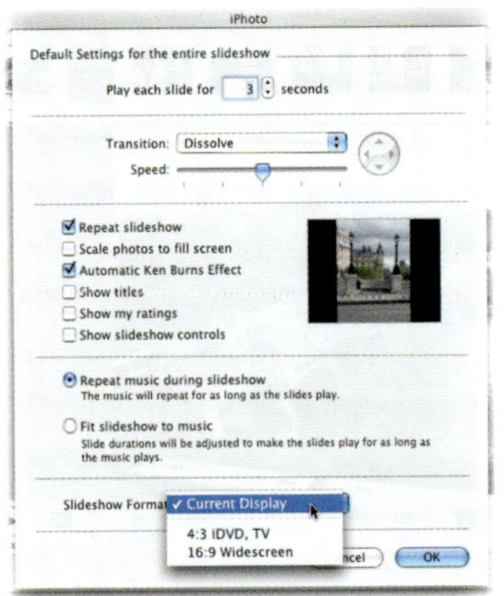

You can also have iPhoto fit the slide show's duration to match the length of its music soundtrack: click the Fit Slideshow to Music option.

And finally, you can have iPhoto create a widescreen (16:9 format) version of your slide show—ideal if you have an Apple Cinema display or want to create a widescreen-format DVD in iDVD. To create a widescreen slide show, choose 16:9 Widescreen from the Slideshow Format pop-up menu.

Adding to a Saved Slide Show

You've crafted a gorgeous slide show and decide you want to add more photos to it. It's easy: just drag the photos to the slide show's item in your Slideshows list. You can even drag photos from the edit view's photo browser into a slide show.

Ken Burns and Transitions

Planning to use the Ken Burns effect in a slide show? There's something you should know about Ken: he prefers the dissolve transition and the fade through black transition.

If you use any other type of transition in a slide show, a Ken Burns move will end right before the transition starts, and won't begin for the next photo until the transition has finished displaying. Having those smooth moves abruptly stop and start before and after each transition can appear jarring with some transitions.

Bottom line: if you're using Ken Burns, lean toward the dissolve or fade through black transitions.

When Just One Song Won't Do

Want more than one song to play back during a slide show? In iTunes, create a playlist containing the songs you want to use. Then, return to iPhoto and choose the playlist's name when assigning music to the slide show or album.

Customizing Basic Slide Shows

Basic slide shows—the kind you see when you click the Play button in the iPhoto window—provide a couple of customizing opportunities.

A song for each album. You can assign a different song to each of your albums. When you view a particular album as a basic slide show, iPhoto plays the song you've assigned to it.

To assign a song to a specific album, select the album in your Albums list. Next, drag a song from the iTunes window into the iPhoto window. iPhoto asks if you'd like to "make the selection your default slideshow music." Click OK. To assign a different song to a different album, repeat this drill.

Custom settings, too. Every album can have its own basic slide show settings—and not just for music. All of the other options that you can adjust in the Slideshow dialog box—transition style, photo scaling, and so on—can also apply on an album-by-album basis. Just select the album whose settings you want to adjust, click the Play button near the bottom of the iPhoto window, make your adjustments, and click Save Settings.

Keep in mind that these tips refer to basic slide shows—the kind I described on pages 178–179. Saved (cinematic) slide shows can obviously have their own settings, too, but you adjust them using the slide show editor.

Add a Slideshow Button

If you frequently create saved slide shows, you might want to add a Slideshow button to iPhoto's window—it's a bit more convenient than using the New Album command. Choose View > Show in Toolbar > Slideshow.

While you're customizing the toolbar, consider adding or removing other buttons to reflect the way you use iPhoto.

Creating Special Effects

You can add some interesting special effects to your slide shows by duplicating photos, modifying the duplicates, then sequencing them in the slide show. For example, you can have a photo start out in black and white and then dissolve or wipe into a color version.

To duplicate a photo, select it, then choose Duplicate from the Photos menu (⌘-D).

Choosing Display Preferences

You can have iPhoto display additional information and other items during a slide show. For a basic slide show, use the Slideshow dialog box. For a saved slide show, use the Settings dialog box.

Display Titles. Each photo's title appears in the upper-left corner of the screen.

Slide Show Keyboard Controls

To Do This	Press
Pause the slide show	Spacebar To resume the slide show, press the spacebar again.
Adjust the speed of the slide show	The up arrow and down arrow keys
Manually move through the slide show	The left arrow and right arrow keys
Rate the currently displayed photo	0 (zero) through 5
Rotate the currently displayed photo	⌘-R (clockwise) or Option-⌘-R (counterclockwise)
Stop the slide show	Esc (or click the mouse button)

Display My Ratings. Each photo's rating appears in the center at the bottom of the screen.

Display Slideshow Controls. The rotation, rating, and deletion tools described on page 181 appear immediately—no need to move the mouse first.

Exporting a Slide Show as a QuickTime Movie

Want to email a slide show to someone or post it on a Web site? Configure the slide show settings as desired, then use the Export command to create a QuickTime movie as described on page 220. Feeling ambitious? Take things a step further: Import the movie into GarageBand and add narration and chapter markers to create a "slide show podcast" (page 376).

Note: If you plan to distribute your slide show's movie, avoid using iTunes Store purchases as soundtracks—the songs won't play on computers that aren't authorized for your iTunes account (for a workaround, see page 229). Note that this restriction does not apply to iTunes Plus purchases, which lack DRM protection.

More Slide Show Tips

Use iPhoto to Create Titles

To earn some extra style points, sprinkle some titles into a slide show. For example, create a set of titles—one for each destination—for your vacation slide show.

You already have a great program for making titles. It comes with pre-designed styles that are ready for your own photos and text. The program is called iPhoto.

By combining iPhoto's greeting card features with the Mac's ability to create a PDF file of just about anything, you can create great-looking titles and add them to your slide shows.

Step 1. Select the photo or photos that you want to be part of your title.

Step 2. Click the Card button at the bottom of the iPhoto window.

Step 3. Choose the Postcard style, then choose a theme. (For details on creating greeting cards, see page 218.)

Step 4. Want text? In the greeting card editor, use the Design pop-up menu to choose a design that allows for text. Type your text and perform any other design tweaks.

Step 5. Choose File > Print.

Step 6. In the Print dialog box, click the From button and be sure that the page range is *1 to 1*. (There's no need to create a PDF of the "back" of your postcard, unless you want to use it in your slide show, too.)

Step 7. Click the PDF pop-up menu and choose Save PDF to iPhoto.

iPhoto and Mac OS X go to work, and a few moments later, your library contains a PDF of your postcard. To see it, click the Last Import item in the Recent list.

Your PDF title is ready for its screen debut. If you've already created a slide show, drag the title to the slide show in your Slideshows list. If you haven't created the slide show yet, add the title to the album where you've stashed the slide show's images.

Variations. To animate your title slides, use the Ken Burns effect. Here's a fun trick: Follow your title with the same photo that you used in the title. Apply the Ken Burns effect to the title so that it zooms in slowly, ending at a point where the photo almost fills the viewing area. Use a cross-dissolve effect between the title and the following photo. When you play your slide show, the title will zoom in, then its background and text will fade away, leaving just the photo.

Here's another way to put Ken to work. Use one of the postcard styles that holds two or more photos, then create a Ken Burns move that slowly pans across the photos.

You can also save a book or calendar page as a PDF and add it to a slide show. Making a slide show of a three-week road trip? Start it with a calendar page whose dates contain photos from the trip. Then, use the Ken Burns effect to pan across the calendar page.

Sharing a Slide Show Using iChat Theater

If you use Mac OS X 10.5 (Leopard), you have yet another way to share a slide show: iChat Theater. This sublimely cool addition to Apple's instant-messaging software lets you broadcast a slide show (among other things) to people with whom you're chatting. They'll see Ken Burns moves and transitions, and will even hear your background music.

And your friends don't have to be using Leopard, either—earlier iChat AV versions can also view iChat Theater broadcasts, as can compatible instant-messaging software for Windows.

Note: iChat Theater can broadcast basic slide shows only; you can't broadcast a saved slide show. (Workaround: Export the slide show as a QuickTime movie, then broadcast the movie using iChat Theater.)

Sharing a Basic Slide Show

Step 1. Choose File > Share iPhoto With iChat Theater.

A media browser appears.

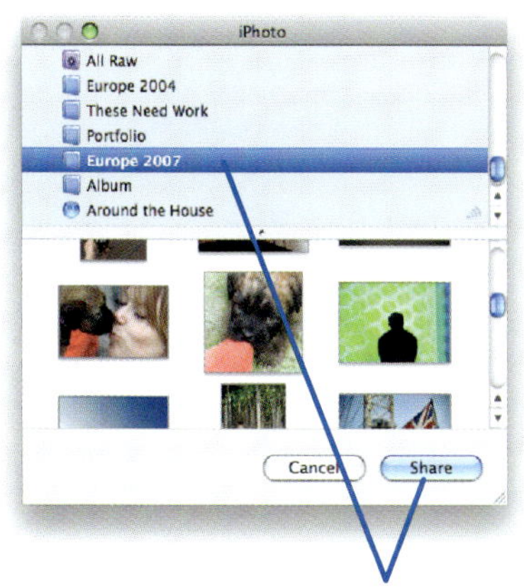

Step 2. In the media browser, select an album, then click Share.

iChat tells you to invite a buddy to a video chat.

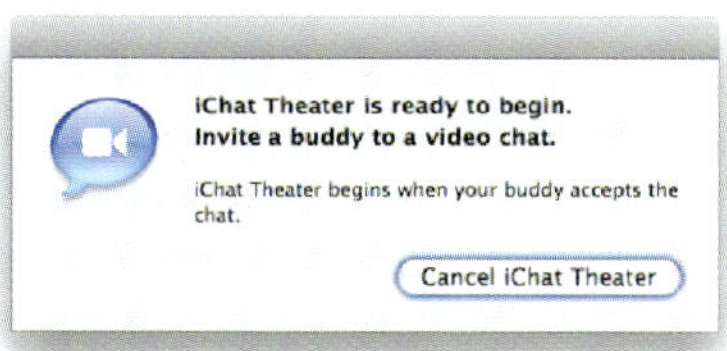

Step 3. Establish a video chat: select a name in iChat's Buddy List window, then click the video camera button (■◂) at the bottom of the window.

As soon as your victim accepts the invitation, the slide show begins.

Your Mac switches to iPhoto, where a window lets you control the slide show.

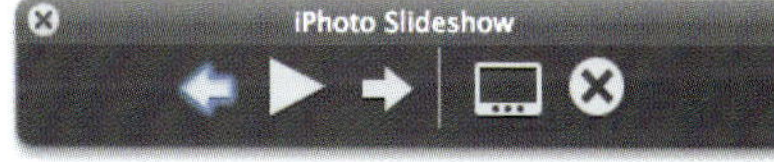

Notes and Tips

Already connected? The instructions above assume that you haven't yet begun a video chat with someone. If you're already in a video chat, skip Step 3.

Sound options. Your chat buddy will hear whatever music you've assigned to basic slide shows (page 179). If your Mac has a microphone, your chat buddy will *also* hear you talk. If you'd rather not broadcast a music soundtrack—maybe you'd prefer to narrate—uncheck the Play Music During Slideshow box in iPhoto's Slideshow dialog box. (You'll need to do this before starting the slide show broadcast.)

Conversely, if you don't want your buddy to hear you type or talk during a slide show, click the Mute button (🎤) in the Video Chat window.

Sharing other items. The iPhoto/iChat connection goes beyond slide shows. Want to broadcast the photos from an event without creating an album? Start a video chat, then drag the event thumbnail into the Video Chat window.

You can also broadcast just a few photos: select them, then drag them into the Video Chat window.

Sharing Photos via Email

Email takes the immediacy of digital photography to a global scale. You can take a photo of a birthday cake and email it across the world before the candle wax solidifies. It takes just a few mouse clicks—iPhoto takes care of the often tricky chores behind creating email photo attachments.

iPhoto can also make images smaller so they transfer faster. Take advantage of this feature, and you won't bog down your recipients' email sessions with huge image attachments.

Normally, iPhoto uses the Mac OS X Mail program to email photos. Using a different email program, such as Microsoft Entourage? Use the Preferences dialog box to specify your email program.

Step 1. Select the Photos

Select the photos you want to email. Remember that you can select multiple photos by Shift-clicking and ⌘-clicking.

Step 2. Click the Email Button

iPhoto displays the Mail Photo dialog box.

Step 3. Specify a Size, then Click Compose

iPhoto can make the images smaller before emailing. (This doesn't change the dimensions or file sizes of your original images, which iPhoto always stores in all their high-resolution glory.)

When you click Compose, iPhoto adds the photos to a new, blank email, which you can complete and send on its way.

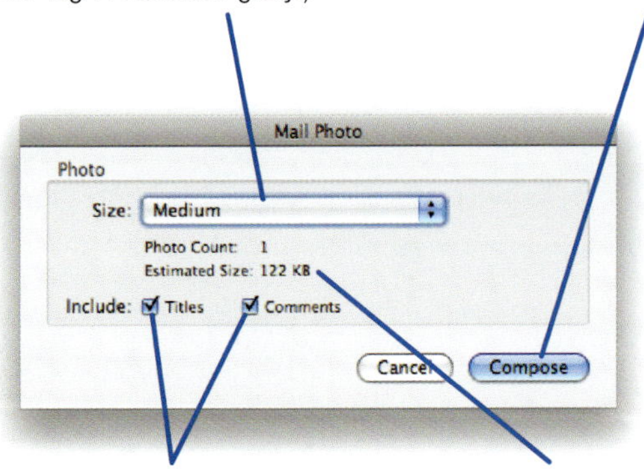

You have the option to include titles and comments along with the images—another good reason to assign this information when organizing your photos.

iPhoto estimates the size of the final attachments. If you're sending images to someone who is connecting using a modem (as opposed to a high-speed connection), try to keep the estimated size below 300KB or so. As a rule of thumb, each 100KB will take about 15 seconds to transfer over a 56 kbps modem.

Exporting Photos By Hand

When you email a photo using iPhoto's Email button, iPhoto uses the name of the original photo's disk file as the name of the attachment. Problem is, most of your photos probably have incomprehensible filenames, such as *200203241958.jpg*, that were assigned to them by your digital camera.

You might want an attachment to have a friendlier file name, such as holidays.jpg. For such cases, export the photo "by hand" and then add it to an email as an attachment. Choose Export from iPhoto's File menu, and be sure the File Export tab is active.

Export the photo as described at right. Save the exported photo in a convenient location, such as on your desktop. (You can delete it after you've emailed it.) Finally, switch to your email program, create a new email message, and add the photo to it as an attachment.

The settings below are good starting points for exporting a photo by hand. Here are a few more details and pointers.

The JPEG format is best for emailing, but you might choose the TIFF format if you're exporting a full-resolution version of a photo for use in a page-layout program.

Higher quality settings mean larger image files. Medium is a good compromise.

When you check this box, iPhoto adds the photo title and any keywords to the image's metadata (see page 229). This is useful if you plan to use the photo with other image-management programs, such as Apple's Aperture or Adobe Lightroom.

For emailing, Medium is a good size. You have additional options, though, including the ability to specify exact pixel dimensions.

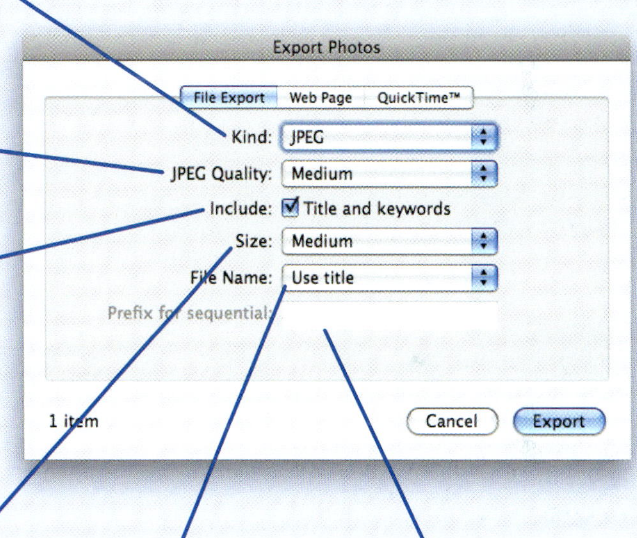

If you titled a photo (page 140), you can have iPhoto use the title as the exported photo's file name. When exporting just one photo, you can choose Filename and then type a name after clicking Export.

Exporting multiple photos? You can choose Sequential from the File Name pop-up menu, and then type a prefix here. iPhoto names the files accordingly. For example, if you type *dog* as the prefix, the files are named *dog1.jpg, dog2.jpg, dog3.jpg*, and so on.

Sharing Photos via Web Galleries

Email is an easy way to share photos over the Internet, but it has its drawbacks. Emailing photos to a large group of friends and family is a chore. And your recipients end up with a collection of photos scattered throughout their email inboxes.

If you have an account with Apple's .Mac Internet service, you have a much better way to share photos over the Internet: *Web gallery albums*. Publish some photos as a Web gallery album, and friends and family can view the photos on the Web. Instead of dealing with clumsy email attachments, they can visit a sharp-looking Web page that makes your photos look their best.

That isn't all. You can set up a Web gallery album with options that no email program can match. Allow visitors to download your photos so they can print them or add them to their own photo collections.

You can even allow visitors to upload their own photos to a gallery album. If the entire family was shooting photos at the reunion, set up a gallery album that lets everyone contribute his or her best shots.

It gets even better. Other iPhoto '08 users can subscribe to your Web gallery albums—much as they would subscribe to a podcast. Add new shots to an album, and they'll automatically appear in someone else's iPhoto. And if you have an iWeb site, you can add your gallery albums to any iWeb page (page 405).

Emailing photos seems kind of old-fashioned, doesn't it?

Creating a Web Gallery Album

Step 1. Select some photos, or better yet, select an album or event.

Step 2. Click the Web Gallery button or choose Share > Web Gallery.

Step 3. Specify your Web gallery options, then click Publish.

To restrict access, choose a different option (see page 190).

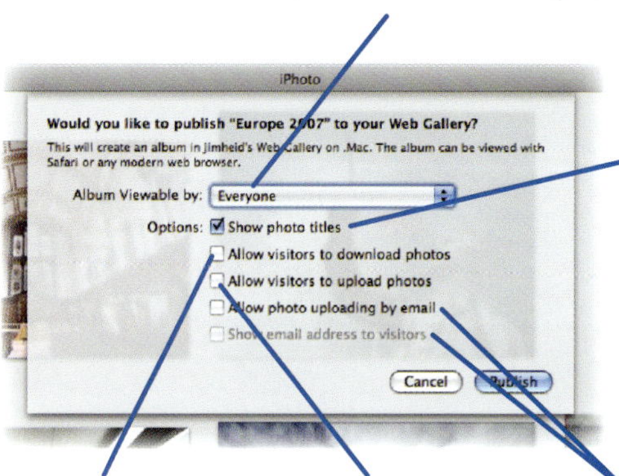

What's in a name? Another good reason to title your best shots (page 142). Didn't add titles? Uncheck the box, lest visitors see names like DSC9843.JPG.

Take-out available? To let visitors download your photos, check this box.

Pitch in? To let visitors upload their own photos, check this box.

Via email? You can add photos to the album by emailing them (see page 190). To let any visitor contribute by email, check the last option, too.

After Publishing

When you click Publish, iPhoto uploads your photos to .Mac. The gallery album appears in the Web Gallery list.

Select this item, and the album's photos appear along with the album's Web address, which you can click (see page 190).

To email someone about your new album, click Tell a Friend.

Working with Gallery Albums

Changing a Gallery Album

You can change a gallery album that you've published—keep it fresh, change settings, and more.

Change the content. To add new photos to the gallery album, drag them to the album in the Web Gallery list. To remove a photo from the gallery album, select the photo and press the Delete key. You can also edit photo titles and change the order of photos.

After making changes, click the update icon ( ) next to the published album's name. iPhoto updates the album on the Web.

Change settings. Changed your mind about allowing downloads? Did you decide to make a public album private? Select the published album, then click the Settings button to access the same options shown on the opposite page.

Collect contributions. If you've allowed others to upload photos to the album, you can update the album to grab the latest additions. Click the update icon; if iPhoto finds new photos, it downloads them.

Delete an album. To completely remove a gallery album from your .Mac account, select the album in the Web Gallery list, and then press the Delete key.

Subscribing to a Gallery Album

You can subscribe to a gallery album that another iPhoto '08 user has created. When you do, the album appears in your copy of iPhoto. You can enjoy and share the photos without having to visit the Web page, and if the creator of the album changes it, iPhoto can update your copy.

On the gallery album page, click Subscribe.

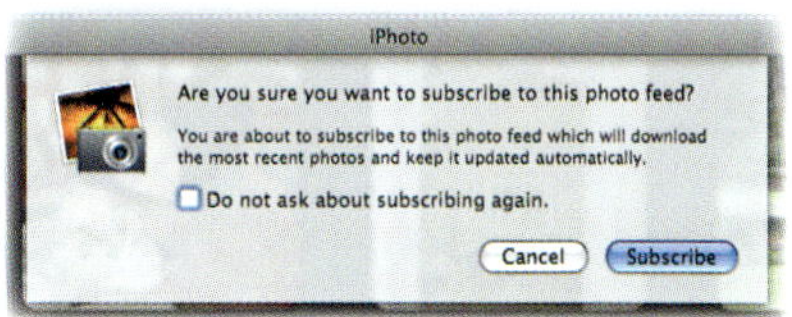

Click the Subscribe button or press Return. iPhoto loads the photos from .Mac and adds the gallery album to the Subscriptions area.

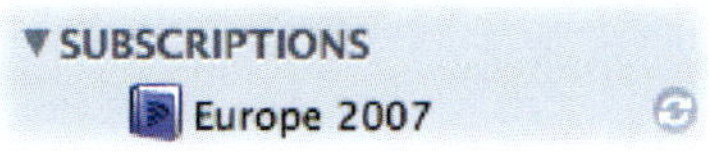

Now what? You can do almost anything with the photos in a subscribed album: print them, use them in slide shows, create calendars, and so on. You can assign titles and keywords and hide the shots you don't like. But you can't edit a photo—not without some simple trickery (see page 190).

Updating. To update an album to which you've subscribed, click the update icon to the right of its name ( ). iPhoto downloads any new photos.

Auto update. To have iPhoto check your subscriptions automatically, choose iPhoto > Preferences, then click Web Gallery. Choose an interval from the pop-up menu.

Unsubscribing. No longer want to subscribe to an album? Select it in the Subscriptions list and press the Delete key. iPhoto gives you the option of moving the photos into your library—if you still want to access the photos but don't care about updating, for example.

Web Gallery Tips

The Gallery Album Page at a Glance

Here's a look at the Web gallery albums your online fans will see, along with a tour of their features.

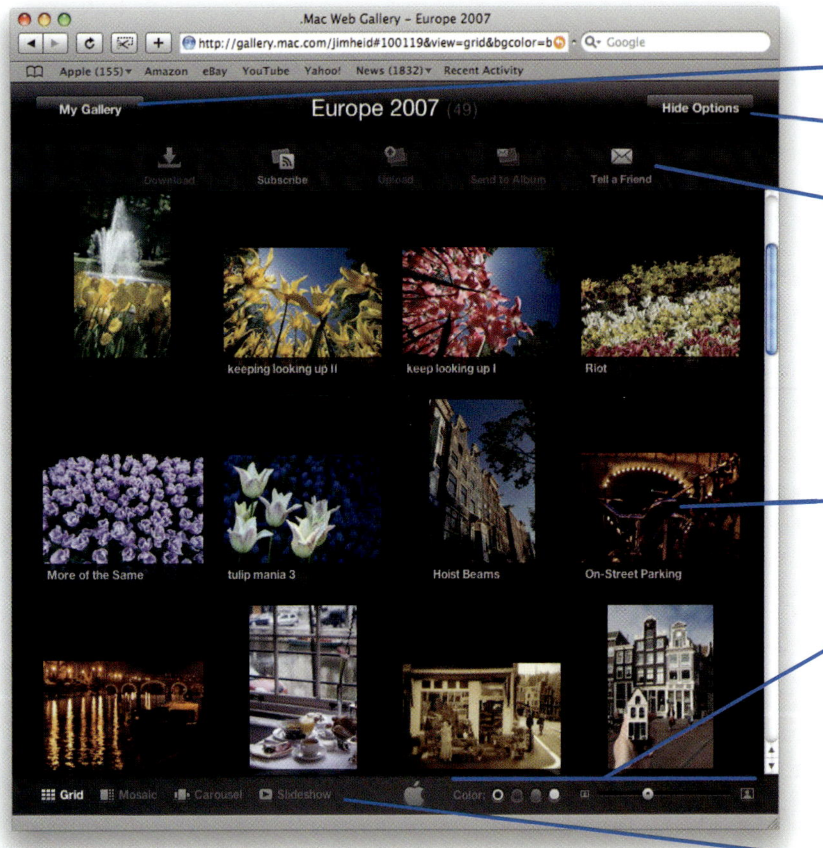

View the gallery index page (below).

Hides (or shows) the toolbar below.

From left to right: Download the album's photos, subscribe to the album, upload photos, email photos to the album, and tell a friend. As shown here, some buttons might be disabled, depending on the album's publishing options.

To view a larger version of a photo, click its thumbnail. When viewing a large version, you have the option to download just that photo (if the publisher has allowed downloads).

Change the album's background color and adjust thumbnail sizes.

View the gallery in different ways. The Mosaic option displays one large photo and many small thumbnails. Carousel resembles the iTunes Cover Flow view. Slideshow displays a full-screen slide show.

Notes and Tips

The index page. Click the My Gallery button on a gallery album, and you see a visual table of contents for all the albums you've published. Each album has its own thumbnail, and you can skim across the thumbnails to see its photos.

Changing the index page name. Is the name "My Gallery" too generic, too dorky, or both? Change it. Choose iPhoto > Preferences, click Web Gallery, then type a name.

Tip: You can also use the Preferences dialog box to stop publishing an album: select it and click Stop Publishing.

iPhone and iPod touch. You can view Web galleries using the Safari browser on an iPhone or iPod touch—they appear in a special format for the small screen.

Controlling Access to Albums

Who gets to see your albums? You decide when publishing the album, or afterwards. Choose one of these options from the Album Viewable By pop-up menu.

Everyone. Any stranger who finds your gallery pages can see the album.

Only me. Only you—to see the album, you must type your .Mac account name and password.

Aunt Fern. Okay, it doesn't say that. But you can specify a name and password that visitors must type to see the album. To create a name and password for the album, choose Edit Names and Passwords. In the next dialog box, click the plus sign, and type a name and password. Give that name and password to everyone who needs to see the album.

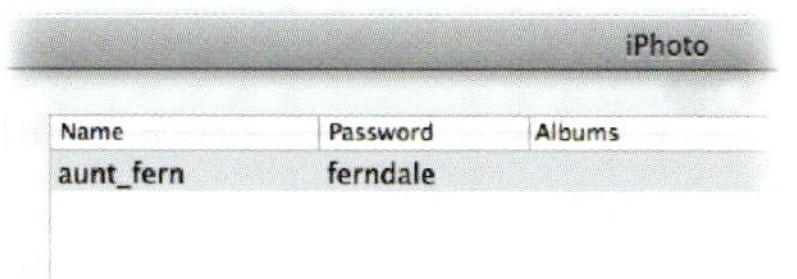

Uploading by Email

When you set up a gallery album to allow uploads via email, .Mac gives you a "secret" email address for that album. To see the address, select the album in your Web Gallery list—the address appears in the upper-right corner of the iPhoto window. Give this email address to your friends, and they can add photos via email.

jimheid-83pq@gallery.mac.com

To upload a photo via email, send the photo as an attachment to the album's secret email address. The email's Subject field becomes the photo title. You can send multiple photos in one email, if you like.

The iPhone angle. You can use the secret email address to upload photos from an iPhone, but there's an easier way that eliminates pecking out the address.

On your iPhone, display the photo you want to upload. Tap the button, then tap Send to Web Gallery. In the next screen, tap the name of the album where you want the photo to be stored.

Editing a Photo from a Subscription

Normally, iPhoto doesn't let you edit a photo from an album that you've subscribed to. If you open the photo in edit view, all the tools are disabled.

The workaround is easy: Add the photo to an album in your iPhoto library. Then, select the photo in that album and open it in edit view.

A Sampling of Web Gallery Ideas

You might simply use gallery albums to share photos with friends and family without having to use email. But the possibilities go beyond that. Here are a few ideas to get you thinking.

Following along. Hitting the road? Set up a gallery album that allows email uploads from you alone, then email photos as you go—from your iPhone, if you like. Friends can follow your progress by visiting the gallery page. And if they have iPhoto '08, they can subscribe to the album and set up iPhoto to update every hour or every day.

A group effort. Attending a party or any event where cameras are out in force? Set up a gallery album that allows email uploads from anyone, then send the "secret" email address to the partygoers. (Better yet, create the album *before* the party, and print the email address on the invitation.)

When the partygoers return home, they can email their favorite shots to the gallery or use the gallery's Upload button. The result: a collaborative album.

A kid's world. Want to share photos of the kid? Create a gallery album with restricted access, then give the name and password to folks who deserve to receive them. Set up the album to allow downloads so that grandparents can make their own prints.

More Internet Sharing Options

Chances are most of the Internet sharing you do will be through email, .Mac Web gallery albums, and iWeb photo albums. But when you're in the mood for something completely different, iPhoto is ready. You can also create custom Web photo albums as well as slide shows that are shared through Apple's .Mac service.

.Mac slide shows are a fun way to share photos with other Mac users. Publish some photos as .Mac slides, and other Mac OS X users can configure their Macs to use those photos as their screen savers.

You might create a custom Web album if you already have your own Web site, perhaps one that is served by your local Internet provider rather than Apple's .Mac service.

If you're a Web publisher, you can modify these pages as you see fit. You might open them in a program such as Adobe Dreamweaver, embellish them with additional graphics or other tweaks, and then upload them to a Web site. It's a lot more work than creating Web albums with iWeb, but has the potential to give you much more control over your designs.

iPhoto's Web pages are on the bland side. To spice up iPhoto's HTML exporting, try an iPhoto add-on called BetterHTMLExport (www.geeksrus.com). BetterHTMLExport provides numerous design templates for you to choose from and modify.

Creating a .Mac Slide Show

Step 1. Select the photos you want to publish. To select an entire album or event, click its name.

Step 2. Choose .Mac Slides from the Share menu.

iPhoto connects to .Mac, then displays a message asking if you're sure you want to publish the slide show.

Step 3. Click the Publish button.

iPhoto transfers your images to your iDisk. When the transfer is complete, a message appears enabling you to send an announcement email. The announcement contains instructions on how users can access the slide show.

To view a .Mac slide show, use the Desktop & Screen Saver system preference.

Tip: If you frequently publish .Mac slides, you can add a button to the bottom of the iPhoto window for doing so. Choose View > Show in Toolbar > .Mac Slides.

Exporting Web Pages

You can export photos and albums as Web pages to post on Web sites or burn to CDs (opposite page). iPhoto creates small thumbnail versions of your images, as well as the HTML pages that display them. (HTML stands for *HyperText Markup Language*—it's the set of codes used to design Web pages.)

To export a Web page, select some photos or an album, choose Export from the File menu, then click the Web Page tab. Specify the page appearance and dimensions of the thumbnails and the images, then click Export. In the Export dialog box, click the New Folder button to create a new folder. (The export process will create several folders, so it's a good idea to stash everything in one folder.)

Check out my Flickr photos.
www.flickr.com/photos/jimheid/

The Flickr of Addiction

If you aren't a .Mac subscriber and you don't want to fuss with Web servers, you have other Web album options. Most online photofinishers provide free Web album features, but given that the primary focus of these sites is to sell prints and photo gifts, your albums tend to be surrounded by ads and e-commerce clutter.

A better choice is a site designed specifically for online photo sharing. I'm a huge fan of Flickr (www.flickr.com), which combines photo-sharing and print-ordering services with an inspiring community of creative photographers who comment on each other's photos.

Flickr is packed with slick features you won't find elsewhere, starting with an uploading tool that lets you transfer photos directly from iPhoto's Export dialog box. (Try out the Flickr export plug-in for iPhoto at www.connectedflow.com.)

You can also assign descriptive tags, such as *beach*, to your photos, and other Flickr users can search for images based on those tags. The Flickr iPhoto plug-in even supports iPhoto titles, comments, and keywords. Titles and comments are displayed along with your photos, and keywords are converted into Flickr tags.

Best of all is Flickr's pervasive support for RSS and newsreaders. Subscribe to another user's photo stream, and small thumbnails appear in your newsreader whenever that user uploads new photos. You can also subscribe to specific tags. Subscribe to the *beach* tag, and your newsreader will display everyone's beach photos as they're uploaded. You can even subscribe to photo feeds using iPhoto itself (see page 230).

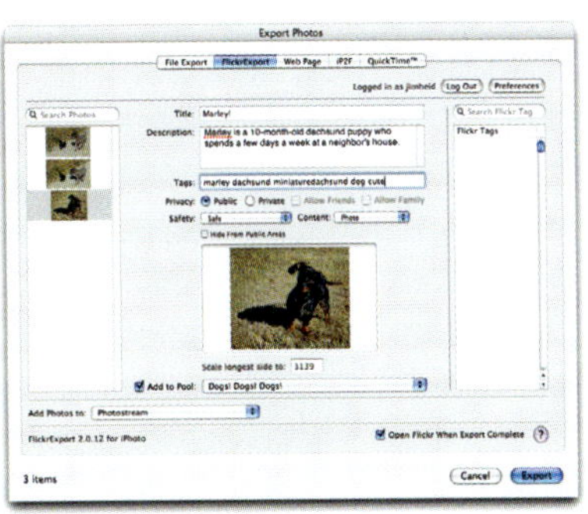

Flickr can also automatically publish, on your blog, your recent photos. It's a happy marriage between photography and the latest geek technologies. A Flickr account is free, although if you upload many photos, you may reach the 100MB-per-month bandwidth limit of a free account. A Pro account costs $24.95 per year and allows for unlimited uploads and much more.

Burning HTML Albums on a CD

Even if you aren't a Web jockey, there's a good reason to consider exporting an album or event as a set of Web pages: you can burn the exported pages onto CDs, and then mail them to others. They can view the album on their Macs or PCs using a Web browser—no attachment hassles, no long downloads.

After exporting the Web page, use the Mac OS X Finder to copy its folders and HTML pages to a blank CD-R disc. Burn the disc, eject it, and you have a photo Web site on a disc.

To view the site, simply double-click on the site's home page file. (This file is named *index.html*.)

And by the way, resist the urge to rename the site's home page file. If you change the name, the links in the Web album won't work.

Similarly, don't rename any image files or move them from their folders.

Sharing Photos on a Network

If you have more than one Mac on a network, you can share each Mac's photo library and make it accessible to the other Macs on the network.

Network photo sharing leads to all kinds of possibilities. Keep your "master" photo library on one Mac, and then access it from other Macs when you need to—no need to copy the library from one Mac to another and worry about which library is the most current.

Don't like centralization? Embrace anarchy: let everyone in the family have his or her own photo library, and then use sharing to make the libraries available to others.

Have an AirPort-equipped laptop Mac? Sit on the sofa (or at poolside) and show your photos to friends and family. Or take your laptop to their house and browse their libraries. Network sharing, a laptop Mac, and AirPort form the ultimate portable slide projector.

You can choose to share an entire photo library or only some albums. And you can require a password to keep your kids (or your parents) out of your library.

Activating Sharing

To share your photo library with other Macs on a network, choose Preferences from the iPhoto menu, then click the Sharing button.

To have the Mac automatically connect to shared libraries it finds on the network, check this box.

You can share your entire library or only selected albums. To share a specific album, click its check box.

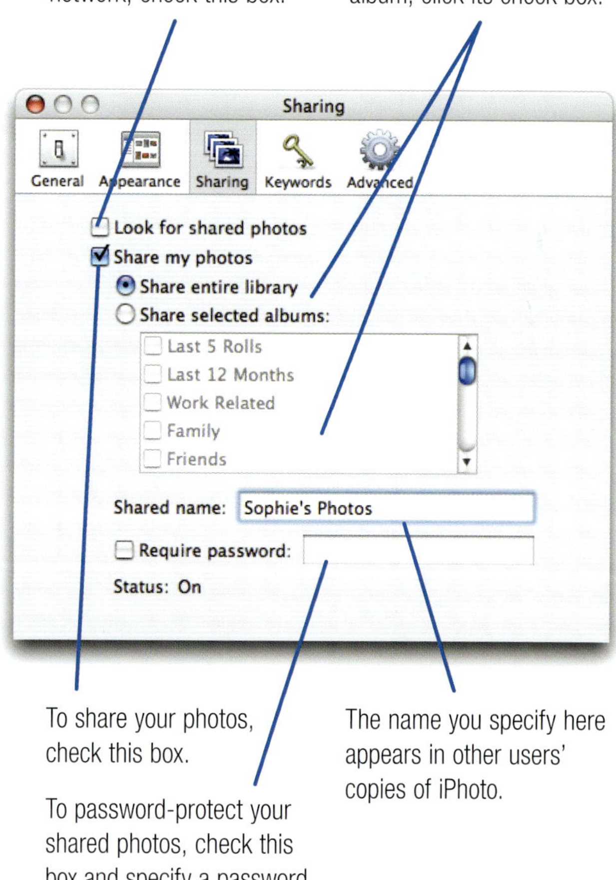

To share your photos, check this box.

To password-protect your shared photos, check this box and specify a password.

The name you specify here appears in other users' copies of iPhoto.

Accessing Shared Photos

To access shared photos, choose Preferences from the iPhoto menu, click the Sharing button, and be sure the Look for Shared Photos box is checked. iPhoto scans your network and, if it finds any shared photo libraries, adds their names to the Shares area of the Library list.

To view a shared library, click its name.

To view albums in a shared library, click the little triangle next to the library's name.

To disconnect from a shared library (perhaps to reduce traffic on your network), click the Eject button.

Working with Shared Photos

Searching Limits

You can use the Search box to look for photos in a shared library—within limits. You can search for text in a shared photo's title or description, but you can't search for keywords. And date searching is an unreliable proposition, at least as of this writing.

Slide Show Music

You can view a slide show of a shared album, but if the shared album has music assigned to it, you won't hear that music. Instead, iPhoto plays its default music, unless you've assigned a different song to your library.

But here's an interesting twist: you can temporarily assign a song or playlist from *your* local iTunes library to a *shared* album. Just use the techniques described on page 179.

When you assign local music to a shared album, iPhoto doesn't save your assignment. If you disconnect from the shared album and then reconnect, it's back to whatever your default song happens to be.

Just Looking

You can view shared photos, and you can email them, order prints, and display a basic slide show. But you can't edit or print shared photos, nor can you send them to iWeb or access them from the photo browsers in the other iLife programs.

To perform these tasks, copy the shared photos you want to your local iPhoto library: select the photos, then drag them to the Library item or to an album.

And what about adding shared photos to saved slide shows, calendars, cards, or books? You can do it: if you drag a photo to one of these items in your Library list, iPhoto imports the photo, adds it to your local library, and then adds it to the item.

Note: If you copy shared photos to your library using any of these techniques, iPhoto does not copy the photos' keywords to your local library. If you want to copy some photos to your local library and preserve this information, burn the photos to a CD or DVD (see page 222) and then copy the photos from the CD or DVD to your library.

Folders and Shared Libraries

If you store albums in folders, as I recommend on page 149, you'll be in for an unpleasant surprise when you connect to your library from a different Mac. iPhoto doesn't display the individual albums within a folder. Instead, it simply displays the name of the folder containing the albums. If you select the folder's name, you'll see the photos in *all* of the albums contained in that folder.

The unfortunate moral: when you want to be able to connect to a specific album from a different Mac, don't store that album in a folder.

Printing Photos

Internet photo sharing is great, but hard copy isn't dead. You might want to share photos with people who don't have computers. Or, you might want to tack a photo to a bulletin board or hang it on your wall—you'll never see "suitable for framing" stamped on an email message.

iPhoto makes hard copy easy. If you have a photo-inkjet printer, you can use iPhoto to create beautiful color prints in a variety of sizes. This assumes, of course, that your photos are both beautiful and in color.

When printing your photos, you can choose from several formatting options, called *themes*. You can produce standard prints, but you can also choose themes with elegant borders and mat designs.

Want event more control? A click of the mouse gives it to you. Adjust a photo's appearance, add a text caption, choose different background styles, and more.

So go ahead and beam your photos around the world on the Internet. But when you want something for your wall (or your refrigerator door), think ink.

Printing Standard Prints

A standard print contains just the photo, with no ornamental borders or mats.

Step 1. Select the photo or photos you want to print.

Step 2. Choose File > Print or click the Print button.

Step 3. Choose printing options, then click Print.

For a look at other printing themes, see the opposite page.

Adjust the photo's appearance, add a caption, and more (see page 198).

If you selected multiple photos, you can preview each print by clicking the arrows.

Choose your printer here.

Choose paper and quality settings. For highest quality, choose an option with Fine in its name.

Specify the size of the paper you're using.

Specify the size of the print you want (see below).

Notes and Tips

Choosing a print size. Most of the time, you'll want a photo to fill the page. But you can also choose a print size that is smaller than the paper size you've chosen. A small image floating within a large expanse is a common framing technique.

Another reason to choose a small print size is to get more than one photo on a sheet of paper—to shoehorn a couple of 4- by 6-inch prints onto a letter-sized sheet, for example (see page 199).

Going borderless. To produce borderless prints, your printer must support borderless printing and you must choose a borderless paper option using the Paper Size pop-up menu.

Beyond Standard Prints

With the print themes in iPhoto, you can produce prints with borders, mats, and more. And by clicking the Customize button in the Print dialog box, you can personalize the themes to match your photos and tastes. For details on customizing print jobs, see the following pages.

Contact Sheet

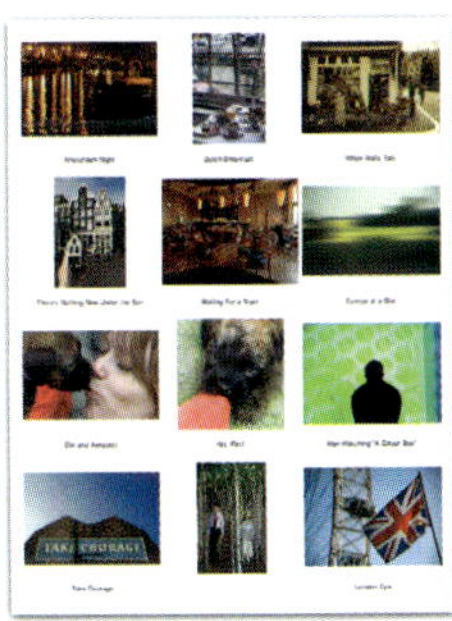

Prints numerous photos on a page—a handy quick-reference to the photos in an event or album. Be sure to select a bunch of photos (or select an entire album or event) before choosing Print.

Customizing: Change the background of the page as well as how many images appear across each row. Print titles, captions, dates, and exposure information beneath thumbnails.

Simple Border

Adds a wide border around the image.

Customizing: Change the border style and choose from several layouts, some with text captions and multiple photos on a page.

Single Mat

Simulates the stiff cardboard mat that a framing shop uses to accent a photo and set it off from its frame. The mat has a bevel-cut opening through which the photo appears.

Customizing: Choose from 26 mat colors and styles. Add a white border inside the mat. Choose from several layouts, some with text captions and multiple photos on a page.

Double Mat

Simulates a framing technique that involves using two mats to provide a richer look. A top mat has a large opening that reveals a bottom mat, whose smaller opening reveals the photo.

Customizing: Choose from 26 mat colors and numerous border styles. Choose from several layouts, some with text captions and multiple photos on a page.

Customizing a Print Job

For creating basic prints, the steps on the previous pages are all you need. But you can go beyond the basics to customize many aspects of a print job.

Change the eye candy. Every print theme lets you add a text caption and choose various design layout options. Even the Standard theme provides customizing opportunities.

Adjust the photo. Here's one of those "local editing" opportunities I discussed back on page 152. You can crop a photo and adjust its exposure, sharpness, and other settings for just a single print—no need to edit the original (and thus change the photo's appearance elsewhere, such as in a slide show).

Print Settings View at Glance

To customize a print job, click the Customize button in the Print dialog box. This opens iPhoto's *print settings view.*

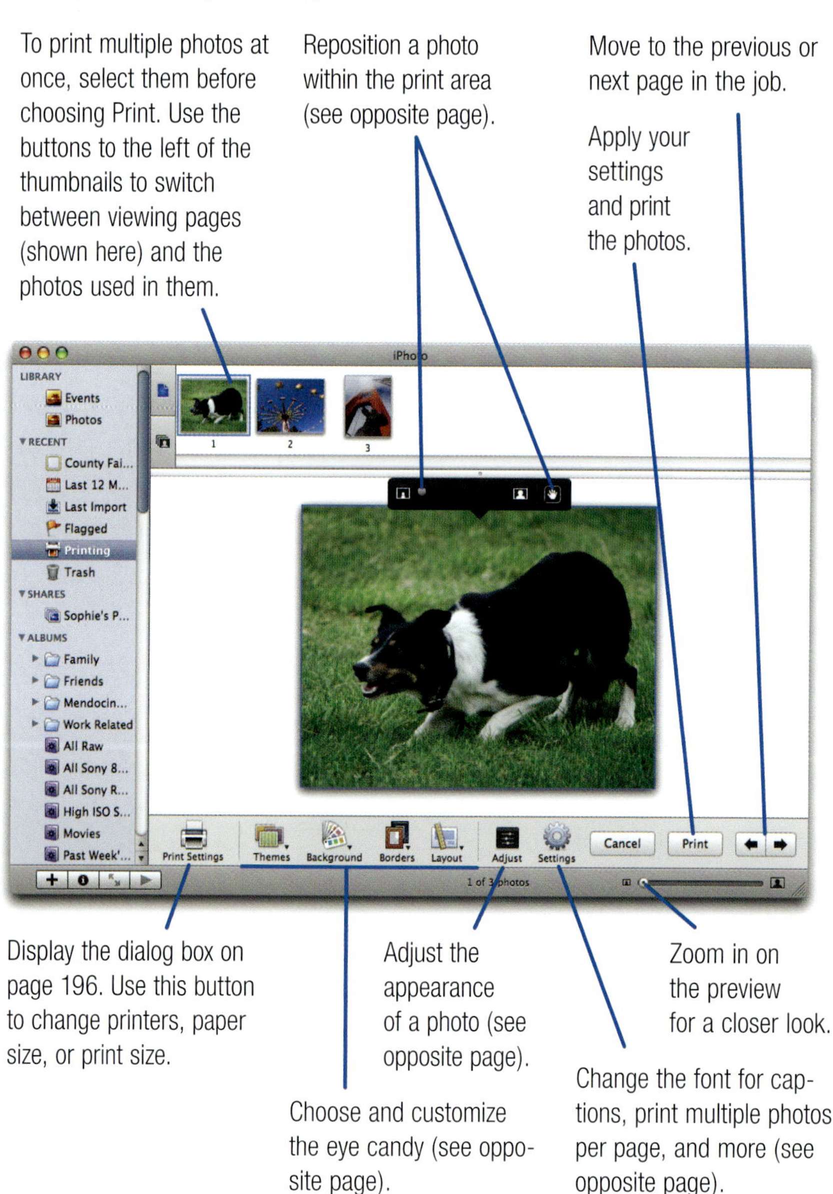
To print multiple photos at once, select them before choosing Print. Use the buttons to the left of the thumbnails to switch between viewing pages (shown here) and the photos used in them.
Reposition a photo within the print area (see opposite page).
Move to the previous or next page in the job.
Apply your settings and print the photos.
Display the dialog box on page 196. Use this button to change printers, paper size, or print size.
Adjust the appearance of a photo (see opposite page).
Zoom in on the preview for a closer look.
Choose and customize the eye candy (see opposite page).
Change the font for captions, print multiple photos per page, and more (see opposite page).
iPhoto
LIBRARY
Events
Photos
RECENT
County Fai...
Last 12 M...
Last Import
Flagged
Printing
Trash
SHARES
Sophie's P...
ALBUMS
Family
Friends
Mendocin...
Work Related
All Raw
All Sony 8...
All Sony R...
High ISO S...
Movies
Past Week'...
Print Settings
Themes
Background
Borders
Layout
Adjust
Settings
Cancel
Print
1 of 3 photos

Perfecting Your Print

Here are the two most common adjustments you can make—ones from which any print job can benefit.

Adjust "cropping." A photo's proportions rarely match the proportions of the paper size you're using. I don't know of any digital camera whose photos perfectly fit an 8.5- by 11-inch sheet.

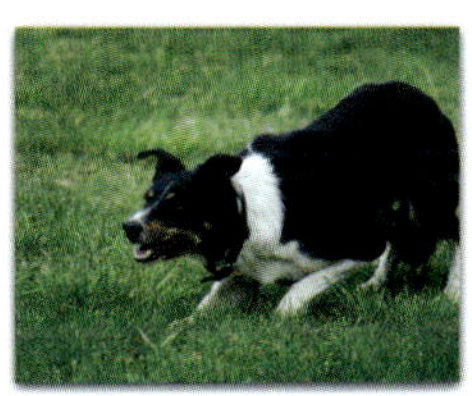

With some programs, mismatched proportions yield prints with uneven borders. iPhoto eliminates that problem by enlarging an image until it fits the dimensions of the print size you chose. That gives you nice, even borders (or a fully borderless print), but at a price: parts of the photo's edges are cut off. In this example, iPhoto cut off part of the dog's legs and tail (ouch).

By positioning a photo within the print area, you can control how the photo is cropped. Click the photo, then use the controls above it to zoom and reposition the photo. You can see the results on the opposite page: I dragged the dog (gently!) to fix the unwanted leg surgery.

Adjust appearance. To adjust exposure, contrast, and other image settings, select the photo and click the Adjust button. The Adjust panel is similar to its counterpart in edit view (pages 160–167), but changes you make here apply only to this print job.

Sharpen up. The single best adjustment you can make is to sharpen. As I said on page 166, ink-jet printers introduce some softness, and sharpening can help. Don't be afraid to crank the sharpness way up—even to 100 percent. Make some before-and-after prints and judge for yourself.

Tip: The one downside of making "local" image adjustments is that iPhoto doesn't save your settings. If you want to make another print a week later using the same settings, you'll have to recreate them by hand. If you anticipate wanting to repeat a print job, jot down the Adjust panel settings you've made.

More Ways to Customize

Use the Background, Borders, and Layout pop-up menus to explore each theme's design options. Here are some tips.

Add a caption. To print a text caption at the bottom of a print, use the Layout pop-up menu to choose a layout with text.

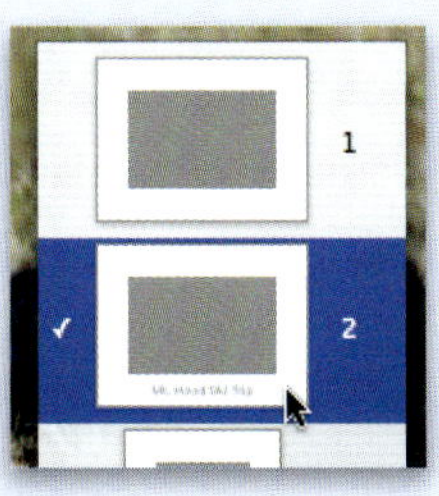

Type the text below the photo. To change the font and size of the entire caption, click Settings. To mix and match fonts within the caption, use the Fonts panel. For details and tips, see page 210.

Multi-photo layouts. Most theme layouts provide options that print two or more photos on a page.

But what if you selected only one photo before choosing Print?

No problem—just add more photos to the print job. When you open print settings view, an item named Printing appears in your Recent list. To add photos to the print job, drag their thumbnails to the Printing item.

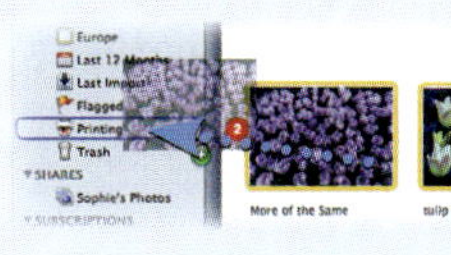

Then, click the Printing item. iPhoto automatically creates additional pages for the new photos, but you can rearrange the photos as you see fit. To remove a photo from a page, select it and press Delete. To see all the photos in the print job, click the button in the thumbnail browser.

Mix and match settings. Normally, when you change a print background or border, iPhoto applies the change to *all* the pages in the print job. But you can also apply changes on a page-by-page basis: just hold down the Option key while choosing a background or border.

Printing Tips and Troubleshooting

Multiple Copies

By tweaking a few print settings, you can print multiple copies of a photo on a single sheet of paper. Have a cute kid photo that you want to send around? Print multiple 4- by 6-inch photos on a letter- or legal-sized sheet, then cut them apart.

Step 1. Select the photo and choose File > Print.

Step 2. Choose the paper size you're using, such as Letter or Legal.

Step 3. From the Print Size pop-up menu, choose a smaller size, such as 3 x 5 or 4 x 6.

Step 4. Click the Customize button.

Step 5. In print settings view, click the Settings button.

Step 6. From the Photos Per Page pop-up menu, choose Multiple of the Same Photo Per Page, then click OK.

Step 7. Click the Print button.

Tips: iPhoto can print guides to help you cut the photos apart. In the Settings dialog box, click the Show Crop Marks box.

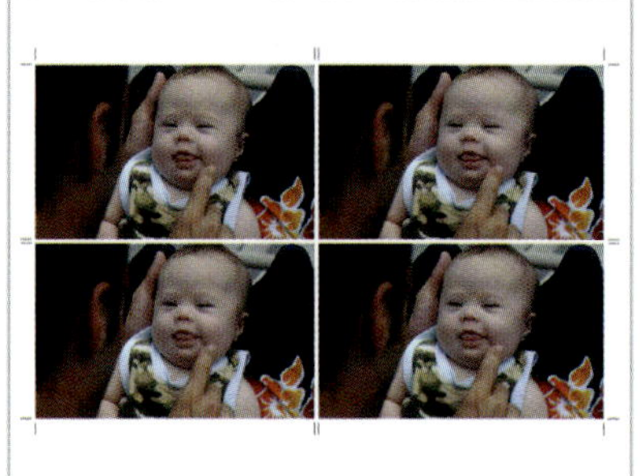

You can also use this technique to print multiple photos (but not the same one) on a single sheet of paper. Select several photos, then perform steps 1–5. In Step 6, choose the option labeled Multiple Photos Per Page.

Kill the Cropping

On previous pages, I discussed how iPhoto prevents uneven borders by enlarging a photo until it fills the paper size you've chosen. And I described how you can use print settings view to zoom and pan a photo to crop it as you see fit.

But what if you don't want any cropping at all? Easy. In print settings view, Control-click on a photo and, from the shortcut menu, choose Fit Photo to Frame Size.

Your print will almost certainly have some uneven borders, but it will contain every precious pixel of your original image. You can trim the borders by hand after printing.

Save a PDF

Remember that you can save a print job as a PDF file and use it elsewhere, such as in an iPhoto or iDVD slide show, a print project, or an iMovie project. After customizing the print job, click the Print button. In the final print dialog box (the one you see when you're actually ready to commit ink to paper), use the options in the PDF pop-up menu to create a PDF. To create a PDF and add it to your iPhoto library in one fell swoop, choose Save PDF to iPhoto.

PDF to photographic print. You can combine this PDF technique with Apple's online print-ordering service (page 202). The result: the ability to design a fancy print and then have it printed by Apple.

Design a print, first making sure to choose a paper size that corresponds to the print size you'll order. (For example, if you plan to order an 8 by 10, choose the 8 x 10 paper size.)

Next, use print settings view to choose mats and borders and adjust the photo as desired. Click the Print button, then choose the Save PDF to iPhoto option.

When iPhoto has finished importing the PDF, select it and click the Order Prints button. Complete your print order as described on page 202.

When Prints Disappoint

When your prints aren't charming, read on.

Verify paper choices. In iPhoto's Print dialog box, be sure to choose the preset that matches the type of paper you're using and the quality you're seeking. It's easy to overlook this step and end up specifying plain paper when you're actually using pricey photo paper.

Check ink. Strange colors? Check your printer's ink supply. Many printers include diagnostic software that reports how much ink remains in each cartridge.

Clean up. The nozzles in an inkjet printer can become clogged, especially if you don't print every day. If you're seeing odd colors or a horizontal banding pattern, use your printer's cleaning mode to clean your ink nozzles. Most printers can print a test page designed to show when the nozzles need cleaning. You may have to repeat the cleaning process a few times.

Preserving Your Prints

After all the effort you put into making inkjet prints, it may disappoint you to learn that they may not last long.

Many inkjet prints begin to fade within a year or two—even faster when displayed in direct sunlight. Most printer manufacturers now offer pigment-based inks and archival papers that last for decades, but pigment-based printers are pricier than the more common dye-based printers.

If you have a dye-based printer, consider using a paper rated for longer print life. Epson's ColorLife paper, for example, has a much higher permanence rating than Epson's Premium Glossy Photo Paper.

To prolong the life of any print, don't display it in direct sunlight. Frame it under glass to protect it from humidity and pollutants. (Ozone pollution, common in cities, is poison to an inkjet print.)

Allow prints to dry for at least a few (preferably 24) hours before framing them or stacking them atop each other.

For long-term storage, consider using acid-free sleeves designed for archival photo storage.

Finally, avoid bargain-priced paper or ink from the local office superstore. Print preservation guru Henry Wilhelm (www.wilhelm-research.com) recommends using only premium inks and papers manufactured by the same company that made your printer.

Is all this necessary for a print that will be tacked to a refrigerator for a few months and then thrown away? Of course not. But when you want prints to last, these steps can help.

To learn more about digital printing, read Harald Johnson's *Mastering Digital Printing, Second Edition* (Muska & Lipman, 2005).

Ordering Prints

Inkjet photo printers provide immediate gratification, but not without hassles. Paper and ink are expensive. Getting perfectly even borders is next to impossible, and getting borderless prints can be equally frustrating.

There is another path to hard copy: ordering prints through iPhoto. Click the Order Prints button, specify the print sizes you want, and iPhoto transmits your photos over the Internet to Kodak's print service. The prints look great, and because they're true photographic prints, they're much more permanent than most inkjet prints.

You can also order prints from other online photofinishers, many of whom also offer free online photo albums and other sharing services. Using these services isn't as straightforward as clicking a button in iPhoto, but it isn't difficult, either. Many services, such as Shutterfly (www.shutterfly.com), offer software that simplifies transferring your shots. The Flickr online photo-sharing site also offers print-ordering services.

And some services offer output options that iPhoto doesn't, such as mouse pads, T-shirts, and even photo cookies. For links to some online photofinishers, see www.macilife.com/iphoto.

To Order Prints

Step 1.

Select the photos you want prints of, then click the Order Prints button or choose Order Prints from the Share menu.

Step 2.

Specify the sizes and quantities you want, then click Buy Now.

The yellow triangle of doom (⚠) indicates that the photo doesn't have enough resolution for good quality at that size; see the sidebar at right for details.

Want a 4 by 6 of every photo you selected? Specify the quantity here.

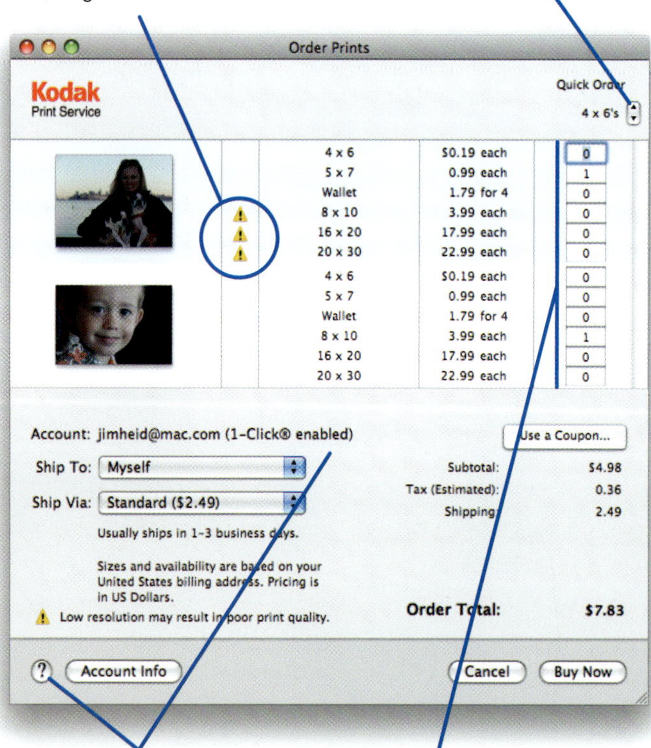

To order prints, you must have an Apple ID account with 1-Click ordering enabled. For help, click the help button.

Specify how many prints you want for each size.

Create a Temporary Album

If you're ordering prints from many different events, create an album and use it to hold the photos you want to print. Give the album an obvious name, such as *Pix to Print.* This makes it easier to keep track of which photos you're printing. After you've placed your order, you can delete the album.

As an alternative to creating an album, you can flag photos you want to print. After you've done so, click the Flagged item, then click Order Prints.

Cropping Concerns

The proportions of most standard print sizes don't match the proportions of a typical digital camera image. As a result, Kodak automatically crops a photo to fill the print size you've ordered.

The problem is, automatic cropping may lop off part of the image that's important to you. If you don't want your photos cropped by a machine, do the cropping yourself, using iPhoto's edit view, before ordering. Use the Constrain pop-up menu to specify the proportions you want.

If you plan to order prints in several sizes, you may have even more work to do. A 5 by 7 print has a different *aspect ratio* than a 4 by 6 or an 8 by 10. If you want to order a 5 by 7 *and* one of these other sizes, you need to create a separate version of each picture—for example, one version cropped for a 5 by 7 and another cropped for an 8 by 10.

To create separate versions of a picture, make a duplicate of the original photo for each size you want (select the photo and press ⌘-D), and then crop each version appropriately.

If you crop a photo to oddball proportions—for example, a narrow rectangle—Kodak's automatic cropping will yield a weird-looking print. If you have an image-editing program, such as Adobe Photoshop Elements, here's a workaround. In the imaging program, create a blank image at the size you plan to print (for example, 5 by 7 inches). Then open your cropped photo in the imaging program and paste it into this blank image. Save the resulting image as a JPEG file (use the Maximum quality setting), add it to iPhoto, and then order your print.

No Questions, Please

Kodak can't print a photo whose file name contains a question mark (?). No digital camera creates files that are so named, but if you scan and name images yourself, keep this restriction in mind.

Resolution's Relationship to Print Quality

If you're working with low-resolution images—ones that you've cropped heavily or shot at a low resolution, for example—you may see iPhoto's dreaded low-resolution warning icon (⚠) when ordering prints or a book.

This is iPhoto's way of telling you that an image doesn't have enough pixels—enough digital information—to yield a good-quality print at the size that you've chosen.

Don't feel obligated to cancel a print job or an order if you see this warning. But do note that you may see some fuzziness in your prints.

The table here lists the minimum resolution an image should have to yield a good print at various sizes.

Print Sizes and Resolution

For This Print Size (Inches)	Image Resolution Should be at Least (Pixels)
Wallet	640 by 480
4 by 6	768 by 512
5 by 7	1075 by 768
8 by 10	1280 by 1024
16 by 20	2272 by 1704

Creating Photo Books

Something special happens to photos when they're pasted into the pages of a book. Arranged in a specific order and accompanied by captions, photos form a narrative: they tell a story.

Put away your paste. With iPhoto's book mode, you can create beautiful, full-color books in several sizes and styles. Arrange your photos in the order you want, adding captions and descriptive text if you like. Choose from a gallery of design *themes* to spice up your pages with layouts that complement your subject.

When you're done, iPhoto connects to the Internet and transfers your book to Apple's printing service, where the book is printed on a four-color digital printing press (a Hewlett-Packard Indigo, if you're curious), and then bound and shipped to you.

iPhoto books are great for commemorating a vacation, wedding, or other special event. They're also open for business: architects, artists, photographers, and designers use iPhoto to create spectacular portfolios, proposals, and brochures.

So don't just print those extra-special shots. Publish them.

Creating a Book: The Big Picture

The most efficient way to create a book is to first add photos to an album, and then tell iPhoto to create a book based on that album. Here's an overview of the process.

Step 1.

Create a new album containing the photos you want to publish (page 146). Arrange the photos in approximately the same order that you want them to appear in the book. (You can always change their order later.)

Step 2.

Select the album in the Albums list, then click the Book button 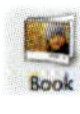

or the Add button [+].

Step 3.

Choose a book type and a theme, then click Choose. For a summary of the types of books you can order, see the sidebar at right.

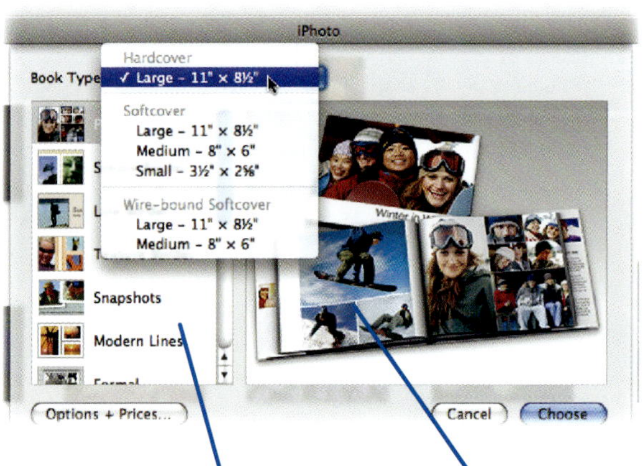

Most book types provide numerous themes. All themes provide coordinated color schemes and several page designs.

Large hardcover books have a dust jacket with a cover and inside flaps that you can customize.

Step 4.

Lay out the book.

You can have iPhoto place the photos for you (the autoflow mode), or you can manually place each photo yourself (see the following pages).

To jump to a page, click its thumbnail. To rearrange pages, drag them left or right (page 209).

Switch between viewing page thumbnails (shown here) or photos that you haven't yet placed in the book (page 208).

To reposition a photo within its book frame, click the photo and drag the size control and/or the photo itself (page 211).

Display your book's pages as a slide show (page 212).

You can view and work with two-page spreads (shown here) or one page at a time (page 209).

Switch themes and page designs and perform other layout and design tasks (pages 208–211).

Many page designs allow for text, whose type style you can customize (page 210).

For more layout options, Control-click on a photo (page 211).

Move to the previous or next page.

Zoom in on a page for proofreading and fine tuning.

Step 5.

Click Buy Book and pay up using your Apple ID (page 15).

Book Types and Sizes

You can create several kinds of books with iPhoto. To preview the books, explore the options in the pop-up menu shown in Step 3 on the opposite page. The cost of a book depends on the type of book you order and on its number of pages; see apple.com/iphoto.

Hardcover. The classiest book option, and the priciest. Also called a *keepsake* book, it measures 11 inches wide by 8.5 inches tall. The book's title is foil-stamped on a suede-like hardcover, and a customizable dust jacket protects the entire affair.

Softcover. Available in three sizes: 11 by 8.5 inches, 8 by 6 inches, and 2.6 by 3.5 inches. The tiniest size is sold in packs of three.

Wire-bound softcover. Available in 11 by 8.5 inch and 8 by 6 inch sizes, this softcover variation has a wire binding that lets the book lay flat.

Planning for Publishing

A book project doesn't begin in a page-layout program. It begins with an author who has something to say, and with photo editors and designers who have ideas about the best ways to say it.

When you create a photo book, you wear all of those hats. iPhoto works hard to make you look as fetching as possible in each of them, but you can help by putting some thought into your book before you click the Book button.

What do you want your book to say? Is it commemorating an event? Or is it celebrating a person, place, or thing? Does the book need a story arc—a beginning, a middle, and an ending? Would the book benefit from distinct sections—one for each place you visited, for example, or one for each member of the family?

And no publishing project occurs without a discussion of production expenses. Is money no object? Or are you pinching pennies?

Your answers to these questions will influence the photos you choose, the book designs you use, and the way you organize and present your photos and any accompanying text. The very best time to address these questions isn't before you start your book—it's before you start shooting. If you have a certain kind of book in mind, you can make sure you get the shots you need.

Here's more food for thought.

Questions to Ask

Here's a look at some of the factors that may influence your choice of book sizes and themes.

What Size Book?

The book size you choose will be dictated by your budget and design goals. On a budget? Use the medium-sized or large softcover formats. Want the largest selection of design options? Go large hardcover. Large book sizes are also best when you want to get as many photos as possible on a page.

Your photos may also influence your choice: for example, if you have low-resolution shots and want to present one photo per page, you may need to choose a medium-sized book to get acceptable quality.

How Much Text?

Most photography books contain more than just photos. Will you want text in your book? If so, how much? Some themes provide for more copy than others.

How Many Photos?

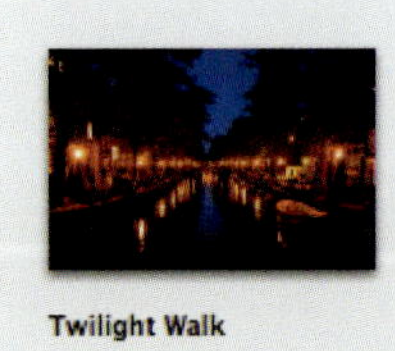

Some themes provide for more photos per page than others. The Travel theme provides up to seven; Picture Book, 16; Folio, only two.

What Design Options?

Each book size and type provides its own set of themes. Each theme has its own design options, including different color schemes; different ways to arrange photos on each page; and special photo effects, such as collages.

Options to Consider

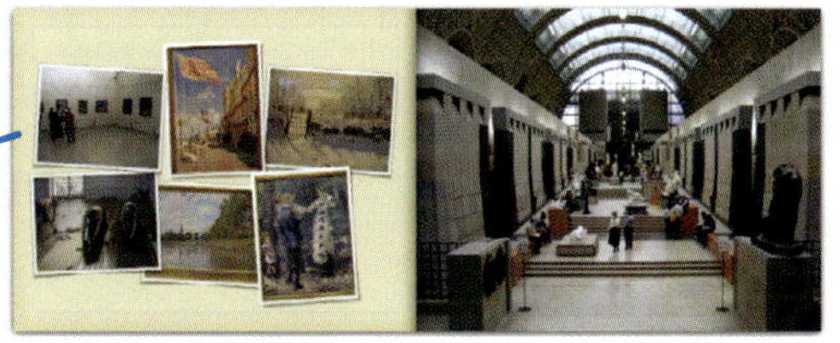

In this spread, which uses the Travel theme, the left-hand page shows works from the Museé d'Orsay, shown on the right-hand page.

Think about ways to have the left- and right-hand pages complement each other.

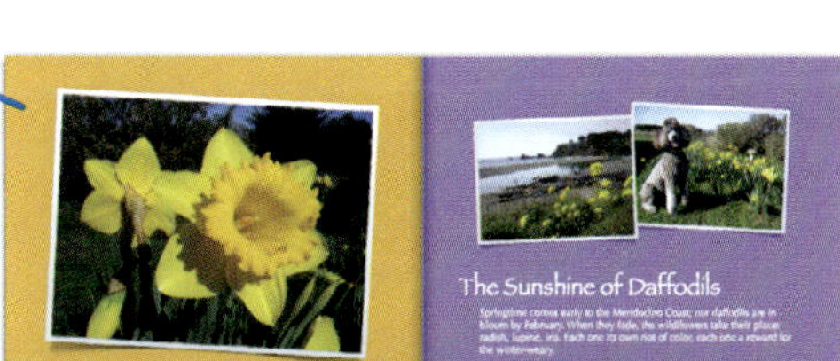

The Family Album theme has a warm, sentimental look—perfect for vintage photos.

Don't have high-resolution photos? Consider a medium or small softcover book, or choose page designs with small photo zones or multiple photos per page.

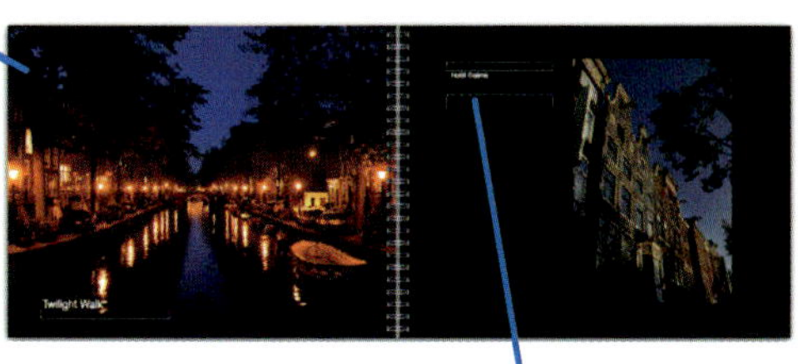

Many themes (including Crayon, shown here) have page designs that allow for text headings and lengthy captions whose formatting you can customize.

Wire-bound books, available in large and medium softcover sizes, lay flat when opened.

In the elegant Folio design, photo titles become headings.

Dust Jacket Decisions

Large hardcover books include a paper dust jacket that can hold text and photos. Besides having front and back covers that you can customize, dust jackets also have inside flaps that tuck behind the front and back covers.

You can customize these flaps, too. In publishing, it's common for the front flap to describe the book, and for the back flap to describe the author. If there's a lot to say about the book or its subject, the text on the front flap may continue on to the back flap.

Each book theme has several flap layouts: just a photo, text and a photo, just text, and blank. When creating a hardcover book, decide how much you want to talk about your book—and yourself—and choose the appropriate layout.

Three Weeks in Europe
The tulip fields of Holland. The bustle of London. The romance of Paris.
Art. Food. Architecture. Food. History. Food. Museums.
And great food, too.
Join us, but try not to drool on the pages.

Book Layout Techniques

Manual or Autoflow?

When you create a book, you can choose to have iPhoto lay out the book automatically by clicking the Autoflow button, or you can take the wheel and drive yourself by dragging photos onto the book's pages. When you create a new book, iPhoto reminds you of these options.

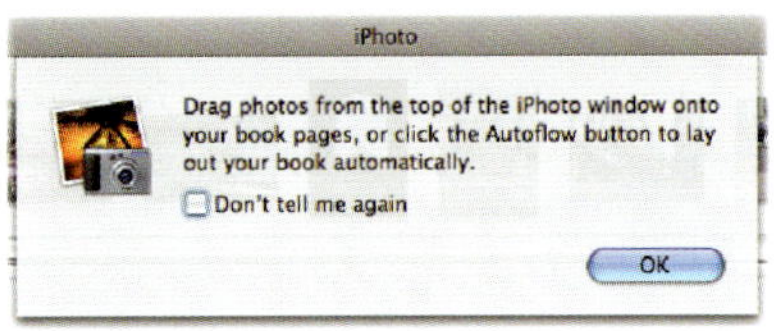

Regardless of the option you choose, iPhoto always creates a book with 20 pages—the minimum a book can contain.

iPhoto also assigns a layout to each page. And that's why I prefer to lay out books manually instead of clicking the Autoflow button. I often want to change the designs that iPhoto has chosen, and if I'm going to do that, I might as well start with a blank slate—why have iPhoto position photos that I'm going to be rearranging anyway?

But that's just me. If you'd rather get immediate results and then fine-tune, click Autoflow. Or mix both approaches. If you want to do something fancy at the beginning of your book—maybe have a full-page photo opposite an introduction text page—lay out those first couple of pages. Then click the Autoflow button to have iPhoto do the rest.

Note that the Autoflow feature adds additional pages to your book if necessary to accommodate the rest of your unplaced photos. Those extra pages will cost you, so if you're watching your production budget, keep an eye on your total page count.

Layout Basics

Each book theme includes numerous *layouts*, each with a different arrangement of text and photos. Some layouts contain just text, some hold just photos, and some hold both.

Choosing a layout. First, navigate to the page you want to change: click the left- or right-arrow buttons or click the page in the thumbnail browser. (If you don't see page thumbnails there, click the button.)

Next, use the Layout pop-up menu to choose a design.

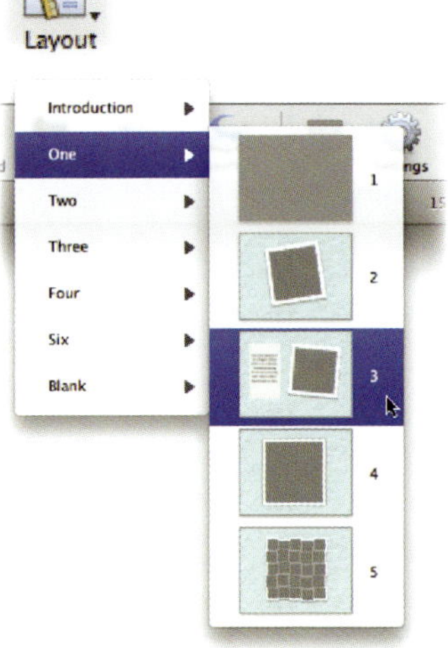

Background options. To change a page's background, use the Background pop-up menu. Background designs vary depending on theme. All themes also let you use a photo as a full-page background; see page 211.

Adding photos. Add photos to the empty frames by dragging them from the thumbnail browser (click the to see photo thumbnails).

Working with Photos

Adding to a full page. If you drag a photo from the photo browser to a page that already contains photos in each photo frame, iPhoto changes the page type, adding an additional photo frame to accommodate the photo.

With some themes and page designs, iPhoto may add more than one photo frame. For example, in the Picture Book theme, the available page types jump from four photos per page to six. If you add a photo to a fully populated four-photo page, iPhoto switches to the six-photo page type. You can either add a sixth photo or ignore the empty frame. iPhoto will omit it when you order your book.

Incidentally, if a page already has the maximum number of photos supported by that theme, iPhoto won't let you add another one.

Moving to a different page. You can move a photo to a different page. Be sure that your page thumbnails are visible (click the button), then drag the photo to its new page. The same points mentioned previously apply: if the destination page is full, iPhoto may change its page type to accommodate the new photo.

Removing a photo. To remove a photo, select the photo and press the Delete key, or drag the photo up to the photo thumbnails browser. iPhoto moves the photo to the thumbnails area.

You can also remove a photo by Control-clicking on it and choosing Remove Photo from the shortcut menu.

To remove the photo's frame, switch to a page type that provides fewer photos, or simply ignore the empty frame—that's what iPhoto will do when you order your book.

Swapping photos. To swap two photos on a page or spread, simply drag one photo to the other one.

Editing a photo. Need to edit a photo that you've placed on a page? Control-click on the photo and choose Edit Photo from the shortcut menu.

Adding photos from your library. To add additional photos to a book, drag them from your library to the book's name in the Projects list.

Adding and Removing Pages

To add a page, click the Add Pages button. If you're viewing two-page spreads, iPhoto adds a full spread, which is two pages. To add just one page, switch to single-page view (click the View button).

Add Pages

To insert a new spread or page between two existing pages, use the page thumbnails browser to select the page that you want to precede the new page. For example, to add a new page between pages 4 and 5, select page 4, then click Add Pages.

When you add a page or spread, iPhoto gives the page or pages a layout from the book's current theme, filled with empty photo frames. Customize the layout as desired.

Removing a page. To remove a page, select it in the pages thumbnail browser and press the Delete key. Or, Control-click on a blank area of the doomed page and choose Remove Page from the shortcut menu.

When you delete a page containing photos, iPhoto moves its photos to the photo thumbnail browser so you can use them elsewhere, if you like.

Rearranging Pages

To reorganize your pages, drag their thumbnails left and right in the page thumbnail browser. If you're viewing two-page spreads, you can move spreads back and forth. In the following example, pages 6 and 7 are being moved so they follow pages 8 and 9.

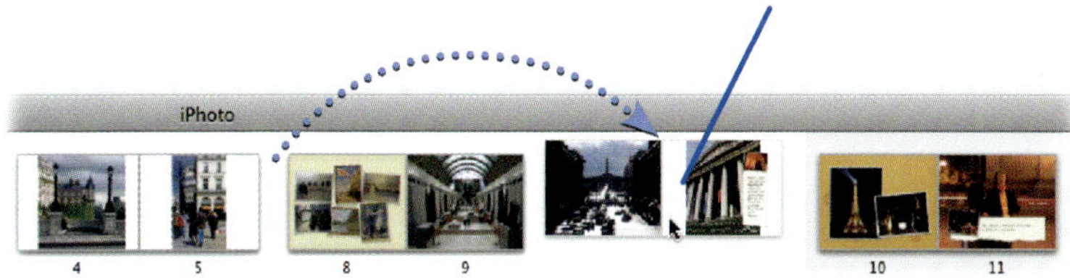

To move individual pages, switch to single-page view. Below, page 4 is being moved so it follows page 5.

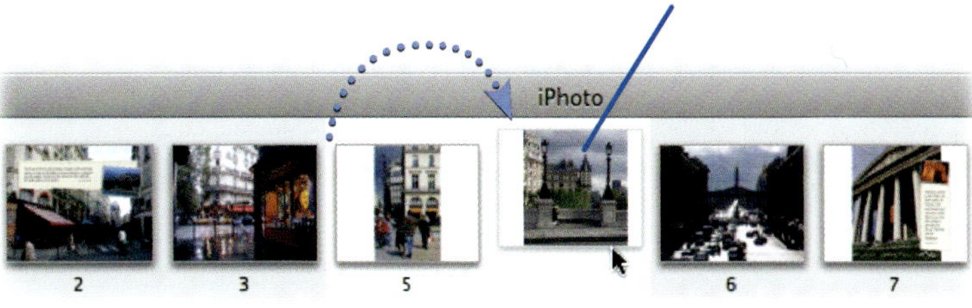

Tips for Creating Books

Formatting Text

You can format your book's text in several ways.

Globally: the Settings button. When you want to change the font iPhoto uses for every occurrence of an element in your book (such as its captions), use the Settings button. **Tip:** Each book theme provides its own text elements, and some provide more than others. The Settings dialog box is a convenient way to see what elements a theme provides.

Locally: the Fonts panel. Typographic consistency is important for a book like the one you're reading, but for a photo book that contains only a few text elements, a bit of variety can be fun. You can format individual text elements—indeed, individual letters, if you want to—by using the Fonts panel. Select the text you want to format, and choose Edit > Font > Show Fonts (⌘-T).

The triangle of doom. You've typed some text or changed text formatting, and suddenly the yellow triangle of doom appears in the text box. iPhoto is telling you that the text won't fit with its current type specs. Either change formatting or delete some text.

I Love Books with Overly Verbose Titles
By Clive Johnson-Farquar III

More Tips for Text

Here are more textual tips.

Low-rent formatting control. All themes provide at least one Introduction layout. But don't feel obligated to write an introduction. You can adapt the Introduction page to other uses, such as a title page. You can also move items around on the page by using the spacebar or Tab key to bump a line of text to the right, and by pressing Return to move text down. These tricks don't provide page-layout precision, but they work.

Consider a word processor. Planning a lot of text in your book? Consider using your favorite word processor to write and format the text. Then, move the text into iPhoto as needed: select the text you need for a given page, and copy it to the Clipboard. Next, switch to iPhoto, click in the destination text box, and paste. iPhoto even retains your formatting.

This approach lets you take advantage of a word processor's superior editing features, not to mention its Save command—something iPhoto lacks.

Controlling paragraph formatting. iPhoto doesn't provide controls for adjusting the spacing between lines (leading) or paragraph indents. Solution: Use your word processor. Format your text in a word processor, then copy and paste it into the text box on your book page.

Saving custom text styles. You've pasted in some custom formatting and would like to save it to apply to future books or to other pages in the same book. Here's how.

First, click within the text box that contains the custom text. Then, Control-click and choose Styles from the shortcut menu's Font submenu. In the dialog box that appears, click the Add to Favorites button. In the *next* dialog box, type a name for your custom style, click both check boxes, then click the Add button.

To use that custom style, select the text you want to format, and Control-click on it to summon the shortcut menu. Choose Styles from the Font submenu, then click the Favorite Styles button. Locate and choose your style in the pop-up menu, and click Apply.

Fun with glyphs. Some of Mac OS X's fonts contain beautiful alternative characters, such as ornamental swashes and flourishes. To explore and use these alternative glyphs, choose Typography from the ⚙▾ pop-up menu at the bottom of the Fonts panel. Then, explore the options in the Typography panel.

For a good example, choose the Zapfino font, then check out the Stylistic Variants portion of the Typography panel. The Apple Chancery font also has some interesting alternate characters.

Also, many fonts have old-style numerals that lend a classic look, as shown here with the Didot font.

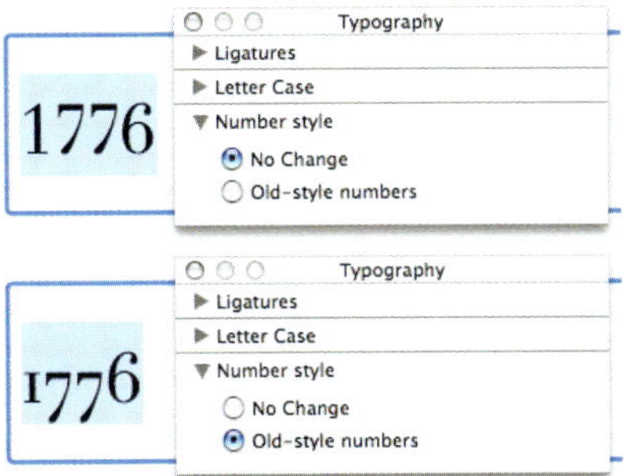

If a font provides old-style numerals, you'll see a Number Style entry in the Typography panel.

Who needs page numbers? Unless you're putting a table of contents or index in your book, you have little reason to print a page number on each page. To remove page numbers, use the Settings dialog box or Control-click on a blank area of a page and make sure that the Show Page Numbers command is unchecked in the shortcut menu.

Adjusting Photos

You can adjust a photo's appearance in the book layout editor. To fine-tune composition, click the photo, then use the controls above the photo to zoom and reposition it.

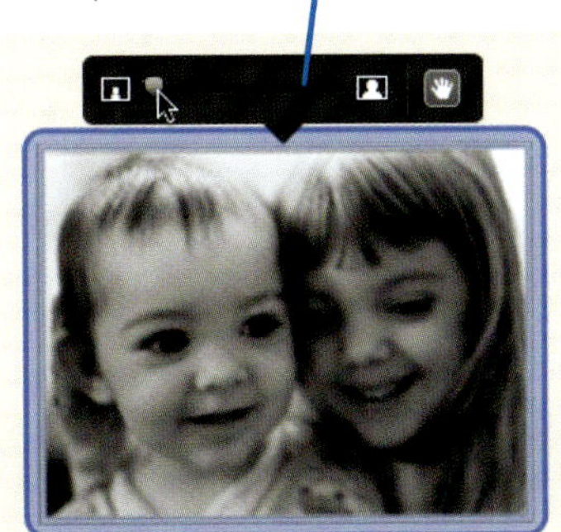

If you zoom in too far for a given photo's resolution, iPhoto displays the yellow triangle of doom to let you know that you won't get good quality at that zoom setting.

To adjust a photo's exposure or add an effect, click the photo, then click the Adjust button. As with inkjet prints, some sharpening can improve quality.

You can, of course, also open the photo in edit view and do your cropping and exposure adjustments there. But doing so changes the photo everywhere you've used it.

Photo as Background

You can use a photo as the background of a page. Put a photo behind the text that introduces your vacation book. Or use a close-up of a garden as the background for a page of weekend-getaway photos.

Start by clicking the Background pop-up menu and choosing the option with a faint palm tree on it:

Next, choose a layout and add photos and/or text to the page, as appropriate.

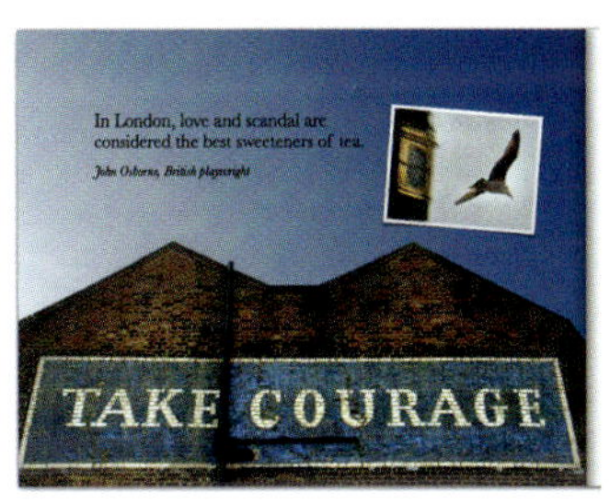

Tip: A busy background photo will overwhelm text or other photos, impairing legibility. Solution: increase the transparency of the background photo. Click the photo, and drag the slider to the right until the photo appears faint.

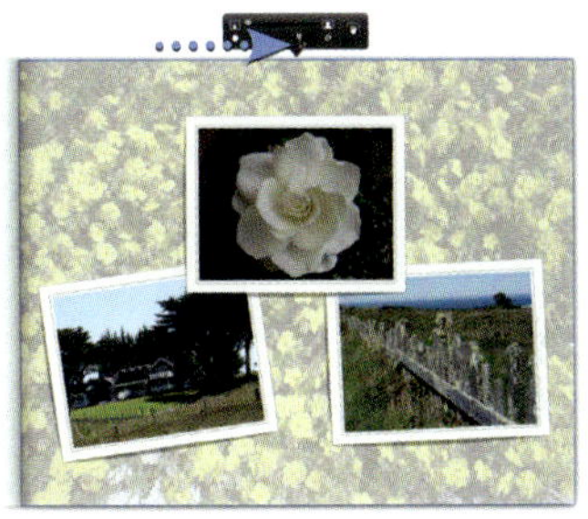

More Tips for Creating Books

Before You Buy

Before you click the Buy Book button to place your order, do one last proofreading pass of any text in your book. And remember, your Mac can help: select the text in a text box, Control-click, and choose Spelling > Check Spelling.

Placeholder text. Also check to see that you haven't left placeholder text on any pages. (This is the stuff iPhoto inserts for you when you choose a page design that supports text. It usually reads *Insert a description of your book.*) But don't sweat it: if your book contains placeholder text and you click Buy Book, iPhoto warns that the placeholder text won't be printed.

Unused photo frames. Don't worry if any pages have unused (gray) photo frames. iPhoto simply ignores them.

Tip: The fact that iPhoto ignores empty photo frames opens up additional design options. For example, say you're creating a book in the Picture Book theme and you want a page with five photos on it—a page type Picture Book doesn't provide. Solution: choose the six-photo page type, but put only five photos on it.

Preview. To preview your book, Control-click on a blank area of a page and choose Preview Book from the shortcut menu. iPhoto assembles the book and displays its pages in Mac OS X's Preview program.

From Book to Slide Show

iPhoto's book editor view provides a Play button that lets you display the pages of your book as a slide show. This opens up some interesting creative possibilities: you can take advantage of iPhoto's book themes and page designs to create "slides" containing multiple images and text. (In the interest of readability, think twice about using a lot of small text.)

You can also send a "book slide show" to iDVD; while in book-edit view, choose Share > Send to iDVD.

Clean Up Your Act

iPhoto provides a somewhat hidden (and completely undocumented) command that helps prepare a book for its voyage to Apple's printing service. The command is called Clean Up Book; to access it, Control-click on the gray area outside of your book's page boundaries to bring up a shortcut menu.

Here's what happens when you choose the Clean Up Book command.

1. iPhoto scans through the book from back to front to find the last-filled photo frame, called the *anchor.*

2. For all pages preceding the anchor, iPhoto removes empty photo frames and changes those pages' page types, if possible.

3. Beginning with the page immediately following the anchor, iPhoto places all unplaced photos by first filling any empty photo frames, then by adding pages.

Because this command can potentially alter your book's formatting (for example, by changing a three-photo page type to a two-photo page type), you might think twice before choosing it. It's better to go through your book yourself for final fine-tuning.

If you do use Clean Up Book and aren't happy with the results, choose Undo before doing anything else to restore your book's design.

Print It Yourself

iPhoto's Print command is alive and well when you're in book view: you can print some or all of your book for proofreading or to bind it yourself.

Tip: If you know that you'll be printing a book yourself and not ordering it through Apple's print service, create the book in single-sided format. In the book editor, click Settings, then uncheck the Double-sided Pages box.

Printing a specific page is a bit cumbersome. Here's the easiest way to do it: in iPhoto's Print dialog box, click the Preview button. When Mac OS X's Preview program starts, display its sidebar (choose View > Sidebar, or, in earlier Mac OS X versions, View > Drawer) to find the number of the page you want to print. Then, while still in the Preview program, choose the Print command and specify that page number.

Single-Sided Books

It's worth noting that you can order hardcover books with single-sided pages—just uncheck the Double-Sided Pages box as noted on the opposite page. In a single-sided book, the left-hand page of each spread is blank. That's unlike any coffee-table book I've ever seen, but if it's what you want, iPhoto can accommodate. (Softcover and wire-bound books always have double-sided pages.)

Mirroring a Photo

Want to flip a photo so that it appears "backwards"? Select the photo in its book frame, then Control-click on it and choose Mirror Image from the shortcut menu.

Here's an easy design trick: Add the same photo to the left and right pages of a two-page spread. Then, mirror one of the photos so that the two photos appear to reflect one another.

Changing Stacking Order

When you have multiple items on a page, you can change the way they overlap. For example, some themes position photos so they overlap. To change the way two photos overlap, Control-click on a photo and choose Move to Front or Send to Back.

Fun with PDFs

You can perform several PDF-related tricks with your books. For more details on these tricks, see www.macilife.com/iphoto.

Combining book designs. You love one of the page designs from the Family Album theme, but you really want to use the Line Border theme for your book. No problem—if you're using Mac OS X Leopard, where the Preview program boasts some powerful PDF-manipulation talents.

Here's the big picture. Create the page that you'll want to add to a *different* book. Preview your book to create a PDF in the Preview program. Extract the page that you want to put in the different book, and save it as a JPEG, with maximum quality. Then, choose Tools > Adjust Size, and specify a width of at least 3,000 pixels. Save this enlarged JPEG, add it to your iPhoto library, and then add it to the book project, choosing a layout that provides one photo per page. The result: two different themes within one book.

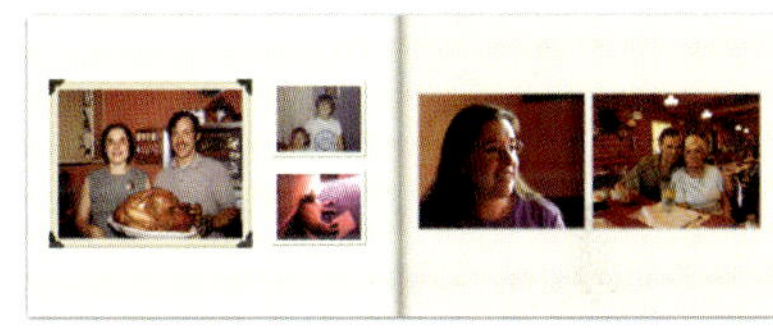

Here's a spread that presents some old photos using the Family Album theme opposite some new photos and the Line Border theme.

Book page to poster. How would you like take one page of a book and turn it into a 20 by 30 inch poster? Create a high-resolution version of a page using Preview as described above, then use edit view to crop it to the proportions of the specific print size you want (such as 20 by 30 inches). Then order a print of the page.

PDFs everywhere. Use the Print command to create a PDF of your book (choose Save as PDF in the Print dialog box). Email the PDF to a friend. Post it on your Web site. Include it in the DVD-ROM portion of an iDVD project (page 312). Or stash it in your iTunes library, if that's your idea of fun (page 86).

Creating a Photo Calendar

Store-bought calendars can be gorgeous, but they lack a certain something: *your* photos. Why build your year around someone else's photos when you can build it around your own?

With the calendar-publishing features in iPhoto, you can create calendars containing as few as 12 months and as many as 24. Choose from numerous design themes, each of which formats your photos and the dates of the month in a different way. Then drag photos into your calendar, fine-tuning their cropping and appearance along the way, if you like.

Commercial calendars usually have national holidays printed on them. Yours can, too—and then some. You can add your own milestones to your calendar: birthdays, anniversaries, dentist-appointment reminders. If you use Apple's iCal software (page 118), you can even import events from iCal and have them appear in your calendar.

When you're finished, click the Buy Calendar button. iPhoto transfers your photos and design to Apple's printing service, which prints your calendar and ships it to you. A 12-month calendar costs $19.99. Each additional month is $1.49.

And you don't have to postpone your foray into calendar publishing until next year. You can have your calendar begin with any month you like.

The Big Picture

Step 1. The most efficient way to create a calendar is to first add the photos you want to publish to an album.

Tip: To further streamline your layout work, sequence the photos in the album in the same general order in which you want them to appear in the calendar.

Step 2. Click the Calendar button. The Themes panel appears.

Step 3. Choose a theme (click its name to see a preview of its design), then click Choose or press Return.

A bigger year. For iPhoto '08, calendars measure 10.4 by 13 inches—70 percent larger than iPhoto '06 calendars.

Step 4. Specify calendar details, then click OK. Here's your first big opportunity to customize the calendar so it contains dates that are important to you.

How many months? Type a number between 12 and 24 or click the arrow buttons.

When? Choose a starting month and a year.

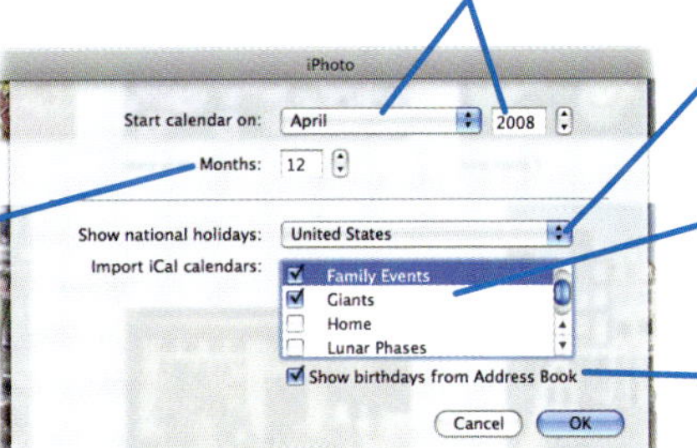

Veterans Day? Deepavali? Queen's Day? Specify your preferred national holiday list, or choose None.

Use iCal? To include iCal dates in your calendar, check the box next to the calendar.

Store birthdays in Mac OS X's Address Book program? You can automatically include them in your calendar.

Step 5. Drag photos into your calendar's pages, or click the Autoflow button.

Switch between viewing calendar thumbnails (shown here) or photos you're using in the calendar (page 216).

Switch views and perform various design tasks (page 216).

Layout for the lazy: click Autoflow, and iPhoto adds photos for you (page 216).

To replace this placeholder text with your own, select the text and type.

View the next or previous month.

Zoom in on a page for proofreading and fine tuning.

Step 6. Step through each month of the calendar, fine-tuning designs and adding custom date items as desired (see the following pages for details and tips).

You can adjust a photo's position within its frame.

Each calendar design offers a variety of photo layouts, some providing space for captions.

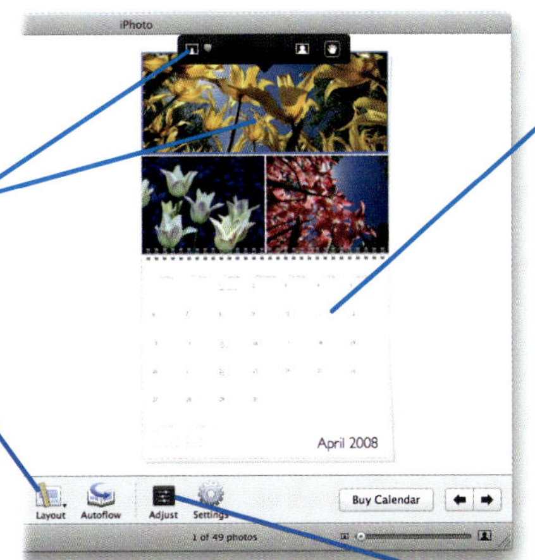

To add text to a date, click its name and type the text in the box that appears. As page 217 shows, you can also add photos and captions to specific dates.

You can adjust a photo's appearance without affecting the original photo.

Step 7. Click Buy Calendar and pay using your Apple ID (page 15).

Tips for Creating Calendars

Choosing Photos

When creating a calendar, try to choose photos that relate to a given month. Use photos of a family member for the month of his or her birthday. If you have some particularly fine holiday shots, use them for the month of December. This sounds obvious, I know, but you'd be surprised how many times I see iPhoto calendars with photos that bear no relationship to the months in which they appear.

Think vivid. I've ordered several calendars, and in my experience, photos with soft, muted colors often print poorly. You're likely to see faint vertical stripes, sometimes called *banding*, in the photos. I get the best results when I use photos that have bright, vivid colors. Black-and-white photos work beautifully, too, provided they have strong contrast.

Layout Techniques

Laying out a calendar involves many of the same techniques behind book creation (pages 204–213). You can add photos by hand, dragging them from the thumbnails area into specific months, or you can click the Autoflow button and have iPhoto sling the photos into your year as it sees fit. As with books, I prefer the manual layout technique for calendars.

How many photos in a month? iPhoto's calendar themes, like its book themes, provide multiple page designs. Some designs provide for just one photo for a given month, while others allow for a half dozen or more.

I like to minimize the number of photos I use each month. Bigger photos have a more dramatic look, and they're easier to see and appreciate when the calendar is hanging on a wall at the opposite end of a room. For most of my calendars, I put just one photo on each month.

That's a rule that begs to be broken, and I do break it now and then. If I have relatively low-resolution photos and iPhoto displays its yellow warning triangle, I'll switch to a page design that has smaller photo frames. Or if I have a series of photos that tells a story about a particular month, I'll choose a page design that lets me use all of those photos.

Top, bottom, or both? Normally, iPhoto's calendar view displays both halves of a given month—that is, the upper portion, where your photos appear, and the lower portion, where the days and weeks are displayed. Between those two halves is the spiral binding that holds the calendar together.

But when you're fine-tuning a calendar's design, you may find it useful to display only the upper or lower portions. The answer? Tear out the spiral binding. Click the single-pages View button (▪), and iPhoto displays only the upper or lower portion of a month.

To switch between viewing the upper or lower portion of a month, display the calendar's page thumbnails (click the ▪ button at the top of the thumbnails area), then click the thumbnail of the page you want to view.

Adding Photos to Dates

When creating a calendar, your photo options aren't limited to just the page above each month. You can also add photos to individual dates. To commemorate a birthday, add a photo to the birthday girl's date. To never forget your anniversary, put a wedding photo on the date. (Another good way to never forget an anniversary is to forget it just once, but this method is not recommended.)

To add a photo to a date, drag it from the thumbnails area of the calendar.

To remove a photo from a date, select the date and press the Delete key.

Don't Forget About the iCal Angle

When creating a new calendar, you can choose to have iPhoto include event information from iCal (discussed on page 222). You can also add iCal data to an existing calendar by clicking the Settings button and checking the appropriate Import iCal Calendars box.

Don't use iCal to manage your life? As I mentioned on page 223, you can download thousands of calendars from iCalShare (www.icalshare.com). Because I like my calendars to include the phases of the moon, I subscribed to a lunar calendar at iCalShare. When I'm creating a new calendar, I simply check the moon-phases calendar and iPhoto does the rest.

Improving Your Calendar Typography

Many of the typographic tips that apply to books (pages 210–211) also apply to calendars.

Global formatting. You can change the fonts that iPhoto uses for various elements of the calendar—its dates and captions, for example—by clicking the Settings button, then clicking Styles. Most of the items in the Settings dialog box are self-explanatory. The two that are less than obvious are Page Text and Comments. The Page Text item controls the font in which dates, days of the week, and the month appear. The Comments item controls the formatting of custom text that you add.

Local formatting. As with books, you can also override iPhoto's font settings and apply formatting to individual text items, but within limits: you can't apply local formatting to a specific date. (For example, you can't have February 14 appear in a bold red font.) You can apply local formatting only to comments and photo captions. To do so, display the item's text box (click on the date, and the text box zooms into view), then select the text and use the Fonts panel as described on pages 210–211.

Curl those quotes. It's common to use apostrophes in calendars: *Sophie's Birthday*, *President's Day*, and so on. But iPhoto commits a cardinal typographic sin by using those heinous "typewriter quotes" instead of true typographer's quotes:

Heinous: Sophie's Birthday

Correct: Sophie's Birthday

Fortunately, it's easy to make your quotes typographically correct. To get a true typographer's apostrophe, press Shift-Option-] (that's the right-bracket key, just above the Return key).

Customizing Photos on Dates

You can customize the way a photo appears on a date.

iPhoto displays the date to which the photo belongs.

To display a text caption adjacent to the photo, check the Caption box. iPhoto uses the photo's title as the caption text, but you can replace that text by selecting it and typing your own. (For details on assigning titles to photos, see page 140.)

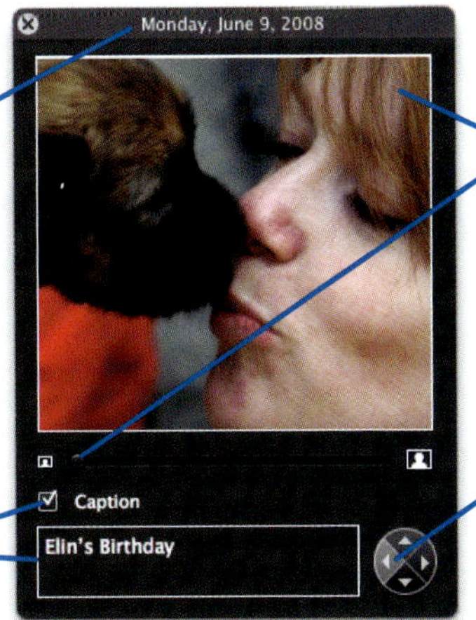

As with slide shows and books, you can fine-tune a photo's composition without having to use the Crop tool. Drag the size slider to zoom in, then drag the photo within its frame until it's positioned as desired.

Photo captions appear on an adjacent date, with an arrow pointing to the photo. To choose where the caption appears, click an arrow. In this example, I've clicked the left arrow, telling iPhoto to display the caption on the date to the left of the photo.

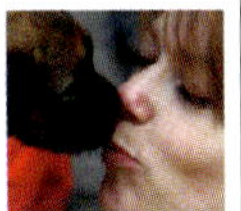

Creating Greeting Cards and Postcards

Let us hereby resolve to never buy a greeting card from a store rack again. Okay, maybe that's a bit strong. But with the greeting card and postcard features in iPhoto, you can definitely curtail your contributions to Hallmark's balance sheet.

An iPhoto greeting card measures 5 by 7 inches, and is of the "tent" variety—folded on its top. (Assuming you use a horizontally oriented photo, that is: if you use a vertically oriented photo, the card's fold is on the left side.) In quantities of 1 to 24, cards cost $1.99 each. Order 25 to 49 cards for $1.79 each; 50 or more cards are $1.59 each.

As for postcards, they measure 4 by 6 inches and cost $1.49 each (1–24), $1.29 each (25–49), or $.99 each (50 or more). The back of a postcard can contain a full block of text or you can use a standard postcard-mailing format, complete with a "place postage here" box.

Greeting cards and postcards are printed on a heavy card stock and include matching envelopes. Even if you order a postcard with a "place postage here" box, you still get an envelope—complete with an embossed Apple logo on its flap.

So forget this era of email and instant messaging, and use iPhoto to create some old-fashioned correspondence. Your recipients will thank you.

Creating a Greeting Card

Step 1. Select the photo that you want on the greeting card.

Step 2. Click the Card button.

Step 3. Choose Greeting Card from the pop-up menu, choose a theme, then click Choose or press Return.

I'm partial to the Picture Card theme, which prints a borderless photo.

Step 4. Replace the card's placeholder text with your own and then fine-tune the design, if desired (opposite page).

Tip: To have the inside of the card appear blank, just leave the placeholder text as is—or, if you're nervous about getting a card that contains the heartwarming message *Insert Title*, delete the placeholder text.

Step 5. Proofread any text you added, then proofread it again. Then, click Buy Card and pay using your Apple ID (page 15).

Creating a Postcard

Step 1. Select the photo you want to include on the postcard.

Step 2. Click the Card button.

Step 3. Choose Postcard from the pop-up menu, choose a theme, then click Choose or press Return.

The themes are similar to their greeting-card counterparts.

Step 4. Replace the card's placeholder text and then fine-tune the design, if desired.

Step 5. Do that proofreading thing you do so well, then click Buy Card and pay using your Apple ID.

Tip: Want to use a book layout as a card? Follow the instructions on page 213, then add the resulting JPEG to a card that uses the Picture Card theme.

Card Design Tips

Switching postcard styles. To switch between a self-mailing postcard and one that tucks into an envelope, select the back of the postcard, then use the Design pop-up menu.

Switching designs and backgrounds. All card themes provide more than one design option for the front of the card. Many themes, for example, provide an option that lets you type some text on the front of the card. To access different designs, select the front of the card, then use the Design pop-up menu.

Many theme designs also offer a selection of background colors or textures. You can access them by using the Background pop-up menu.

Fine-tuning photos. As with books, slide shows, and calendars, you can adjust the appearance and positioning of a photo without having to edit the original. Simply click on the photo, then use the slider to zoom in as desired. To position the photo within its frame, drag it.

To fine-tune the photo's exposure, click the Adjust button.

Fun with fonts. As with books and calendars, you can customize the font formatting of your card in two ways: by using the Settings button, or by bringing up the Fonts panel (⌘-T). The latter option lets you format text on an individual word (or character, if you want to taunt the design police) basis.

And while you're having fun with fonts, note that the text-formatting tips outlined on pages 210–211 also apply to cards.

Print it yourself. As with books, you can print greeting cards and postcards on your own color inkjet printer. Just choose the Print command while the card editor is visible. Note that if you plan to use both sides of the card, you'll need to use inkjet paper designed for double-sided printing.

Kill the apple. Ever conscious of brand recognition, Apple prints its logo on the back of a greeting card. If you'd rather not provide the free advertising, click the Settings button and uncheck the box labeled *Include Apple logo on back of card.*

More Ways to Share Photos

By using the Export command in the File menu, you can turn a photo album—or any set of photos that you've selected—into a portable slide show.

iPhoto can combine a series of photos into a QuickTime movie, complete with a music soundtrack from your iTunes library. You can publish the resulting movie on a Web site, burn it to a CD, or bring it into iDVD and burn it to a DVD. Think of an iPhoto QuickTime movie as a portable slide show. It will play back on any Mac or Windows computer that has QuickTime installed.

As you know, you can create two kinds of slide shows in iPhoto—basic and saved (see pages 178–185). You can export either type as a QuickTime movie. If you export a saved (cinematic) slide show, the resulting movie will have all your Ken Burns moves and custom transition and duration settings. On the other hand, if you simply export an album or selection of photos as a movie, each photo is always separated by a dissolve transition. You can't use the other transitions, such as Cube, that iPhoto's Slideshow dialog box provides, nor will your movie have any automatic Ken Burns moves. When your sweet tooth craves eye candy, you'll want to create a saved slide show and export it.

Looking for still more ways to share? Redecorate your Macintosh desktop with your favorite photo. Or, use a set of photos as a screen saver.

It's obvious: if your digital photos aren't getting seen, it isn't iPhoto's fault.

Exporting a Saved Slide Show Movie

Step 1. In the Slideshows list, select the saved slide show that you want to export. **Note:** If you plan to distribute your slide-show movie, don't use songs from the iTunes Store; see page 228.

Step 2. Choose Export from the File menu, and specify export settings.

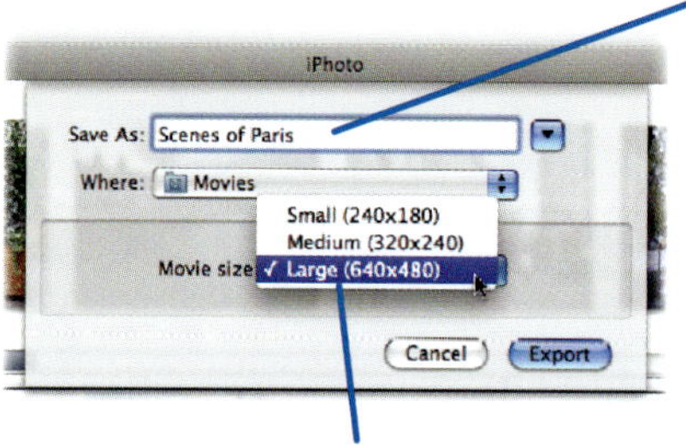

Name your movie. iPhoto normally stores exported movies in your Movies folder, but you can store them anywhere you like.

Choose a movie size. For a movie destined for email or a Web site, choose the Small or Medium option. If you plan to import your movie into iMovie, choose Large—and read the bad news below.

Portable slide show: An iPhoto-created QuickTime movie playing back in the QuickTime Player program.

Tips

Heading for iDVD? If you want to include a cinematic slide show in an iDVD project, you have an alternative to the Export command: just choose Send to iDVD from the Share menu. iPhoto creates a movie version of your slide show and sends it directly to iDVD.

Heading for iMovie? Want to add your exported movie to an iMovie project? Alas, at this writing, iMovie '08 won't let you. There is a workaround; see www.macilife.com/imovie. Or just make your slide shows directly in iMovie.

Exporting a Basic Slide Show Movie

Step 1.
Select a set of images, an event, or an album, then choose Export from the File menu.

Step 2.
To access movie-export options, click QuickTime.

Specify the duration for each image to display.

You can specify that iPhoto add a background color or background image to the movie. The color or image appears whenever the dimensions of the currently displayed photo don't match that of the movie itself. (For example, in a 640 by 480 movie, the background will be visible in photos shot in vertical orientation.) The background will also be visible at the beginning and end of the movie—before the first image fades in and after the last image fades out.

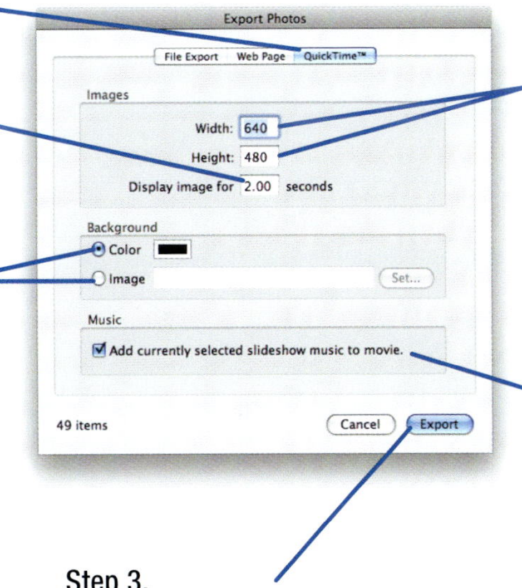

Specify the desired dimensions for the movie, in pixels. The preset values shown here work well, but if you specify smaller dimensions, such as 320 by 240, you'll get a smaller movie file—useful if you plan to distribute the movie over the Internet.

iPhoto uses the song or playlist assigned to your photo library or to the current album (see page 182). To create a silent movie, uncheck this box. **Note:** If you plan to distribute your slide-show movie, don't use songs from the iTunes Store; see page 228.

Step 3.
To create the movie, click Export and type a name for the movie.

Using Photos as Desktop Images and Screen Savers

iPhoto lets you share photos with yourself. Select a photo and choose Share > Set Desktop, and iPhoto replaces the Mac's desktop with the photo you selected.

If you select multiple photos or an event or album, your desktop image will change as you work, complete with a cross-dissolve effect between images. It's an iPhoto slide show applied to your desktop.

Another way to turn an iPhoto album or event into a desktop screen saver is to use the Desktop & Screen Saver system preference—choose the album in the Screen Savers list (right).

Warning: Using vacation photos as desktop images has been proven to cause wanderlust.

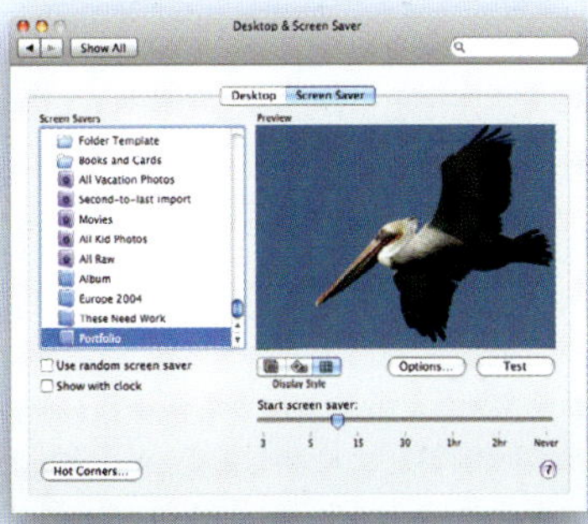

Burning Photos to CDs and DVDs

The phrase "burning photos" can strike terror into any photographer's heart, but fear not: I'm not talking about open flames here. Fire up your Mac's burner, and you can save, or burn, photos onto CDs or DVDs. You can burn your entire photo library, an album or two, some favorite events, a slide show, or even just one photo.

iPhoto's burning features make possible all manner of photo-transportation tasks. Back up your photo library: burn the entire library and then stash the disc in a safe place. Move photos and albums from one Mac to another: burn a selection, then insert the disc in another Mac to work with them there.

iPhoto doesn't just copy photos to a disc. It creates a full-fledged iPhoto library on the disc. That library contains the images' titles and keywords, any albums that you burned, and even original versions of images you've retouched or cropped. Think of an iPhoto-burned disc as a portable iPhoto library.

That's all grand, but your burning desires may be different. Maybe you want to burn photos for a friend who uses Windows, or for printing by a photofinisher. That's easy, too.

So back away from that fire extinguisher—we've got some burning to do.

Burning Basics

Burning photos involves selecting what you want to burn, then telling iPhoto to light a match.

Step 1. Select items to burn.

Remember that you can also select multiple items by Shift-clicking or ⌘-clicking on each one (page 147).

You can also select multiple books, folders, and slide shows—iPhoto can burn them, too. Indeed, burning a disc is the only way to move a book or saved slide show from one Mac to another.

Step 2. Choose Burn from the Share menu.

iPhoto asks you to insert a blank disc.

Tip: If you burn discs frequently, you can have iPhoto display a Burn button in its toolbar. Choose View > Show in Toolbar > Burn.

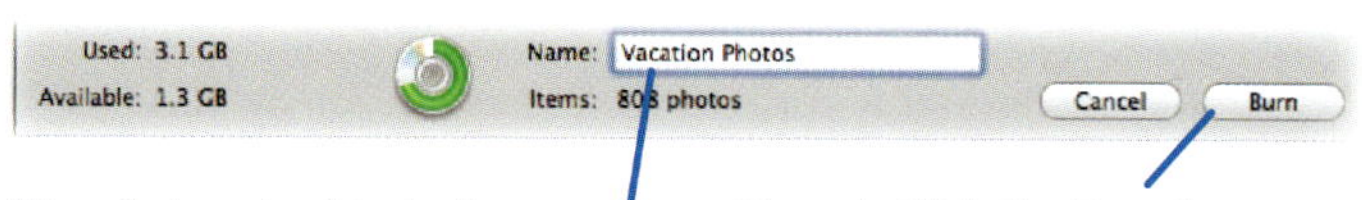

Step 3. Insert a blank disc and click OK.

iPhoto displays information about the pending burn. You can add photos to or remove them from the selection, and iPhoto will update its information area accordingly.

Tip: Give your disc a descriptive name by typing in the Name box.

Step 4. Click the Burn button.

iPhoto displays another dialog box. To cancel the burn, click Cancel. To proceed, click Burn.

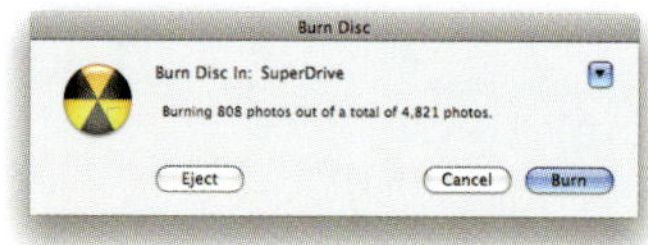

iPhoto prepares the images, then burns and verifies the contents of the disc.

Working with Burned Discs

When you insert a disc burned in iPhoto, the disc appears in the Shares list. To see its photos, select the disc's name. Note that the disc's photos aren't in the iPhoto library on your hard drive—they're in the iPhoto library on the disc.

A small triangle appears next to the disc's name. To view the disc's items, click the triangle.

You can display photos on a disc using the same techniques that you use to display photos stored in your iPhoto library. You can also display basic slide shows, email photos, and order prints.

However, you can't edit photos stored on a burned disc, nor can you create an iWeb photo album, a Web gallery album, a saved slide show, a book, a calendar, or a greeting card. To perform these tasks, add the photos to your photo library as described at right.

Copying Items from a Burned Disc

To modify an item that's stored on a burned disc, you must copy it to your iPhoto library.

To copy an item, select it and drag it to the Events or Photos item in the Library area.

Note: When copying a book or saved slide show to a different Mac, be sure that the destination Mac contains the same fonts or music used in the book or slide show.

Burning for Windows or Photofinishers

Here's how to burn photos for a friend who uses Windows, or for printing by a photofinisher. You can also use these steps to burn a disc for a fellow Mac user who doesn't use iPhoto.

Step 1. Prepare a disc. Insert a blank CD or DVD in your Mac's optical drive. The dialog box below appears.

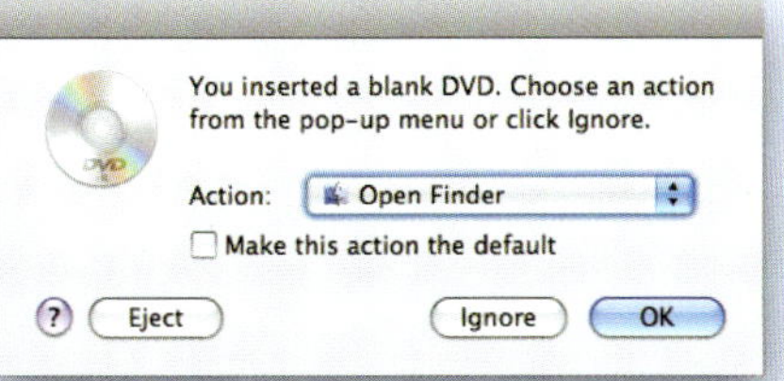

Type a name for the CD and click OK. The blank disc's icon appears on your desktop.

Step 2. Copy the photos. Position the iPhoto window so that you can see it and the blank disc's icon. Drag the photos that you want to burn to the icon of the blank disc.

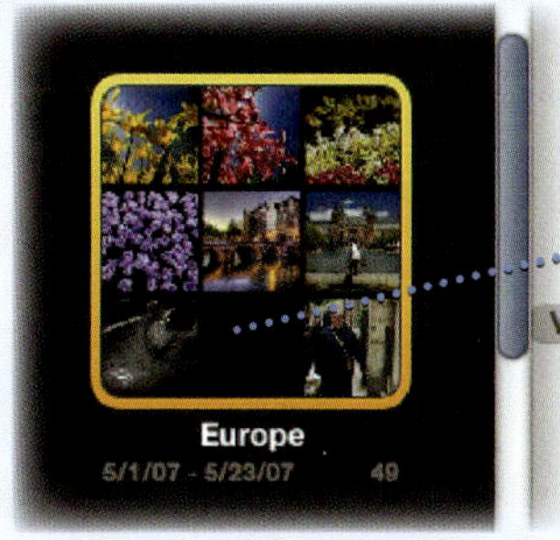

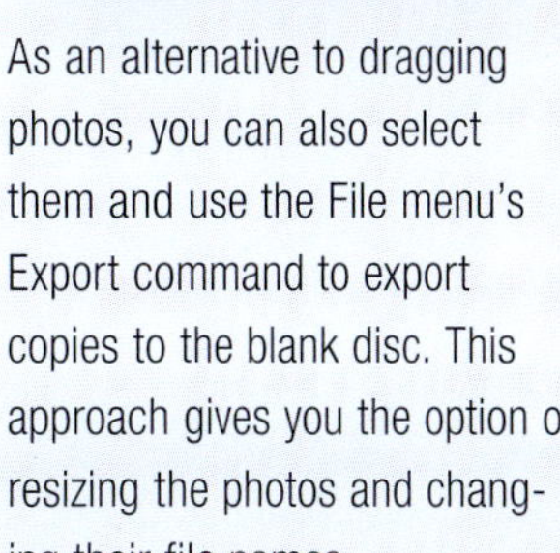

As an alternative to dragging photos, you can also select them and use the File menu's Export command to export copies to the blank disc. This approach gives you the option of resizing the photos and changing their file names.

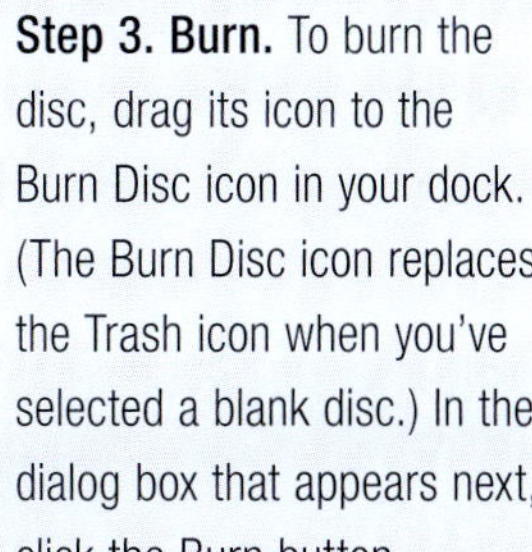

Step 3. Burn. To burn the disc, drag its icon to the Burn Disc icon in your dock. (The Burn Disc icon replaces the Trash icon when you've selected a blank disc.) In the dialog box that appears next, click the Burn button.

Creating and Managing Photo Libraries

As your photo library grows to encompass thousands of photos, locating specific images can be cumbersome. A huge photo library is also more difficult to back up, since it may not fit on a CD or even a DVD.

One solution: create more photo libraries. iPhoto lets you have multiple photo libraries and switch between them. If your photo library has reached gargantuan proportions, back it up and create a new, empty one.

How often should you create a new library? That depends. You might base your decision on disk space: if you back up your library by burning it to a DVD-R, create a new library each time the size of your current library reaches about 4GB (or, if you burn to dual-layer discs, 8GB). That way, you can always be sure your library will fit on a DVD. (To see how much space your library uses, select the Events or Photos items in the Library area, then look in the Information pane.)

Or, you might prefer a chronological approach. If you take hundreds of photos (or more) every month, consider creating a new library each month. Then again, maybe a subject-oriented approach is best for you. Use one iPhoto library to hold your family shots, and another to hold work-related shots.

The latest iPhoto versions are fast enough to manage tens of thousands of photos. But if dividing your photo collection across multiple libraries makes managing and backing up photos easier for you, here's what you need to know.

Creating a New Library

Before creating a new library, you may want to back up your existing library by dragging your iPhoto Library to another hard drive or to a blank CD or DVD. For some backup strategies, see the sidebar on the opposite page.

Step 1. Quit iPhoto.

Step 2. Locate your iPhoto Library and rename it.

To quickly locate the library, choose Home from the Finder's Go menu, then double-click the Pictures folder, where you'll find the iPhoto Library.

Step 3. Start iPhoto.

iPhoto asks if you want to locate an existing library or create a new one.

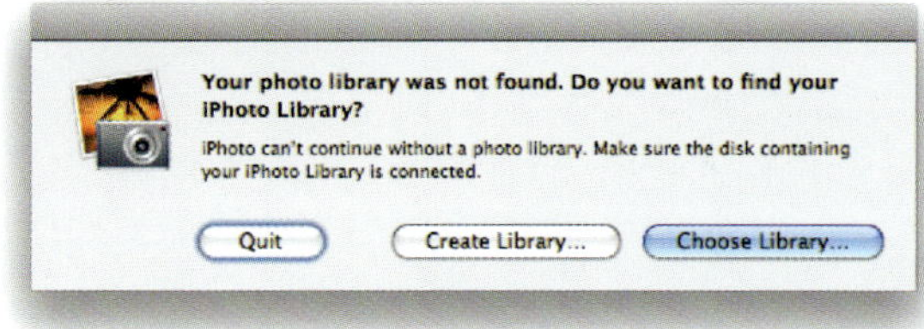

Step 4. Click Create Library.

iPhoto proposes the name iPhoto Library, but you can type a different name if you like.

You don't need to store your library in the Pictures folder; see the sidebar below.

Step 5. Click Save, and iPhoto creates the new, empty library.

Switching Between Libraries

There may be times when you want to switch to a different iPhoto library—for example, to access the photos in an older library. Here's how.

Step 1. Quit iPhoto.

Step 2. Locate your current iPhoto Library and change its name.

Step 3. Start iPhoto.

iPhoto asks if you want to find an existing library or create a new one.

Step 4. Click Choose Library. The Open Photo Library dialog box appears.

Tip: You can also display the Open Photo Library dialog box by pressing the Option key while starting iPhoto.

Step 5. Select the library you want to use and click the Open button.

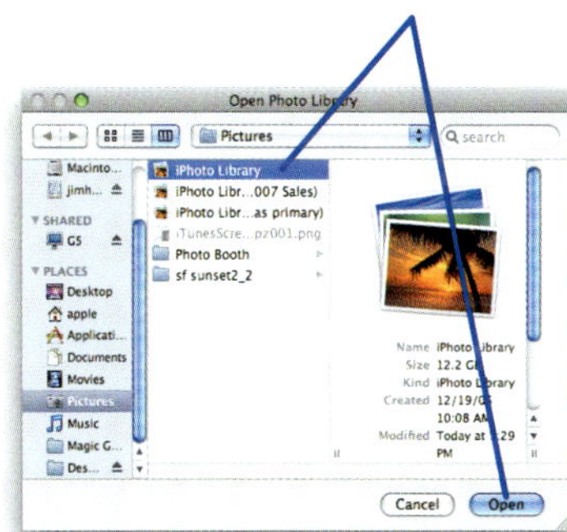

Managing and Backing Up Your Library

Storing Photos Elsewhere

Normally, iPhoto stores your photo library in the Pictures folder. You might prefer to store your library elsewhere, such as on an external FireWire hard drive.

To store your photo library elsewhere, quit iPhoto, then simply move the iPhoto Library wherever you like. If you're copying the library to a different disk, delete the original library after the copy is complete. Restart iPhoto, click the Choose Library button, and use the Open Photo Library dialog box to aim iPhoto in the right direction.

Backing Up

In the film days, you had to fall victim to a fire or other disaster in order to lose all your photos. In the digital age, it's much easier to lose photos; all it takes is a hardware failure or software glitch.

Please don't let photo loss happen to you. Take the time to back up your iPhoto libraries.

If your library will fit on a single blank disc, use iPhoto's burning features to back up.

If your library won't fit on a single disc, buy an external FireWire hard drive and drag your iPhoto Library over to it. Repeat this procedure every now and then.

You can also use backup software. Apple's own Backup, included with a .Mac membership, can copy photos to CDs, DVDs, or hard drives. Many other backup programs are available, including Dantz Development's powerful Retrospect and Econ Technologies' friendly ChronoSync. And Apple's Mac OS X 10.5 (Leopard) has an automatic backup system called Time Machine.

Getting Old Photos into iPhoto

You love your digital camera and the convenience of iPhoto, and it would take an act of Congress to force you to use film again.

And yet the past haunts you. You have boxes of negatives and slides that you haven't seen in years. If you could get them into iPhoto, you could organize them into albums and share them through Web albums, slide shows, prints and books, and even movies and DVDs.

To bridge the gap between pixels and print, you need a scanner. Here's an overview of what to look for, and some strategies for getting those old photos into iPhoto.

Scanning the Options

Before you buy a scanner, take stock of what types of media you'll need to digitize. Do you have negatives, prints, slides, or all three? Not all scanners are ideal for every task.

Flatbed scanners. If you'll be scanning printed photos, a *flatbed scanner* is your best bet. Place a photo face down on the scanner's glass, and a sensor glides beneath it and captures the image.

Repeating this process for hundreds of photos can be tedious. If you have a closet full of photos, you may want to look for a scanner that supports an automatic document feeder so you can scan a stack of photos without having to hand-feed the scanner. Some flatbeds include photo feeders that can handle up to 24 prints in sizes up to 4 by 6 inches. Other scanners accept optional document feeders. Just be sure to verify that the document feeder can handle photos—many can't.

Film scanners. A print is one generation away from the original image, and may have faded with time or been poorly printed to begin with. Worse, many photos are printed on linen-finish paper, whose rough texture blurs image detail when scanned. Bottom line: you'll get better results by scanning the original film.

Many flatbed scanners include a film adaptor for scanning negatives or slides. With some scanners, the adaptor snaps on to the scanner's bed. A more convenient option is a scanner with the adaptor built into the lid, such as Epson's Perfection V750-M Pro. Like many high-end flatbed units, this scanner can scan negatives, mounted slides and, unlike many flatbeds, medium-format film, such as the 120 format popular in old cameras.

A flatbed scanner with a film adaptor is a versatile scanning system, but a *film scanner* provides much sharper scans of negatives and slides. Unfortunately, this quality will cost you: film scanners cost more than flatbeds.

Many film scanners provide a dust- and scratch-removal option called Digital ICE (short for *image correction/enhancement*). Developed by Kodak's Austin Development Center (www.asf.com) and licensed to numerous scanner manufacturers, Digital ICE does an astonishingly good job of cleaning up color film. However, it doesn't work with black-and-white negatives.

Scanning Right

Whether you use a flatbed or film scanner, you'll encounter enough jargon to intimidate an astronaut: histograms, tone curves, black points, white points. Don't fret: all scanners include software that provides presets for common scanning scenarios, such as scanning for color ink-jet output. Start with these presets. As you learn about scanning, you can customize settings to optimize your exposures.

The right resolution. A critical scanning setting deals with how many dots per inch (dpi) the scanner uses to represent an image. Volumes have been written about scanning resolution, but it boils down to a simple rule of thumb: If you're using a flatbed scanner and you plan to print your scans on a photo inkjet printer, you can get fine results with a resolution of 180 to 240 dpi. If you plan to order photographic prints from your scans, scan at 300 dpi. Scanning at more than 300 dpi will usually not improve quality—but it will definitely use more disk space.

Film scanners are different. A film scanner scans a much smaller original—for example, a 35mm negative instead of a 4 by 6 inch print. To produce enough data for high-quality prints, a film scanner must scan at a much higher resolution than a flatbed. The film scanner I use, Minolta's Scan Elite 5400, scans at up to 5400 dpi.

This difference in approach can make for even more head scratching when it comes time to decide what resolution to use. Just do what I do: use the presets in the scanning software. I typically choose my film scanner's "PhotoCD 2048 by 3072" option, which yields a file roughly equivalent to a six-megapixel image.

Special circumstances. If you plan to apply iPhoto's or iMovie's Ken Burns effect to an image, you'll want a high-resolution scan so you can zoom in without encountering jagged pixels. Experiment to find the best resolution for a specific image and zoom setting.

In a related vein, if you plan to crop out unwanted portions of an image, scan at a higher resolution than you might normally use. Cropping discards pixels, so the more data you have to begin with, the more cropping flexibility you have.

Format strategies. Which file format should you use for saving images? The JPEG format is *lossy:* it sacrifices quality slightly in order to save disk space. If this is the last time you plan to scan those old photos, you may not want to save them in a lossy format. When scanning my old slides and negatives, I save the images as TIFF files.

Photos, Meet iPhoto

Once you've scanned and saved your photos, you can import them into iPhoto.

Filing photos. To take advantage of iPhoto's filing features, you may want to have a separate iPhoto event for each set of related photos. In the Finder, move each set of related photos into its own folder, giving each folder a descriptive name, such as *Vacation 1972*. Next, drag each folder into the iPhoto window. iPhoto gives each event the same name as its corresponding folder.

You can delete the folders after you've imported their shots, since iPhoto will have created duplicates in iPhoto Library. (If you prefer to retain your existing filing system, you can set up iPhoto to not copy the photos to the iPhoto Library; see page 135.)

Turn back the clock. To make your iPhoto library chronologically accurate, change the date of the photos and events to reflect when the photos were taken, not when they were imported (see page 141).

Time for retouching. You can use iPhoto's Retouch tool to fix scratches and dust specks, and its Enhance button and Adjust panel to fix color and exposure problems. For serious retouching, though, use Photoshop Elements or Photoshop. To learn more about digital retouching, I recommend Katrin Eisman's *Photoshop Restoration and Retouching, Third Edition* (New Riders, 2005).

Plug in to photo enhancement. Old photos do fade away, typically acquiring a blue or red tint as their dyes, well, die. If you have patience and a good eye for color, you can improve an old photo's color using iPhoto's Adjust panel or Photoshop.

If you have $99, you can buy a Photoshop plug-in that does the job for you. Digital ROC Pro, from Kodak, does an amazing job of improving faded photos. Digital ROC also works in Photoshop Elements. You can download a trial version of it, and more, at www.asf.com.

iPhoto Tips

Tinting a Black-and-White Photo

You can use the Adjust panel's color-adjustment sliders to apply a color tint to a black-and-white photo. After converting the photo to black and white (and improving on it using the tip on page 165, if you like), save the photo. Then reopen it in edit view and drag the color sliders.

Purchased Songs and Slide Shows

You can use songs from the iTunes Store for slide show soundtracks. But if you plan to export the slide shows as QuickTime movies, note that the songs will play only on computers authorized for your iTunes account. The workaround: burn the songs to an audio CD, then re-rip them into iTunes, and use those unprotected versions for your soundtracks.

Note that this limitation does not apply to iTunes Plus songs, which are not copy-protected.

Controlling the Camera Connection

Normally, when you connect a camera or an iPhone, your Mac plops you into iPhoto. You might prefer that it didn't—it can be annoying when you're simply syncing your iPhone, for example.

To control what happens when you connect a camera to your Mac, choose iPhoto > Preferences. Click the General button, and in the Connecting Camera Opens pop-up menu, choose No Application.

Keywords for Movies and Raw Photos

Normally, assigning keywords to photos is your job (page 142). But iPhoto automatically assigns keywords to two types of items that you import: movie clips and raw-format images.

Movies get the keyword *Movie*, and raw images get the keyword *Raw*. Remember, you can use smart albums to quickly display items with one or more keywords. For example, to see all the movies in your iPhoto library, create a smart album whose criterion is Keyword is *Movie*.

Entering Custom Crop Proportions

With the Constrain pop-up menu in edit view, you can tell iPhoto to restrict cropping rectangles to standard proportions (page 155). If you want non-standard proportions, choose Custom from the Constrain pop-up menu and enter the proportions in the boxes that appear. Note that you can't enter fractional values: 8.5, for example, is rounded up to 9.

Hiding Event Titles

If you're browsing your photo library in Photos view, you can have iPhoto hide event titles and show your entire library as one massive set of thumbnails. In Photos view, choose View > Event Titles. It's a cumbersome way to view your library, but you might find it useful when assigning keywords or renaming photos.

To restore some sanity to Photos view, choose View > Event Titles again.

Rebuilding Your iPhoto Library

If iPhoto is acting up—for example, taking forever to launch, running unusually slowly, or not displaying photo thumbnails—try rebuilding your iPhoto library. Quit iPhoto, then hold down the ⌘ and Option keys while starting iPhoto. A dialog box appears asking if you're sure you want to rebuild your library and giving you several options for doing so.

If your image thumbnails appear gray or blank, try selecting the first two options. If iPhoto crashes or refuses to load photos when you first launch it, try the third option. If some of your photos seem to have disappeared, try the "recover orphaned photos" option. And if iPhoto is misbehaving in several ways, check all five options.

Important: To avoid the risk of making a bad situation worse, consider backing up your iPhoto Library before trying to rebuild your library.

Get links to iPhoto add-ons and additional online photo services.
www.macilife.com/iphoto

Non-Destructive Editing and Older Libraries

On page 152, I discussed how iPhoto '08 has non-destructive editing that maximizes quality by always applying your edits to the original version of an image.

There's an exception to this rule, and it concerns older iPhoto libraries that you've upgraded to work with iPhoto '08. Specifically, if you edit a photo that you previously edited using an older iPhoto version, iPhoto '08 applies your latest changes to the *edited* photo, not to the original. Thus, you don't have the full advantage of non-destructive editing.

The solution? If you want to edit a photo that you've already edited using an older iPhoto version, revert to the original version of the photo. Choose Photos > Revert to Original (or, for raw images, Reprocess Raw). This discards edits you made in the past, and new edits will be applied to the original version of the photo.

Inside the iPhoto Library

With previous iPhoto versions, the iPhoto Library item was a folder: you could open it and change its contents—and doing so was a good way to damage your photo library and to lose photos.

In iPhoto '08, the iPhoto Library item is a *package*—a special kind of Mac OS X folder. If you double-click the iPhoto Library item, your Mac simply starts or switches to iPhoto.

But there *is* a way to get inside if you must. Control-click on the iPhoto Library item and choose Show Package Contents from the shortcut menu. Inside, you'll find a bevy of folders and files that constitute your library.

Leave them be. Always use iPhoto to add or remove photos to or from your library: drag photos into and out of the iPhoto window.

EXIF Exposed: Getting Information About Photos

Digital cameras store information along with each photo—the date and time when the photo was taken, its exposure, the kind of camera used, and more. This is called the *EXIF* data. It's also often called *metadata*.

iPhoto saves this EXIF data when you import photos. To view it, select a photo and choose Photos > Show Photo Info (⌘-I).

Not all of this information will be useful to you, but some of it might. If you have more than one digital camera, for example, you can use the window's Photo tab to see which camera you used for a given shot. And as I mentioned on page 150, you can use smart albums to search for various metadata items. At the very least, you can see what kind of exposure settings your camera is using.

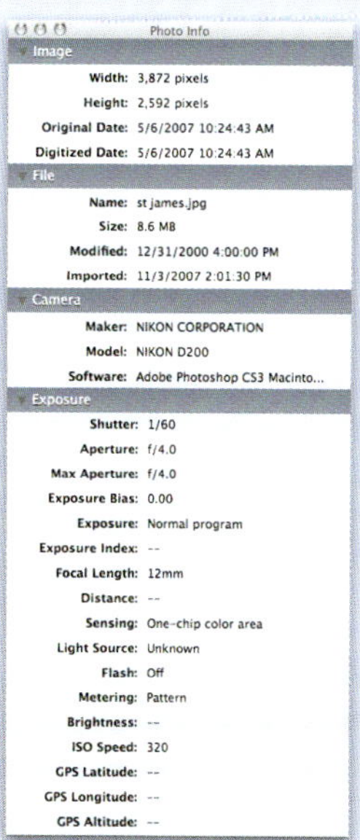

More iPhoto Tips

Including Photos in Documents

You may want to include photos in documents that you're creating in Microsoft Word or other programs. It's easy: just drag the image from iPhoto into your document.

If you use Apple's iWork software—Keynote, Pages, and Numbers—your job is even easier. All three programs provide media browsers much like those in the iLife programs: access your photo library directly, search for a photo, and then add it to a document by dragging it from the media browser.

If you drag an image to the Finder desktop or to a folder window, iPhoto makes a duplicate copy of the image file. Use this technique when you want to copy a photo out of your library.

What Happened to Photocasts?

If you used iPhoto '06, you may remember the photocast feature. It allowed you to publish an album that others could subscribe to using iPhoto or an RSS newsreader—similar to a Web gallery album, but geekier.

Photocasts were cool, at least according to the 16 people who used them. I'm exaggerating, but it's true that relatively few iPhoto users created or subscribed to photocasts. The Web gallery albums in iPhoto '08 provide many of the same automatic updating advantages, but are easier to create and far nicer looking.

iPhoto '08 can't create photocasts, but it can subscribe to them. Simply get the Web address of the photocast and copy it to the Mac's Clipboard. Then, choose File > Subscribe to Photo Feed and paste the address into the dialog box.

The Flickr angle. The Subscribe to Photo Feed command has another use: you can use it to subscribe to photo feeds created by the Flickr online photo sharing service (page 193). Subscribe to a feed, and its photos appear directly in iPhoto. You can view slide shows, make prints, and more. Alas, Flickr provides the photos in low resolution, so you won't be able to make very large prints, and even slide shows will appear chunky. Still, it's good geek fun.

Here's how to do it. Say you'd like to subscribe to my photo feed. (I'm flattered!) Go to my Flickr page (www.flickr.com/photos/jimheid), scroll to the bottom of the page, and locate the Subscribe links. Control-click on the one that reads *Latest,* then choose Copy Link from the shortcut menu.

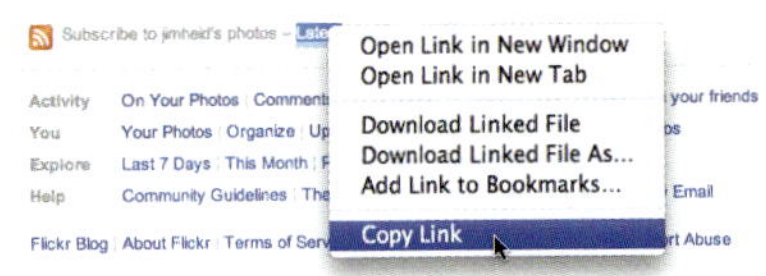

Next, switch to iPhoto, and choose File > Subscribe to Photo Feed. Choose Edit > Paste, then press Return.

My photo feed is added to your Subscriptions list, and iPhoto loads thumbnails of my most recent posts.

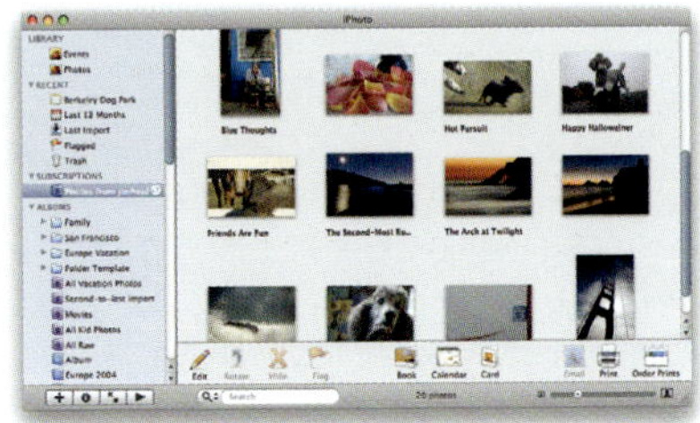

And remember, Flickr generates feeds for just about everything, including groups. Want to keep an eye on photos added to the Standard Poodle group? Subscribe to its feed. And by the way, you're my kind of person.

Emailing Movies

iPhoto can store movie clips that your digital camera takes, but it can't email them. When you select a movie, the Email button is disabled.

The workaround is easy. Start a new, blank email message, then position the iPhoto window so you can see the movie thumbnail and your message. Finally, drag the movie thumbnail from the iPhoto window into the blank email message.

Fun with Mosaics

What's better than a great photo? Dozens or hundreds or even thousands of great photos combined into a photo mosaic.

Here are a few ways to make mosaic magic.

Use Leopard's screen saver. The screen saver in Mac OS X 10.5 (Leopard) has a dazzlingly cool mosaic option. A full-screen version of a photo appears, then grows gradually smaller as other photos appear around it. As the photos get ever tinier, you see what's going on: they're forming a mosaic of yet another photo. The process then repeats with a different photo—it's mesmerizing.

Open the Desktop & Screen Saver system preference, click the Screen Saver button, then choose the Mosaic display style.

Make a life poster. With Zykloid Software's Posterino, you can turn a collection of photos into a full-page poster. Choose from a variety of layout options and templates, then add the poster to iPhoto and order a print or make your own. Or use the poster in an iMovie project, and pan across a year's worth of photos with the Ken Burns effect.

Make a photo mosaic. With a free program called MacOSaiX, you can create a stunning photo mosaic—a single photo made up of thousands of separate photos, each chosen by the software to match the color and tonal qualities of part of the original photo.

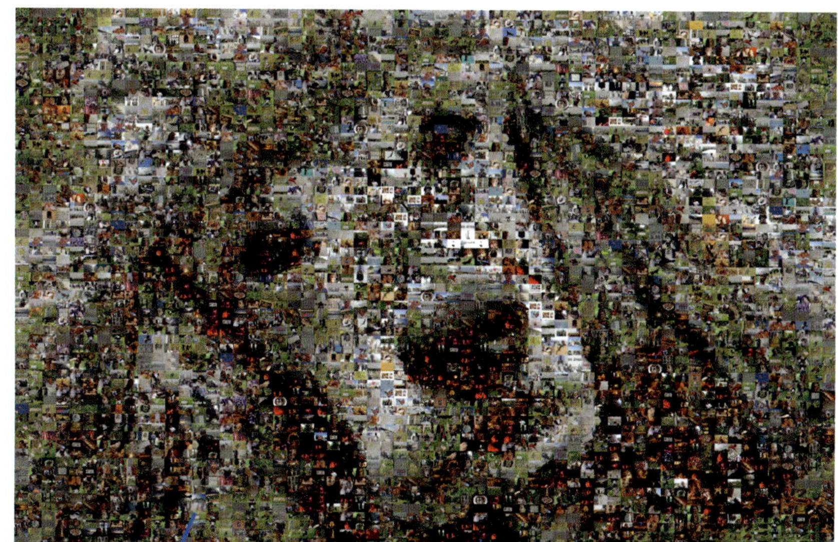

This mosaic, created by the free MacOSaiX software, is made up of over 1200 photos. To see and download the original, visit my Flickr photos (www.flickr.com/photos/jimheid) and search for *mosaic*.

Mastering Your Digital Camera

Resolution Matters

Always shoot at your camera's highest resolution. This gives you maximum flexibility for cropping, for making big prints, and for the Ken Burns effect in iPhoto and iMovie. You can always use iPhoto to make photos smaller (for example, for emailing or Web publishing).

Shutter Lag

Many digital cameras suffer from a curse called *shutter lag*—a delay between the time you press the shutter button and the moment when the shutter actually fires.

Shutter lag occurs because the camera's built-in computer must calculate exposure and focus. If you're shooting fast-moving subjects, it's easy to miss the shot you wanted.

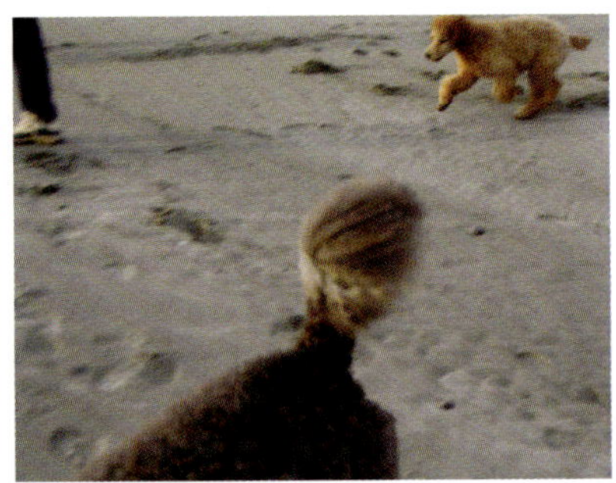

The solution: give your camera a head start. Press and hold the shutter button partway, and the camera calculates focus and exposure. Now wait until the right moment arrives, then press the button the rest of the way.

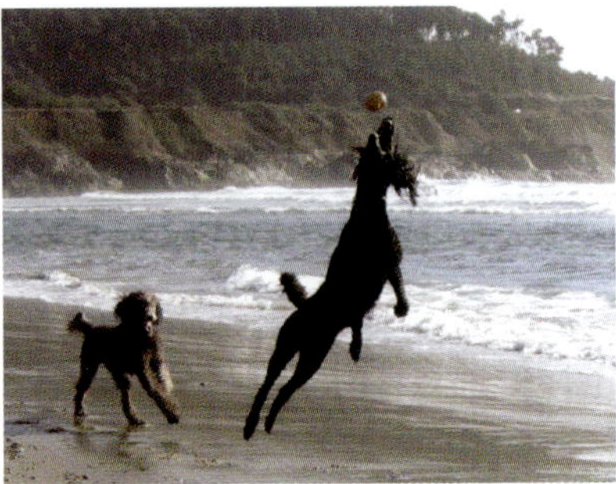

ISO Speeds

In the film world, if you want to take low-light shots, you can buy high-speed film—ISO 400 or 800, for example. Fast film allows you to take nighttime or indoor shots without the harsh glare of electronic flash.

Digital cameras allow you to adjust light sensitivity on a shot-by-shot basis. Switch the camera into one of its manual-exposure modes (a common mode is labeled *P*, for *program*), and then use the camera's menus to adjust its ISO speed.

Note that shots photographed at higher ISO speeds—particularly 400 and 800—are likely to have digital *noise*, a slightly grainy appearance. For me, it's a happy trade-off: I'd rather have a sharp, naturally lit photo with some noise than a noise-free but blurry (or flash-lit) photo.

Higher ISO speeds can also help you capture fast-moving action by day. The higher speed forces the camera to use a faster shutter speed, thereby minimizing blur. That shot on this page of Mimi leaping into the air? Shot at ISO 400.

White Balance

Few light sources are pure white; they have a color cast of some kind. Incandescent lamps (light bulbs) cast a yellowish light, while fluorescent light is greenish. Even outdoors, there can be light-source variations—bluish in the morning, reddish in the evening. Each of these light sources has a different *color temperature*.

Our eyes and brains compensate for these variances. Digital cameras try to do so with a feature called *automatic white balance*, but they aren't always as good at it. That's why many cameras have manual white balance adjustments that essentially let you tell the camera, "Hey, I'm shooting under incandescent (or fluorescent) lights now, so make some adjustments in how you record color."

White balance adjustments are usually labeled WB, often with icons representing cloudy skies ☁, incandescent lamps ☼, and fluorescent lighting ⚏. You'll probably have to switch to your camera's manual-exposure mode to access its white balance settings.

Sharpness and Color Settings

Digital cameras do more than simply capture a scene. They also manipulate the image they capture by applying sharpening and color correction (including white balance adjustments).

Some photographers don't like the idea of their cameras making manipulations like these. If you're in this group, consider exploring your camera's menus and tweaking any color and sharpness settings you find.

For example, many cameras have two color modes: "standard" and "real." The "standard" mode punches up the color saturation—something you can do yourself with iPhoto. I'd prefer to capture accurate colors and make adjustments later. A "real" mode—or its equivalent on your camera—gives you more-natural color. You can always punch it up in iPhoto if you must.

The same applies to sharpness. Most cameras offer a variety of sharpening settings, and when I'm shooting JPEG images, I like to reduce the camera's built-in sharpening. If I feel an image needs some sharpening later, I'll do the job in iPhoto or Photoshop.

And of course, remember that for maximum control, you should shoot in raw mode, in which the camera doesn't apply any color or sharpness adjustments.

Custom White Balance

Most cameras also let you create a custom white-balance setting. Generally, the process works like this: put a white sheet of paper in the scene, get up close so the paper fills the viewfinder, and then press a button sequence on the camera. The camera measures the light reflected from the paper, compares it to the camera's built-in definition of *white*, and then adjusts to compensate for the lighting.

If you're a stickler for color and you're shooting under strange lighting conditions, creating a custom white balance setting is a good idea.

Better still, shoot in raw mode if your camera allows it. Then you'll have complete control over color balance.

Stay Sharp

A camera's built-in LCD screen is great for reviewing a shot you just took. But the screen is so tiny that it's often hard to tell whether the photo is in sharp focus.

Most cameras allow you to zoom in on a photo while displaying it. I like to zoom in and verify that my photo isn't blurred—especially if the subject is still in front of me and I have another chance.

If your camera has an electronic viewfinder, it can be a superior alternative to the LCD screen for reviewing your shots, especially in bright light.

Your Camera's Histogram

If you read through pages 162 and 163, you've seen the value that a histogram display can offer for making exposure adjustments.

Many mid-range and all high-end cameras can display a histogram, too, which you can use to adjust exposure settings *before* you take a photo.

With your camera in one of its manual-exposure modes, activate the histogram display. Then adjust your exposure settings—shutter speed, ISO speed, and aperture—so that the histogram's data is as far to the right-hand side of the graph as possible without introducing white clipping. (Remember, white clipping means lost highlight detail.)

Photography gurus call this technique *exposing to the right*, and it ensures that you're getting as much image data as your camera is capable of capturing.

Photographer Michael Reichmann, publisher of the magnificent Luminous Landscape site, has written an excellent tutorial on using histograms when shooting. I've linked to it on www.macilife.com/iphoto.

Learning More

To learn more about digital photography and Photoshop, I heartily recommend *Real World Digital Photography* by Katrin Eisman, Seán Duggan, and Tim Grey (Peachpit Press, 2004).

Tips for Better Digital Photography

Get Up Close

Too many photographers shy away from their subjects. Get close to show detail. If you can't get physically closer, use your camera's zoom feature, if it has one. If your camera has a macro feature, use it to take extreme close-ups of flowers, rocks, seashells, tattoos—you name it. Don't limit yourself to wide shots.

Vary Your Angle

Don't just shoot from a standing position. Get down into a crouch and shoot low—or get up on a chair and shoot down. Vary your angles. The LCD screen on a digital camera makes it easy—you don't press your eye to the camera to compose a shot.

Changing your angle can be a great way to remove a cluttered background. When photographing flowers, for example, I like to position the camera low and aim it upwards, so that the flowers are shot against the sky.

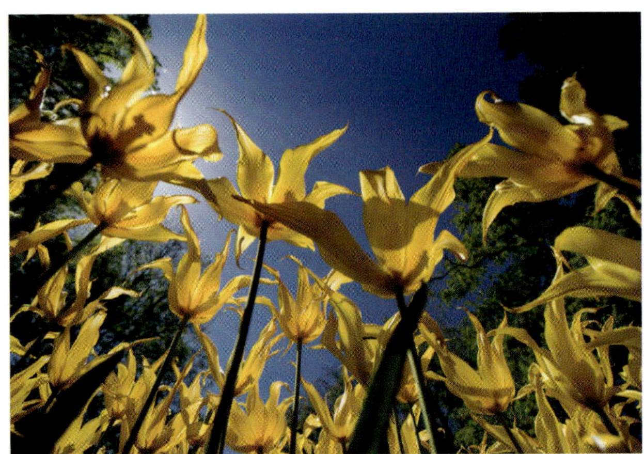

Avoid Digital Zooming

Many digital cameras supplement their optical zoom lenses with digital zoom functions that bring your subject even closer. Think twice about using digital zoom—it usually adds undesirable artifacts to an image.

Position the Horizon

In landscape shots, the position of the horizon influences the mood of the photo. To imply a vast, wide open space, put the horizon along the lower third of the frame and show lots of sky. (This obviously works best when the sky is cooperating.) To imply a sense of closeness—or if the sky is a bland shade of gray—put the horizon along the upper third, showing little sky.

This rule, like others, is meant to be broken. For example, if you're shooting a forlorn-looking desert landscape, you might want to have the horizon bisect the image to imply a sense of bleak monotony.

Crop Carefully

You can often use iPhoto's cropping tool to fix composition problems. But note that cropping results in lost pixels, and that can affect your ability to produce high-quality prints. Try to do your cropping in the camera's viewfinder, not iPhoto.

Kill Your Flash

I turn off my camera's built-in flash and rarely turn it on. Existing light provides a much more flattering, natural-looking image, with none of the harshness of electronic flash.

Dimly lit indoor shots may have a slight blur to them, but I'll take blur over the radioactive look of flash any day.

Beware of the Background

More accurately, *be aware* of the background. Is a tree growing out of Mary's head? If so, move yourself or Mary. Are there distracting details in the background? Find a simpler setting or get up close. Is your shadow visible in the shot? Change your position. When looking at a scene, our brains tend to ignore irrelevant things. But the camera sees all. As you compose, look at the entire frame, not just your subject.

Embrace Blur

A blurred photo is a ruined photo, right? Not necessarily. Blur conveys motion, something still images don't usually do. A photo with a sharp background but a car that is blurred tells you the car was in motion. To take this kind of shot, keep the camera steady and snap the shutter at the moment the car crosses the frame.

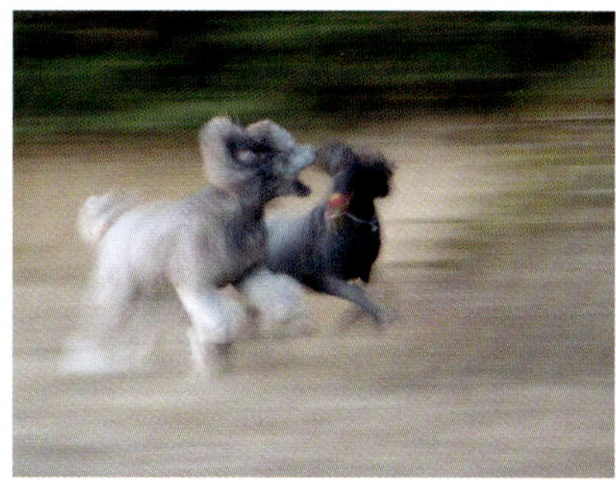

You can also convey motion by turning this formula around: If you pan along with the moving car as you snap, the car will be sharp but the background will be blurred. A canine-oriented example is above.

Compose Carefully

Following a couple of rules of thumb can help you compose photos that are more visually pleasing.

First, there's the age-old *rule of thirds*, in which you divide the image rectangle into thirds and place your photo's subject at or near one of the intersections of the resulting grid.

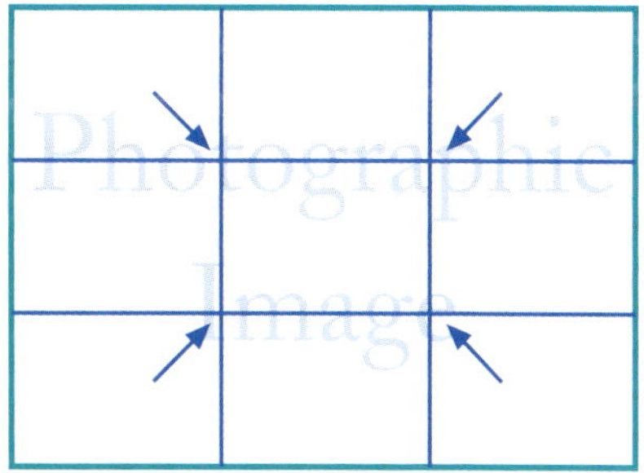

Place your photo's subject at or near these intersections.

This composition technique yields images that are more visually dynamic. The Crop tool in iPhoto's edit view makes it easy to crop according to the rule of thirds (page 155).

A second technique is to draw the viewer's eyes to your subject and add a sense of dynamism by using diagonal lines, such as a receding fence.

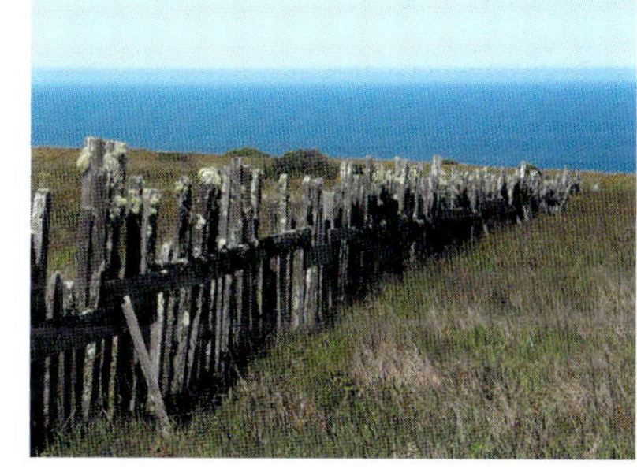

No Tripod?

If you want to take sharp photos in low light, mount your camera on a tripod. If you don't have a tripod handy, here's a workaround: turn on your camera's self-timer mode—the mode you'd usually use when you want to get yourself in the picture—then set the camera on a rigid surface and press the shutter button. Because you won't be holding the camera when the shutter goes off, you won't risk getting a blurred shot.

The Macintosh
iLife'08

iMovie at a Glance

Video editing is the process of assembling video clips, still images, and audio into a finished package that tells a story, conveys a message, and keeps your audience from falling asleep.

iMovie lets you edit video, but it also lets you *manage* it. Just as iPhoto helps you store and organize photos, iMovie helps you keep track of the video you shoot.

That's important, because we're shooting more video than ever. New, tiny video cameras make it easy to capture memories wherever we go. Many new camcorders don't even use tape, instead recording movies on built-in hard drives or on memory cards like those used by your digital camera. And speaking of digital cameras, many of them can shoot video clips, too.

iMovie keeps track of your video in a central place called the *Event library.* You can browse your Event library and relive memories with just a couple of mouse clicks. Don't have time to edit a finished movie? That's fine. Just browse your events and watch your life flash before your eyes.

When you want to assemble some clips into a finished project, iMovie is ready—and indeed, it lets you edit video quickly and efficiently. Create as many projects as you like, and switch between them with a click. Add titles and scene transitions, then share your final product on the Web, on a DVD, or on your iPod or iPhone.

Quiet on the set.

iMovie: A Video Program in Transition

iMovie '08 is dramatically different from its predecessors. Its video-editing tools work differently, and its Event library and video-management tools are completely new. iMovie '08 is a much better program than earlier iMovie versions.

But the road of change often has bumps. There are things that the older iMovie HD could do that iMovie '08 can't. And many people had years of experience with the old version's way of doing things.

In recognition of both realities, Apple has made iMovie HD available as a free download for iLife '08 users. To get it, visit www.apple.com/support/imovie and look for the "iMovie HD Support" area of the page.

Best of both worlds. Even if you've never used the old iMovie, you still might want to grab the free download. That's because iMovie HD has some talents that, at this writing, iMovie '08 lacks. iMovie HD lets you create chapter markers to help DVD viewers navigate your movie. iMovie HD also has a large variety of video effects that iMovie '08 lacks, including stylish motion-graphics themes, slow-motion effects, and video filters for creating special effects.

Does that mean you have to choose one program over the other? Not at all. As I describe on page 285, you can combine both programs to get the best of both worlds.

Free program, free book chapter. But how do you learn the older version? Easy. Head to my Web site, and you can download the entire iMovie HD chapter from the previous edition of this book—over 60 pages of tutorials and tips in PDF form. You'll even find some video tutorials there to help you get going.

Download your free iMovie HD chapter.
www.macilife.com/imovie

Your edited movie projects appear in the Project Library.

Add text titles to your movies (page 274).

The *playhead* indicates the current playback location. You can *skim* video clips by moving the mouse pointer over them (page 248).

Add background music from your iTunes library (page 264).

Add sound effects and narration (pages 264–271).

Your video plays in the *Viewer*, which is also a work area for some adjustments.

From left to right: Add music (page 264); add photos (page 258); create a title (page 274); create a transition (page 272).

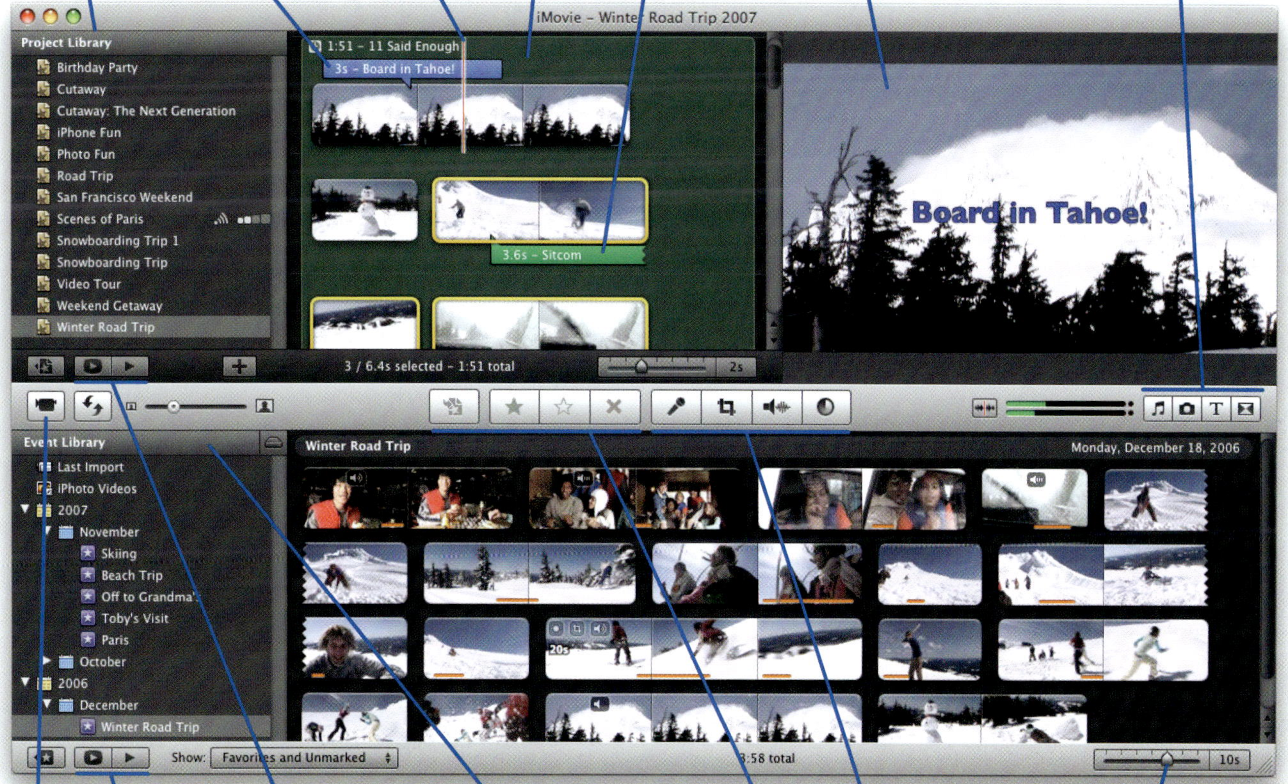

Play an event's video.

Import video from a camcorder (pages 242–245).

Play your project within iMovie's window, or full-screen.

The Event library gives you fast access to the video you've imported. Select an event, and its video appears in the Event browser to the right.

Work with audio, video, and photos.

Mark snippets of video for later use or deletion (page 250).

View each clip as a single thumbnail image, or "unroll" it into a *filmstrip* (page 248).

A Short Lesson in Video Formats

If you have a standard, miniDV camcorder and you're anxious to start making movies, feel free to skip this little lesson and move on to page 242. But if you want to use video from a different kind of device—or you're curious about one of iMovie's most intriguing capabilities—read on.

Just as music and photos can be stored in a variety of digital formats, video also comes in several flavors. And, as with music and photos, each video format takes its own approach to organizing the bits and bytes that make up your media.

In early iMovie versions, projects were based on one video format: DV. You could import other formats into iMovie, but iMovie would convert that footage into DV format. DV was iMovie's native tongue, and using other formats meant a translation step that took time, used up disk space, and often compromised video quality.

Times change. New types of video devices have appeared, and iMovie has evolved to keep pace: iMovie '08 provides native support for several video formats. iMovie '08 is multilingual, and as a result, you have the flexibility to edit video from a wider variety of video devices, ranging from Apple's iSight (which is built into many Mac models) to many digital camera models to the new breeds of high-definition HDV cameras from companies such as Sony, Canon, and JVC.

iMovie's basic operation is identical regardless of which video format you use. There are some subtleties to some formats, and I'll share them as we go. But first, let's look at the video languages iMovie understands.

How Square Are Your Movies?

Many of the differences among video formats aren't visible at first glance, but one of the differences definitely is: the *aspect ratio* of the video frame.

We encountered the concept of aspect ratio when looking at iPhoto cropping techniques (page 155). The phrase simply describes how square or rectangular an image frame is.

Early iMovie versions were limited to one aspect ratio: the standard 4:3 ratio used by most TV sets, DV camcorders, and digital cameras.

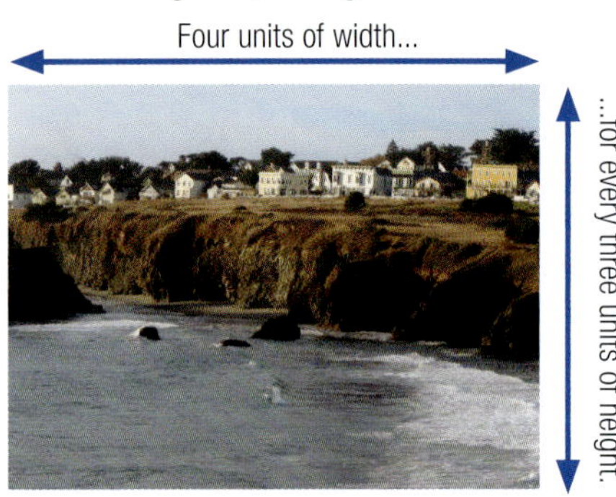

Going wide. iMovie also features the ability to work with and create widescreen video in the 16:9 aspect ratio—the format common in high-definition TV sets.

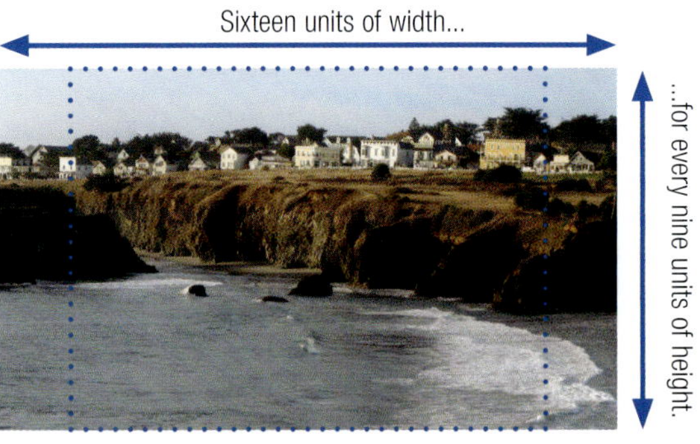

The widescreen format provides a more cinematic experience.

Pronunciation guide. Making video small talk at the local coffee shop? The expressions *4:3* and *16:9* are usually pronounced "four by three" and "sixteen by nine." Technically, "four *to* three" and "sixteen *to* nine" are more accurate, since these expressions are ratios. After all, when was the last time you heard a bookie describe "2 by 1" odds on a horse?

In this chapter, look for the **HD** for information specific to HDV editing.

Choosing a Video Format

One of the quiet, yet revolutionary, features of iMovie '08 is that it doesn't care much about which video format you throw at it. You can stick with one format throughout a project, mix formats within the same project, or apply an aspect ratio that's different from the original footage.

That said, iMovie can't read *everything*: uncompressed HD, for example, remains in the realm of professional tools, such as Final Cut Pro. Here's a look at the formats you can use with iMovie '08.

DV. By far the most common format used by digital camcorders. Now that the era of high-definition TV is upon us, the DV format is often described as a *standard definition* format.

DV Widescreen. Most DV camcorders can shoot in widescreen mode, often by simply cropping the top and bottom of the video frame. (To shoot in this mode, use your camcorder's menus to activate 16:9 mode.) You don't get the picture quality of high-definition TV, but you do get that cinematically wide image.

HDV 1080i and HDV 720p. High definition (HD, for short) TV is gradually gaining momentum, and the new breed of HDV camcorders is helping. The HDV format brings high-definition videography to advanced amateurs and budget-minded professionals (and, as prices come down, to the rest of us). HDV always uses a 16:9 aspect ratio. The images below illustrate the difference between DV and 1080i resolution.

MPEG-2 and MPEG-4. Many digital cameras shoot their movie clips in these formats, as do a growing number of compact video cameras that connect via USB.

AVCHD. This high-definition video format is based on MPEG-4; it's used by camcorders that record 1080i footage directly to a built-in hard disk, removable memory cards, or DVDs.

iSight. Apple's iSight camera is built into some current Mac models and used to be available as a separate camera. (You'll still find them on eBay.) The iSight is designed for video chatting using iChat, but makes a great low-budget TV camera, too.

1080i (HDV and AVCHD): 1920 by 1080 pixels

DV: 720 by 480 pixels

Importing DV and HDV Video

The first step in an iMovie editing project usually involves importing video that you've shot. If you're using a miniDV or HDV camera, you can connect the camera to your Mac's FireWire jack and use iMovie's camera mode to bring in your video. (If you're using a camera that connects using USB, your import procedure will be a bit different; see page 244).

With camera mode, you can control your camera using the transport buttons in iMovie's Import window. There's no need to grope for the tiny buttons on your camera when you need to rewind, fast-forward, stop, or play. Click the on-screen transport buttons, and iMovie sends the appropriate signals to your camera through the FireWire cable. Video professionals call this *device control.*

When you import video, the footage is organized into events—much as iPhoto organizes photos. You can create a new event or have iMovie store footage in an existing event. As in iPhoto, you can browse events by skimming across them, and you can assign keywords to help you locate footage later.

The first step in editing a movie may be importing video, but another step should come first: making sure you have enough free disk space. Digital video eats disk space like I eat Oreos: for miniDV video, you'll need about 200MB of free space for each minute of video. For HDV video, you'll need a few times that amount. Bottom line: think about buying an external hard drive and using it for your video endeavors.

Importing from a FireWire Camera

Step 1. Connect your DV or HDV camera to your Mac's FireWire jack.

Step 2. Be sure the camera is turned on and in its VCR mode (called VTR on some cameras).

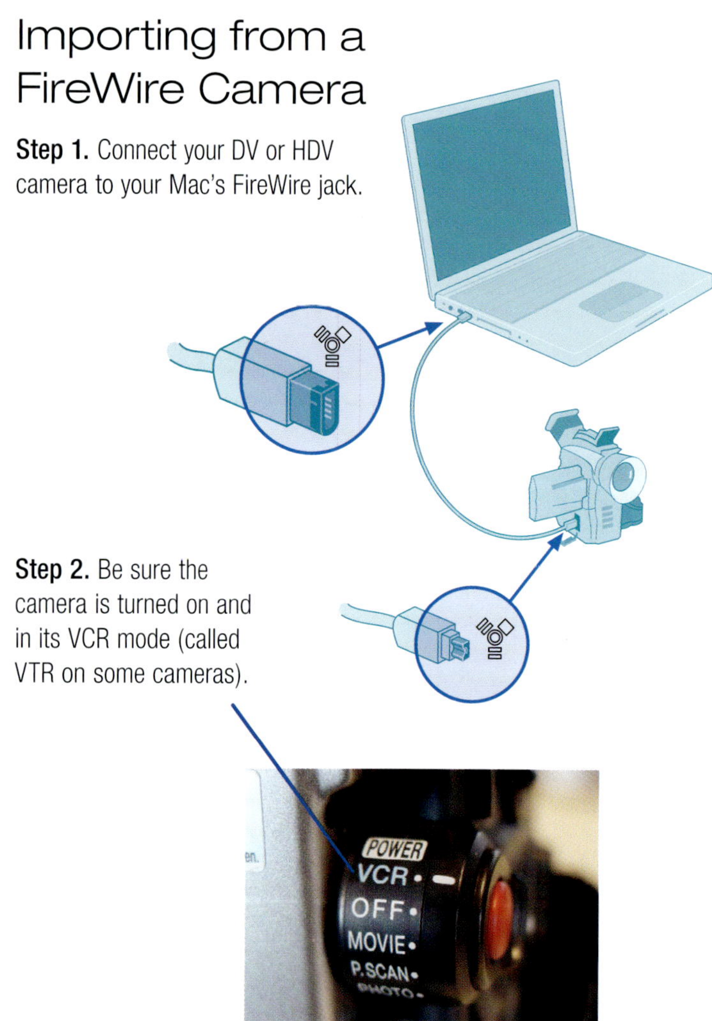

Tip: To store imported video on an external hard drive, simply create the video's event on the external drive. If you've already started the project and it's on your internal drive, quit iMovie and open the Movies folder in your home folder. Next, open the iMovie Events folder, locate the folder for the Event you want to move, and copy that to the iMovie Events folder on the external drive. When you launch iMovie again, it will rebuild the Event's thumbnails and you'll be set.

Step 3. To start importing, click Import or press the spacebar while the tape is playing back.

The playback buttons control your camera.

Automatic mode rewinds the tape and imports all footage. Manual mode lets you choose which clips to import.

If more than one camera is attached, choose your camera from the Camera pop-up list.

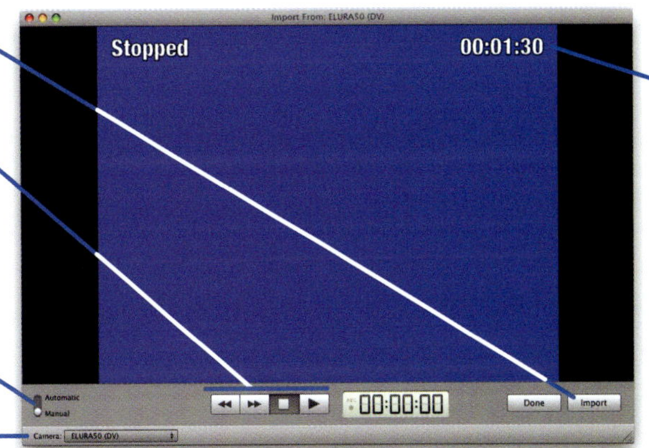

iMovie displays the time code that your camera recorded on the tape. This can help you keep track of where you are on a tape as you fast-forward or rewind.

Step 4. Type a name for the new event. To add video to an existing event, choose the event; see page 248.

iMovie displays each clip you import in the Event browser.

Note: As your camera plays back, you'll see its video in the Import window.

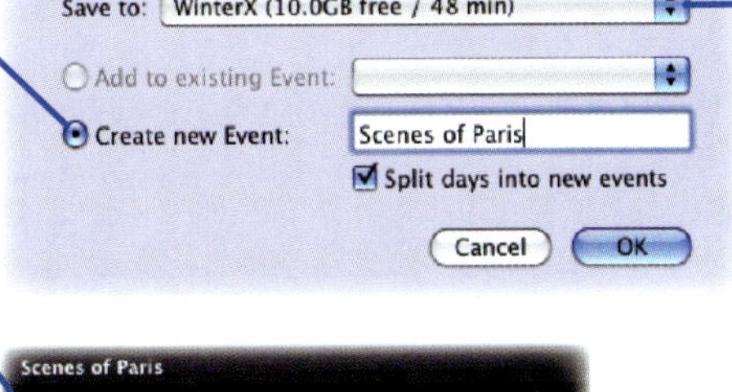

If you have more than one hard drive, you can use the Save To pop-up menu to specify where you want the footage to be stored.

HD Differences

Importing from an HDV camera? Under some circumstances, you may experience an odd delay as the video comes in: the tape may finish playing, but you'll still see video being displayed in iMovie's Import window. The video's motion may also appear jerky.

This occurs because your Mac must transcode (convert) the HD video into a format that allows for fast editing. This process occurs more or less in real time, depending on whether you're running other programs that may be fighting for their share of processor power.

To minimize the delay, close other applications. And if you're running Mac OS X 10.5 (Leopard), consider turning off its Time Machine backup feature while importing.

One ramification: it's a bit harder to tell when to stop importing, since your Mac may be displaying footage that the camera actually played back seconds or minutes earlier.

For more precise control when selectively importing HD footage, view the footage on your camera's LCD screen during the import, and use your camera's buttons to stop and start playback.

Importing Video from Other Sources

Camcorders have come a long way in a short time. All camcorders used to capture footage to tape—many sizes and formats of tape, but always to cassettes of magnetic tape.

Thanks to the onward march of technology, tape may soon be the exception rather than the rule. A growing number of cameras record footage directly to DVDs, solid-state memory cards like the ones your digital camera uses, or internal hard disks.

The benefits? No more rewinding or fast-forwarding to find a scene—and no more stacks of tapes sitting on the shelf and waiting to be digitized.

The shift isn't just a matter of media. The new tapeless formats compress video in various ways to save significant amounts of storage space.

iMovie can import clips from most tapeless cameras. (Apple has published a list on its Web site; I've linked to it at www.macilife.com/imovie.) The import process is a bit different—and more convenient—than the steps outlined on the previous pages.

iMovie can also import movies stored in your iPhoto library or elsewhere on your hard disk. And if you're an iMovie veteran with older iMovie HD projects, iMovie '08 can import them, too—to a degree.

Note: To import AVCHD footage, you need a Mac with an Intel processor. However, a utility called Voltaic (www.mac1080hd.com) can convert the raw AVCHD video files on PowerPC-based (or Intel-based) Macs. Also, if your camera records AVCHD video to DVDs, you must use iMovie under Mac OS X 10.5 (Leopard).

Importing from a Tapeless Camera

Step 1. Connect your camera to the Mac's USB port. (Even if your camera includes a FireWire port, iMovie recognizes tapeless formats only via USB.)

Step 2. Be sure that the camera is turned on and set to its PC Connect mode.

Step 3. In the Import window, choose an import mode. Automatic grabs all clips in the camera's memory. Want to be selective? Choose Manual, then click the checkboxes beneath each clip that you want to import. (You may want to click Uncheck All and then select the clips.)

Step 4. Click Import All or Import Checked, as appropriate.

Step 5. Name the new event. To store the footage in an existing event, choose the event's name (see page 248).

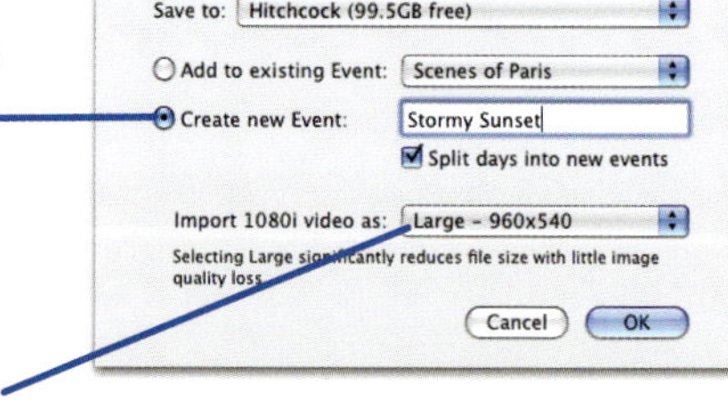

If you're importing high-definition 1080i video, choose a size. The full size retains the camera's highest dimensions (typically 1920 by 1080 pixels, but some cameras capture only 1440 by 1080); the Large option reduces the dimensions to 960 by 540 pixels. For advice on which size to choose, see the sidebar on the opposite page.

Step 6. Click OK and take a break while iMovie copies the footage and transcodes it into the editable AIC (Apple Intermediate Codec) format. When it's finished, click Done.

Importing Footage from Your Hard Disk

Step 1. Choose File > Import Movies.

Step 2. Locate the movie file and choose an event (or create a new event). For HD video, specify the Large or Full size option.

To have iMovie move the video file to your movie library, choose the Move Files option; to have iMovie make a duplicate of the video file, choose Copy Files.

Step 3. Click Import or press Return.

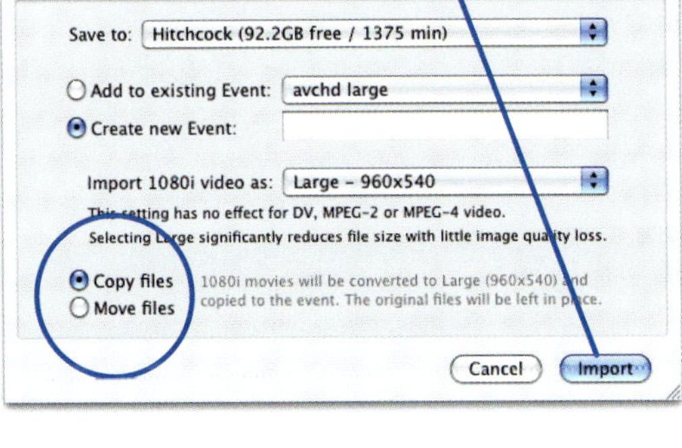

Importing from Elsewhere

From an iMovie HD project. iMovie '08 can import projects created in iMovie HD, but the results aren't pretty. Effects, titles, and music tracks are discarded, and all transitions are converted to Cross Dissolve transitions. Clips in the Clip viewer are put into a new event, and any clips in the timeline go into a new project. If all those trade-offs sound acceptable, choose File > Import iMovie HD Project, locate the project, and click Import. Otherwise, finish your old projects in iMovie HD and use iMovie '08 for new movies.

Recording using an iSight. If you own a Mac with a built-in iSight camera, or you own an old external iSight, you can record directly in iMovie. Open the Import window and choose the iSight from the Camera menu. Click Capture to specify an event and start recording (smile!). To end recording, click Stop.

Large versus Full HD

HD You paid good money for the extra pixels that HD video gives you, so why reduce the size by importing footage at the Large size? The answer depends on what you're shooting. For most home uses, reducing the size to 960 by 540 won't produce a noticeable difference in the video quality—but it does ease the processor strain on iMovie when throwing around full-resolution HD video, not to mention reducing the amount of disk space consumed (13 GB for one hour of footage compared to 40 GB for the full quality, according to Apple).

In fact, the term *full quality* is a bit misleading. To make the footage easier to handle, iMovie tosses out some of the image information (specifically, one field of interlaced video).

If you're concerned about getting the absolute highest quality possible, a program such as Final Cut Express or Final Cut Pro is a better choice.

Creating a Video Slide Show

You've imported some video from your camera and maybe you also imported some movies that were already on your hard drive. Now what?

If you're the obsessive-organizer type, you might want to start organizing your video—managing events, marking clips as favorites or rejects, and maybe even assigning some keywords to help you file your footage. If this sounds like the most exciting way to begin exploring a personal movie studio, feel free to turn the page and dive in.

But if you'd rather *make* something out of the video you've imported, stay tuned. Here's a little lesson that introduces the basic techniques and tools for editing in iMovie.

We're going to make a "video slide show"—a series of video clips, each four-seconds long, accompanied by some background music. In the interest of immediate gratification, I'll skip over the details and just give you the big picture.

Making a Movie

Step 1. Choose File > New Project, type a name for your project, and choose the aspect ratio that matches that of the video you imported.

Step 2. In the Event Library, select the event containing your video. The event's video footage appears in the Event browser.

Step 3. In the Event browser, skim the mouse pointer over a clip. When you see a scene you'd like to add to the slideshow, click on the clip.

When you click a clip, iMovie automatically selects four seconds' worth of video, starting at the spot where you were pointing. The yellow border marks the selected footage.

Step 4. Click the Add Selection to Project button, or simply press the E key, its keyboard shortcut.

iMovie adds the selected four seconds to your project.

Step 5. Repeat Steps 3 and 4 a few times.

Skim over a clip until you see something you like, click the clip, then add the clip to your project.

After clicking a clip, try dragging it from the Event browser to the project—that's a very common way of working in iMovie.

Tip: Want to see more of each clip in your event? Drag the slider at the lower-right corner of the Event browser.

Step 6. Add a background music soundtrack.

Display the Music and Sound Effects Browser by clicking its button. Find a tune, then drag it to the background of your project; the entire background turns green.

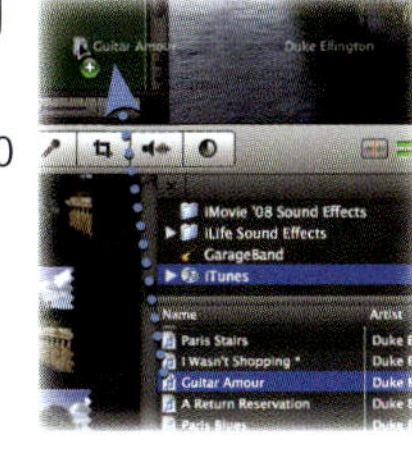

Step 7. Play your movie.

Click one of the two play buttons below the Project Library. The button on the left plays the movie full-screen.

Step 8. Add transitions.

Let's add a cross-dissolve transition between each clip in your movie. Choose File > Project Properties. Check the box labeled Add Automatically, then click OK. Another message appears; click OK to that one, too.

The Project Properties dialog box controls overall project settings: its aspect ratio, durations of transitions and photos, and more.

Step 9. Play your movie again.

Each clip now dissolves into the next one. In the Project browser, little transition symbols now appear between each clip.

It's that easy to assemble a quick movie: Click a clip, add it to the project, and repeat. There's much, much more you can do, of course, and the rest of this chapter tells all.

Essential Notes and Tips

Never destructive. When you assemble a project in iMovie, you're never altering your original source video (the footage you imported). This isn't old Hollywood, where editors cut and spliced film and unwanted footage fell to the floor. iMovie simply keeps track of which parts of each clip you want to use, and in what order. You're always able to change edits and use footage that you didn't use the first time around.

At the same time, some housekeeping features let you delete unwanted footage and free up disk space (see page 250).

Full-screen controls. When playing a movie full-screen, try moving the mouse—controls appear that let you jump to a specific spot in the movie.

How many seconds? If you like iMovie's click-and-add editing technique, you may want to customize how much video iMovie selects when you click a clip. Choose iMovie > Preferences, and drag the slider labeled Clicking in Events Browser Selects. Want to create a fast-paced video? Choose a short duration, such as two seconds. Creating a leisurely montage of scenic shots? Think longer.

Selection tips. Clicking a clip is just one way to select some of its footage. You will also frequently select video by dragging across a clip. This lets you select a *specific* amount of footage: as you drag, the thumbnail and the Viewer display the frame currently under the playhead. A little time readout also appears next to the clip; it shows how many seconds you've selected.

To select an entire clip in the Event browser, press Option while clicking the clip.

To select more than one clip at a time, ⌘-click on each clip, or Shift-click to select a range of clips—standard Mac selection maneuvers.

Clip details. As you work, you might want to display information about a clip. Choose View > Playhead Info. A little banner appears above the playhead containing information about the current clip.

Keyboard shortcuts abound. As you get familiar with iMovie, start exploring its keyboard shortcuts—there are lots of them, and they can help you edit efficiently. (For a list, choose Help > Keyboard Shortcuts.)

Browsing Your Video Library

iMovie isn't just about editing video; it's also about managing it. Indeed, one of the great strengths of iMovie '08 is that it lets you organize and keep track of the video you import. You might say that iPhoto has taught iMovie a thing or two about organization.

And as with a photo library, the more accessible and organized your video library is, the more likely you'll spend time exploring and enjoying it.

Here's a look at the basic explorer's tools iMovie '08 provides. We'll explore more video-management tools on the following pages.

Browsing Events

iMovie stores video you import as a series of events, which appear in the Event library area. To browse the footage in an event, select the event.

Skimming and playing. It's easy to browse your iPhoto library: all the photos are there for you to see. Video, however, involves time—what you see at the beginning of a clip is just a hint of what happens later, requiring you to watch the entire thing (or keep it all in your head).

iMovie's skimming feature lets you conquer time.

Move the mouse pointer over a clip to quickly scan the footage. As you skim, the frame beneath the playhead appears in the Viewer.

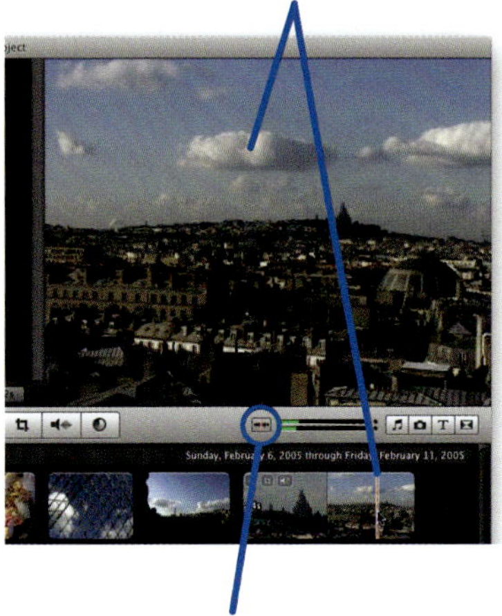

Don't want to hear audio as you skim? To quiet things down, click the Audio Skimming button (or press ⌘-K).

Play time. To play video at actual speed, point to the spot on a clip where you want playback to begin, then press the space bar. You can also double-click a clip.

To watch all the footage in an event, select the event in the Event Library, then click the Play or Play Full Screen button.

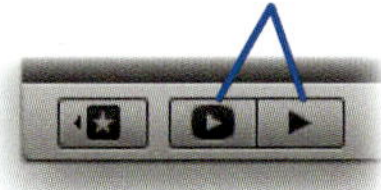

Using the Event Browser

The Event browser shows the clips in an event. You can customize how those clips appear.

The big picture. When you want to see as many clips as possible in the Event browser, drag the clip size slider all the way to the right, until the word All appears next to it. In this view, you see just one frame per clip. When you're assessing some newly imported footage or just reliving some memories, this is an efficient way to view clips.

A closer look. When you're editing, you'll want to see more of each clip in the Event browser. It's essential for selecting which portions of clips you want to use in your project.

And seeing more of the clips is easy: just "unroll" your clips into *filmstrips* by dragging the clip size slider to the left. The further to the left you drag, the more frames you see. At the leftmost setting, iMovie displays a thumbnail for every half-second of video—great for precision work.

Thumbnail sizes. To control the size of the clip thumbnails, drag the thumbnail size slider above the Event library. Want to see as many clips as possible on the screen? Make the thumbnails small. Need to see the differences between similar-looking clips? Make the thumbnails big.

The thumbnail setting applies to clips in both the Event browser and the Project browser.

Working with Events

Renaming an event. To change the name of an event, double-click its name, type a new name, and press Return.

Splitting an event. For organization's sake, you may sometimes want to split one event into two. Maybe you have an event containing footage from a morning hike with the kids and a nighttime poker game with friends. Those are very different events, and you might like your movie library to reflect that.

To split an event, click the clip that you want to be the first clip of the new event. (In this example, that would be the first poker game clip—the clip where you tuck the ace up your sleeve.) Then, choose File > Split Event Before Selected Clip.

Merging Events. At other times, you might decide that two or more events really constitute just one. Maybe you have several events containing footage from your Paris vacation, and you'd like to see them stored as just one.

Select the events you want to combine, choose File > Merge Events, and give the new event a name.

Tip: You can also Control-click on selected events and use the shortcut menu to merge them.

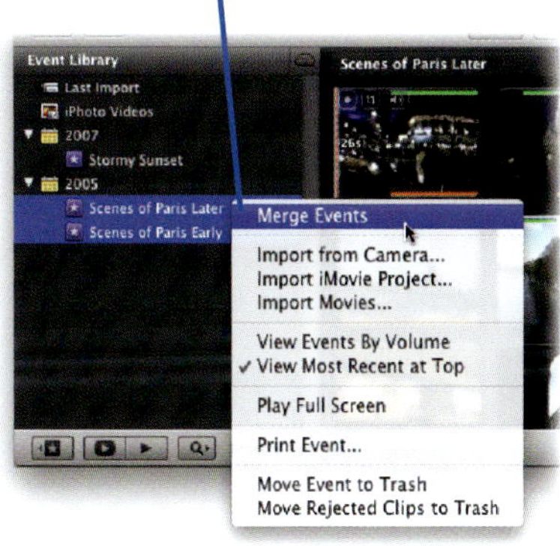

Moving footage between events. Sometimes, you might want to move a clip from one event to another. Maybe your latest import revealed some new-puppy footage that you forgot was in your camera, and you'd like to move those clips into the New Puppy event that contains the rest.

Begin by selecting the event that contains the clips you want to move. Next, select the clips you want to move (use the Shift-click and ⌘-click maneuvers to select multiple clips). Finally, drag the selected clips to the event where you want them.

More Ways to View the Event Library

You can customize the way events appear in the Event Library.

To see your library displayed according to the hard drives that contain it, click the Volumes button (or choose View > Events by Volume). When a disk is disconnected or otherwise offline, it doesn't appear in the list.

iMovie organizes events into years. If you shoot a lot of video, you might want more viewing precision: choose View > Events by Month.

Want to see each day of an event displayed separately? Choose View > Separate Days in Events. To see the clips organized from newest to oldest, choose View > Most Recent Days at Top.

Managing Video

Just as iPhoto provides features for organizing and keeping track of photos, iMovie provides features for managing the video in your Event library.

And just as with iPhoto, you don't have to use any of these features. But as your video library grows, you may find that locating specific clips becomes cumbersome. You may also find yourself running low on hard drive space.

iMovie's video-management tools can help on both counts.

Keep or Trash? Marking Video

Your first job after importing some video will probably be to sit back and enjoy it —to watch the footage, smile at the good stuff, and cringe at the bad. As you watch, you may get ideas for ways to edit the video into a finished project.

As you audition your footage, you can *mark* sections of it to reflect your smiles and grimaces. The best stuff? Mark it as a favorite. The stuff your enemies may use against you someday? Mark it for deletion.

Playing favorites. To mark a clip, start by selecting part or all of the clip. (See page 247 for details on selecting clips.) Then, turn to the toolbar.

Thumbs up: mark the selection as a favorite (keyboard shortcut: press the F key).

Not sure: unmark the selection (press U).

Thumbs down: reject the selection (press R).

Favorite footage is indicated by a green line.

By skimming, selecting, and tapping the keyboard shortcuts for each of these buttons, you can very quickly group your footage into these best, worst, and "I'll decide later" categories.

Controlling what you see. Using the Show pop-up menu below the Event Library, you can control what iMovie displays in the Event browser.

Normally, iMovie shows your favorite footage and anything that you haven't marked. To see only your favorite footage, choose Favorites Only. iMovie hides unmarked and rejected footage.

To see everything, choose All Clips. And to see only the awful stuff, choose Rejected Only. iMovie indicates rejected footage with a red bar.

Advanced Marking

As you become accustomed to marking footage, you might want to take advantage of a more powerful marking mode. Choose iMovie > Preferences, and check the Show Advanced Tools box.

The marking tools now work differently. Click the Mark as Favorite button, for example, and then drag across the range of frames to be marked. When you're done, the tool is still active, so you can drag across another clip and mark it—saving you a couple of clicks.

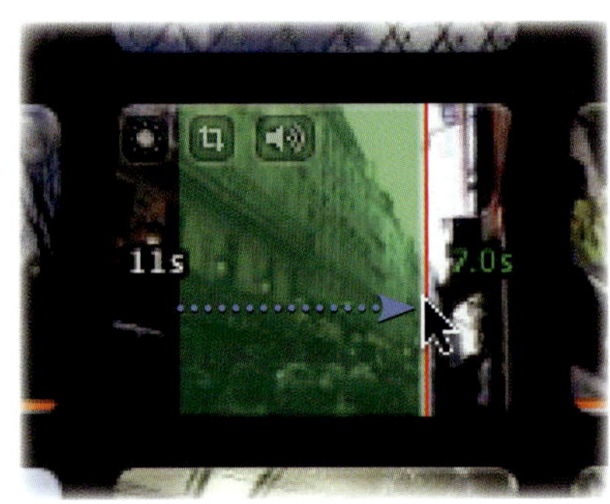

Deleting Footage

Frames that you've marked as rejected remain in the Event library, even if they're not visible. If you *know* you'll never use those clips and want to free up some disk space, choose Rejected Only from the Show pop-menu, then click the Move Rejected to Trash button.

iMovie moves rejected footage to the Finder's Trash, which you can then empty.

Organizing Footage with Keywords

Like iPhoto, iMovie lets you assign descriptive *keywords* to video: Dog, Beach, Vacation, Paris, and so on. You can then organize and search based on keywords.

Note: To access iMovie's keywording features, you must turn on the Advanced Tools option in the Preferences dialog box.

Creating Keywords

Like iPhoto, iMovie has a small set of keywords already defined. They're a good start, but you'll want to create your own keywords to reflect the subjects in your footage.

Begin by displaying the Keywords window: click the toolbar's Keywords button.

To create a keyword, click in the New Keyword box, type the keyword, then press Return. The new keyword appears in the Keywords window.

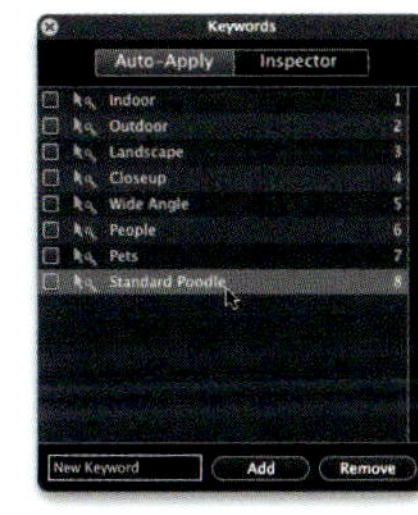

The first nine keywords get a single-key shortcut—a numeral 1 through 9. If you want a keyboard shortcut for a particular keyword, drag it so that it's one of the first nine in the Keywords window.

To delete a keyword, select it and click Remove.

Assigning Keywords

To assign keywords to some footage, again summon the Keywords window. Next, check the boxes next to the keywords you want to assign. (You can also tap the single-key number shortcuts for keywords that have them.)

Finally, select the footage that you want to mark with those keywords. Below, I'm assigning a few keywords to some footage of a famous dog.

Tip: You can also select a range of footage, click the Keywords button on the toolbar, and *then* choose the keywords in the Keywords Window.

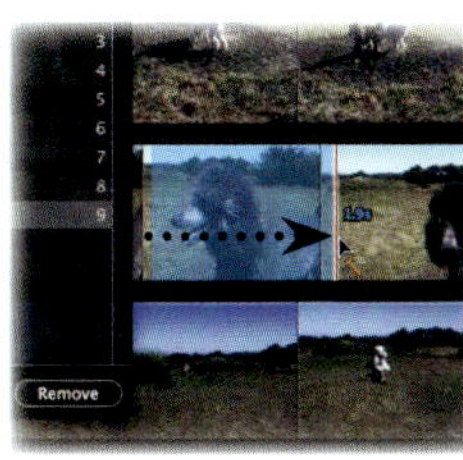

Sorting by Keywords

Here's where your organizational fortitude pays off. You can view your footage by keyword.

First, click the Keyword Filtering button (🔍). This displays the Keyword Filtering pane.

Next, check the box next to each keyword you want to search for. Use the buttons at the bottom of the pane to specify how you want to search. To search for all the keywords you've checked, click All. (Example: "Show me all the footage with the keywords Paris, Outdoor, and Close-up.") To search for any of them, click Any. ("Show me anything that has Paris or Outdoor or Close-up.")

With the Exclude button, you can hide footage that has the keywords you've selected. ("I don't want to see any close-ups from Paris right now.")

The results of all this clicking appear in the Event browser. Here, I'm searching for any footage that has the Travel keyword.

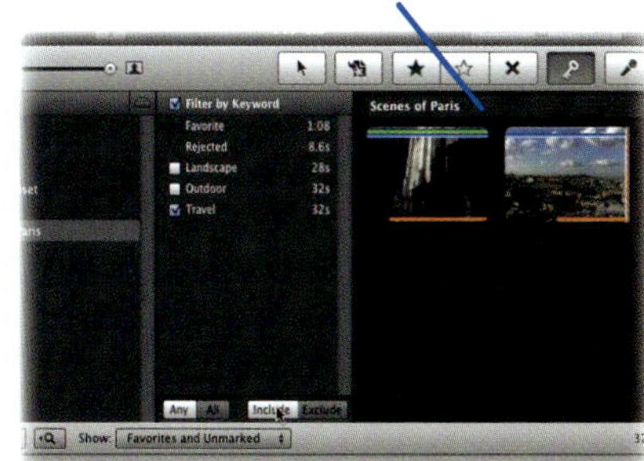

Creating a Movie Project

One of the many beauties of iMovie '08 is that you don't actually have to do any editing in order to enjoy your video. You can relive those memorable events by simply browsing footage that you've imported into your Event library—just as you can enjoy your photos in iPhoto without having to publish a book.

But as we saw with iPhoto, something special happens when you turn raw material into a finished, polished product. An iPhoto book (or any other iPhoto project) shows your photos at their best and lets you tell a story.

The same applies when you create a project in iMovie. Select just the best parts of an event, and then sequence them in a way that tells a story, brings a laugh, or simply recalls good times. Then share your project in a variety of ways.

iMovie lets you create as many projects as you like. Your projects appear in the Project Library, and you can switch from one project to another with the click of a mouse. iMovie even automatically saves your work as you go along.

Here's how to get started.

Creating a New Project

Step 1. Click the New Project button (or choose File > New Project or press ⌘-N).

The New Project dialog box appears.

Step 2. Type a name for your project, choose its aspect ratio (see page 240), then click Create or press Return.

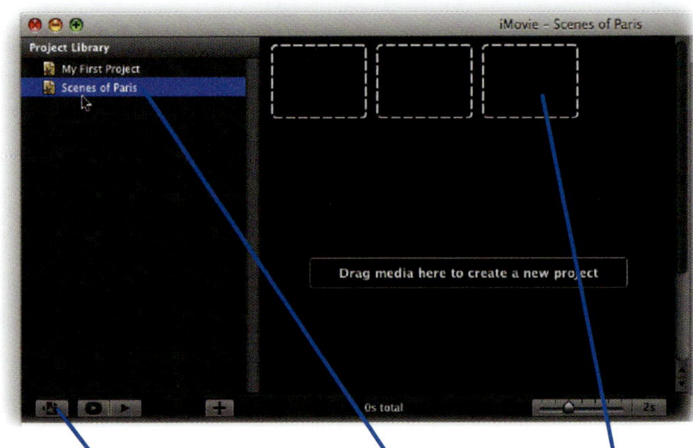

Want more screen space to work on your project? Hide the Project Library list (see the sidebar on the opposite page).

Your movie appears in the Project Library.

iMovie displays placeholder rectangles in a new, empty project.

Notes and Tips

Renaming. To change a project's name, double-click it in the Project Library, then type a new name and press Return.

Deleting. To delete a project, select it and press ⌘-Delete. Change your mind? Choose Edit > Undo Delete Project—and do this before you do anything else.

Duplicating. To make a duplicate of a project, Control-click on the project's name and choose Duplicate Project from the shortcut menu. This is a great way to experiment with different editing approaches.

Format flexibility. You can change the aspect ratio of a project at any time: choose File > Project Properties (⌘-J). You can combine this flexibility with the Duplicate Project command to create, for example, one version of a movie for your 16:9 widescreen TV, and another version for your 3:2 iPhone: duplicate a completed project, then select the duplicate, and change its aspect ratio.

Adding Clips to a Movie

A clip in the Event Library is like a baseball player on the bench. To put the clip on the playing field, you must add it to a project.

Select part or all of a clip using the techniques described on page 247, then drag it into the Project area.

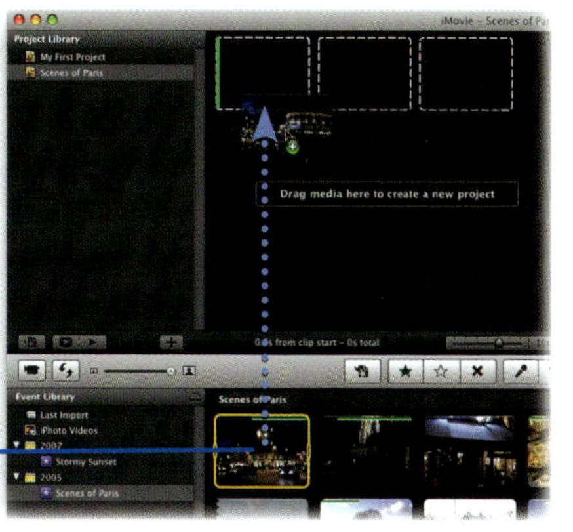

Tip: Want to insert a clip between two clips that are already on the timeline? Just drag the clip between them—a green vertical line appears between the clips to indicate the insertion.

Other Ways to Add Clips

Usually, you work with one clip at a time, dragging it to the project as you sequence your movie. But there's more than one way to work with clips.

Drag several at once. You can add multiple clips to a project at once. Select each clip by ⌘-clicking on it, then drag the clips to the project as a group.

Add to Project button. With a clip or range of frames selected in the Event browser, click this button or simply press E. iMovie adds the selected footage to the end of your movie.

This can be a fast and efficient way to build a movie: select some footage, press E, select more footage, press E, and so on.

Paste from the Clipboard. You can also add a clip to a project using the Paste command. Select a clip in the Event browser—or a clip that's already in your movie—and cut or copy, then paste. You can even paste clips from a different iMovie project.

Using the Add to Project tool. Here's another great rapid-fire editing technique. In iMovie's preferences dialog box, check the Show Advanced Tools box.

This changes the workings of the Add to Project button. Click it and select some footage in the Event browser—the footage is immediately added to the end of your project.

Here's the best part: the tool is still active and ready for action. Drag across some more footage in the Event browser, and iMovie adds it to the project. Try it—you'll be impressed with how fast it lets you sling footage into your project.

More Room to Work

When you're in the throes of editing, you may not need to see your list of projects or even your Event library. You can hide both to free up space in iMovie's window: just click the hide button below each. To show them, click the buttons again.

To gain even more work space for your project's timeline, swap the position of the event and project panes: click the Swap Events and Projects button.

iMovie also provides a few preset window arrangements: to explore them, choose Window > Viewer. You might prefer the Large setting when cropping footage or photos, or when using the Ken Burns effect (page 258). When you're working mostly in the timeline and Event browser, the Small setting gives you more room.

And finally, you can change how iMovie divides its window by clicking and dragging any blank area of the toolbar. Take advantage of these interface-customizing features. You'll spend less time scrolling and more time editing.

Editing Techniques

In a well-edited video, the cuts between scenes occur at exactly the right moments. In movies, the action cuts between two actors as they converse, reinforcing both the dialog and the drama. Every moviegoer has experienced this, probably without even thinking about it.

iMovie provides several features that let you edit with precision. You can trim the start or end point of a clip within the project timeline or, for more precision, by using a separate window called the *trimmer*.

You can change which part of a clip appears without changing the clip's overall duration—a technique called a *slip edit*.

When you're just slinging together some favorite pieces of footage, you probably won't need these advanced editing techniques. But when you need to cut with precision, iMovie can be a surprisingly sharp scalpel.

Here's a tour of these tools, along with some details on how you can adjust the appearance of the video footage and photos in your projects. For more editing tips, see the following pages, as well as pages 282–285.

Trimming Techniques

Trimming is the process of changing where a clip starts and ends. You might need to trim clips when editing dialog or when timing clips to match a musical background or narration.

Trimming directly. To trim a clip directly in the project, drag across a clip to specify the range of frames you want to keep. Then, choose Edit > Trim to Selection (⌘-B).

Alternatively, you can drag to select frames you want to remove, then press the Delete key.

In either case, iMovie doesn't delete the footage you've trimmed; it simply hides it. You can restore the footage by using the trimmer.

Using the trimmer. For more trimming precision, use the trimmer. Select the clip you want to trim, then choose Edit > Trim. (You can also click the tiny clock icon on the clip.)

Your project's timeline is temporarily replaced by the trimmer.

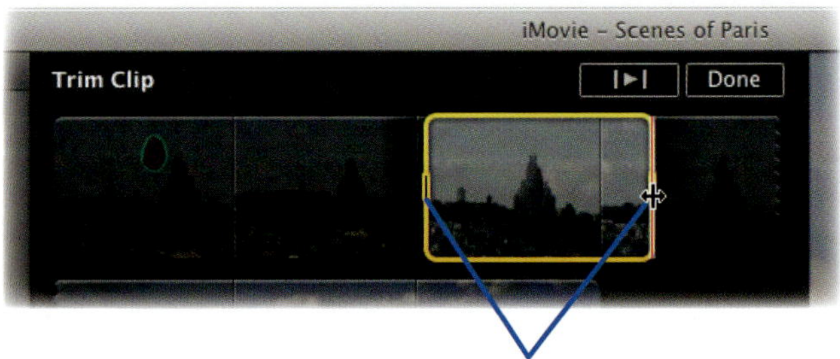

To change the clip's start point or end point, drag the left or right handle. As you drag, the Viewer displays the current frame. To preview the trim, click the trimmer's Play button. When you're finished, click Done.

Tip: To trim in single-frame increments, point to the handle you want to trim, then press Option along with the left- or right-arrow key.

Editing Tips

Slip editing. You may sometimes want to use a different part of a clip that you've added to a project. Maybe you have a five-second shot of a beach, and you realize that a different part of the original source clip looks better.

Open the clip in the trimmer, then drag the entire yellow selection border left or right (the mouse pointer looks like a hand with an arrow on it). This tells iMovie to use a different part of the source clip, but to keep the duration the same. This is called a *slip edit.*

Splitting a clip. There are times when you might want to split one clip into two—to insert a photo, for example. To split a clip, drag to select some frames, then choose Edit > Split Clip.

More precision in the Project browser. To edit with single-frame precision in the Project browser, point to the left or right edge of a clip, then hold down the ⌘ and Option keys. An orange outline appears that lets you drag the edge in one-frame increments, up to one second.

Tip: Like this option? Choose iMovie > Preferences, and check the Show Fine Tuning Buttons box. Now when you select a clip, tiny fine-tuning buttons appear at the left and right side of the clip. Click the appropriate button to change the start or end point of the clip.

Cropping and Rotating Video

iMovie lets you crop and rotate not only stills (page 258), but also video clips.

Select a clip, then click the toolbar's Crop button or the tiny Crop button on the clip's thumbnail.

To crop the clip to improve its composition, click the Crop button in the Viewer, then resize the crop rectangle.

To rotate a clip, click one of the rotation arrows. You might rotate a clip if you accidentally thought your camcorder was a still camera and shot a scene in vertical orientation—or if you want to present a scene upside-down.

To preview your work, click the Viewer's Play button. When you're finished, click Done.

Adjusting Color, Exposure, and More

In addition to changing a clip's duration and dimensions, you can adjust its color to fix lighting problems or to create special effects. Select a clip (or a photo), then click the toolbar's Adjust Video button.

To have iMovie optimize the clip's levels, click Auto.

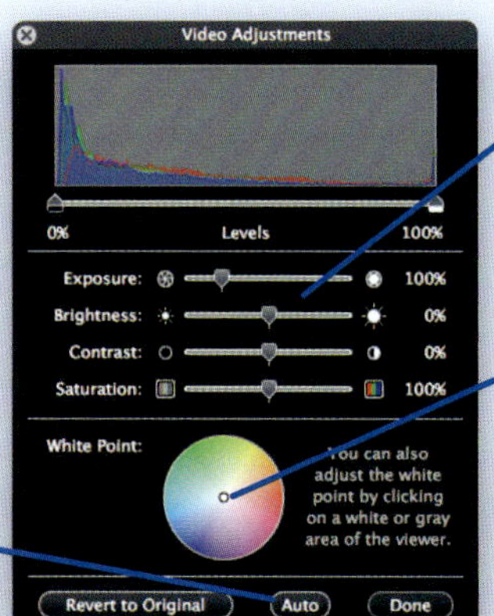

Otherwise, use the sliders to adjust the clip's appearance; they work much like the ones in iPhoto (page 160).

If a clip's color is off, try clicking something in the scene that's supposed to be white or gray. Or drag the circle inside the White Point color wheel.

Tips: To make the clip black and white, drag the Saturation slider to zero. To create strange video effects, experiment with all the sliders. To add more color-adjustment sliders, activate the advanced editing tools in the Preferences dialog box. To apply the identical adjustments to other clips, use the Paste Adjustments command (page 282).

Creating Cutaways

A *cutaway* is a common video-production technique. Think of Barbara Walters nodding solemnly while Fabio describes what kind of tree he'd like to be. Or maybe the video changes to show a close-up of Grandma's garden as she talks about it.

Try it yourself. Want to experiment with cutaways? Go to www.macilife.com/imovie and download the Cutaway Example Footage archive. Double-click the archive after downloading it, then open the folder named Cutaway Footage and read the instructions inside.

Step 1. Get Your Shots

Begin planning cutaway shots when shooting your video. After Grandma talks about her garden, shoot some close-ups of the plants she talked about. While you're shooting the school play, grab a couple of shots of the audience laughing or clapping. Or after you've shot an interview, move the camera to shoot a few seconds of the interviewer nodding. (In TV news, this kind of shot is called a *noddie*.)

Tip: Still have an old VHS or 8mm camcorder? Dust it off, pop it on a tripod, and use it to shoot short cutaway shots. Dub the footage to your current camcorder, then import it into iMovie. The video quality won't match exactly, but your viewers may never notice. And your cutaways will be authentic rather than staged.

Step 2. Set Up for the Edit

With your footage imported, you're ready to set up for the edit. With cutaway shots, you retain the audio from the primary clip and discard the audio from the cutaway shot.

Add your primary footage to the Project browser, and then click it to select the clip.

Next, some trickery. To keep the audio of the primary audio clip intact, you're going to import just the audio from the source clip. Choose Edit > Reveal in Event Browser; the selected footage from the source clip is highlighted in gray. Next, hold the ⌘ and Shift keys and drag the clip again from the Event browser to the Project browser, dropping it at the beginning of the video clip; the audio appears as a green audio clip.

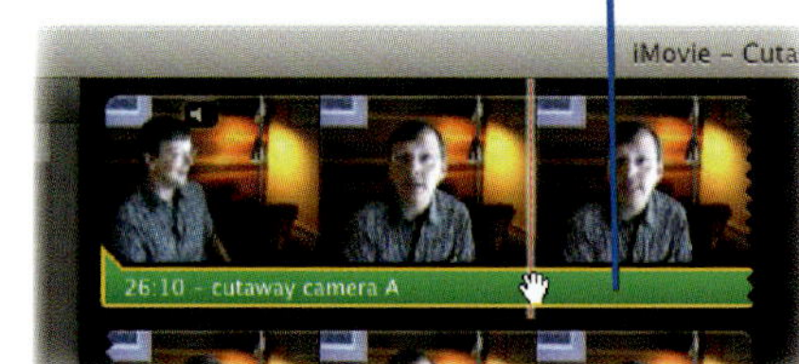

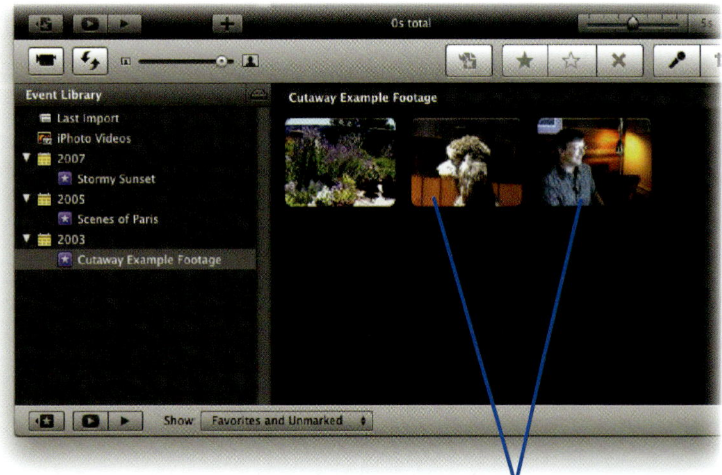

Make sure your primary and cutaway footage exist as separate clips.

Step 3. Silence the Source

Set the video clip's audio to zero (click the Adjust Audio button and drag the volume slider to 0%) so only the green audio clip is audible.

Step 4. Copy the Cutaway

In the Event Browser, drag to select the cutaway footage and choose Copy from the Edit menu (⌘-C).

Step 5. Insert the Cutaway

In the Project browser, navigate to the spot where you want the cutaway to begin and choose Edit > Paste. Next, use the Audio Adjustments window to mute the audio of the cutaway clip.

Step 6. Fix the Sync

Adding the cutaway throws off the primary clip's audio synchronization. To fix that, make note of the duration of the cutaway, then remove an equal amount of footage from the beginning of the primary clip that follows the cutaway. For example, if the cutaway is three seconds long, select three seconds of the clip that follows the cutaway, then choose Edit > Cut.

Cutaway Notes and Tips

You may find that cutaways are easier to wrangle if you view clip durations as timecode instead of as seconds. Choose iMovie > Preferences and check the Display Timecodes box.

If your video and audio have gotten hopelessly out of sync, you can fix it without fussing with the cutaway edits. Highlight the portion of your primary footage before the cutaway and choose Reveal in Event Browser, then ⌘-Shift drag that portion of the clip back to the Project browser, aligning it with the start of the primary clip. Finally, extend the end of the audio clip to cover the length of the cutaway.

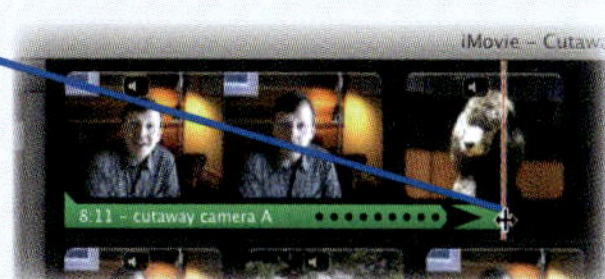

Adding Photos to Movies

Photographs are mainstays of many types of movies, especially montages and documentaries. With the Photos browser in iMovie, you can add photos from your iPhoto library to your movies. You can also add photos that aren't stored in your iPhoto library by dragging them into iMovie.

When adding photos to movies, consider taking advantage of iMovie's *Ken Burns* effect to add a sense of dynamism to your stills. Why name a feature after a filmmaker? Think about Ken Burns' documentaries and how his camera appears to move across still images. For example, a shot might begin with a close-up of a weary face and then zoom out to reveal a Civil War battlefield scene.

That's the Ken Burns effect. Now, Ken Burns himself would probably call it by its traditional filmmaking terms: *pan and scan* or *pan and zoom*. These terms reflect the fact that you can have two different kinds of motion: panning (moving across an image) and zooming (moving in or out).

Whatever the effect's name, its result is the same: it adds motion and life to otherwise static images.

Adding a Photo from Your iPhoto Library

Step 1.

Click the Photos button, or press ⌘-2.

To view a specific album, choose its name from the list.

Step 2.

Select the photo. You can select multiple photos by Shift-clicking or ⌘-clicking on them.

Step 3.

Drag the photo to the project. To insert the photo between clips, drag to the space between clips, as shown here.

Step 4.

To customize the Ken Burns move, click the Crop button in the photo's thumbnail, or click the Crop tool in the Toolbar and select the photo in the project. Adjust the move as described below, then click Done.

To pan-zoom a photo, specify the start and finish settings for the move: that is, how you want the photo to look when it first appears, and how you want it to look at the end of its duration.

iMovie automatically applies the Ken Burns effect. To switch modes, click Fit or Crop (see below).

Tip: You can change the default mode using the Initial Photo Placement pop-up menu in the Project Properties dialog (choose File > Project Properties or press ⌘-J).

Specify the desired starting setting by resizing (drag the corners or sides) and moving the green Start box.

Reverses your settings—for example, turns a zoom in into a zoom out.

Specify the last frame of the move by resizing and moving the red End box.

The yellow arrow indicates the direction of the pan.

Preview the Ken Burns effect.

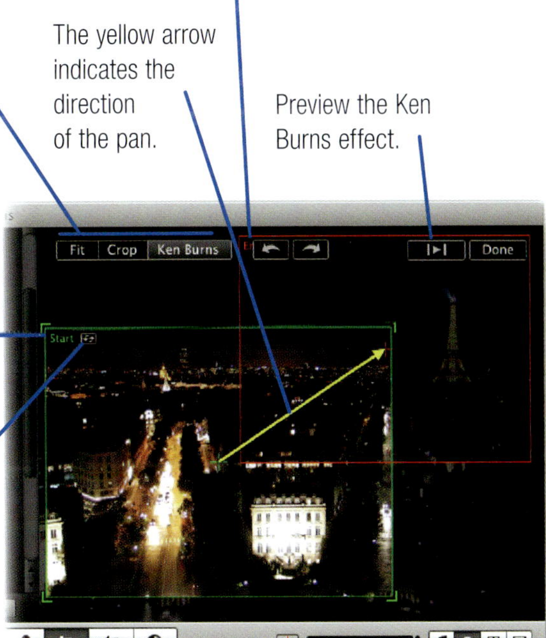

Cropping and Fitting

Don't want Ken Burns? You can choose to fit the entire static photo in the frame (you may see black bars at the edges, depending on the aspect ratio of the photo) or to fill the screen with the photo (cropping some of the image).

Cropping also lets you focus on part of an image to improve its composition—or remove the unwanted tourist spoiling the shot.

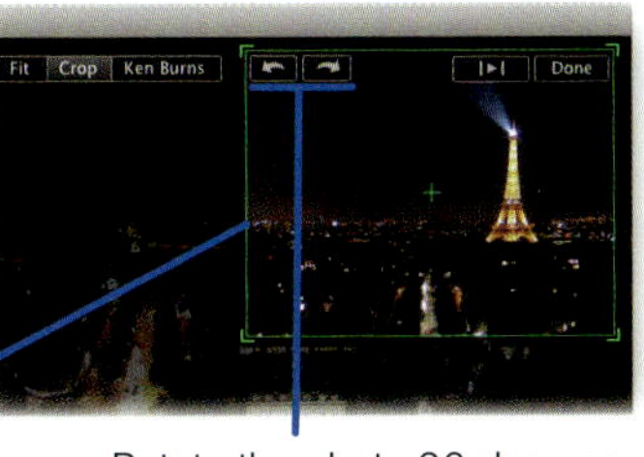

Rotate the photo 90 degrees.

Photo Tips

Photos from elsewhere. You can also use photos that aren't stored in your iPhoto library. To access a folder of photos, drag the folder to the top of the Photos browser; it appears in a folder named Folders (what folderol!). You can also drag an image file from the Finder directly to the project. The Photos browser also shows pictures from Photo Booth and from Apple's Aperture software, if you have them.

Change photo duration. Click the Duration button (the tiny clock) on a clip, or choose Edit > Set Duration. Enter a new value, and specify whether the new duration applies to the selected photo or to all photos in the project.

Adding a photo overlay. Instead of dropping a photo in the space between clips, drop it directly onto a clip. The image appears as a blue bar above the filmstrip (much like a title; page 274), complete with its own cross-dissolve transitions at the start and end. This approach lets you keep the video's audio while a photo appears, without having to trim the video clip.

For even more fun, create an image with transparency, save it as a PNG file, and add it to a movie using this technique. The underlying video shows through the transparency, while the opaque pixels of your image appear overlaid on top. (For example, you could make a logo appear in a corner without obscuring the entire screen.)

Tips for the Ken Burns Effect

Video Formats and Photo Proportions

iMovie's support for multiple video formats introduces some special Ken Burns considerations.

4:3 formats. Working in a standard (4:3) format, such as DV? If you plan to show a photo at actual size, be sure your photos' proportions match the 4:3 aspect ratio of these formats. Otherwise, the photos won't completely fill the video frame: they will have black borders.

Most digital camera photos have a 4:3 aspect ratio. If the photos you want to use don't have these proportions, you have two options. The easiest option is to simply crop in iMovie: in the Viewer, click the Crop button. A green crop area appears; its aspect ratio matches that of your project. To change which part of the photo appears, resize the crop area.

The more drastic option is to crop your photos in iPhoto. From the Constrain pop-up menu in iPhoto's edit view, choose 4 x 3 (DVD). Remember, cropping alters the photo in your library and anywhere else it appears. If you want an uncropped (or differently cropped) version of a photo, duplicate the photo before cropping it.

HD **HD format.** Photos can look beautiful in high-definition format, but in their original form, they will definitely not fill the video frame. Instead, they'll appear *pillarboxed*, with fat black borders on their left and right edges.

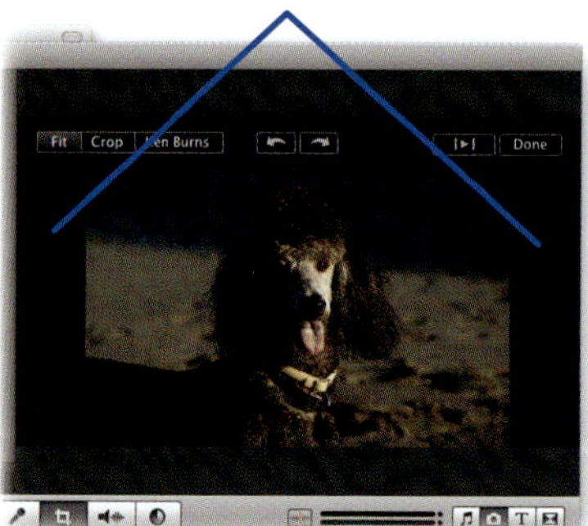

Simply use iMovie's Crop tool to crop the photo to match your project's 16:9 aspect ratio. If you'd prefer to give iMovie cropped photos to begin with, use iPhoto's Constrain pop-up menu to specify a custom crop proportion of 16 x 9 (HD).

Changing Settings

You've applied the Ken Burns effect and now decide that you want to change the clip's pan or zoom settings. Select the clip in the project timeline, then click the Crop button on the clip or on the toolbar. Now make the desired adjustments in the Viewer and click Done.

Starting over. If you don't like the way you've set up a Ken Burns move or a crop, it's easy to restore the photo to its original state. First, click the photo's Crop button or select the Crop tool and then click the photo in the project timeline. Next, click the Fit button in the Viewer.

Image Resolution and Zooming

iMovie imports photos at their full resolution. This lets you zoom in on part of a photo and still retain image sharpness.

However, if you zoom in on a low-resolution image or one that you've cropped heavily in iPhoto, you will probably notice some chunky-looking pixelation. So think twice about zooming in on low-resolution images unless you want that pixelated look.

HD If you're working in a high-definition format, you may find that you can't zoom in very far on photos that have relatively low resolution (for example, two megapixels), at least not without seeing ugly visual artifacts.

Searching for Photos

The Photos browscr in iMovie contains a search box, which lets you search for text present in a photo's title, description, or keywords. You can also focus your search on only keywords or star ratings; use the pop-up menu in the search box.

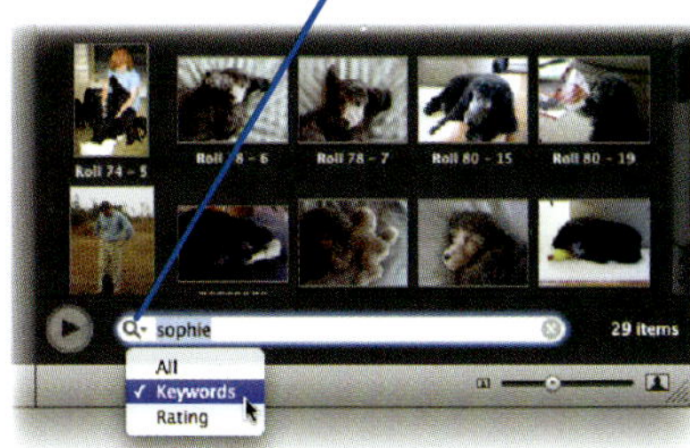

Zoom to Tell a Story

Creative use of zooming can help tell your story. When you zoom in, you gradually focus the viewer's attention on one portion of the scene. You tell the viewer, "Now that you have the big picture, this is what you should pay attention to."

When you zoom out, you reveal additional details about the scene, increasing the viewer's sense of context. You tell the viewer, "Now that you've seen that, look at these other things to learn how they relate to each other."

Go Slow

Unless you're after a special effect, avoid very fast pans and zooms. It's better to pan and zoom slowly to allow your viewers to absorb the changes in the scene.

Onc way to control the speed of the zoom is to extend the duration of the clip. A ten-second Ken Burns move is smoother than a two-second one.

Another way to control the speed of the zoom is to simply zoom less. A gentle zoom is less visually jarring anyway.

Vary Your Zoom Direction

Variety is the spice of zooming. If you're creating a photo montage and zooming each image, consider alternating between zooming in and zooming out. For example, zoom in on one image, then zoom out on the next. If you add several photos at once, iMovie automatically sets up their Ken Burns moves this way.

A fine example of this technique lives elsewhere within iLife: iPhoto's automatic Ken Burns effect alternates between zooming in and zooming out. So does the screen saver in Mac OS X.

Cropping for Composition

Cropping is a good way to make a photo fit the aspect ratio of a project, but that isn't its only application, of course. You can also crop to simply improve photo's composition.

No Rendering Needed

If you've used earlier iMovie versions, you're probably used to waiting a lot. For example, when you created a Ken Burns move, iMovie would have to generate, or render, each of the video frames necessary to create the move.

iMovie '08 eliminates the need to render by taking advantage of the graphics power in Mac OS X. As a result, you have more freedom to experiment—and less waiting to do.

Advanced Ken Burns Techniques

Ken Burns has some limitations. One is that you can't "hold" on a certain frame. You might want to have a 10-second clip in which the photo zooms for the first eight seconds and then remains static for the last two. Or maybe you want to zoom in part way, freeze for a couple of seconds, and then continue zooming.

Ken can't do that.

Another limitation is that you can't combine multiple moves in a single clip. For example, you might want to pan across a photo and then zoom in on part of it.

Ken can't do that, either.

At least not without a little finessing. It's actually possible to accomplish both of these tasks in iMovie. Here's how.

Holding on a Frame

To hold on a frame, start by adding a photo to the project timeline.

Step 1.

Set up the Ken Burns effect as desired and then apply it, as described on page 259.

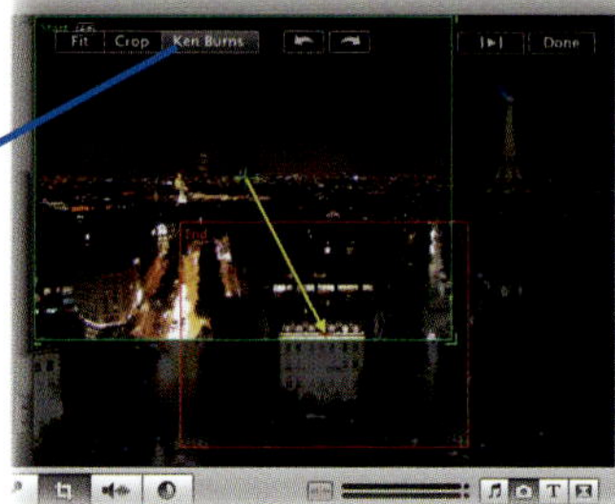

Step 2.

Copy the clip (press ⌘-C) and then paste it (⌘-V) to create a duplicate right after the original.

Step 3.

Click the Crop button to edit the Ken Burns settings, and then select the End state (the red box). Click the Reverse button to set the end state as the start state.

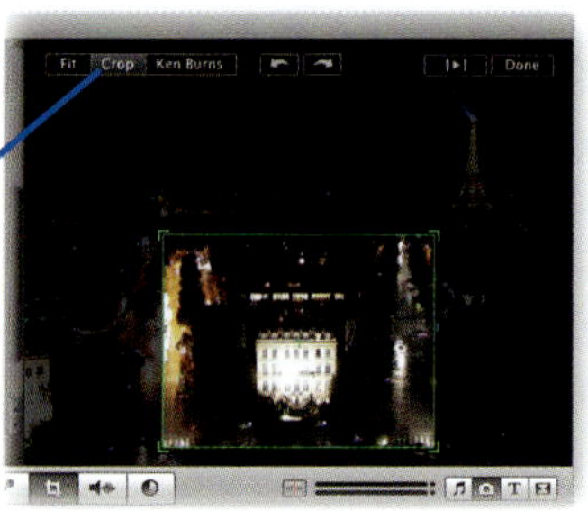

Step 4.

Click the Crop button to remove the Ken Burns effect but retain the same cropping as the last frame of the original clip.

Step 5.

Copy and paste the second—cropped—clip and click the Ken Burns button. The cropped area becomes the Start box.

Step 6.

Configure the Ken Burns settings for the clip, then click Done. If you like, adjust each clip's duration settings to set the timing you want. **Tip:** You can also start by holding on a frame, and then panning and zooming. First, apply the Ken Burns effect, then copy and paste the clip. Set the second photo's state to Crop, and position it before the Ken Burns clip.

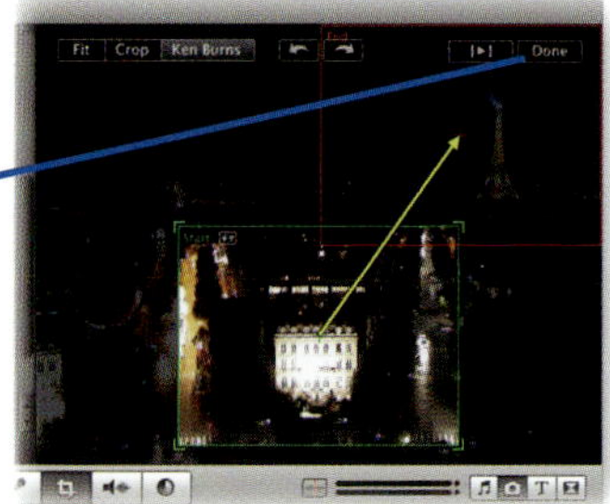

Combining Moves

Combining two kinds of moves involves importing the same photo twice and applying different Ken Burns settings each time.

Step 1.

Set up the first Ken Burns move as desired and then apply it.

Step 2.

Select the clip and choose Edit > Copy or press ⌘-C.

Step 3.

Drag a fresh copy of the photo from the Photos browser.

Step 4.

Select the new copy and choose Edit > Paste Adjustments > Crop.

Step 5.

Click the Crop button to edit the photo, and click the Reverse button.

This reverses the Ken Burns settings that you set up for Step 1: its end point becomes the new start point.

Step 6.

Specify the End settings for the second Ken Burns move and then click Done.

Beyond Ken Burns: Other Pan-Zoom Tools

Ken Burns isn't the only game in town. Other pan-zoom tools are available that work with iMovie.

Photo to Movie. Photo to Movie by LQ Graphics (www.lqgraphics.com) makes it very easy to create pan-zoom effects. Create your effect in Photo to Movie, export it as a QuickTime movie, and then bring it into iMovie and add it to your project.

Photo to Movie's results are superior to those created by the Ken Burns effect. Photo to Movie does a better job of what animators call *ease in* and *ease out*: rather than motion abruptly starting and ending, the motion starts and ends gradually. The results have a more professional appearance.

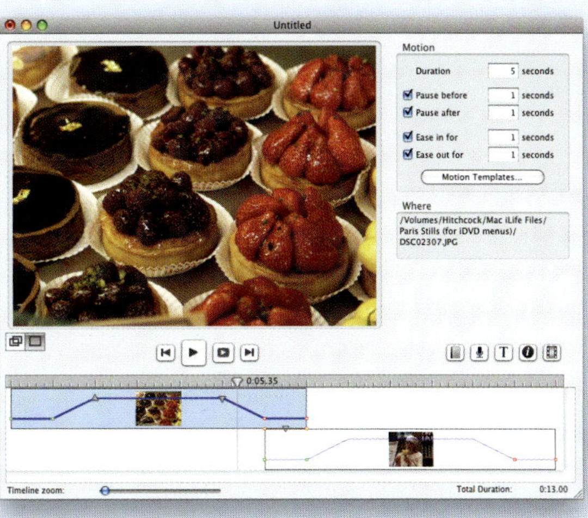

Motion Pictures HD. This scaled-down version of Photo to Movie is included with Roxio's Toast.

Adding Audio to Movies

In movie making, sound is at least as important as the picture. An audience will forgive hand-held camera shots and poor lighting—*The Blair Witch Project* proved that. But give them a noisy, inaudible soundtrack, and they'll run for the aspirin.

Poor quality audio is a common flaw of home video and amateur movies. One problem is that most camcorders don't have very good microphones—their built-in mikes are often located on the top of the camera where they pick up sound from the camera's motors. What's more, the microphone is usually far from the subject, resulting in too much background noise. And if you're shooting outdoors on a windy day, your scenes end up sounding like an outtake from *Twister*.

If your camcorder provides a jack for an external microphone, you can get much better sound by using one. On the following pages, you'll find some advice on choosing and using microphones.

If you've already shot your video or you can't use an external mike, there is another solution: don't use the audio you recorded. Instead, create an audio *bed* consisting of music and, if appropriate, narration or sound effects (see page 267).

iMovie provides several features that you can use to sweeten your soundtracks. Take advantage of them. And if they don't do the job, consider bringing your movie into GarageBand for additional sonic seasoning (page 376).

Importing Music from Your iTunes Library or GarageBand

Use the Music and Sound Effects browser to bring in music from your iTunes library or GarageBand.

Step 1.

Click the Music and Sound Effects button in the toolbar, or press ⌘-1.

Step 2.

Select iTunes or GarageBand in the list of audio sources.

Note: In order to be able to preview a GarageBand project in the media pane, or add the song to your movie, the project needs to be saved with an iLife preview.

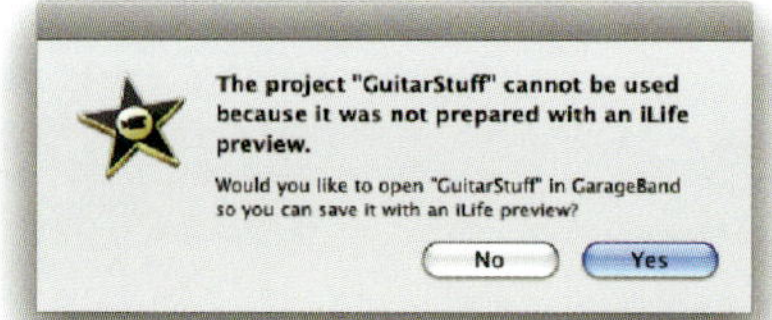

For details, see page 361.

Step 3.

Locate the song you want to import.

You can choose a specific playlist from the list of sources.

Use the Search box to quickly locate a song based on its name or its artist's name.

To play a song, select it and click this button, or simply double-click the song's name.

Step 4.

Drag a song to your project. Where you drop the song determines how iMovie treats it.

Background music. Drag the song to the edge of the background area of your project (the background turns green). The song becomes a background music track that plays behind the audio of the video footage.

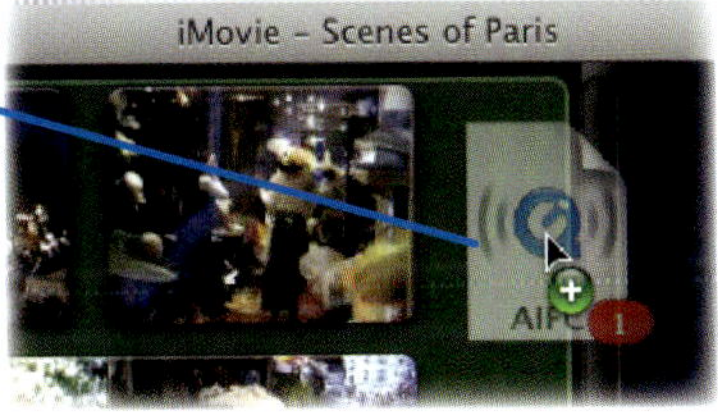

Audio clip. To tie the audio to a specific video clip, drop the audio onto the clip, positioning it at the frame where you want playback to begin. The audio is locked to that video clip: move the video, and the audio moves with it.

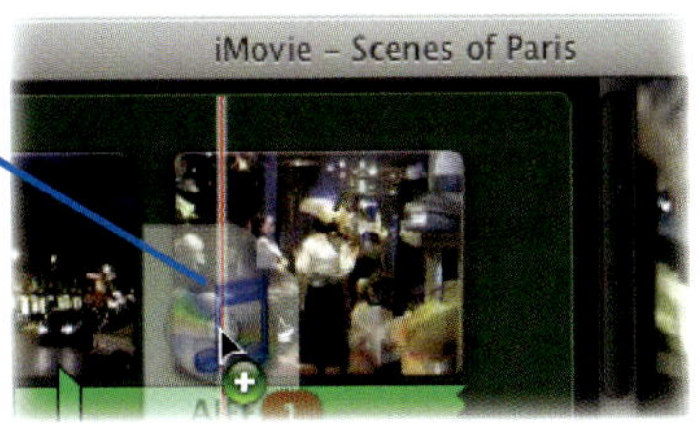

Tip: You can stack as many audio clips as your ears can bear. For details on managing audio, see page 268.

Recording an Audio Narration

You can record narration directly within iMovie.

To begin recording, click the Voiceover button in the toolbar (or press O) and then click the point in your movie where you want to begin recording. iMovie gives you a three-second countdown and then starts recording. To stop recording, click again in the browser. (To cancel recording, press Esc.) When you're done, close the Voiceover window.

As you record, iMovie adds your narration to the filmstrip (as a purple audio clip), positioning it at the playhead's location.

Setting levels. For the best sound, you want to record loud, but not too loud. At its loudest, your voice should illuminate iMovie's volume meter as mostly green. If you push the levels into the red, your sound will be distorted.

Good

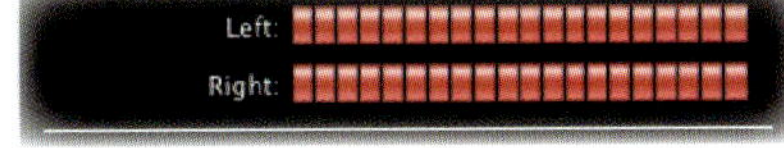

Bad

Tips. The Voiceover window has some controls that can improve recording quality. To reduce background noise, such as room echo, use the Noise Reduction slider. To add aural "punch" to your recording, click the Voice Enhancement check box.

Tips for Recording Better Sound

Upgrade Your Microphone

To get better sound, get a high-quality external microphone and place it close to your subject.

Before you buy an external mike, determine whether your camcorder can accept one. Some inexpensive camcorders don't provide a jack for an external mike; others may require an adapter that connects to the bottom of the camera. Most mid-range and all high-end camcorders have external mike jacks. On most cameras, it's a ⅛-inch stereo minijack.

Clip-on. Microphones come in all sizes and designs. Some are specialized—for example, a *lavaliere* mike, which clips to a lapel or shirt, is great for recording a single voice, such as that of a teacher (or TV host). But a lav mike is unsuitable for recording a musical performance.

Shotgun approach. When you can't get the mike close to your subject but still want to reduce extraneous noise, consider a *shotgun* mike. In a shotgun mike, the microphone capsule is mounted within a long barrel designed to reject sound coming from the side of the mike. Shotgun mikes are popular in TV news and movie making. They're sensitive enough to be located out of the video frame, and their highly directional sensitivity means they won't pick up noise from cameras and crew members.

A shotgun mike works best when mounted on a *boom*, a long pole (often hand-held) that allows the mike to point down at the subject. When you see a video crew with one person who appears to be holding a fishing pole with a long tube on the end of it, you're seeing a shotgun mike (and a sound technician) in action.

Two in one. The most versatile mike you can buy is a *single-point stereo* mike. A stereo mike crams two microphone capsules into a single package. Each capsule is precisely positioned relative to its companion, thus eliminating one of the biggest challenges of stereo recording: getting accurate balance and separation between the left and right channels. I use the AT822 from Audio-Technica (www.audio-technica.com).

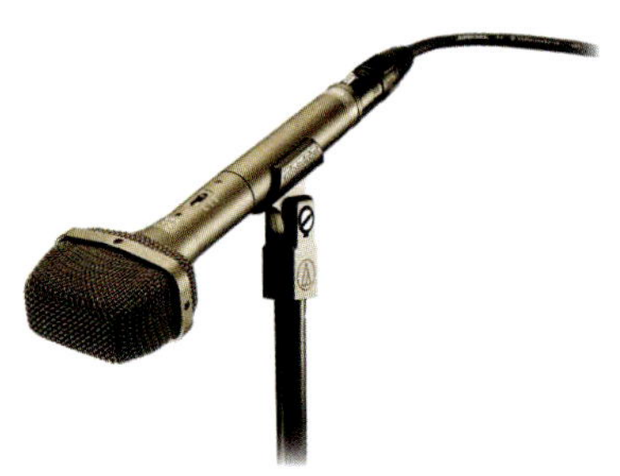

With high-quality extension cables, the mike and camera can be up to about 25 feet apart. At greater distances, you risk losing some high frequencies and picking up hum and other electrical noise.

A balanced alternative. When you need to run cables longer than 25 feet or so—or when you want the best possible quality and are prepared to pay for it—consider a *balanced* mike. All of the aforementioned mikes are available in balanced and unbalanced versions. A balanced mike is wired in a way that reduces electrical noise and allows for cable runs of up to 100 feet or so. Balanced mikes cost more than unbalanced ones, but professionals and serious amateurs prefer balanced mikes due to their resistance to electrical noise and their support for longer cable runs.

A balanced mike typically uses an *XLR* connector, and only high-end camcorders have XLR jacks. But there is a way to connect a balanced mike to an unbalanced miniplug jack: the DXA-2 adaptor from BeachTek (www.beachtek.com). A compact metal box that attaches to your camera's tripod mount, the DXA-2 requires no external power supply and has built-in knobs for adjusting volume levels.

Placement is Everything

To do justice to any mike, position it properly. For that school play or recital, use a mike stand and position the mike high, pointing down toward the stage at about a 45-degree angle. If you can't set up your own mike stand, just try to get the mike at least a few feet off the stage and as close to center stage as possible.

How close should the mike be? That depends on what you're recording (see the table at right). The closer the mike is to a sound source, the less room noise and reverberation it picks up.

But if the mike is too close, stereo separation is exaggerated—some sounds come only from the left speaker, others only from the right, and sounds in the center are louder than they should be. Move the mike too far away, and you get a muddy-sounding recording with too much room reverb.

When recording a live performance, try to show up for rehearsals so that you have time to experiment with different mike distances. If your camera has a headphone jack, connect a good pair of headphones—ones whose cups surround your ears and thus block out external sounds. Record a test, play it back, and listen.

For recording narrations, consider assembling a makeshift sound booth that will absorb room echo and block computer and hard drive noise. Glue some sound-absorbing acoustical foam onto two sheets of plywood or foamcore. (See www.soundsuckers.com for a wide selection.) Position the two sheets in front of you in a V shape, with the mike at the narrow end. If you're on a tight budget, use blankets, pillows, carpet remnants, or even a coat closet. The idea is to surround yourself, and the mike, with sound-absorbing material.

Another major microphone manufacturer, Shure, has published some excellent mike-placement tutorials. Download them at www.shure.com.

A Field Guide to Mike Placement

Scenario	Ideal Mike Position
Solo piano	About a foot from the center of the piano's harp, pointed at the strings (open the piano's recital lid).
Wedding ceremony	As close to the lovebirds as possible. Many wedding videographers attach a wireless lavaliere mike to the groom or the officiator. (Bridal gowns tend to rustle too much.) A mike hidden in a flower arrangement may also work.
Narrator	6 to 9 inches from the speaker's mouth, angled downward. To avoid plosive problems, use a windscreen and position the mike just off to the side, pointing at the mouth. Alternative: a lavaliere mike.
Choral group	1 to 3 feet above and 2 to 4 feet in front of the first row of the choir.
Birthday party around a table	On an extended floor stand, angled downward. Alternative: on a tabletop desk stand, pointing at the birthday kid.

Creating an Audio Bed

If you weren't able to get good audio when you originally shot your video, consider muting your video's audio track and just putting a music bed behind your shots. Create a montage of shots, using bookmarks and direct trimming to help you time your edits to the music.

And finally, a related tip: If you're shooting scenes where the audio is mostly ambient sound—the waves at the beach, the din of a party—shoot a few minutes of uninterrupted video, keeping the camera stationary. After importing the video, you can use only the clip's audio. In iMovie, hold ⌘ and Shift while dragging the clip into your project; it appears as an audio clip below the filmstrip. Now mute the audio of the other clips (see page 268). This technique eliminates jarring sound changes between shots.

Working with Audio

Adjusting the volume of an audio track is a common task. And when you combine audio in any way—mixing music, sound effects, dialog, and background sounds—you almost always need to adjust the relative levels of each sound to create a pleasing mix.

iMovie provides several ways to work with sound levels. You can reduce the volume of an entire sound clip. You might do this if you're mixing music with the sound of the surf, and don't want the waves to drown out the music.

You can also vary a track's volume level over time. When combining music and narration, you might want the music to start at full volume, fade when the narrator talks, then return to full volume when she stops—a feature called *ducking*.

Just as with video, you can change the duration of audio clips. You can trim directly in the project timeline or, for more precision, summon the trimmer, which has the added benefit of displaying audio *waveforms*. A waveform looks a bit like the penmanship of an earthquake seismograph. Back-and-forth lines indicate the intensity of the shaking—in this case, of the sound wave. Being able to see your sound is a big help when trimming audio tracks.

Making Audio Adjustments

To control audio levels, use the Audio Adjustments window. Click the toolbar's Audio Adjustments button (or press A), then, in your project, click the clip that has the audio you want to adjust. (Shortcut: Click a clip's Audio Adjustments button—the tiny speaker.)

Quiet down (or speak up): Change the volume of the selected clip.

Pipe down for a moment: to have iMovie reduce the volume of concurrently playing audio (such as background music), check Ducking. The selected clip's volume is unchanged, but other audio gets quieter. The higher the setting, the quieter the other audio gets.

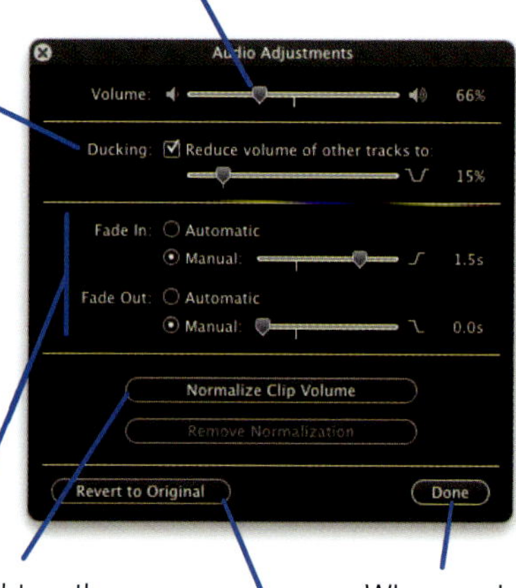

Fades: To have a clip's audio fade in or fade out, click Manual, then drag the slider to specify the fade duration, in seconds. For no fade at all, drag all the way to the left.

All together now: iMovie can make volumes consistent across multiple clips. Click Normalize, then select another clip and click Normalize again. Repeat for each clip.

Change your mind? Click to restore the clip's original levels.

When you're finished, click Done.

Managing Background Music

Adding background music to a project is easy, but there's more to the story. You can have multiple songs in a project—just drag them to the project's background, as shown on page 265. When you add multiple songs to the background, they play one after the other, separated by a one-second crossfade.

Rearranging background music. To change the playback order of your project's songs, choose Edit > Arrange Music Tracks.

Drag the songs to change their playback order, then click OK.

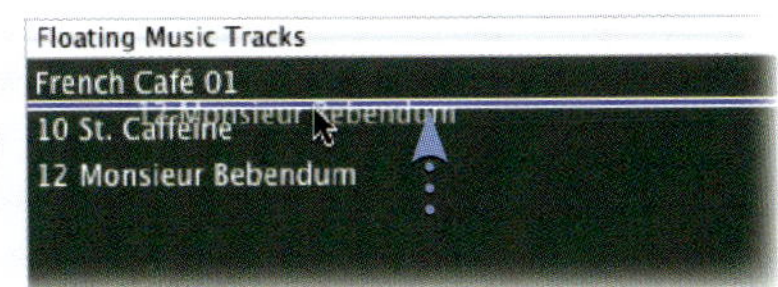

Pinning audio. You can *pin* a background song to a specific clip so that it begins playing when that clip appears—and so that it moves along with the clip as you edit and change your project.

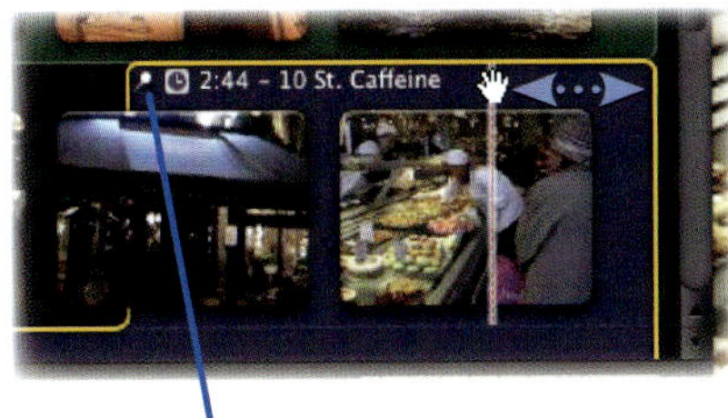

To pin a background song, drag the song until the little pin is above the video frame where you want playback to begin. The green background icon turns purple.

To make the song float again, select it and choose Edit > Un-Pin Music Track.

Tips: For projects with several pinned tracks, it's often easier to use the Edit menu's Arrange Music Tracks command to unpin tracks.

If you pin a music clip and then add another background song, the new song fills in any gap between the last floating song and the pinned clip.

Trimming Audio

To change the duration of an audio clip, trim it—either directly in the project or in the trimmer.

In the project. To trim audio in the browser, point to the beginning or end of the clip and then drag left or right.

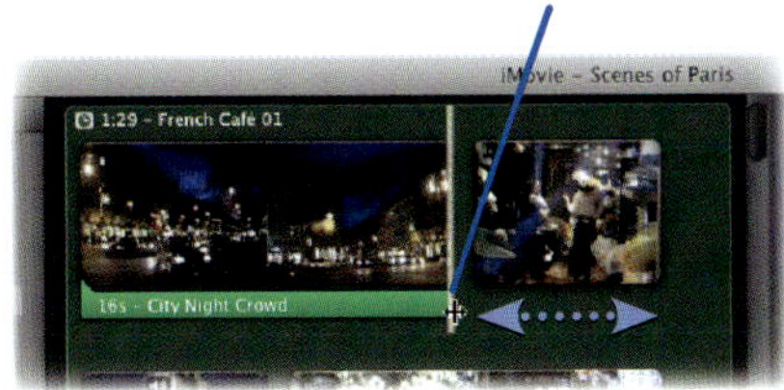

In the trimmer. For more control, use the trimmer: select the song and choose Edit > Trim Music (⌘-R).

Preview your work.

The audible portion of the clip.

To change the clip's duration, drag the yellow handle at the beginning or end of the clip.

Slipping audio edits. Sometimes, you may want to keep the duration of a clip the same, but change which part of it plays—maybe you need 50 seconds of a song behind some footage, but you want a *different* 50 seconds.

Easy: in the trimmer, drag within the middle of the audible portion to perform a *slip edit.*

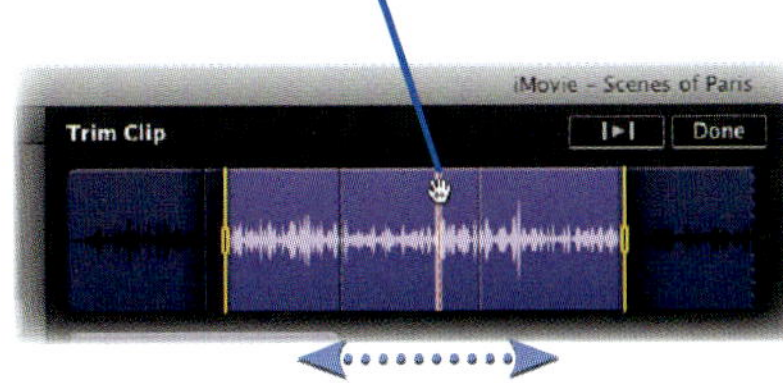

More Sound Advice

Waveform Tip

To work with more precision when viewing waveforms in the Trimmer, zoom in: drag the thumbnail slider to the right, and drag the clip size slider to its leftmost position (the half-second setting).

Trimming Audio

You can trim the start and end of an audio clip using the same techniques described on page 255. As with video clips, you can reclaim audio that's outside of a clip's boundaries by resizing the clip.

Scrubbing Audio

Here's a handy way to locate the exact spot to trim or split an audio clip. First, be sure that audio skimming is on: choose View > Audio Skimming (⌘-K). Next, open the clip in the trimmer, and slowly skim across its waveform. Your audio plays back, but is slowed down. The sound even plays backwards when you skim to the left. (Beatles fans: import some *White Album* songs from your iTunes library and have fun.)

Extracting Audio

At times, you may want to use only the audio portion of a clip. For example, you're making a documentary about your grandmother's childhood and you'd like to show old photographs as she talks.

To do this, hold the ⌘ and Shift keys while dragging the clip to your project. iMovie adds just the audio portion of the clip.

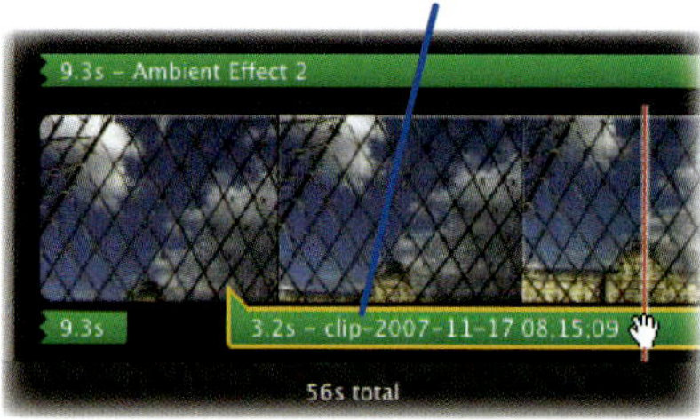

You can now position still images and other clips in the space above the audio in the filmstrip. You can also drag the audio elsewhere in the timeline.

Tip: Another way to get the same result is to drag pictures from the Photos browser onto a video clip in the filmstrip. This overlays the photos on top of the video without disrupting the audio.

Repeating Sound Effects

You might want some sound effects to play for a long period of time. For example, iMovie's Hard Rain sound effect is less than 10 seconds long, but maybe you need 30 seconds of rain sounds for a particular movie.

For cases like these, simply repeat the sound effect by dragging it from the Music and Sound Effects browser to the project as many times as needed. You can also duplicate a sound by Option-dragging it in the project. If the sound effect fades out (as Hard Rain does), overlap each copy to hide the fade.

You can build magnificently rich sound effect tracks by overlapping sounds. To create a thunderstorm with a bit more punch, for example, drag the Thunder and Rain sound effect so that it overlaps Hard Rain. And don't forget to use iMovie's audio controls to fine-tune the relative levels of each effect.

Camcorder Sound Settings

Most miniDV camcorders provide two sound-recording settings: 12-bit and 16-bit. Always record using the 16-bit setting. If your sound and picture synchronization drift over the course of a long movie, it's probably because you recorded using 12-bit audio.

Get links to sources of sound effects and music.
www.macilife.com/imovie

Copying Audio Adjustments

You've adjusted an audio clip and would like to apply the same adjustments to other audio clips. Select the adjusted clip and choose Edit > Copy. Then select other clips and choose Edit > Paste Adjustments > Audio.

When you don't want to use the audio from a series of video clips, this is the easiest way to mute the clips. Mute one, choose Copy, select the others (⌘-click on each one), then paste the adjustment.

Sources for Sound Effects and Music

Sound Effects

iMovie's library of built-in sound effects, accessed through the audio section of the Media browser, covers a lot of aural ground.

But there's always room for more sound, and the Internet is a rich repository of it. One of your first stops should be FindSounds, a Web search engine that lets you locate and download free sound effects by typing keywords, such as *chickadee*. SoundHunter is another impressive source of free sound effects and provides links to even more audio-related sites.

Most online sound effects are stored as WAV or AIFF files, two common sound formats. To import a WAV or AIFF file, use the File menu's Import command or simply drag the file directly to the desired location in the timeline viewer.

Managing Sound Effects

If you assemble a large library of sound effects, you might find yourself needing a program to help you keep track of them. You already have such a program: it's called iTunes. Simply drag your sound effects files into the iTunes window. Use the Get Info command to assign descriptive tags to them, and you can use iTunes' Search box to locate effects in a flash. You might even want to create a separate iTunes library to store your sound effects.

Music Sources

You'll find a symphony's worth of music on the Internet. For private, non-commercial projects, try Freeplay Music (www.freeplaymusic.com). You can download and use its music clips for, yes, free. For commercial projects, however, be sure to carefully read the company's rate card and licensing requirements.

Plenty of music is also available from sites such as SoundDogs, KillerSound, and Award Winning Music. These sites have powerful search features that let you locate music based on keywords, such as *acoustic* or *jazz*.

Loopasonic is another cool music site. It offers hundreds of music loops—repeating riffs—that you can assemble into unique music tracks and use in GarageBand (which, of course, you can use to compose your own movie music).

And for building custom-length music tracks, you can't beat SmartSound's Sonicfire Pro software. Sonicfire Pro provides an expandable library of songs, each of which is divided into blocks that the software can assemble to an exact length.

Adding Transitions

Visual transitions add a professional touch to your project. Transitions also help tell a story. For example, a cross-dissolve—one clip fading out while another fades in—can imply the passage of time. Imagine slowly dissolving from a nighttime campfire scene to a campsite scene shot the following morning.

Similarly, iMovie's wipe transitions, where one clip pushes another out of the frame, are each a visual way of saying "meanwhile..." Imagine using a wipe transition between a scene of an expectant mother in the delivery room and a shot of her husband pacing in the waiting room, chain-smoking nervously. (Okay, so this is an old-fashioned maternity movie.)

The Fade Through Black and Cross Dissolve transitions are "desert-island" transitions—the ones you'd want when stranded on an island (perhaps while editing an episode of *Survivor*). But unless you are stranded on an island, don't limit yourself—experiment with other types of transitions.

Like effects, transitions are visual spice. Season your video with them, but don't let them overpower the main course: your subject.

Creating a Transition

To add a transition between two clips, first display the Transitions browser: click the Transitions button, choose Window > Transitions, or press ⌘-4.

To see a preview of a transition, point to it (don't click) in the Transitions browser.

To add the transition, drag it between two clips in the timeline or clip viewer.

In the project, each transition style has its own icon so you can identify it at a glance.

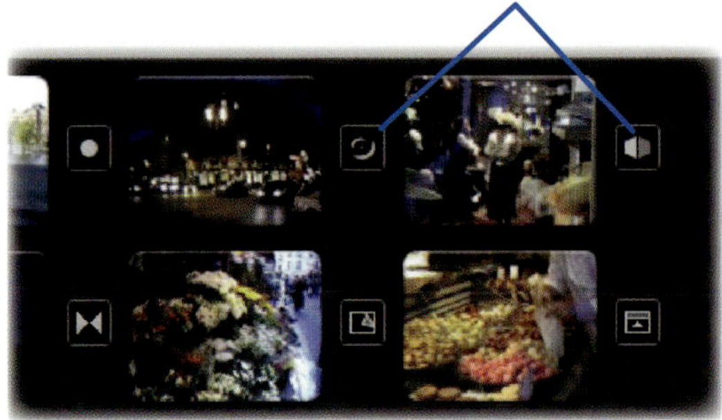

Changing a Transition's Duration

After adding a transition, you can change its duration: select it and choose Edit > Set Duration from the Edit menu (⌘-R). Enter a new duration in seconds, and specify whether the new duration applies to just that one transition or to all transitions in the project. Finally, click OK.

Testing the Transition

To see the finished transition, select it and choose View > Play Selection (or press the forward-slash key).

If you aren't happy with the transition, you can delete it (press the Delete key) or choose Undo.

Inserting a Clip at a Transition

When you create a transition between two clips, you establish a connection between those clips.

If you need to insert a new clip between those two clips, simply drag it to either side of the transition, and iMovie drops it into place.

Changing a Transition

Change your mind about using a particular transition style? To change an existing transition, grab a new transition from the browser and drop it directly onto the old one.

Adding a Transition Between All Clips

You can have iMovie automatically add a transition between every clip in your project. This can be a nice way of adding visual polish to a "video slide show"-style project.

To begin, choose File > Project Properties (⌘-J).

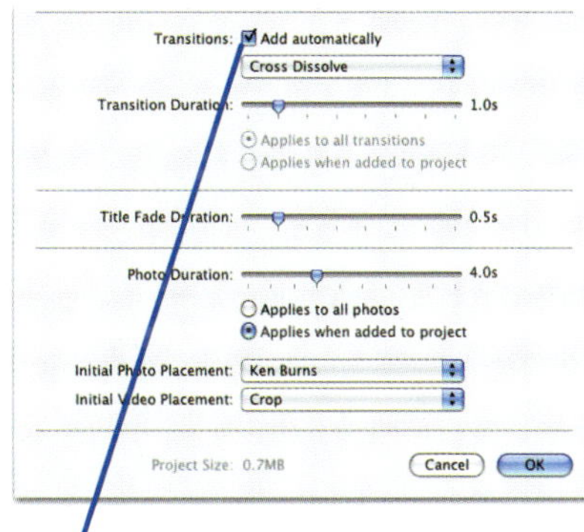

In the Transitions area, check the Add Automatically box, choose a style from the pop-up menu, and click OK.

Next, iMovie asks how you'd like to apply the transitions—and it asks using two very verbose and not entirely clear options.

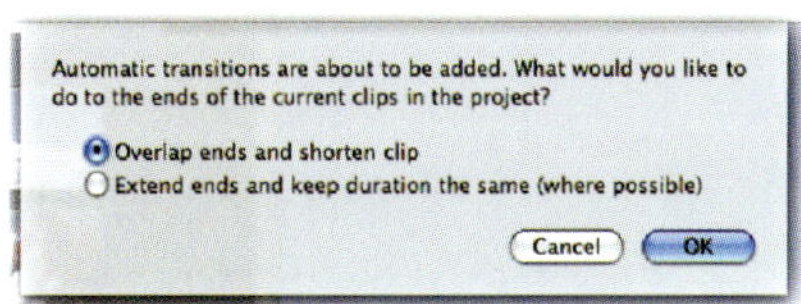

The first option works well when you want to guarantee that the footage you selected before the transition is the footage that's seen, regardless of what it does to the project's overall duration.

Choose the second option if you've already edited the video to synchronize with an audio clip (such as background music) and don't want the project's overall duration to change. The risk with the latter choice is that frames you deliberately edited out could become visible during the transition—your awesome rollerblade jump becomes less awesome when the viewer sees that you polished the pavement half a second after your initial edit.

After you've activated auto transitions, iMovie continues to add transitions when you add new clips to the project.

Removing auto transitions. If that's too much lockstep conformity, return to Project Properties and uncheck Add Automatically. After you click OK, you have another choice to make: whether to keep the footage that was used by the transitions; to maintain the clips' durations; or to leave all the transitions in place so you can remove or edit them individually.

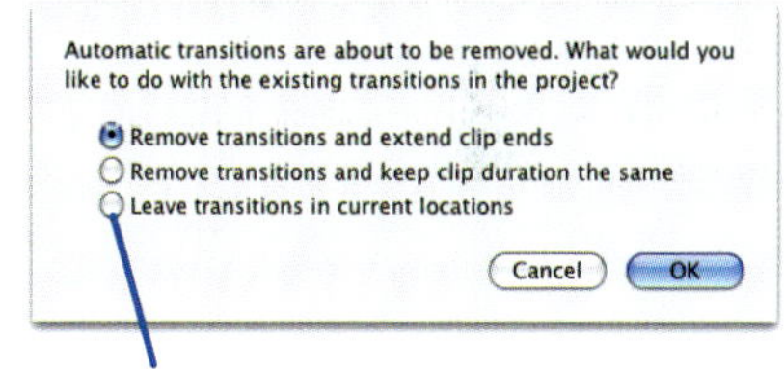

The last option is handy if you want to customize some of the transitions (something iMovie doesn't let you do with automatically added transitions). Turn off auto transitions, but tell iMovie to leave the transitions in place. Then, customize the transitions you want to change, and manually delete the ones you don't want.

Creating Titles

What's a movie without titles? Incomplete. Almost any movie can benefit from text of some kind: opening and closing credits, the superimposed names of people and places, or simply the words "The End" at, well, the end.

iMovie's Titles browser is your ticket to text. There are a dozen title styles, and you can customize their text in a variety of ways.

Regardless of the style you choose, you'll get the best results with sturdy fonts that remain legible despite the limited resolution of television. For example, at small text sizes, Arial Black often works better than Times, which has ornamental serifs that can break up when viewed on a TV set.

You'll also get the best-looking titles if you choose colors conservatively. Avoid highly saturated hues, especially bright red, which can "bloom" when viewed on a standard-definition TV set. High-definition formats are less prone to these problems, but since your video may still end up being viewed on standard-definition TVs, a conservative approach is smart.

Roll the credits.

To Create a Title

Creating a title involves choosing the title style, dragging the title to the project, and then editing the text and its formatting.

Step 1. Click the Titles button to display the Titles browser.

Step 2. Choose the title style you want and drag its icon into your project. You can superimpose title text over a video or photo clip or have it appear against a black background.

Superimposing. To superimpose text over a clip, drop the title onto the clip. As you drag the title near the clip, a purple highlight indicates where the title will appear: over the first half of the clip, the last half, or the entire clip. (You can change this later.)

Over black. To have the title text appear on a solid black background, drop the title between two clips.

Step 3. Specify the title text and font settings.

See the opposite page for an overview of title settings.

Step 4. Click the Done button in the Viewer.

Changing a Title

Need to change an existing title? In the project, select the title. Next, make your changes in the Viewer. Finally, click the Done button.

To move a title, drag it within your project. To change its duration, drag either of its edges.

Tip: If you want to change the title style, you must delete the existing title and add a new one. But you can at least retain any special text formatting you've already done. Select the existing title's text and choose Edit > Copy. Next, delete the old title, add a new title in its place; then paste the text.

Play a preview of the title.

Show or hide the Fonts window.

Use the Fonts window to format text. Select the text, then choose a font, size, or style. You can also control alignment and character spacing, and you can move text up or down.

Type or paste the title's text here. In title styles that provide multiple text boxes, you can jump from one box to the next by pressing the Tab key.

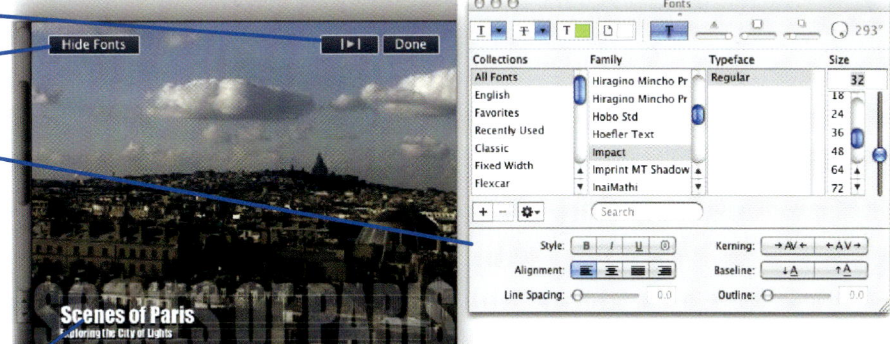

Tips for Titling

Choosing Colors

To choose a color for title text, click the Color button in the Fonts window. Click on the color palette to choose your hue. To match a color that appears in a clip, click the magnifying glass icon, position the pointer over the color you want to pick up, and then click.

Photoshop Titles

You can use Adobe Photoshop or Photoshop Elements to make gorgeous, full-screen titles. You can add photos, create color gradients, shadow effects, and more.

To create a title in Photoshop, specify an image size appropriate to your project's video format. For DV-format projects, use 720 by 528; for DV Widescreen, use 869 by 480. For iSight and MPEG-4 formats, use 640 by 480. For 720p HD, use 1280 by 720, and for 1080i HD, use 1920 by 1080.

Next, create your title, and avoid putting any text in the outer ten percent of the screen. (It might get cut off when the title appears on a TV set.) And to avoid flicker, make the thickness of any horizontal lines an even number of pixels (for example, 2, 4, 6). Save the file as a JPEG or PNG.

To add the title to your movie, simply drag the file's icon directly to the timeline. Be sure to add it as a new photo clip. Don't drag it onto a video clip as you would add a title; iMovie won't recognize the dimensions properly if you do.

Because you added the title as a photo, you can apply the Ken Burns effect to it. Indeed, you can combine a Photoshop graphic with iMovie's built-in title styles to create titles with text superimposed over a moving background. Create a background graphic, then import it and apply a slow pan. Superimpose a title over the graphic.

You could also extract a page from an iPhoto book using the technique on page 213 and use it as a title background.

Stay Title-Safe

TV sets generally cut off the outer edges of a video frame, and that can cause problems with some of iMovie '08's title styles. If you plan to send your project to iDVD, avoid using the subtitle lines of any of the title styles except for Centered—they're likely to be cut off when you view your video on a TV set. And if you use any of the left-aligned title styles, bump the text to the right a bit by pressing the spacebar a few times.

Sharing to .Mac, YouTube, and iTunes

First things first: the Internet isn't the best medium for sharing digital video. The huge size of digital video files means that anything but a very short movie will take a long time to transfer, particularly over a modem line.

But if you have made a short movie—or you have a fast Internet connection and expect that your viewers will, too—you can use iMovie to prepare your work for cyberspace.

From the Share menu, you can publish a movie to your .Mac Web Gallery (if you're a .Mac subscriber), upload it to YouTube, or prepare it for a video-capable iPod, iPhone, or Apple TV. For Internet movies, iMovie compresses the movie heavily to make its file size smaller. In the process, you get an introduction to The Three Musketeers of Internet video: jerky, grainy, and chunky.

A movie compressed for the Internet contains fewer frames per second, so motion may appear jerky. The movie's dimensions are also much smaller—as small as 176 by 144 pixels, or roughly the size of a matchbook. And depending on the options you choose, the sound quality may not be as good as the original.

The best way to watch a movie is on a big screen. (That's where Apple TV shines: share your movie to iTunes, and you can sync it to Apple TV and watch it on your widescreen TV set.) But if you're willing to trade some quality for the portability of an iPod or the worldwide reach of the World Wide Web, iMovie is ready.

Publishing to a .Mac Web Gallery

Step 1. Choose Share > .Mac Web Gallery. Specify the settings shown below, then click Publish.

Name your shared movie.

Tell us about it: the description you write appears on the Web Gallery page.

Click the checkbox for each size you want to publish. Offering more than one size lets you accommodate various Internet speeds. The blue dots indicate which Apple devices and services work best at those sizes—but note that the Large size yields huge downloads with lengthy movies.

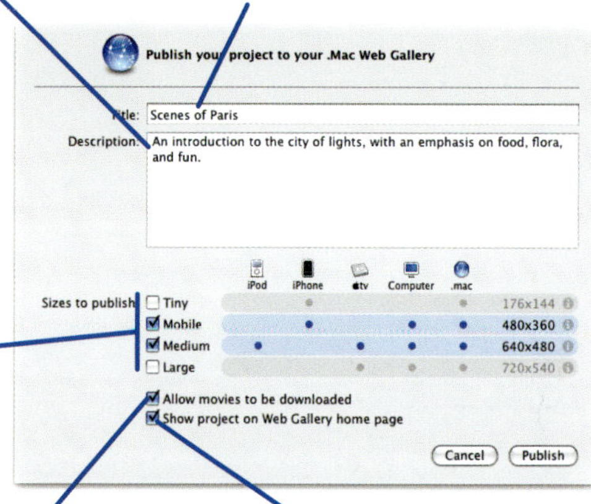

For keeps? To allow viewers to download the movie to their hard drives, check this option.

To add the movie to your Web Gallery index page (page 190), check this box.

Step 2. iMovie compresses the movie and uploads it to your .Mac Web Gallery. When that's done, a dialog box lets you view the page or tell a friend.

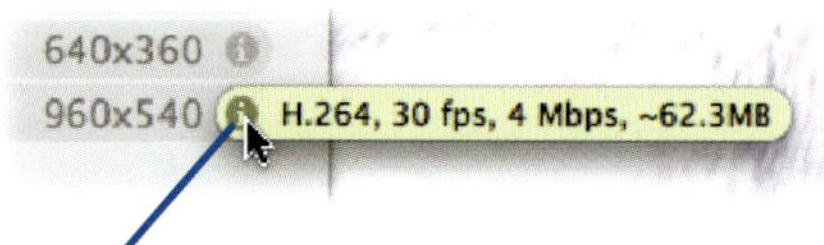

Tip: Point to the ⓘ icon at the right end of each setting, and iMovie shows some details about how the movie will be encoded—and estimates its file size. Here, we see that a two-minute movie will yield a 62MB file in the Large setting—on the big side.

Sharing to YouTube

iMovie can upload movies directly to the popular and addictive YouTube video sharing site. (You'll need a free account; sign up at www.youtube.com.)

Step 1. Choose Share > YouTube.

Step 2. Type a title and description, but don't stop there. Choose a category and enter keywords in the Tags field—make your video easier to find in searches.

Click this option to restrict who views the movie.

Step 3. Click Next to review the YouTube Terms of Service (welcome to the entertainment business!), then click Publish to upload the movie.

Sharing to iTunes

Sharing your movie to iTunes is the key to getting your movie to an iPod, iPhone, or Apple TV.

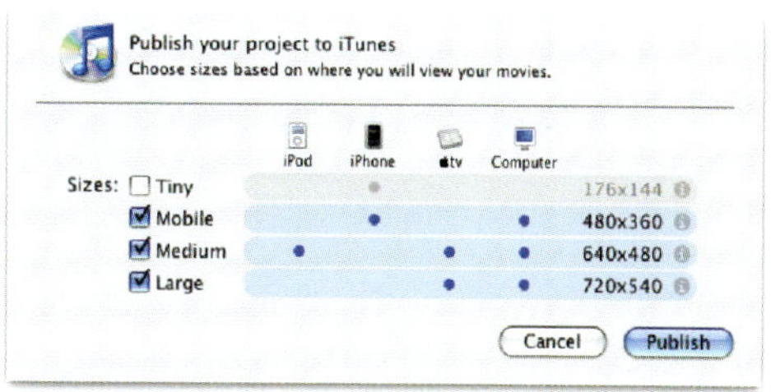

Step 1. Choose Share > iTunes.

Step 2. Choose the sizes you want to share.

After iMovie compresses the movie, it copies the movie to your iTunes library. Use iTunes to sync the movie to your iPod, iPhone, and Apple TV (page 108).

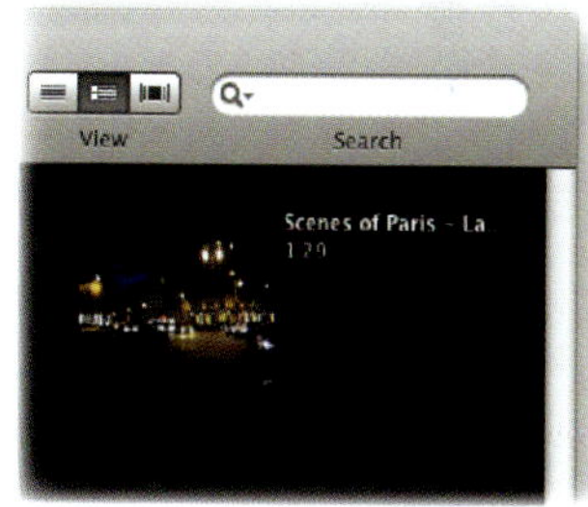

Note: 16:9 movies don't cleanly fit the proportions of the iPod's screen; the movie will be letterboxed with borders above and below the image.

After the Sharing

After you've shared a movie, an icon to the right of its name in the Project Library shows which sizes are published, and a bar at the top of the Project browser indicates where it's been shared.

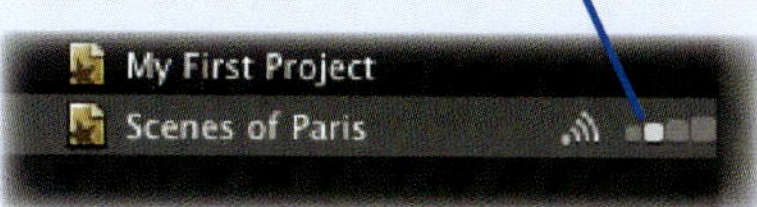

If you change a shared movie, iMovie warns you that the shared version is out of date.

Don't want to share anymore? Choose the appropriate Remove command in the Share menu.

More Ways to Share Movies

Most of iMovie's sharing features are directed to specific outlets, such as YouTube or iTunes. But your movies can play in other venues, too. Want to add a movie to an iDVD or iWeb project? Share it to the Media browser, and it becomes available to any program that offers a Media browser—not only iDVD, iWeb, and GarageBand, but Apple's iWork applications, too.

You can also export a movie in a way that gives you access to the full range of QuickTime compression settings. Normally, iMovie's sharing features insulate you from compression technicalities, but when you want to get your hands dirty, iMovie provides the gardening tools.

iMovie can also export a Final Cut XML file, which is a plain text file containing instructions for Final Cut Pro or Final Cut Express to build a project based on your edits. It's the easiest way to move from a rough cut in iMovie to finer finishing work in Final Cut.

Sharing to the Media Browser

When you share a project to the Media browser, the movie becomes available in the Media browsers of other iLife programs, such as iDVD and iWeb, not to mention other software that supports Apple's Media browsers.

Step 1. Choose Share > Media Browser.

Step 2. Click the checkboxes for the sizes you want to create. The table indicates which sizes are appropriate for which devices and services.

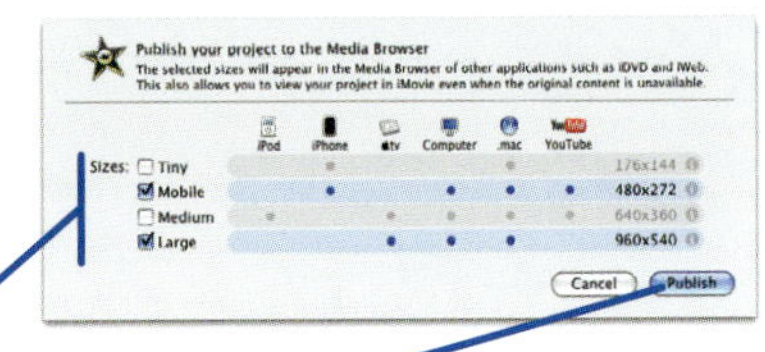

Step 3. Click Publish.

iMovie encodes the movie and makes it available to other applications. You can then import the movie into iWeb (page 409); GarageBand (page 376); or iDVD (page 296).

Exporting a Movie File

You can export a movie using iMovie's friendly presets without having to send the movie to iTunes. Choose Share > Export Movie, then choose a size.

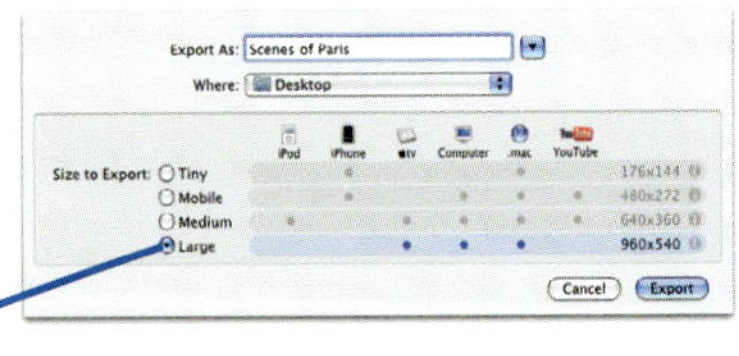

Why bother? Here's one way you might use this feature. Say you're creating a DVD containing some video. How about also including a standalone version of the video, encoded for viewing on an iPod or iPhone? Export the movie to your hard drive, then add it to your DVD's DVD-ROM folder (page 312). Instruct your DVD's recipients that they can insert the DVD in their computers, copy the mobile version of your movie to their iTunes library, and then carry it with them.

You might also use the Export Movie command to create a movie file that you'll upload to a Web server. Use the Tiny preset, and you can even create a movie file small enough (more or less) to email to someone.

Exporting a QuickTime Movie

To export your project as a QuickTime movie, choose Export Using QuickTime from the Share menu.

Choose a preset from the pop-up menu.

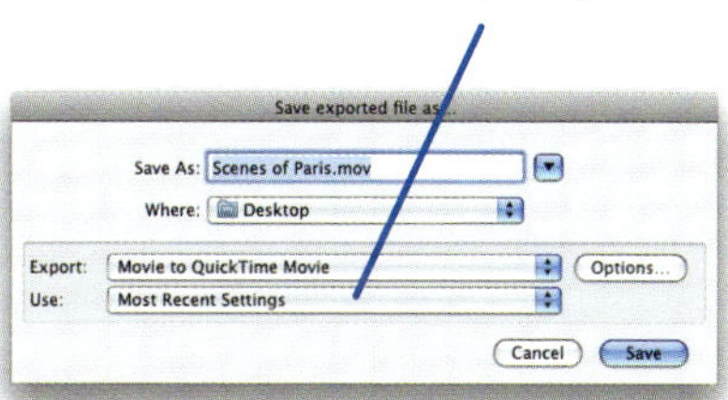

Now what? iMovie's Tiny, Mobile, Medium, and Large sharing presets deliver great results for most uses. The additional presets in the Export dialog box give you even more options. But to really plumb the depths of QuickTime's exporting options, choose Movie to QuickTime movie from the Export pop-up menu, and then click the Options button. This leads to an increasingly technical maze of dialog boxes that let you adjust everything from the video frame size to the sound sampling rate. Unless you know your compression, you're best off leaving the settings to iMovie.

Filter fun. There is one fun and easy thing to explore. Click the Filters button, and you can access some filters, including one that adds an old-movie effect to your footage—dust specks and scratches. (The freely downloadable iMovie HD 6 provides friendlier access to this filter and more; see page 238.)

To learn about compression, see *iMovie '08 & iDVD '08 for Mac OS X Visual Quickstart Guide*, by Jeff Carlson (Peachpit Press, 2008). For more QuickTime resources, see www.macilife.com/imovie.

Exporting as Final Cut XML

If you're accustomed to working in Apple's intermediate and advanced video editing applications, but want to take advantage of iMovie's Event library and fast cutting capabilities, there's an easy bridge between iMovie and Final Cut Pro or Final Cut Express.

But first, a few caveats. This feature transfers only the basic cut information (start and end points); any transitions you've added are converted to cross dissolves; and only the audio levels of video clips are retained. Titles, audio clips, video adjustments, cropping, and Ken Burns effects are ignored. So, use iMovie to whip up a rough assembly and then hand it off to Final Cut for finessing. The file references the iMovie Event's source files, so you're not creating new versions and duplicating content on your hard disk.

To export for Final Cut, choose Share > Export Final Cut XML, and then specify a name and location for the file. Finally, import that file from within Final Cut.

Fun with Freeze Frames

You see it all the time in movies and TV shows: a scene begins with the action frozen, and suddenly the still image springs to life. The frozen image often has a special effect, too—maybe it's been altered to look like a faded photograph. When what appears to be an old photo suddenly turns Technicolor and starts moving, the effect can be magical.

In Hollywood, they use expensive equipment and expensive artists for cinematic tricks like this. You can do it for free using iMovie, and it's a cinch. Simply save a still image from the very beginning of a particular clip, then apply one or more video adjustments to it. Once you've altered the freeze frame, it just takes a few clicks to complete the effect.

This effect can be a fun way to introduce an event that just screams nostalgia—a kid opening presents, a family sitting down to a Thanksgiving feast, or some kids hitting a slope for some sloppy sledding. Start your scene with this effect, superimposing some title text if you like, and you've instantly gone beyond a run-of-the-mill home movie.

Step 1. Trim as Needed

Once you've chosen a video clip for this project, trim its start point so the clip begins at the most appropriate spot. For example, if there are a few seconds of jerky camera movement before Junior starts opening presents, trim the clip to remove the bad footage.

Step 2. Create a Still Frame

Next, point to the very first frame of the trimmed clip, Control-click, and choose Add Still Frame to Project from the shortcut menu.

iMovie adds a still frame to the very end of the project.

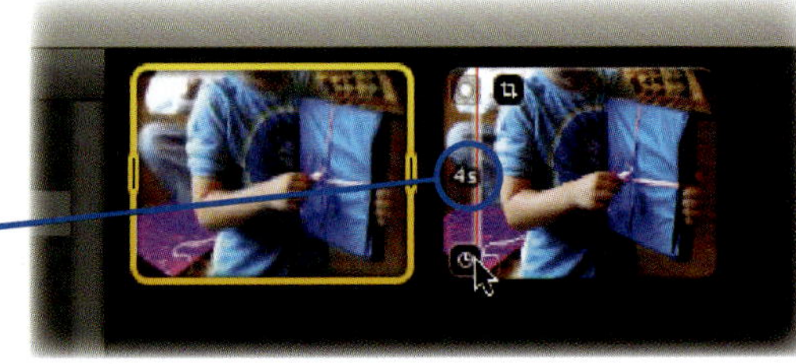

A still frame always has a duration of four seconds. To change its duration, click the clip's Duration button and specify a new value in the Duration dialog box.

Play it back if you like: select it and press the forward-slash key (the shortcut for the Play Selection command).

Step 3.
Position the Still Frame in the Project

Before applying the effect, move the freeze-frame clip by dragging it to the space just before the video clip.

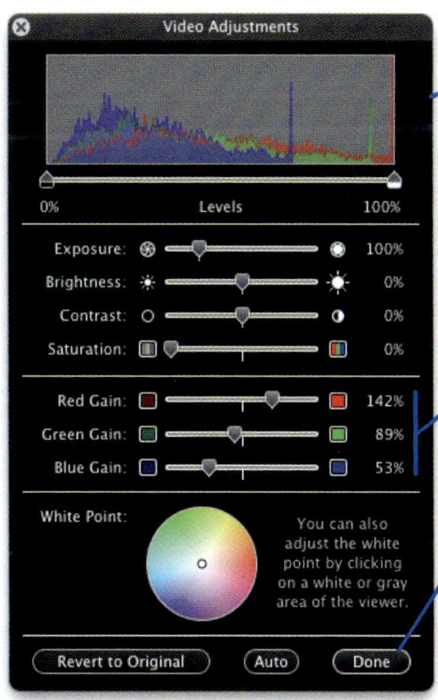

Step 4.
Add the Effect

Now you're ready to alter the appearance of the freeze frame. If you're after a nostalgic look, try giving the clip a sepia tone.

First, make sure iMovie's advanced tools are enabled in the Preferences dialog box—this gives you access to all of iMovie's color-adjustment features.

Next, click the clip's video adjustment button to open the Video Adjustments window.

Adjusting the color setting. In the Video Adjustments window, set the Saturation slider to zero (making the image black and white). Next, adjust the gain sliders like so: Red to 143%, Green to 89%, and Blue to 53%.

To apply the effect, click Done.

Adjusting the transition. For this project, you want the effect to fade away shortly before the end of the clip; this enables the freeze frame to blend cleanly with the live-action clip that will follow it.

To accomplish this, add a Cross Dissolve transition between the two clips. To change the transition's duration, select it and choose Edit > Set Duration (⌘-R), then specify a duration.

Now sit back and admire your work. Click the Play Project from Beginning button (normally or using the Full Screen button).

The thumbnail doesn't display video adjustments, but the effect is visible in the Viewer.

Optional steps. Want to jazz up your effect even more? Apply the Ken Burns effect so that the freeze frame first appears zoomed in a bit, then zooms out to its actual size just before the dissolve.

To add a title to the freeze frame clip, use the Titles browser as described on page 274.

Variations on a frozen theme. You can also turn this trick around: have a scene suddenly freeze and then turn into an old movie frame. This can be a fun way to end a scene.

To do it, save a frame from the last frame of a clip. Then, put the modified freeze frame after the clip from which it came and add the transition between the two.

iMovie Tips

Copying and Pasting Clips

You can make additional copies of a clip by copying it to the Clipboard and pasting it into the Project browser (you can't paste into the Event browser). If you want to experiment with different effects or cropping schemes, select the clip and choose Edit > Copy, then choose Edit > Paste. Another way to duplicate a clip is to press the Option key while dragging the clip.

You can even move clips from one project to another by copying and pasting them. You aren't using additional disk space when you do—you're simply making additional references to the source footage in your Event library.

Copying and Pasting Adjustments

Just as you can copy and paste clips, you can also copy and paste the *adjustments* that you apply to clips. For example, if you've used the Video Adjustments window to brighten a murky clip, you can apply the same settings to other clips shot at the same time. You can copy and paste video adjustments, audio adjustments, and cropping settings, including the Ken Burns effect.

First, select an adjusted clip and choose Edit > Copy. Next, select the clip or clips to which you want to apply the adjustment. Finally, sprint up to the Edit menu and choose the appropriate command from the Paste Adjustments submenu: All (⌘-Shift-V), Video (⌘-Option-I), Audio (⌘-Shift-U), or Crop (⌘-Shift-R).

Pasting replaces any previous adjustments you may have made to the clips.

Customizing the Media Browsers

When you open the Music and Sound Effects browser, iMovie presents the contents of your iTunes library in a list. To customize the columns that appear, Control-click on the list, then use the Show Columns submenu to change which information appears.

And if you're a visual-memory person? Check out the Display as Icons option—it displays each track as an icon with its album art.

Customizing the Photos browser. Want to see larger (or smaller) photo thumbnails? Drag the size slider to the right (or left). To see photos displayed as a list, Control-click in the photo thumbnails area and choose Display as List from the shortcut menu.

And if you don't need to see the list of albums and events all the time, drag the divider between the albums and the photos toward the top of the browser; the source list becomes a pop-up menu. This tip applies to the Music and Sound Effects browser, too.

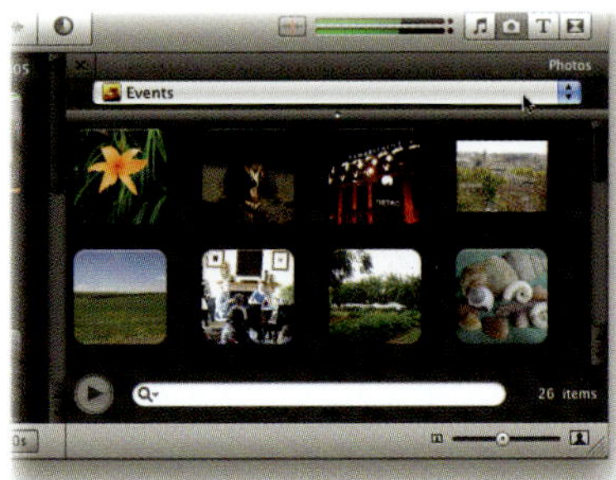

Print Your Movie

No, that isn't a mistake. iMovie can print your video (on paper) as a handy visual reference. Select either a project name or an event (or multiple events) and choose Print Project or Print Event from the File menu. Choose a number from the Preferred Number of Pages pop-up menu and choose whether to include the colored bars for event metadata, such as favorites or keywords (but not, alas, the keywords themselves).

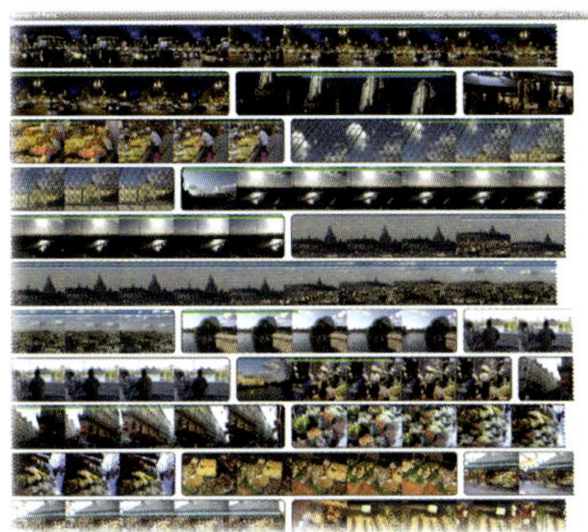

Click Print, and iMovie runs off a copy for you. The Clips Size slider determines how many thumbnails appear on the page.

Movies from Your Digital Camera

You can add movie clips taken by a digital camera to your iMovie projects. If a movie you want is in your iPhoto library, you can locate it by clicking the iPhoto Videos item in the Event Library. If the movie isn't in your library, simply locate its icon on your hard drive and drag it into the Event Library.

But let's step back and look at the greater question: why bother? Compared to the quality you get from a real video camera, the movies from most digital cameras look genuinely awful.

And yet there are some good reasons to consider using a digital camera movie in an iMovie project.

It's all you have. If you don't have a camcorder but want to include some video in a movie project (as opposed to still photos and Ken Burns clips), use your digital camera. Adjust its menu settings to get the largest frame size and highest quality your camera is capable of. iMovie enlarges the video frames to fill the screen, so you'll get better results from larger movies.

For a special effect. Video producers often spend big bucks to get video that looks pixilated and has jerky motion. With digital-camera movies, those "effects" are standard equipment. Have a video camera? Shoot some footage using it and your digital camera's movie mode. Then cut between the two for a cool effect.

For the sound. When I was in Paris, I wanted to capture the sound of the many street musicians who play in Metro stations. I shot digital camera movies and imported them into my iPhoto library. In iMovie, I added still photos of the street musicians to the timeline and applied the Ken Burns effect to the photos. Then, I added the audio portions of the digital camera movies by holding ⌘-Shift while dragging the movie to the Project browser. The result: a montage of still photos with an authentic soundtrack.

Navigation Tips

Play Around Playhead

When you make an edit, you'll often find yourself moving the playhead a few seconds before the edit to replay that section and see how it turned out.

Rather than back up and play by hand, press the bracket keys to play *around* the playhead. Pressing [plays one second before and after the playhead's location; pressing] plays three seconds on each side.

Control-Click

Remember that you can Control-click on just about anything to bring up a shortcut menu that lets you perform relevant tasks. Try Control-clicking on a clip in the Event browser, and on audio and video clips in the Project browser.

More iMovie Tips

Saving Disk Space

Hard disk filling up? Get another one. Or, in the meantime, consider using iMovie's Space Saver command. Space Saver can mark clips as rejected if they aren't added to any project, not marked as a favorite, or both. You won't be able to dig into your archives for unused footage later, but you will free up space.

Choose File > Space Saver, choose which type of footage to reject, and then click Reject and Review.

The Rejected Clips view appears in the Event browser, where you can verify that you do want to get rid of the nixed footage. To delete the clips from the Event library, click the Move Rejected to Trash button. Finally, switch to the Finder and empty the Trash.

Accessing Your Project's Media

In older iMovie versions, a movie project was stored in a *package*, a special kind of Mac OS X folder, and its media assets, reference movies, and shared movies were stored within it.

iMovie '08 works differently. Its files are freely accessible in the Finder—making it easier to find source files, but also increasing the risk of damaging a project by removing or altering files you shouldn't.

Project files are located in a folder called iMovie Projects; it's located in the Movies folder of your Home directory. The file names end in the extension .rcproject. (Those files, incidentally, are packages that contain the editing data as well as the thumbnails iMovie generates.)

Your imported source footage is stored in the iMovie Events folder in your Movies folder, with each event in its own folder. When working in iMovie, you can Control-click a clip and choose Reveal in Finder to locate the media file directly.

If you specified an external hard disk as the location for an event while importing (see page 244), you'll also find an iMovie Events folder at that disk's top-level directory. Even if you use footage from an external hard disk, the project files remain saved in your Home directory.

Normally, you shouldn't have to delve into any of these folders—let iMovie manage their contents for you. But should you have the need or urge to go spelunking, now you have a map.

Exporting Sound

There may be occasions when you want to export part or all of the audio track of your project. Maybe you want to bring it into an audio-editing program, such as SoundStudio or Amadeus, for fine-tuning. Or maybe you recorded a music recital and you'd like to bring the performance into iTunes or GarageBand.

To export your project's soundtrack, choose Export Using QuickTime from the Share menu. In the Save dialog box that appears, choose Sound to AIFF from the Export pop-up menu. Click Options, then choose the desired audio settings.

If you'll be bringing your audio back into iMovie, use the default options. If you'll be importing the audio into iTunes or GarageBand, choose 44.1 kHz from the Rate pop-up menu.

Burning Movies to CD and Video CD

The best way to share a finished movie on a shiny platter is to burn it to a DVD. But you can also burn a movie to a CD that will play on any Mac or Windows computer that has QuickTime. You might take this route if you want to send a movie to a friend who has a computer, but no DVD player. (While you're at it, make a note to buy a cheap DVD player for your friend.)

To start, choose Share > Export Movie, choose the Mobile option, and click Export. Next, insert a blank CD into your Mac's optical drive and copy the movie to the CD.

If you have Roxio's Toast software, you can also create a Video CD. This video format is very popular in Asia, and somewhat obscure everywhere else. But most stand-alone DVD players can play Video

Get more iMovie tips.
www.macilife.com/imovie

CDs, as can all current personal computers. (To play Video CDs on a Mac, use Mireth Technology's MacVCD X software, available at www.mireth.com. And if you don't have Toast Titanium, you can also make Video CDs using Mireth Technology's iVCD.)

Video on a Video CD is compressed in MPEG-1 format. The image quality is a far cry from that of the MPEG-2 format used on DVDs; Video CD image quality is more akin to that of VHS videotape. One reason is because the video frame size is smaller—352 by 240 pixels, instead of DVD's 720 by 480. Another reason is that the video itself is compressed more heavily—about 90:1, compared to roughly 30:1 for MPEG-2. But on the plus side, a Video CD can shoehorn about an hour of video onto a CD-R disc.

A variation of the Video CD format is called *Super Video CD*, or *SuperVCD.* On a SuperVCD, video is stored in MPEG-2 format, yielding better quality than a Video CD. The SuperVCD format also allows for many DVD-like features, such as alternate language tracks. Its video quality still falls short of a DVD's, however.

Video CD and SuperVCD are second-best alternatives to DVDs, but any alternative is better than none. For background on the Video CD and SuperVCD formats, see www.vcdhelp.com.

Combining iMovie '08 and iMovie HD

As I mentioned at the start of this chapter, iMovie is a program in transition, and iMovie '08 represents only the first frames of that grand cross-dissolve. The older iMovie HD can do things that iMovie '08 can't, and that's why Apple has made it a free download for iLife '08 owners.

You can combine both programs to exploit each one's strengths. Edit a project in iMovie '08, then export it to iMovie HD to add DVD chapter markers or apply a visual effect to part of the movie.

Or go the other way: use iMovie HD to create a special effect, a theme motion graphic, or a clip with tricky editing requirements that benefited from bookmarks. Then export that footage and add it to an iMovie '08 project.

Here's how to get the two programs on speaking terms. Be sure your aspect ratios match—for example, if you're exporting a 16:9 project from iMovie '08, be sure to import it into a 16:9 project in iMovie HD. And don't forget to get your free iMovie HD chapter at www.macilife.com/imovie.

iMovie '08 to iMovie HD. Choose Share > Export Using QuickTime. In the Export dialog box, choose Movie to DV Stream from the Export pop-up menu. Save the file somewhere convenient, such as on your desktop, then drag it into iMovie HD's Clips pane. You can delete the exported movie from your desktop, since iMovie HD makes a copy in your project file.

Notes: Be sure you export the movie's audio using a 48 kHz sample rate (to verify, click Options in the Export dialog box). Make sure your video resolutions match, too: if you're exporting 1080i HD footage, for example, be sure to import it into a 1080i project in iMovie HD. And finally, you may notice a slight loss of video quality, though in my tests, the difference was negligible.

iMovie HD to iMovie '08. Choose Share from the Share menu, then choose the Full Quality setting. Save the movie on your desktop for easy access. In iMovie '08, choose File > Import Movies, locate the exported movie, and add it to your Event library. When that's done, delete the copy on your desktop.

Tips for Making Better Movies

Editing takes more than software. You also need the right raw material. Advance planning will help ensure that you have the shots you need, and following some basic videography techniques will make for better results.

Plan Ahead

Planning a movie involves developing an outline—in Hollywood parlance, a *storyboard*—that lists the shots you'll need to tell your tale. Professional movie makers storyboard every scene and camera angle. You don't have to go that far, but you will tell a better story if you plan at least some shots.

Consider starting with an *establishing shot* that clues viewers in on where your story takes place—for example, the backyard swimming pool. To show the big picture, zoom out to your camcorder's wide-angle setting.

From there, you might cut to a *medium shot* that introduces your movie's subject: little Bobby preparing to belly flop off the diving board. Next, you might cut away to Mary tossing a beach ball. Cut back to Bobby struggling to stay afloat, and then finish with a long shot of the entire scene.

Keep in mind that you don't have to shoot scenes in chronological order—sequencing your shots is what iMovie is for. For example, get the shot of Mary's throw any time you like and edit it into the proper sequence using iMovie.

Steady Your Camera

Nausea-inducing camera work is a common flaw of amateur videos. Too many people mistake a video camera for a fire hose: they sweep across a scene, panning left and right and then back again. Or they ceaselessly zoom in and out, making viewers wonder whether they're coming or going.

A better practice is to stop recording, move to a different location or change your zoom setting, and then resume. Varying camera angles and zoom settings makes for a more interesting video. If you must pan—perhaps to capture a dramatic vista—do so slowly and steadily.

And, unless you're making an earthquake epic, hold the camera as steady as you can. If your camera has an image-stabilizing feature, use it. Better still, use a tripod or a monopod, or brace the camera against a rigid surface. Keeping the camera steady is especially critical for movies destined for the Internet—because of the way these videos are compressed, minimizing extraneous motion will yield sharper results.

Compose Carefully

The photographic composition tips on page 234 apply to movie making, too. Compose your shots carefully, paying close attention to the background. Get up close now and then—don't just shoot wide shots.

Record Some Ambient Sound

Try to shoot a couple of minutes of uninterrupted background sound: the waves on a beach, the birds in the forest, the revelers at a party. As I've mentioned previously, you can extract the sound from this footage and use it as an audio bed behind a series of shots. It doesn't matter what the camera is pointing at while you're shooting—you won't use the video anyway.

After importing the footage, extract its audio, as described on page 270.

Shooting with Compression in Mind

If you know that you'll be distributing your movie via the Internet—either through a Web site or email—there are some steps you can take during the shooting phase to optimize quality. These steps also yield better results when you're compressing a movie for playback on a mobile device, and they even help deliver better quality with iDVD.

First, minimize motion. The more motion you have in your movie, the worse it will look after being heavily compressed. That means using a tripod instead of handholding your camera, and minimizing panning and zooming. Also consider your background: a static, unchanging background is better than a busy traffic scene or rustling tree leaves.

Learn more about digitizing old tapes and movies.
www.macilife.com/imovie

Second, light well. If you're shooting indoors, consider investing in a set of video lights. A brighter picture compresses better than a poorly lit scene. To learn about lighting, read Ross Lowell's excellent book, *Matters of Light and Depth* (Lower Light Management, 1900).

Vary Shot Lengths

Your movie will be more visually engaging if you vary the length of your shots. Use longer shots for complex scenes, such as a wide shot of a city street, and shorter shots for close-ups or reaction shots.

Be Prepared, Be Careful

Be sure your camcorder's batteries are charged; consider buying a second battery so you'll have a backup, and take along your charger and power adapter, too. Bring plenty of blank tape or media cards, and label them immediately after ejecting them. To protect a tape against accidental reuse, slide the little locking tab on its spine.

Don't Skimp on Tape

Don't just get one version of a shot, get several. If you just shot a left-to-right pan across a scene, for example, shoot a right-to-left pan next. The more raw material you have to work with, the better.

Converting Analog Video and Movies

Somewhere in your closet is a full-sized VHS camcorder—the kind that rested on your shoulder like a rocket launcher. You want to get that old VHS video into your Mac.

If you have a DV camera, chances are it has a *pass-through* mode that enables you to use it as an analog-to-digital converter. Connect the video and audio output jacks on the VHS deck to your DV camera's video and audio input jacks. If your VHS deck and camcorder each provide S-video jacks, use them to get the best picture.

Next, put your camera in VCR or VTR mode, and read its manual to see if you have to perform any special steps to use its pass-through mode. With some cameras, you must make a menu adjustment. With others, you simply need to remove the tape.

After you've made the appropriate connections and adjustments, you can play your VHS tape and click iMovie's Import button to record the converted footage coming from your camera.

Analog-DV Converter

A faster way to get analog video into your Mac is through a converter, such as those sold by Formac Electronics, DataVideo, Sony, and others. These devices eliminate the time-consuming process of dubbing VHS tapes to DV format. Connect a converter to your Mac's FireWire jack, then connect your old VHS rocket launcher to the converter's video and audio inputs. Then, launch iMovie and use its import features to bring in VHS video.

When importing VHS video, you may notice a thin band of flickering pixels at the bottom of the image. Don't worry: these artifacts won't appear when you view your finished video on a TV screen.

Converting Films

As for those old Super 8 film-based flicks, you'll need to send them to a lab that does film-to-video transfers. Many camera stores can handle this for you. The lab will clean your films, fix bad splices, and return them along with videotapes whose contents you can bring into the Mac. If you have a DV camcorder, be sure to use a lab that will supply your converted movies on DV cassettes—you'll get much better image quality than VHS provides. Some labs also offer optional background music and titles, but you can add these yourself once you've brought the converted video into the Mac.

I wrote a feature article on digitizing old tapes and movies for *Macworld* magazine's June 2004 issue. The article is available online; I've linked to it at www.macilife.com/imovie.

The Macintosh

iLife'08

iDVD at a Glance

iDVD lets you burn movies and photos to DVDs, complete with menus you can fully customize.

Designers and photographers can use iDVD to assemble digital portfolios that they can hand out like brochures. Filmmakers and advertising professionals can distribute rough cuts of movie scenes and commercials to clients and colleagues. Businesspeople can create in-house training discs and video archives of corporate meetings. Videographers can offer DVDs of weddings and other events. And home-movie buffs can preserve and share family videos and photographs.

Creating a DVD involves choosing and customizing a menu design and adding the movies and photos you want to include on the DVD. You can perform these steps in any order and preview your work along the way. When you've finished, you can commit the final product to a shiny platter.

Starting a New iDVD Project

Creating a DVD with iDVD involves creating a new project document, choosing and customizing a menu design theme, and adding content. Here's how to get started.

Step 1. Choose File > New or click the Create a New Project button.

Step 2. Name your iDVD project, choose an aspect ratio, then click Create.

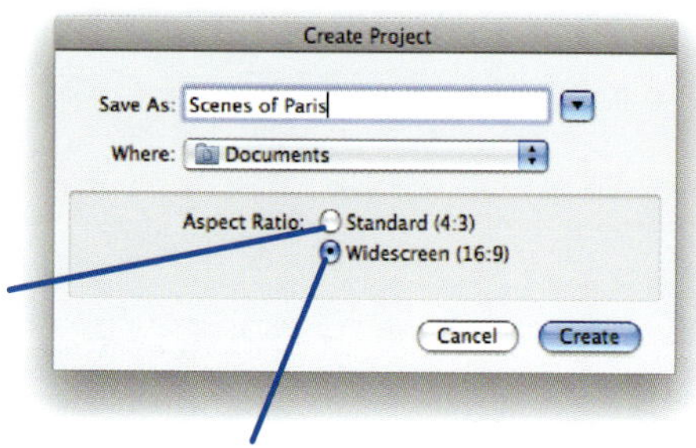

Standard is the best choice if your DVD will contain 4:3 video (page 240) or will be shown mostly on 4:3 televisions.

Go wide if the DVD contains 16:9 video and you'll be viewing the DVD on widescreen TVs. Widescreen is also great for photos.

Note: You can change the aspect ratio later if you like.

Step 3. Now what?

Choose a theme and fine-tune it if you like (pages 292–295). Add movies to your DVD (page 296). Create slide shows containing your photos (pages 298–301). Explore the authoring and menu-customizing features described later in this chapter. Preview your work as you go (page 293), then burn the final product (page 316).

A Short Glossary of DVD Terms

authoring The process of creating menus and adding movies and images to a DVD.

button A clickable area that plays a movie or slide show, or takes the user to another menu.

chapter A video bookmark that you can access from a menu or with a remote control. Creating chapters in a movie lets viewers jump to specific sections.

DVD-R The blank media that you'll use most often when burning DVDs. A DVD-R blank can be burned just once.

DVD-RW A type of DVD media that you can erase and reuse.

menu A screen containing clickable buttons that enable users to access a DVD's contents.

motion menu A menu whose background image is an animation or movie, a menu that plays background audio, or both.

MPEG-2 The compression format used for video on a DVD. MPEG stands for *Moving Picture Experts Group.*

Many themes have *drop zones*, special areas into which you can drag photos or a movie (pages 293–295).

To add a movie to your DVD, drag it into iDVD's window (page 296). iDVD creates a button, whose appearance you can customize (page 307).

To create a custom menu background, drag an image from iPhoto or another program to the iDVD window (page 301).

Each menu on your DVD has a title, whose position and formatting you can customize (page 307).

Many themes have several menu designs, ideal for a DVD containing multiple menus (page 304).

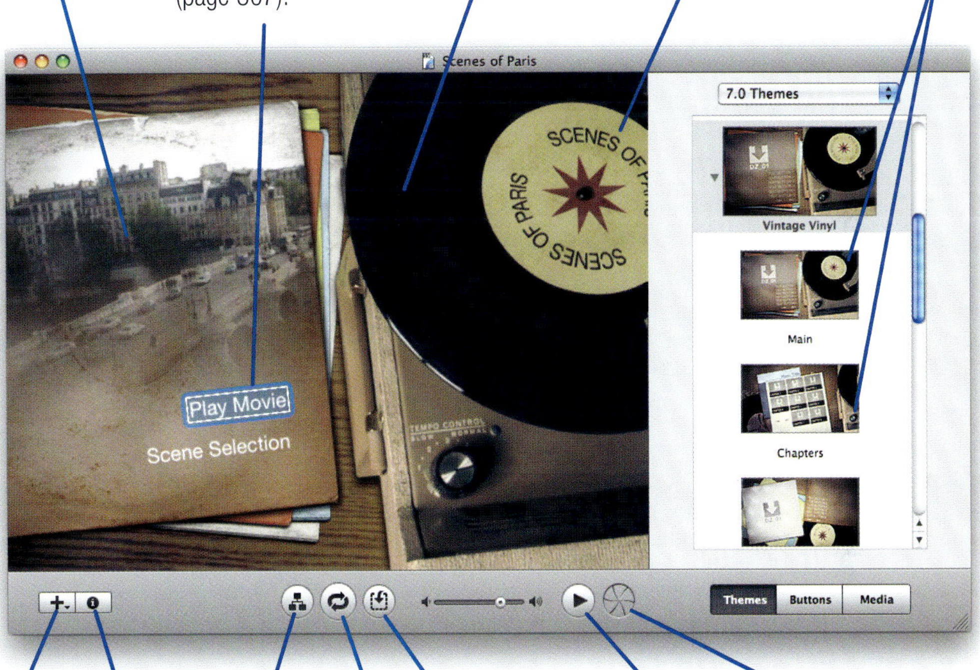

Add a new menu (page 305), movie (page 296), or slide show (page 298).

View your DVD's menu structure and modify its content in Map view (page 310).

Change the contents of drop zones (page 295).

Preview your DVD before burning it (page 293).

To burn your finished DVD, click Burn (page 314).

Preview menus containing motion or background audio.

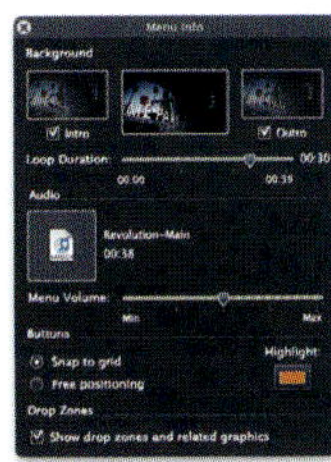

Display the Menu Info window (left), a floating window for setting options.

Choosing and Customizing Themes

A big part of creating a DVD involves choosing which menu theme you want. iDVD includes menu themes for many types of occasions and subjects: weddings, parties, vacations, kids, and more. Many of these themes have motion menus containing beautiful animations and background music.

In iDVD, all themes are designed for widescreen presentation. Although iDVD can't yet burn high-definition discs, you can take advantage of the more cinematic 16:9 aspect ratio if you shot widescreen video. You can also create your project in the older 4:3 aspect ratio, if that better suits your movie formats and TV set.

Your design options don't end once you've chosen a theme. Many of iDVD's themes provide *drop zones*, special areas of the menu background into which you can drag photos or movies. Drop zones make it easy to customize a theme with your own imagery.

Most drop zones have special effects that iDVD applies to the photos or movies that you add to them. For example, the Reflection White theme puts your imagery in a set of 3D panels that glide like a moving art gallery. The Road Trip theme puts your imagery in a scrapbook—and if you look closely, you'll see that the pages cast shadows on each other.

Most themes provide "dynamic" drop zones that move around the screen. And as the following pages describe, you have more options for managing the contents of drop zones.

Choosing a Theme

Step 1.

If the list of themes isn't visible, click the Themes button.

Step 2.

Choose the theme you want by clicking it.

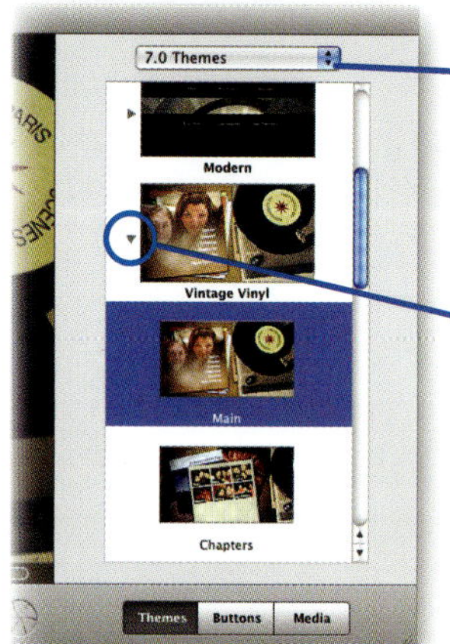

Use the pop-up menu to access themes from older versions of iDVD.

Click the disclosure triangle next to a theme family to reveal specific menu themes.

Tip: When you select a new theme, iDVD may ask if you want to switch between a widescreen or standard-definition aspect ratio. If you get tired of this nagging, click Do Not Ask Me Again before clicking Keep or Change.

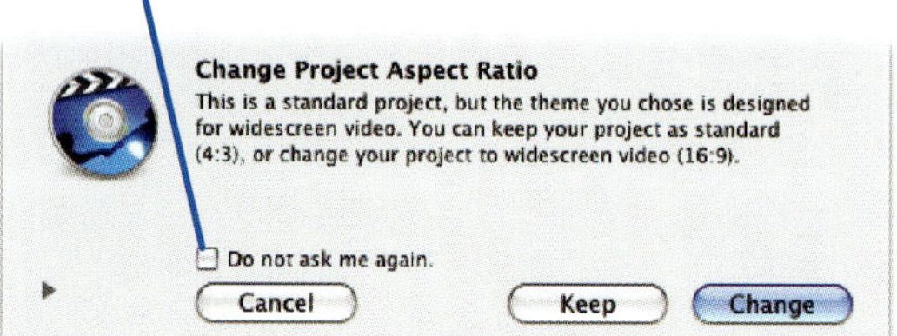

Note: In order to see a theme's motion, you must have motion turned on. To turn motion on or off, click the Motion button. As you work on your DVD, you'll probably want to turn motion off since iDVD performs better this way.

Adding Items to a Drop Zone

iDVD provides several ways to add items to drop zones. Here's the technique you're likely to use most often. For details on more drop zone techniques, see the following pages.

Step 1.

Click the Media button. Then, to access photos in your iPhoto library, click the Photos button. To access movies, click Movies.

Step 2.

In the photo or movie media browser, select the item or items you want to add. You can select multiple photos or an entire album. If you add multiple photos to a drop zone, iDVD displays them successively as the menu is displayed. You can add up to 99 items to a drop zone.

Step 3.

Drag the selected items into the drop zone.

As you drag into a drop zone, a dotted line indicates the drop zone's boundaries.

Step 4.

To fine-tune an item's position within the drop zone, hold the ⌘ key and drag it using the hand pointer.

Previewing and Testing Your Work

As you work on a DVD, you'll be anxious to see how the final product will look. To find out, use iDVD's preview mode. Click the Preview button, and iDVD turns itself into a DVD player and starts playing your DVD.

In preview mode, an on-screen remote control lets you navigate—choose menu buttons, jump to chapters, and watch the movies and slide shows you've added to your DVD.

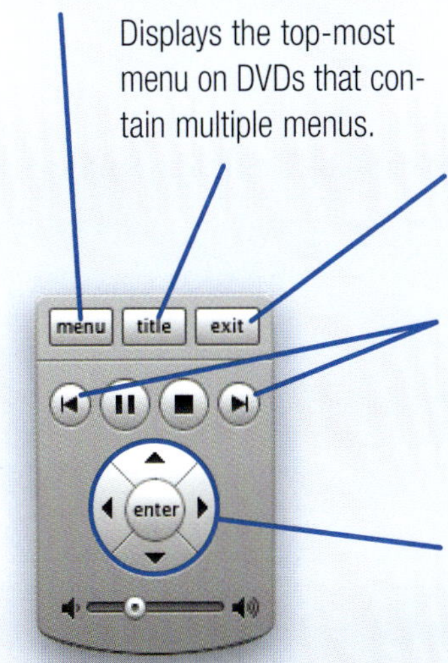

Displays a movie's menu.

Displays the top-most menu on DVDs that contain multiple menus.

Exits preview mode.

Jumps to the previous or next chapter in a movie, or to the previous or next photo in a slide show.

Click the arrows to navigate. Click Enter to choose the highlighted menu button.

Preview mode plays back whatever is displayed in iDVD's window. If your main menu is visible, that's what plays back. If you're working on a slide show, the slide show begins playing.

Using iDVD's preview mode is a great way to check your work, but you shouldn't rely on it as your only testing tool. As you near the end of your project, create a disc *image* and use Mac OS X's DVD Player program to test it (see page 316). Then burn a disc and test it in your DVD player.

Working with Drop Zones

Here are some tips for working with drop zones.

Drop Zones Versus Menu Buttons

It's important to understand the difference between drop zones and buttons. A drop zone is merely an area of imagery within a DVD menu—it isn't a clickable button that your viewers can use to watch your DVD. A drop zone is a piece of eye candy; a button is a navigation control that plays a movie or slide show, or jumps to another menu.

How to tell the difference. As you drag items into the menu area, how can you tell whether you're dragging into a drop zone or creating a button? Easy: When you're dragging into a drop zone, a dotted-line pattern appears around the edges of the drop zone, as shown on the previous page.

If you don't see this pattern, you aren't in the drop zone, and you'll end up creating a button or changing your DVD's background image. If that happens, head for the Edit menu and choose the Undo command.

Navigating Dynamic Drop Zones

In most themes, drop zones are *dynamic*—they move around on the screen or they appear and disappear as a motion menu plays.

How do you add items to a drop zone that's behind another drop zone or not even visible?

Use the motion playhead. At the bottom of iDVD's menu area is a horizontal motion playhead that lets you scrub through a menu: drag the playhead left and right, and iDVD plays the motion menu, displaying its drop zones. Simply drag the playhead until the drop zone you want is visible.

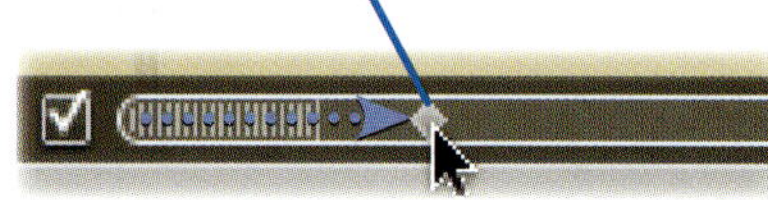

(If you don't see the motion playhead, choose Show Motion Playhead from the View menu.)

Use the drop zone editor. Double-click on any drop zone, and iDVD displays the drop zone editor. You can add photos and movies to drop zones by dragging them into the editor.

You can also display the drop zone editor by choosing Edit Drop Zones from the Project menu.

Autofill. Want quick results? Let iDVD do the work. Choose Project > Autofill Drop Zones, and iDVD fills all drop zones with images from the media in your DVD. You can fine-tune the results if you like.

Older themes. Both the motion playhead and drop zone editor also work with iDVD's older themes.

Introductory Animations

Many iDVD themes provide introductory animations. For example, in the Vintage Vinyl theme, the stack of album sleeves slides into position before the menu buttons become visible.

These animations are cute, but you might not always want to use them. They're fine on a DVD's main menu, but on a submenu (such as a scene selection menu for a movie), they slow down your DVD's users, who must wait for the animation to finish before they can access the menu's buttons.

Solution: Turn off the introductory animations when you don't want them. Just click the little check box at the left edge of the motion playhead. Or, display the Menu Info window and uncheck the Intro or Outro boxes.

Other Ways to Add Items

You can also add items to a drop zone by dragging them from the Finder: simply drag the items' icons into the drop zone or drop zone editor. And you can drag photos from iPhoto and other programs directly into a drop zone.

Another way to add items is from the shortcut menu: Control-click within a drop zone, and choose the Import command; or, choose Fill with Content to grab media used elsewhere in the project.

Removing and Rearranging Items

To remove the contents of a drop zone, drag the item out of the drop zone. When you release the mouse button, the item disappears in a puff of smoke. As an alternative to dragging, you can also Control-click within the drop zone and choose Clear Drop Zone Contents from the shortcut menu.

What if you have a drop zone containing multiple items and you want to remove a few of the items—or even just one? Here's how. Double-click the drop zone to display the drop zone editor, then double-click the entry for the drop zone that you want to edit. iDVD displays the drop zone photos editor, where you can delete individual items.

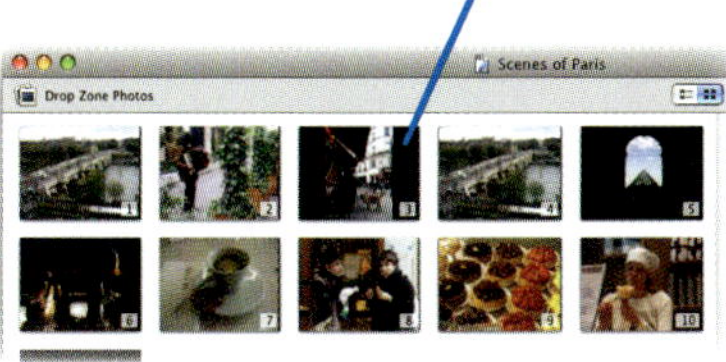

You can also use the drop zone photos editor to rearrange the order in which items in a drop zone are displayed: just drag the items around. And you can add items to a drop zone by dragging them into its editor.

Adding Movie Clips from iMovie

In the Media pane, click the Movies tab and select an iMovie project that's been shared to the media browser. Drag the shared movie into a drop zone.

What if you want to use just part of a video clip in a drop zone? You can't use iMovie's cropping or trimming features to indicate which portion you want to keep. That's because these features don't actually delete any video; they simply tell iMovie which parts you want to use. If you drag a cropped clip into an iDVD drop zone, the entire clip plays in the drop zone.

To control how much of the movie plays in the drop zone, click on the drop zone that contains the movie. iDVD displays a set of crop markers above the movie; drag the markers left and right to specify which portion of the movie should play.

Browsing a Drop Zone

If you have a drop zone that contains multiple items, you can quickly scan through the drop zone's contents without having to open up the drop zone editor. Click on a drop zone, and a small slider pops up; to scan through the drop zone's items, drag the slider back and forth. If, while browsing, you decide to rearrange the drop zone's contents, click the Edit Order button below the slider.

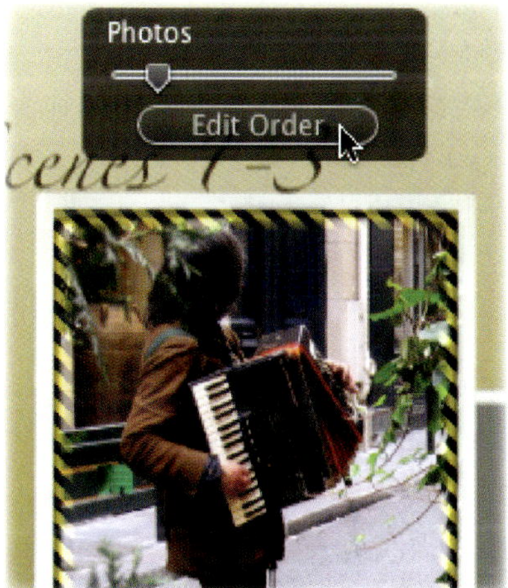

Preview Glitches?

When you've added movies or high-resolution photos to a menu's drop zones, you may see and hear some problems when you preview the menu: the drop zones' motion may appear jerky, and the menu's background audio may break up as it plays.

Not to worry—these problems won't occur on your final DVD. Indeed, the problems often go away once the menu has had a chance to play through once.

Adding Movies to Your DVD

iDVD's job is to integrate and present assets from other programs. The assets you're most likely to add to your DVDs are movies you've created in iMovie or another video-editing program, such as Apple's Final Cut Express or Final Cut Pro.

You can add movies to your DVDs using a couple of techniques. iDVD can accept movies in just about any QuickTime-compatible format (for some examples of movies you can't use, see page 318). You can also use 16:9 movies in either HDV or DV Widescreen format. If you use high-definition movies, however, note that iDVD will convert them to standard-definition for display—not because it wants to, but because it has to. Today, the high-definition DVD landscape is still in flux, with a couple of standards vying for acceptance.

In the meantime, your high-definition movies will still play in all their widescreen glory if you play your DVD on a widescreen TV set. On a conventional TV, they'll play in letterboxed format.

Video on a DVD is compressed, or encoded, into a format called MPEG-2. As the sidebar on the opposite page describes, iDVD performs this encoding either as you work or after you click the Burn button.

Adding a Movie Using the Movie Browser

Step 1.

Click the Media button, then click the Movies button.

iDVD lists movies contained in iMovie as well as your Movies folder, iPhoto, and iTunes. To have iDVD list movies located elsewhere on your hard drive, choose Preferences from the iDVD menu, click the Movies button, and add additional folders to the list.

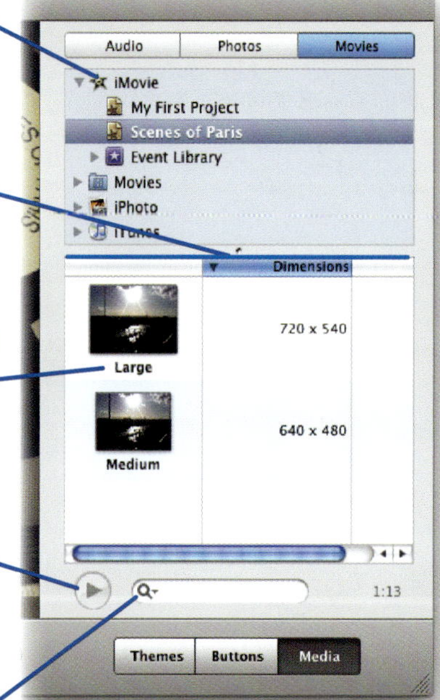

Available movies appear here.

For best quality, use the Large version of iMovie projects that you've shared to the media browser (see page 279)

To preview a movie in the movie browser, select the movie and click this play button, or simply double-click the movie.

Use the Search box to locate a movie in the browser.

Step 2.

Drag the desired movie into your DVD's menu area.

iDVD adds the movie to your DVD and creates a menu button for it.

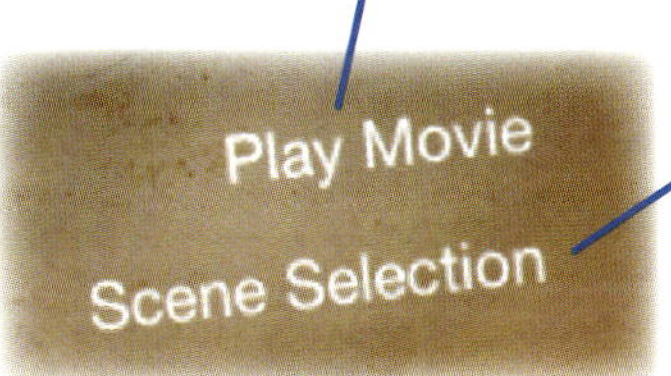

If the movie contains DVD chapter markers, iDVD creates two buttons: one named Play Movie and another named Scene Selection. If the movie lacks DVD chapters, iDVD simply creates one button, giving it the same name as the movie itself. To rename any button, select it and edit the name.

Tip: If you don't want iDVD to create a chapter submenu—or if you'd like iDVD to ask if you want one—use the options in the Movies portion of the Preferences dialog box.

Other Ways to Add a Movie

You can also add a movie by dragging its icon from the Finder into the iDVD window, or by choosing File > Import > Video. These techniques are convenient if you store your movies on an external hard drive and you don't feel like adding the drive to the movie browser using the Preferences command.

You can also use the media browser to add video clips from your iTunes or iPhoto libraries (although you can't burn your video purchases from the iTunes store). For more details on using digital camera movies in iDVD projects, see page 318.

Tips for DVD Movies

Encoder Settings

You can have up to two hours of video on a disc—four hours, if you have a dual-layer DVD burner (see page 316). By adjusting iDVD's encoder settings, you can control how much video will fit as well as the quality of the video itself. Choose iDVD > Preferences, click Projects, and cast your eyes on the Encoding pop-up menu. (You can also change encoding settings for an individual project as described on page 319.)

The Very Best

If you have more than one hour of video—or you want the best quality iDVD is capable of—choose Professional Quality. In this mode, iDVD puts on its thinking cap and analyzes your video twice, with the goal of compressing it as little as possible.

You get great quality and two (or four) hours on a disc, but be patient. Encoding upwards of two hours of video may take several hours, even on speedy modern Macs.

The Next Best

For high quality in less time, choose High Quality. iDVD analyzes your video like the Professional Quality setting does, but it performs just one pass instead of two.

The Very Fastest

If you have under an hour of video, consider the Best Performance option. The video still looks great and encoding is much faster. When you choose Best Performance, iDVD encodes while you work.

For more encoding insights, see page 317.

Using Movies from Final Cut

iDVD can also encode Final Cut Pro or Final Cut Express movies. Export the movie by choosing QuickTime Movie from the File menu's Export submenu. (In older Final Cut versions, this command is Final Cut Movie or Final Cut Pro Movie.) If the movie has chapter markers, be sure to choose the Chapter Markers option in the Markers pop-up menu of the Save dialog box.

Creating DVD Slide Shows

iDVD slide shows are a great way to share photos. Even low-resolution photos look spectacular on a television screen, and they can't easily be copied and redistributed—a plus for photographers creating portfolio discs. (You can, however, opt to include the originals on the disc, as described in "The DVD-ROM Zone" on page 312.)

iDVD provides a few ways to create a slide show. You can use iDVD's photo browser to drag a few photos or an entire album or event into the iDVD window. You can also use the Send to iDVD command in iPhoto to send an album, an event, a selection of photos, or a saved slide show to iDVD. And you can manually drag photos from iPhoto (or anywhere else) into iDVD's slide show editor.

As the following pages describe, you can give your slide shows background music from your iTunes library and fine-tune other aspects of their appearance. You can also choose to have transitions between images; iDVD gives you twelve transition styles from which to choose (see page 300).

Each image in a slide show can be any size and orientation; however, vertically oriented images will have a black band on their left and right edges.

Slide shows aren't even limited to still images. Sprinkle movies into them, too. Make a slide show containing just movies if you like. Try *that* with your slide projector.

Creating a Slide Show Using the Media Browser

Step 1.

In iPhoto, create an album that contains the photos you want in the slide show, sequenced in the order you want them to appear (see page 146). You can also create a slide show from an entire event's worth of photos.

Step 2.

In iDVD, click the Media button, then click the Photos button.

Your iPhoto library and its events and albums appear here. To display more photos or albums, drag the horizontal separator below the album list up or down.

The photos in your library or a selected album appear here.

To search for a photo based on its title, type part or all of its title here.

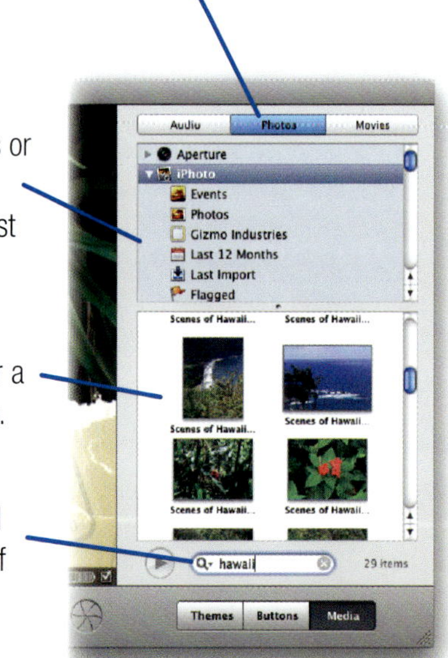

Step 3.

Locate the desired album or event and drag it into the iDVD menu area.

Tip: Be sure you don't drag the album or event into a drop zone; see "Working with Drop Zones" on page 294.

iDVD creates the slide show and a menu button for displaying it. iDVD gives the button the same name as the album or event, but you can rename the button to anything you like.

Creating a Slide Show Within iPhoto

You can send photos to iDVD from within iPhoto, and with a couple of different options.

Saved slide show. If you've created a saved (cinematic) slide show, you can add it to iDVD and retain its custom Ken Burns moves and other goodies. In iPhoto, select the saved slide show in your Slideshows list. Then, choose Send to iDVD from the Share menu. iPhoto creates a video version of the slide show and ships it off to iDVD.

If you need to revise the slide show, first delete it from your iDVD project. (Select its button and press Delete.) Then, return to iPhoto, make your changes, and choose Send to iDVD again.

If you create a 16:9 (widescreen) slide show in iPhoto, iDVD displays it in wide-screen format.

Basic slide show. Here's the technique to use if you don't need Ken Burns moves and you'd prefer the advantages of a DVD slide show (for example, more efficient use of disc space and the ability to easily include original images on your disc). In iPhoto, select an album or a series of photos. Then, choose Send to iDVD from the Share menu.

You can revise this type of slide show directly within iDVD using the techniques on the following pages.

Creating a Slide Show from Scratch

You can also create a blank slide show and then manually add photos to it. You might use this technique to add photos that aren't stored in your iPhoto library.

Step 1.

Choose Add Slideshow from the pop-up menu or choose Project > Add Slideshow (⌘-L).

iDVD adds a button named My Slideshow to the currently displayed menu. Rename this button as desired.

Step 2.

Double-click on the button that iDVD just created. The slide show editor appears.

Step 3.

Drag photos (or a folder containing photos) into the slide show editor. Or, display the photo browser and drag photos from your iPhoto library.

Tip: You can add a movie to a slide show, too—just drag it into the editor from the movies browser or elsewhere.

Refining a Slide Show

When you create a DVD slide show, you can fine-tune it using the slide show editor. To display the editor, double-click the slide show's menu button or icon in Map view.

When checked, this box superimposes arrows over the images as a hint to viewers that they can move back and forth in the slide show using their DVD remote controls.

Check this box, and the slide show will repeat until the cows come home—or at least until your DVD's viewer presses the Menu or Title button on his or her remote control.

Switch between list view and thumbnail view.

To display these options, click the Settings button.

To have iDVD store the original images on the DVD, check this box. (For details, see page 312.)

To edit a photo's title or comment, click its text. If Show Titles and Comments is checked, the text appears during the slide show.

If you've added movies to the slide show, check this box to quiet the background music while a movie plays.

To change playback order, drag images. You can select multiple images by Shift-clicking and ⌘-clicking.

You can specify a duration for the images, or have the slide show timed to match its soundtrack. If the slide show has a soundtrack, the Manual option isn't available.

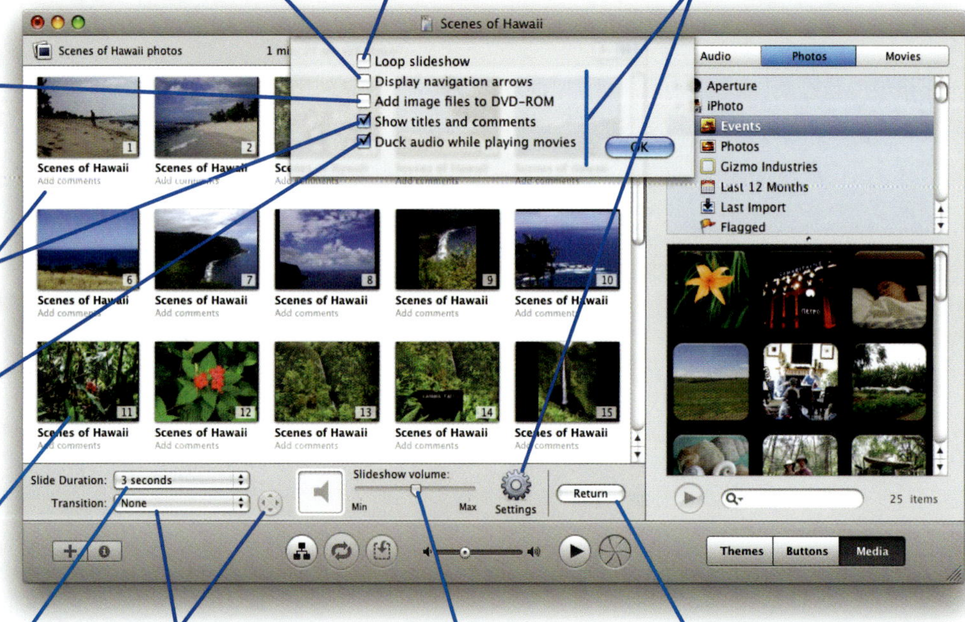

You can have transitions between photos. For some transition styles, you can also specify a direction, such as a left-to-right wipe.

- None
- Cube
- ✓ Dissolve
- Droplet
- Fade Through Black
- Flip
- Mosaic Flip Large
- Mosaic Flip Small
- Page Flip
- Push
- Reveal
- Twirl
- Wipe

Adjust the volume of the slide show's soundtrack.

Return to the menu that leads to this slide show.

Tip: To delete a photo from the slide show, select it and press the Delete key. This doesn't delete the photo from your hard drive, it just removes it from the slide show.

Adding Music to Slide Shows

You can add a music track to a slide show. One way to add music is by using the iTunes browser in iDVD. Click the Media button, then click the Audio button. Locate the song you want (use the search box if need be), then drag it to the Audio well. To add an entire playlist, drag it to the Audio well.

You can also drag a song directly from the iTunes window or, for that matter, from any folder on your hard drive. And you don't even have to drag an *audio* file: if you drag a QuickTime movie to the Audio well, iDVD will assign its audio to your slide show.

If you create a slide show by dragging an iPhoto album into the iDVD window (or by choosing Send to iDVD while an album is selected in iPhoto), the slide show will retain whatever song was assigned to it in iPhoto. (For details on assigning songs to albums, see page 182.)

Music and timing. How iDVD matches your soundtrack to your slides depends on the option you choose from the Slide Duration pop-up menu. If you choose a specific duration, such as five seconds per slide, iDVD repeats your soundtrack if its duration is shorter than the slide show's total length. If the soundtrack is longer than the slide show, iDVD simply stops playing the soundtrack after the last slide displays. (To have the music fade at the end of the slideshow, use the Slideshow portion of the Preferences dialog box.) And if you choose the Fit to Audio option, iDVD times the interval between image changes to match the soundtrack's duration.

To remove a slide show's background music, drag the icon out of the Audio well. When you release the mouse button, the icon vanishes in a puff of smoke.

Slide Show Tips

TV-Safe Slide Shows

Normally, when you view a slide show on a TV screen, you don't see the outer edges of each photo. This is because TV screens typically crop off the outer edges of an image. If you want to see your images in their full, uncropped glory, choose iDVD's Preferences command, click the Slideshow button, and check the box labeled Always Scale Slides to TV Safe Area. When this option is active, iDVD sizes images so they don't completely fill the frame—thus eliminating cropping.

Beyond 99 Slides

The DVD specification limits the number of images in a slide show to 99. Fortunately, iDVD lets you work around this limitation. You can drag more than 99 photos into the slide show editor, and, thanks to some clever technical trickery, iDVD is able to present them as one slide show.

What iDVD can't do is make your viewers patient enough to sit through all those shots.

Making a Magic iDVD

When you want to create a DVD in a hurry, use the Magic iDVD feature.

Magic iDVD presents you with a single window containing a list of menu themes, a set of drop boxes for holding movies and photos, and a media browser for accessing your audio, photos, and movies.

Choose a theme, then drag movies into the drop boxes. To create DVD slide shows, drag photos to the drop boxes. Drag an entire event or album from iPhoto or build a slide show one photo at a time by dragging individual photos into the same box. Want a music soundtrack for a slide show? Drag an audio track into the slide show's drop box.

When you're done, preview your work by clicking the Preview button and using iDVD's standard preview features (page 293). Then click the Burn or Create Project buttons, and iDVD builds your project for you, even creating chapter submenus for movies containing DVD chapters (page 297).

Magic iDVD may be all you need for many projects. And if you need to customize or enhance the DVD it creates, you can bring the rest of iDVD's authoring features to bear. Indeed, Magic iDVD is a great way to rough out a project that you plan to refine later.

Here's how to make DVD magic.

Magic iDVD versus OneStep DVD

iDVD provides two ways to go from zero to DVD with very few steps. Which method should you use, and when?

When to go OneStep. Use OneStep DVD when you want to burn just one movie to a DVD and you don't need navigation menus. When you use OneStep DVD, you don't have the opportunity to customize menu designs—there aren't any. As page 305 describes, OneStep DVD creates an *autoplay*, or *kiosk-mode*, DVD: the disc begins playback as soon as you insert it into a computer or DVD player.

When to go Magic iDVD. Use Magic iDVD when you want navigation menus and more than one piece of content on your DVD—for example, a couple of movies and some slide shows.

To Make a Magic iDVD

Step 1. Choose File > Magic iDVD.

Step 2 (optional). Edit the DVD title.

Step 3. Choose a theme for the DVD by clicking one of the theme thumbnails. (To access additional themes, use the pop-up menu above the row of thumbnails.)

Step 4. To add video to the DVD, click the Movies button in the Media pane, then drag one or more movies into the drop boxes.

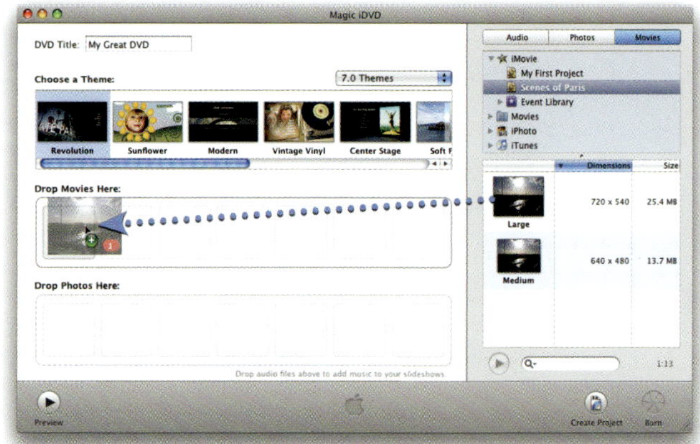

Tips: You can also drag movies directly from folders on your Mac's hard drive. (To have iDVD list movies from other folders in its media browser, use the Preferences command as described on page 296.)

Need to add multiple movies? Simply Shift-click or ⌘-click on each one to select the movies, then drag them as a group, as shown on the opposite page. When you release the mouse button, each movie appears in its own drop box.

Step 5. To add a slide show to the DVD, drag photos into the photos drop boxes. Each box represents a different slide show.

Tips: You can drag albums or events from iPhoto, or folders of photos from your hard drive or a CD. If you like to overwork, you can drag individual photos to a drop box, one at a time. You can also combine approaches. For example, you can drag an entire album or event to create a slide show, then drag individual photos to that slide show's drop box to add them to the show.

And just as you can add multiple movies at once, you can create multiple slide shows at once. Shift-click or ⌘-click on each event or album in the Photos media browser, then drag the items as a group. Each item becomes its own slide show.

Step 6 (optional). To add music to a slide show, drag an audio file from the Audio media browser (or elsewhere on your hard drive) to the slide show.

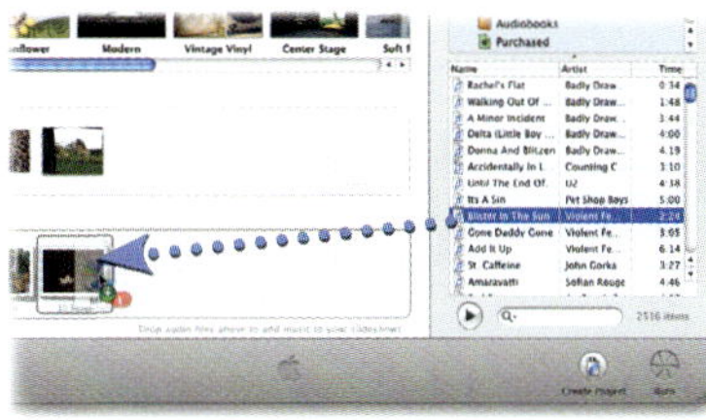

A speaker icon appears on the slide show's thumbnail to indicate that it has a soundtrack.

Step 7. Preview or finish up.

Check your work. To preview the DVD, click the Preview button. When you exit preview mode, you return to the Magic iDVD window.

Ready to bake. If you're happy with the job Magic iDVD has done, click the Burn button. iDVD creates a project containing your content, then immediately switches into burn mode. (For burning details, see pages 314–317.)

Further refinement. If you want to refine the project—for example, to customize some menus or refine your slide shows—click the Create Project button. iDVD creates a project that you can customize using the techniques described throughout this chapter.

Behind the Magic

Here's a look at how Magic iDVD does its design. And remember, you aren't locked into its magical decisions. You can customize anything in the projects that Magic iDVD creates.

Main title. The name you type into the DVD Title box becomes the title of your main menu.

Submenus. Your DVD's main menu will contain buttons that link to submenus for playing the DVD's movies and slide shows.

Chapter menus. Similarly, if you add a movie containing DVD chapter markers, you get a submenu for accessing those chapters. For themes that have separate chapter menu designs (as do all of the new iDVD themes), iDVD uses the chapter menu design for the chapter menu.

Drop zones. iDVD automatically adds movies to the drop zones of whatever menu theme you choose. If your DVD contains only slide shows, iDVD uses photos from the slide shows for the drop zones.

Planning and Creating Menus

When creating a DVD, you're also designing a user interface. If your DVD contains a couple of movies and a slide show, the interface will be simple: just one menu containing a few buttons.

But if your DVD will contain a dozen movies and another half-dozen slide shows, it will need multiple menus. And that means that you'll need to think about how to structure a menu scheme that is logical and easy to navigate.

As you plan a complex DVD, consider how many buttons each menu should have. In iDVD, a menu can have up to 12 buttons. That's a lot—too many choices for a main menu. If you have several movies and slide shows to present, it's better to create a set of *submenus* that logically categorize your content.

It's a balancing act: create too few menus, and you present your viewers with a daunting number of choices. Create too many, and you make them spend time navigating instead of viewing.

All of the new themes in iDVD '08 are designed with submenus in mind. You don't have to use these themes for projects containing submenus, but at least note their underlying philosophy: it's a good idea for a submenu to share some common design traits with the menus that lead to it.

Planning Your DVD

If your DVD will be presenting a large number of movies or slide shows, you need to plan how you will make that content available to the DVD's user. How many menus will you need? How will you categorize the content in each menu? This process is often called *information design*, and it involves mapping out the way you want to categorize and present your content.

A good way to map out a DVD's flow is to create a tree diagram depicting the organization of menus—much as a company's organizational chart depicts the pecking order of its management.

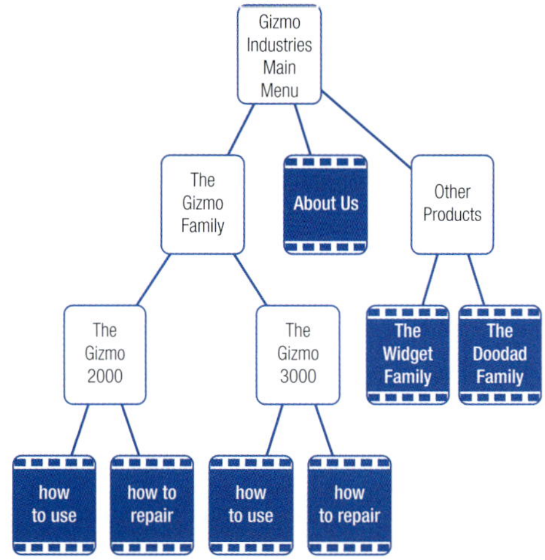

The chart shown here depicts the flow of a DVD a company might create to promote its new Gizmo product line. A main menu contains three buttons: two lead to other submenus, while the third plays a promotional movie about the company.

The submenu "The Gizmo Family" leads to two additional submenus, one for each Gizmo model. The "Other Products" submenu leads to two movies that promote other fine products.

Creating Additional Menus

To create a submenu, choose Add Submenu from the + pop-up menu or choose Project > Add Submenu.

To design the new menu and add content to it, double-click its button. You can customize the look of each submenu independently of other menus.

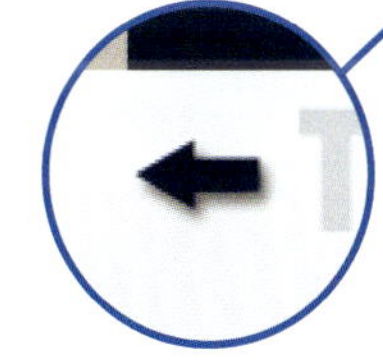

Each submenu has a return button that, when clicked, returns the user to the menu that led to the submenu.

A DVD in OneStep

If you just want to slap some video onto a DVD and you don't want menus, chapters, or slide shows, check out the OneStep DVD feature.

Insert a blank DVD in your Mac's optical drive, connect your DV camera via FireWire, and choose OneStep DVD from the File menu. iDVD rewinds your tape, captures video until it reaches the end of the tape, and then encodes the video into MPEG-2 format and burns it to disc. When you insert the burned disc in a DVD player, the video begins playing back immediately. You can also create a disc from a movie file instead of an attached camcorder; choose File > OneStep DVD from Movie.

OneStep DVD is a fast way to create a DVD, but it isn't a perfect method of backing up a tape—you don't have as much flexibility to edit the video in the future. You can't extract the video from a DVD without some effort (see page 321), and even then, the quality won't be as good as the original, since the video will have been compressed.

OneStep Tips

Controlling the capture. Normally, OneStep DVD rewinds a tape to the beginning and then begins capturing video. If you begin capturing from the middle of the tape, press your camera's Stop button during the rewind process, then immediately press its Play button. iDVD will begin capturing at that point.

Similarly, to stop the capture before the tape reaches the end, press your camera's Stop button, and iDVD burns what you captured up to that point.

Beware of breaks. If your tape contains a lengthy gap between scenes—a segment of blank tape with no timecode—OneStep DVD will probably stop importing video when it encounters that gap.

Reclaiming disk space. OneStep DVD stores your captured video in a hidden folder on your hard drive (to see where, choose iDVD > Preferences, then click Advanced). These files are deleted the next time you restart your Mac.

Customizing Menus

The design themes built into iDVD look great and, in some cases, sound great, too. But you might prefer to not use off-the-rack designs for your DVDs.

Maybe you'd like to have a custom background screen containing your company logo or a favorite vacation photo. You might like the background image of a particular iDVD theme, but not its music or its buttons' shape or typeface. Or maybe you'd just like to have the title of the menu at the left of the screen instead of centered.

You can customize nearly every aspect of your DVD's menus and navigation buttons. With the Buttons pane and the Menu Info window, you can modify buttons, add and remove background audio, change a menu's background image, and more.

You can also create text labels—for example, some instructions for DVD newbies or a few lines of commentary about the DVD's subject.

iDVD '08 provides more menu customizing options than did earlier versions. You can even have a different shape and style for *each* button on a menu. As with all design tasks, restraint is a virtue. Have fun with your menu designs, but don't lose sight of the menu's main purpose: to provide convenient access to your DVD's contents.

Moving Items Around

Normally, iDVD positions buttons on a fixed grid. This keeps them lined up nicely, but you can also manually specify a button's location—perhaps to line it up with a custom background image.

Simply drag buttons (or other objects) wherever you like.

When you drag a button or other object, iDVD displays positioning guides to help you align items. (You're free to ignore these guides.) If you want to return to the fixed grid, click the Inspector button, then, in the Menu Info window, click the Snap to Grid.

Changing Menu Durations

You like a particular motion menu but you don't want to use all of it. Maybe you don't need all eight drop zones in the Reflections themes. Just shorten the menu's duration. Go to the Menu Info window, then drag the Loop Duration slider until the menu is the desired length.

This technique works best with themes that don't have background music, so either choose a theme that lacks music or delete the music (see page 308).

Adding Text

To add descriptive text, captions, or instructions to a menu, choose Add Text from the Project menu (⌘-K). A text area appears; drag it to the desired location, then click within that text area, and type. To start another line, press Return.

To format the text, choose a font and size from the pop-up menus that appear below it, or use the Inspector window; see the opposite page.

Kill the Watermark

iDVD displays the Apple logo watermark on each menu screen. To get rid of it, choose Preferences from the iDVD menu, click the General button, and then uncheck the Show Apple Logo Watermark box.

Staying TV Safe

TV sets omit the outer edges of a video frame—a phenomenon called *overscan*. To make sure buttons and other menu elements will be visible on TV sets, choose the Show TV Safe Area command in the View menu, and avoid putting buttons or other elements in the shaded area.

Get links to more iDVD menu themes.
www.macilife.com/idvd

Changing the Background Image

To change the background image of an iDVD menu, simply drag an image into the menu area. For the best results, be sure to use a photo with proportions that match your project's aspect ratio: 4:3 for standard television or 16:9 for widescreen or HD television. You can ensure these proportions when cropping in iPhoto: from the Constrain pop-up menu, choose 4 x 3 (DVD) or 16 x 9 (HD).

Tips: Some photos make better backgrounds if you reduce their brightness and contrast so the image doesn't overwhelm the buttons. In iPhoto, duplicate the image and then adjust the brightness and contrast of the duplicate.

If you replace the background on a theme that has a drop zone, the drop zone remains. To remove drop zones after replacing a background, go to the Menu Info window and uncheck the Show Drop Zones and Related Graphics box.

Want a plain white background? You can download one from www.macilife.com/idvd. You can also make your own patterned or solid-colored backgrounds in a program like Photoshop Elements. Create a graphic with dimensions that are 640 by 480 pixels (854 by 480 pixels for widescreen), save it as a JPEG image, and then drag it into iDVD.

If your project contains several menus, you can apply one menu's custom design to other menus in the project; see page 309.

And, if you decide you'd rather just have the theme's original background, simply drag the custom background's image thumbnail out of the Background well (above the Loop Duration slider) in the Menu Info window.

Customizing Button Shapes

To change a button's shape, select it and display the Buttons pane.

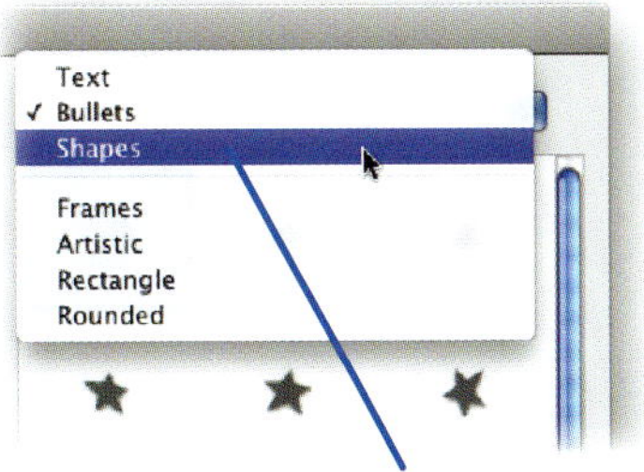

The first three options in the pop-up menu control formatting of text-only labels; the categories below them offer buttons with video or photo previews. Click a shape to choose it.

You can also control the size of the buttons by dragging the Size slider.

Changing Button Text Labels

When you choose a button shape, your buttons consist of text labels and little thumbnail images or movies. In the Button Info window, you can change where a button's text labels appear in relation to the button's thumbnail image.

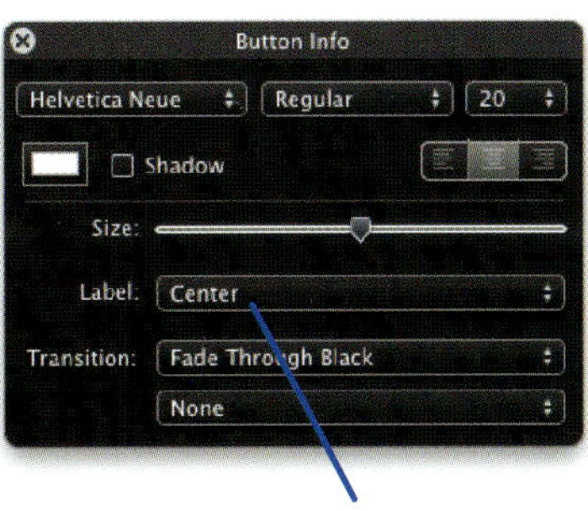

To customize button labels, choose an option from the pop-up menu.

To add a soft shadow to some text, select the button or label and click the Shadow box.

Each button style has its own style of highlight, which appears when a user selects the button. To change the highlight color, click the Highlight Color well.

You can also change the font, font color, and type size for button text and for the menu's title and any text you've added. If you don't like the results, choose the Undo command as many times as needed to get back to where you started.

Tip: To format all of a menu's buttons at once, select them all first. Click on one button, then press ⌘-A. Similarly, to select every text item you've added, click one item and then press ⌘-A.

To return the buttons to the theme's style, select them and choose Advanced > Reset Object to Theme Settings.

More Design Tips

Adding Transitions

You can have a transition between menus. For example, when your DVD's viewers choose a button to go to a movie, you can have the menu appear to peel away to reveal the movie.

You can choose from a dozen different transition styles. For menu transitions, I'm partial to cube, page flip, or wipe—each conveys the notion of moving from one area to another.

You create menu transitions by assigning them to buttons. You can assign a different transition to every button in a menu, but in the interest of good taste, it's better to stick with just one or two different transition styles. For example, you might choose the cube transition for buttons that go from one menu to another, and the fade through black transition for buttons that lead directly to movies and slide shows.

To assign a transition to a button, select the button and then choose the desired transition from the Transition pop-up menu in the Button Info window. Some transitions, such as cube, also allow you to specify a direction—set this by choosing from the second Transition pop-up menu.

Varying the direction of transitions can be a nice way to add variety without resorting to using a lot of different transition styles. For example, when a viewer chooses a button to go to a slide show, you might have a cube that rotates to the left. For a different button that leads to another menu, you might have a cube transition that rotates downward.

Tip: If you've mixed and matched transitions and decide you'd prefer to use just one transition style, you don't have to change the transitions one button at a time. Just use iDVD's map view to change the transitions in one fell swoop; see page 311.

Note: A menu transition is, unfortunately, a one-way street. That is, a transition appears only as you drill *down* into a DVD's menu structure. If you navigate from a submenu back to a main menu, you don't see a transition.

Moving Buttons Between Menus

To move a button from one menu to another, select the button and choose Cut. Next, move to a different menu (use map view to get there in a hurry), then paste.

You can also *copy* a button instead of pasting it. You might do this to provide access to a piece of content from several different menus.

For example, say you've created a series of online help screens in the form of a slide show. To make the online help available from every menu in your DVD, copy its button and then paste it into each menu.

New Menu from Selection

After adding numerous items to a DVD, you realize that a particular menu has too many buttons. The solution: move some of those buttons to a new menu. But don't wear out your wrists cutting and pasting. Just select the buttons you want to move (Shift-click on them), then sprint up to the Project menu and choose New Menu from Selection. iDVD removes the selected buttons and stashes them in a new menu.

Silencing Motion Menus

You might like the look of a motion menu, but maybe you don't want any music or sound effects to play. To silence a motion menu, go to the Menu Info window and drag the Menu Volume slider to its leftmost position. If you change your mind, raise the volume level. To silence the menu for good, drag the icon out of the Audio well, and it disappears in an animated puff of smoke.

Audio-Only Menus

Conversely, maybe you would like some background audio to play, but you don't want motion in your menus. First, choose a theme that lacks motion, or replace an existing motion theme's background with a static image. Next, drag an audio file, iTunes playlist, or QuickTime movie into the Menu pane's Audio well. To hear the audio, click the Motion button. A menu can play for up to 15 minutes before it loops.

Motion Buttons

In many themes and button styles, iDVD also applies motion to your movie buttons: small, thumbnail versions of the movies play back when the menu is displayed.

You can even specify which portion of the movie plays: just drag the slider that appears above the movie or in the Button Info window.

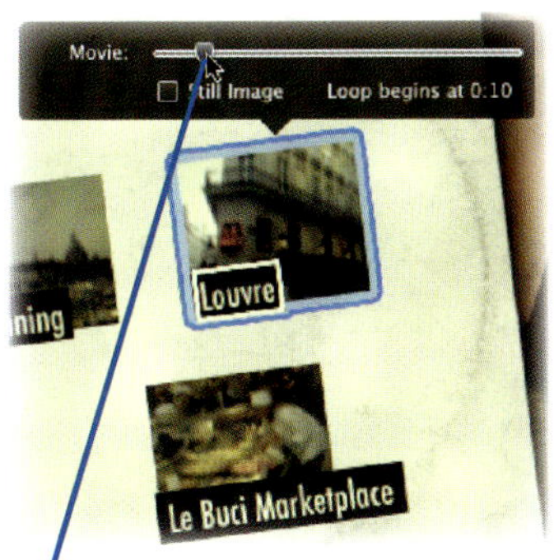

To specify how much of a movie plays in a motion button, drag the Loop Duration slider in the Menu Info window.

There are times when you might not want a movie's button to be a thumbnail movie. Maybe the movie thumbnail distracts from the motion menu's background. In any case, simply enable the Still Image checkbox. Now use the slider to choose a static thumbnail image for the movie.

If you're using a theme that has text-only buttons, you can add motion or thumbnail buttons by choosing a different button style in the Buttons pane.

Copying Custom Menus

Your project contains several menus and you've customized one of them. Now you decide you'd like to apply your design to all the menus in your project. Easy: choose Apply Theme to Submenus from the Advanced menu.

Conversely, if you've customized a submenu and want to apply that design to the project's other menus, choose Apply Theme to Project.

Copying Button Styles

You've changed a button's text and color, and would like to apply that formatting to other buttons. Easy: select the formatted button and choose Edit > Copy Style. Then select one or more other buttons and choose Edit > Paste Style.

Saving a Theme Design

Happy with the results of a menu-design session? Save your customized theme as a "favorite," and you can apply it to future projects with one mouse click.

Choose Save Theme as Favorite from the File menu. If you have multiple user accounts on your computer, you can make the custom theme available to all users: check the Shared For All Users box.

The new theme appears in the Themes pane. To see it, choose Favorites or All from the themes pop-up menu. On your hard drive, saved themes are stored in your home directory in the following path: Library > Application Support > iDVD > Favorites. Shared themes are stored in the same path at the root level of the drive.

Fading Menu Audio

To have a menu's audio fade out at the end of the menu loop, enable that feature in the General portion of the Preferences dialog box.

More Themes

Want to go beyond the themes that are built into iDVD? Try out some of the themes from DVDThemePak (www.DVDthemepak.com). The company offers more than a dozen theme and button collections. They look great and are inexpensive.

Navigating and Authoring with Map View

iDVD's map view lets you see the organization of your DVD project using a display that looks a lot like the organizational chart depicted on page 304.

In map view, you can see at a glance how your project is organized. More to the point, you can get around quickly. By double-clicking the icons in map view, you can jump to a specific menu or preview a slide show or movie. Need to drill down into a deeply nested submenu to do some design work? Display the map, then double-click the submenu's icon.

Map view is about more than just seeing the big picture. You can use it to rearrange submenus, change menu themes, create menu transitions, and add content to your DVD. You can also use map view to loop a slide show or movie so that it plays over and over again. And you can use map view to have a movie or slide show start automatically when your DVD is played.

To switch to map view, click the Map button. To exit map view, click the Map button again, double-click an icon in the map, or click the Return button in the lower-right corner of the map.

Customizing Your View

When you're on the road, sometimes you need the big picture and sometimes you need street-by-street details. Map view provides this flexibility, and then some.

Switch between left-to-right (shown here) and top-to-bottom views.

To scroll quickly, press the Option key and drag within the map.

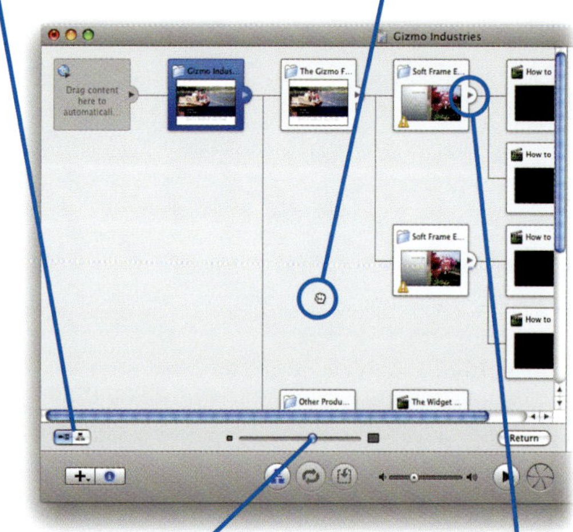

To zoom in and out on the map, drag the size slider. When zoomed out, you see only icons representing folders, slide shows, and movies.

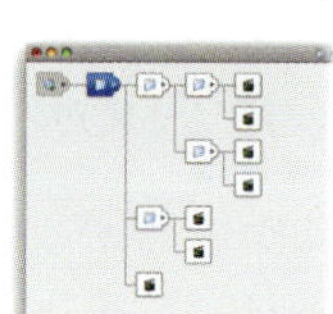

When you zoom in, iDVD displays small thumbnail images as well as names of menus and other content.

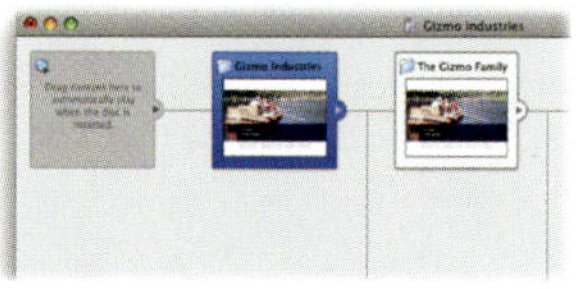

If you don't need to see a particular set of icons, click the right-pointing triangle to hide them and free up viewing space.

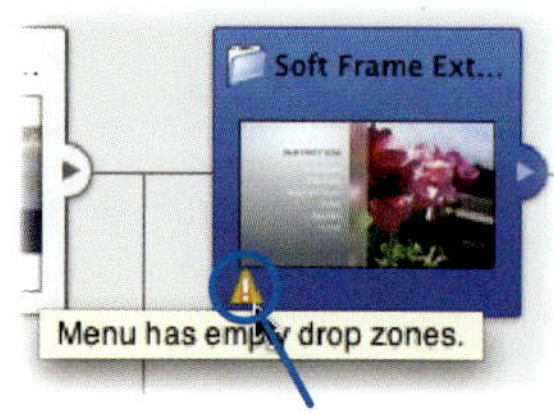

See a warning triangle? Point to it, and iDVD displays details about the problem.

Authoring in Map View

Customizing Menus

To customize a menu in map view, select the menu by clicking it once. To change the menu's theme, use the Themes panel. To change the menu's background, audio, drop zones, or text formatting, use the Menu Info window. To change the appearance of all buttons on a menu, use the Buttons pane; to set a transition, use the Button Info window.

Here's the best part: you can customize multiple menus at once. Just Shift-click on each menu you want to change, and then use the panes to make your changes.

Note: When you use map view to specify a transition for a menu, every button on that menu will use the same transition. If you want a different transition for some of the menu's buttons, assign a transition to each button individually as described on page 308.

Rearranging Your Project

Want to move a slide show or other item to a different menu? Simply drag the item's icon to another menu.

Checking Transitions

To see which transitions a menu uses, point to the menu's icon, and a description of the transition appears.

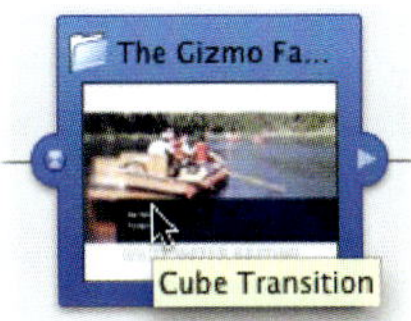

Adding Content to a Menu

To add content to an existing menu, drag it from the media browser or the Finder to the menu's icon.

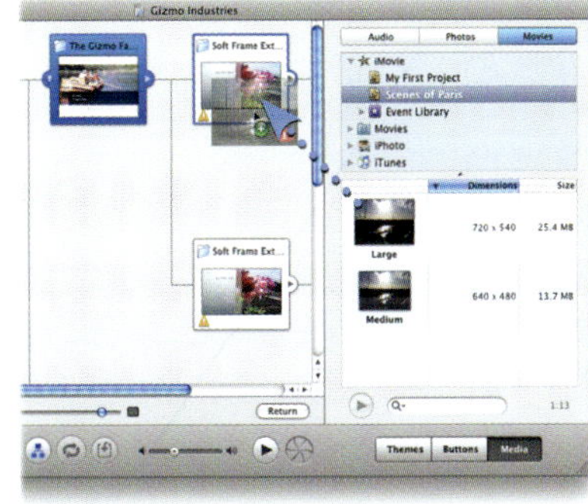

If you drag a movie or iPhoto album to an existing menu, iDVD creates a button for that item.

You can also change a menu's background image using the map: just drag a single image to the menu's icon. (For more details on customizing menu backgrounds, see page 307.)

Looping a Movie or Slide Show

To have a movie or slide show *loop* (play over and over), select its icon and choose Loop Slideshow from the Advanced menu.

(When you aren't in map view, you can specify looping by selecting a movie's or slide show's menu button and choosing Loop.)

Adding AutoPlay Content

On many DVDs, a movie appears when the DVD begins playing—an FBI warning, for example, or a movie-studio logo.

You can use map view to add this *AutoPlay* content to your DVD. Simply drag a movie, a photo, a set of photos, or an entire iPhoto album to the project icon.

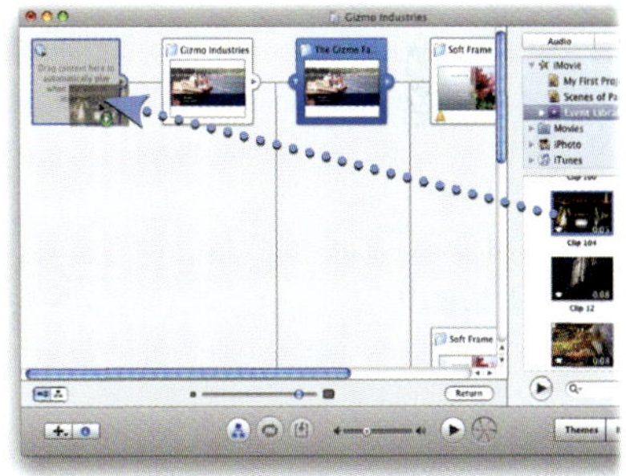

If you drag photos to the project icon, you can double-click the project icon to open the slide show editor where you can specify transitions and add background music (page 300).

Don't want an AutoPlay item after all? Just drag it out of the project icon, and it disappears in a puff of pixel smoke.

Creating a Kiosk DVD

Want a movie or slide show to play automatically and continuously? Drag it to the project icon and then, with the project icon still selected, choose Loop from the Advanced menu.

Adding DVD-ROM Content

One of the reasons why the DVD format is so versatile is that it can accommodate not only video, sound, and pictures, but also any disk files that you may want to distribute.

Here's the scoop on this aspect of DVD authoring, along with a peek under the hood to see how MPEG-2 compression manages to squeeze up to two hours of video onto a 4.7GB DVD.

The DVD-ROM Zone

A DVD can hold more than video and slide shows; it can also hold "computer files"—Microsoft Word documents, PDF files, JPEG images, and so on. You might take advantage of this to distribute files that are related to your DVD's content.

If you've created an in-house training DVD for new employees, you might want to include a PDF of the employee handbook. If you've created a DVD containing a couple of rough edits of a TV commercial, you might also include some PDFs that show the print versions of your ad campaign. If you've created a DVD promoting your band, you might include some audio files of your tunes.

When a DVD-Video disc also contains files intended to be used by a computer, it's said to have a *DVD-ROM* portion. If users play the DVD in a living-room DVD player, those files are invisible. However, if they use that same DVD with a personal computer, they can access the files.

Including Photos

As described on page 300, when creating DVDs containing slide shows, you can have iDVD copy the original images to the DVD-ROM portion. In the slide show editor, click Settings, then check the box labeled Add Image Files to DVD-ROM.

This option is ideal for photographers who want to distribute high-resolution versions of their images along with slide shows. You might also find it a useful way to back up a set of digital photos. The slide shows serve as a handy way of viewing the images, while the original, high-resolution files are archived in the DVD-ROM portion of the disc.

Note: If your slide show includes raw-format photos from iPhoto, iDVD includes both the raw-format originals and the JPEG stand-ins that iPhoto created. If you'd rather not include the raw originals (or the JPEGs), save your DVD as a disc image and edit the contents of the disc image as described on page 317.

Tip: If you *always* want to include a slide show's original images on your DVD, choose Preferences from the iDVD menu, click the Slideshow button, then check the box labeled Always Add Original Photos to DVD-ROM Contents.

Including Other Content

To add other types of files to your DVD, choose Edit DVD-ROM Contents from the Advanced menu. Use the DVD-ROM Contents window to manage and organize the contents of the DVD-ROM folder.

Your DVD will contain a folder with the name of your project plus *DVD-ROM Contents.*

To add files to the DVD-ROM area, drag them into the DVD-ROM Contents window, or use the Add Files button. To delete a file from the DVD-ROM area, select it and press the Delete key.

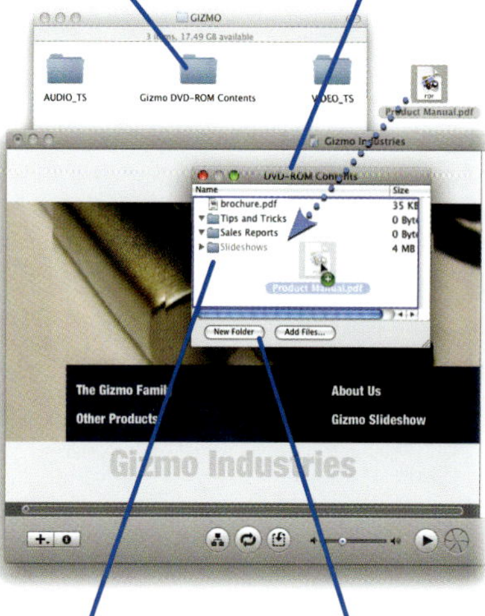

If you've added photos from one or more slide shows to the DVD-ROM area, they appear in a folder named Slideshows. You can't rename this folder or move it to another folder. To delete it, return to the slide show editor and uncheck its DVD-ROM box.

You can create additional folders within the DVD-ROM folder, and you can drag files or other folders into it.

MPEG: Compressing Space and Time

One of the jobs iDVD performs is to compress your movies into MPEG format, the standard method of storing video on DVD-Video discs. Like image and audio compression, MPEG is a *lossy* format: the final product lacks some of the quality of the original. But as with image and audio compression, the amount of quality loss depends on the degree to which the original material is compressed.

Like JPEG, MPEG performs spatial compression that reduces the storage requirements of individual images. But video adds the dimension of time, and MPEG takes this into account by also performing *temporal compression*.

The key to temporal compression is to describe only those details that have changed since the previous video frame. In an MPEG video stream, some video frames contain the entire image; these are called *I-frames*. There are usually two I-frames per second.

An I-frame describes an entire scene: "There's a basketball on a concrete driveway."

Sandwiched between those I-frames are much smaller frames that don't contain the entire image, but rather only those pixels that have changed since the previous frame.

"It's rolling toward the street."

To perform temporal compression, the video frame is divided into a grid of blocks, and each square is examined to see if anything has changed. Areas that haven't changed—such as the stationary background in this example— are simply repeated in the next frame.

This is why video with relatively little motion often tends to look better than video that contains a great deal of motion. When little changes from one frame to the next, the quality of each frame can be higher.

Burning Your DVD

You've massaged your media and made your menus. What's next? Burning the final product onto a blank DVD. Simply click iDVD's Burn button and insert a blank disc. But before you burn, read the following tips.

Preview First

Before you insert that pricey blank DVD, preview your work by clicking iDVD's Preview button. Use the iDVD remote control to step through your menus and spot-check your video, slide shows, and any menu transitions you've added. And don't forget to proofread your menu titles and button text.

Consider a Disc Image

Before you burn, consider creating a *disc image*, a kind of virtual disk that can be extremely useful for testing and burning. You'll find full details on working with disc images on page 316.

If your DVD has a lot of menus, transitions, and content, consider creating a disc image and using Mac OS X's DVD Player program to test it. And if you have a slower Mac—or just seem to have trouble burning reliably—creating and burning a disc image can be a great way to increase your success rate.

Note: If you will be burning a dual-layer DVD, do not try to burn it from a disc image. For details, see page 316.

Run Lean

When burning a DVD, avoid running complex programs that put a lot of demands on your system. Recording a track in GarageBand while also burning a DVD is not a good idea, for example. Also, consider turning off file sharing and quitting any disk-intensive programs.

What Kind of Media?

Several types of writable DVD media exist: DVD-R, DVD-RW, DVD+R, and DVD+RW. Previous versions of iDVD could handle the DVD-R format only, but iDVD is now much more versatile. It can burn any of the aforementioned formats, assuming your DVD burner supports them. Most of the SuperDrives in today's Macs can; older SuperDrives support the DVD-R and DVD-RW formats only.

The differences between the "minus" and "plus" camps are technical ones and don't have much bearing on your burning endeavors. The more important difference deals with R and RW: an RW disc can be erased and reused roughly 1,000 times. If you insert an RW disc that already contains data, iDVD even offers to erase it for you.

RW discs are great for testing, although as the following page describes, you're more likely to encounter playback problems on some DVD players. Also, RW discs are more sensitive to damage and aging than write-once discs.

If you're interested in the technical details between the minus and plus formats, read Jim Taylor's superb DVD FAQ at www.DVDdemystified.com.

Dual-Layer Differences

Many of today's Macs include SuperDrives capable of burning on dual-layer DVD+R media. With a dual-layer drive, you can burn nearly 8GB, or about four hours' worth of video.

To see if your Mac is capable of dual-layer burning, choose Project > Project Info, and click on the DVD Type pop-up menu. If you have a dual-layer drive, you'll have the option of specifying dual-layer media.

Incidentally, if you have a single-layer SuperDrive but would like to double your pleasure, you can buy external dual-layer burners that work just fine with iDVD. But note that more is not always better. Dual-layer burned discs often do not play in standalone DVD players, and may lack the longevity of single-layer discs.

DVD Type ✓ Single-Layer (SL) - 4.2 GB
Double-Layer (DL) - 7.7 GB

Will It Play?

You've burned a disc and are ready to show it off to your boss. You pop the disc into the conference room DVD player and proudly press the play button—and nothing happens.

Welcome to The Incompatibility Zone. The sad fact is, some DVD players and personal computer DVD drives are unable to read burned DVD media. Generally, older DVD players and drives are most likely to have this problem, but you may encounter it in newer players, too.

Roughly 85 percent of DVD players can read DVD-R and DVD+R discs, and about 80 percent can read DVD-RW and DVD+RW discs. Those are good numbers, although they won't be of much solace if your player—or your boss's—is in the minority.

The picture is much more bleak when it comes to dual-layer DVD burning: a large percentage of DVD players have trouble playing dual-layer burned DVDs. If you're shopping for a new DVD player, be sure to verify compatibility with the type of media you plan to burn. And diplomatically inform your friends, family, and colleagues that if they have problems playing your DVD, the fault probably lies with their players.

Making More

You can burn multiple copies of a DVD using iDVD, but you might find the job easier with Roxio's Toast or Popcorn software, both of which provide copying features. Or, make a disc image and use Mac OS X's Disk Utility program to burn multiple copies (see page 316).

If you need to have more than a few copies of a disc—for example, 2,000 training DVDs for a large company—you'll want to work with a replicator. Most replicators will accept a burned DVD as a master.

One excellent source for low-volume replication is CreateSpace (www.createspace.com), which also provides e-commerce and shipping services.

Archiving Projects for Burning Elsewhere

iDVD provides an archiving feature that saves a project and all of its assets in one self-contained file.

Archiving enables you to author on one Mac, then burn on another. Move projects between home, school, or work. Start a project on a cross-country flight, then archive and transfer your project when you land.

To archive a project, choose Archive Project from the File menu.

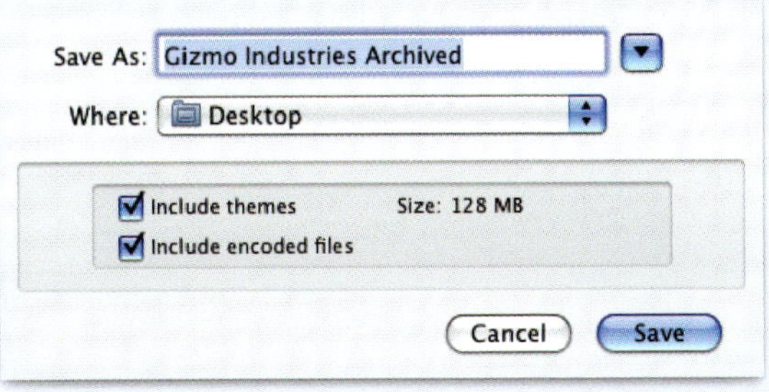

If you created customized themes for the DVD—or if you want to be certain that your themes will be available in a future version of iDVD—check the Include Themes box. If you're using standard themes and aren't obsessed about future compatibility, you can uncheck this box and your archive file will be a bit smaller.

If iDVD has already encoded the DVD's content, you can include those encoded files in the archive by checking the Include Encoded Files box. Doing so will make your archive file quite a bit larger, however.

After you specify archive settings and click Save, iDVD goes to work, copying everything in your project into a file. You can transfer this file to another Mac using a fast network, a FireWire hard drive, or the Fire Wire disk mode that laptop Macs provide.

Burning Tips

For many projects, one click of the Burn button is all it takes to commit your work to plastic. But sometimes it's better to take the roundabout route: creating a *disc image* and then using it as the basis for your burns.

If you've downloaded software from the Internet, you're probably already familiar with the concept of disc images. But if you haven't heard the term before, it can seem confusing.

And for good reason: a disc image isn't a disc or an image. It's a file on your hard drive. The bits and bytes in this file are organized in the same way that they would be on a disc. If you double-click a disc image file, the Mac's Finder reads the disc image and creates an icon on your desktop—as if you'd inserted a disc.

iDVD lets you create a disc image for a DVD project. You can then test your DVD on your Mac, or use other software to burn it.

In a bigger hurry? Save the project as a VIDEO_TS folder. You can test your project by opening this folder with the DVD Player program.

Important: If you plan to burn a dual-layer disc, note that Apple recommends burning the disc directly from iDVD, rather than creating a disc image and then burning from that image. To quote from iDVD's online help, "double-layer discs burned from a disc image may cause playback issues in some DVD players, such as freezing during playback."

Creating a Disc Image

Step 1.

Choose Save as Disc Image from the File menu (Shift-⌘-R).

Step 2.

Give your disc image a name and click Save.

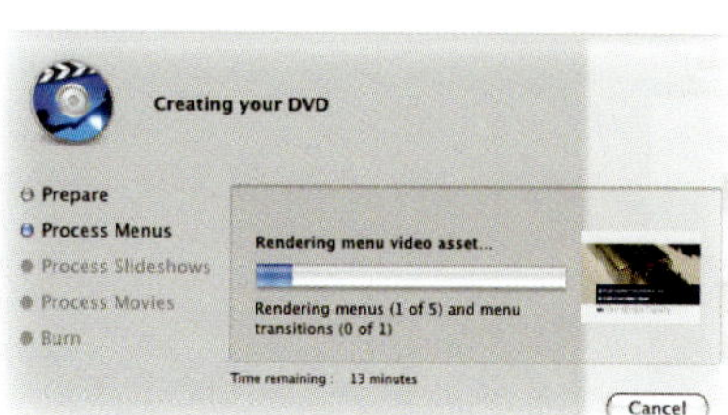

iDVD compresses your video, encodes your menus, and then saves the resulting data in the disc image file. The file's name ends in .img.

Testing a Disc Image

To test your DVD using Mac OS X's DVD Player program, begin by double-clicking the disc image file to create an icon on your desktop.

If you double-click this icon to examine its contents, you'll see two folders: AUDIO_TS and VIDEO_TS. (If you added DVD-ROM content to the DVD, you'll see a third folder.) Those awkward names are required by the DVD standard, as are the even more awkward names of the files inside the VIDEO_TS folder.

(The AUDIO_TS folder will always be empty, but don't try to create a DVD that lacks one; the DVD may not play in some players. And if it ever comes up in a trivia contest, TS stands for transport stream.)

To test your disc image, start DVD Player and choose File > Open DVD Media. (In pre-Tiger Mac OS X versions, choose File > Open VIDEO_TS Folder.) Navigate to your disc image, select its VIDEO_TS folder, and click Choose or press Return. Now press the spacebar or click DVD Player's Play button, and your faux DVD will begin playing back.

Burning a Disc Image

If you found a problem when testing your disc image—a typo, for example, or a missing piece of content—you haven't wasted a blank DVD. Simply trash the disc image, make your revisions in iDVD, then create and test another disc image.

And if you're ready to burn? If you're burning a single-layer DVD, don't bother with iDVD's Burn button—use the disc image instead.

First, start up Mac OS X's Disk Utility program. (It's located in the Utilities folder within your Applications folder.) Next, click the Burn button in the upper-left corner of Disk Utility's window. In the dialog box that appears, locate and double-click the disc image file. Disk Utility displays another dialog box. Before you click its Burn button, click the little down-pointing arrow to expand the dialog box.

What's the hurry? You can get more reliable burns—and increase the chances that your DVD will play in other players—by burning at your drive's slowest speed.

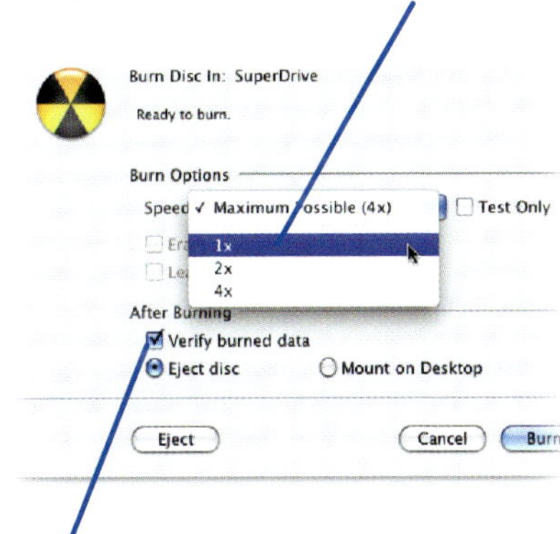

In a hurry? If you uncheck Verify Burn, your disc will be ready sooner. On the downside, you won't know if data was written inaccurately until you try to play the disc.

Other Ways to Burn

If you have Roxio's Toast Titanium software, you can drag your disc image's AUDIO_TS and VIDEO_TS folders into Toast and burn your disc there. If you've installed Toast's Toast It shortcut menu, the job is even easier: Control-click on your disc image icon and choose Toast It from the shortcut menu. (Use Toast's Preferences command to install the Toast It shortcut menu plug-in.)

You can also use Toast to fine-tune any DVD-ROM content you've added—for example, removing the raw versions of the photos that you've included in a slide show (see page 312).

Toast also gives you a choice of burning speeds. For critical projects where you need the broadest compatibility, burn at 1x speed.

Encoding Insights and Tips

You don't have to know how iDVD encodes MPEG-2 video, but if you're curious, here are the details.

High Quality. When you choose High Quality in the Encoder Settings area of the Preferences dialog box, the bit rate depends in part on how much media is in your project. Data rates will vary from a low of 3.5 megabits per second (Mbps) to 7 Mbps. With high-quality encoding, iDVD uses variable bit rate (VBR) encoding: the bit rate of a video stream changes according to the complexity of the scene. Motion-intensive scenes get a higher bit rate, while scenes containing little motion get a lower rate.

Professional Quality. New to iDVD '08, Professional Quality performs the same VBR calculations as High Quality, but it does the job in two passes.

Best Performance. When you choose Best Performance, iDVD encodes at a fixed bit rate of 8 Mbps.

Tip: If you've burned a DVD using high-quality or professional-quality encoding and you delete some content from the project, you may be able to improve the video quality of the remaining content by having iDVD encode it all over again. Choose Delete Encoded Assets from the Advanced menu, then burn the project again.

iDVD Tips

Make It Last

Burned discs don't last forever. To improve their reliability and longevity, don't use peel-and-stick labels. If a label isn't perfectly centered, the DVD will be off-balance when it spins, and that could cause playback problems. If you want to label your DVDs, use an ink-jet printer that can print on DVD media.

Label discs with a Sharpie or other permanent marker. Write small and be brief—the solvents in permanent ink can damage a DVD's substrate over time.

Keep burned DVDs in jewel cases, and store them in a cool, dark place. Be careful to never flex the disc—a DVD is comprised of several different layers, and flexing a disc can cause the layers to separate. To remove a disc from a jewel case, press the center button of the case, then lift the disc out—don't simply pull the disc by its edges. (This advice applies to all optical media, by the way.)

Which Movie Formats Work with iDVD?

You can include digital camera movies in an iDVD project—just drag them into the iDVD window. If the movies are in your iPhoto library, you can use iDVD's photo or movies browsers to access them.

Indeed, you can burn nearly any kind of QuickTime movie onto a DVD, including movies you've downloaded from the Web or copied from an old CD-ROM.

If a movie is smaller than the DVD standard of 720 by 480 pixels, iDVD enlarges it to fill the screen. This results in a loss of sharpness, but enlarged movies can still look good when viewed on a TV. It's better to have shared a blurry movie than never to have shared at all.

You can't use movies stored in MPEG-1 or MPEG-2 formats. Sony digital cameras use the MPEG format for their movies, and many of the movies that have been posted on file-sharing networks are in MPEG format.

There are free or cheap utilities that enable you to convert MPEG movies into a format that iDVD (and iMovie) can use. I've written up instructions on my site; see www.macilife.com/imovie. You can also use Toast Titanium's Export Video command, as described at right.

Incidentally, this MPEG prohibition does not apply to MPEG-4 movies created by digital cameras or to iMovie projects created in MPEG-4 format. Those movies work just fine in iDVD.

Reverting Your Project

You've made some modifications that you don't like. Many programs, including GarageBand, have a Revert command that lets you get back to the last version you saved. iDVD lacks a Revert command, but you can simulate one: just reopen the project by choosing its name from the Open Recent submenu in the File menu. Click Don't Save when iDVD asks you if you want to save changes before reopening the project.

Extracting Video

You burned some cherished video to a DVD, then lost the original tape—and now you want to edit it in iMovie.

You can extract video from a DVD and convert it into DV format, but you will lose some quality in the process. If you have Toast Titanium, click its Video button and drag your DVD's VIDEO_TS folder into the Toast window. Locate the clip you want to extract, select it, and click the Export button.

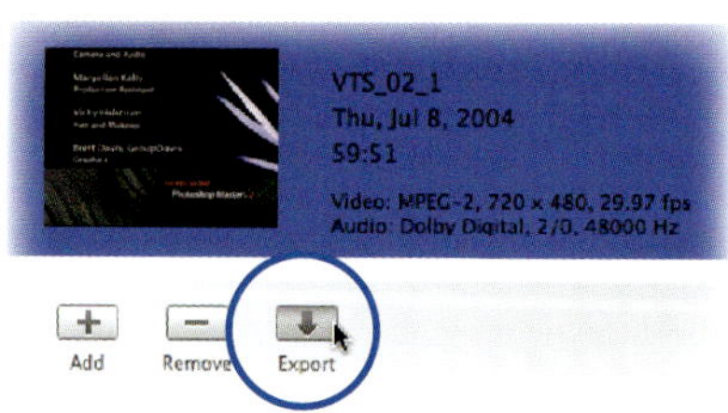

You can also extract video using any of several free or cheap utilities. Video guru Matti Haveri has published a fine tutorial on his Web site; I've linked to it at www.macilife.com/iDVD.

Get more iDVD tips.
www.macilife.com/idvd

Project Management Tips

When you add a movie or set of images to iDVD, the program doesn't actually add those files to your project file. Rather, iDVD simply links to the existing files on your hard drive.

If you need to move a project from one Mac to another, create an archive of the project using the Archive Project command in the File menu. As described on page 315, this command copies all of the project's assets into one file.

If you copy just the project file—or if you delete an asset that you added to the project—iDVD displays broken-link icons for buttons whose assets are missing.

When you open a project containing broken links, iDVD displays an error message.

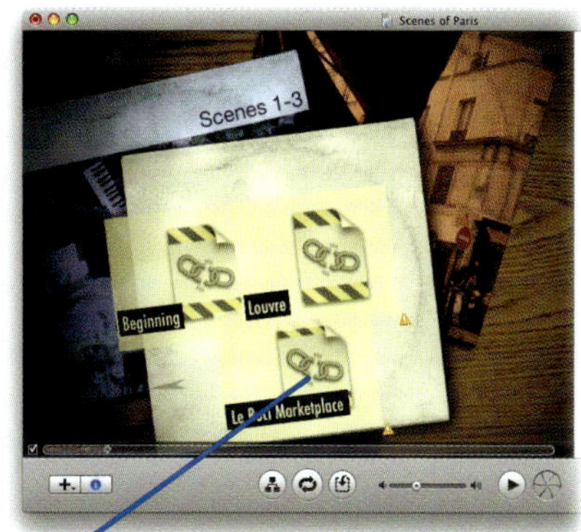

You can avoid the hassle by not moving assets once you add them to a project, or by creating an archive of the project to gather all its assets in one place.

To get the big picture of a project, choose Project Info from the Project menu.

Use these options to change a project's video format and encoding settings.

To reconnect to a missing file, double-click its entry, then locate the file and double-click its name.

You can change the DVD's name here. This doesn't change the name of your project file; rather, it changes the name of the final DVD. The DVD specification doesn't permit a disc name to have spaces in it; iDVD replaces any spaces with underscores, as in HAWAII_SCENES.

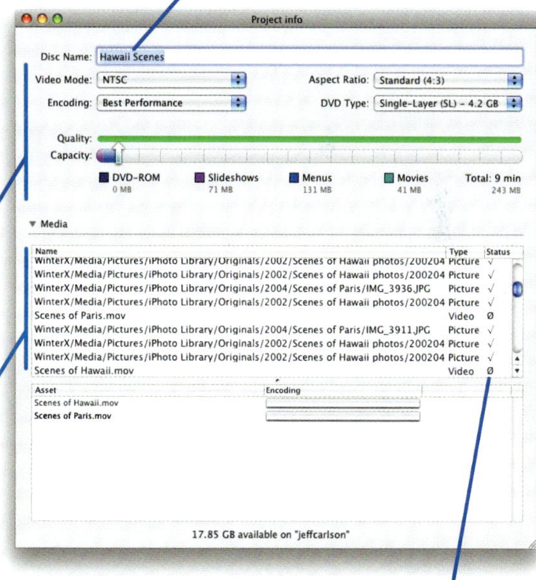

The Project Info window displays a list of the project's assets; its Status column indicates if any assets are missing (Ø).

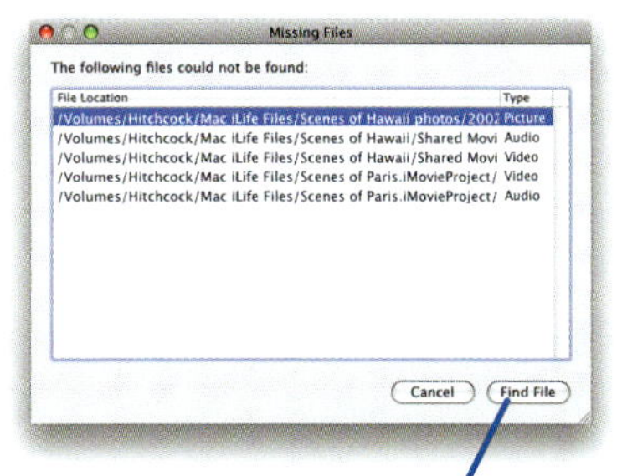

If you've moved a file to a different folder or drive, you can aim iDVD in the right direction: click Find File, then locate and double-click the file.

More iDVD Tips

Copy and Paste Drop Zone Contents

If you've assembled a great set of photos for a drop zone and you'd like to use that same set elsewhere in the project, it's easy to duplicate it. Control-click the drop zone and choose Copy Drop Zone Contents from the shortcut menu. Then, go to the destination drop zone and choose Paste Drop Zone Contents from the shortcut menu.

Browsing Other Folders

You can use the Preferences command to tell iDVD to search other folders and hard drives when displaying its movie browser (page 296). You can expand your browsing options for audio and photos, too. Just drag a folder from the Finder into the appropriate media browser.

This also works for the movie browser—and it's a handy alternative to the Preferences dialog box.

Hacking iDVD Themes

Previous versions of iDVD stored the themes within the application itself, but starting with iDVD 6, Apple moved them to a more sensible location: Computer > Library > Application Support > iDVD > Themes.

Each theme (which ends with the text .theme) is also a *package*—to explore it, Control-click on its icon and choose Show Package Contents from the shortcut menu. Double-click the Contents folder and then the Resources folder, and you'll find background movies and audio loops. To extract an item—for example, to grab the background audio from the Revolution-Main theme—press Option while dragging the item's icon out to the desktop. This makes a duplicate of the item, leaving the original theme unchanged.

Take care to not throw away or alter any resources whose purpose you don't understand, lest you have to reinstall the iDVD application.

From PDF to DVD

An iDVD slide show isn't restricted to the JPEG image format. A slide show can display numerous graphics formats, including PDF.

iDVD's PDF support means that you can display just about any document in a slide show. Want to put a Microsoft Word document or a Web page in a slide show? Create a PDF version of the document: choose Print from the File menu, then click the Save as PDF button. Drag the PDF into the iDVD slide show editor, and iDVD creates a slide containing the contents of the PDF's first page. (If you have a multi-page document, save each page as a separate PDF or use the Preview application to extract specific pages, as described in the following tip.)

Before making a PDF of a document, you might want to choose the Page Setup command and click the landscape-orientation button. That way, your PDF will have the same horizontal orientation as a slide. If you make the PDF in portrait orientation, your slide will have black borders on either side of the page.

Think twice about using a PDF that contains lots of text, especially in font sizes below 14 point. Small text looks fuzzy on a TV screen.

From iPhoto Book to Slide Show

On page 213, I discussed a method for saving an iPhoto book as a PDF and then extracting pages for printing. Here's a variation of that technique that lets you include iPhoto book pages in iDVD slide shows.

After saving your book as a PDF, open the PDF in Mac OS X's Preview program. Next, open Preview's sidebar (choose Sidebar from the View menu). In the sidebar, locate the page that you want to turn into a slide. Select the page and choose Copy from the Edit menu.

Next, choose the New from Clipboard command from the File menu. The Preview program creates a new document and pastes the page you copied into it. Save the page as a new PDF file.

Get links to background animations and other iDVD add-ons.
www.macilife.com/iDVD

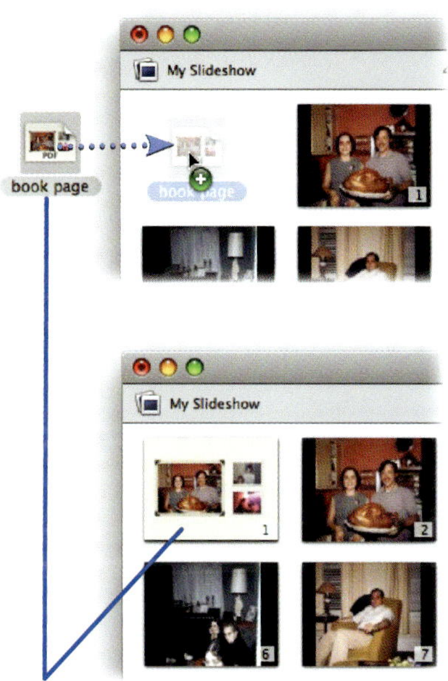

Now add that page to your slide show. Drag the PDF file from the Finder into the iDVD window.

Making Custom Motion Menus

You aren't limited to the motion menus that accompany iDVD. You can make any QuickTime movie a motion menu background: just drag the movie to the Background well in the Menu pane.

If your motion menu movie is smaller than full-screen, iDVD enlarges it to fit. For the best video quality, use a movie whose dimensions are 640 by 480 pixels or 720 by 480 pixels.

As for what to put in your own custom menu, that's up to you. If the star of your DVD is an iMovie production, you might use a two- or three-minute excerpt of your movie. Copy and paste a few clips from your movie into a new iMovie project. Then, use iMovie's Video Adjustments tools to increase the brightness and make the footage appear faint. That way, buttons and text labels will still be easy to read. Share the movie to the Media Browser, return to iDVD, and drag the movie from the Media pane to the Background well in the Menu Info window.

Smooth looping. A motion menu loops until a user chooses a menu option. To avoid a visually jarring loop point, try this: In iMovie, create a still frame of the very first frame of your menu movie. Add this still frame to the very end of the movie, and put a fairly lengthy (say, two-second) dissolve between the end of the movie and the still frame. Finally, trim the clip to make the remainder of the still frame as short as possible. (In the trimmer, drag its right edge to the left until it's right next to the dissolve in the timeline.) Now, when your movie loops, its last frame will appear to gradually dissolve into its first frame.

If you're after something more abstract, you can buy royalty-free libraries of animated backgrounds that you can use as motion menus. Two sources are ArtBeats (www.artbeats.com) and Digital Juice (www.digitaljuice.com). If you have Final Cut Pro or Final Cut Express, you can use its LiveType program to create rich animated textures.

A motion menu in iDVD can be up to 15 minutes long. But keep in mind that menu video uses disc space just like any other video clip.

Automating iDVD

iDVD provides thorough support for AppleScript, the automation technology that's built into Mac OS X. iDVD's AppleScript support enables you to create scripts that automate the creation and layout of DVDs.

In Mac OS X 10.5 (Leopard), you can use the Automator program to build *workflows* that put iDVD on autopilot. For example, you could create a workflow that prompts a user for a movie and some photos, then builds a DVD containing the results.

To learn more about Automator, visit www.automator.us.

Back to the Top

If you have a DVD containing several levels of submenus, you might want to offer your viewers a button that lets them get back to the uppermost, or title, menu. To do so, choose Project > Add Title Menu Button.

GarageBand: Music, Podcasts, and More

The Macintosh

iLife '08

GarageBand at a Glance

GarageBand turns your Mac into a musical instrument and a multitrack recording studio. Not a musician? The Magic GarageBand feature builds songs for you on a virtual bandstand. It's a great way to see and hear what GarageBand is about.

Feeling creative? Explore GarageBand's library of pre-recorded musical phrases, called *loops*. Assemble the loops you like into a tune. For extra credit, change the pitch of some loops by *transposing* them.

If you play the piano, plug a music keyboard into your Mac and go to town—GarageBand's *software instruments* enable your Mac to mimic instruments ranging from pianos to guitars to drums and beyond. Use loops to create a rhythm section, and then play along. Edit your performance to make it shine.

If you sing or play an instrument, connect a microphone, electric guitar, or other audio input to your Mac and hit the Record button. Create a three-part harmony by laying down vocal tracks one at a time. Or record multiple tracks at once.

As you compose, you may want to enhance certain tracks with *effects*. Refine your mix as you go. When you're finished, export to iTunes or burn a CD.

Here's how to become a one-Mac band.

The Loop Browser

To locate and audition loops, use the loop browser. Find loops by clicking buttons or typing search terms, such as *conga* (page 333). To hear a loop, click its name.

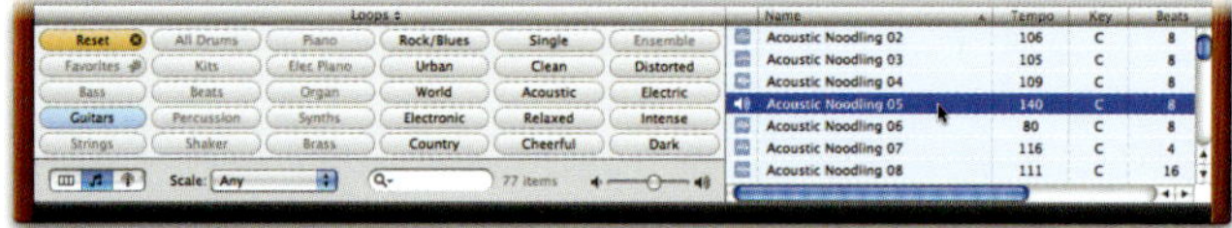

The Track Editor

Refine your performance using the track editor.

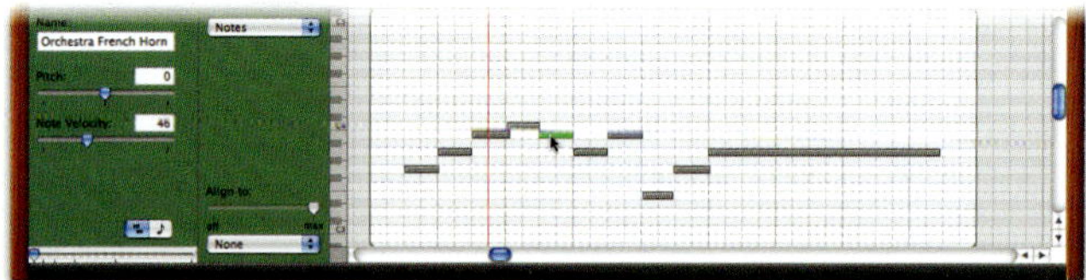

Editing notes. With the track editor for software instruments, you can edit individual notes, either in piano-roll format (above) or in standard music notation (below); see page 340.

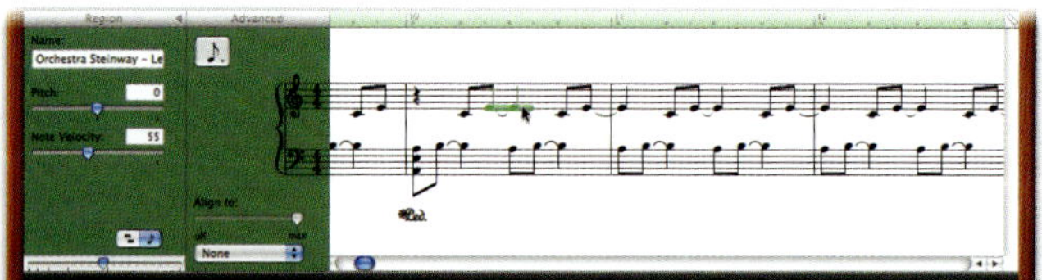

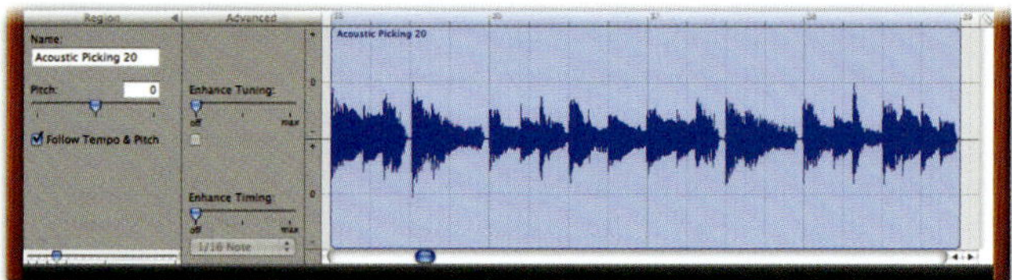

Editing audio. With the track editor for real instruments, you can modify recordings (page 347).

Each track is a member of your virtual ensemble. Each track has controls for muting, adjusting volume, and more.

Use the track mixer to adjust a track's overall volume and left-right stereo position (page 354).

Use the Arrange track to define different sections of a song (page 350).

The moving playhead shows the current playback location; drag the playhead to move around within a song.

The *beat ruler* shows beats and measures. To move the playhead to a specific spot, click the ruler.

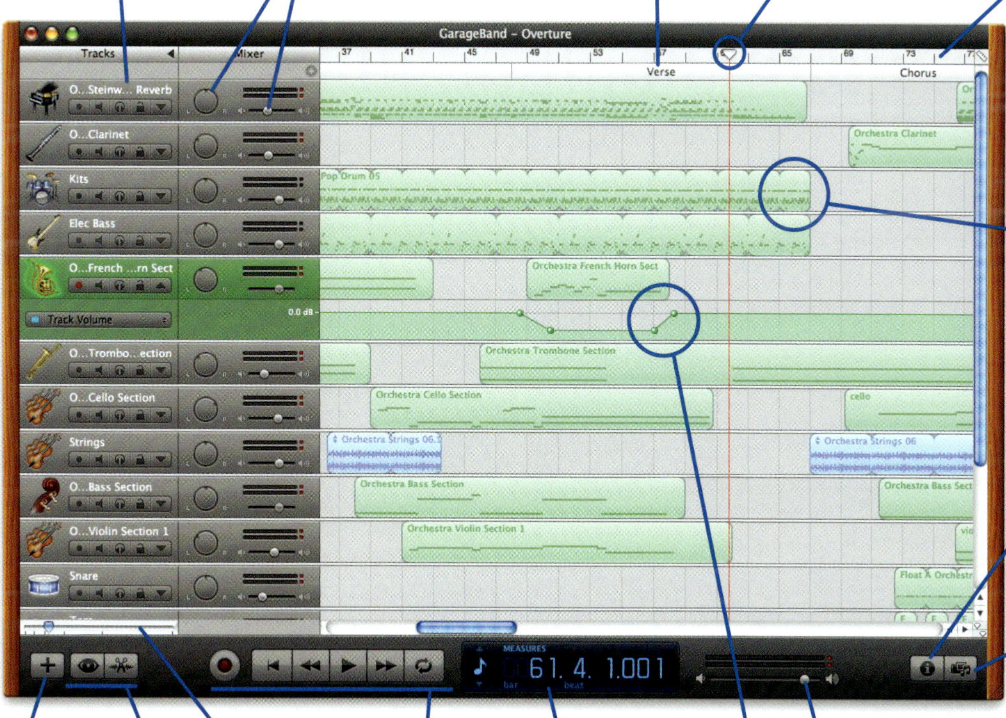

By repeating and modifying loops in the *timeline*, you can assemble everything from rhythm sections to entire arrangements (page 332).

Display the Track Info pane (pages 338 and 344).

Display the media browser, for accessing your other iLife media (pages 370 and 376).

Create a new track.

Display the loop browser and the track editor —essential tools for building and editing songs (opposite page).

Drag the zoom slider to zoom in and out on the timeline.

Transport controls: record, play, rewind, and cycle playback (page 335).

The LCD displays the position of the playhead and more (page 329).

Monitor and adjust the overall song volume.

To control volume and panning over time, create automation curves (page 354).

Podcasts, too. You can also use GarageBand to produce podcasts (see page 368).

How to Be a Songwriter

How you use GarageBand depends on your musical experience and your musical tastes. Here's a look at a few different paths you can take. And note that you aren't restricted to just one route—you might move from path to path as a song comes together.

Start a New Project

Specify the key, tempo, and time signature for your song. You can change any of these details later. You can even adjust tempo while your song is playing back.

Composing with Loops

Use the loop browser to locate a loop that sounds interesting (page 332).

Playing a Keyboard

Create a software instrument track and choose the desired software instrument (page 338).

If you like, customize the instrument to create a unique sound (pages 352 and 364).

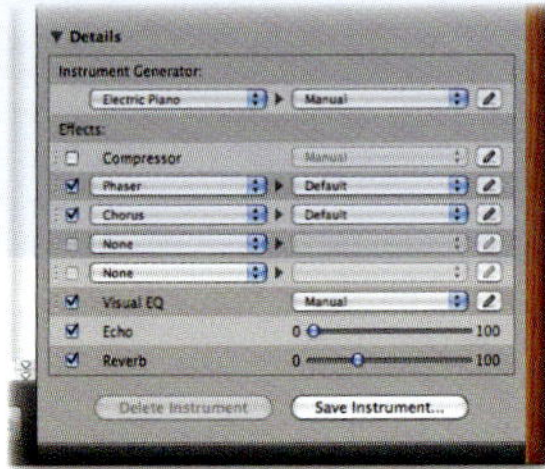

Recording Audio

Create a real instrument track and choose the desired effect settings (page 344).

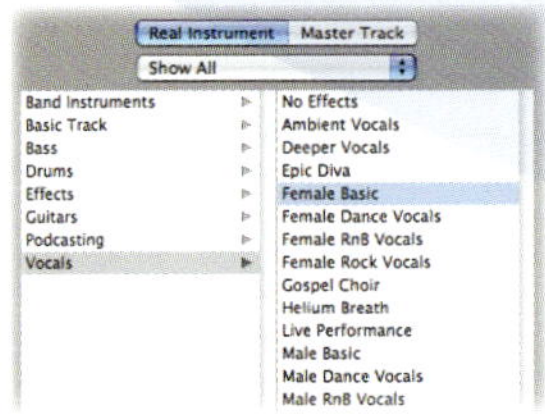

Adjust volume levels to get a loud, but not distorted, signal (page 344).

Use the Instrument tuner to get in tune (page 345).

Drag the loop into the timeline to add it to your song; drag the loop pointer to repeat the loop as desired (page 333).

Refine as desired: split and transpose regions (page 336), edit them (pages 340–343), and change the track's effects (page 352).

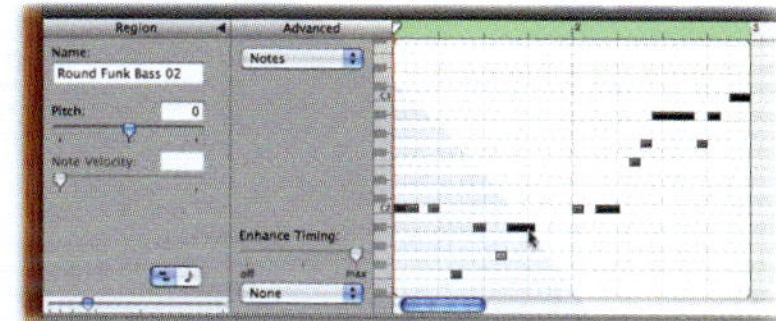

Record your performance, using GarageBand's Count In command and metronome to keep you in tempo (page 338).

Refine and arrange: modify and move regions (page 334), apply effects (page 352), and fix mistakes (pages 340–343).

Record your performance, laying down multiple takes if you like (page 344).

Edit your recording—rearrange it, change its effects, enhance its tuning or timing, or combine the best parts of several takes into a single track (page 347).

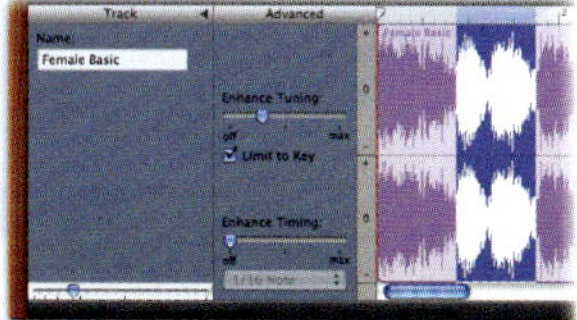

Mix

Adjust each track's volume levels and panning, optionally adding a set of final-mastering effects and a fade-out (page 356). When you're finished, export the song to your iTunes music library.

Instant Music: Magic GarageBand

If you aren't a musician—and even if you are—your first moments with GarageBand might be a bit intimidating. Software designers call it the "blank canvas syndrome" —you see GarageBand's empty window and wonder what your first steps should be.

If you're new to GarageBand, your first steps should be magic. Try out the Magic GarageBand feature: it lets you build a song in one of nine genres in just a couple of mouse clicks. Use a virtual bandstand to customize the instrumentation of your song, choosing between different guitar, bass, drum, and keyboard combinations. All told, there are over 3,000 combinations in each genre.

When you're done, GarageBand builds a song to your specifications. Play it back. Record your own solo or vocals. Practice along with it. Use parts of it in your own projects. Along the way, you'll learn how GarageBand works its magic. And you'll be hooked.

Using Magic GarageBand

Step 1. Choose File > New, and click the Magic GarageBand button.

The Magic GarageBand screen appears.

Step 2. Choose a genre by clicking its button.

Step 3 (optional). To preview the genre's song, click the Play button. The button to its left lets you preview a short snippet or the entire song.

Shortcut: You can preview any genre by simply double-clicking its button.

Step 4. Click the Audition button.

The bandstand appears, and it's where the fun happens. Move the mouse pointer over each instrument. When you do, a spotlight illuminates it.

Step 5. To change an instrument, click it, then choose a different instrument.

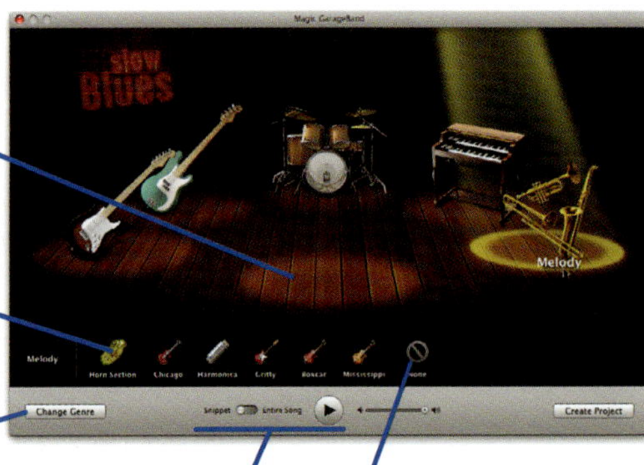

Your turn: If you'll want to solo or sing along, click here and choose an instrument.

Choose from several instruments for each band member.

Start over with a different genre.

Preview the song as you audition different band members.

You're off the gig: to remove a particular instrument from the band, click None.

Step 6. Work your way across the bandstand, choosing a different instrument for each player, if you like. Explore how different instrumentation creates a completely different sound.

Step 7. When you're done, click Create Project.

GarageBand creates a song containing the tracks of each part.

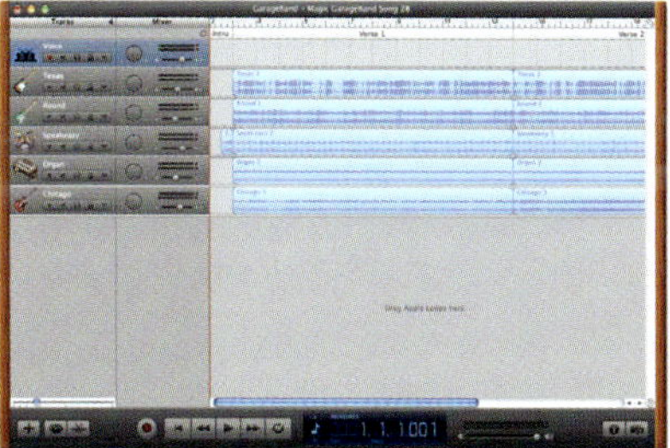

Now What?

Your GarageBand canvas is no longer blank. What next? Here are a few ideas.

Record a solo. If you set up the song to have your own part, your turn has arrived. Use the techniques on later pages to record your own performance.

Get acquainted. Experiment with each track's controls to get a feel for working in GarageBand. Adjust levels, and mute or solo some tracks (page 334). Pan instruments to change their position in the stereo mix (page 354). Change effects settings (page 352).

Rearrange. Magic GarageBand builds songs that have arrange regions (page 350). Try rearranging the song: click a region heading (for example, Verse 1), and drag it elsewhere in the song.

Change the tempo and key. This is a good time to get familiar with GarageBand's LCD (see the sidebar below). Choose the Project option, then choose a key. Speed up the tempo or slow it down.

Go beyond. Already know your way around GarageBand? Use Magic GarageBand to create building blocks for your own songs. Copy and paste regions from a Magic GarageBand project into your own. Build a song by creating several Magic GarageBand tunes, then copy the solos out of each one into another song. With this technique, you can combine some of the great solos that are part of each Magic GarageBand template—for example, copy a horn solo from one project and then paste it into another project, placing it after a guitar solo.

The regions in each Magic GarageBand template also make great Apple Loops. You can add them to your loop library using the steps on page 362.

Get to Know the LCD

GarageBand's LCD is a counter and control center. Use its pop-up menu to switch between functions.

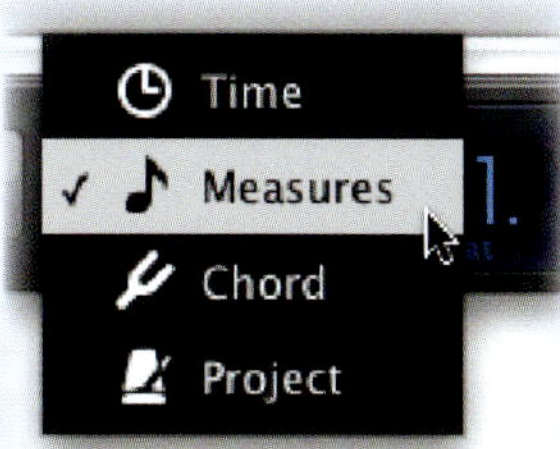

Time. Shows the playhead's position in absolute time (hours, minutes, seconds, and fractions thereof). Ideal for podcasting and movie scoring, where beats and measures are less important than minutes and seconds.

Measures. Shows the playhead's position in bars and beats. Ideal for music projects.

Chord/Tuner. See chords as you play them (page 358), or use the instrument tuner (page 345).

Project. View and change a song's key, tempo, and time signature.

You can change numeric values in the LCD by dragging across them or by double-clicking them, then typing. For example, to jump to measure 33, you can drag up or down on the bar readout, or double click it (its numerals flash) and then type *33* and press Return.

Two Types of Tracks

When you compose in GarageBand, you work with two very different types of tracks: *real instrument* tracks and *software instrument* tracks. The loops that GarageBand provides also fall into these two broad categories: loops with a blue icon are real instrument loops, and loops with a green icon are software instrument loops.

But what's the difference between a real instrument and a software instrument? The answer lies in the fact that today's Macs are powerful enough to generate sound using more than one technique. In fact, GarageBand is able to generate sound using multiple techniques *at once*.

Here's a look a how GarageBand makes its noise—and at what it all means to you.

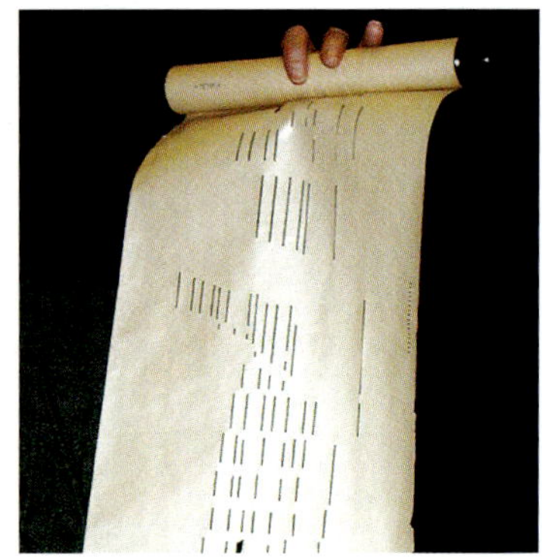
Photographic Historical Society of Canada

Real Instruments: Recorded Sound

A real instrument track holds a digital audio recording—a riff played by a bass player, some strumming on an acoustic guitar, a phrase played by a string section, or a vocal that you record.

A real instrument track is blue, and a real instrument loop has a blue icon. Notice that the track and the icon depict a waveform—a graphical picture of sound, similar to what we saw back on pages 44 and 268.

Variations. When you record an audio source, its regions are purple. If you import an audio file, its region is orange. See page 347 for all the colorful details.

Software Instruments: Sound on the Fly

A software instrument track doesn't hold actual sound. Instead, it holds only *data* that says what notes to play and how to play them. The sounds you hear when you play a software instrument track are being generated by your Mac as the song plays back.

A software instrument track is a bit like the music rolls that a player piano uses—just as the holes in the music roll tell the piano which notes to play, the bits of data in a software instrument track tell your Mac which notes to generate.

A software instrument track is green, and a software instrument loop has a green icon. Instead of depicting a waveform, a software instrument region shows individual notes—why, it even looks a bit like an antique player piano roll (see photo, left).

Comparing Approaches

Each type of track has advantages and capabilities that the other lacks.

The real advantage. When it comes to realism, you can't beat real instrument tracks. Listen to the Orchestra Strings loops that come with GarageBand. They don't just sound like a string section—they *are* a string section. Compare their sound to that of the software instrument loop named 70s Ballad Strings 02.

Another advantage of real instrument tracks is that they can hold *your* digital audio. When you plug a microphone into your Mac and belt out *My Way,* your voice is stored in a real instrument track.

The software advantage. The primary advantage of software instrument tracks is versatility. Because software instrument tracks store individual note data, you can edit them in almost any way imaginable. You can even change the instrument entirely. Want to hear how your bass line would sound when played by a synthesizer instead of an electric bass? Just double-click on the software instrument track's header and choose a synth.

On the down side, software instrument tracks make your Mac work harder than real instrument tracks—it's harder to generate sound on the fly than it is to play back a recording.

Common ground. Although real instruments and software instruments work differently, you can do many of the same things with both types of tracks. You can repeat loops within both types of tracks, and you can apply effects to both types. You can even transpose both types of tracks, including audio that you've recorded. However, you can't transpose audio regions across as wide a range as you can software instruments—they'd sound too artificial.

By supporting audio recordings (real instruments) and also being able to generate sound on the fly (software instruments), GarageBand gives you the best of both worlds.

How Apple Loops Work

The loops that come with GarageBand are stored in *Apple Loop* format. If you've played with GarageBand, you've experienced the program's ability to adjust the pitch and tempo of loops to fit your song. Here's how that works.

Apple Loops contain more than just sound. They also contain *tags*—tidbits of data—that describe the sound, starting with the key and the tempo in which the loop was originally recorded. The tags also contain information about the *transients* in the recording. A transient is a spike in volume—such as occurs when a drumstick slaps a drumhead. Transients denote where beats occur, and GarageBand uses this information when changing the playback tempo of an Apple Loop.

When GarageBand transposes an Apple Loop to a different key, it's performing a process called *pitch shifting.* When GarageBand changes a loop's tempo, it's *time stretching.*

Apple Loops also contain descriptive tags, such as *Guitar* and *Jazz.* These tags are what you use to sift through loops by clicking on the buttons in the loop browser.

The green loop difference. Finally, it's important to know that software instrument loops (the green ones) contain more than just "piano roll" note data. They also contain audio, just as real instrument loops do. This lets you use them in real instrument tracks—and thus lighten the load on your Mac; see pages 351 and 366.

Working with Loops

For many GarageBand musicians (including yours truly), a composing session often begins with some loops: a bass line, some percussion, a repeating synthesizer riff, or maybe all three.

The gateway to GarageBand's library of loops is the loop browser, whose buttons and search box let you quickly home in on loops of specific instruments or specific styles.

Once you find a loop that sounds interesting, you can add it to your song by dragging it into GarageBand's timeline. Once that's done, you can repeat the loop over and over, edit it, and transpose it.

GarageBand lets you audition loops even as your song is playing back—simply click on a loop in the loop browser. This is a great way to hear how a particular loop will fit into the arrangement you're building.

Working with loops is as easy as clicking and dragging. But as you master GarageBand, there's a powerful subtlety behind loops that you may want to take advantage of. Specifically, you can use software instrument loops in real instrument tracks in order to lighten the load on your Mac's processor.

If that makes no sense to you now, don't worry. When your arrangements become complex and you want to wring every bit of performance out of your Mac, you'll find all the details on pages 351 and 366.

Adding a Loop to a Song

To display the loop browser, click or use the ⌘-L keyboard shortcut. To add a loop to a song, drag the loop into the timeline.

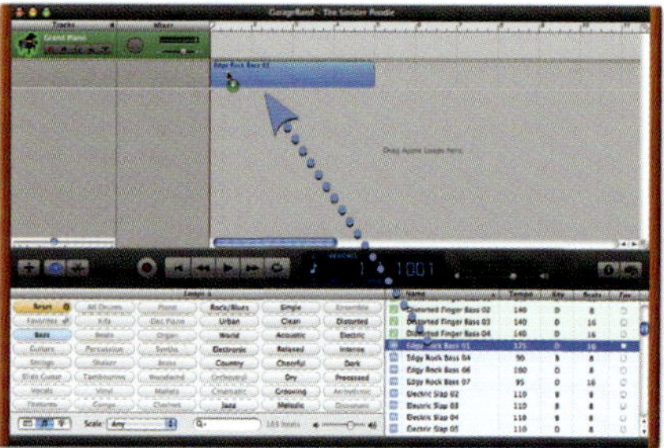

Creating a new track. When you drag a loop into an empty area of the timeline where there is no existing track, GarageBand creates a new track for the loop. The vertical bar indicates where the loop will begin playing. To move the loop after you've added it, drag it left or right (if the loop is too tiny to drag, zoom in).

Adding to an existing track. You can add a loop to an existing track. Mixing loops within a track is one way to add variety to a song.

Tip: You can drag a software instrument loop into a real instrument track, but not vice-versa. For more details, see page 351.

Variations. Many loops include several variations, and are named accordingly. To change to a different loop from the same family, click the tiny arrows in the upper-left corner of the loop, then choose a different loop.

Looping a Region

When you add a loop to a track, you create a *region* that you can modify without changing the original loop. The most common kind of modification you'll perform is to loop a region so that it plays repeatedly.

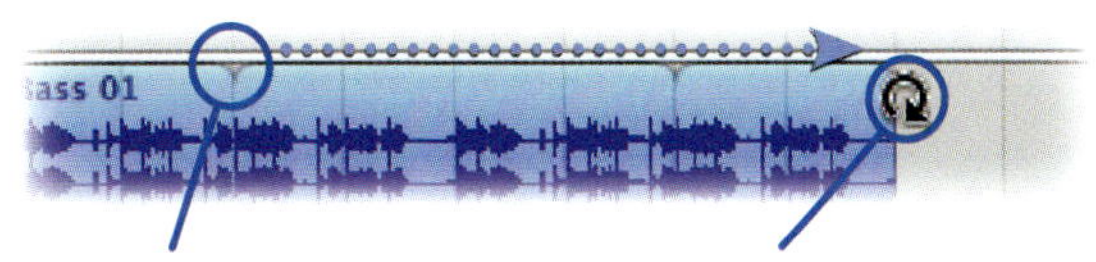

The notches show the beginning and end of each repetition of the loop.

To loop a region, point to its upper-right corner and drag it to the right.

Using the Loop Browser

Resets the loop browser, clearing any search text and deactivating any keyword buttons you've clicked.

Have lots of loops? Use the Loops pop-up menu to focus on specific collections (page 363).

To view more loop keywords, enlarge the loop browser by clicking here and dragging upward.

Tip: You can customize the loop browser buttons. To reorganize buttons, drag them around. To change a button's keyword, Control-click on the button and choose a keyword from the pop-up menu. To restore the original buttons, use the Preferences command.

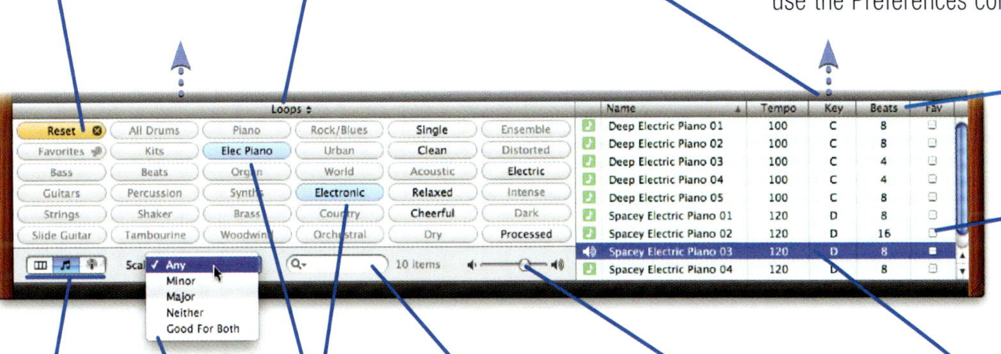

To sort the loop list, click any column heading.

Love that loop? Click the Fav check box to add it to your Favorites list. To display your favorites, click the Favorites button (it's under the Reset button).

Switch between column view, music loop view (shown here), and podcast sounds view (page 370).

Click the keyword buttons to home in on specific instruments or styles.

Many loops use major or minor scales. You can use this menu to filter the list of loops to only those that complement your song.

To search by keyword, type some text and press Return. You can search for instruments (for example, *piano* or *guitar*) or styles (*jazz*, *funk*).

If you're auditioning a particular loop and it's overwhelming the rest of your arrangement, use this slider to turn down the loop browser's volume.

To audition a loop, click it. To hear how the loop sounds with the rest of your song, begin playing the song before you click the loop.

Working with Tracks and Regions

Tracks can be a lot easier to work with than musicians. Tracks never show up late for a gig, they always play in tune, their sense of timing is impeccable, and they never trash the hotel room.

Nonetheless, there are some important points to know about working with tracks and the regions that they hold. (A *region* is a set of notes or a snippet of sound. When you drag a loop into the timeline or record a performance, you create a region.) For starters, when creating multitrack arrangements, you should rename tracks so you can tell at a glance which parts they hold: the melody, a solo, an alternate take of a solo.

As you compose, you may want to silence, or *mute*, certain tracks. Maybe you've recorded a few versions of some background strings, each on its own track, and you want to audition each one to hear which sounds best.

On the other hand, there may be times when you want to *solo* a track—to mute all the other tracks and hear only one track. Soloing a track can be useful when you're fine-tuning a track's effects settings or editing a region in the track.

A big part of creating an arrangement involves copying regions within a track or from one track to another. And as you move regions around, you often have to work with the beat ruler at the top of GarageBand's timeline. By fine-tuning the ruler's *snapping* feature, you can have your regions snap into place on exactly the right beat.

Here's how to get along with the members of the band.

Soloing, Muting, and More

The *track header* contains the track's name and controls.
Your turn: enable the track for recording (pages 338 and 344).
Lock up: prevent changes and help performance (page 366).
Detailed Drums
Quiet: mute the track. Keyboard shortcut: M.
Only you: solo the track. Keyboard shortcut: S.
Over time: create volume and pan curves (page 354). Keyboard shortcut: A.

Renaming a Track

Normally, GarageBand names a track after the instrument you've assigned to it. When you have multiple tracks that use the same instrument, it's hard to tell the tracks apart. Give your tracks descriptive names, such as *Third Verse Strings.* To rename a track, click its name in the track header, hold the pointer over the name for a moment, and, when the name is highlighted, type a new name.

Track Tips

You can move tracks up and down by dragging their headers. Consider grouping related tracks together—put all your rhythm section tracks together, then all your solo tracks, and so on.

When a track header is selected, you can use your keyboard's up- or down-arrow keys to select the track above or below the current track. This shortcut teams up nicely with those described above.

Play It Again: Cycling

When you're rehearsing, mixing, or recording, it's often useful to have part of a song play over and over. To do this, click the Cycle button and then drag in the area just below the beat ruler to indicate the region that you want to repeat.

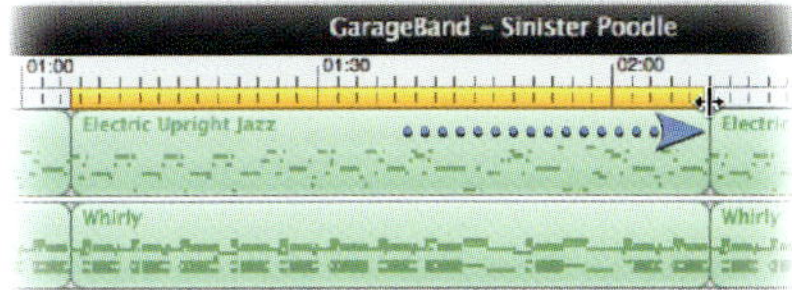

The yellow region repeats until time comes to an end or your parents pull the plug, whichever comes first. To resize the region, drag its left or right edge. To move the region, drag it left or right.

When cycling is on, playback always begins at the start of the cycle region.

Turning cycling on is also the first step to using GarageBand's multiple-take recording feature (page 348).

Duplicating a Track

You can make a duplicate of a track: a new, blank track with the same instrument and effect settings as the original. Select the track's header, then choose Duplicate from the Track menu (⌘-D).

Duplicating a track is another way to record multiple takes of a part: record each take in its own track, then copy and paste the best parts into a single track.

Copying Regions

Copying a region is a common task, and GarageBand provides a couple of ways to accomplish it. You can copy and paste: select a region, choose Copy, move the playhead to the destination, and paste. You can also press the Option key while dragging the region you want to copy.

Note: If you want to copy a region to a different track, the tracks must be of the same type. You can't copy a software instrument region to a real instrument track, or vice-versa.

Zooming tip: When you're moving regions over a large distance, use GarageBand's zoom slider to zoom out for a big-picture view. And use the keyboard shortcuts: Control-left arrow zooms out, while Control-right arrow zooms in.

Copying Versus Looping

You can repeat a region by either looping it or copying it. So which technique should you use? Looping is the fastest way to repeat a region over and over again: just drag the loop pointer as described on page 333.

The advantage of copying a region is that each copy becomes an independent region that you can edit without affecting other copies. With a repeating loop, if you edit one note in the loop, that edit is present in each repetition.

Snap to the Beat

When moving a region, you almost always want to move it to the exact beginning of a particular measure or beat. GarageBand's *timeline grid* supplies this precision: when the grid's snapping feature is active, GarageBand automatically snaps to beats and measures as you drag regions, move the playhead, drag loops to the timeline, and perform other tasks.

Normally, GarageBand adjusts the sensitivity of its grid to match the way you're viewing your song. If you're zoomed all the way out, GarageBand assumes you're performing fairly coarse adjustments, such as dragging a region from one part of a song to another. In this case, GarageBand's grid will snap to the start of each measure.

If you're zoomed all the way in, GarageBand figures you must be making precise adjustments, so it adjusts its grid to snap in sixty-fourth-note increments.

You can override GarageBand's automatic grid sensitivity: just choose the desired value from the grid menu.

Click the timeline grid button (▧) to display the grid menu.

The "swing" options delay every other grid point. This lets you maintain a swing feel when dragging regions. The amount of delay is greater with the "Heavy" options.

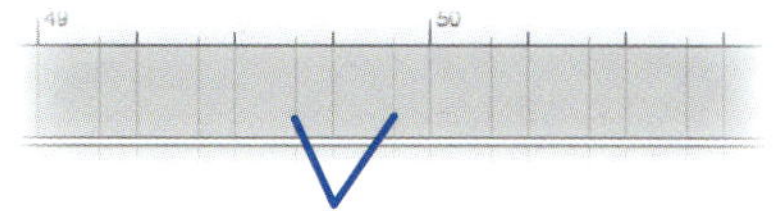

Every other grid point is delayed slightly.

Transposing and Creating Chord Changes

Unless they're from the soundtrack of *Wayne's World*, most songs aren't built around just one chord. Most songs contain chord *changes* or *progressions*—variations in key that add harmonic interest. Chord changes can be simple, such as those of a 12-bar blues, or they can be complex, such as those of Billy Strayhorn's jazz classic, *Lush Life*.

You can build chord changes in a couple of ways. For fast results, use the master track to create a *pitch curve* that transposes every track in your song (with two exceptions, noted at right).

When you want more control, transpose individual regions as described on the opposite page. This approach lets you be selective about what you transpose. For example, you can transpose some piano or guitar chords while keeping your bass track at the root key of your song. You can also edit individual regions to better fit your song's chord changes.

Transposing with the Master Track

Creating a pitch curve in the master track is the fastest way to "program" chord changes.

Step 1. Choose Show Master Track from the Track menu (⌘-B).

Step 2. In the master track header, choose Master Pitch from the pop-up menu.

Step 3. In the timeline, click at the point where you want to create a chord change—for example, at the beginning of a measure.

Step 4. Drag the control point up or down to transpose in increments of one *semitone* (one half-step). For example, to program the first chord change in a blues, drag up five semitones.

Notes and Tips

Audio limitations. A pitch curve will *not* transpose any audio regions that you recorded (purple regions) or imported (orange ones). To transpose purple regions, see the opposite page. To transpose orange regions, convert them into purple ones first; see page 347.

Changing a change. To remove a control point, select it and press the Delete key. To change its pitch, drag the control point up or down. To change the point when the chord change occurs, drag the control point left or right.

Adjusting precision. The point in time when GarageBand places control points is determined by the current timeline grid setting (see the previous page). If you want more precision in placing or adjusting a control point's position in time, zoom in or choose a smaller note value from the timeline grid button.

Unlock first. If you've locked any tracks (page 334), you can't adjust the pitch curve. If you try, GarageBand displays a dialog box that lets you unlock all locked tracks.

Transposing Individual Regions

This method is more work than creating a pitch curve, but as I noted on the opposite page, it offers more options and creative control.

The fastest way to use this technique is to repeat a loop for the entire duration of a verse (for example, 12 measures), split the loop at each point where you need a chord change, and then transpose the appropriate regions. This is a quick way to lay down a bass track.

If you'd like to follow along with the steps below, create a new song in GarageBand and add the loop named Woody Latin Bass 01 to it.

Step 1. Drag a loop into the timeline and use the loop pointer to drag it out to the desired length.

Step 2. Split the loop at the start of the change.

Drag the playhead to the beginning of the measure that needs to be transposed, then choose Edit > Split (⌘-T).

Step 3. Split the loop at the end of the change.

Drag the playhead to the *end* of the measure that needs transposing, and choose Split again. You now have an independent region that you can transpose.

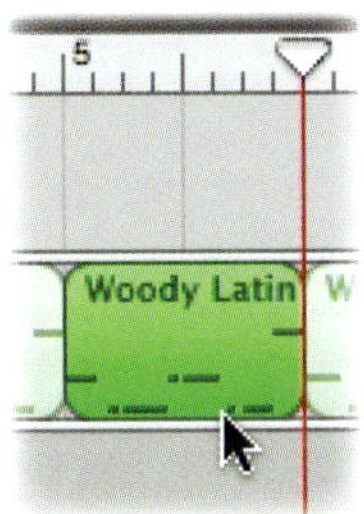

Step 4. Prepare to transpose.

Select the region you just created and open the track editor by clicking the track editor button (▦). Shortcut: Double-click the region to open it in the track editor.

Step 5. In the track editor, drag the Pitch slider or type a value in the box.

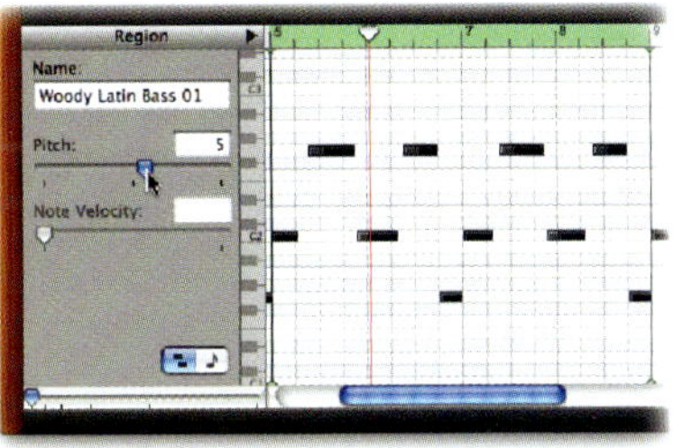

You can transpose in one-semitone increments. In the timeline, GarageBand indicates how far you've transposed a region.

Notes and Tips

Editing a region to fit the changes. Building a bass line from software instrument loops? You can build a better bass line by editing regions so that they complement your chord changes. For example, if you're going from F to C, you might make the last note of the F measure a C# or a B. That way, the bass will "lead in" to the new chord change. Edits like these can also take some of the repetitiveness out of tracks built from loops.

First, double-click the region you want to edit. Then, in the track editor, drag the last note of the region up or down to the desired note. GarageBand plays the note as you drag it, making it easy to determine where the note should be.

For details on editing software instrument tracks, see pages 340–343.

Transposing real instrument regions. You can also transpose regions in real instrument tracks, but within a narrower range: one octave in either direction, as opposed to three octaves for software instrument tracks. And although you can't change individual notes as you can with software instrument tracks, you *can* perform some edits to regions in real instrument tracks; see page 347.

Recording Software Instruments

When you connect a music keyboard to your Mac, you unlock a symphony's worth of software instruments that you can play and record. There are pianos and keyboards and guitars of all kinds. There are synthesizers, strings, a flute, and some horns. And there are some drums you just can't beat.

As the following pages describe, you can edit your recordings and use effects to refine your tracks. You can even create completely new instruments of your own design.

If you don't have a music keyboard and don't want to spend a fortune on one, check out the offerings from M-Audio (www.m-audio.com). Its Keystation 61es is a 61-key (five octave) keyboard that sells for under $200. Its "semi-weighted" action gives it a piano-like feel, and its keyboard is *velocity sensitive:* it measures how hard each key is pressed. Most of GarageBand's software instruments respond to this velocity information, changing their loudness and other characteristics to allow you to play (and record) with expression.

You can also use a costlier keyboard that requires a separate MIDI interface. (MIDI stands for *Musical Instrument Digital Interface*, and is a standard for interconnecting electronic instruments and computers. Think of it as USB with a music degree.) Pricier keyboards often provide *weighted action*—their keys respond like a piano's instead of like an organ's, and thus feel more natural to experienced pianists. You'll also find more keys—up to 88 of them.

Recording a Software Instrument

Step 1. Create a new track. Click the New Track button (+) or choose New Track from the Track menu (Option-⌘-N).

Step 2. In the New Track dialog box, click Software Instrument, then click OK or press Return.

Step 3. Select a category, and then select an instrument.

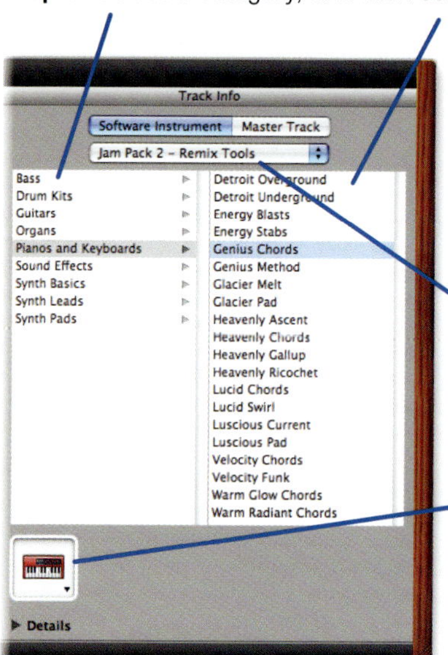

Tip: You can use the up- and down-arrow keys to move from one instrument to the next.

You can use the pop-up menu to choose from a specific instrument collection (see page 363).

Optional: choose an icon to appear in the track header.

Tip: You can try out the selected instrument by playing keys on your music keyboard or by clicking the on-screen keys in GarageBand's Keyboard or Musical Typing windows (see page 359).

Step 4. Get ready. Position the playhead a few measures before where you want to begin recording. To give yourself time to get ready, choose Count In from the Control menu.

Step 5. Hit it. Click the Record button (●) or press the R key. To stop recording, press the spacebar or click the Play button (▶).

Notes and Tips

Watch your playing. As you record, GarageBand displays the new region (and its notes, in piano-roll style) in the timeline. Display the track editor for the current track, and your performance appears as you play—even in music notation.

Recording in an existing track. The instructions at left assume you're starting a brand-new track. You can, of course, also record in an existing software instrument track. Just select the track's header to enable it for recording. To change the track's instrument—before or after you record—double-click the track header to display the Track Info pane.

Multitrack recording. You can record one software instrument track and some real instrument tracks at the same time: record a vocal while you play, or record a couple of acoustic instrumentalists. For details, see page 346.

Multiple-take recording. By turning cycling on, you can record take after take, and then choose the best one; see page 348.

Anatomy of a Music Keyboard

Like many keyboards, M-Audio's Keystation 61es contains no sound-generating circuitry. When you play, the keyboard transmits MIDI data that describes which keys you pressed, how hard, and for how long. Keyboards that lack sound-generating circuitry are often called *controllers*.

Most keyboards can accept an optional foot pedal that plugs into the back of the keyboard and acts like a piano's sustain pedal. If you frequently play piano software instruments, you'll want a pedal. Some keyboards also accept a volume pedal that many software instruments respond to, giving you more expressive options.

On the Keystation 61es, the volume slider controls the volume of the currently selected software instrument track.

All music keyboards provide two controls that allow for more creative expression when you play.

A *pitch bend wheel* lets you do something no acoustic piano permits: bend notes the way guitar players do. The pitch bend wheel pairs up well with guitar and synthesizer instruments.

A *modulation wheel,* or *mod wheel*, lets you vary the sound of an instrument, usually by adding a vibrato-type effect. In Apple's Symphony Orchestra Jam Pack, the mod wheel also lets you obtain different articulations (see page 362).

Adjust Your Sensitivity

If your keyboard seems overly sensitive—even a relatively light touch triggers a software instrument's louder sounds—use the Audio/MIDI portion of the Preferences dialog box to turn down the sensitivity. Conversely, if you have to really pound to get louder sounds, increase the sensitivity.

Keyboard Sensitivity:
Less
Neutral
More

Editing Software Instrument Regions

Editing Software Instrument Regions

We've already encountered one form of software instrument region editing: transposition (page 337). That's just the beginning. There's almost no end to the ways you can edit MIDI data, and unlike when you're onstage, you can always undo any disasters.

You can edit regions you record or regions that you create by dragging loops from the loop browser. And you can edit in either of two views: the piano roll-style *graphic* view or music-notation view. In either view, you can change notes, modify their duration, change their velocity values, draw new notes, and more. And in notation view, you can print a track's music.

To switch views, click the button in the lower-left corner of the track editor.

Selecting Multiple Notes

You often need to select multiple notes—for example, prior to duplicating them or adjusting their velocity. To select more than one note, Shift-click on the notes or drag a selection rectangle around them.

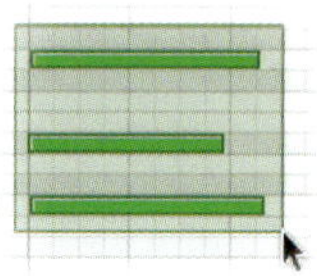

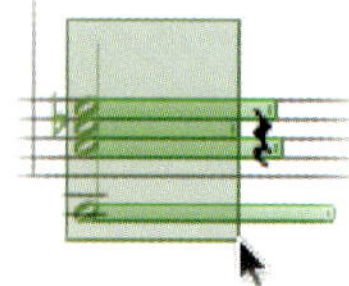

Editing in Graphic View

Editing is easy in the graphic view's piano-roll display.

Fixing wrong notes. To fix a wrong note, drag it up or down until it becomes the right note. If the note is very high or low, scroll the track editor or make it taller by dragging the area to the left of the Record button.

If you fumbled and accidentally hit two keys when you meant to hit just one, delete the extra wrong note: select it and press the Delete key.

Moving a note in time. To move a note backward or forward, drag it left or right. To zoom in for more precision, drag the track editor's zoom slider to the right. You may also want to adjust the track editor's grid sensitivity by using its grid ruler button. Or turn the grid off entirely (⌘-G).

Changing a note's duration. To make a note longer or shorter, drag its right edge to the right or to the left.

Drawing a new note. To draw a new note, press ⌘ and then drag within the track, using the little vertical piano key legend (and your ears) as guides.

Notes and Tips

Improving expression. By editing the velocity values of some notes, you can improve expression and realism. This is especially true for software instruments, such as Classical Acoustic, that change dramatically depending on how hard you play a note.

To edit a note's velocity, select it and then specify the desired velocity in the Note Velocity box. To change the velocity of a range of notes, select the notes first.

Velocity values can range from 1 (quiet as a hoarse mouse) to 127 (way loud). To give you a visual hint at a note's velocity, GarageBand uses shading:

Soft — Loud

Under 32 | 33 to 63 | 64 to 95 | 96 to 127 (maximum)

Chords in a hurry. You can create chords by duplicating notes: press the Option key, click on a note, and then drag up or down by the desired note interval. This also works on a range of notes: select the notes, then Option-drag them.

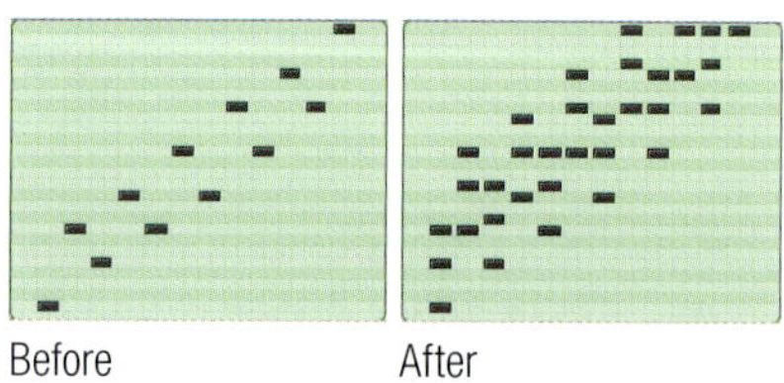

Before — After

Tip: Want to create a cinematic string section? Record a series of single notes, then duplicate them and drag the duplicate up seven semitones (a musical fifth). For some heavy metal action, try this with the Big Electric Lead guitar instrument. Just warn me first.

Editing in Notation View

Read music? Want to learn? Notation view is for you. It's also an ideal place to draw new notes and edit or create sustain-pedal information.

The techniques on the opposite page also apply to notation view, with the following differences.

Adjusting grid precision. When working in notation view, you'll want to use the grid ruler pop-up menu in the track editor to specify the degree of precision you want. For example, to move a note in quarter-note increments, choose 1/4 note. If you choose a small grid increment, you may see a lot of strange and small note or rest values, such as sixty-fourth notes.

Using the arrow keys. You can move notes by selecting them and pressing the arrow keys on your keyboard. To move selected notes back or forward one full measure, press Shift-left arrow or Shift-right arrow. Similarly, to transpose notes up or down one octave, press Shift-up arrow or Shift-down arrow. You can also drag notes with the mouse.

Changing a note's duration. To change a note's duration, select the note, then drag the green duration bar left or right. The duration bar works exactly like the piano roll-style notes in graphic view: drag to the left to shorten the note, and drag to the right to lengthen it.

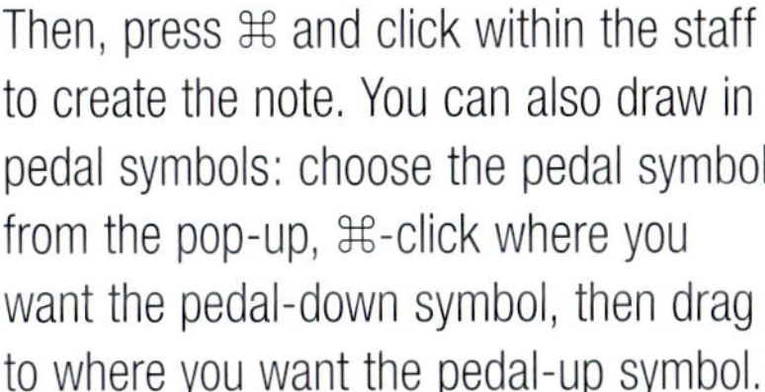

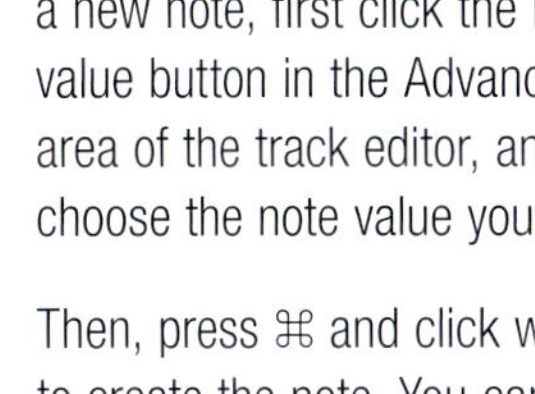

Drawing new notes. To draw a new note, first click the note value button in the Advanced area of the track editor, and choose the note value you want.

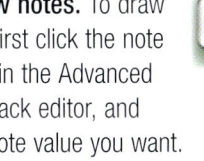

Then, press ⌘ and click within the staff to create the note. You can also draw in pedal symbols: choose the pedal symbol from the pop-up, ⌘-click where you want the pedal-down symbol, then drag to where you want the pedal-up symbol.

Enlarging the notes. To make the notation view larger, make the track editor taller: drag the area to the left of the Record button upwards. Similarly, to increase the horizontal spacing between notes, drag the track editor's zoom slider.

Notation Notes

Choosing a clef. Normally, notation view displays both the bass and the treble clef. That makes sense for instruments with a broad note range, such as piano. But for instruments with a narrower range—such as bass or piccolo—you may not need to see both clefs.

To make a choice appropriate to the instrument, click the clef at the left edge of the notation display, then choose the clef you want.

Here's a bass line as it should appear.

Printing music. You can print a track's contents as sheet music. Select the track's header, then be sure that the note grid is displayed at a setting that makes sense for hard copy. If you have it set for a very fine, sixty-fourth-note resolution, for example, you'll have strange-looking notation with lots of short-duration notes. To adjust the resolution, use the grid ruler pop-up menu in the track editor.

To control how many measures appear in each row of music, drag the zoom slider in the lower-left corner of the track editor. Generally, you'll want to drag the slider to the left and zoom out.

To print the music, choose File > Print. To preview the sheet music first, click Preview in the Print dialog box. GarageBand adds little niceties to your hard copy: the song name at the top of the page, the tempo, instrument name, and your name (as it's stored in the My Info portion of the Preferences dialog box).

More Region Editing Techniques

More Controller Editing Options

Modulation and sustain are just two forms of MIDI controller data that you can edit. Here's a look at more controller editing options.

Pitch bend. A music keyboard generates pitch bend data when you move its pitch bend wheel. You can edit this data or draw your own.

Expression. True to its name, expression data lets you increase or decrease the loudness of a region. You might draw in expression data to create a crescendo or decrescendo. Try recording a chord with a horn section instrument, then adding an expression curve to it.

With Apple's Symphony Orchestra Jam Pack, moving the pitch bend wheel generates expression data.

Tip: If you have a volume (expression) pedal connected to your music keyboard, you can have GarageBand respond to and record the data it transmits. Be sure your keyboard is transmitting the pedal's data as expression data (MIDI controller #11), not volume data (MIDI controller #7).

Foot control. Apple's Symphony Orchestra Jam Pack uses foot control data to control articulation for some of the orchestral instruments, such as strings.

Doubling a Track

You can create a duet by duplicating a region in a different track. Create another track of the same type (software instrument or real instrument), then Option-drag the region into that track. (You can also copy and paste.) To start with the same instrument and effect settings, duplicate a track: select it and press ⌘-D.

Next, refine your duet. If it's a software instrument track, experiment with different instruments. You might also transpose one of the tracks to create a harmony or put each part an octave apart. You might also experiment with different effects, panning, and volume settings.

Tip: One way to add richness to a duet is by very slightly offsetting the second track's region. Turn grid snapping off (⌘-G), zoom in on the region, then nudge it ever so slightly to the left or right. This way, the regions won't play back at exactly the same time, strengthening the illusion of multiple musicians.

Importing MIDI Files

GarageBand can also import files created in standard MIDI format. Most sequencers can create MIDI files, and thousands of them are available on the Internet. (Jazz lovers: check out www.thejazzpage.de. Classical buffs: go to www.classicalarchives.com, especially if you have Apple's Symphony Orchestra Jam Pack. Downloading a MIDI file usually involves Control-clicking on it and choosing Download Linked File from the shortcut menu.)

A standard MIDI file's name ends with *.mid*. To import the file into GarageBand, simply drag it into the timeline. GarageBand reads the file, creates tracks, and assigns instruments to them.

You may have to fine-tune the results of an importing session. I often have to transpose the bass track up by one octave and reassign software instruments.

Still, importing a MIDI file is a great way to move a song created in a different sequencer into GarageBand. It's also a fun way to practice and create songs: download a MIDI file, drag it into GarageBand, then remix it, change its tempo, or play along.

Fixing Timing Problems

You can have GarageBand *quantize* a region—move its notes so that they fall exactly on the beats in the beat ruler.

Before quantizing a region, choose a note value from the Enhance Timing pop-up menu in the Advanced area of the track editor. If you're quantizing a walking bass line in 4/4 time, try the quarter-note (1/4 Note) setting. If you're quantizing a more nuanced performance, use a higher resolution. For jazz or other syncopated styles, try one of the swing settings.

With all settings, you can "dial down" the quantization by dragging the Enhance Timing slider to the left. Experiment with different settings. If the results sound strange, try again or choose Undo.

You can also quantize individual notes within a region: select the notes, then perform the above steps.

Quantizing can be a mixed bag; it works well with extremely mechanistic music styles (such as dance and even some classical), but expect disappointing results when quantizing a jazz piano solo or any musical form that plays somewhat fast and loose with beats. Experiment. If you don't like the results, choose None from the pop-up menu to turn quantizing off.

Tip: You can also quantize a track as you record it. Select a track but don't select any notes or regions in the track. Choose a note value from the pop-up menu to have GarageBand quantize to that value as you record. This is handy for drum parts.

Editing Controller Information

Not all MIDI data deals with notes. A keyboard's pitch and modulation wheels also generate data, as does a sustain pedal. You can edit and create this *controller data* in the track editor's graphic view.

Editing controller data involves working with *control points* similar to those of pitch, volume, and panning curves. By adjusting this data, you can change the expressiveness applied by a pitch or mod wheel, adjust your pedal work, and more.

Say you have a software instrument whose sound timbre "sweeps" when you move the modulation wheel (examples include Star Sweeper, Aquatic Sunbeam, Cloud Break, and Falling Star). If you want that sweep to change over a specific number of measures, create a *modulation curve*.

To create controller data from scratch, choose the controller type from the pop-up menu in the Advanced area of the track editor. ⌘-click to create control points, then drag them as needed.

You'll find an example of this on my Web site, at www.macilife.com/gbandexamples.zip. Expand the archive by double-clicking it, then open the folder. Check out the GarageBand project named Modulate Me. It contains two regions, each playing the identical note. But in the second region, I drew a modulation curve to create a precisely timed sweep.

As for editing sustain data, you can clean up sloppy pedal work by fine-tuning the position of the control points that represent each pedal push: just drag the control points left or right.

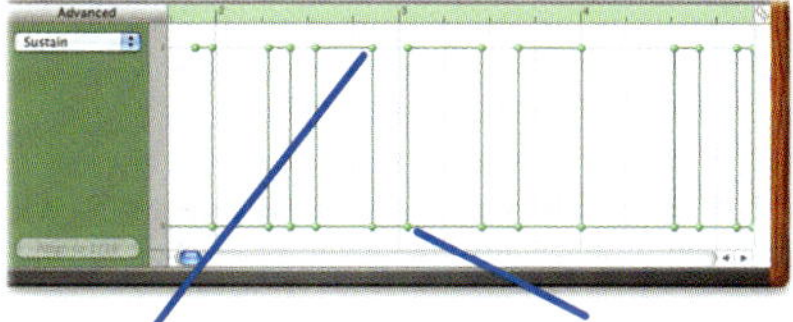

Pedal is pressed (sustain is on).

Pedal isn't pressed (sustain is off).

And if you don't have a sustain pedal, you can draw your own sustain data. Check out the project named Add Sustain in the aforementioned examples folder. I recorded the first region without using my sustain pedal. Then I duplicated the region and added sustain data to the duplicate.

Press the pedal: ⌘-click to create a control point.

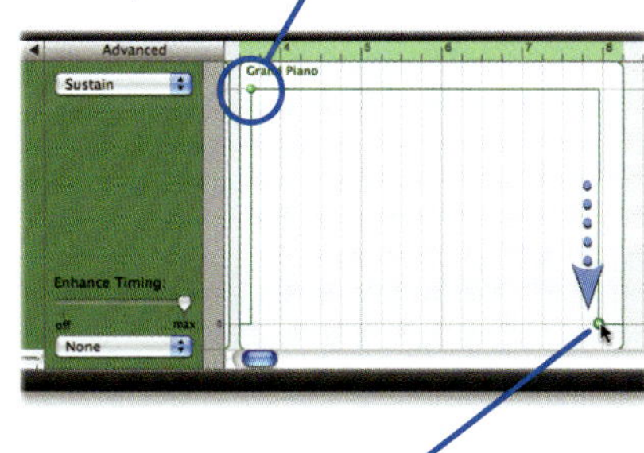

Release: ⌘-click where you want the pedal release, then drag down to the bottom of the grid. Drag control points left and right as needed to fine-tune timing.

I wouldn't want to draw in sustain data for a Billy Joel ballad, but for the occasional sustained arpeggio, it works.

Recording an Audio Source

If you sing or play an instrument—sax, guitar, kazoo—GarageBand provides yet another dimension to explore. Connect a microphone or other sound source to your Mac, and you can record a performance in a real instrument track.

Most mikes and guitars don't produce a loud-enough signal for the Mac, which works best with a *line-level* signal like that of a cassette deck, for example. No problem—products aplenty await your wallet. M-Audio, MOTU, and others sell first-rate audio interfaces for the Mac. Guitar players on a budget (and aren't they all?) might consider SoundTech's LightSnake, a cable that connects between a guitar or bass and the Mac's USB port.

GarageBand lets you apply effects to audio that you record. You can even have GarageBand simulate the sound of a vintage guitar amplifier. But your audio is always recorded and saved with no effects—unprocessed, or *dry*. GarageBand applies its effects as your music plays back, so you can experiment with effects settings.

Before recording a real instrument track, be sure your audio hardware is properly configured. You may need to visit the Sound system preference and GarageBand's Preferences dialog box to ensure that the audio input is set to the hardware you plan to use. And be sure you have plenty of free disk space before you start—your recording will use 10MB per minute for a stereo track.

Recording to a New Track

Step 1. Create a new track. Click the New Track button (+) or choose New Track from the Track menu (Option-⌘-N).

Step 2. Click the Real Instrument Track button and click Create or press Return.

Step 3. Choose an instrument.

When you select an instrument, you're choosing a set of effects that GarageBand will apply when playing back the track. You can change this setting later if you like: double-click the track header and choose a different setting in the Track Info pane.

Select a category, then select an instrument within the category.

Don't want to apply any effects to the track? Select No Effects.

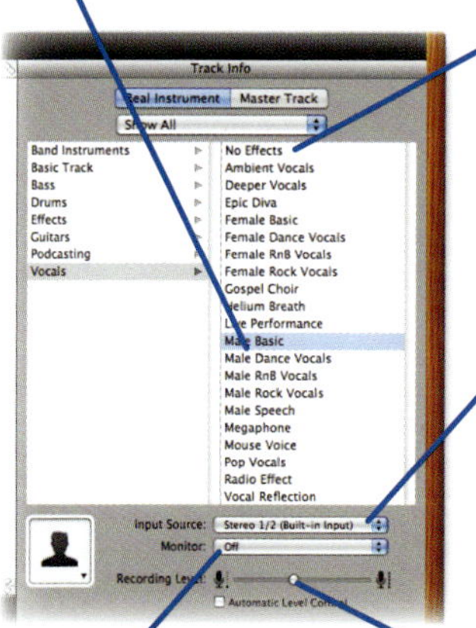

If you've connected a stereo microphone or device, choose Stereo 1/2. Otherwise, choose the channel that your sound source is connected to (see page 346).

When monitoring is on, you can hear your instrument or microphone. This can be great with a guitar or bass, but with a mike, you're likely to get loud feedback when monitoring is on. This is why monitoring is turned off by default. If you're using a mike, you might want to plug headphones into your Mac when monitoring.

To adjust recording levels, use the Volume slider. To have your Mac adjust levels for you, click Automatic Level Control.

Tip: To quickly create a real instrument track with no effects, choose Track > New Basic Track.

Explore some audio-interface options.
www.macilife.com/garageband

Step 4. Adjust recording levels.

Sing or play some notes, and watch the level meters in the track's header. If the clipping indicators light (see below), ugly distortion looms. Lower the volume of your input source—for example, lower the Volume slider in the Track Info pane, or, if you're using a mixer or audio interface, adjust its volume controls.

Step 5. Get ready.

Move the playhead a few measures before where you want to start recording, or use the Count In command in the Control menu to give yourself time to get ready.

Step 6. Press Record (●) and make us proud.

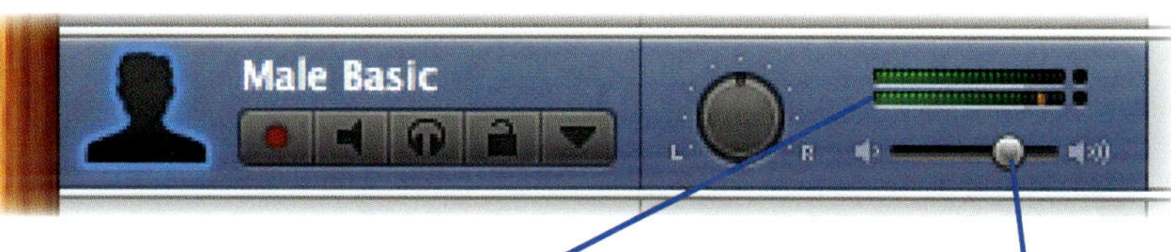

The meters should illuminate fully during loud passages, but the two clipping indicators (the tiny circles) shouldn't light up. If they do, lower the input volume as described above.

Tip: When the clipping indicators light, they stay lit until you click them. This is GarageBand's way of telling you that clipping occurred while your eyes were closed as you belted out *My Way*.

When you're setting levels, this *isn't* the volume control to use. This slider adjusts the track's playback volume, not its recording input level. See for yourself: turn down the track volume while singing or playing, and you'll see that the meters still move. Here's the rule: To adjust *playback* volume, use the track mixer. To adjust *record* volume (technically, input gain), follow the instructions in Step 4, above.

Get In Tune with the Instrument Tuner

Is your axe in tune? GarageBand can help. Its instrument tuner listens to the audio coming into a real instrument track and displays its note value.

This works with single notes only, not with chords. However, the LCD can display chords that you play using a software instrument; see page 358.

To use the instrument tuner, select the track for the instrument you want to tune and make sure that its Record button is enabled. Then, click the icon on the left side of the LCD and choose Tuner, or choose Control > Show Instrument Tuner (⌘-F).

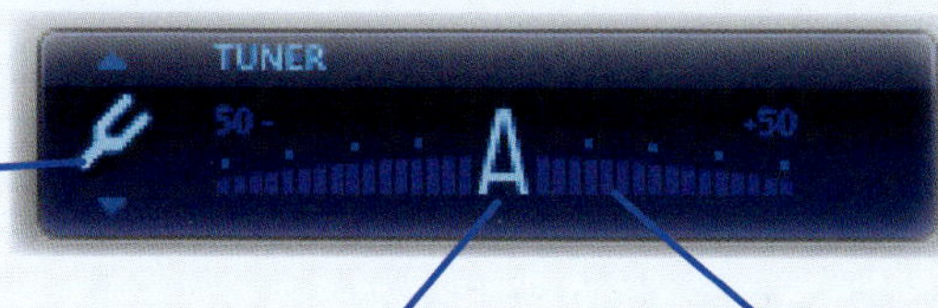

The tuner displays the note you're playing.

If the note is flat, the indicator moves to the left of center. If the note is sharp, the indicator moves to the right. When you're in tune, the indicator is centered, as shown here.

More Audio Techniques

Multitrack Recording

GarageBand is a great tool for musicians who labor alone. But what if you want to record a couple of musicians simultaneously and put each performer on a different track? Or what if you'd like to record yourself singing a vocal while strumming a guitar or playing a MIDI keyboard?

If your Mac has a basic stereo input, you can record two real instrument tracks simultaneously, *plus* one software instrument track: two singers and some GarageBand piano, for example. Connect multichannel audio hardware, and you can record up to eight real instrument tracks and one software instrument track: a real garage band.

Here's how to record two simultaneous audio tracks using your Mac's built-in audio input or a basic adaptor, such as Griffin's iMic. These basic steps apply to more ambitious multitracking tasks, too.

Get jacked up. Your Mac's built-in audio input can accommodate two signals: left channel and right channel. When multitrack recording, forget left and right: you're using one channel for one audio source (say, a mike), and the other channel for another source (for example, an electric guitar).

Use a splitter cable or Y-adaptor that has a ⅛-inch stereo miniplug on one end and two audio jacks on the other. Those two audio jacks can be RCA phono jacks, ¼-inch mike jacks—whatever meshes with the gear you plan to connect.

Connect each audio source to one of the splitter's input jacks.

Assign channels. Next, assign one input channel to one track and the other channel to a different track. Double-click a real instrument track's header (or create a brand-new track), and use the Input pop-up menu in the Track Info panel to assign the input to Channel 1. Adjust your audio device's level to get a good input level as described on the previous page.

Next, repeat this process for the other track, assigning it to Channel 2.

Arm the tracks. Make sure that the two tracks are enabled for recording: click the red Record button in their track headers. If you want to record a software instrument along with the two real instrument tracks, now's the time to create that track and enable it for recording, too.

Get down. Set up the metronome and count-in as desired, and record.

Notes and Tips

Panning your tracks. The technique I've described here creates two mono audio channels. And yet when you play your recording, you'll hear each channel coming from *both* speakers. To control each track's position in the stereo field, use the track's panning knob in the track mixer. For panning advice, see page 355.

Hard drive labor. Recording two simultaneous audio tracks puts your Mac's hard drive to work, especially if you're also playing back some existing real instrument tracks. If you have a slower Mac—or a laptop Mac or Mac mini, all of which have slower hard drives—you might need to mute some existing real instrument tracks to lighten the load on your hard drive and to avoid an error message.

The same applies to software instrument tracks that you've locked (see page 366): if GarageBand displays an error message while recording, try muting those tracks.

Multi-take recording. GarageBand's multi-take recording feature works with real instrument tracks, too. In fact, it even works when you're doing multitrack recording. Turn on track cycling, and each band member gets as many takes as he or she needs to get the part right. For details on multi-take recording, see page 348.

Working with Real Instrument Regions

You can modify real instrument regions—either ones you've recorded or those you created by dragging blue loops into the timeline—in several ways.

Copy, paste, and dupe. You can duplicate a region by copying and pasting or by simply Option-dragging it. Duplicating a lengthy region doesn't use any additional disk space.

Digital splicing. You can also do some basic editing. Maybe you belted out a *yeah* that sounded more like Howard Dean than James Brown. Double-click on the region to open it in the track editor.

You can also copy and paste part of a region: select it in the track editor, then choose Copy. Now paste it at a different position or in a different real instrument track.

Tip: To "double" a vocal and add a richer sound, offset the duplicate slightly using the technique on page 342. And pan each member of your chorus to a different position (see page 354).

Enhancing tuning and tempo. Singer sour? Drummer dragging? Use the track editor's Enhance Tuning or Enhance Timing slider. Every track is different, so drag the slider until things sound good.

Drag across the offending utterance (zoom in and turn off grid snapping for more precision), then choose Delete from the Edit menu.

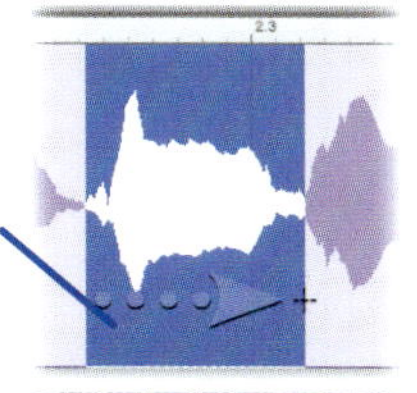

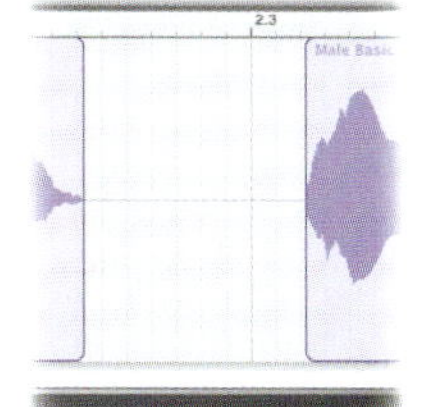

When adjusting pitch, you can have GarageBand limit enhancement to the song's key (check the Limit to Key box) or to the chromatic scale (uncheck the box). And to try your hand at an effect first popularized by Cher back in the last century, crank Enhance Tuning all the way up.

Track editor tips. Want to turn a selection into an independent region? Just click within the selection.

And with some strategic mouse positioning, you can move, resize, and loop regions directly within the track editor—no need to journey up into the timeline. To move a region, position the pointer near its upper-left corner. When the mouse pointer changes to a ◂|▸, drag left or right.

To resize a region within the track editor, point to its lower-left corner and drag. To loop a region, point to its upper-right corner and drag.

Orange Loops: Imported Audio and More

You can import audio from iTunes and the Finder: just drag the audio file into the timeline. GarageBand accepts AIFF, WAV, Apple Lossless, MP3, and AAC formats.

(You can't import a song purchased from the iTunes Store. The workaround: burn the song to a CD, then rip it back into iTunes and import that version. This limitation doesn't apply to iTunes Plus purchases.)

GarageBand displays imported audio regions in orange.

05 Love Is Here To Stay.1

You can't shift the tempo of orange audio regions, nor can you transpose them—at least not without a little trickery. If you know that your song's tempo and key match those of the orange region (or if you don't care—maybe you just want to slow down a solo to figure it out), here's the secret: select the orange region, press Control-Option-G, and then click elsewhere in the timeline. GarageBand "stamps" the region with your project's key and tempo settings and turns the orange region into a purple one. Now you can transpose it and stretch its tempo. This is great for doing remixes of iTunes tracks.

Incidentally, if you open a project created in GarageBand 1.x, its once-purple regions will be orange. Use the Control-Option-G trick to convert them.

Recording Multiple Takes

Sometimes it takes more than one try to get a performance just right. If you're like me, it may take dozens of tries. If at first you don't succeed, GarageBand makes it easy to try, try again. With the multi-take recording feature, you can record a passage over and over again—without having to start and stop, or click buttons, between attempts. GarageBand records each try as a separate *take*.

Multi-take recording is easy to set up, and as I mentioned on previous pages, it works with software instruments and real instruments alike. Indeed, you can even do multi-take recording when you're doing multi*track* recording—each member of the band gets multiple takes. (Keep in mind that recording multiple takes on multiple real-instrument tracks will gobble up disk space.)

After you record multiple takes, you can switch among them and choose the one you like best. And, armed with the region-editing skills you picked up on previous pages, you can pick and choose the best parts of each take and edit them into a perfect performance.

Here's how to keep on trying.

To Record Multiple Takes

Step 1. Turn cycling on by clicking the ( ) button.

Step 2. Adjust the size of the yellow cycling bar to match where you want the recording to start and end.

For more details on cycling, see page 335.

Step 3. Enable one or more tracks for recording, then start recording—and start playing.

When the playhead reaches the end of the cycling region, it returns to the beginning and GarageBand starts recording another take.

It's that easy. Keep recording takes until your hands fall off, your voice turns into gravel, your hard disk fills, or you never want to hear the song again, whichever comes first.

Then what? When you stop recording, check out the region that you recorded: the tiny number in its upper-left corner shows how many takes you recorded.

The region displays the very last take you recorded. To switch to a different take, click the tiny number and choose the take you want.

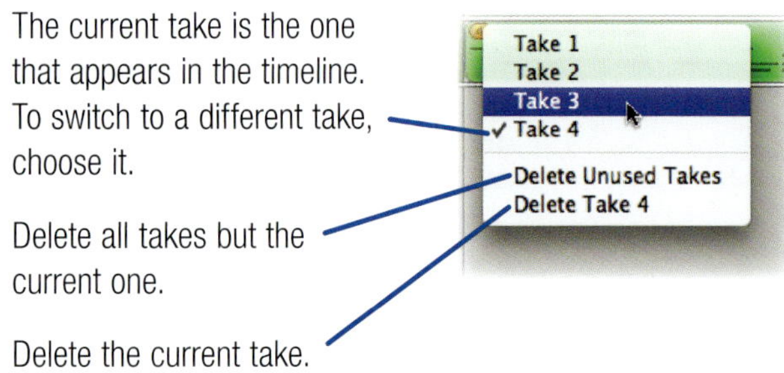

The current take is the one that appears in the timeline. To switch to a different take, choose it.

Delete all takes but the current one.

Delete the current take.

Notes and Tips

Regions and takes. When you use multi-take recording, each region in a track can have its own set of takes. Indeed, if you use the Split command to split a region containing multiple takes, you'll see that each region retains all the takes. This makes possible some slick take-management tricks. For example, you can split a multiple-take region into two regions, and then delete all but one of the takes from one of the regions.

Merging takes. When you're recording multiple takes on a software instrument track, you have an additional option: the ability to merge each take into a single region.

This option is great for building up a drum track. Record the bass drum on your first take, the hi-hat on the second take, ride cymbal on the third, snare on the fourth, and so on. When you're done, you'll have a full drum track contained in one region.

To activate this option, choose GarageBand > Preferences, click the General button, and click the oh-so-wordy option named Automatically Merge Software Instrument Recordings When Using the Cycle Region.

Note: You must activate this option *before* recording the takes.

More Multiple-Take Options

Multi-take recording is great, but it doesn't let you pick and choose parts of each take to build a single track containing the best parts. To do that, you have a few options.

Record on separate tracks. Use the Duplicate Track command to create multiple duplicates of a track, and record each take on its own track. Then, use the region editing techniques covered on previous pages to copy and paste the best parts of each track into one.

Splitting a multi-take region. Say you like the first part of Take 1 and the last part of Take 3. Display Take 1, then move the playhead to the spot just before it goes bad. (If you need extra playhead precision, zoom in and use the Control menu to turn off grid snapping.) Choose Edit > Split; GarageBand splits the region into two. Finally, in the second region, use the tiny pop-up menu to display Take 3.

Multiple takes to one track. Use the multi-take recording feature to record as many takes as you like. Next, use the Duplicate Track command to create *one* duplicate of the track. Now return to the track containing all the takes, and switch from one take to another, copying and pasting the best parts into the duplicate track.

Max Headroom for Sound: The 24-bit Advantage

Back on page 173, I talked about the advantages of 16-bit imaging: it captures a scene more accurately and gives you more headroom to make adjustments without sacrificing image quality.

There's a similar advantage in the audio world. Normally, GarageBand records in 16-bit mode—it uses 16 bits of data to describe each of the 44,100 snapshots of sound that it takes every second.

Many audio interfaces support 24-bit audio. Those extra eight bits make a difference: instead of being able to represent roughly 65,000 different volumes, a 24-bit recording can measure over 16 million.

If you have an audio interface that supports 24-bit audio, you can have GarageBand record at this higher resolution. Choose GarageBand > Preferences, and click the Advanced button. From the Audio Resolution pop-up menu, choose Better or Best. Both options record at 24-bit resolution. If you choose Best, GarageBand also *exports* songs at 24-bit resolution. (At the Better setting, GarageBand exports 16-bit audio.)

Make space. Note that recording in 24-bit mode uses roughly 50 percent more disk space. (Remember, this applies to real instrument tracks only.) Is the extra disk space worth it? Do some tests and let your ears decide. But, in general, more bits are always better in the computer biz, so if your audio hardware supports 24-bit recording, you might as well take advantage of it.

Adding Structure with the Arrange Track

Songs typically have structure: an introduction, verses, a chorus or bridge, and an ending. You can see this in the tunes created by the Magic GarageBand feature (page 328).

With GarageBand's arrange track, you can create *arrange regions* that define these elements in your projects. Once you do, you can perform all manner of arranging tricks. Build the arrangement for a verse—the rhythm tracks, chords, background vocals, and so on—and then copy it as many times as needed throughout your song. (You can edit each copy, too, to add variety.)

By adding structure to your song, you also have more opportunity to experiment. Should the chorus repeat twice at the end of the tune? How about a different intro treatment? Without the arrange track, questions like these are harder to answer, requiring a lot of copying and pasting and dragging of regions.

With the arrange track, the creative answers you seek are a few clicks away.

Using the Arrange Track

To work with arrangements, start by displaying the arrange track: choose Track > Show Arrange Track.

Defining Arrange Regions

Step 1. In the arrange track, click the Add Region button (⊕).

GarageBand creates an eight-bar region.

Step 2. To change the duration of the arrange region, drag its left and right edge.

Step 3. To name the region, double-click it and pause until the name is highlighted, then type a name.

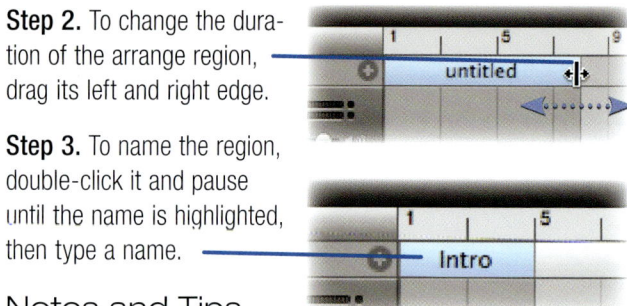

Notes and Tips

You can also create an arrange region by simply dragging within an empty area of the arrange track—no need to click the little plus sign first.

To resize an arrange region, drag its left or right edge. But note that if you lengthen a region, the region that follows it will be shortened accordingly. For example, if you add four bars to an intro that is followed by a verse, the verse is shortened by four bars. To avoid that, move the adjacent region to create some empty measures between it and the one you want to lengthen.

Working with Arrange Regions

After you've defined one or more arrange regions, you can work with them in several ways.

Moving a region. To move an arrange region to a different spot in your song, click its heading and then drag left or right in the arrange track. When you move a region, everything in the region—notes, automation curves, and so on—moves accordingly.

Duplicating a region. To duplicate a region, press Option and drag the region elsewhere in your song. If you position a region between two existing ones, the region to the right moves to accommodate the region that you're dragging.

Tip: Get in the habit of renaming duplicates after you create them, lest you end up with region names like *Verse Copy Copy Copy*—a great name for the Xerox corporate anthem, but not all that descriptive otherwise.

Deleting a region. Don't want that second chorus after all? Click the arrange region's header to select the region, then press Delete.

Splitting regions. To split an arrange region into two, select the region, position the playhead at the point where you want to split the region, then choose Edit > Split (⌘-T).

Joining regions. You can also join adjacent arrange regions. Shift-click on each region's header to select it, then choose Edit > Join.

Selecting multiple regions. You can duplicate, move, or delete more than one region at once: just Shift-click on each region before using the techniques above.

To select every single region in the song—maybe to add the intro that you just decided your tune needs—click the track header of the arrange track; it's the blank area directly below the word *Tracks*.

A Closer Look at Software Instrument Loops

On page 331, I mentioned that software instrument loops contain more than just piano-roll MIDI notes—they also contain audio. To see this for yourself, drag a green loop into a real instrument track—instead of the usual piano-roll notation within a green region, you'll see a waveform display within a blue region.

Two in one. How does this work? A software instrument loop is really two loops in one. It contains not only the MIDI note data that can be used by a software instrument track, but also a *rendered* version of the loop—an actual audio recording, complete with effects.

Here's another way to see this for yourself. Use the Finder's Find command to locate a software instrument loop, such as Southern Rock Guitar 01. You'll notice the loop's file name ends in .AIF—it's an audio file in AIFF format. You can open and play this file using QuickTime Player or iTunes. You can even drag it into iMovie or iDVD. But embedded within the AIFF file is MIDI note data that GarageBand can use.

The fact that software instrument loops also contain audio data has an important ramification: As I mention on page 366, if you plan to use a software instrument loop as is, you can lighten the load on your Mac's processor by using the loop in a real instrument track.

If you haven't yet created the track for the loop, take advantage of the following shortcut: press the Option key while dragging a green loop into the timeline, and GarageBand creates a real instrument track for it.

If you frequently use software instrument loops without changing them, you can use the Loops portion of the Preferences dialog box to have GarageBand *always* create real instrument tracks when you drag green loops into the timeline.

The downsides. There are some downsides to using a green loop in a real instrument track. You can't edit individual notes or change instrument or effect assignments, since all these things are part of the audio recording. Also, you can't transpose an audio region over as large a range. But for those times when you want to use a green loop as is, adding it to a real instrument track is a great way to improve GarageBand's performance.

Refining Your Sound with Effects

Effects can be just as important to your final arrangement as the notes you play. With effects, you can add richness to a track—or brain-liquefying distortion, if that's your idea of fun. You can add some spice to a track, or change it beyond recognition.

Effects alter the "color" of sound. Some effects simulate real-world phenomena, such as reverberation and echo. Other effects let you sculpt your sound to enhance certain frequencies, much like the equalizer in iTunes. Still other effects process (and sometimes mangle) audio in ways that could only exist in the digital world.

Recording studios have racks of hardware effects boxes. GarageBand's effects exist in software: by applying complex math to your sound, GarageBand can simulate the reverb of a concert hall, the characteristics of an old guitar amplifier, and much more. Best of all, you can customize GarageBand's effects in a limitless number of ways to create sounds that are yours alone.

You can apply GarageBand's effects to software and real instrument tracks alike. And as I've said previously, GarageBand never alters your original audio; effects are applied as your song plays. This lets you experiment with effects until you arrive at just the right amount of sonic seasoning.

Here's a look at how GarageBand applies its effects and how you can customize them.

Effects Basics

All of GarageBand's software instruments employ effects to some degree. Similarly, when you create a real instrument track and choose an instrument, GarageBand assigns a collection of effects to that track (page 344). And as I describe on page 356, a song's master track can apply effects to your entire song.

To examine and change a track's effects settings, double-click the track header, then click the Details button in the Track Info pane.

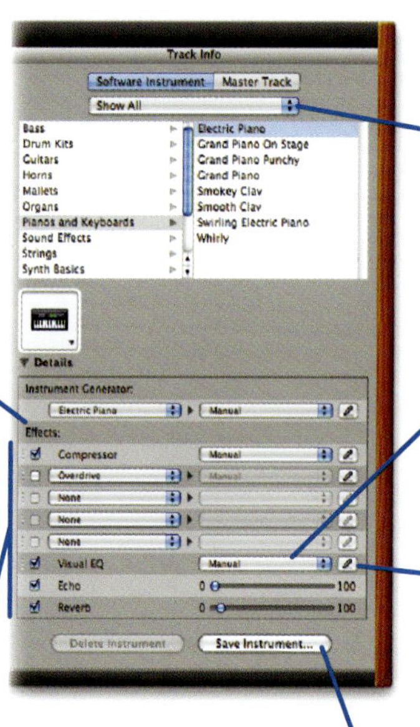

If you create your own presets (opposite page), you can view them by choosing My Settings from the pop-up menu.

You can drag effects up and down to change the order in which GarageBand applies them (see page 358).

Choose effect presets from these pop-up menus.

To create your own settings for an effect, click the pencil (see opposite page).

For software instruments, standard effects include Compressor, Visual EQ, Echo, and Reverb. (Real instrument tracks provide these same effects, and they add a *noise gate* effect, which removes noise from silent portions of a recording.) You can choose four additional effects by using the four pop-up menus.

Like what you've come up with? You can save the customized version of the instrument and use it again in future songs (see opposite page).

The Fab Four

Compressor, Visual EQ, Echo, and Reverb are mainstay effects, the salt and pepper of sonic seasoning.

Compressor. A compressor is a kind of automatic volume control that adjusts volume thousands of times per second. Most popular music is heavily compressed, and FM radio stations often compress it even more. Compression can add punch to drum tracks and vocals, but too much compression can add an annoying "pumping" quality to sound.

Visual EQ. Visual EQ is a sophisticated equalizer for adjusting bass, mid-range, and treble. It's described on page 358.

Echo. Also called *delay,* the echo effect simulates evenly timed sound reflections. **Tip:** GarageBand's echo repeats at a rate that matches your song's tempo. Try applying echo to vocal or synthesizer "stabs" in a dance, electronica, or hip-hop tune. To have different echo rhythms on each track, use the Track Echo effect.

Reverb. A distant cousin to echo, reverb consists of thousands of randomly timed sound reflections. Reverb simulates the sound of an acoustic space: a concert hall, a small lounge, a stadium. GarageBand provides a reverb effect that is controlled by the master track (page 356). A separate Track Reverb effect lets you apply different reverb to a specific track.

Customizing Effects

You can customize effects in several ways.

Turn them off. Maybe you love GarageBand's Arena Run synth, but you don't like the way it echoes every note. Just turn off the Echo effect by unchecking its box.

Turn them on. GarageBand's most intriguing effects lurk within the four pop-up menus in the Effects area. Want to add a rich, swirling texture to a track? Try Flanger, Phaser, or both. Want to liquefy your listeners? Unleash Distortion, Bitcrusher, or Amp Simulation. Want a track to continuously pan between the left and right channel? Try the Tremolo effect's Circular Structure setting. Want to turn a male singer into a female—or a chipmunk? Try the amazing Vocal Transformer.

Automate them. You can automate an effect so it changes as your song plays—have the reverb get stronger, increase and decrease the amount of tremolo, and so on. For details, see page 361.

Try different presets. Many of GarageBand's effects have an assortment of presets that you can apply with a click.

Create your own presets. Click the little pencil ( ) next to an effect's Preset pop-up menu, and a dialog box appears where you can adjust the effect's parameters.

To create a new preset containing the current settings, open the pop-up menu and choose New Preset.

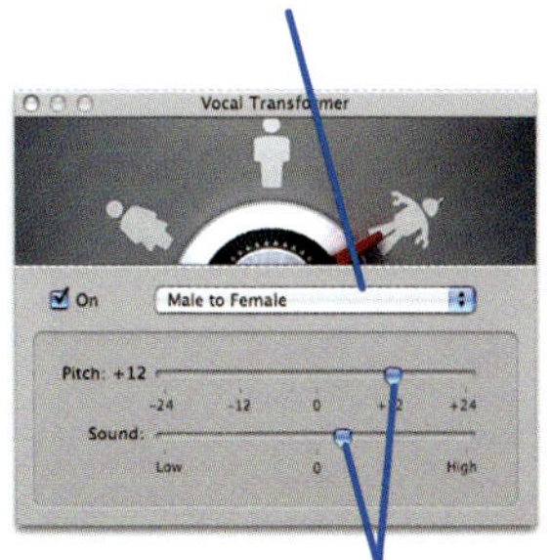

Each effect has a unique set of parameters that you can adjust.

Saving Instruments

When you change a track's effects, you're customizing the way GarageBand has defined that software or real instrument. If you switch to a different instrument or effect preset, GarageBand asks if you want to save the changed instrument before switching.

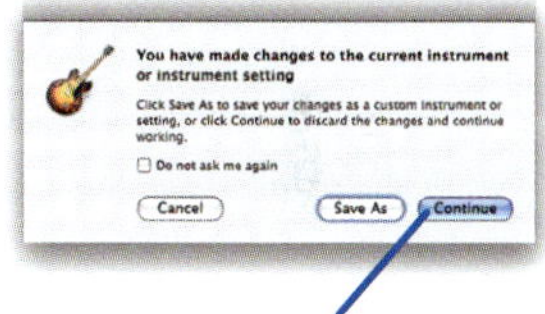

If you click Continue (or just press Return), GarageBand discards your settings. If you think you'll want to use them again, click Save As, then type a name for your newly customized instrument.

If you like tinkering with effect settings and you don't want GarageBand pestering you about saving them all the time, check the Do Not Ask Me Again box. You can also use GarageBand's Preferences command to control this paranoia mode.

For more details on creating instruments, see page 364.

Refining the Mix: Volume and Panning

A good song has a pleasing mix of melody, chord changes, and maybe lyrics. A good *recording* of a song has a pleasing mix between instruments. It's possible to have a poorly mixed version of a great song, and as a spin of the radio dial will confirm, it's also possible to have a well-mixed version of a lousy song.

As a GarageBand-based recording engineer, the job of mixing is yours. Adjust each track's volume so all the tracks mesh—no single instrument should overwhelm the others, but important instruments or voices should be louder than less important ones.

And to create a rich stereo field, pan some instruments toward the left channel and others toward the right. You'll find some tips for panning on the opposite page.

To adjust a track's playback volume level and panning position, use the Mixer area of GarageBand's window. If the Mixer isn't visible, display it by clicking the little triangle at the top of the Tracks area or by choosing Show Track Mixer from the Track menu (⌘-Y).

To have a track's volume or panning change as the song plays, create a *volume curve* or *panning curve*—a set of control points that tell GarageBand how to change volume or panning over time.

Note: If you've edited a track's volume or panning curve, you can't drag the volume slider or turn the panning knob. Instead, make volume or panning adjustments to the curve.

Adjusting Volume

To adjust a track's playback volume, drag the slider.

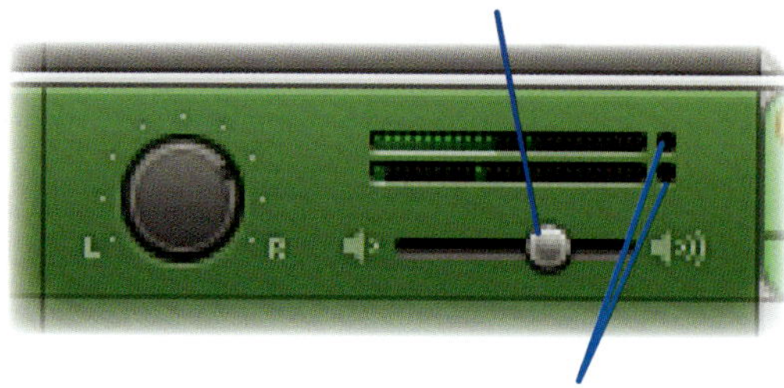

To avoid distortion, lower the volume if the clipping indicators light.

Editing a Volume Curve

To create fades, add expression, or mute a track for part of a song, edit the track's volume curve.

Step 1. Click the triangle next to the track's Lock button or select the track header and press the A key.

Step 2. Choose Track Volume from the pop-up menu and click the little box at the left edge of the pop-up menu to turn on the curve for editing.

Step 3. The horizontal line represents the track's volume. Click the line to create a control point where you want the volume change to begin.

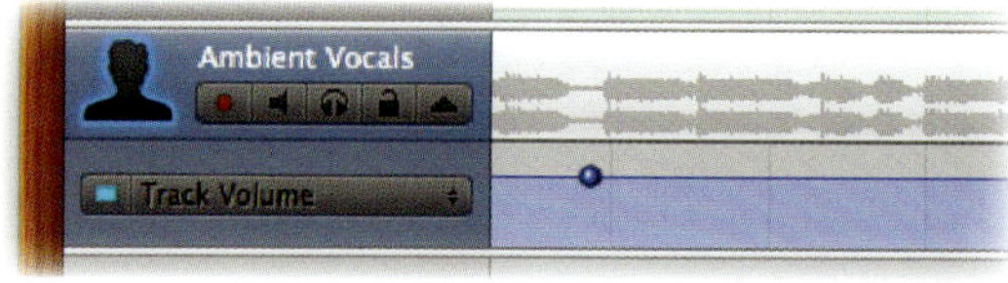

Step 4. Click at a different point on the line to create a second control point, then drag it down to lower the volume, or up to raise it.

To turn off a volume or pan curve without deleting its control points, click the little blue indicator.

Adjusting Panning

To pan a track, drag its pan knob to turn it clockwise (toward the right speaker) or counterclockwise (toward the left). To return to dead center, Option-click the knob.

Editing a Pan Curve

To pan a track from one channel to the other as the song plays, edit the track's pan curve. Display the track's curve by clicking its triangle or pressing A. Then, choose Track Pan from the pop-up menu and click the little box at the left edge of the pop-up menu to turn on the curve for editing.

Next, create control points and drag them. To pan toward the left channel, drag a control point up. To pan toward the right, drag a control point down.

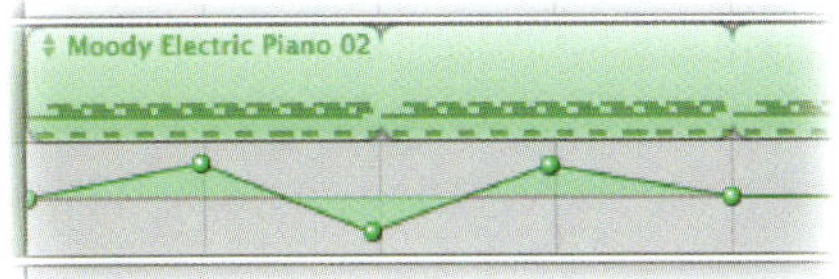

Tips for curves. To adjust a control point's location in time, drag it left or right. To delete a control point, click it and press the Delete key. To delete or move multiple control points at once, select them by Shift-clicking or dragging across them.

If you move regions within your song, any curves you created for them don't move along with the regions. To fix that, choose Control > Lock Automation Curves to Regions. Now, when you move a region, any automation curves beneath it will go along for the ride.

Mixing Tips: Panning

By sweating the details of your stereo mix, you can make your song more aurally interesting. Two ears, two speakers—take advantage of them.

Sit right. Your position relative to your speakers will affect how you hear a stereo mix. When refining your track panning, sit directly between your speakers. Test your mix with headphones if you like, but don't rely exclusively on them—your listeners won't.

Panning hard. Think twice about panning tracks *completely* to the left or right. In the real world, sound reaches both ears even when a musician is at the far side of the stage. Of course, some songs have little to do with the real world, so feel free to bend this rule.

Panning for realism. If you're after a realistic stereo mix, visualize your ensemble and pan accordingly. In a jazz combo, the drums might be slightly to the left, bass in the middle, piano slightly to the right, and sax further right.

Panning a duet. If your song contains a vocal duet or two instruments that trade solos, pan one of the vocalists or instruments somewhat left (about 10 o'clock on the pan wheel) and the other somewhat right.

To simulate backup singers, record each part on a separate track and pan the tracks near each other on one side of the stage—for example, one track at 9 o'clock and the other at 10 o'clock.

Panning similar instruments. If your song contains multiple instruments that have a similar frequency range—for example, a solo guitar and a rhythm guitar—pan each instrument to the opposite side of center. The 10 o'clock and 2 o'clock positions are good starting points.

Consider your effects. If you've applied an effect that enhances a track's stereo—for example, Chorus, Flanger, or Tremolo—think twice about panning that track heavily to one channel. You'll lose many of the benefits of the effect.

Panning percussion. If you've built up a drum kit by recording different drums and cymbals on different tracks, pan the tracks to increase realism. Put the snare and kick drum dead center. Pan the hi-hat slightly right, and the ride and crash cymbals slightly left. If you're using tom-toms, pan them according to their pitch: high-pitched toms slightly right, low-pitched toms slightly left. This layout mirrors the typical layout of a drum kit: the hi-hat is on the drummer's left and the floor tom is on his or her right.

Creating the Final Mix

In a recording studio, once each track has been recorded and refined, the final mix takes place. Everyone settles into the control room and takes a seat between monitor speakers as a golden-eared recording engineer adjusts the levels and left-right panning of each track.

Then they make decisions about the entire song. If it is to fade out, at what point should the fade take place, and how long should the fade be? Which effects should be applied to the entire mix to add punch and clarity?

The producer and everyone involved with the song listens, tweaks, and listens again. When the song is mixed to their satisfaction, it's released.

In GarageBand, these jobs are yours. But GarageBand helps. It contains dozens of mastering presets aimed at most every musical genre. Use a preset as is, and you've applied a golden-eared engineer's knowledge to your work. Or customize it to suit your ears.

When that's done, you can release your tune by exporting it in a variety of formats. Have fun at the release party.

Echo Presets

Reverb Presets

Working with the Master Track

GarageBand's *master track* is a special kind of track that doesn't hold notes or regions, but instead controls certain aspects of your entire mix. Specifically, you can transpose the entire song (page 336) and you can apply effects to the master track and create a volume curve to have your song fade in or fade out.

To show the master track, choose Show Master Track from the Track menu (⌘-B).

Applying mastering presets. GarageBand includes dozens of final-mastering presets for common musical genres. To use them, double-click the master track's header. In the Track Info pane, choose a genre on the left, then a preset. And, of course, you can customize the presets and create your own final-mix presets using the techniques I've described on previous pages.

Creating a fade. To fade a song, choose Track > Fade Out. GarageBand adds a multi-point volume curve to the master track. **Tip:** To create a musically appealing fade, edit the volume curve so that the fade *ends* at the very beginning of a verse or measure. Don't have a fade end in the middle of a measure—it feels abrupt.

Customizing reverb and echo. As described on page 352, GarageBand provides reverb and echo on both a master level and a track level. To adjust the echo and reverb parameters that GarageBand applies to an entire song, use the master track's Track Info pane.

GarageBand's dozens of reverb and echo settings (shown at left) are worth exploring. The reverb presets are spectacular—everything from a living room to a large cathedral, with some offbeat stops in between. Explore them to add just the right sonic ambience to your track. And if you're into dance and electronic music, you can while away a weekend trying out and customizing GarageBand's echo presets.

Exporting Your Project

With the commands in the Share menu, you can burn your project to a CD. You can also export the project, post it on your iWeb site, add it to your iTunes library, and more.

Optimizing loudness. Before exporting your project, adjust GarageBand's master volume slider to get loud (but not distorted) playback levels. Play back the loudest parts of your project, and make sure the master volume slider's clipping indicators don't light. Check the levels of individual tracks while you're at it (page 354).

To have GarageBand optimize loudness levels of the exported project, choose GarageBand > Preferences, click Advanced, then check the Auto Normalize box. GarageBand will export the project at an optimum level (a process, incidentally, that's a bit like iTunes' Sound Check feature, and identical to the Normalize Clip Volume option in iMovie's Audio Adjustments window).

Exporting Techniques

When you export a project, GarageBand mixes your tracks down to two stereo channels. What happens next depends on your destination.

To CD. To burn an audio CD of a song, choose Share > Burn Song to CD, then insert a blank CD.

Tip: Normally, GarageBand burns a project as one CD track. To define multiple tracks, choose Track > Show Podcast Track and add a chapter marker at each spot where you'd like a new track to begin. For details on chapter markers, see page 373.

To disk. Choose Share > Export Song to Disk to export a project in any of a few audio formats (see below).

To iTunes. Export a project to iTunes, and you can add it to playlists and burn CDs—and sync it to your iPod, iPhone, or Apple TV. Choose Share > Send Song to iTunes. Edit the song information if you like (see "Customizing Tags," at right).

Format options. To export an uncompressed AIFF file, uncheck the Compress box. For a smaller file size with great audio quality, choose the AAC Encoder and Higher Quality options. For a recap of audio format options, see page 22.

To iWeb. To post your project on your iWeb site, choose Share > Send Podcast to iWeb. Choose an audio format, keeping in mind that higher-quality settings mean bigger downloads. For details on blog and podcast publishing in iWeb, see page 400.

Notes and Tips

Customizing tags. To customize how your song is categorized in iTunes—artist name, album name, and so on—use the My Info portion of GarageBand's Preferences dialog box.

Exporting an excerpt. At times, you may want to export only part of a song. Maybe you want to email it to a collaborator or mix it down in order to bring it back into GarageBand (see page 367). To export a portion of a song, turn on cycling and then resize the yellow cycling region in the beat ruler to indicate the portion you want to export.

GarageBand Tips

A Closer Look at Visual EQ

GarageBand's Visual EQ is a powerful four-band equalizer for optimizing the bass, mid-range, and treble portions of a track or your entire project. With Visual EQ, you can add punch to bass parts, add brightness and clarity to vocals, reduce sibilant "S" sounds, and much more.

Visual EQ lives in the Effects area of the Track Info window. Like other effects, it sports a pop-up menu containing a large selection of presets aimed at specific sonic enhancements. And as with other effects, you can customize the presets and create your own.

To do that, click the tiny pencil button to the right of Visual EQ's pop-up menu. The Visual EQ window appears.

Choose a preset from the pop-up menu, and notice how the window changes: the graph depicts how certain frequency ranges will be boosted or attenuated.

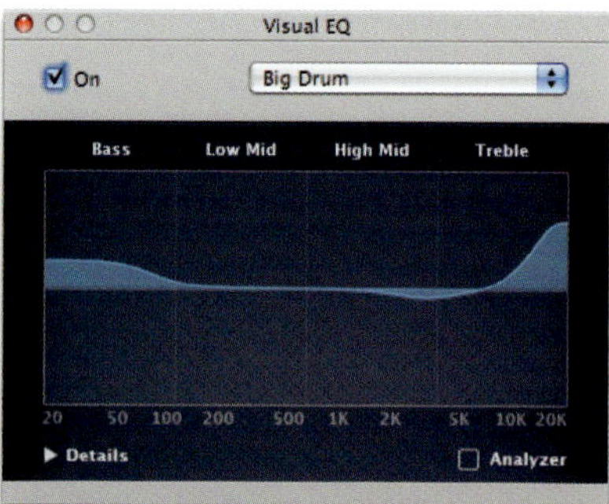

Here's the fun part: drag across the graph, and you can adjust the EQ curve. Drag up and down to increase or attenuate a certain frequency range, and left or right to define which frequency range you want to change.

Here's the even-more-fun part: you can make these adjustments while your song plays back. Try it.

If your heart can take even more joy, click the Analyzer checkbox during playback. Visual EQ displays a real-time graph that depicts the frequency curve. Besides being cool, the curve can help you determine which frequency ranges may need boosting or attenuating. **Tip:** The analyzer uses a lot of processor power, so turn it off when you aren't using it.

To make precise adjustments, click the Details triangle. You can then drag up or down on the frequency and decibel values to change them, or double-click them and type exact values.

As with many effects, you can apply Visual EQ to individual tracks, to the master track, or to combinations of both.

Changing Effects Order

Speaking of effects, GarageBand lets you rearrange the order in which some effects are applied to a track. By changing the order of the *effects chain* or *signal chain,* as engineers call it, you can obtain different sounds. For example, if you place the Distortion effect *after* the Track Echo or Chorus effect, you get a very different sound than if you place Distortion before those effects. Give it a try and you'll immediately hear what I mean.

GarageBand's effects chain goes from top to bottom in the Track Info window: the effect at the very bottom is applied last, and thus affects every effect that precedes it. To change the order of the effects chain, drag effects up or down in the Track Info window.

The Web contains some useful articles on effects chains. I've linked to some on www.macilife.com/garageband.

Compacting a Project

If you have a project containing real instrument recordings you've made, you can reduce the disk storage requirements of the project by compacting it. You'll sacrifice some sound quality, but the resulting project file will be smaller—helpful if you're collaborating with someone and emailing project files around.

Choose File > Save As, and in the Save dialog box, check the Compact Project box. Choose an audio quality option from the pop-up menu.

What Chord?

When a software instrument track is selected, you can have GarageBand show you what chord you're playing on a music keyboard. In the LCD, choose Chord from the pop-up menu, or choose Control > Show Chord in LCD. Now play a chord, and GarageBand tells you what it is.

If you like the chord display, check out Wonder Warp Software's SimpleChord, an inexpensive and incredibly powerful chord utility.

Playing GarageBand's Keyboards

GarageBand provides two on-screen keyboards that let you audition (and even record) software instruments without having to reach for (or even have) a music keyboard.

Keyboard window. To view this simulated piano keyboard, choose Window > Keyboard (⌘-K).

The current track's instrument appears here.

C3 is middle C on a piano.

To display a different range of notes, click the little keyboard.

Scroll and resize the Keyboard window.

The keyboard is velocity sensitive: the closer you click to the bottom edge of a key, the louder the note.

Musical Typing window. Play notes by pressing keys on your Mac's keyboard. Choose Window > Musical Typing (Shift-⌘-K).

Note: When the Musical Typing window is visible, some of GarageBand's keyboard shortcuts—such as pressing Home to move to the beginning of the song—aren't available.

Add pitch bend, modulation, or sustain by pressing the number keys or Tab key.

Change the octave range by pressing Z or X or by clicking the little keyboard at the top of the window.

Play chords by pressing more than one key at once.

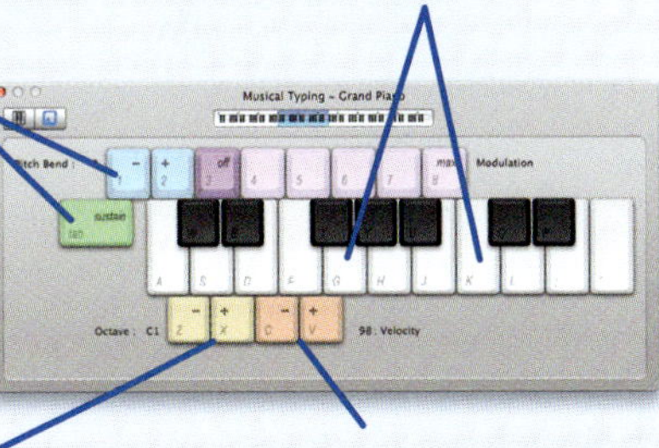

Change velocity by pressing C or V.

Arranging Tips

More Ways to Work with Regions

I've already mentioned the most common tasks you're likely to perform with regions: looping them, moving and copying them, splitting them, transposing them, and editing them.

There's more. Here are a few additional ways you might work with regions.

Resizing a region. To extend a region—make it longer—point to its lower-right corner and drag to the right.

Why extend a region? Say you recorded a riff that you want to loop. If your recorded region doesn't end at the proper measure boundary, the region won't loop properly. By extending the region, you can have it loop.

Another reason to extend a region is to be able to draw in additional notes or controller data using the track editor. Yet another is to add some silence before a region's content repeats.

To make the region shorter, drag its lower-right corner to the left. You might shorten a region in order to "crop out" some unwanted notes—possibly as a prelude to rerecording them. When you shorten a region, you don't delete the notes in the hidden portion of the region. To restore the notes, lengthen the region.

You can also resize a region from its beginning by dragging its lower *left* corner. This enables you to add silence to the beginning of a region (drag to the left) or to crop out audio from the beginning of a real instrument recording (drag to the right).

Joining regions. You've transposed a set of loops using the Split technique from page 337, and now you want to transpose the entire verse to a different key. Select all the loops and choose Join from the Edit menu (⌘-J). GarageBand turns all the regions into one region that you can transpose.

When you join real instrument regions that you've recorded, GarageBand combines those regions into a single audio file.

Adding Variety

When you're working with loops, it's easy to create overly repetitious arrangements. Fortunately, it's also easy to add variety.

Vary loops. Many of the bass and drum loops that come with GarageBand and Apple's GarageBand Jam Packs have variations that sound similar but not identical. Rather than relying on just one loop for a bass or drum track, switch between some different but similar-sounding ones. To switch loops within the same family, click on the tiny arrows in the upper-left corner of a loop region, then choose another loop (see page 332).

Edit some loops. Make your own loop variations. Make a copy of a software instrument loop and edit it—delete a few notes or transpose others. For real instrument loops, select part of the loop, copy it, and then paste it elsewhere.

Another way to edit loops is to change the instrument played by a software instrument loop. Try assigning an electric piano or clavinet to a bass loop.

Record your own bass track. Use bass loops to sketch out an arrangement and choose instruments, then replace the loops with your own bass line.

Take breaks. Add a *drum break* now and then—silence your drums for the last beat or two of a measure or for an entire measure. You can split the region and then delete part of it. Or you can edit the region if it's a software instrument drum track. Or leave the region alone and create a volume curve that plunges the track's volume down all the way, then brings it back up.

Add fills. Don't want to edit a drum loop? Create a new track that uses a software instrument drum kit. Use this track to hold drum fills, such as an occasional cymbal crash or tom-tom fill. Want a kick drum to mark the beat during a drum break? Put it in this track.

Vary the percussion. Add one or more percussion tracks to some verses—shakers, tambourines, claves, congas, bongos.

Add a pad. A *pad* is a note, a series of notes, or a chord that forms a sonic background for a song. It's often a lush string section or an atmospheric synthesizer that plays the root note or a fifth (for example, G in a song written in C).

One way to add variety to an arrangement is to have a pad play throughout one verse. Stop the pad at the start of the next verse, or add another track with a pad that uses a different instrument.

Add Tempo Changes

A song doesn't have to have the same tempo throughout. Add a *ritard* (a gradual slowing of the tempo) to the end of a song, or kick up the beat during a solo.

To add tempo changes, use the master track. Choose Tracks > Show Master Track. In the master track header, choose Master Tempo from the pop-up menu, then add control points and drag them up (to increase the tempo) or down (to decrease it). As you drag a control point, GarageBand displays its tempo, in beats per minute.

GarageBand applies tempo changes gradually. For a sudden tempo change, add two control points and position one directly above or below the other.

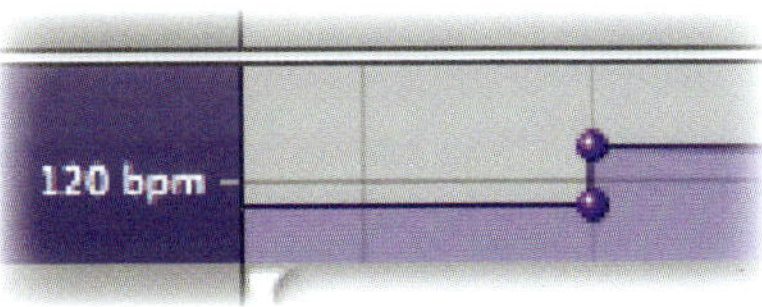

For more details on working with control points, see page 355.

Automate Effects

Another way to add variety is to change how an instrument's effects sound over time. For example, you might want a synthesizer solo to start out mellow, then get more gnarly as the solo builds in intensity. One way to do this is to add the Distortion effect to the track, then automate it.

To add automation to a track, click the triangle in its header (▲), or select the header and press the A key. From the automation pop-up menu, choose Add Automation. A dialog box lists the types of items that you can automate, given the instrument and effects in use. Click the triangle in the dialog box to show automation options, then check the one you want to automate.

Next, choose those options from the track automation pop-up menu, and add control points.

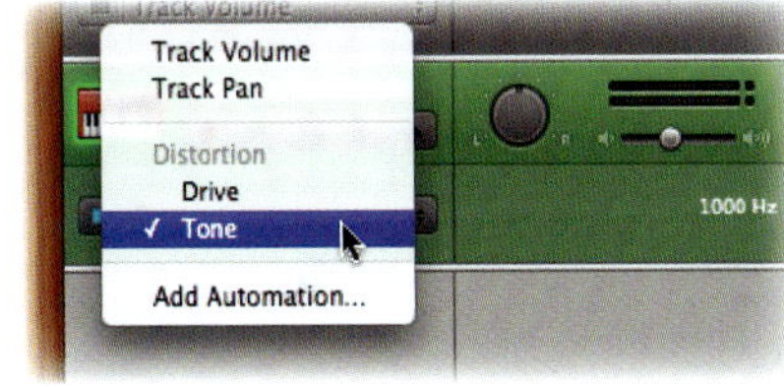

Saving a Preview

You can save an audio "preview" along with a project. A preview is simply a stereo mix of the song, stashed inside the project file.

Saving a project with a preview makes possible a couple of tricks. For one thing, you can access the project using the media browsers in the other iLife programs—use a song in an iPhoto slide show or in an iMovie project, for example.

Another benefit to saving a preview along with the project is that you can import one song into another, as described on page 358. And if you use Mac OS X 10.5 (Leopard), saving a preview lets you preview the song in the Finder's Quick Look feature and in Time Machine.

To have GarageBand always create a preview when you save a project, choose GarageBand > Preferences, click General, and check the Audio Preview box.

This feature greatly increases the time required to save a project, since GarageBand must create a stereo mix of your song. For this reason, you might want to leave this feature turned off as you're working on a song—a time when you are (or should be) using the Save command all the time. Then, when you've finished the tune, turn on the preview feature and save the project again.

Expanding Your Loop Library

For a GarageBand musician, loops are like groupies: you can't have too many. A large loop library is a source of creative inspiration. A few minutes of clicking in the loop browser is often all it takes to get the song-writing juices flowing.

There's no shortage of loop collections for GarageBand. Apple offers several great collections of its own: the GarageBand Jam Pack series includes not only thousands of loops, but some ear-stunning software instruments and effects, too (see the opposite page).

Many other companies have also created loop packages for GarageBand; you can sample many of them through GarageBand community sites, such as iCompositions (www.icompositions.com).

GarageBand can also work directly with loops in the ACID format. (ACID is a pioneering loop-based music program that debuted on Windows computers back in 1998.) There are more ACID loops available than you can fit on your hard drive.

GarageBand also lets you create your own loops. Record a riff or edit an existing loop, then—with a few mouse clicks—turn it into a new loop. Try it—create a Magic GarageBand project and turn your favorite regions into loops that you can use in your own songs.

Creating Your Own Apple Loops

You can turn any region into a loop with a few mouse clicks.

Step 1. If necessary, resize or split a region to make it the proper length of your custom loop.

Step 2. Drag the region to the loop browser or select it and choose Add to Loop Library from the Edit menu.

Step 3. Specify information about the loop, then click Create.

For rhythmic regions, choose Loop; this enables GarageBand to shift the loop's tempo to match the song in which it's used. If the region won't require tempo shifting —maybe it's a recording of a single dog bark—choose One-shot.

Type a name for the loop.

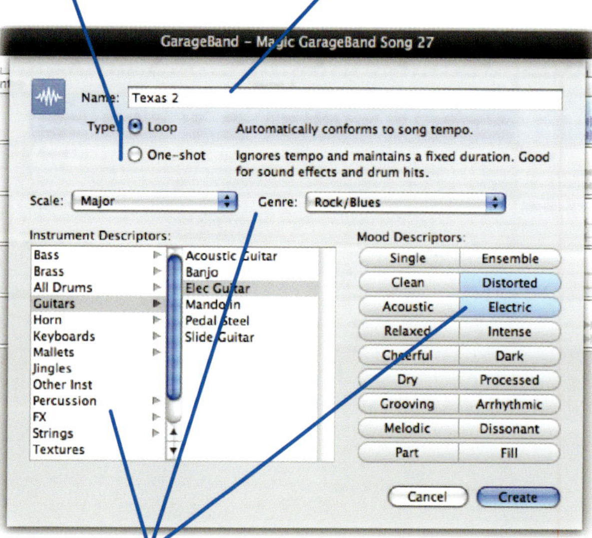

Assign as much information to the new loop as you like. The more information you specify, the easier it will be to locate the loop in future searches.

Narrowing Down Your Choices

If you've installed multiple Jam Packs and other loop collections, there may be times when you want to browse for loops from one specific collection.

To focus on a specific loop collection in the loop browser, point to the word Loops (Loops), hold down the mouse button, and then choose a collection.

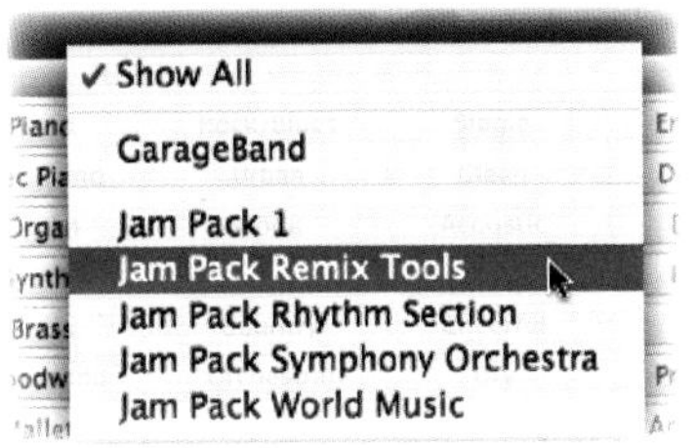

To switch back to browsing your entire loop library, choose Show All. To view GarageBand's original, factory-installed loops, choose GarageBand.

As I've described previously, GarageBand provides a similar feature when you're assigning an instrument to a track.

Importing ACID Loops

To add ACID loops to your loop library, simply drag a folder containing the loops into the loop browser. The loops remain in ACID format, but GarageBand indexes them in a way that lets you search using the loop browser's buttons and search box.

Jam Packs: More than Just Loops

Here's an overview of each Jam Pack; you can learn more at www.apple.com/garageband.

Remix Tools. If the turntable on the box doesn't give it away, the sounds will: this Jam Pack is aimed at dance, hip-hop, and electronica composers. Its loops lean toward drum beats and bass lines, synthesizer patterns, and special effects (including, of course, vinyl scratches). Several vintage drum machine software instruments and a sizzling assortment of synthesizers round out the collection.

Rhythm Section. Let the beating begin: this two-DVD set contains roughly 1,000 drum loops in a variety of styles, as well as another 1,000 bass lines and guitar and keyboard loops. Software instruments include drum sets ranging from jazzy brushes to steel drums, as well as basses and guitars of all kinds—from acoustic to electric, and from Dobro to banjo.

Symphony Orchestra. iPhoto and iMovie have the Ken Burns effect; Symphony Orchestra gives you the John Williams effect. It's a jaw-dropping collection of symphonic orchestra loops and software instruments—the most ambitious Jam Pack of them all.

Its beautifully recorded symphonic loops are an aural feast, but what really sets this Jam Pack apart are its software instruments. By moving the modulation and pitch-bend wheels of your music keyboard—or by creating controller data in the track editor—you can vary the way an instrument plays to obtain amazing realism. To create crescendos and decrescendos of a sustained note or chord, move the pitch bend wheel. To obtain different articulations, such as staccato or legato, adjust the modulation wheel. And don't miss the accompanying PDF documentation, which includes interesting backgrounders on orchestral history and arranging.

World Music. Go global: this Jam Pack includes a collection of ethnic percussion, wind, and string instruments—from tabla drums to bagpipes to Native American flutes, Peruvian panpipes, Persian santoors, Spanish Flamenco guitars, and much more. Completing your travels are over 3,000 loops recorded by pros from around the planet.

Voices. Sing it: the Voices Jam Pack adds 1,500 vocal loops, mostly in the R&B, blues, and hip-hop genres. Also included are a variety of vocal software instruments: choral ensembles, choirs, shouts, and more.

Creating Your Own Instruments

In GarageBand, a software instrument is based on a foundation called a *generator*, and every generator has settings that you can tweak. You can create your own software instrument by picking a generator and then adjusting its settings.

For example, say you want to create an instrument that has a funky electronic synthesizer sound. Here's one way you might approach the task.

Step 1. Create a new software instrument track, and pick an instrument—any instrument.

Step 2. Double-click the track's header and examine the Generator pop-up menu.

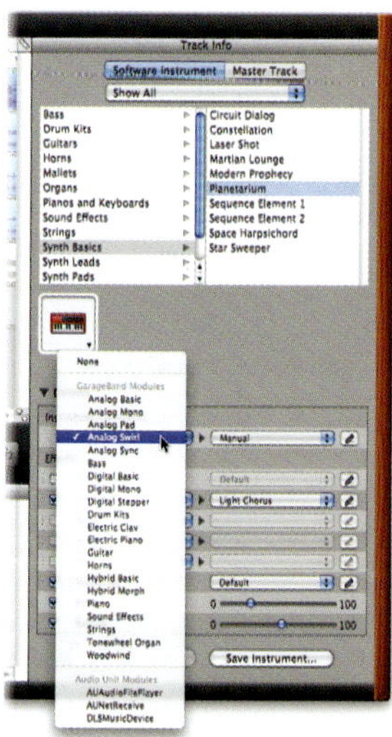

Some generators are based on short recorded *samples* of actual instruments, such as piano and guitar. Other generators create their sound "from scratch," based on sound synthesis techniques.

Step 3. Choose a generator.

Step 4. Examine the generator's presets. Try them out—you might find one you like.

Step 5. Click the pencil to the right of the generator's preset pop-up menu. This displays the settings that apply to the generator you chose.

Many generators let you customize what's often called the *ADSR envelope*. You can dramatically change a sound's percussive qualities by changing its envelope.

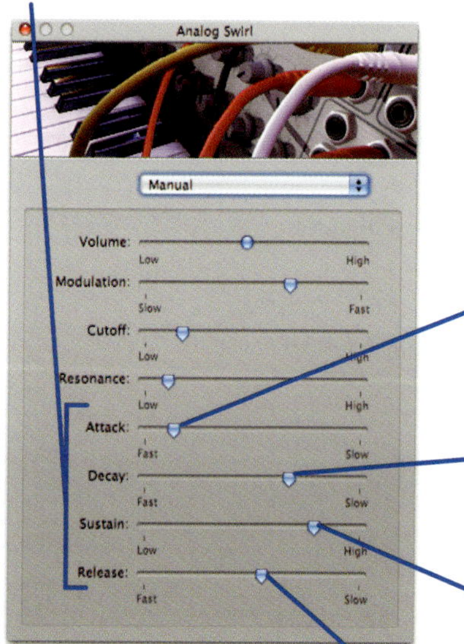

Tip: To get a feel for the kinds of settings each generator provides, drag the settings window so that you can see it and the Track Info pane at the same time. Then paw through the generators and their presets, and watch the settings window change.

Step 6. Play with the settings until you arrive at a sound you like. While you're at it, adjust effects as desired—they're stored along with the generator settings.

Step 7. Click the Save Instrument button in the Track Info pane and type a name for the new instrument. GarageBand saves the instrument settings on your hard drive (see the sidebar on the opposite page).

How quickly should the note sound when a key is pressed? A piano has a fast, or *sharp*, attack (as the hammers hit the strings). A flute has a slower attack.

How quickly should the sound volume fade or drop to the sustain level?

Should the sound sustain when a note is pressed and held down? A piano note decays over time; an organ note doesn't.

What happens when the key is released? With a fast release, the sound ends immediately. With a slower release, the sound fades gradually after the key is released.

Adding Audio Unit Instruments

You can expand GarageBand's sound-generating and effects capabilities with software plug-ins called *Audio Units.* Some absolutely stunning software instruments are available in Audio Unit format. My favorite is Native Instruments' B4, which mimics the legendary Hammond B3 organ with frightening realism. And yes, it runs within GarageBand.

I'm also a big fan of Pluggo from Cycling '74 (www.cycling74.com). Pluggo is a collection of more than 100 synthesizers and effects, and it lets you run software instruments that use other plug-in formats, such as the popular VST format.

High-end software instruments like B4 cost several times what iLife '08 costs. If you don't want to spend that much, there are some great-sounding Audio Unit instruments and effects that don't cost a dime. To explore what's available, go to www.icompositions.com or do a Google search for *audio units*. Don't expect to get any work done for a while.

Where they live. Commercial Audio Unit plug-ins usually include an installer program that puts things where they belong, but some free Audio Units don't have these installers. So for the record, Audio Units are stored in Library > Audio > Plug-Ins > Components. They can also reside in your home directory, in the same path.

Adding Effects

There's also a large selection of Audio Unit effects, and the aforementioned sites are great places to find them.

You might also explore ChannelStrip from Metric Halo (www.mhlabs.com). This legendary set of mastering effects has long been popular among recording professionals, and now it's available for GarageBand.

And while most people think of Apple's Jam Packs as being primarily a source of loops and software instruments, they're also a source of effects.

If you have a Jam Pack and would like to see what additional effects it provides, double-click any track's header, then choose the Jam Pack's name from the pop-up menu at the top of the Track Info pane. Next, choose an effect and explore its pop-up menu of presets.

How GarageBand Stores Instruments

GarageBand stores a software instrument as a file with a name that ends with .cst—for example, if you named your instrument *Wacko*, its file will be Wacko.cst. GarageBand stores its instrument files deep inside your hard drive's Library folder.

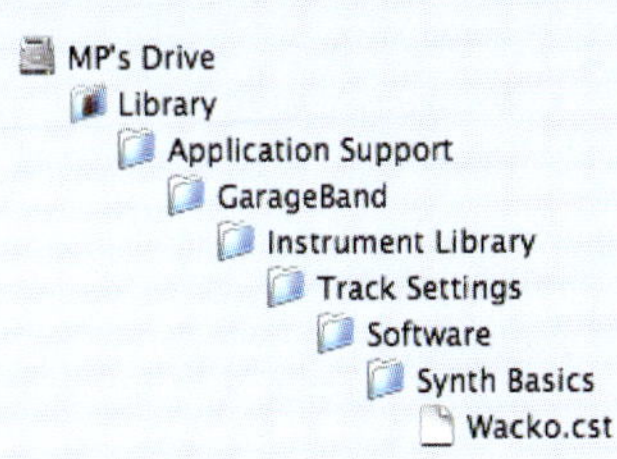

Tip: To put your custom instrument in a different category in GarageBand's Track Info pane, move its file into the appropriate category folder. For example, to move an instrument from the Synth Leads category to the Bass category, move its file from the Synth Leads folder to the Bass folder.

- Bass
- Choir
- Drum Kits
- Guitars
- Horns
- Mallets
- Organs
- Pianos and Keyboards
- Strings
- Synth Basics
- Synth Leads
- Synth Pads
- Woodwinds

Optimizing GarageBand's Performance

With apologies to the great James Brown, GarageBand is the hardest-working program in show business. It synthesizes sound, plays back audio tracks, generates effects—and never skips a beat.

Of course, this assumes that your Mac is fast enough. On slower Macs—for example, older G4 iMacs or iBooks—GarageBand can stumble and display an error message if it isn't able to perform its duties. GarageBand works hard to avoid stopping the music. For instance, if your Mac starts working up a sweat during playback, GarageBand defers scrolling the screen and updating its time readout.

To let you know how hard it's working, GarageBand changes the color of its playhead: from white (don't worry, be happy) to yellow (I will survive) to orange (the thrill is gone) to red (the sound of silence). If you see the red playhead, anticipate an error message—GarageBand is on the verge of maxing out your Mac.

But as I tell my guitar player friends, don't fret. You can do a lot to bring the music back—besides buying a faster Mac.

Performance Tips

Lock tracks. If your song has numerous software instrument tracks or real instrument tracks that use a lot of effects, locking some tracks should be your first step. For details, see the opposite page.

Add memory. A memory upgrade will improve your Mac's overall performance.

Quit other programs. Let your Mac devote all its attention to GarageBand.

Quit and relaunch. Clear GarageBand's head: quit the program and then launch it again.

Use the audio in software instrument loops. If you plan to use a software instrument loop as is (that is, you aren't going to edit the loop or change its instrument or effects assignments), you can lighten the load on your Mac by dragging the loop into a real instrument track. For more details, see the sidebar on page 351.

Tweak preferences. Choose GarageBand's Preferences command and click the Advanced button. There you can examine and change settings that GarageBand normally makes automatically. Try reducing the number of voices per instrument. Note that this restricts the number of simultaneous notes you can play.

Simplify your song. Mute some tracks and turn off some effects. The Amp Simulation effects are particularly power hungry. You *can* greatly lighten GarageBand's burden by unchecking Reverb and Echo in the Master Track's Track Info pane, but doing so will eliminate the ability to use these effects in your song. Still, you might find this a worthwhile price to pay for extra tracks. You can always transfer your song to a faster Mac to get the polish that good reverb provides.

Use an external drive. A high-performance external FireWire hard drive may be able to keep up with multiple real instrument tracks better than your Mac's built-in drive, especially if you have a laptop Mac or Mac mini.

Optimize laptop performance. If you're using a laptop Mac, open the Energy Saver system preference and choose Highest Performance from the Optimize Energy Settings pop-up menu.

Turn off FileVault. Mac OS X's FileVault feature can dramatically slow the reading of data from the Home directory of your hard drive. Turn off FileVault using the Security system preference, or store your songs outside your Home directory.

Bouncing to Disk

If the measures I've described here don't do it for you, there's still hope: an update of a technique that us old fogies—people who grew up with analog multitrack recording—know about all too well.

Back in the analog multitrack days, when you approached the limit of your four-track cassette deck, you would mix down the three tracks you had already recorded and put them on the fourth track. After the mix-down, you could erase and re-use the original three tracks.

This technique was often called *bouncing*, and it's alive and well in GarageBand. Say you've laid down a sweet rhythm section groove—some drums, some bass, and maybe a keyboard or synthesizer pad.

You want to play a synth solo over this, but your PowerBook doesn't have the power.

Solution: save your project with an iLife preview (page 361), then add the project to a new GarageBand project.

Fine-tune your mix. Adjust every setting—panning, volume, effects, everything—until your mix sounds exactly as you want it.

Save with preview. Use the Preferences command to activate the save-with-preview feature, as described on page 361. Then, save the project. GarageBand creates a stereo mixdown of your tune and saves it along with the project.

Start over. Start a new GarageBand project. Be sure to set the key signature and tempo to match your song's settings. Locate your song in the GarageBand media browser, then drag it into the new project.

Add tracks and have fun. Because your rhythm groove is now one audio track—not a whole bunch of different, system-taxing tracks—your Mac can devote its energy to the new tracks.

Making changes. If you decide to change your rhythm groove, just open up your original project, make your changes, and save again. Because GarageBand maintains a link between the two projects, your changes will be incorporated in the second project when you reopen it.

The Key to Locking Tracks

If your Mac is choking during playback, try locking one or more tracks. To lock a track, click the padlock button in the track's header. Then, play the song from the beginning. GarageBand renders the locked track to disk: it creates an audio file containing the track's audio.

When the song begins playing, GarageBand plays back that audio file instead of making your Mac's processor do the heavy lifting involved in generating sounds and effects in real time.

Locking candidates. The best candidates for locking are software instrument tracks (particularly ones that use the Symphony Orchestra Jam Pack) and real instrument tracks containing complex effects, such as the guitar amp simulators.

Harder on the hard drive. Alas, locking tracks makes your hard drive work harder. If you have a laptop Mac or a Mac mini—computers that have slower hard drives than other Macs—you may find that locking a lot of tracks causes playback problems. When you lock tracks, your project also uses more disk space.

Extracting a locked track. You can use the Finder to extract the audio from a locked track. Control-click on your project's icon and choose Show Package Contents from the shortcut menu. In the window that appears, open the Freeze Files folder: it will contain the audio files that GarageBand has rendered. You can open these files in other programs (including iTunes), but you can't import them into GarageBand.

To avoid corrupting a project, don't rename or delete any files in the project's Freeze Files folder.

Unlocking a track. You can't edit a locked track or change its instrument or effects settings. (You can make volume and panning adjustments, however.) To change a locked track, unlock it by clicking the padlock button again.

Creating a Podcast at a Glance

I've already described how you can use iTunes and your iPod to listen to podcasts of all kinds (pages 34–37). With GarageBand, you can go from listener to producer.

GarageBand turns your Mac into a radio studio—with broadcast engineer. Connect a microphone to your Mac or use the built-in mike that most Macs provide. You can also use the microphone built into Apple's standalone iSight video camera. GarageBand contains audio filters that optimize the sound produced by an iSight or built-in Mac mike.

Record your rants, vacation dispatches, family interviews—whatever you like. You can even record remote interviews with iChat users. Your audio is recorded into real-instrument tracks, so you can edit it using the same techniques described earlier.

Need theme music? Compose your own or use one of the many royalty-free music jingles included with iLife '08. Use the *ducking* feature to have GarageBand automatically lower and raise the music volume when you start and stop talking—just like the radio.

But don't stop there. Consider creating an *enhanced podcast*. Add chapter markers that enable listeners to conveniently jump around through your show. Add artwork that appears during playback in iTunes and on any iPod that can display photos. And add Web URLs that let iTunes users jump to specific Web pages as your show plays.

When you're finished, send your completed production to iWeb for publishing on the Internet. Here's how to become a podcaster.

Pick a Background

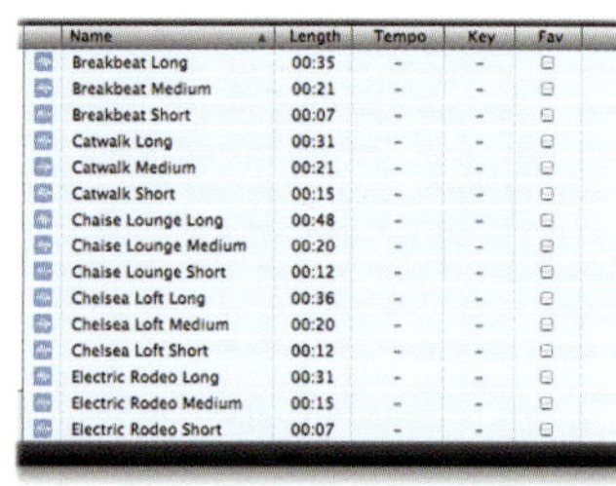

Use the loop browser to explore and choose from more than 100 jingles, including many sets that provide the same song in lengths of 7, 15, and 30 seconds. You can also choose from hundreds of sound effects and music *stingers*—and even use the Musical Typing window to play them as you do your show (page 359).

Add Visuals

Use the media browser to add photos (page 372) or movies (page 376). Use the search box to quickly locate what you need.

Add Web Connections

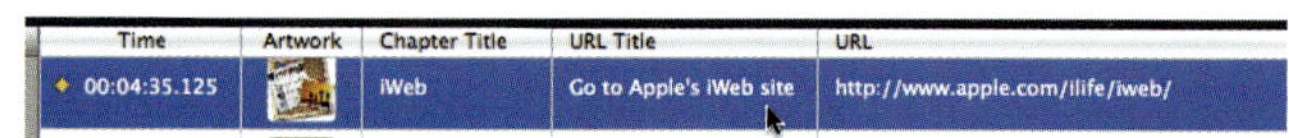

Want your listeners to be able to jump to Web pages that relate to your subject? Add Web addresses (URLs) to your markers (page 373).

When you create a new podcast, GarageBand gives you a standard set of tracks for common elements. You can customize these tracks and add more.

Use the *podcast track* to view and edit marker regions—for example, to synchronize a piece of artwork with a specific section of your show (pages 372–373).

Control how a track's volume is affected by the ducking feature. Click the down-pointing arrow for a background music track (page 371). Customize the ducking effect if you like (page 374).

Preview the appearance of your enhanced podcast as it plays back (page 371).

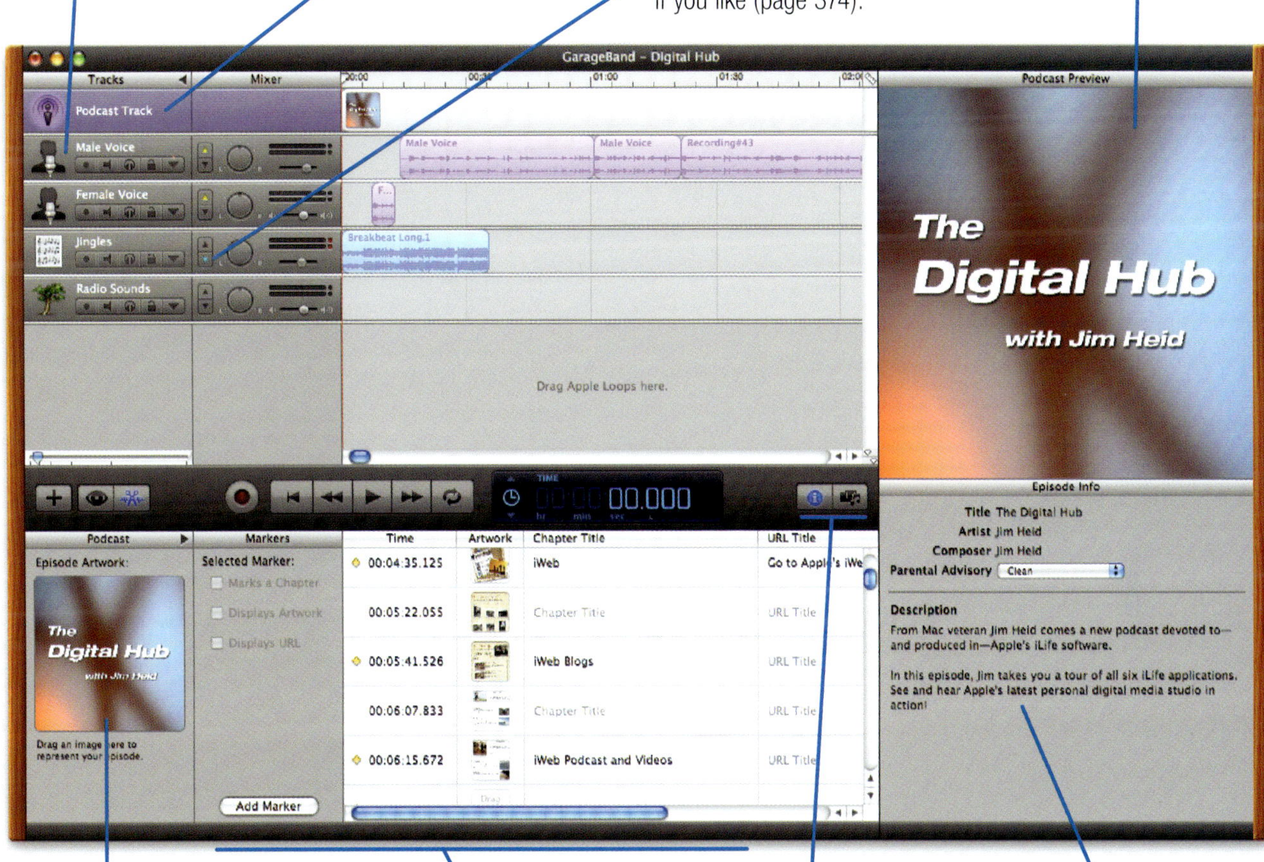

Drag an image here to add *episode artwork* to your podcast (opposite page and page 373).

Create, edit, and manage the markers in your enhanced podcast (page 373).

Switch between displaying the Media browser (opposite page) and Track Info pane, where you can refine your sound.

Specify episode information, which appears in iTunes and iWeb.

Podcast Production Techniques

Plan

There are as many types of podcasts as there are types of songs. But no matter what topic you cover, you have a common set of planning and production options to consider.

Script (or at least sketch). You don't have to script every word of your podcast, but at least sketch out the structure of your show. And because they're the critical bookends for your barking, consider scripting your introduction and conclusion.

How long? Around 20 to 30 minutes is a good balance between depth and reasonable download times, not to mention listener attention span.

How much? You can record one non-stop rant, but I'm unlikely to listen to it. Consider covering several topics, limiting each to five minutes or so.

What's the theme? Start your podcast with an introductory music jingle. Compose your own or use the ones that come with GarageBand. To explore them, display the loop browser, then click the button.

GarageBand's jingles come in several durations. Consider using a 30-second version for your intro and a seven-second version as a separator, called a *bumper*, between topic segments.

Tip: Don't waste time by letting your intro music play and play. Your listeners want to hear *you*, so let the music play for just a few seconds, then start your intro. Use GarageBand's automatic ducking feature to lower the music's volume when you start talking.

Who else? Will you have guests? A variety of voices makes for more interesting listening. You can record guests via phone or iChat (page 374) or, ideally, in person, with a second microphone.

Produce

Get started. As shown on the previous pages, when you click Create New Podcast Episode while creating a new GarageBand project, you get a set of tracks for male and female voices. You also get jingles and radio sounds, such as sound effects and *stingers*, which are short, sonic spices of the kind you hear on the radio before traffic and weather reports.

If you'll need additional tracks—perhaps to record a guest with a second microphone, or some music using a software instrument and your music keyboard—add the tracks using the techniques described earlier in this chapter.

Prepare for recording. Record in a quiet location and with the best microphone you can use. (For advice on obtaining good sound, see page 266.) If you're using multiple mikes or audio sources, assign inputs to each track (page 348). Adjust your recording levels (page 347).

Cue the band. When should you add music to your podcast? I recommend waiting until after you've recorded and refined the core content of your podcast. Save the music for the post-production phase. The way GarageBand lets you drag audio regions around makes it easy to time where you want the music to come in.

On the air. To begin recording, click the Record button or press the R key. Make a mistake? Pause for a second or two, then pick up at a point before your blunder. You can edit out the flub later using the techniques on page 339.

Polish

Optional: Adjust effects. The male and female tracks that GarageBand provides in a new podcast project are fine for most efforts. But you might want to open the Track Info pane and explore some of GarageBand's effects and audio-enhancement options. Double-click on the track header for the track you want to tweak, then click the Details button in the Track Info pane.

The Speech Enhancer effect can sweeten a voice in several ways. Explore the presets in the pop-up menu, then click the pencil button to view all your options. If you're using an iSight camera's mike or the mike built into your Mac, you can choose options that will optimize sound quality. You can also apply a noise-reduction filter.

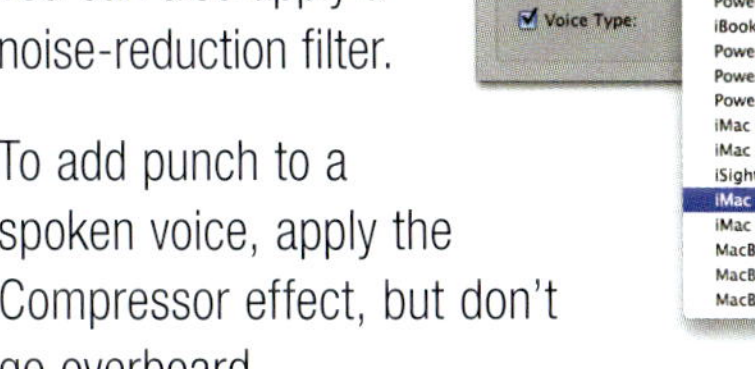

To add punch to a spoken voice, apply the Compressor effect, but don't go overboard.

Add music and refine timing. Now's the time when I like to add theme and bumper jingles and refine the timing of my podcasts. To take advantage of GarageBand's volume-ducking feature, be sure the down-pointing arrow is active in the Jingles track (or other music tracks you may have added) and the up-pointing arrow is active in your primary voice track or tracks.

Optional: Enhance your podcast. If you're creating an enhanced podcast—one with artwork, chapter markers, URL markers, or any combination thereof—add those items now. See the following pages.

Publish

Preview and proofread. Before exporting the final podcast, play it all the way through. If you've added artwork, chapter, or URL markers, use the Podcast Preview pane to verify that they appear when they should. Click any URL markers to ensure that they go to the proper Web address. (If the Podcast Preview pane isn't visible, double-click on the track header for the Podcast track.)

Make sure there are no odd audio glitches caused by editing. Adjust volume levels as necessary to deliver a strong signal with no clipping. Adjust ducking settings for the best balance of voice and background (page 374).

Export your podcast. Use the Share menu to send your podcast to iWeb or iTunes, or save it to disk. Choose the MP3 or AAC formats, and choose an audio quality setting.

You can also burn your podcast to an audio CD. For details, see page 357.

Enhancing Your Podcast

With enhanced podcasts, your options go beyond sound to include photos, chapter markers, and URL markers. You can use just one of these enhancements in your podcasts, or you can use all three.

By adding images to the podcast track, you can add photography and artwork that appears in the iTunes window or on photo-capable iPods. Create a training podcast that illustrates the steps involved in performing a task. Or an art history podcast that shows famous works as you talk about them. Or a vacation travelogue that shows your stops.

With chapter markers, you can add convenient navigation to your podcast. When your podcast is played in iTunes, a chapter menu appears that allows listeners (and viewers) to jump to sections of interest. When playing your podcast on an iPod, your audience can navigate the chapters using their click wheels or touch screens.

With URL markers, you can add the immediacy of the Internet. Create links to pages that relate to your subject. The link appears in the iTunes window, and your podcast's audience can jump to the link's URL by clicking it.

The one downside to an enhanced podcast is that you must deliver it in the AAC audio format, which means that the podcast will play only in iTunes and on iPods and Apple TV. If you're planning to deliver your podcast in MP3 format to reach the broadest possible audience, keep your podcasts unenhanced.

Adding Artwork

Step 1. Display the media browser by clicking its button.

Step 2. In the media browser, click the Photos button, then locate the photo you want to add.

Step 3. Drag the photo to a location in the podcast track.

Step 4. To fine-tune the amount of time the artwork appears, drag the edges of its region left or right.

You can also drag the entire artwork region left and right, just as you can other GarageBand regions. **Tip:** To have regions snap toward each other as you drag, choose Control > Alignment Guides. This helps prevent you from accidentally replacing part of a region by dragging another region over it.

Notes and Tips

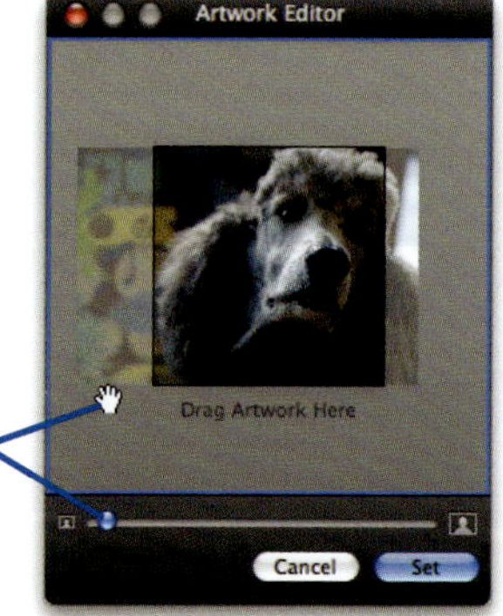

Editing art. To adjust an item's zooming and cropping, double-click the item's thumbnail in the Artwork column. Use the Artwork Editor to zoom in and adjust which part of the art is visible, then click Set.

You can also replace an image by dragging a new image to the editor.

Art from elsewhere. You can also add an image to the podcast track by dragging it from the Finder. You can even add an image from a Web page by dragging it from the Safari browser.

More than just art. An artwork region can also represent a chapter marker and a URL marker. For example, maybe you'd like a chapter to begin when a particular image appears. In the podcast track, select the image. Next, in the podcast track editor, click in the Chapter Title box and type a name for the chapter. For more details, see the opposite page.

Adding Chapter Markers

Step 1. Position the GarageBand playhead at the point where you want the marker to appear, then click the Add Marker button in the podcast track editor.

Tip: You can click Add Markers to add markers as your podcast plays back.

Step 2. In the podcast track editor, select the marker's *Chapter Title* placeholder text in the Chapter Title column, then type a title.

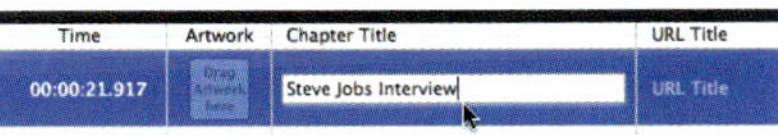

In iTunes, a Chapters menu appears in the menu bar when the podcast plays.

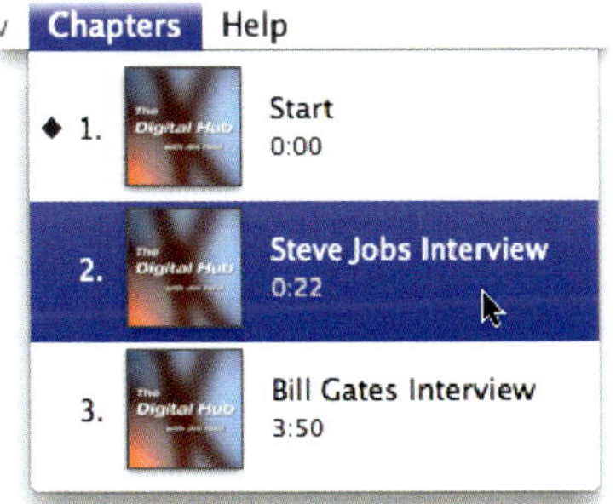

Tip: As noted on the opposite page, you can use an artwork region as a chapter marker by simply typing a title in the region's Chapter Title box.

Adding URL Markers

As with chapter markers, you can assign a URL to a region that contains artwork; just skip to Step 2 below.

Step 1. Position the playhead at the point where you want the marker, then click the Add Marker button in the podcast track editor.

Step 2. In the podcast track editor, type the URL title and address.

Type the address of the Web page here. You can also copy an address from the Safari location bar and paste it here.

The URL title is displayed in the artwork area of the iTunes window.

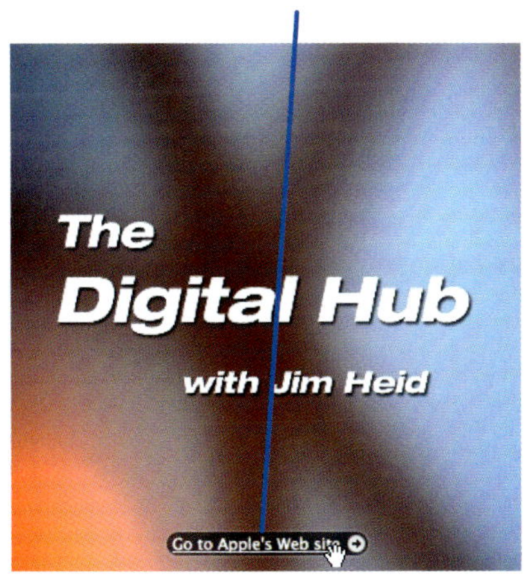

Adding Episode Artwork

Episode artwork is a single image that appears in iTunes while your podcast is playing. iWeb also uses episode artwork when you add a podcast to a Web page (page 400). You might use episode artwork to display your company logo, a favorite photo from your vacation podcast, or a graphic created in Photoshop or Photoshop Elements that contains a few words about the podcast's topic.

If your podcast also contains artwork regions as described on the opposite page, the regions replace the episode artwork as the podcast plays back. When those artwork regions end, the episode artwork reappears.

To add episode artwork, drag an image from the media browser (or elsewhere) to the Episode Artwork well at the left edge of the podcast track editor. To tweak the cropping of the artwork, double-click it in the Episode Artwork well, then use the Artwork Editor as described on the opposite page.

Podcasting Tips

Adjusting Ducking

GarageBand's ducking feature makes it easy to create a podcast in which you talk over background music. Activate ducking, and GarageBand lowers the volume of the music when you talk, then brings it up again during pauses. There's no need to manually create volume automation curves that adjust the music's volume.

But the ducker may not always lower the volume as much as you'd like—and as any boxer will tell you, partial ducking just isn't enough.

If your voice is still getting a left hook from your background music, adjust the ducker. Double-click the header for the master track, turn to the Track Info window, and choose one of the presets from the Ducker pop-up menu.

The presets let you choose how quickly music volume is lowered and restored, and to what degree. You can also create a custom preset by clicking the tiny pencil button next to the pop-up.

Stamp Your Podcast

Many podcasters like to begin each episode with a very brief announcement of the podcast's name and date: *This is The Digital Hub, Episode 3, for August 17, 2008.* This little "stamp" is handy for listeners who are using iPods. It lets them immediately verify that they're listening to the right episode—without having to take their eyes off the road.

The Leopard angle. In Mac OS X 10.5 (Leopard), iChat can record audio and video chats, provided all chat participants are using Leopard. After starting the chat, click the Record button in iChat. iChat notifies the participant that he or he is about to be recorded.

When you're done, locate the recording. (You'll find it in Documents > iChats, unless you've changed your preferences.) Drag it into GarageBand. If you recorded a video chat but you want only the audio, simply choose Track > Show Podcast Track after you import the video. GarageBand discards the video but keeps the audio.

If you want to record within iChat but your chat participant isn't using Leopard, check out Ecamm Network's Conference Recorder, an iChat add-on that can record audio and video chats conducted with pre-Leopard iChat versions—and even with Windows audio-video chat programs.

Recording iChat Interviews

If you use Mac OS X 10.4 Tiger or a later version, you can use Apple's iChat conferencing software to record audio interviews with distant guests. GarageBand stores each participant's voice in its own track. And if you're conducting a video conference, GarageBand grabs a still shot of each participant when he or she begins speaking and adds that image to the podcast track.

To record iChat interviews, you must initiate the audio or video conference—that is, *you* must be the one to invite the other guests to the conference. Do that, and then chat with your guests for a minute or two to make sure that your Internet connection, and the Internet as a whole, are behaving themselves. I've had best-laid interview plans shattered by Internet difficulties that were out of my control. Use this testing time to remind your guests that you'll be recording them.

When you're ready to begin recording, click GarageBand's Record button or press the R key. GarageBand asks if you want to record the chat.

Click Yes, and GarageBand begins recording. Now grill your guests and grill them hard.

In my experience, you need a fairly fast Mac to get good results when recording iChat conferences. My 1.67GHz PowerBook G4 sometimes stumbles, but a G5 or Intel Duo system does a good job. And needless to say, a fast Internet connection is a must, particularly for multi-guest interviews.

The Leopard angle. In Mac OS X 10.5 (Leopard), iChat can record audio and video chats, provided all chat participants are using Leopard. After starting the chat, click the Record button in iChat. iChat notifies the participant that he or he is about to be recorded.

When you're done, locate the recording. (You'll find it in Documents > iChats, unless you've changed your preferences.) Drag it into GarageBand. If you recorded a video chat but you want only the audio, simply choose Track > Show Podcast Track after you import the video. GarageBand discards the video but keeps the audio.

If you want to record within iChat but your chat participant isn't using Leopard, check out Ecamm Network's Conference Recorder, an iChat add-on that can record audio and video chats conducted with pre-Leopard iChat versions—and even with Windows audio-video chat programs.

Recording Phone Interviews

iChat interviews can be fun, but you might prefer to back away from the cutting edge and conduct your interviews the way many radio stations do: via telephone.

You have a few options for recording a telephone call. Radio Shack sells several phone-recording adaptors for under $30. Connect the adaptor to your phone and attach it to your Mac's microphone jack, and you're underway.

The problem with inexpensive recording devices, though, is that *your* voice also sounds like it's coming over the phone (which, from your Mac's standpoint, it is). What you want is for your voice to be recorded by that high-quality microphone that you were smart enough to buy. For this, you need a specialized piece of hardware called a *telephone hybrid.*

A telephone hybrid is a box that contains jacks for the telephone line and your microphone. Connect your mike and your phone to the hybrid, then connect the audio output of the hybrid to your Mac's microphone jack. Some hybrids also have volume knobs that let you adjust the mix between your mike and your guest's phone.

A good source for telephone hybrids is JK Audio (www.jkaudio.com). The company's least expensive device, the AutoHybrid, sells for under $200. A Google search for *telephone hybrid* will yield more sources.

The Skype angle. If you use the Skype software to make Internet phone calls, you can conduct interviews via Skype and record the results. You can use Rogue Amoeba Software's Audio Hijack Pro to record Skype calls, but many podcasters swear by Ecamm Network's Call Recorder, a simple and inexpensive utility designed specifically for the task.

Music Rights and Wrongs

Thinking of doing a music podcast? Note that you can't legally publish a podcast containing commercial recordings—at least not without paying for the rights to do so.

To learn the latest about the frequently changing world of digital music licensing, do some Google searches for *podcast music licensing* and *podcast music rights.*

Tune Into Magnatune

You might also investigate music sources that permit rebroadcasting and podcast use. A great stop is Magnatune (www.magnatune.com), which has refreshingly simple policies for podcasters: "Magnatune is one of the only record labels on the planet whose music you can legally use in your podcast, without paying for a licensing agreement. Because we work directly with artists, we can legally do this."

And you have to love a record label whose corporate slogan is "We are not evil."

Scoring Movies with GarageBand

iMovie's audio features are adequate for many projects, but your soundtrack options don't end there. You can bring video into GarageBand and apply GarageBand's audio and music-making features to the movie's soundtrack.

GarageBand's video features aren't for editing the picture; that's a job for iMovie. Rather, you bring a finished edit into GarageBand for additional sonic seasoning. Punch up the sound with GarageBand's effects. Record and edit narration with more precision than iMovie provides. Or compose your own music soundtracks by using loops and by recording your own performances. When you're finished, send the final movie to iTunes, iWeb, or iDVD.

You might also use GarageBand's video features to create a *video podcast*: a podcast that adds the dimension of motion. As with GarageBand's audio podcasting features, you can add chapter and URL markers to the video. When you're done, you can send your final product to iWeb or save it for manual uploading to a Web server.

You'll need a fast Mac with a fast hard drive for movie scoring. If you have playback problems, consult the advice on page 366 to optimize GarageBand's performance.

Refining an iMovie Soundtrack

Step 1. In iMovie, finish your edit, then share the movie to the media browser (Share > Media Browser; see page 278).

Step 2. In GarageBand, display the media browser, click the Movies button, then locate your movie and drag it into the tracks area of the GarageBand window.

iMovie imports the movie and displays it in the video track (opposite page).

Step 3. Enhance to your ears' content: add tracks, record narration, apply effects, or add chapter and URL markers for a video podcast.

Step 4. Use the commands in the Share menu to send your finished movie to iTunes, iWeb, or iDVD, or to export it as a QuickTime movie (opposite page).

Notes and Tips

Chapters for iDVD. iMovie '08 doesn't let you create chapter markers for a DVD, but you can use GarageBand to do the job. In iMovie, share your project to the media browser, choosing the Large quality setting. Bring the movie into GarageBand as described above.

Next, select the movie track and click the track editor button. Use the track editor to add chapter markers. Give each chapter a title—iDVD will use it to label each chapter's button.

Finally, choose Share > Send to iDVD. iDVD creates a new project and adds the movie to it, creating a Scene Selection menu for accessing the chapters.

Movies from elsewhere. In addition to using the media browser to add a movie to GarageBand, you can also simply drag a movie's icon from any location on your hard drive into the GarageBand window.

Working with Movies

When you've brought a movie into GarageBand, here's what you see—and what you can do.

Your movie's video frames appear in the video track. The more you zoom in on the timeline, the more sequential frames you see. When you want to position a region (for example, a sound effect) so that it begins when a specific frame appears, zoom in until you see that frame.

The video track editor works much like the podcast track editor: you can add chapter markers and URL markers.

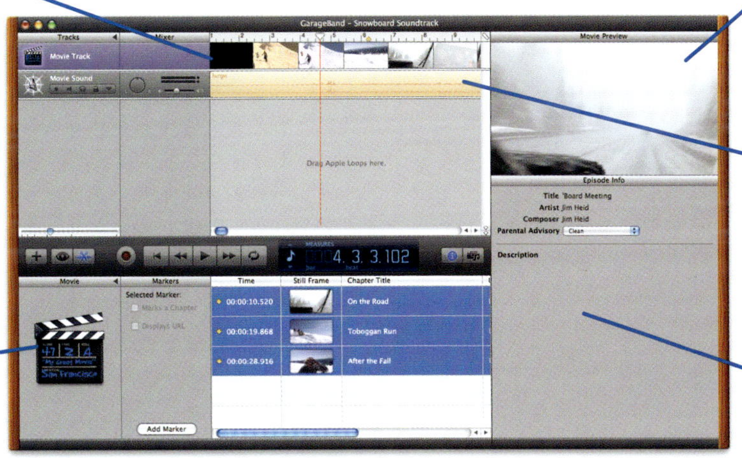

When you play the project, the movie plays here.

Your movie's soundtrack appears as an imported audio region. You can add filters or effects to this track using the techniques described earlier in this chapter.

Creating a video podcast? Use this area to type a description for the podcast.

Tips for Video

Enhancing narration. If you've recorded a voice-over or other narration in GarageBand (or, for that matter, in iMovie), consider applying GarageBand's audio effects to it. For example, use the Compressor effect to add punch to a narration. Use the Speech Enhancer filter to reduce noise and optimize male or female voices.

Exporting your final effort. When you've finished refining a movie's soundtrack, you can use the Share menu to send your final effort to iTunes, iWeb, or iDVD.

You can also export the project as a QuickTime movie. Choose Share > Export Movie to Disk, and choose a quality setting from the pop-up menu.

To customize export settings, choose the Expert option, then adjust the settings in the subsequent dialog box. Your options are identical to those described on page 278.

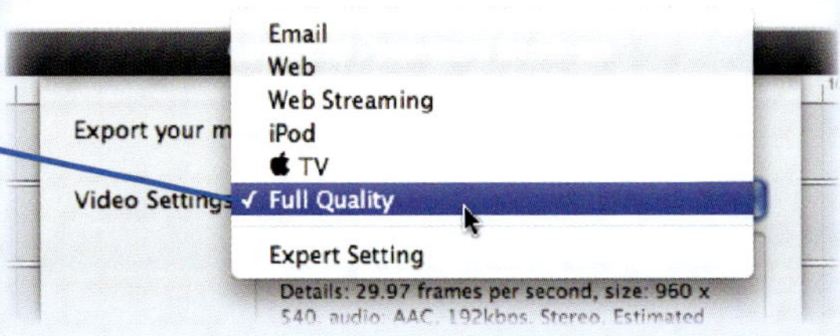

iWeb: Your World on the Web

The Macintosh
iLife '08

iWeb at a Glance

With iWeb, you can put your world on the Web. You can create Web sites containing text, photos, movies, podcasts, and more. iWeb insulates you from Web publishing technicalities, such as markup languages and servers.

Start by choosing one of the site design *templates* that are built into iWeb. Many of those designs have counterparts in other iLife '08 programs. For example, the Travel template in iWeb resembles the Travel theme in iPhoto and iDVD. Thus, you can create a Web site about your vacation and have it match your iPhoto books and calendars, and the DVD containing your video and travel slide shows—a consistent visual identity, as the marketers would say.

Each iWeb template provides several types of pages. As you create a site, you simply add new pages as needed to accommodate what you want to publish.

Decided on a design? Just add content. Replace the placeholder photos and text with your own. Use the page design as is, or use iWeb's formatting tools to customize it to your own liking. You can add maps and ads from Google, as well as .Mac photo galleries, with a few clicks, too. If you've used Apple's Pages or Keynote software, you'll feel at home with iWeb's formatting features.

iWeb also simplifies creating blogs and podcasts. Creating a new blog or podcast entry is as easy as creating a new email message. iWeb also manages the chores of creating archive pages and RSS feeds.

When you're finished, one click publishes your site to Apple's .Mac service.

A Gallery of Web Pages

Each iWeb template provides eight page styles, each aimed at a specific type of content. Not shown here: the Blank style, which shares the template's background and color scheme, but lacks placeholder text and graphics.

Welcome
An introductory home page, ideal for welcoming visitors and stating the purpose of your site.

About
A good place to describe yourself, your business, your organization—whatever your site is about.

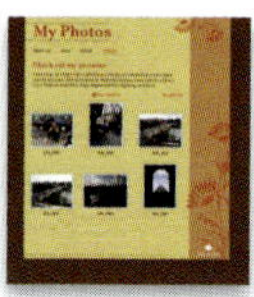

Photos
A photo album, with small photo thumbnails and a button for displaying photos as a slide show. You can also create a photos page from within iPhoto (page 394).

My Albums
An index page that acts as a gateway to photos and movie pages. Drag iPhoto albums and movies here to quickly publish them (pages 394–399).

Movie
A page designed to present a QuickTime movie (page 409).

Blog
Your blog's main page, with links to individual blog entries. You can also create a blog entry from within iPhoto (page 400). A similar page style holds podcasts.

The *sidebar* lists the sites you create and their pages. You can create multiple sites with iWeb, and even move pages between sites.

Change the theme of the current page.

As you create pages, iWeb creates a *navigation menu* that your site's visitors will use to get around. iWeb updates your navigation menu as you rearrange and expand your site.

Create your pages on the *webpage canvas*. Drag text and graphics around, add and remove text boxes and photos, type and format text, add shapes, and more.

Add photos from your iPhoto library or another source (page 394).

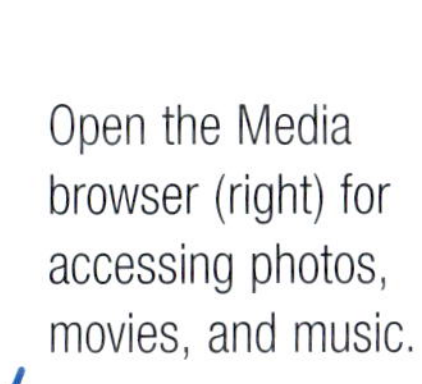

Open the Media browser (right) for accessing photos, movies, and music.

Open the Adjust panel (right) for image tweaking, such as in iPhoto (page 389).

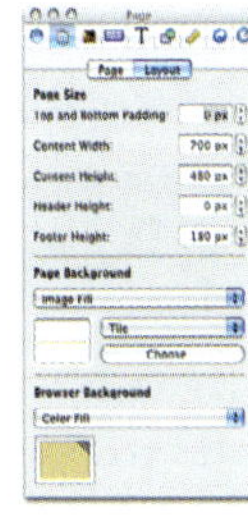

Open the Inspector (right) for precise formatting, linking, and more.

Add a new Web page (page 383).

Send the site to .Mac for all—or only some—to see (page 406).

Open the published version of the site in your Web browser.

Add text boxes (page 386) and shapes (page 391); insert ads, maps, and other items (page 404); and refine layouts (page 388).

Your .Mac account appears here.

Add a *hit counter* to count the visitors to your site, and an email link to allow visitors to contact you (page 408).

Creating a Web Site

What do you want to publish? A few iPhoto albums? The occasional movie? A podcast? Or a full Web site containing numerous pages as well as photo albums, a blog, and a podcast?

iWeb can handle any of these tasks. If you're planning an ambitious site, though, consider sketching out the site's structure on paper before you start. You might want to draw an organizational chart, with the home page at the top and other pages beneath it—much like the DVD menu diagram on page 304. This kind of advance planning can help you map out your site and organize your thoughts.

After you've planned your attack, perform it. Start by creating a new site and choosing a page template for its design. Then replace the placeholder content with your own text and graphics. Tweak the text formatting if you like, but be careful—the "wrong" kinds of formatting can cause iWeb to create large pages that load slowly (page 386).

As your site comes together, you'll add additional pages and create links to connect them. You might also create links to other sites on the World Wide Web. You'll add graphics and adjust their appearance. And then you'll publish your site on Apple's .Mac service.

I cover each of these phases, and more, in the pages that follow. Here's how to get started.

Creating a New Site

First Time Here?

The first time you start iWeb, it presents its list of templates and page styles.

Step 1. Choose the template that best matches what you have in mind for your site. Remember, you can customize your pages.

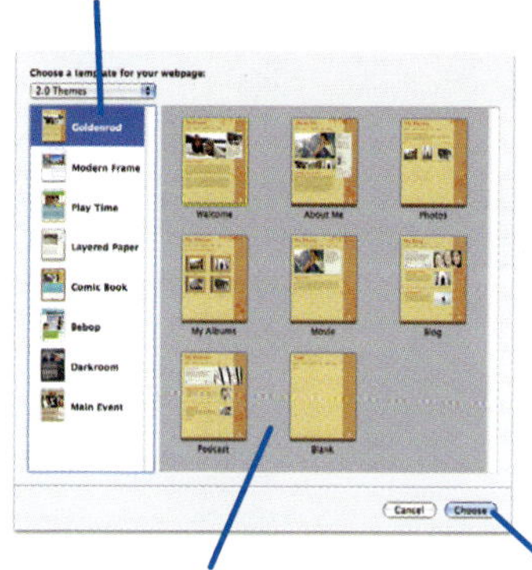

Step 2. Choose a page style. The Welcome and About Me styles are good starting points for general-purpose pages, while the remaining styles are tailored for specific tasks (page 380).

Step 3. Click Choose or press Return.

Repeat Customer?

You can create multiple Web sites and switch between them with the click of a mouse. When you want to create a new site, choose New Site from the File menu (Shift-⌘-N), then choose a template and page style as described above.

Renaming Sites and Pages

To change the name of a site or page, double-click it in the sidebar, then type a new name.

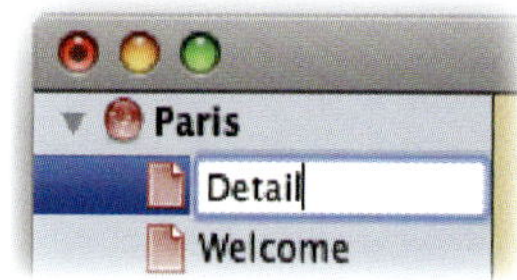

Brevity rules. Unless you specify otherwise (page 385), iWeb adds a navigation menu link for a new page. If you use a wordy page name, the link may not display correctly—and it will definitely look hokey.

Note that if you use spaces in page names (as in *Main Menu*), iWeb will translate them into underscores (for example, *Main_Menu*) when you publish your site. The links will still work, but they'll look unwieldy and will be hard to recite over the phone. For the tidiest page addresses, avoid spaces.

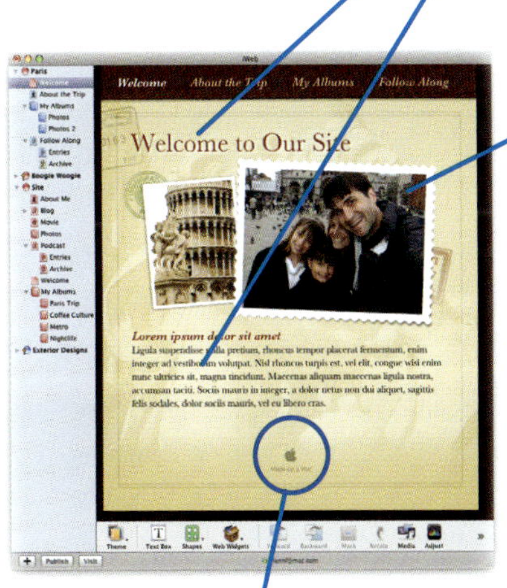

Kill the advertising. To remove the "Made on a Mac" graphic, select it and press the Delete key.

Creating a Page: The Basics

After you choose a page style, iWeb gives you a page filled with placeholder graphics and text. By replacing this placeholder content with your own, you can create an attractive Web page.

Here's a look at the basic techniques behind iWeb page design. In the following pages, I describe how you can tailor a page design to your tastes.

Replacing placeholder text. To replace a section of placeholder text, select it and begin typing.

Adventures in Paris

Replace placeholder photos. To replace a placeholder photo with one of your own, drag the photo from the media browser or from any folder on your hard drive to the placeholder folder.

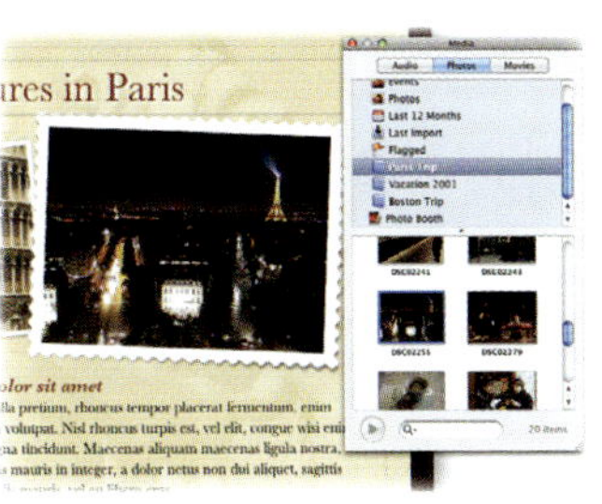

Creating Additional Pages

To add a new page to a site, choose New Page from the File menu or click the + button. Choose a template and page style as described on the opposite page.

Off the menu. Normally, iWeb includes a new page in your site's navigation menu. In some cases, you may not want this—maybe you plan to use a text link or other button to provide access to that page. Use the Inspector to remove a page from the navigation menu; see page 385.

Where iWeb Stores Your Sites

iWeb stores all of your sites and their pages in one place: a file named *Domain* tucked deep within your hard drive. Specifically, the Domain file lives in your home directory, within Library > Application Support > iWeb.

Get in the habit of backing up the Domain file now and then. If you use Apple's Backup 3, included with a .Mac subscription, you can have this done automatically. Time Machine, part of Mac OS X 10.5 (Leopard) will also automatically back up the Domain file unless you specifically exclude a folder that contains that file.

Page Design Basics

If you aren't a tailor, it's better to buy off the rack than to try to make your own suit. And if you aren't a Web designer, it's a good idea to stick with the built-in page styles that each iWeb template provides.

But the temptation to tinker may beckon. Maybe a certain page style requires a few more graphics to meet your needs, and maybe one of those graphics could use some work. Maybe you'd like to use a different type font, or adjust the line spacing of some text. Maybe a page needs another block of text, or a different background color.

You can perform many design tweaks directly on the webpage canvas. Click and drag blocks of text or graphics to move them around. Resize an item by selecting it and then dragging one of its selection handles.

For other design tasks, you'll turn to iWeb's Inspector. This small floating window is actually numerous control panels in one; you display the Inspector you need by clicking a button at the top of the Inspector window. With the Inspector, you can specify paragraph formatting, add and remove page backgrounds, create special graphics effects, and more.

For still other tasks, you'll use menu commands and the tools at the bottom of the iWeb window. Add additional text boxes to a page. Add shapes, such as lines and boxes. Control how objects overlap, specify colors and fonts, insert Web widgets, modify images, and more.

Here's a tour of your design studio.

Moving an Object

To move an object (for example, a text box or a graphic), click and drag it to the desired location.

iWeb displays *alignment guides* when an object you're dragging is centered on the page or aligned with another object on the page. To customize the alignment guides, use the Preferences command (page 409).

As you drag an item, iWeb displays its location on the page, in pixels. Here, the photo is 91 pixels from the left edge of the page and 203 pixels from the top.

Notes and Tips

Go straight. If you press the Shift key while dragging, iWeb constrains the item's movement to horizontal, vertical, or a 45-degree angle.

Keyboard control. To nudge an item in one-pixel increments, select the item and then press one of the arrow keys on your keyboard. To nudge in 10-pixel increments, press Shift along with an arrow key.

Have another. To duplicate an item, press the Option key while dragging the item.

Resizing an Object

To resize an object, select it and drag one of its selection handles. If you resize a text box, its text reflows to fit the new size.

To resize an item in just one direction, drag a side handle.

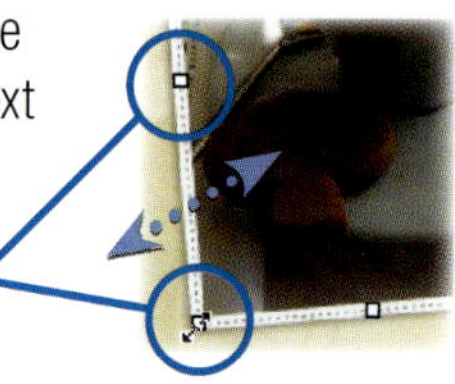

Tip: To avoid changing the proportions of a text box or shape when resizing it, press the Shift key while dragging.

Anatomy of a Page

Each page style in an iWeb template has four regions. Each region serves its own purpose, and by changing the dimensions of the regions, you can change the appearance and dimensions of a Web page.

To see each of the four regions, choose Show Layout from the View menu (Shift-⌘-L). iWeb displays faint gray lines between each region.

Some page styles use some regions, but not others. For example, the page styles in the Travel template lack header regions. You can add those regions, however, by using the Page Inspector as described at right.

The *header* appears at the very top of the page.

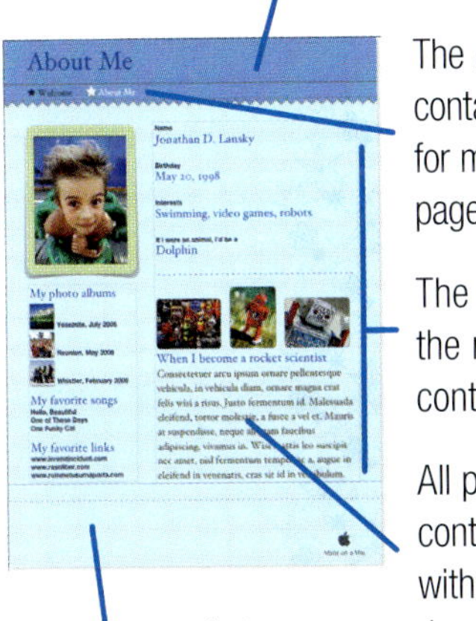

The *navigation bar* contains the menu for moving from page to page.

The *body* holds the main page content.

All page styles contain *text boxes* with placeholder text that you can replace or delete. You can also add additional text boxes.

The *footer* is at the very bottom of the page and typically holds the "Made on a Mac" graphic along with other optional elements, such as page counters and "email me" buttons (page 408).

Introducing the Inspector

The Inspector is the gateway to many design and formatting tasks in iWeb. To display the Inspector, click the Inspector button near the lower-right corner of the iWeb window, or choose Show Inspector from the View menu (Option-⌘-I).

If you don't want a page to appear in your site's navigation menu, uncheck this box.

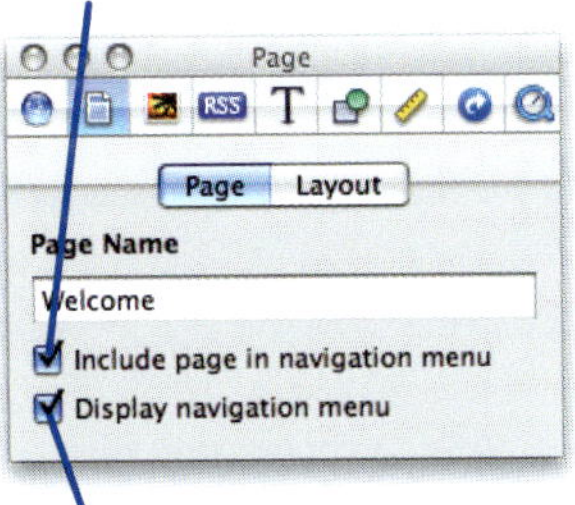

To prevent the navigation menu from appearing on the page, uncheck this box.

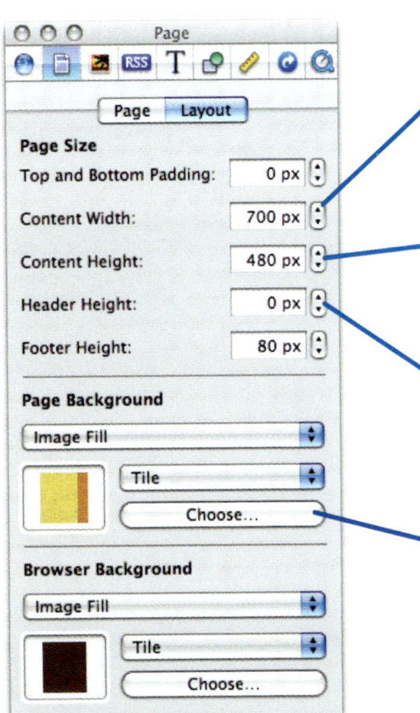

Changing Pages: The Page Inspector

iWeb's page styles tend to have short pages that your site's visitors can scroll through with just a click or two. That's convenient, but maybe you have more content than will fit within a page's confines. As long as your design is uncluttered (and your content interesting), there's nothing wrong with having a longer Web page.

To change a page's dimensions, use the Page Inspector. Display the Inspector, then click the Page button to display the Page Inspector.

The Page Size values determine the dimensions of a page and each of its regions.

You can make a page wider by increasing the value in the Content Width box, but don't go overboard: you don't want your site's visitors to have to scroll horizontally to read the entire page.

To make a page longer, increase the Content Height value by clicking the arrows or typing a new value. (The values are in pixels.)

Want to add a header region to a page style that lacks one? Specify a value here.

With many page styles, you can customize the page background here (see page 392).

Working with Text

To state the obvious, text plays a large role on Web sites. iWeb gives you plenty of text control. You can use the fonts that Apple has used for page templates, or you can summon the Fonts panel and format as you prefer.

But there's a peril to this typographic freedom. If you use fonts that aren't commonly available on Macs and Windows PCs, or if you perform some non-standard formatting (as I describe on the opposite page), iWeb renders that text as a graphic. Instead of getting a full page of fast-loading text, you get a large "picture of text" that makes your Web page load slowly. And because the text won't *really* be text, if your site's visitors try to print the page, they'll get poor-quality hard copy.

The best way to avoid this problem is to format large passages of text conservatively: stick with the fonts in iWeb's templates, or with fonts that are common on Macs and Windows PCs, such as Verdana. If you want a headline in a fancy font, create a separate text box for it.

Finally, because Web sites aren't Web sites without hyperlinks, you can turn a word or series of words into a link that whisks your visitors off to another page—elsewhere on your site or elsewhere in the world.

Text Basics

Mind your placeholder. iWeb's page styles have placeholder text boxes, but you don't have to fill every box with text. If you don't need a particular box, select it and press the Delete key. Note that you can't delete the text boxes on the blog and podcast page styles.

You can always recognize a text box that iWeb won't let you delete: when you select it, its selection handles are gray. On objects that you *can* delete, selection handles are white.

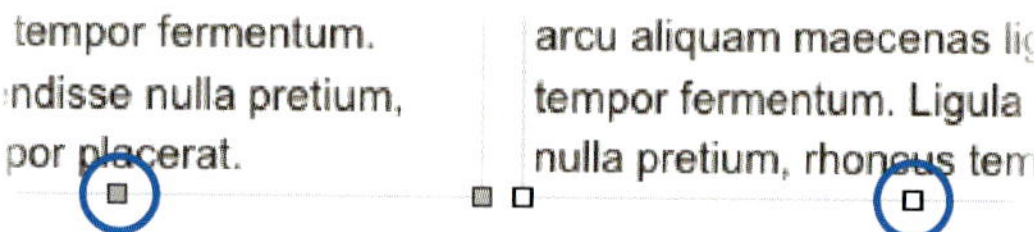

Adding a text box. You can also add a new text box to a page by clicking the Text Box button or choosing Insert > Text Box.

Linking to another page. It's easy to turn a word or phrase into a hyperlink that connects to another Web page. Select the word or phrase, then turn to the Link Inspector. Click the button, then, in the Inspector, click .

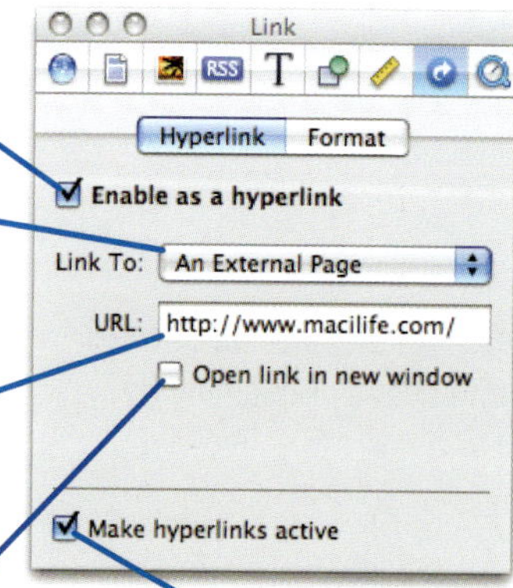

Check the box. (To turn a hyperlink into ordinary text, uncheck the box.)

You can link to another page on your site, a page elsewhere on the Web, a file, or an email message (page 408).

For an external link, type the Internet address here. If you don't type the *http://* part of the address, iWeb adds it for you.

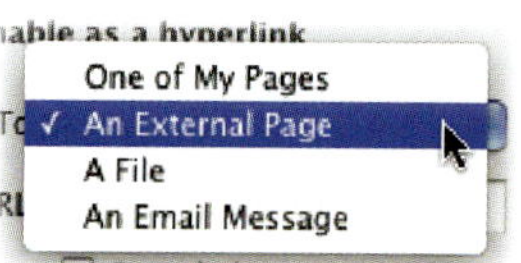

If this box is checked, the link will open in a new browser window.

When this box is checked, hyperlinks work as they will when you publish your site. To be able to click on text for editing, uncheck this box.

Text Formatting Techniques

Formatting characters. To change your text's font, size, and style, use the Fonts panel. To display the panel, click the Fonts button or choose Format > Font > Show Fonts (⌘-T). Select the text you want to format, then use the Fonts panel to do the job. **Important:** Avoid using the text shadow feature available in the Fonts panel. Adding a text shadow to even one character causes iWeb to render the entire text box as a graphic.

Formatting paragraphs. You can also apply paragraph-level formatting: line spacing, alignment, and so on. For these tasks, use the Text Inspector. Click the Inspector button, then, in the Inspector, click T.

Copying and pasting style. To copy one text box's formatting to another, select the formatted text and choose Format > Copy Text Style. Then select the text you want to format and choose Format > Paste Text Style.

iWeb can automatically flow text around another shape, such as a photo or graphic (page 389).

You can format a series of paragraphs as a bulleted or numbered list.

Control whether the text is positioned at the top of its box, centered within the box, or positioned at the bottom.

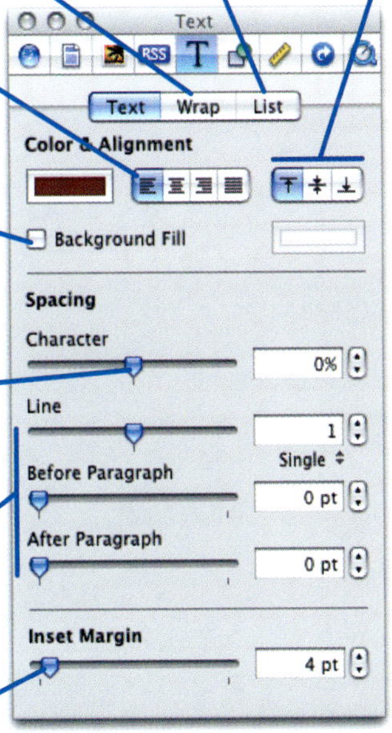

Specify margin alignments. Think twice about using justified text (even left and right margins); it's difficult to read on screen.

Add a background color to a text box.

Control the spacing between characters. Tightening up large text can improve its appearance, provided characters don't actually touch.

Control line spacing. The values are in points, of which there are 72 in an inch.

Control how much space is around the text.

Lose the text, keep the style. You may prefer to write your text in a word processor, then paste it into iWeb when you're done. At the same time, though, you may want to retain the existing font formatting of some placeholder text. No problem. After copying your text to the Clipboard, switch back to iWeb, select the text box where you want your new text to reside, then choose Edit > Paste and Match Style. iWeb pastes the new text but gives it the formatting of the old.

Resizing and rotating. You can resize text boxes using the mouse or the Metrics Inspector. You can also use the Metrics Inspector to rotate text, but note that iWeb will turn the text into a graphic.

Opacity and more. To change the opacity of text—for example, to make it appear faint—use the Graphics Inspector (page 388). You can also add a solid or dotted border around a text box.

Formatting links. To format the text links on your page, use the Format portion of the Link inspector. Removing underlining from text links can make your page's text easier to read. I like to disable underlining except when the mouse is pointing at a link (the rollover state). Just be consistent across your site.

Working with Graphics

Essential Photo Techniques

Words are important, but a picture can be worth at least few of them. iWeb makes it easy to add images to your pages. Just drag them from the media browser (or from any location on your hard drive) to the webpage canvas.

Then, you can modify the photos—make them larger or smaller, crop them, and more. You can also use iWeb's layering controls to change how the photos stack with other objects on the page.

Chances are most of the images you'll be adding will be photos, but you might also add non-photo graphics: your company's logo, an elaborate headline created in Photoshop, and so on.

Basic formatting. You can resize an image by dragging its selection handles (see page 384). For more precision, click the Inspector's button. This summons the Metrics Inspector, where you can specify exact pixel dimensions. (To squish or squeeze a photo, uncheck the Constrain Proportions box.)

You can also use the Metrics Inspector to rotate images and specify their exact location on the page. And you can use the Graphics Inspector to add shadows, reflections, borders, and more. To make the image faint so you can superimpose text over it, use the Graphic Inspector's Opacity slider.

Fixed versus inline. When you add a photo to a page, its location is fixed at the point where you drag it. However, you can also insert a photo *inside* a text box. That's called an *inline graphic*, and because it lives among the letters, it moves when you move them. It also moves within the text box as you edit and format.

Use inline graphics for images that need to stay close to specific pieces of text—a photo of a business executive next to her biography; or the photos or illustrations in a report, an educational page, or a lengthy travelogue.

To add a photo as an inline graphic, press the ⌘ key while dragging the photo into a text box. As you drag, position the vertical insertion point where you want the graphic to appear—for example, just before the first letter in a paragraph. When you release the mouse button, iWeb inserts the photo, which you can resize as needed. You can also cut (⌘-X) a photo that's already on a page, click the insertion point in a text box, and paste (⌘-V).

You can also use the Text Inspector to have iWeb wrap the text around the graphic (see the opposite page).

Replacing a placeholder image. iWeb's placeholder images remind me of those photos of strangers that are tucked inside new wallets. To replace an iWeb stranger, drag a photo to the placeholder photo.

Make it link. You can turn a graphic into a button that, when clicked, takes your site's visitors to another Web page. Select the graphic, display the Link Inspector, and specify the link details (see page 386).

Forward and Backward: Layering Controls

As you add items to a page, you may have objects that overlap. For example, in the Travel template's Welcome page, two photos overlap each other, and the photos themselves overlap a couple of design elements (the passport stamps).

When you add a new object to a page, it appears at the top of the "stack." You can control how objects overlap by using the Forward and Backward buttons at the bottom of the iWeb window, or the commands in the Arrange menu.

For example, to change the layering order so that a dog photo appears atop a cat photo, select the dog photo and click Forward, or select the cat photo and click Backward.

I guess you can tell: I'm a dog person.

A Gallery of Image Techniques

Cropping a Photo

In iWeb's world, cropping is called *masking*. To crop out part of an image, you must adjust the size of the image's mask. (You can also mask an image with a shape; see page 390.)

Step 1. Select the image.

Step 2. Click the toolbar's Mask button ( ) or choose Format > Mask.

Beneath the image, the sizing and mask editor appears.

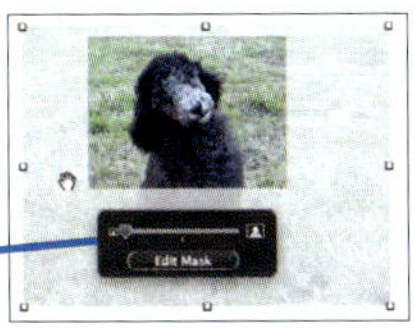

Step 3. Click Edit Mask.

Drag the mask and its selection handles to indicate the part of the image you want to retain. You can also nudge the mask using the keyboard's arrow keys and zoom the photo in and out by dragging the slider.

Step 4. When you're finished, click outside of the image, press Return, or click Edit Mask again.

iWeb hides the portion that was outside of the mask. To remove the cropping, click the Unmask button in the toolbar or choose Format > Unmask.

Adjusting a Photo

iWeb's Adjust panel works much like its counterpart in iPhoto, with one big exception: your original photo isn't altered. iWeb simply applies your adjustments to the copy of the photo that you add to the page.

Tip: Windows computers often display photos darker than Macs do, so you might consider using the Adjust panel to lighten dark photos slightly so they don't appear too murky when viewed on Windows computers.

Wrapping Text Around a Photo

For inline graphics, you can set up a *text wrap* so that text flows around vertical and horizontal boundaries of the photo.

After adding a photo as an inline graphic, as described on the opposite page, select the photo and open the Text Inspector. Click its Wrap button, and check the Object Causes Wrap box.

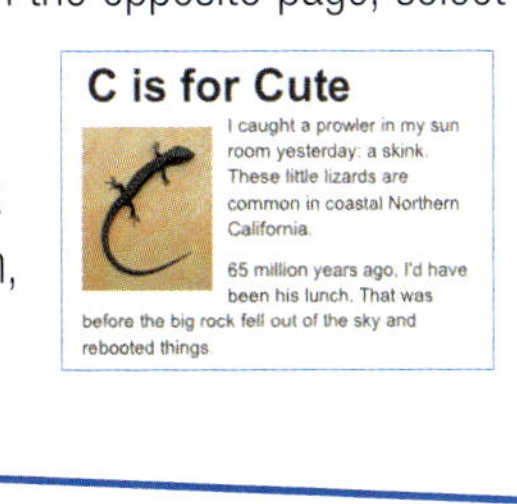

The object can appear at the left or right edge of a paragraph.

You can add extra space around the image.

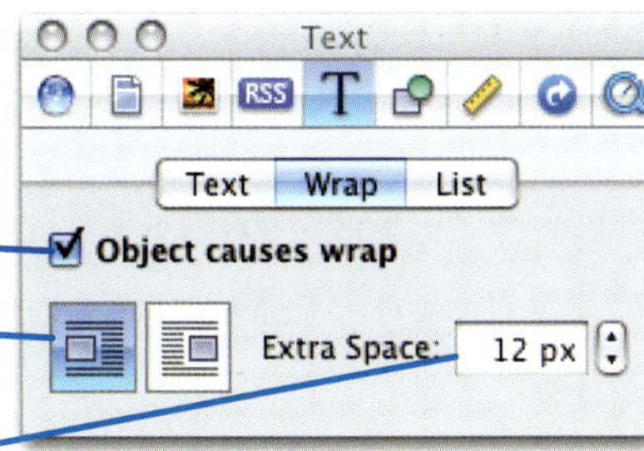

Reflections, If You Must

In some of iWeb's page styles, photos have a reflection effect, as though they're suspended over a piece of frosted glass.

You can apply the reflection effect to photos that you add, too—but don't overdo it.

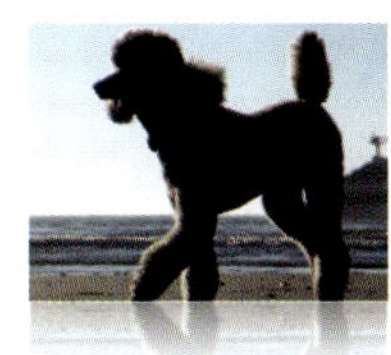

Select the photo, then display the Graphic Inspector ( ). Check the Reflection box. To adjust the intensity of the reflection, drag the slider.

To remove the reflection in an iWeb template that uses it, select the graphic and uncheck the Reflection box.

More Graphics Techniques

Rotating Images

In some iWeb page styles, photos are slightly askew to add visual interest. You can rotate photos you add: press the ⌘ key while dragging a photo's corner handle.

For more precision, type a value in the Metrics inspector. You can also twiddle the little Rotate dial in the Metrics inspector.

Behind the scenes, iWeb creates a new version of the image, with transparency enabled to let the background show through. iWeb also creates a separate image for a reflection if you've added one.

Adding Shapes

With the Shapes pop-up menu, you can endow a page with anything from straight lines to comic-book speech bubbles.

You can turn a shape into a hyperlink, and you can resize and modify shapes using the Graphic Inspector, the Color window, and the techniques discussed throughout this chapter.

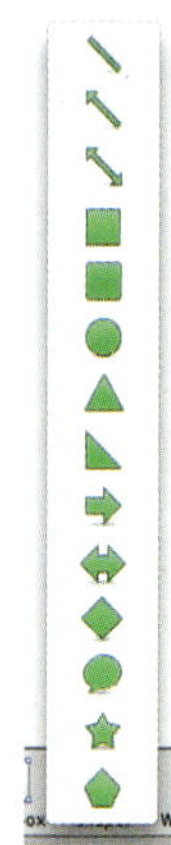

Some shapes have settings panels for specifying details, such as the number of points in a star.

Inline shape. To insert a shape as an inline graphic, first click within a text box at the spot where you want the shape to live.

Text in a shape. You can type text within a shape: double-click in the shape, and start typing. If you type more text than will fit in the shape, a little plus sign (+) warning appears at the bottom of the shape.

Masking a photo with a shape. When you add a photo to an iWeb page, the photo has a mask—a rectangle. You can use other shapes to mask a photo, however, and doing so gives you more creative options for breaking away from all the rectangles and straight lines that you see on Web layouts.

To mask a photo with a shape, select the photo, then choose Format > Mask With Shape > *the shape you want.*

Adjust the mask and the photo's position within it using the techniques described on the previous pages.

If you've already added a photo and a shape to a page, you can marry the two: select both (Shift-click on each one), then choose Format > Mask with Selected Shape (⌘-Shift-M). Finally, drag the photo to the shape.

Don't want the mask shape after all? Select the masked photo and click the Unmask button (or choose Format > Unmask or press ⌘-Shift-M).

Using Instant Alpha

With Instant Alpha, you can selectively remove the background of an image. Instant Alpha (which is also part of Apple's Pages program) replaces the often tedious process of painting out the background of an image.

You might use Instant Alpha when you want to seamlessly blend an image into the background or have part of an image appear over or behind some text. You can also combine two photos to remove a background and place the subject of the photo into another scene.

Instant Alpha is easy to use: just drag across the color you want to remove. As you drag, iWeb masks out similar colors. The phrase "similar" is key: you'll get the best results with large areas of solid color. It's easier to remove a blue-sky background than a crowded city street background.

Step 1. Drag a photo onto a page or select a photo that's already on the page.

Step 2. Choose Format > Instant Alpha.

A crosshair pointer appears when you point to the photo.

Step 3. Slowly drag across the area you want to remove.

As you drag, the selection grows to encompass areas that use the same color.

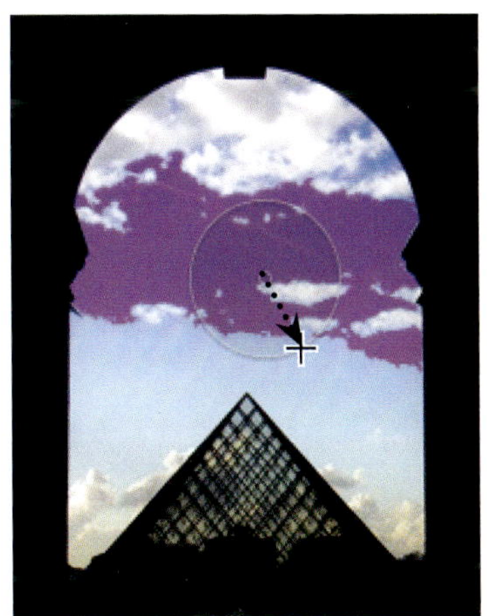

Tip: For more precision, make the photo temporarily larger: drag one of its selection handles. When you're finished making your alpha mask, you can restore the photo's previous size.

Step 4. To remove a differently colored area, repeat step 3. Each time you click, you get a new selection, and can select more color.

Step 5. When you're finished, press Return.

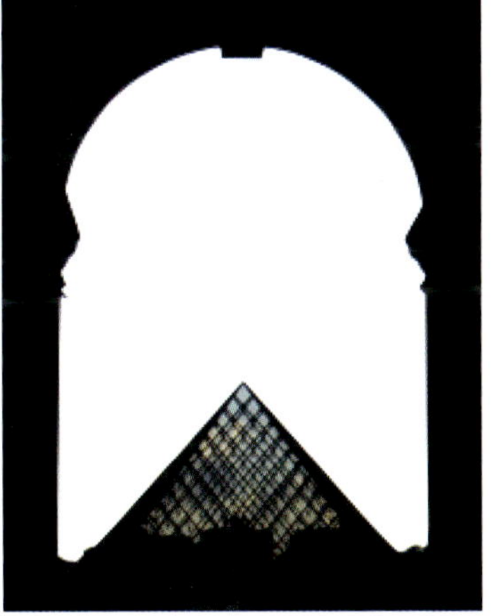

The page background now shows through the areas you've masked.

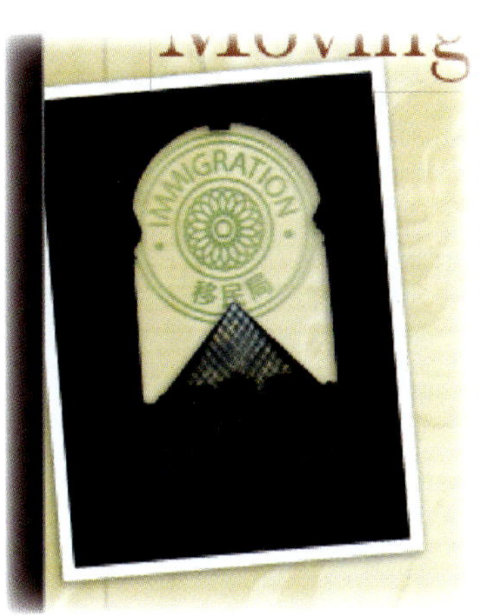

Notes and Tips

Removing Instant Alpha. To remove Instant Alpha, select the photo to which you've applied it, and choose Format > Remove Instant Alpha.

Creating a new background for a photo. To create a different background for a photo, use Instant Alpha to remove the background of one shot, then position that shot over another one, using the Forward and Backward buttons as needed to have the photos stack properly.

Original photo

With Instant Alpha

With a new background

Customizing Page Backgrounds

Many of iWeb's page templates have background images or patterns. By using the Page Inspector, you can customize the backgrounds of Web pages in several ways. Open the page that has the background you want to customize, then display the Layout portion of the Page Inspector. Choose one of the following options from the pop-up menu in the Page Background area.

Color Fill. Give the page a solid background color. After choosing Color Fill, click the color well (located below the pop-up menu), then choose a color.

Gradient Fill. Add a *gradient* (a gradual shift from one color to another). After choosing this option, use the controls below the pop-up menu to fine-tune the gradient.

Specify the start and end colors of the gradient. To swap the two colors, click the double-headed arrow.

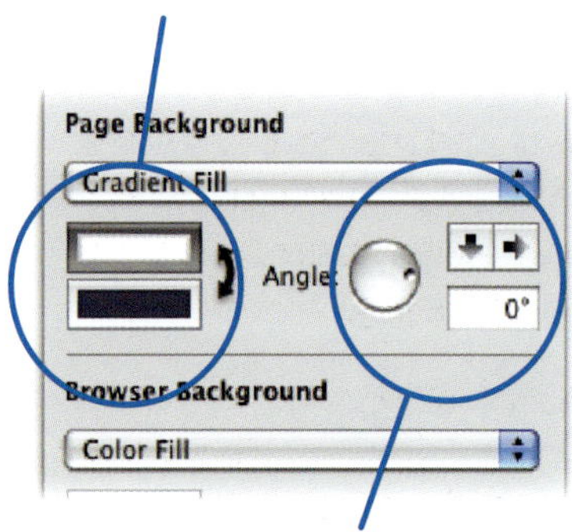

Control the angle of the gradient by dragging the Angle dial, by clicking the arrows, or by typing a value.

Image Fill. Add a photo or other graphic to the background. Use the controls below the pop-up menu to fine-tune the fill (see "Using Background Images," at right).

Tinted Image Fill. Similar to Image Fill, this option lets you add a color tint to the background image. To make the color more or less transparent, use the Opacity slider in the Colors window.

Changing the Browser Background Color

At the bottom of the Page Inspector are options for customizing the background color of the browser window. This is the area outside the dimensions of your Web page: if you imagine your Web page as a sheet of paper, the browser background color is the color of the desk on which the paper rests.

Visitors to your site who have relatively small displays may not even see the browser background color, but those lucky folks with 30-inch Apple Cinema Displays are quite likely to.

Normally, the browser background color is white, but you can change the color. Choose Color Fill from the pop-up menu, click the color well, and pick a color.
Tip: To pick up a color that is present elsewhere on your Web page, click the magnifying glass in the Colors window, and then click on the color you want to match. This trick works in any Mac program that uses the Colors window.

Background Textures

Web browsers have a cool capability: they can repeat, or *tile*, a small image so that it completely fills the background of the Web page.

Web designers take advantage of tiles to create page backgrounds that have interesting textures or patterns. Because a Web browser can tile a small image, the Web designer doesn't have to worry about creating a massive background graphic that's big enough to accommodate any size of browser window.

You can download an astronomical quantity of free page-background textures from a variety of Web sites. Do a Google search for *web page backgrounds*, and prepare to spend a lot of time exploring.

Once you've found a pattern you like, drag it to your desktop. In the Page Inspector, choose Image Fill from either the Page Background or Browser Background pop-up menu, depending on which background you want to change. Finally, drag the image into the Page Background or Browser Background image well.

You'll find a lot of garish, busy background patterns out there. Avoid them—they'll make your page look amateurish and will impair the legibility of your text.

Using Background Images

Adding a background image or texture to a Web page can be a nice way to dress it up—provided that the image or texture doesn't impair the legibility of the page's text.

To add a background image to a page, choose Image Fill from the Page Background or Browser Background pop-up menu in the Page Inspector. Then add the image and specify how you want iWeb to display it.

Here, I'm dragging a photo from the media browser, but you can also drag an image from any location on your hard drive. You can also click the Choose button and locate the image in the subsequent dialog box.

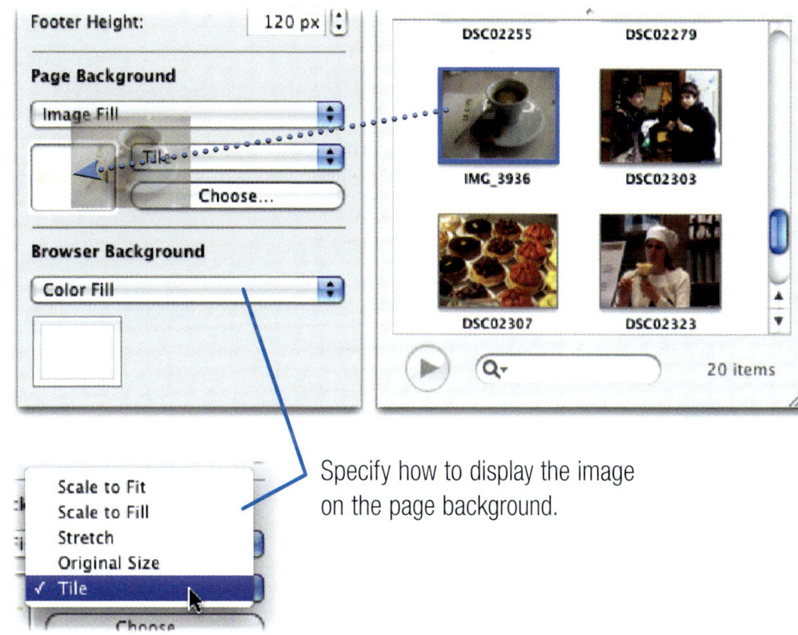

Specify how to display the image on the page background.

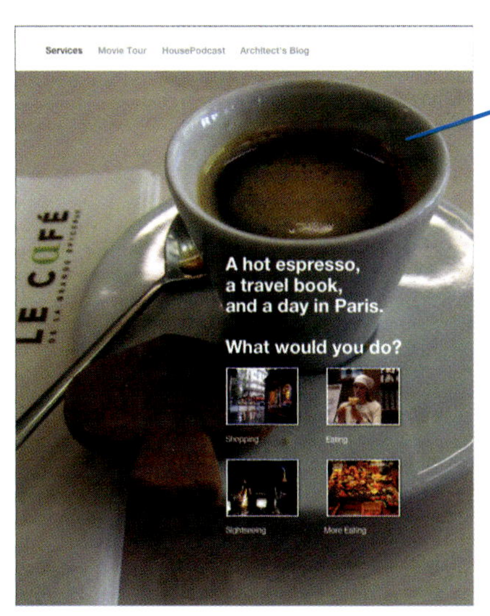

Here's a look at each image-fill option; note that only the Original Size and Tile options are available for the browser background.

Scale to Fill. iWeb enlarges the image to fill the page dimensions; the outer portions of the image are cropped off. This is the most useful option when you want an image to fill a page.

For this example, I added a solid white shape to the navigation bar so that its text didn't appear superimposed over the image.

Scale to Fit. iWeb displays the entire image, with no cropping. With horizontally oriented images, this option is likely to leave large borders above and below the image.

Stretch. iWeb fills the page with the image, altering the image's proportions to avoid any cropping. The image is likely to have a squished or stretched appearance.

Original Size. iWeb displays the image at its original size. For large images, such as digital camera photos, you're likely to see only a small part of the image on the page.

Tile. iWeb repeats the image across the background. Use this option to create background textures, as described on the opposite page.

Creating a Photos Page

With iWeb photos pages, you can create online photo albums with a few mouse clicks. The album pages contain rows of small thumbnail images that your visitors can click to see larger versions. They can also view a slide show. You can even allow visitors to add comments.

Thanks to the way the iLife programs work together, you can start your foray into photos pages in either iPhoto or iWeb. In iPhoto, stash some photos in an album and then sequence them in the order you want them to appear. Then use the Share menu to send the photos to iWeb.

Prefer to start in iWeb? Create a new page and choose a Photos page style. Then drag photos into the placeholder area, or better yet, drag an entire event or album from the media browser. Have lots of photos pages? Create a My Albums page to act as a table of contents for all of them (see page 398).

iWeb places a caption beneath each thumbnail image. And here's another good reason to use iPhoto to assign titles to your photos (page 140): iWeb uses a photo's title as its caption.

A photos page in iWeb can contain up to 500 photos. You can customize numerous aspects of a photos page: how many columns of thumbnail images to display; how much room to leave for text captions; the kind of frame you want to appear around each thumbnail; and more. And you can apply all the other design techniques described earlier in this chapter: add text, change backgrounds, and tweak formatting.

Creating a Photos Page within iPhoto

Step 1. Stash the photos you want to publish in an album. If you're lazy, you can also simply select a series of photos in your library.

Step 2. Choose Share > Send to iWeb > Photo Page.

Step 3. In iWeb, choose a template, then click Choose or press Return.

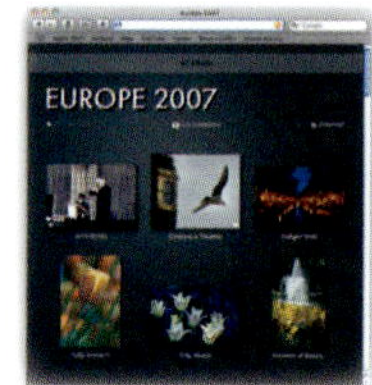

Creating a Photos Page within iWeb

Step 1. Choose File > New Page or click the + button in the lower-left corner of the iWeb window.

Step 2. Choose a template, then select its Photos page style, and then click Choose or press Return.

Step 3. Drag photos into the thumbnails placeholder area. Here, I'm using the media browser to add an entire iPhoto album.

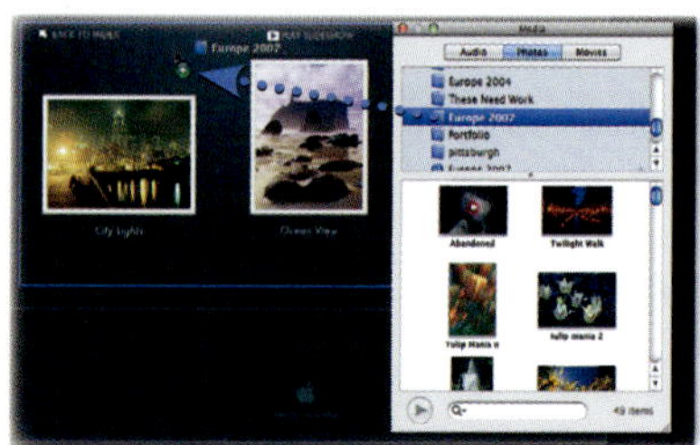

Notes and Tips

Mix and match. You can mix and match approaches: create a photos page using iPhoto, then switch to iWeb to add additional photos to the existing page. You can't take the opposite route, however—when you send photos from iPhoto to iWeb, the photos are always added to a *new* photos page.

Rearrange and refine. To change the order of the photos in a photos page, simply drag the photos. To remove a photo, select it and press the Delete key. To change a photo's caption, click it and start typing.

Photos Page Tips and Techniques

Photos page or Web gallery album? iPhoto creates lovely Web gallery albums (page 188), so why bother with photos pages? Control. Photos pages offer far more formatting options, and they allow visitors to comment on your photos.

Want to share some photos quickly and enable other iPhoto users to subscribe to them? Create a Web gallery album. Want full control over your design, along with goodies like comments, fancy slide show options, and RSS support? Create a photos page.

And it isn't an either/or proposition. You can publish the same iPhoto album or event as *both* a Web gallery album and a photos page. And as the following pages describe, you can add Web gallery albums that you've already created to your iWeb site.

Movies, too. Don't let the name fool you: a photos page can also hold movies. Just drag movies from the media browser or any location on your hard drive into the thumbnail grid.

How it Looks and Works

When visitors click a thumbnail on a photos page, they see a *detail page*. This page contains a large version of the photo, as well as controls for downloading the photo and displaying other photos in the album. If you've enabled photo comments (see the following page), a link appears that allows visitors to add their two cents' worth.

A visitor can weigh in on the photo and include an optional name and web site. The security text prevents spammers from using your site to do their dirty work.

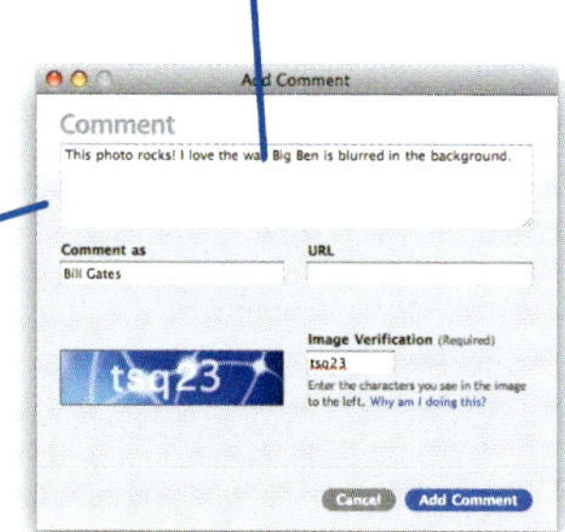

1 COMMENT
BILL GATES
This photo rocks! I love the way Big Ben is blurred in the background.
SATURDAY, DECEMBER 1, 2007 - 06:18 PM

Comments appear below the photo.

Customizing a Photos Page

iWeb's photos pages look great right off the rack, but if you'd prefer to tailor your photos pages, here's your sewing machine.

Customizing the thumbnail grid. To customize the grid of thumbnail photos on a photos page, select any thumbnail. The Photo Grid window appears.

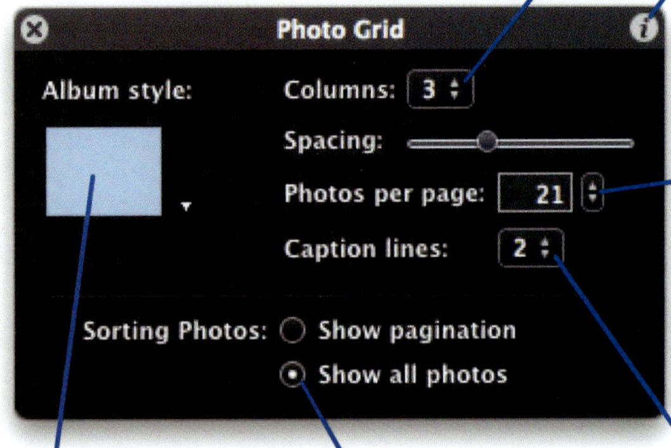

Specify how many columns of thumbnails you want and the spacing between thumbnails. I like a two-column grid; its thumbnails are larger.

Display the Photos Inspector (right).

How many photos per page? If the number of photos in the photo grid exceeds this value, iWeb creates additional pages for you, complete with navigation buttons that let visitors move from page to page.

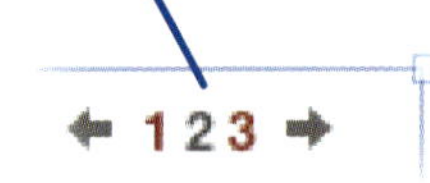

Frame shop: choose the frame style you want.

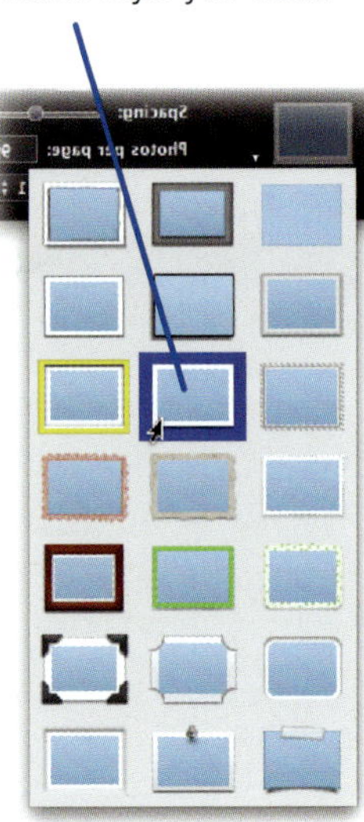

Choose your view: if your settings result in a multi-page album, you can choose to view the actual pages in iWeb or to see every single photo on just one page. The latter option is handy when you're sequencing photos and writing captions. (If all your photos will fit on a single Web page, these two options don't appear.)

Specify how many lines of text you want to allow for each caption. Don't want captions? Choose 0.

Customizing the page. With the Photos Inspector, you can customize the photos page and its slide show.

To enable visitors to subscribe to a photos page in their RSS newsreaders, check this box. (For background on RSS, see page 10.)

Visitors can download photos; choose the size you'd like to offer here.

Customize or disable the slide show (see opposite).

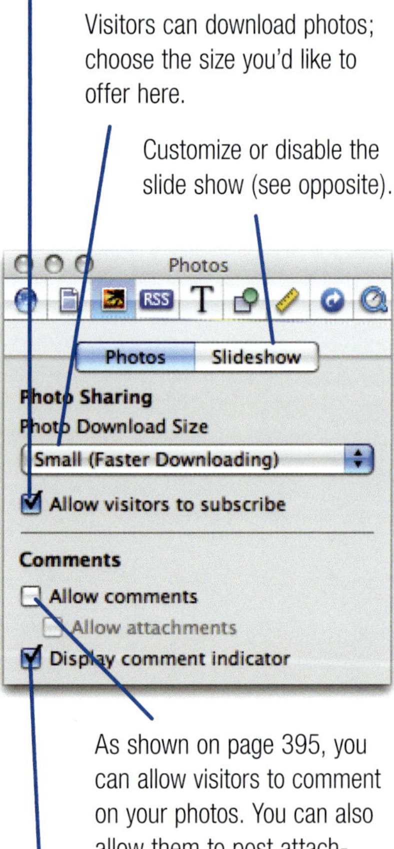

As shown on page 395, you can allow visitors to comment on your photos. You can also allow them to post attachments—for example, to share their version of a scene you photographed.

To have a tiny badge appear on photos that have comments, check this box. The badge lets visitors know someone had something to say about the photo.

Customizing the slide show. To customize (or disable) the slide show, click the Slideshow button in the Photos Inspector.

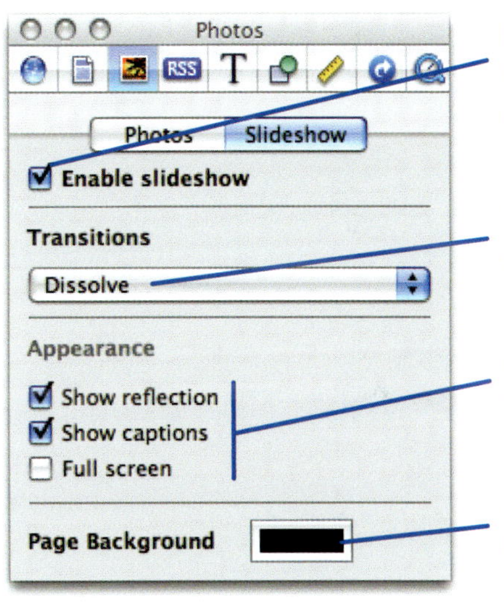

No show tonight? To disable the slide show option, uncheck this box.

You can choose one of several transition styles.

Control the appearance of the slide show.

Customize the slide show's background color.

Customizing captions. To customize the appearance of the captions beneath photo thumbnails, use the Text Inspector and the Fonts panel. For example, you can have the captions be left-aligned beneath each thumbnail instead of centered, and you can change the font.

To be sure that iWeb applies your formatting changes to every caption, select the thumbnail grid but not any thumbnails within it. Click near one of the edges of the grid. If you end up selecting a thumbnail, too, ⌘-click it to deselect.

Customizing photo borders. By selecting the photo grid and then displaying the Graphic Inspector, you can add a drop shadow behind photo thumbnails, customize the color of the border around the thumbnails, and more.

Managing Comments and Attachments

If visitors comment on your photos, how do you know? Choose File > Check for New Comments. If someone commented on a photo, iWeb adds the comment to the photo's detail page.

Sometimes, you might want to delete a comment. Maybe someone posted a large attachment, and you don't want it taking up space on your iDisk. Or maybe someone posted something inappropriate.

You can delete a comment in two ways.

In iWeb. Use the sidebar to go to the page containing the comment. Scroll down until you see the comment, then click the X that appears in its upper-right corner. If you're connected to the Internet, iWeb deletes the comment immediately; you don't have to republish the site.

In Safari. Fire up Safari, go to the page containing the comment, and click the lock icon.

Manage Comments

Select All

Bill Gates
Great capture!

A page appears asking for your .Mac name and password. Supply them, and the Manage Comments page appears, where you can select individual comments for deletion, or delete all comments on that photo.

Creating a My Albums Page

If you like to publish photos on your iWeb site, you'll quickly create a lot of photos pages. If you're into iMovie, you'll create a lot of movie pages, too. You could let iWeb create a link in your site's navigation bar for every single media page that you create, but your navigation bar will get big and unwieldy.

A book has an index that lets people find and jump to the page they need. iWeb provides *My Albums* pages that perform the same role. A My Albums page is an index page, a jumping-off point that consolidates access to your media pages.

A My Albums page can have up to 99 albums on it. You can create as many My Albums pages as you like—one for your vacation photos, another for your vintage family photos, and another for movies. Each albums page provides elegant animation effects, including a skimming feature that lets visitors preview the photos in a photos page. You can let visitors subscribe to the page in their RSS newsreaders, and you can customize the look of the page.

You can create an albums page after you've published a lot of media pages, or before. In fact, if you anticipate creating a lot of media pages, you can save yourself some time by creating an albums page first. Then, you can create new photos pages or movie pages by simply dragging photos or movies to the My Albums page.

Creating a My Albums Page

Step 1. Choose File > New Page or click the [+] button.

Step 2. Choose a template, then select its My Albums page style.

Step 3. Click Choose or press Return.

iWeb names the page My Albums, but you can rename it in the sidebar.

Now What?

You can build your albums page in any of several ways.

Adding existing media pages. If you've already created some photos or movies pages, you can add them to the albums page by dragging them within the sidebar.

You can also click the My Albums page, and then drag photos or movies pages from the sidebar into the albums page.

Creating new media pages. To create a new photos page and add it to the My Albums page all in one step, display the My Albums page, then drag photos into it.

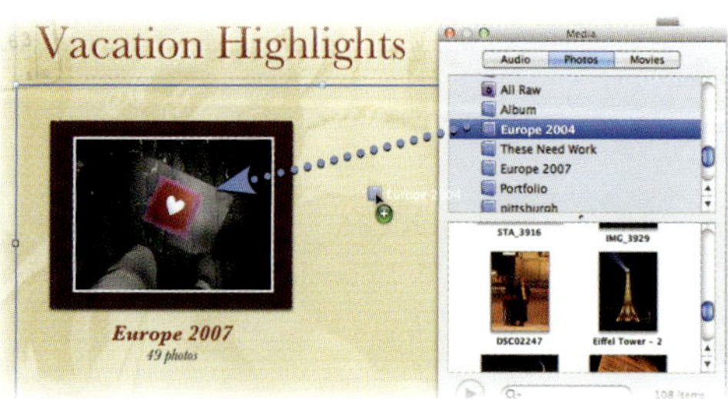

iWeb creates a photos page and adds it to the My Albums page. To customize the photos page, see page 396.

You can also create a blank photos page: select the albums page in the sidebar, then create a new photos page.

To create a new movies page, the drill is similar: drag a movie from the media browser or any location on your hard drive to the My Albums page.

Customizing the My Albums Page

You can customize the look of your My Albums page using many of the same techniques described on previous pages.

Tweak the grid. Each photos page and movies page on a My Albums page has its own thumbnail. To customize the grid of thumbnails, click one of the thumbnails. The Media Index window appears.

Choose how you want each thumbnail to be framed. There are 17 styles available, and even more in the Graphic Inspector.

You can choose to show or hide the name of each media page (which you can edit on the page) and, for photos pages, and the number of photos.

To not offer an RSS subscription option for your My Albums page, uncheck this box.

Display the Graphic Inspector, where you can choose more frame styles.

Choose how many columns of thumbnails you want and the space between them. Like large thumbnails? Choose a 1-column format.

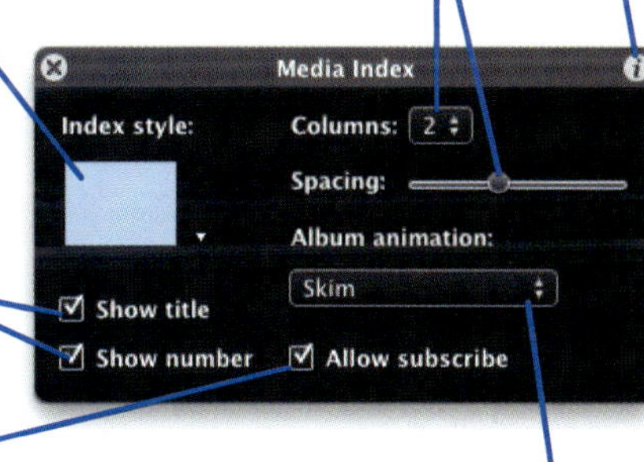

Each thumbnail animates when a visitor points to it. The skim animation is the most useful: it lets visitors preview your photos. To disable animation, choose None.

Customizing Notes and Tips

Offering a subscription option. You can let visitors subscribe to your My Albums page in their RSS newsreaders or in Safari. Indeed, if you frequently add photos pages to your site (or change existing ones), it makes more sense for folks to subscribe to your My Albums page than to individual photos pages.

iWeb adds the Subscribe link automatically. If you'd rather not offer a subscription option, uncheck the box in the Media Index window or in the Photos Inspector's Photos tab.

Customizing the album frame. If you don't like the faux album frame styles, you can turn the frame off. In the Media Index window, choose the upper-left style from the Index Style pop-up menu.

To have a line as a border, select the album region, open the Graphic Inspector, and choose Line from the Stroke pop-up menu. You can choose a color, style, and thickness. The Graphic Inspector also offers a wider set of frame choices.

Reorganizing albums. You might want to change the order of the album thumbnails in the My Albums page. Easy: Just drag the thumbnails. You can also change their order by dragging your media pages up and down in the iWeb sidebar.

Formatting flexibility. As with any iWeb page, you can change the font formatting of a My Albums page. The techniques are identical to those described on page 397.

Adding a Web Gallery album. If you've published some Web gallery albums using iPhoto (page 188), you can add them to your My Albums page, too. Display your My Albums page, then choose Insert > .Mac Web Gallery > *the album you want.*

Creating a Blog

The term *blog* sounds like something that would make you reach for the stain remover, but it's actually a corrupt contraction of the words *Web log*.

My *Webster's* defines *blog* thusly: "A personal Web site that provides updated headlines and news articles of other sites that are of interest to the user; also may include journal entries, commentaries and recommendations compiled by the user."

I'll build on that definition to add that a blog's contents, called *postings* or *entries*, are generally presented in reverse chronological order: the most recent entry appears first. I'll also add that blogs almost always use RSS to let readers subscribe and have new postings delivered to their RSS newsreaders.

And I'll amend the definition to remove the word *personal*. It's true that blogs are often personal journals. But businesses of all kinds have embraced blogging, too, relying on blogs to conduct conversations with their customers and engage in a dialog that's often more honest than the public relations people would like (see *Publish & Prosper: Blogging for Your Business*, by DL Byron and Steve Broback, New Riders, 2006).

iWeb makes it easy to create a basic blog. Apple's .Mac service even allows visitors to leave comments and search your blog.

The process of publishing podcasts is nearly identical to that of publishing blogs; simply choose the Podcast page style instead of Blog. For details on podcast production, see the previous chapter.

Creating a New Blog

Step 1. Choose File > New Page or click the [+] button.

Step 2. Choose a template, click its Blog page style, then click Choose or press Return.

The Entries page appears.

To add a new blog entry, click Add Entry. iWeb creates a new page, which appears below the list of entries.

Take it back: to delete a blog entry, select the entry and then click Delete Entry. Change your mind? Choose Undo to resurrect it.

Each blog entry appears here. To edit an entry, select it. To change an entry's title, double-click it.

Create your blog entry here. You can replace placeholder text and graphics and perform all the other design tasks described earlier in this chapter.

To resize the list of entries, drag the horizontal separator up or down.

The Elements of a Blog

In the course of managing a blog, iWeb creates and manages three types of pages.

Blog Page

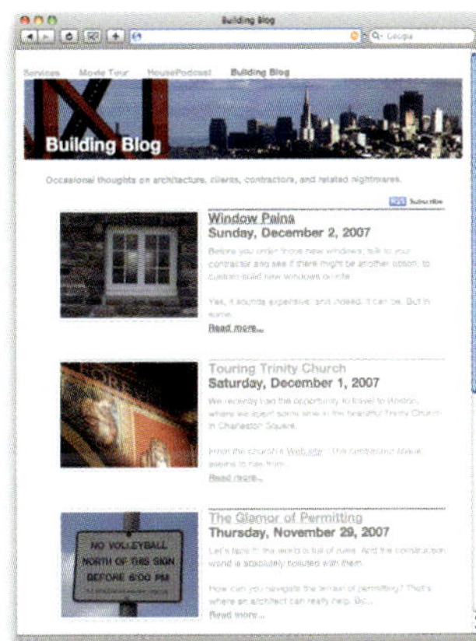

The blog page is the main lobby for your blog. Visitors see excerpts of up to 50 of your most recent entries, and each excerpt has a link that lets them read the full entry. (You can customize the number and size of excerpts as described on the following pages.)

In the sidebar, the main blog page has the name *Blog*, although you can rename it as you can any iWeb page.

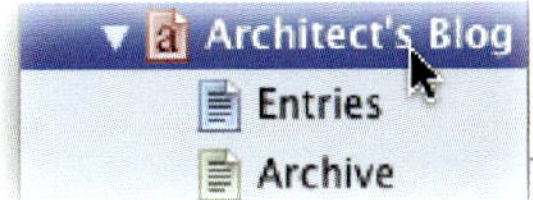

Entry Pages

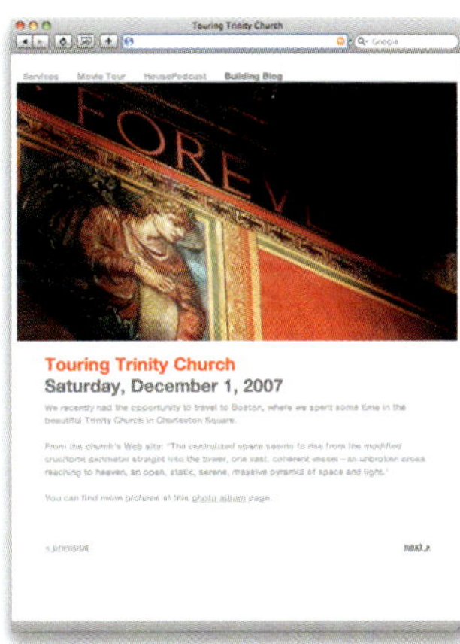

An *entry page* contains one blog posting: your rant of the day (or the hour). Each entry page also contains links, labeled *Previous* and *Next*, that allow your site's visitors to step through each of your blog entries. You can delete these links if you'd prefer that your visitors use your blog and archive pages to navigate.

Archive Page

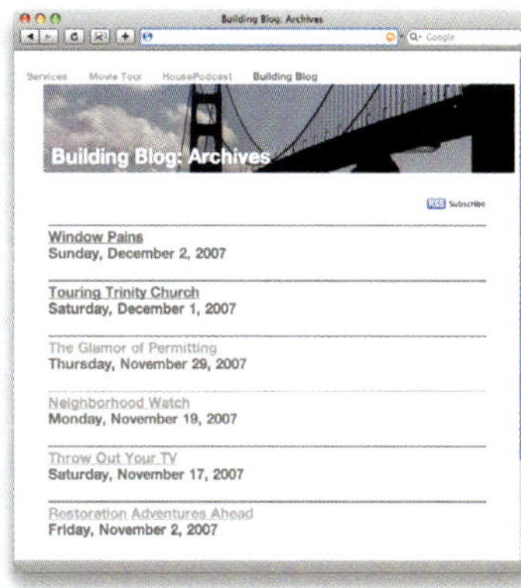

The *archive page* is the dusty newspaper morgue where old back issues live; that is, it's where visitors can access all of your blog posts, not just recent ones.

Notes and Tips

Today's the day. It's common for each entry in a blog to be stamped with the day of its posting. When you create a new blog entry, iWeb gives it the current date.

However, you can bend time to your will. To change the date of a blog entry, double-click the entry's date—either in the list of blog entries or on a blog entry page itself—then choose a new date (and date format, if you like).

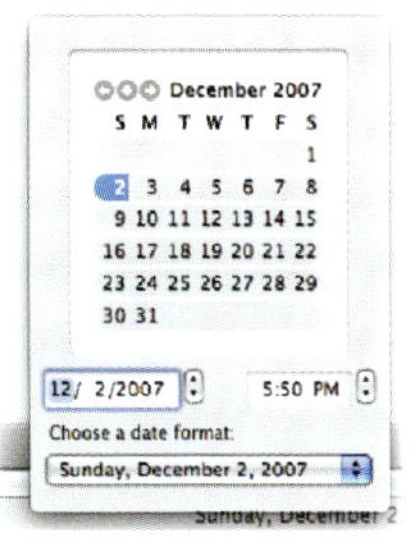

Room for everyone. You can have as many blogs and podcasts within a Web site as you like. Have several family members (or colleagues) with something to say? Each one can have his or her own blog.

Customizing Your Blog

As with all of the pages that iWeb creates, you can use blog pages as they are or customize them to suit your tastes and needs.

Some of your customizing options involve the structure of the blog: how many excerpts appear on the main page, for example, whether an RSS subscription button is available, and whether you want to allow visitors to comment on your blog entries and to search your blog.

Other customizing options are design-oriented. With the Blog Summary window, you can customize many aspects of your blog's layout.

Here's a look at your blog customizing options.

Customizing the Main Page

You can use the Blog & Podcast Inspector to specify how many excerpts appear on your blog's main page as well as the length of each excerpt.

In the sidebar, select the blog's main page, then display the Inspector and click its RSS button.

You can show as few as one excerpt or as many as 50. To avoid creating a huge, slow-loading page, think twice about showing more than five or 10 excerpts.

Control how much of each entry iWeb excerpts. If you drag the slider all the way to the left, your visitors will see only the entry title and the *Read More* link.

Tip: Want to reduce the amount of clicking your visitors must do to read your latest dispatch? Show only one excerpt, and drag the Excerpt Length slider all the way to the right. Your latest entry will appear by itself, in its entirety, on the blog's main page.

Create a two-way conversation by enabling visitors to leave comments. You can also let them add attachments to their comments.

Tip: To check for and manage comments, use the techniques described on page 397.

To allow visitors to search your blog (a nice convenience), check this box.

The RSS Angle

Normally, iWeb adds a Subscribe button to your blog's main page. Visitors to your site can use this button to subscribe to the RSS feed that iWeb creates for your blog. If you don't want to offer an RSS subscription option, delete the Subscribe button.

Excerpts and RSS. The excerpts that iWeb creates for each entry are also what subscribers see when they update your subscription. If you want to deliver the entire blog post to your subscribers—a nicety that many newsreader users appreciate—drag the Excerpt Length slider all the way to the right.

Note: Your blog must be hosted on .Mac in order to provide comments and searching.

Customizing Your Blog's Layout

You can customize the layout of your blog summary page (the main page that visitors to your blog see).

To begin, select your blog's name in the iWeb sidebar. The Blog Summary window appears.

Choose from several different layouts; each one positions the photo differently in relation to the text.

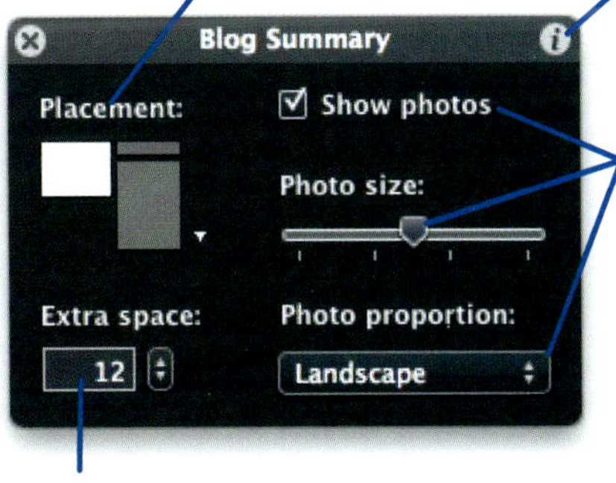

Add or remove space between the photo and text.

Display the Blog & Podcast Inspector, described on the opposite page.

Photo controls. To omit photos from the summary page, uncheck the box. To control the size of photos, use the slider. To choose a photo proportion, use the pop-up menu. (Some proportions may cause photos to appear cropped on the summary page.)

Customizing Entry Page Formatting

You can also customize the formatting of your blog entry pages. Don't like the font or size that an iWeb template uses? Change it. Want shorter lines of text so you can place photos in the margins? Resize the text box that holds the entry's main text.

To change the formatting of an item on an entry page, display that entry page, select the item, then use the Fonts panel as described on page 387. You can also add graphics and other embellishments using the techniques described earlier in this chapter.

If you change formatting in one entry page, iWeb does *not* change other entries in your blog. So what if you want to use your new design for all future blog entries? It's easy. When you're ready to create a new blog entry, select the entry with the formatting you modified, and choose Edit > Duplicate. iWeb makes a duplicate of the entry. The duplicate is now your newest blog post: just edit its date (page 401) and update its content.

Each time you want a new blog post, duplicate one of your specially formatted entry pages.

The Podcast Angle

As I mentioned on page 400, publishing a podcast with iWeb is similar to creating a blog. In the template chooser, pick the Podcast page style. Then, drag the podcast that you exported from GarageBand into the entry page.

The Blog & Podcast Inspector does provide some podcast-specific options. To see them, click its Podcast button.

To submit your podcast to the iTunes store, be sure that the Allow Podcast in iTunes Store box is checked, then choose File > Submit Podcast to iTunes. In the dialog box that appears, specify copyright and category information, then click Publish and Submit.

Maps, YouTube, and More: Web Widgets

With Web widgets, you can endow your site's pages with special features: Google maps, Google ads, YouTube videos, .Mac Web gallery albums, and more.

With the Google Maps widget, you can insert a map of any location you choose. Provide directions to your business, show the address of the park where you took your latest photos, or share a satellite view of your favorite tourist spot. You can customize a map's appearance, scale, and size.

With the Google AdSense widget, you can add advertisements to your site. Google uses its industrial-strength search technology to match ads that it thinks are appropriate to the content of a given page—and when visitors click an ad on your site, you make a tiny sum.

Finally, with the HTML Snippet widget, you can add HTML code to your pages. (HTML, you'll recall, is the markup language used to create Web pages.) You'll use this widget to embed YouTube videos in your iWeb sites.

The Web is filled with HTML widgets that you can add. With just some copying and pasting, you can add news tickers, games, RSS readers, and much more to your iWeb pages. Start your exploration at SpringWidgets (www.springwidgets.com). And check out the iTunes widgets I describe on page 408.

And if you're an HTML jockey, you can write your own code to add effects or features that are difficult or impossible to create with iWeb's built-in features.

Adding a Google Map

Step 1. From the Web Widgets button, choose Google Maps. (Or choose Insert > Google Map.)

A placeholder appears on the page, and the Google Map window appears above it.

Step 2. In the Google Map window, type an address and click Apply.

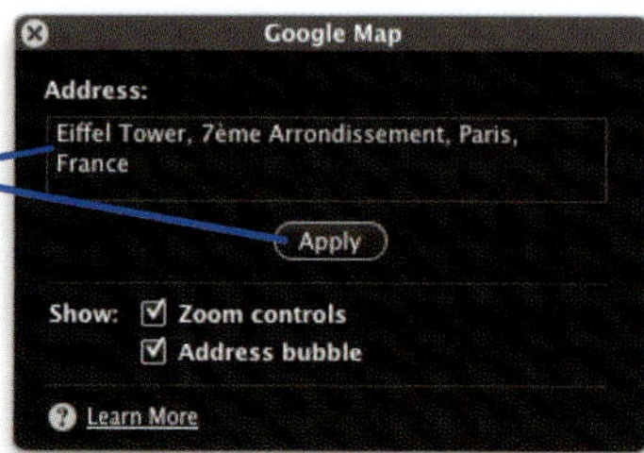

The Google map appears on your page. You can place as many maps as you want on a page.

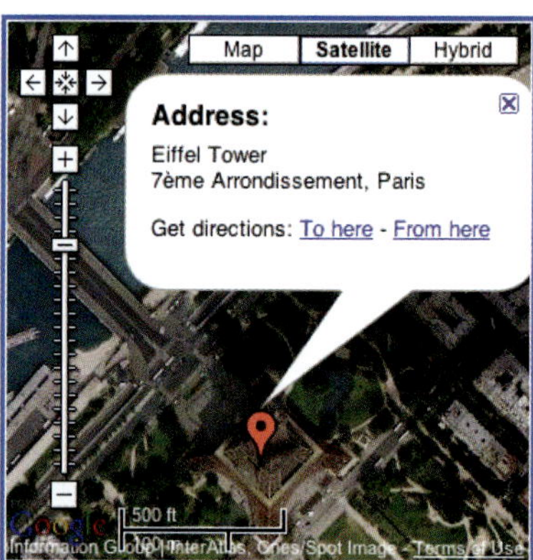

Customizing Tips

To resize the map, drag its selection handles. To hide the address bubble and zoom controls, uncheck their boxes in the Google Map window.

To fine-tune the area shown by the map, drag within it. To switch between map, satellite, and hybrid views, click their buttons in the map.

Find Web widgets galore.
www.macilife.com/iweb

Adding Google AdSense Ads

Google's AdSense program lets you display ads on your site. You can choose from three categories—text ads, text and image ads, and text links—and each category provides several sizes of ads.

Step 1. From the Web Widgets button, choose Google AdSense Ad. (Or choose Insert > Google AdSense Ad.)

Step 2. If you already have an account with Google, click I Already Have an Account and follow the steps provided. No account yet? Enter your preferred email address, then click Submit.

The Google AdSense Ad window appears.

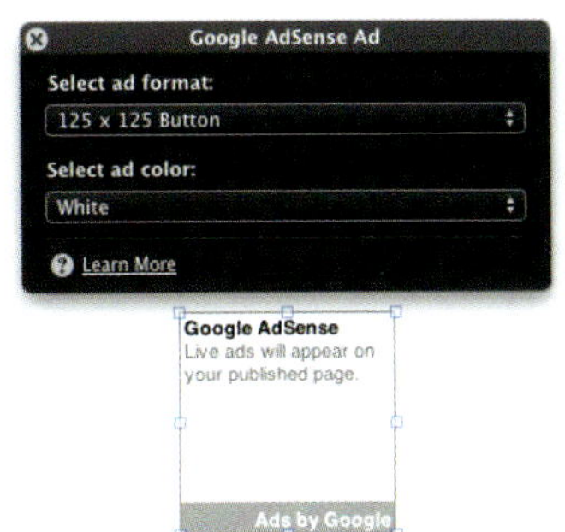

Step 3. Choose an ad format and color.

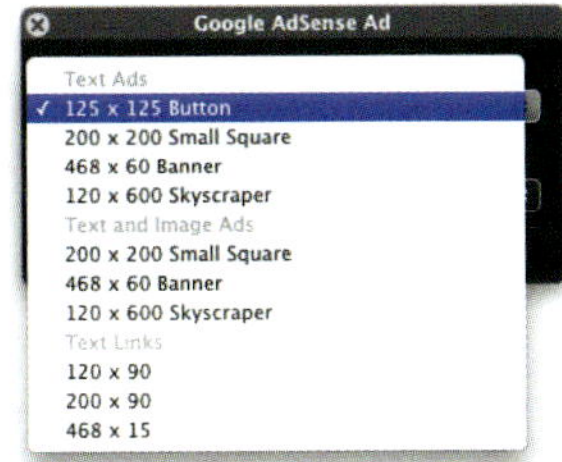

Note: You can't resize AdSense ads.

Adding YouTube Clips

To add a YouTube video to a page, use the HTML Snippet widget.

Step 1. Go to the YouTube page containing the video you want to embed.

Step 2. On the YouTube page, select all of the HTML code in the Embed box, then choose Edit > Copy.

(To customize how the video will appear in your page, click the Customize link first.)

Step 3. From the Web Widgets pop-up menu, choose HTML Snippet.

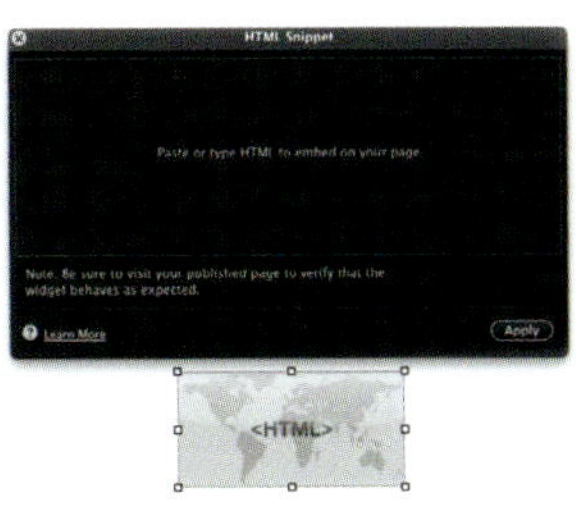

Step 4. Click in the large box at the top of the HTML Snippet window to create a blinking insertion point, then choose Edit > Paste.

Step 5. Click the Apply button.

The YouTube video loads and appears on your page.

Tip: Even though YouTube videos are movies, you don't have to use the Movie page style. The Movie page style is for QuickTime movies; YouTube videos are delivered in the Adobe Flash format.

Adding a .Mac Web Gallery Album

As described on previous pages, you can insert a .Mac Web Gallery album on any page. Choose .Mac Web Gallery from the Web Widgets button (or the Insert menu), then choose a gallery you've published.

An animated thumbnail of the Web gallery appears. You can change the position of this thumbnail, but not its size.

Publishing Your Site

When your site is ready for its debut, you'll *publish* it on Apple's .Mac service. Click iWeb's Publish button, and iWeb translates your designs into HTML (Hypertext Markup Language, the coding language used to describe the appearance of Web pages). iWeb also prepares your graphics, and then transfers everything to Apple's servers, which dish it out the world.

Similarly, when you change your site—create a new blog entry, fix a typo, or add an entire set of pages—you must publish it in order for your changes to become available. When you publish a site that you've updated, iWeb transfers only those pages that changed since the last time you published the site.

Normally, the sites you publish are available for anyone to see. But you can also post a guard at the door: using the Site Inspector, you can specify a user name and password that visitors must specify before they can see your site.

iWeb meshes best with .Mac, but you can also publish your sites to a folder on your hard drive. You might take this path if you plan to transfer your site to a different Internet provider or burn your site to a CD or DVD.

Important: As mentioned on previous pages, in order to have comments, blog and podcast searching, password protection, and hit counters, your site must be hosted on Apple's .Mac service.

To Publish on .Mac

Before publishing your work, be sure that you've signed up for a .Mac account and entered your user name and password in the .Mac system preference.

Then, choose File > Publish to .Mac or click the Publish button.

A dialog box lectures you to verify that you have the rights to publish your material. To avoid this legal nag in the future, check the *Don't show this again* box, then click Continue.

iWeb publishes the site while you get onto other tasks, and then alerts you when it's done. You can then choose to visit the site or send an announcement email containing the site's address. **Tip:** To visit a specific page, select it in the iWeb sidebar, then press the Option key while clicking the Visit button.

In the sidebar, published pages have blue icons, while blog archive pages appear green. Modified or new pages have red icons.

Assigning a Password

To protect a site with a password, select the site in the sidebar, open the Inspector, click the button, then click the Password button.

Use the Site panel to change a site's name, update the contact email address, and monitor your iDisk usage.

Hire the guard: check the box.

Train him: specify the user name and password that visitors must enter. Every visitor will have the same user name for a given site; you can't specify different names for different visitors.

Get more tips for iWeb publishing.
www.macilife.com/iweb

Publishing Tips

Where Your Sites Live

iWeb stores your sites on your iDisk, the virtual storage locker that is included with your .Mac subscription. To view your iDisk, switch to the Finder, then choose Go > iDisk > My iDisk.

Within your iDisk is a folder named Web, and within that folder is folder named Sites. Your iWeb-created sites are in the Sites folder.

Publish Everything

When you publish to .Mac, iWeb transfers only those pages that you added or changed since you last published. However, you can force iWeb to transfer everything: press the Option key, then choose File > Publish All to .Mac. (You can't choose to publish just certain sites or pages.)

If you notice that links between your iWeb sites aren't working, try this technique to fix the problem.

Publishing to a Folder

To have iWeb publish your site on your hard drive, choose File > Publish to a Folder. A dialog box appears that lets you specify a location for the published site. Normally, when you publish to a folder, iWeb saves the site in the Sites folder within your home folder.

Note: If you'll be uploading the site to a Web server and your site contains RSS links, be sure to enter your site's URL in the Publish to a Folder dialog box. iWeb uses this URL to build the RSS feed to your site.

Each time you publish a site to a folder, iWeb generates every page in the site, whether the page changed or not. That can make it tricky to figure out which pages you need to upload to a Web server. Some iWeb users have developed cumbersome but serviceable workarounds for this; for links to them, see my Web site.

Clear Your Cache

You've changed a page and published it, but the page looks the same when you visit your site. That's probably because your Web browser has retained the previous version of the page in its *cache*. A browser keeps recently loaded graphics in its cache to avoid having to load them again should you revisit a page.

If you're using the Safari browser, you can empty the browser cache by choosing Safari > Empty Cache. If you'd rather not empty the entire cache, you can force Safari to reload the entire page by pressing the Shift key while clicking Safari's [C] button.

Your Own Domain Name

Normally, when you publish your site on .Mac, your Web site's address begins with web.mac.com. However, if you've registered your own domain name (for example, www.jimheid.com), you can set up .Mac to use your domain name. It adds a professional touch to your Web site.

To set up a personal domain name in iWeb, choose File > Set Up Personal Domain. Your browser will take you to .Mac. Log in to your account, and click the Personal Domain button, and follow the instructions.

The process involves modifying your domain information with the company where you registered your domain—for example, Domain Direct. It's a straightforward process that usually involves visiting the company's site, logging in, and adjusting a setting called CNAME. If you get stuck, contact your domain registrar's technical support department.

When you set up a personal domain, your site is still being published on .Mac. You simply set up an alias that lets your domain name point to your pages on .Mac.

iWeb Tips

Adding Goodies

You can add several kinds of goodies to your pages.

It's a hit. A *hit counter* is a Web odometer that displays how many times a particular page has been viewed. To add a counter to a page, choose Insert > Button > Hit Counter. iWeb inserts the hit counter.

You can position the hit counter wherever you like, but be sure it fits entirely within the webpage canvas.

Notes: A hit counter works only if you serve your site through Apple's .Mac service. To reset the hit counter to zero, delete the hit counter, publish the page, then add a new hit counter and publish the page once more.

Keep in touch. Want to provide a convenient way for your site's visitors to email you? Add an Email Me button: choose Insert > Button > Email Me. When a visitor clicks that button, his or her email program will open a new message addressed to you.

To specify your email address, open the site inspector, click the Site button, and complete the Contact Email field.

If you want incoming email messages to go to a different address, create a text or graphic hyperlink and, in the Link Inspector, choose An Email Message from the Link To pop-up menu. Specify the address and subject for the email in the boxes that appear.

Date and time. It's common for a Web page to contain a date listing when the page was last modified. When you want to date-stamp your pages, don't look at your calendar—let iWeb do the work. Click within a text box to create a blinking insertion point, then choose Insert > Date & Time. A dialog box appears giving you a choice of date and time formats. Select the one you want, then click Insert or press Return. If you'd like the date and time to be updated whenever you launch iWeb, check the Automatically Update box.

If you've worked on a page and would like to update its date or time stamp, Control-click on the date and time and choose Update Date & Time Now from the shortcut menu. You can also double-click the date and time to change its display format and the date and time shown.

Playlists. Want to share a list of your favorite tunes with your site's visitors? Drag an iTunes playlist from the media browser into the webpage canvas. iWeb creates a set of links for each song.

Blues in the Airport
Spring Tones
Moorefield Mojo
Blue Ice Cubes
Winter Tones
Boomph!
Saying Goodbye
You Don't Even Know
Air Mobile
Same Old Blues (vocal)
Wondering Blues (vocal)

When visitors click song links (or their link arrows), they'll be taken to those songs on the iTunes Store, where they can buy, buy, buy.

By the way, you can also link to any item on the iTunes Store by simply dragging the item from iTunes into the webpage canvas.

Your iTunes widgets. Make that My iTunes widgets. Whatever. You can create flashy widgets that list your most recent iTunes purchases, favorite artists, and reviews.

In iTunes, choose Store > View My Account, and sign in. Click the Manage My iTunes button, then choose the widgets you want. iTunes supplies their HTML code, which you can paste into iWeb (page 405).

Beyond Apple's Templates

Want to go beyond the templates that are built into iWeb? Go visit Suzanne Boben. A graphic designer who's apparently also a glutton for punishment, she hacked her way through iWeb's templates to figure out how they work. Then she wrote documentation describing how to modify them, and came up with her own line of templates—some of which are free.

Check out her amazing contributions to the iWeb world at www.11mystics.com.

Customize Your Guides

With the Preferences command, you can customize the alignment guides that iWeb displays as you drag items on the webpage canvas. You can change the color of the guides and you can have iWeb display guides at the edges of an object as well as at its center.

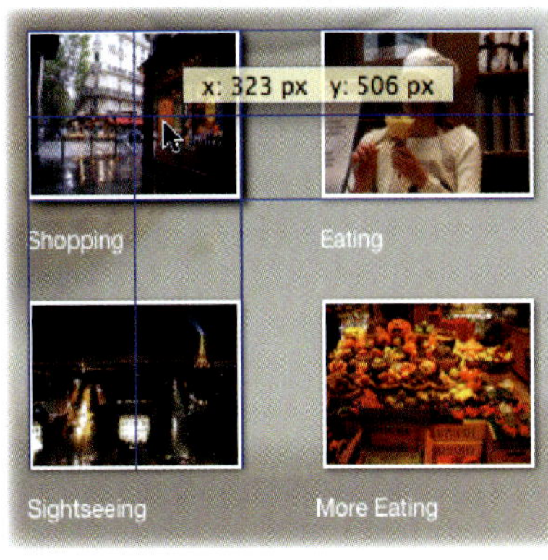

Activating this second option can make it easier to align items. (Apple's iWork '08 programs provide a similar convenience.)

From iWork to iWeb

Speaking of iWork, it's worth noting that you can paste elements created in Keynote or Pages into iWeb. Need a chart or a price list table on your Web page? Create it in Pages or Keynote, then select it, copy it, and paste it into iWeb.

Adding QuickTime Movies

Each iWeb template provides a page style designed specifically for holding a QuickTime movie. But you aren't restricted to just that page style. You can add a QuickTime movie to any iWeb page: simply drag it from the media browser or any location on your hard drive. If the movie is larger than 10MB, iWeb warns you that it may take a lifetime to download on slower connections.

As with graphics, movies can stand alone on a page or they can be in line with text. You might format a movie as an inline object if you want to have text wrap around it. For details on working with inline objects, see page 388.

If you drag a movie to the image placeholder in a blog entry, the movie becomes a video podcast.

Controlling movie display. To customize how a movie plays, select the movie and open the QuickTime Inspector. You can control the start and stop point and pick the poster frame that appears before the movie plays.

To have the movie play when the page loads, check the Autoplay box. To have it play over and over, check Loop. Don't want to give your visitors any playback controls? Uncheck the Movie Controller box. But think twice about this measure—friendly Web sites give visitors control.

Audio only. You can also add an audio file to a Web page by dragging it from the media browser or any location on your hard drive.

Dealing with Blog URLs

When iWeb creates a blog entry page, it gives the page a fairly long URL. If you try to email that URL to a friend so he or she can read a specific entry, the link may not work—email programs are notorious for breaking links that take up more than one line.

The solution? TinyURL. Go to www.tinyurl.com, where you can paste a lengthy link and have it turned into a small one that you can email.

Index

Index

E

F

G

Index

Index

J

K

L

M

Index

Q

R

S

T

Reviewers and readers rave—
praise for previous editions of
The Macintosh iLife

The book you're holding is the sixth edition of the original Macintosh digital hub book. Since its debut, *The Macintosh iLife* has become the top-selling book on iLife. Wonder why? Here's a sampling of what reviewers and readers have said about previous editions.

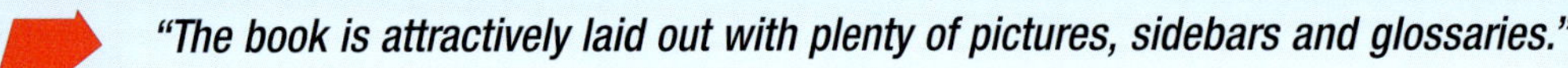

"The book is attractively laid out with plenty of pictures, sidebars and glossaries."

—Leander Kahney, Wired News and author, The Cult of Mac

"Jim Heid has created the best 'how to' book I have seen."

—Arthur Arnold, Alaskan Apple Users Group

"Jim Heid has been writing and teaching about the iLife applications for quite a while, and his expertise is visible on every page. If you want a great book that splendidly covers all the iLife applications, don't ask questions, just buy this book."

—Tim Robertson, MyMac.com

"The beautiful color illustrations jump out at you, making this book so enjoyable to read and so easy to follow at your computer."

—Maria Arguello, Main Line Macintosh User Group

"The layout of the book is highly accessible. Rather than imposing pages of unrelenting text, the book is filled with screenshots, diagrams and all sorts of helpful, easy-to-follow instructions. Even with all the pictures, this book is no lightweight. There is a wealth of information on all the iLife products."

—R.C., on Amazon.com

"Jim has done a great job distilling these feature rich applications down to their essence."

—J.H., on Amazon.com

"What a refreshing style of presentation!"

—E.B.

"This book is incredibly helpful for people just beginning on the Mac. It sets up each program separately and also shows you how to get the best use of all of them together."

—A.P., on Amazon.com

Lesson Plans

Mini-lessons

Lessons

The Macintosh iLife in the Classroom Mini-lessons

Like a recipe for a 30-minute meal, mini-lessons are quick, are easy, and often have just a few ingredients. However, they're still satisfying educationally. These mini-lessons are a great way to do a fast project with iLife, iWork, some recommended software, and the included tools on every new Mac. These lessons are relatively easy to accomplish, but they aren't simplistic. You can easily modify each mini-lesson to enhance an in-depth project for any curricular area that meets any level of learner. Most of all, these easy projects will give teachers and students a fast and meaningful way to learn the tools on a Mac.

Recipe Name: The Story of the Runaway Shape

Description: In this lesson, students create a short, engaging story about a runaway shape. Each collaborative group can choose a specific shape, or the teacher can assign them. For younger students, the class can focus on a single shape and do a group story. In the story, students must visualize places they see that shape in the classroom and schoolyard. They write about those places and take digital photos to show the shape. The digital photos and text of the story are combined in an iPhoto picture book or a Comic Life project.

Ingredients:

- TextEdit, Pages, or other word processor
- A digital camera or the built-in iSight camera with Photo Booth
- iPhoto or Comic Life
- Color printer (if printing the project)

Steps:

1. In a group, discuss where we find specific shapes around us and provide examples.
2. In smaller groups, students look around the classroom to find everyday objects that have the chosen shape in them (for example, rectangles can be found on the white board, the door, or the desktop). Students can take time to brainstorm where they see rectangles both in the classroom and in the schoolyard.
3. Students write a story about where this shape is hiding around the classroom and school. Depending on the age level of the students, it can be a simple story or more complex. The following is an example of a simpler story: "Once upon a time, the classroom rectangle ran away. We searched all around the room and outside. Samantha found it on the handball court, but it got away again. Joseph searched for it in the classroom and saw the rectangle on the board. He moved too quickly and scared it away. We knew we'd find it because we knew what we were looking for … four right angles and four sides."

   Note: No digital camera? No problem. Students can use the built-in iSight camera with Photo Booth to take photos of objects around the classroom (if they have laptops). Or students can bring the objects to the iSight camera to take snaps of it.

4. Students import the photos into iPhoto and organize them into an album. To create an album, click the plus symbol, name the album, and click the Create button. Students can also create a new album by navigating to the File menu and selecting New Album. To add photos to the album, drag and drop images in the iPhoto Library into the new album. If images are selected prior to creating a new album, they will be placed in the album if the message, "Use selected items in new album" is activated. Alternatively, you can highlight photos, navigate to the File menu, and choose New Album from Selection, which will create a new album with the selected images.

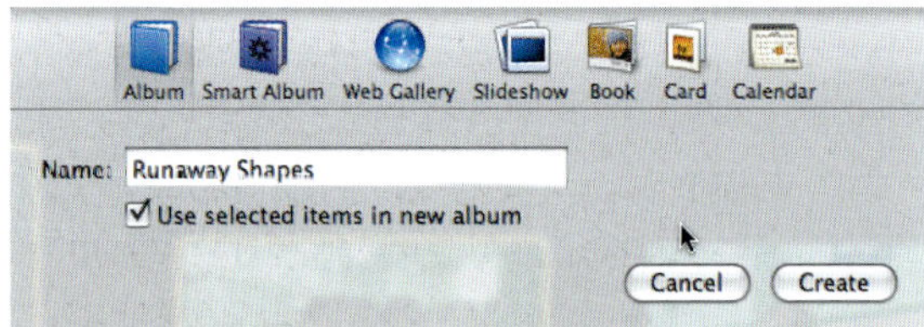

5. Highlight the shape album, and click the Book button to create a picture book. Students can also create a new book by selecting an album, clicking the plus symbol, choosing Book, deciding on a theme (Picture Book works well), and clicking Choose.

6. When students get to the inner pages of the book, they can choose from several layout options. To explore all the inner pages, click the Layout button.

   Tip: Because there might be a lot of text in this book, it's best to select the layout of one image on one side and a text page on the other.

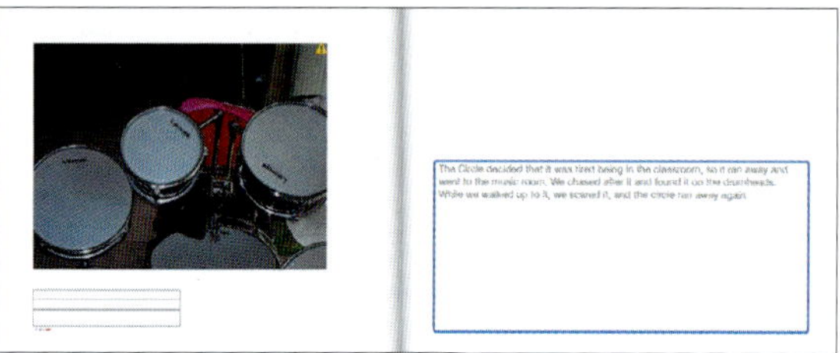

7. Drag the images to the different drop zones of the book.
8. Copy the segment of the story for each picture on the side with the large text box.

   Note: Users can zoom in to the text by using the Zoom slider located under the Buy Book button.

9. Continue adding images and text until the book is complete.
10. Print the iPhoto picture book on a color printer, or click the Buy Book button to get a bound version.

Extras:

Alternatively, the students can use Comic Life to create a comic book with their pictures and words. Comic Life is integrated with the iPhoto library, so it features simple drag-and-drop creation of comic books. For more information on learning how to use Comic Life, download the PDF tutorial at *http://plasq.com/help/Comic_LIfe_manual.pdf.* As a comic book, the steps to this project are essentially the same as with the iPhoto picture book. The main difference is that students will be working with templates for the photo layout, and they will use creative titling, captions, and speech bubbles to tell the story.

Other options for this project include creating an enhanced podcast with the narration and images or using a video camera to create a movie.

Recipe Name: Dear Mom

Description: For most students in any grade level, developing descriptive language in writing is a never-ending process. Regardless of the writing project (be it expository, narrative, persuasive, or friendly letters), teachers are always asking for more details in the work. This lesson focuses on descriptive writing through a friendly letter. Students use Photo Booth to take altered digital images of their face. Through iPhoto, students use these images to create a greeting card for their mom (or dad) to explain what happened to their face.

Note: This project is a funny gift for Mother's Day.

Ingredients:

- TextEdit, Pages, or other word processor
- Built-in iSight camera with Photo Booth
- iPhoto
- Color printer

Steps:

1. Launch Photo Booth.
2. Click the Effects button, and select an effect from the second page of options. These are the effects that alter the image with distortions that include bulge, twirl, squeeze, fish-eye, and stretch.

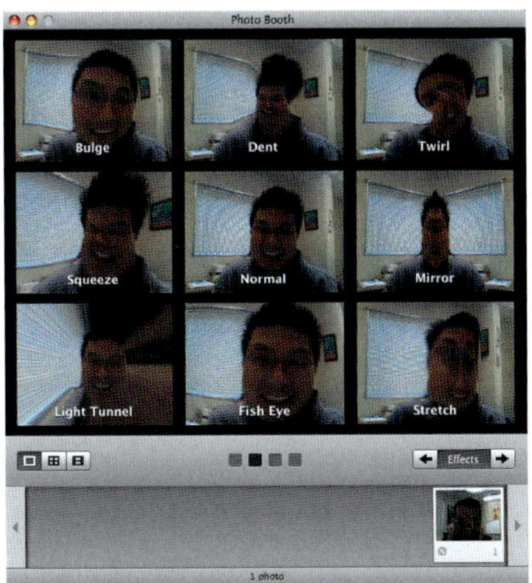

3. Students should move their heads and bodies around until the special effect alters their face to their liking. Click the red camera button in the middle of the interface to take an image. There will be a 3-second countdown before the photo is taken.
4. Select the photo from the bottom of the window, and click the iPhoto icon in Photo Booth to import the image into iPhoto.

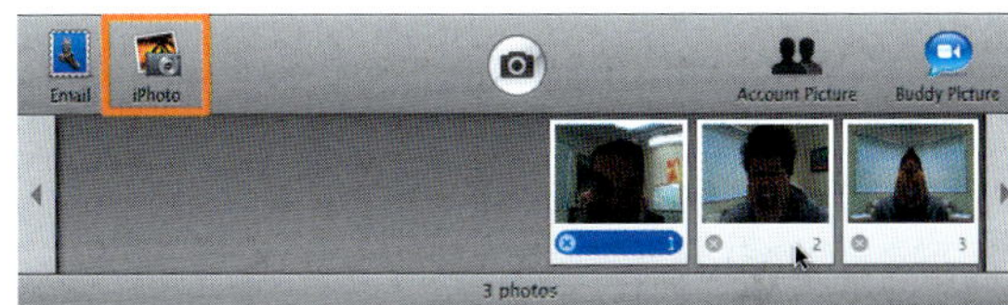

5. In TextEdit or Pages, have the students type a letter to Mom explaining how their face became that way. Students should be creative in their explanation of how their face was changed. Pay attention to the number of words. On its default setting, the interior of the card can fit approximately 200 words of centered text. However, the settings can be changed. By decreasing the font size of the text in the body of the card, students can fit more words.
6. In iPhoto, select the newly imported image, and click the Card icon to create a greeting card. Students can choose from several templates. It's best to select a card layout with a single photo. Alternatively, students can also click the Add symbol and select Card from the choices.

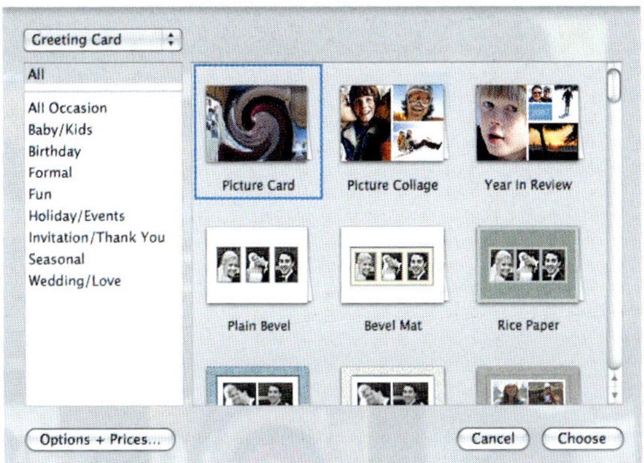

7. The image will be located on the outside of the card, and the text will be on the inside.
8. Students will copy their text from Pages or TextEdit and paste it to the body section of the card interior. To change the default size of the font so that more text will fit, click the Settings button, and change the font size of the text for the body to a lower number.

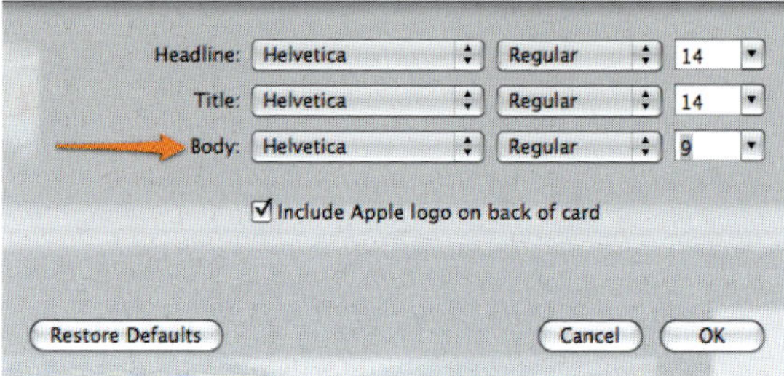

9. Print the two sides of the card with a color printer, and assemble the card to give to Mom.

   Note: In iPhoto, the default printing for the card may be 5" x 7". This sometimes causes errors when trying to print to 8.5" x 11" paper. However, if you only have 8.5" x 11" paper, then preview the card before printing, and it will be able to print on that size paper.

Extras:

This project can, of course, be modified for Father's Day or any other holiday. To extend this lesson and adapt it for older students, this project can be connected to descriptive vocabulary being taught in language-arts lessons. You can also modify it to different curricular areas. For example, this could be a greeting card from a famous scientist describing a new discovery.

Recipe Name: Problem-of-the-Week Podcast

Description: The majority of students are visual learners. By adding images to a mathematical problem of the week, many students conceptualize and comprehend word problems more readily. The teacher or students record a math-problem-of-the-week podcast with GarageBand and enhance it with appropriate images. Additionally, through an archive of podcasts, students will have a way to return to a mathematical concept for easy review and reinforcement.

Ingredients:

- TextEdit, Pages, or other word processor
- GarageBand
- Safari
- iPhoto
- Digital camera
- Keynote (optional)

Steps:

1. Students select an appropriate word problem that focuses on a concept being studied in mathematics. Alternatively, the teacher or students can write one. The script for the word problem can be typed in TextEdit, Pages, or any other word processor.

   Tip: If students create the problem of the week, it will help them comprehend word problems more easily because they will practice using the language of mathematics. As all teachers know, when students are required to express themselves or teach others, they are more likely to master the curriculum.

2. Students should find appropriate images that will help them visualize the problem. The images should help reinforce the concept in the word problem and provide scaffolding for struggling learners. For example, if the problem of the week has to do with two trains, find copyright-friendly images of two different trains. If the problem of the week focuses on monkeys in a tree, then images of a tree and monkeys will be necessary. Students can use Safari to search for copyright-friendly image from sites such as *http://pics4learning.com* or *http://kitzu.com*. However, they can also take their own images with a digital camera.

   Tip: Avoid thumbnail images, and find the largest size possible.

3. Download the images to the computer. To download an image, either drag and drop it to the desktop or Control-click the image and select Add Image to iPhoto Library or one of the Save options.

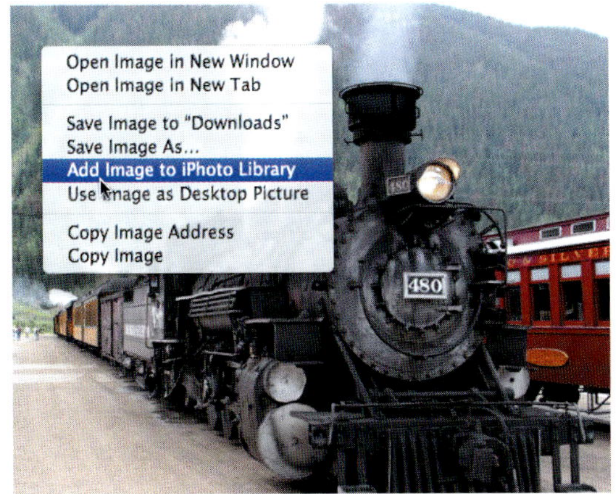

4. Import the images into iPhoto (if they were saved to the desktop or a downloads folder), and organize them into an album so that they can be accessed through GarageBand's Media Browser. To organize them in an album, select all the images for the problem, navigate to the File menu, and select New Album from Selection.

5. Launch GarageBand, and click Create New Podcast Episode. Name it appropriately, and click Create.

   Note: GarageBand automatically opens the last project worked on. To get the Project window, navigate to the File menu, and select New. This will open the Project window where students can select the Create New Podcast Episode option.

6. When the project finishes loading, the basic podcast layout will launch, and the Media Browser will display by default. Students can close the Media Browser by clicking the Show/Hide Media Browser button. This is especially helpful on laptops where screen "real estate" is limited.

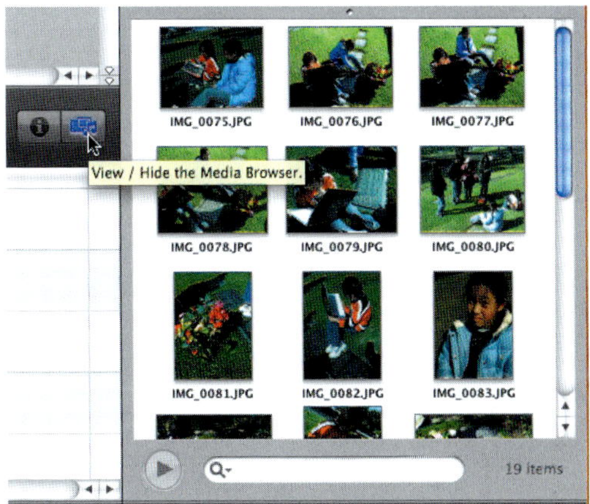

7. Select a vocal track (either a male or female voice will do), click the big red button to record, and narrate the problem of the week.

   Tip: Before clicking the Record button, it's recommended that students test the audio level to make sure their recording is not too loud or soft. To adjust audio sensitivity, show the track information for that voice, and adjust the microphone input by using the Recording Level slider.

Note: The Automatic Level Control check box is new to GarageBand '08. With this check box selected, microphone sensitivity will increase and decrease automatically depending on the volume of the input. However, people who can maintain a steady volume will not need this feature.

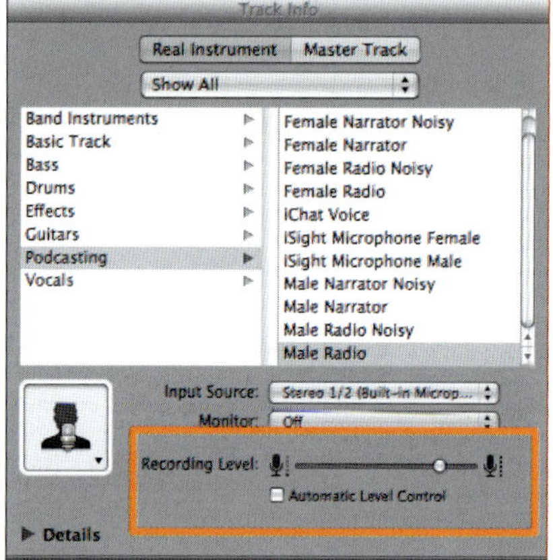

8. Open the Loop Browser (the button with the eyeball icon), and add appropriate music and sound effects (if needed). To add sounds, drag and drop from the Loop Browser to the track area where you see the words "Drag Apple Loops here."

   Tip: Drag each new sound effect under all the other audio to create a new track. By having each jingle, stinger, or sound effect on a separate track, you can adjust individual audio levels to achieve a better final mix.

9. Open the Media Browser (if it was hidden earlier), and select the album of images for the word problems. Students will enhance the audio by dragging images to the podcast track in GarageBand where the interface displays the words "Drag Artwork here."

   Tip: Start from the beginning of the recording, listen to the audio, and pause before dragging each image to the podcast track. Don't allow any gaps between images, or the message "No Artwork Available" will be displayed during playback.

10. Share the podcast to iTunes by navigating to the Share menu and selecting Send Song to iTunes.

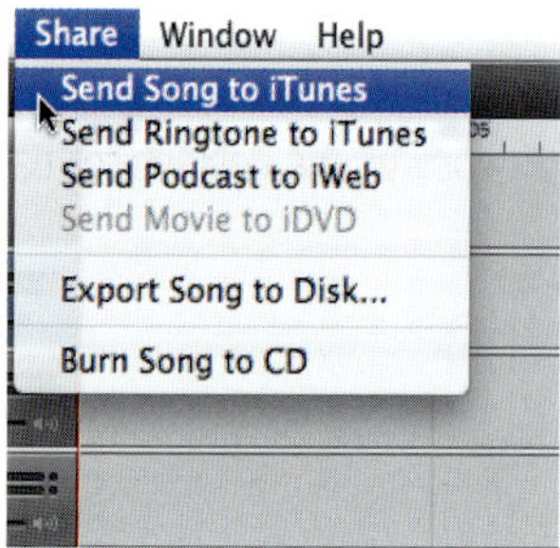

11. In the following window, enter the information for the artist, composer, and album.

    Note: The most important entries are for the Artist and Album.

    Click Share when the information has been entered. Additionally, the default playlist that the podcast will export to is the user's playlist in iTunes. If students want to create a new playlist in iTunes for the Problem of the Week, they can replace the default playlist name with a new one.

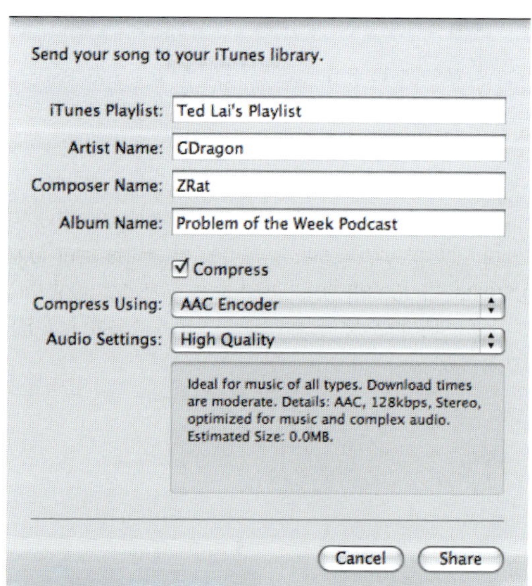

12. Finally, post the podcast to a .Mac account, school server, or independent podcast host.

    Tip: If you're using a server or podcast host to post work, drag the audio file from iTunes to the desktop. This will create an extra copy on the desktop for easier uploading.

Extras:

If you want to include text with each image or text-only slides, students can use Keynote to combine the photos with words. For each new image or phrase, a new slide would be used in Keynote. Additionally, by bringing images into Keynote prior to adding them to GarageBand, students can utilize arrows, lines, and other shapes in their slides to highlight a concept. All the Keynote slides can be exported as images by navigating to the File menu and choosing Export. In the next window, select Image, and choose the quality of the image.

Tip: It helps if you create a folder on the desktop for the exported images. You can drag this whole folder on top of the iPhoto icon on the Dock to import the images into iPhoto. Once in iPhoto, these slides are just like any other image file and are accessible through GarageBand's Media Browser.

Another extension is to use iWeb to create a podcast page with all the problems of the week. Like several members of the iLife suite, iWeb has a Media Browser that accesses all the photos in iPhoto, audio files in iTunes, and videos in the Movies folder. All the exported podcasts will be in the computer's default playlist (usually named after the user login). This podcast page can be posted to a .Mac account through one-click publishing, or it can be uploaded to the school or classroom server.

Recipe Name: My Goals

Description: It's important to set attainable goals in work, school, hobbies, and life. In this fun project, the teacher and students get to know each other and get some hands-on experience with some hardware and software they will be using throughout the school year. Students select an academic or personal goal at the beginning of the school year, write about how they will achieve that goal, and visualize it through digital images. The mini-lesson is culminated in a Pages document, iPhoto book, or Comic Life project to describe their goal for the year. Through the use of digital images, students are able to include a picture representing their goal.

Ingredients:

- TextEdit, Pages, or other word processor
- Digital camera or computer with built-in iSight camera
- Photo Booth (if using the iSight camera)
- Pages, iPhoto, or Comic Life
- Color printer

Steps:

1. Students brainstorm some different academic or personal goals they have for the school year.

   Note: It is important to be specific in the goal. For example, instead of writing "I will get better in math," students could write, "I will memorize my multiplication facts through the 12s."

2. Each student selects a single goal and writes a few sentences describing that goal and how they will achieve it. Students should focus on the steps that they will take to improve.
3. Each student takes a photo of him or herself achieving that goal. Alternatively, they can take a photo of an object that represents that goal. For example, if a student wants to memorize the gases in the periodic table, then the student could use an image of the periodic table.

4. Import the images into iPhoto. Students should take time to update the information of their photo and change its title so that it can be found more easily. Alternatively, a single album of the goal images can be created with all the students' photos.
5. Students launch Pages and begin a blank document. They type or copy and paste the text onto their page. They should take a moment to format the text so it fills up the page and is pleasing to the eye.

   Note: Text can easily be enlarged by selecting the text box or highlighting the text and pressing the keystroke ⌘+= (command key and equal key) combination. This increases text by 1 point with each press.
6. To access the image of themselves, students will open the Media Browser, navigate to or search for their image, and drag the photo onto their open Pages document.
7. Students should resize and recenter the image to fit the page better. To resize the image, click the picture and drag one of the small squares surrounding the image. If the image is too large to see the small squares, then the photo can also be resized in the Metrics Inspector. Click the Inspector button, and select the Metrics Inspector (ruler symbol). Resize by changing the values for the width or height.

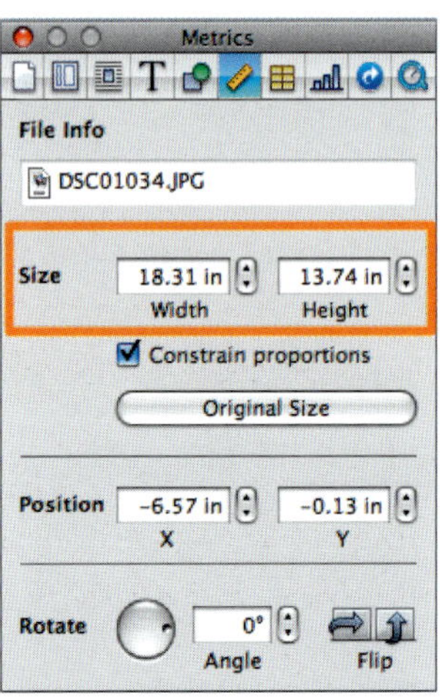

   Tip: If students want to zoom in on one detail of their image, they can do so by inputting a larger number for width or height and recentering their image by clicking and dragging it.
8. With the Graphic Inspector, they will change the opacity of the image to about 40 percent so it is more transparent.

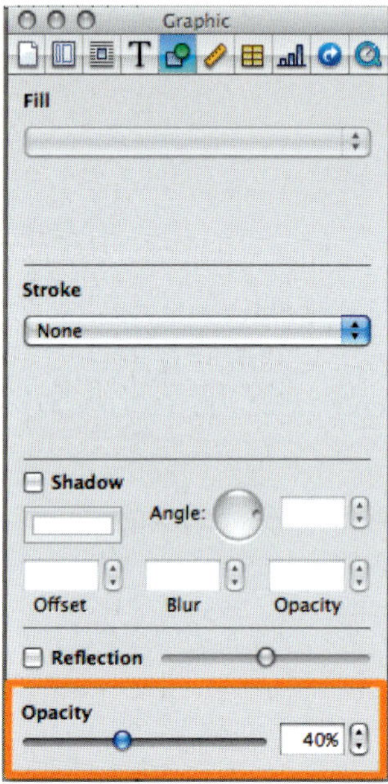

   Note: Depending on the colors of their image, students should set the opacity to whatever level makes the text most legible.
9. Pages is a layout program that works in layers. The most recently added object will be on the frontmost layer. Because the image was added after typing the text, it is actually on a layer further forward than the text. To make the text clearer, it is important to arrange the image behind the text. With the image selected, navigate to the Arrange menu, and select Send to Back so that the photo becomes the background for the page and the text is on the layer in front.

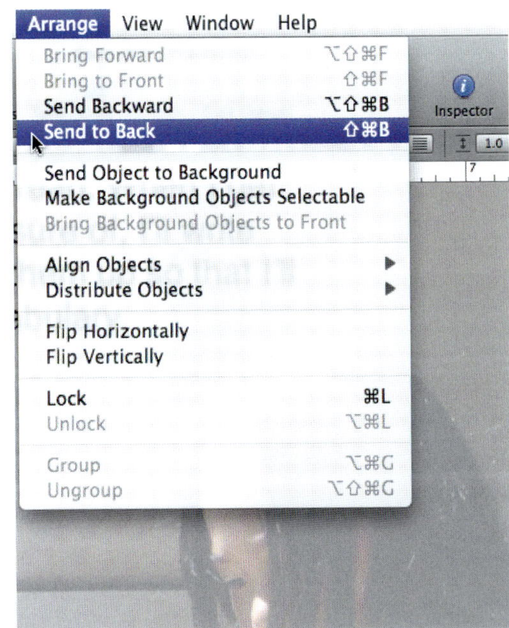

10. Print the project, and post it on a wall or place it in a classroom book of goals.

Extras:

If Pages is unavailable, then this project can also be completed in iPhoto as a picture book or in Comic Life as a comic book. In iPhoto, select the album with the goal images, and click the book icon. Make sure the picture book option is chosen. Select the single image layout for the interior pages with a text page on the opposite page. Drag and drop each student's image into the book, and copy and paste the corresponding text on the text page on the opposite side.

As a comic book, use a simple one-panel template. The Built-in: Basic templates are a good start. There's one template with a single panel that fills the whole page. Alternatively, the user can drag a single panel to the interface and expand its size to fill most of the page. Students can add a colorful title, captions, and speech bubbles to their comic book page.

Tip: Their prewritten paragraph for their goal should be added with the speech bubbles or captions, not with the titling.

Finally, as an extension activity, students can also create a comic book with more than one panel per page, displaying a series of images that would show them achieving their goal. Although this extension would take more time and planning, it would also empower students to be more creative in how they show their goal. The use of visual literacy in this way is a 21st-century learning skill.

Recipe Name: Poetry Slam Podcast

Description: In every grade level, the language-arts curriculum will contain a poetry unit. In this project, students create a class poetry slam podcast by recording their self-written poems with GarageBand. Using the built-in tools in GarageBand, students enhance the podcast with images and chapter markers. The use of chapters creates bookmarks for easy browsing of the podcast. The majority of parents will want to hear their child first, so they'll be able to use the chapters to skip straight to a specific student.

Ingredients:

- Pages, TextEdit or other word processor
- Safari (optional)
- Digital camera or built-in iSight camera with Photo Booth
- iPhoto
- GarageBand

Steps:

1. Each student uses TextEdit, Pages, or another word processor to write a poem.

   Note: Depending on the age, grade, and ability level, the teacher can choose to have students write their poem with a partner, in a small group, or as a whole class.

2. Students take photos of themselves to represent their poem visually. Alternatively, they can take a digital image that symbolizes their writing. Another option is to search the Internet for an appropriate image. Their image can even be an avatar (a cartoon image of their face). Dookyweb (*http://dookyweb.com/avatars.swf*) is one Web site to create avatars. Dookyweb is a Flash site that has many tools for creating a cartoon likeness of you.

   Note: The e-mail option does not function properly. Students will need to do a "selection grab" to save their image (a keystroke of Command+Shift+4).

3. Import the image into iPhoto so that all student images can be organized in a single album.

4. Students take turns recording their poem in GarageBand. Although each student can record their own podcast individually, in this project, a single computer will be used to compile all the poems into one group podcast so that chapter markers can be added.

5. Click the Media Browser to access the images that will be used to visually represent each poem. Drag each image to the appropriate poem.

   Tip: It's much easier to start from the beginning and listen to the podcast, pausing at each new poem to drag the appropriate image to the podcast track.

6. Click the Show Track Editor button (the scissors icon by the eyeball).

7. To add bookmarks to the podcast, just enter a chapter title next to the image. A new chapter will be created for each title added.

Tip: Depending on your district's Acceptable Use Policy and Internet safety measures, it's recommended that students list or say only their first name for any digital work. To add a measure of safety, use the chapter title area for the name of the poem, not the name of the student.

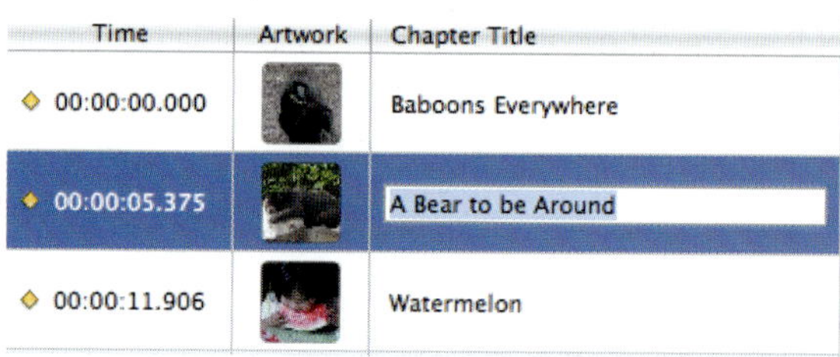

Time
Artwork
Chapter Title
00:00:00.000
Baboons Everywhere
00:00:05.375
A Bear to be Around
00:00:11.906
Watermelon

8. When all images and chapters have been added to the podcast, navigate to the Share menu, and select Export to iTunes to complete the podcast. Fill out the appropriate information and click on share to send the podcast to iTunes.

9. The audio file will be exported to the computer playlist. To make the podcast accessible to parents, the file should be uploaded to a podcast host or posted on a class Web site or school server.

Extras:

Students don't need to stop at a single image. To adapt this lesson for older students, multiple images can be used to visually enhance each stanza or line. This extension provides further support for English-language learners, special-needs students, and all visual learners.

Note: Each image does not need to be a separate chapter. In GarageBand, students can use multiple images in a single chapter, so they would still type only one chapter title at the beginning of each student's poem.

Recipe Name: Go West, Young Student

Description: In this mini-lesson, students simulate the journey west along the famed Oregon Trail by creating a daily journal of the different events that could happen to a pioneer on the trip. By reliving the experience with photos and words, students learn what it was like to leave their home and travel more than 2,000 miles by foot, horse, and wagon. Through the use of iPhoto, students create a visual calendar/diary of their day-to-day travels with all the trials and tribulations they might have encountered along their adventure. One result of this lesson is that students will make the curriculum more relevant by synthesizing it through words and images.

Note: The Oregon Trail (*www.isu.edu/~trinmich/Oregontrail.html*) is a fact-filled Web site with interesting information, genuine journal entries, and historic sites along the trail. There are quite a few enlightening facts on how the travelers spent their free time. Another site with information and images is America's Story by the Library of Congress (www.americaslibrary.gov). Information can be browsed by famous people, times, states, activities, and multimedia.

Ingredients:

- Safari
- iPhoto
- Pages, TextEdit, or other word processor
- Digital camera or built-in iSight camera with Photo Booth (optional)
- Period costumes (optional)
- Color printer

Steps:

1. Using Safari, students find copyright-friendly images depicting things they might have encountered on a journey west along the Oregon Trail. For example, they might have images of rock formations, prairies, wagon trains, musical instruments, mountains, rivers, and any animals that would be typically found throughout the regions of the United States. These are some possible sites for finding images:
   - Pics4Learning at *http://pics4learning.com.*
   - Kitzu at *http://kitzu.com.*
   - Calisphere at *http://calisphere.org*. Calisphere is easy to navigate, but it is predominantly high-quality primary source material that focuses solely on California's history.

     Tip: Download the largest, highest-quality image possible. Avoid thumbnails and smaller images.
   - American Memory at *http://memory.loc.gov/ammem/browse*. American Memory is a collection of images by the Library of Congress.
2. After downloading the images, students should import and organize them in iPhoto. If all the images are imported at the same time, they will be part of the same event. Students can also create a new album with their westward expansion images. Having all the images in a single event or album will help facilitate searching for them when creating the project. To create an album, select all the images that are going to be part of the album, and click the plus symbol, choose Album, and name it.
3. In collaborative groups, students use a word-processing application to write mock journal entries of their travels. Details and attention should be made on the different problems and daily life of the travelers on the Oregon Trail.
4. In iPhoto, highlight the images that will be used in the project. With all the images selected, click the Calendar button on the bottom of the interface to add a new calendar.

   Note: If all the images are already in an album or an event, students can click the album or event before clicking the Calendar button.

5. Select a calendar style such as the Picture Calendar or Travel Calendar, and rename it if necessary. The option to import calendars from iCal can be ignored if students wrote their entire script in a word processor.

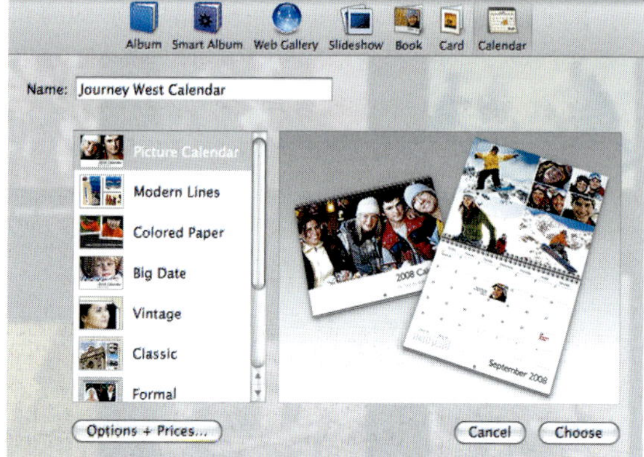

6. To add images to the calendar, the photos can be dragged into the large placeholders. Images can also be dragged to the squares with the dates, and they will automatically resize to fit the squares.
7. The diary entries can be added to any of the squares by clicking the date and copying the text of an entry.

   Note: The squares will fit approximately 120 characters per date with the default font size of 8 points. Text can be changed to 6 points by clicking the Settings button and navigating to the Style tab. The font size for the comments can be reduced to as little as 6 points using this menu.

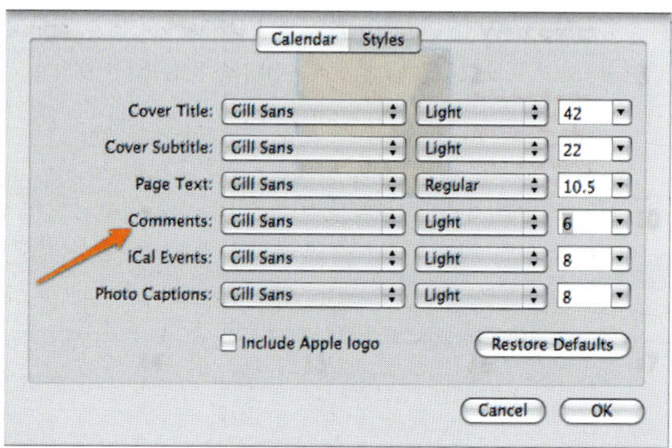

8. The students don't need to have text entries every day. They can mix in appropriate images with captions as well. However, the diary should last as long as the journey would actually take (for example, depending on the weather, settlers on the Oregon Trail could have traveled for five or six months).

   Tip: Have students create story arcs in their diary so their entries are related. For example, they could have entries on the difficulties of hunting or the search for fresh vegetables.
9. Print and compile the calendar pages when the project is complete. Through iPhoto, professionally printed calendars can be ordered for a high-quality keepsake or portfolio.

Extras:

You could create several alternative projects to enhance learning about traveling out west. These include a multimedia diary in Pages, a comic book of the journey in Comic Life, and a visual and auditory diary created in GarageBand. As a Pages project, photos, videos, and audio clips can all be combined to create a dynamic, multimedia journal of a pioneer. This is an effective project for differentiated learning because ELL students and kids with a reading or writing disability will still be able to express themselves through images and audio.

In Comic Life, students can create more of a story with their journal by dragging in several images for each day and adding dialogue. This is more appropriate for in-depth learning and simulation. Although the comic book could have a panel for each day, this would be a better medium for writing a detailed single day or week in the life of someone on the Oregon Trail.

As a way to develop voice and reading fluency, a GarageBand recording enhanced with images is another alternative for this project. Students would have to pay more attention to writing a narrative with descriptive vocabulary and avoid a diary with a bulleted list of events. These recordings could be exported and posted as enhanced podcasts to culminate a unit on the Oregon Trail.

Finally, you could modify this type of lesson for any part of the curriculum where a journey takes place. Following the life of a gold miner, simulating a soldier during a war, and detailing the life of an indentured servant are all different options for a calendar/diary project.

Recipe Name: Temperamental Tempos

Description: One of the keys to changing the feel of music is altering the tempo. Although most people can tell when music gets faster or slower, they might not think about how that change affects emotions and mood. In this lesson, students use the Magic GarageBand feature to quickly create a song, and then they explore how the mood in a musical piece can be manipulated by varying its tempo. This mini-lesson can be completed individually or in small groups.

Ingredients:

- GarageBand
- iTunes
- Pages, TextEdit, or other word processor (optional for journal writing)

Steps:

1. Launch GarageBand, and select Magic GarageBand in the project window. The Magic GarageBand feature is new in iLife '08. It is a fast and easy way to work with a song in the GarageBand interface. The user selects a genre of music on which to base their piece. There are nine different musical selections from rock to blues to reggae to jazz. Students can preview any of the tunes by clicking the Play button. The name of the piece will default to Magic GarageBand with a number appended to it (the number will change depending on how many previous Magic GarageBand projects have been created). This name will be changed in iTunes later.

   Note: For the purposes of this lesson, it is not necessary to play an entire song; a snippet will do.

2. To listen to selections, choose a genre, and click the Play button (symbolized by a single triangle). When a genre of music has been decided upon, the students will click the Audition button to begin modifying it.

3. When the song finishes launching, the Magic GarageBand interface will display five different default instruments to represent the tracks in the piece. To change the default instrument, click a part and select a different one from the options.

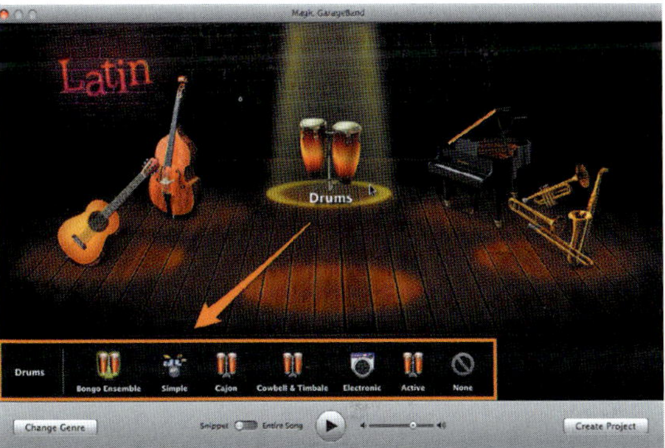

   Note: Although the instrument choices won't matter in this lesson, if the teacher wants to give the students time to explore this feature, then students should be allowed to audition the different instruments.

4. When the students are happy with the instruments they've chosen for their piece of music, they click the Create Project button. This will create a GarageBand project with each of the instruments in a different track.

5. This first version of the song will be left intact. To create an audio file of this piece, navigate to the Share menu, and select Send Song to iTunes. After filling in the appropriate ID3 information (album name, artist, and so on), click the Share button. When the file is finished encoding, the audio will begin playing in iTunes. Pause the song before moving onto the next step.

Note: If students want their songs in a separate playlist, they just need to enter a new name for the playlist, and one will be created for their newly shared song.

6. Before going back to GarageBand, the name of the song should be changed. The default name of the song will be Magic GarageBand. Click the name of the file in the iTunes interface. Just like renaming a folder or file on the desktop, the name of the track will be highlighted in blue with a black rectangle around it. Begin typing the new name of this song.

   Tip: In this project, it's a good idea to name the file with the first name or initials of the student, the song genre, and the tempo of this song (slow, fast, or regular). A song I create might be called "Ted Reggae Unchanged." Students can also change the name in iTunes by clicking the song, navigating to the File menu, selecting Get Info, and altering the appropriate box. The great part about the Info window is that students can type short comments as well.

7. Once the file has been renamed, it's time to change the tempo of the song. Back in GarageBand, navigate to the Control menu, and select Show Tempo in LCD. Another option is to click the left side of the LCD display (the default symbol is a musical note) and select the Project option with the metronome symbol. This will change the LCD display and give the user an option for altering the key, tempo, and time signature. The Tempo setting displays how many beats per second this song will play at.

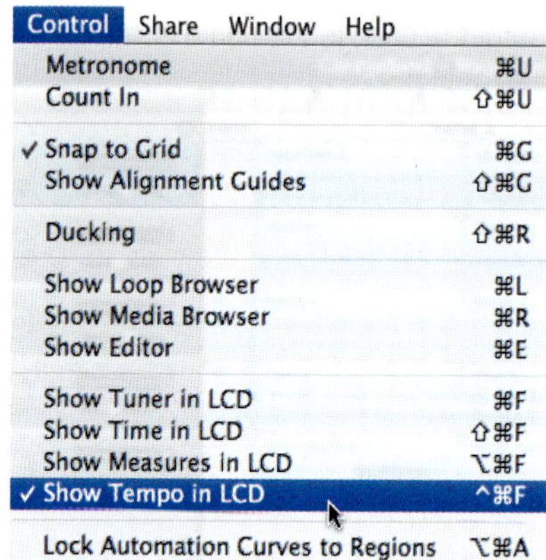

8. To speed up the music, click the Tempo LCD once, and a slider will appear. Click and drag the slider up to increase the tempo.

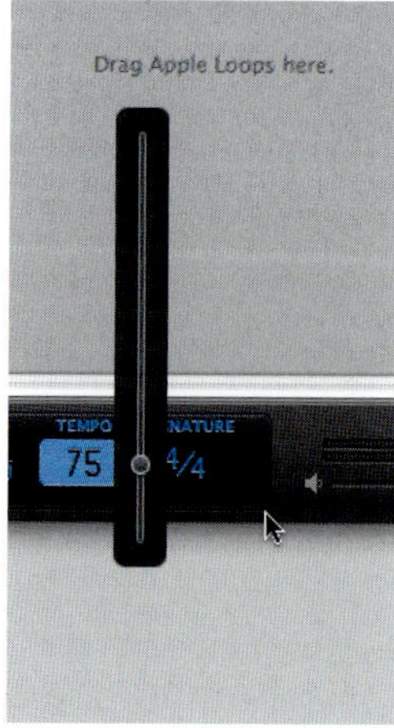

Note: Students can change the tempo while they are listening to the song. Sometimes hearing the difference helps accentuate the relationship between the beats per minute and how the song sounds. It's best to wait for the song to finish changing before altering it again.

9. Repeat the steps to share the song to iTunes, and change the name.

   Note: Don't forget to use the same naming protocol as the first song (first name or initials of the student, the song genre, and the tempo).

   Note: Don't forget to change the name of the file to reflect which version this is (fast).

10. Back in GarageBand, navigate to the LCD controls, and click the Tempo LCD again. This time, decrease the tempo of the song so it sounds slower than the first version.

11. Repeat the steps to share the song to iTunes and change the name.

    Note: Don't forget to change the name accordingly so that its tempo is reflected as well.

12. With all the songs exported to iTunes, students can listen to them and reflect on how each one sounds. Special attention should be put on how the change in the tempo affects their mood. Some possible journal ideas to write about are as follows:

    – What do you think about when you listen to the piece with the fastest tempo?

    – How do you feel when you listen to the slowest song?

    – If you could draw pictures to go with each song, what would they look like?

    – If you were sad, which version of the song would you most likely listen to and why?

Extras:

Students can combine all the versions of their songs very easily. GarageBand's Media Browser can access songs in iTunes. To do so, start a new Music project from the Project window. Name the project, and click the Create button. When the interface finishes launching, open the Media Browser. Select Audio from the buttons at the top of the Media Browser window, and choose iTunes as the library to browse. There is a search area on the bottom of the Media Browser where students can type the name of their file. They can also select the playlist where all their songs are organized. To bring them into the GarageBand project, they click and drag each song onto a track in the timeline.

Note: It's important to drag and drop each song to the end of the previous version. This compilation can be exported to iTunes and will include all three versions. Students can also add a basic track and record their thoughts on tempo directly into this compilation.

Recipe Name: Presenting Mr. Potato Head for President

Description: Politics and elections are as much about the speeches as they are about the people. In this lesson, students learn about presentation and public speaking as they take common cartoon characters and toys and create a campaign to elect their pop-culture icon as president. Through the use of Keynote, students design an engaging presentation to speak on behalf of their character and persuade the public (their fellow students) to vote for their candidate. This lesson focuses on the electoral process with cross-curricular connections of language-arts and communication.

Ingredients:

- Pages, TextEdit, or other word processor
- Digital camera
- Safari
- Keynote
- Pages or Comic Life for creating a flyer (optional)
- Color printer (optional)

Steps:

1. To gain background knowledge of the democratic process, students can research presidents, politics, or leadership. Some possible Web sites to learn about the presidents and democracy include the following:
   - The PBS Kids Democracy Project at *http://pbskids.org/democracy/*. This site has a lighthearted interactive simulation where the students can pretend to be the president.
   - The PBS By the People Educator site at *www.pbs.org/elections/kids/educators.html*.
   - The Miller Center of Public Affairs site on the American President at *www.millercenter.virginia.edu/academic/americanpresident/*.
2. In cooperative learning groups, or as a whole class, students brainstorm and list some of the qualities that are present in a good leader or president.
3. The groups select a cartoon character, action toy, or other childhood icon. Some possible choices are Mr. Potato Head, Strawberry Shortcake, Wonder Woman, Superman, or any other pop culture icon. The students should be urged to select one that actually has definable characteristics. For example, Yoda has an entire storyline and background that can be used for a campaign, but Hello Kitty doesn't have as much history.
4. If students own that toy or action figure, they can take digital images of their character. They can also visit Web sites of their character and download images of him or her. These images should be imported into iPhoto so that they can be accessed more easily in the Media browser in Keynote.
5. Students brainstorm the different qualities of their fictional character, and they consider how those characteristics would result in positive traits of a political candidate. For example, Mr. Potato Head is always prepared for a variety of situations, he's a classic character through the years, and he is loyal to his mate. Strawberry Shortcake is kind, considerate, and a friend to all in her land.
6. Groups launch Keynote and select a theme for their presentation.

   Tip: The theme is not permanent, so teachers might opt to have students select a generic white or black background and then change it after the information has been input into the Keynote.
7. Follow the onscreen instructions to add text (Keynote has the instructions to "Double-click to edit"). To add more slides, click the Add button.
8. If students want a different slide layout than the default bulleted list (for the second slide and beyond), then click the Master button to select a different slide layout.
9. Students finish typing information highlighting all the positive attributes of their characters and why they are deserving of the students' votes.

   Note: The number of slides will vary depending on the age of the students, but try to have at least one slide per major point.
10. Relevant images of their character can be added to the slides through the Media Browser. With the Media Browser open, drag and drop images onto the slide and resize as necessary.
11. Teachers need to emphasize that a presentation should contain only snippets of information. The slides should merely summarize what the students will present, and they will provide more information when they are speaking in front of the classroom.

    Note: Some teachers might require students to write out an entire script to their presentation speech. Keynote has a very useful tool called Presenter Notes. To add notes, navigate to the View menu, and select Show Presenter Notes. These notes can also be activated through the View button on the toolbar.

12. As an option, students can add transitions between slides or builds (movement) to any text or object. These options are located in the Inspector.
13. Student groups divide the parts of their presentation and rehearse what they will say. They present in front of their classroom. To play the slide show, select the first slide, and click the Play button.

Extras:

There are many different extensions to this lesson. One of the most fitting modifications is to end with an election day where all the students get to vote for the character they think would make the best president. This can be expanded by having students do their presentations in the cafeteria or auditorium for any other classes that want to take part in the voting process.

Political posters are another fun adaptation that emphasizes visual literacy. Using Pages, an iPhoto picture book, or Comic Life, students can create colorful campaign posters with eye-catching phrases or single words that emphasize the positive traits of their candidates. These campaign posters can be posted around the school as part of a larger election.

One extension for students is to visit Garr Reynold's tips on presenting at *http://garrreynolds.com/presentation*. A professional presenter, Reynolds provides tips on organization, delivery, and slide design. His slide design tips are especially helpful for Keynote users.

Keynote has a great new feature called Record Slideshow. With this option, students can record their entire presentation. After navigating to the File menu and selecting Record Slideshow, the presentation begins playing and records any sound made near the computer. Students perform their entire presentation, and Keynote records audio and timing. When the presentation is done, Keynote will save the recorded audio and timing with the file. Each time the presentation is played thereafter, Keynote will include their entire audio presentation as well. This finished presentation can be exported as a QuickTime movie or to the iPod to make a compressed video for use as a podcast.

Note: Students can delete the audio recording by navigating to the File menu and selecting Clear Recording.

Recipe Name: Flexible Sorting

Description: Students study a set of photos, sort them into groups, and organize those batches into iPhoto albums. This open-ended sorting lesson utilizes digital tools to compare and contrast items. Students are empowered to think of their own sorting criteria instead of relying on a predetermined structure. By creating their own albums to represent their thought process, students are taught to analyze a set of photos and creatively identify what's similar or different about each photo.

Ingredients:

- A set of images gathered by the teacher or students.

  Note: It is beneficial to use images of things that deal with the curriculum that's being studied (for example, different types of triangles or angles, matter in its three states, animals by phylum, leaf structure, shapes, gold-mining methods, or fictional characters).
- iPhoto.
- Safari or digital camera (if student are required to gather or create the sets of images).
- Color printer (optional).

Steps:

1. The teacher or students gather images that pertain to a topic they are studying. These could be assorted digital images of shapes, animals, or anything in their curriculum.

   Note: The sets don't have to contain a great amount of images. Ten digital photos will be enough to begin the project. These photos should be in iPhoto for easier viewing.

2. Students examine the image set and brainstorm how these photos can be sorted. What are some of the attributes of the things represented in the images? For example, if these were shape images, perhaps some have angles, and some don't. Students should be thinking about the differences and similarities of the things represented in the images.
3. In iPhoto, create two or more albums that focus on the different attributes of the images. To add new albums, click the plus symbol on the bottom left of the interface. In our example, this is an Angles album and a No Angles album. If the subject were the Gold Rush, maybe the images would be the different gold-mining methods, and the sorting criteria would result in an album of mining methods that require less than four people and one for four or more people.

   Tip: Be sure to name the albums.
4. Click the Photo Library or event where the full set of photos reside, and drag and drop each image into its respective albums.
5. Students should take a moment to explain their sorting method through the information section of each album. To access this text area, click an album that was created, and then click the Show Information button symbolized by a letter *i*. This will open the information section for the album. Text can be typed in the Description section so that students can explain their criteria for this album.

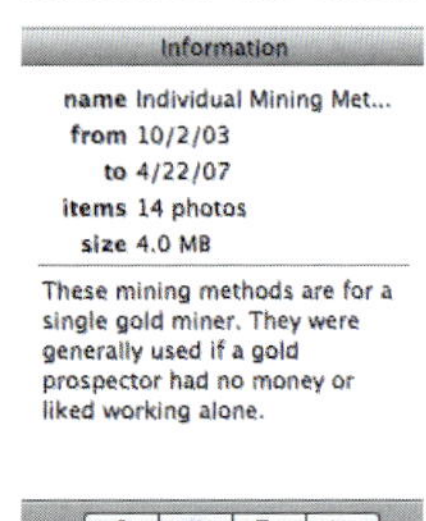

   Tip: Before typing a description in the text box, make sure the album is selected, not a specific photo.

Extras:

After creating their filtered albums of images, students can add more photos to their sorting. Using a digital camera, students take images of other things that would fit into their different albums. An alternative would be to use Safari to find copyright-friendly images on the Internet that would also fit the criteria that the students have created.

Older students can explore the use of keywords to tag their photos. To find the keywords, navigate to the View menu and select Keywords. Under each image, there will now be an area to type keywords for each photo. As each keyword is typed, press return to add another keyword. Students can search for photos that contain specific keywords, or they can create Smart Albums that can include images with specific keywords.

Recipe Name: Developing Reading Fluency with GarageBand Recordings

Description: This is a teaching and learning tool. Students develop fluency in reading when they practice reading more. Improvement can be heard when a single passage or story is read repeatedly. One of the new features in GarageBand '08 is the ability to record multiple takes when the Cycling mode is active. Instead of overwriting each successive take, like in previous versions of the application, GarageBand records each one for playback or selection. In this lesson, students use this feature to learn that re-reading passages can help them develop fluency and comprehension.

Ingredients:

- A short passage of reading that can be easily segmented
- A computer with a built-in microphone (iMac, eMac, or laptop)
- GarageBand
- iTunes
- USB or line-in microphone (optional)

Steps:

1. Before beginning GarageBand, it's important to prepare the reading material. Segment the passage into one or two sentence blocks.

   Tip: Err on the side of shorter passages than longer. If a student is truly struggling, then longer passages will serve to frustrate rather than motivate.

2. Launch GarageBand, and select Create New Podcast Episode. Name the file, and click Create.

   Note: A possible naming format could be the student's first name followed by the title of the reading passage.

3. Highlight either the Male Voice or Female Voice track to enable the recording mode.

4. Click the Cycle button. This button is located in the same group of master controls as the Play button.

   A yellow bar will appear at the top of the interface under the time ruler. When the playhead reaches the end of the yellow bar during playback or recording, it will automatically return to the beginning of the yellow region and play or record again over the same area.

5. Lengthen or shorten the yellow cycling region by clicking and dragging the ends of the yellow bar. The length of the yellow bar should be a little longer than the first segment that the student will be reading.

   Tip: It's always better to give more time than less time at first.

   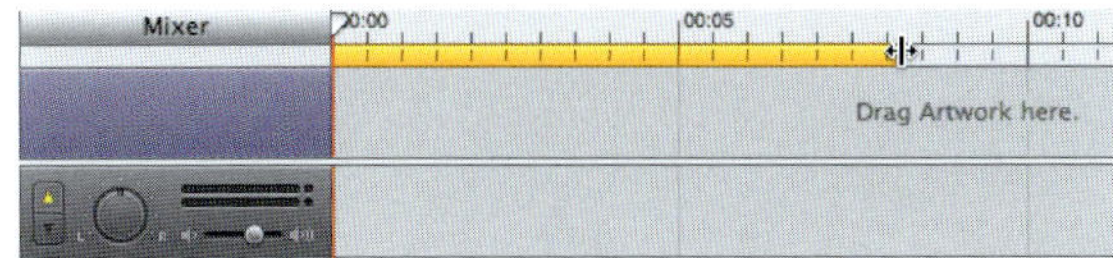

6. Click the Record button (the big red button), and begin reading the passage.

7. When the playhead cycles back to the beginning of the recorded region, the student should begin reading the same passage again. The student can continue re-reading the sentence(s) each time the playhead cycles back to the beginning of the recording area. This can be continued until fluency has noticeably improved (three to five times). Press the spacebar to stop recording. The number of takes recorded will display at the top of the audio segment. The current take that is being played will be in a yellow oval.

   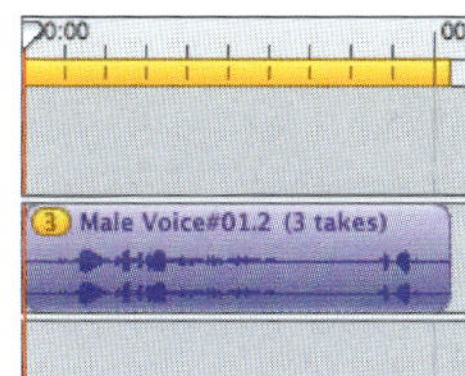

8. Students can spend a moment listening to each recorded take to make note of the improvement in fluency. To play back a different take, click the number of the take on the audio segment. A drop-down menu will appear with different options for playing back or removing the different takes. Play a different take, and listen to it.

   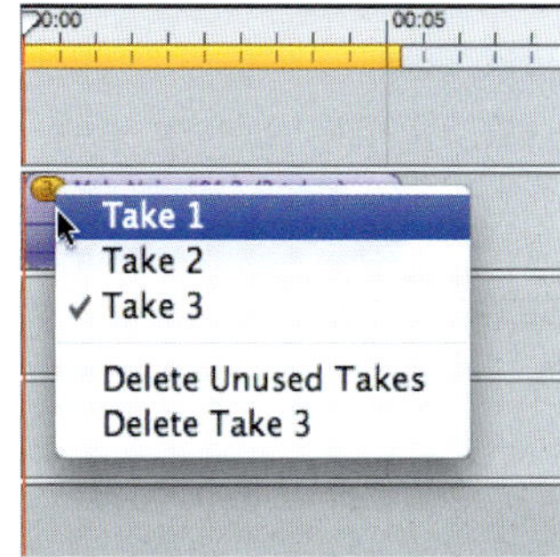

9. To begin recording the next segment, move the playhead to the end of the recorded area, and move the yellow cycle region so that its left side is aligned with the playhead. By moving the yellow cycle region, the next region recorded will not overwrite the first segment.

   Note: The playhead is the white triangle with the red vertical line.

10. Click and drag the right side of the yellow bar to shorten or lengthen the cycling region as needed (depending on the length of the passage to be read).
11. Click the Record button, and read the next sentence(s) with the multitake feature. Don't forget to wait for the playhead to cycle back to the beginning of the yellow area before re-reading the passage. Press the spacebar when this segment has been repeated a few times and there's apparent improvement.
12. Continue this process until all segments have been recorded.
13. After listening to each take again, select the most fluent recordings for each segment, navigate to the Share menu, and select Send Song to iTunes to export a recording with the greatest fluency displayed.

    Note: If there is an excess of empty space after a reading a passage, the segment can be shortened to match the reading by navigating to the bottom right of the recorded region and clicking and dragging the right side inward.

Extras:

To analyze the progression of reading fluency, students can select what they think are their worst takes for each segment and export the project to iTunes. After that, they can select their best takes and export that series to iTunes as well. These two audio files can be compared to show growth. The audio file with the better takes can be used as a student's fluency goal for how they want to sound when reading.

Teachers can use these audio files as part of a digital portfolio, parent-teacher conference, or IEP. If students create these recorded passages throughout the year, the portfolio can showcase growth in reading fluency.

Recipe Name: Modernizing Masterpieces

Description: Finding copyright-friendly, royalty-free music can be difficult. This lesson empowers students to create their own musical arrangement for use in any classroom multimedia project. Although the default software instrument in GarageBand is a Grand Piano (when creating a new music project), it doesn't need to stay that way. In this activity, students who know how to play piano use a MIDI keyboard to play a piece of classical music in GarageBand. Another student in the group changes the track to a more modern-sounding software instrument. Students continue modernizing their song by adding a beat track, other supporting instruments, or special effects. The final song is a copyright-friendly musical arrangement that can be utilized in any multimedia project.

Ingredients:

- GarageBand
- MIDI controller (Several different USB keyboards are available. Select a MIDI controller, such as the M-Audio Keystation 49e, because it will be able to control all the software instruments that come with GarageBand.)
- Sheet music or piano book
- A student able to play a short piece of music accurately to a tempo on the keyboard
- iTunes
- Blank CDs

Steps:

1. Begin the mini-lesson by launching GarageBand. From the opening Project window, select Create New Music Project, and name the piece. Change the key, tempo, and time signature to match the piece the student will play. Click the Create button.

2. When GarageBand finishes loading, connect the MIDI controller to the computer. A dialog box will pop up asking whether you want to use this detected MIDI input. Click to accept this as the instrument of choice.

   Note: Apple includes a tool called Musical Typing that transforms your computer keyboard into a MIDI controller. For complicated musical arrangements that require two hands, Musical Typing will seem limiting, but for simple melodies, it will work. To access Musical Typing, navigate to the Window menu, and select Musical Typing.

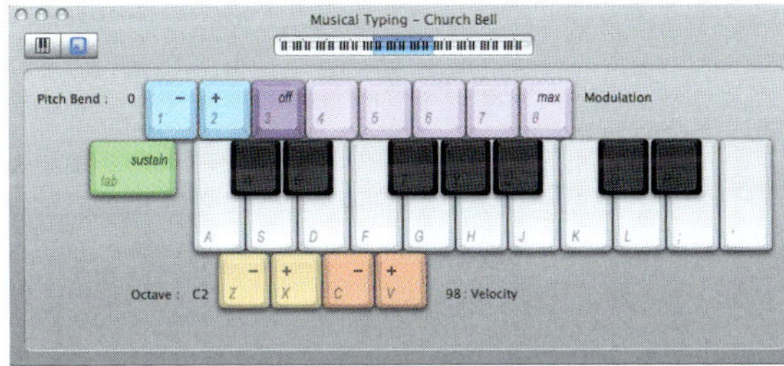

3. To record the piece of music, click the Record button (the big red one in the main controls), listen for the tempo of the metronome, and play the musical piece. Press the spacebar when finished recording.
4. Rewind to the beginning of the recording by clicking the Rewind to Beginning button or by dragging the playhead to the start. Press the Play button or spacebar to begin playing back the piece. Delete and re-record if necessary.

   Tip: It is essential to play to the correct tempo. If students are having trouble playing to the tempo of the metronome, the beats per minute can be slowed down. To do so, navigate to the Control menu, and select Show Tempo in LCD. Click to display the tempo slider. Click and drag the slider to slow down or speed up the tempo. Once the song is recorded, the tempo can be increased to reflect a faster speed.

5. To change the instrument to a more modern sound, click the View/Hide Track Info button represented by the letter *i*. This will reveal the Track Info window where the software instrument can be changed and effects can be added to the track.

6. To change the instrument, first select the family of instruments on the left column of the Track Info window, and then choose the specific instrument to which you want to change it. For example, in the Guitars family, users can select a Clean Electric guitar as the specific instrument.

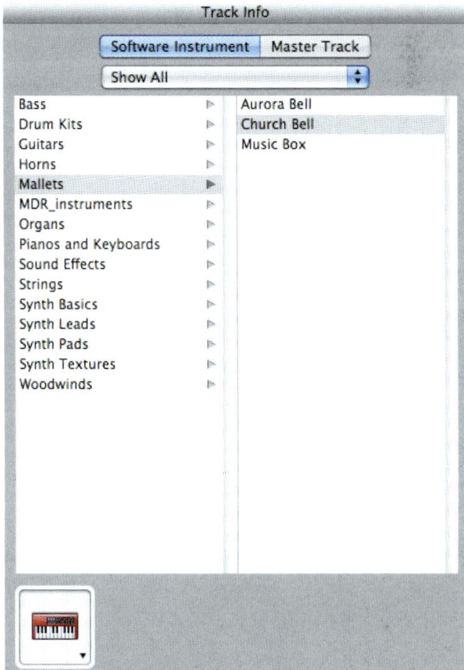

   Note: If the Cycle button is activated, students can play their song and change the instrument while it plays. By doing this, they can hear each instrument in real time.

7. The Track Info panel is also the area to add different filters and effects. To access the effects and filters, click the little triangle by the word Details. This will open a hidden area of the track information. The Effects area

has a compressor, visual EQ, echo, reverb, and four drop-down menus to add more effects. Move the Echo or Reverb slider to add those effects, or click one of the drop-down menus to select a different effect.

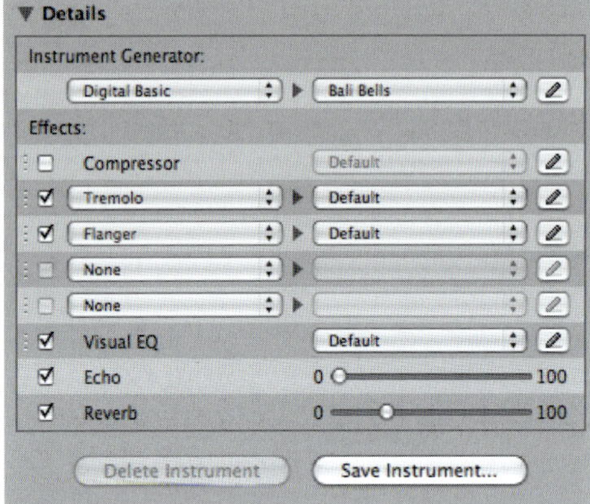

Note: When the instrument changes and effects have been made, you can add loops to the musical piece. Although each loop has a specific key and tempo, GarageBand automatically transposes the loops to match the key of the piece. The tempo isn't a problem either with beat matching. In other words, as long as the user entered the correct key signature at the beginning and recorded to the correct metronome beat, then any loop should sound like it matches the piece.

8. To add loops, click the button to view the Loop Browser (the eyeball icon). This opens the Loop Browser on the bottom of the GarageBand interface. To search for a loop, select the instrument and genres by clicking the buttons. The left side controls the instruments, and the right side refines a search by a style of music.

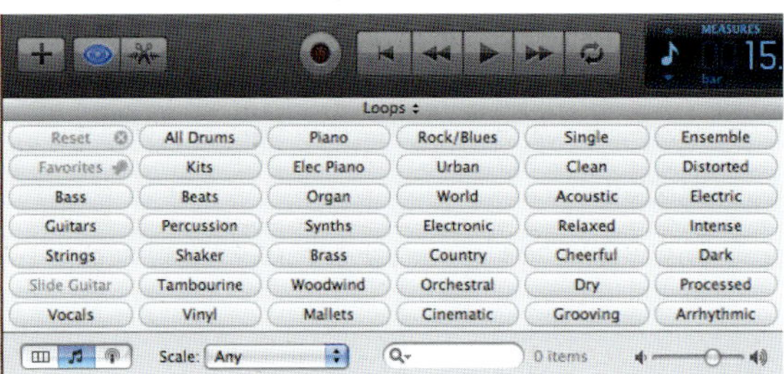

Loop names will appear on the right side of the Loop Browser. To sample a loop, click its name in the Loop Browser. To make it stop, click it one more time. To use a loop, drag and drop it below the recorded instrument to the area that displays the words "Drag Apple Loops here."

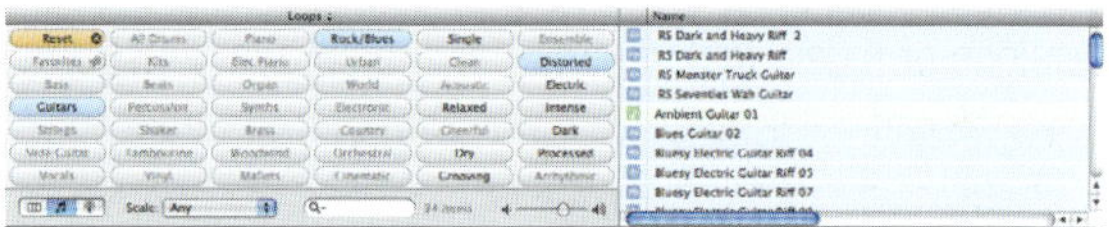

9. Move and lengthen the loops to match your recording. To lengthen the loop, move the pointer to the top right of the blue or green loop. A small, circular arrow will appear. If you click and drag to the right, the loop will repeat.

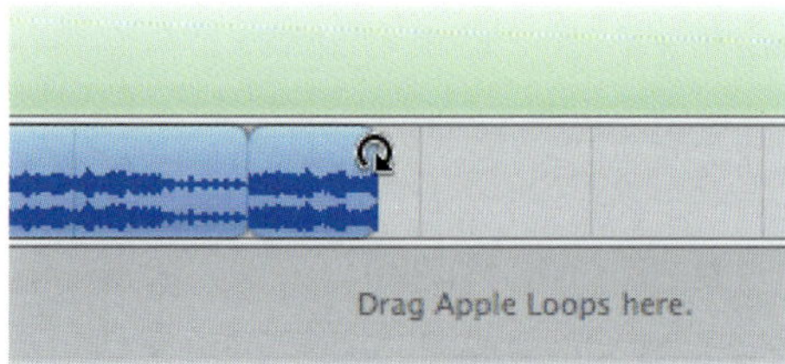

Tip: Just adding a cool beat to classical music will make it sound more modern.

10. When all effects and loops have been added, navigate to the Share menu and export the song to iTunes.

Tip: Be sure to listen to the entire piece before exporting it.

Extras:

In iTunes, students can add a playlist and create a mix CD of all their favorite class tunes. To do so, they launch iTunes, add a new playlist with the Plus button, go back to the Music Library, and drag the songs they want into their new playlist. Alternatively, they can highlight all the songs they want to select by Command-clicking each one, and then they navigate to the File menu and select New Playlist from Selection. After creating the new playlist, they should name it. To burn a CD, they insert a blank CD, select their playlist, and click the Burn CD button located on the bottom right of the iTunes window.

If none of the students has a background in musical keyboarding, or they're too young to play accurately to a tempo, then you can download free classical MIDI files and import them into the GarageBand project. MIDI files are electronic versions of music that separate all the software instruments. GarageBand displays each instrument in a different track. Students can change each instrument and add effects or other loops. The following are two sites with free classical MIDI files:

- mfiles at www.mfiles.co.uk/midi-classical.htm
- Kunst der Fuge at http://kunstderfuge.com/

MIDI files can be downloaded as easily as images. Control-click the MIDI file link, and select Download Linked File. You can also save the MIDI file by Option-clicking the link. To import a MIDI file into GarageBand, position the Finder window over the GarageBand interface, and drag and drop the MIDI file onto an open track. GarageBand will do the rest, separating each instrument for editing and modifying.

Recipe Name: Color Me Happy

Description: In art, instructors often talk about the temperature and mood of a photo. Different colors convey different information and emotions. Authors and artists often use colors to symbolize and communicate feelings in their work. An example of how artists use color to communicate can be found in the work of Pablo Picasso during his Blue Period. Using the effects in iPhoto, students change the temperature, tint, and saturation of their image to change its mood in a subtle way. In this lesson, students learn how to edit iPhoto images with the Adjust palette. They also gain experience in using a digital camera or Photo Booth with the built-in iSight camera. In the curriculum, students will learn how different elements of art, such as color, can communicate feelings. They will also study how color symbolism can change from one culture to another.

Ingredients:

- Computer with a built-in iSight camera
- Photo Booth
- Digital camera
- iPhoto
- Safari
- Color printer (optional)

Steps:

1. Students learn about color symbolism and design. The following are three possible Web sites to visit to learn about color and design:
   - Picasso's Blue Period at Art Knowledge News, *www.artknowledgenews.com/blueperiod*.
   - An interactive lesson from the Poynter Institute on color, contrast, and dimension, *http://poynterextra.org/cp/index.html*.
   - Princeton Online lesson about cultural differences in color symbolism with a variety of links on color, *www.princetonol.com/groups/iad/lessons/middle/color2.htm*.
2. Using a digital camera or the built-in iSight camera and Photo Booth, students take pictures of themselves.

   Note: For the purposes of this lesson, students using Photo Booth should take an image with no effects.
3. Select the image in Photo Booth, and click the iPhoto button to import it into iPhoto. If using a digital camera, connect the camera to the computer via USB, turn it on, and follow the onscreen instructions to import it into the iPhoto Library.
4. Find the image in the iPhoto Library, and select it by clicking it once.

5. Click the Edit button to gain access to the different editing tools.

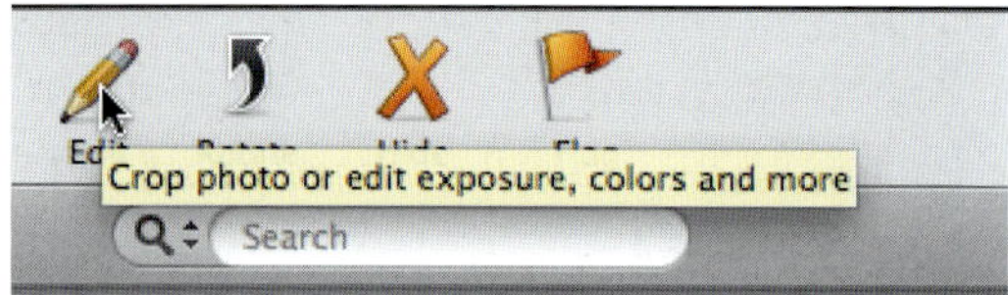

6. Click the Adjust button to launch the gray Adjust window. In this floating palette, students can change the temperature, saturation, and tint of the picture. Students can also adjust the brightness and contrast if necessary. Experiment by using the different sliders to change the values of the saturation, temperature, and tint.

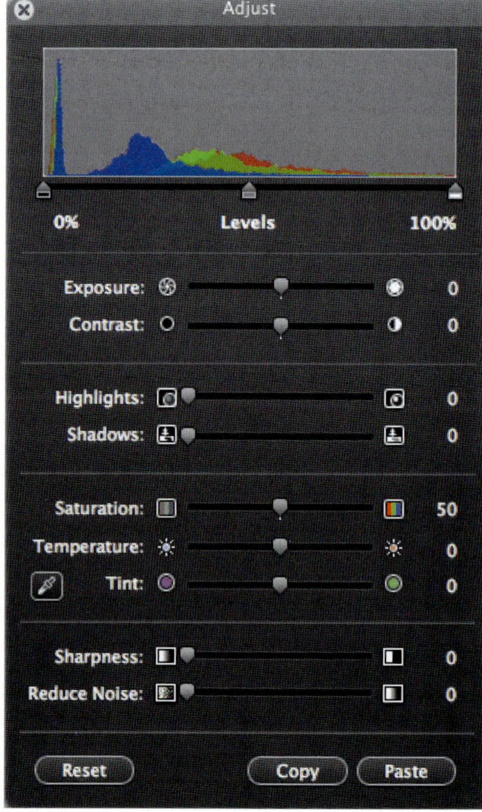

Note: To change the image back to the default, selecting the Reset button will remove all changes.

7. When all the adjustments have been made, students can click the Done button.

Extras:

Prior to any adjustments, students can duplicate their image multiple times and change each one to a different color to compare and contrast how mood and emotion varies depending on the color. To duplicate an image, select it, navigate to the Photos menu, and choose Duplicate. Command+D is the keystroke to duplicate an image quickly.

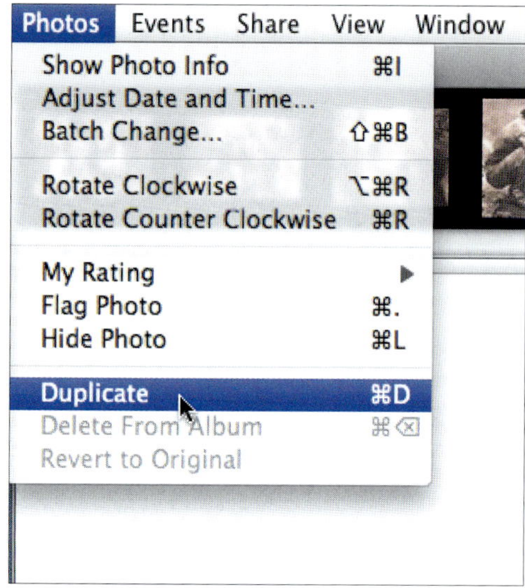

Students can create picture books to showcase all the different emotions. For example, a Happy Book can be created to showcase all the colors and tones that convey a feeling of happiness. The same can be done for any of the emotions. Students can add poetry or expository writing on text pages of the book to further emphasize the emotion.

For an open house or any special school day, students can play slide shows of their altered images sorted by emotional themes. They can also use iMovie to create videos with their images and add music that further reinforces the emotions.

Recipe Name: Voyage to the Bottom of the Intestines

Description: Students take an adventurous journey through the digestive system. With digital images and a script of information, students create a multimedia voyage from the mouth through the intestines, stopping at all the different organs. Students easily add titles, effects, and transitions to their video as they showcase what they know about the digestive process. Students will also be able to use the Ken Burns effect to add motion to an image by panning vertically or horizontally or zooming in or out. Motion in an image can serve to highlight details or provide a sense of traveling, emphasizing the idea of the journey that food takes.

Ingredients:

- TextEdit, Pages, or other word processor
- Safari
- iPhoto
- iMovie
- Digital camera or an iSight camera with Photo Booth
- GarageBand (optional)
- Comic Life (optional)

Steps:

1. After studying about the journey that food takes through digestive system, students write a story describing the voyage of food. They can pretend to be the food, speak in the voice of the organs, or act as tour guides for the food. Teachers should remind students to write details about each organ and its function in the digestive system. This writing will be the scripted narration for their movie.
2. Students find and download images to represent the different parts of their journey. Some photos can be taken with a digital camera (for example, the mouth, teeth, or tongue), but many images will need to be found on the Internet (such as the esophagus, stomach, and small and large intestines). Teachers should try to steer students toward copyright-friendly Web sites like the following:
   - Pics4learning, *http://pics4learning.com.*
   - kitZu, *http://kitzu.com.*
   - The Wikimedia Commons is a resource of copyright-friendly or public domain images, audio, and video that is featured on Wikipedia. One caveat about using Wikimedia: not all the images are kid-friendly. However, teachers can download the images for the students. You can search for Wikimedia Commons images with the Mayflower media search engine at *http://tools.wikimedia.de/~tangotango/mayflower/.* Virtually all media at the Wikimedia Commons is in the public domain or has a Creative Commons license.
   - Most video streaming or online encyclopedia subscriptions. Although they aren't free, services such as CaliforniaStreaming, Discovery Education Streaming, WorldBook, and EBSCOhost all have a variety of information and images that can be used in educational projects.
3. Import the images into iPhoto, and create an album or event to organize the photos in one place.

   Tip: Be sure to put all the photos into the same event or album for more convenient access.
4. Students finish planning their movie with storyboards. This step does not have to be intensive. The most important concept of a storyboard is to make sure students know what words will go with each image.

   Note: If students use Pages, there is a storyboard template where students can drag and drop each image and copy and paste the words that they will say for that image. Students can also use Comic Life to create storyboards. There are several templates with four to six panels, and they can use captions for the narration.

5. Launch iMovie, and access the photos by clicking the Camera icon to show the Photos Browser. The Photos Browser provides access to all the photos organized in iPhoto. Students can search the entire iPhoto Library or specific events and albums.

6. To use an image, drag and drop it to the project area (it's between the Project Library and the Project Viewer). Continue adding all the images in the order they should appear in the movie.

   Note: Each image will display for 4 seconds as a default amount, but its duration can be lengthened by clicking the tiny clock symbol located on the lower left of each image clip.

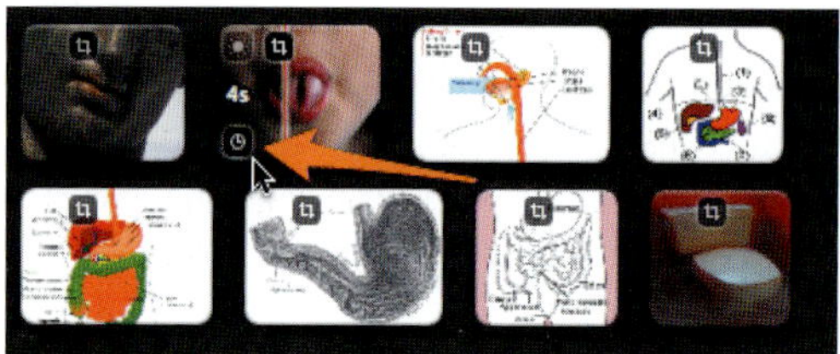

Students can modify the duration of each image in the appropriate area of the pop-up window.

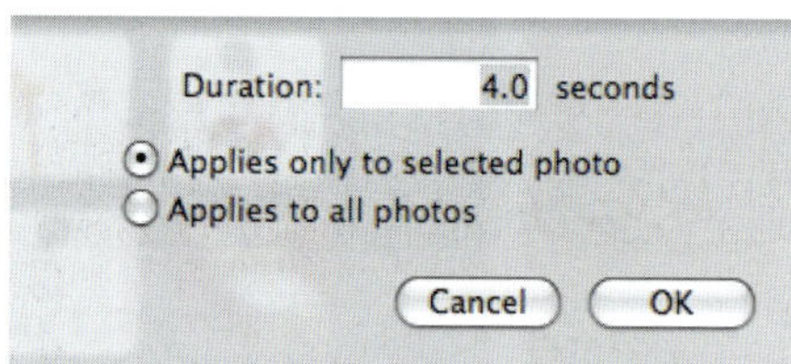

7. To add narration, click the Voiceover button (it's the microphone icon). A semitransparent box (the Voiceover window) will appear, prompting the user to click the image they want to narrate. Once a clip is selected, there is a 2-second delay before the recording begins.

   Tip: The recorded narration cannot be longer than the total duration of all the images, so it is better to lengthen the time of a clip more than needed, record the narration, and then shorten the length that the image will be to match the voice.

8. The Ken Burns effect is a good way to add motion to still images, highlighting important details or simulating travel. To activate the Ken Burns effect, click the Crop symbol in the middle controls or on the individual clip. In iMovie '08, a green rectangle shows the starting point for the Ken Burns effect. The red rectangle displays what the image will look like when the Ken Burns effect is completed. Students can even add downward motion

by panning vertically on images of the esophagus. To remove all motion, set the green and red rectangle to be identical.

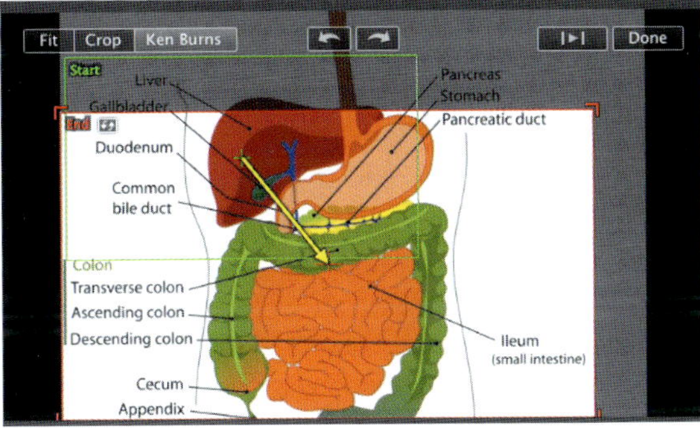

9. With the different icon buttons, students can add music, titles, transitions, and image colors.

Note: Scrolling credits are found in the Titles panel and can be used to cite all resources used.

10. When everything is complete, preview the entire movie to check for any errors. To export the movie, navigate to the Share menu, and select one of the different sharing options.

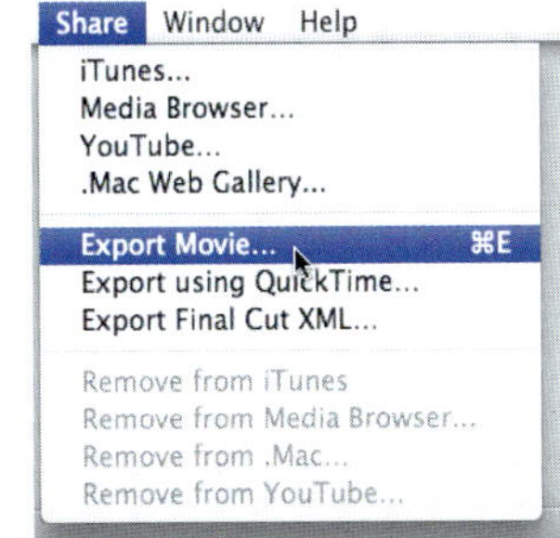

Note: To see the export presets that were present in previous versions of iMovie, select Export Using QuickTime.

11. In iMovie '08, there is a much simpler interface than previous versions for exporting video in four different sizes. Students can see a visual relationship between video size and purpose.

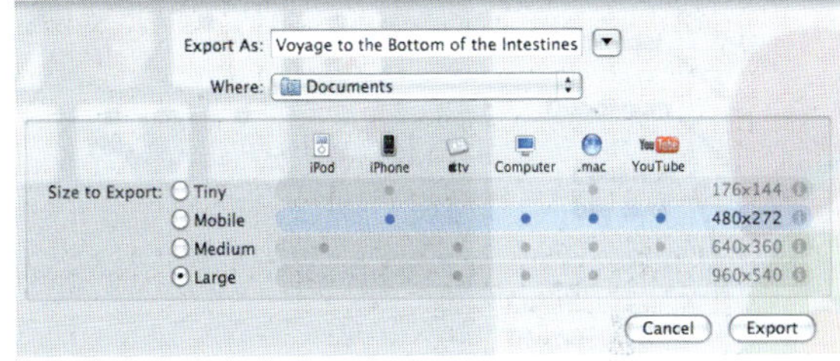

Extras:

This lesson is in the form of an iMovie, but video projects, as worthwhile as they are, often tend to take more time in post-production than other types of multimedia assignments. A few of the alternatives for slightly simpler projects would be an enhanced podcast in GarageBand, a picture book in iPhoto, or a comic book in Comic Life. However, with these projects, students will not be able to easily show motion to enhance the journey.

With a podcast, the students record their narration first and add the images to the appropriate places. Make sure there are no gaps between images on the podcast track. GarageBand's multiple audio tracks make layering different sound effects and music easier. Although it's usually faster to create an enhanced podcast instead of a video, there are some downsides. The images will be static (no motion), and transitions and titles cannot be added as easily.

An iPhoto picture book project would be the easiest because images would be dropped into the book and the text would be copied into the caption areas of the book. Text pages can also be used for the paragraphs. A comic book would be similar, but there are more controls for altering the images and text.

For example, the same image can be dragged into two different panels, but one of them can be zoomed in and recentered to focus on a slightly different part of the image. Titles, captions, and speech bubbles can all be used for the script.

This mini-lesson is also a good template for projects that focus on other systems of the body such as the central nervous system or the cardiovascular system.

Recipe Name: This Class in History, the Blog

Description: What are the notable events that have happened in the history of the world? What will be the most memorable events that happen in the classroom throughout the year? Using iWeb, students connect the past to the present by writing an ongoing blog about important events that have happened in the past as well as something they learned in the present. Students will learn how to use iWeb's blog feature to summarize the historical things that have happened and compare them to classroom current events.

Ingredients:

- Safari
- iWeb
- .Mac account or other Web server
- Digital camera (optional)
- Pages, TextEdit or other word processor (optional)
- Streaming video or online encyclopedia subscriptions (optional)

Steps:

1. Students explore calendars, Web sites, and encyclopedia software with historic facts of things that have happened on that date. The following are some possible sites to visit for more information on each date:
   - This Day in History by the History Channel site (*www.history.com/this-day-in-history.do*) features a multimedia video of events that have happened in our world every day. There is also a This Day in History Newsletter to which the teacher can subscribe.
   - The Wikipedia date in history feature has active links for all the historical events that it lists. To access this feature, enter *http://en.wikipedia.org/wiki/<month_day>* in the browser (for example, if you want to see what happened on December 11th in history, enter *http://en.wikipedia.org/wiki/December_11*).
   - The Library of Congress American Memory site (*http://memory.loc.gov/ammem/today/*) showcases the notable events in American history. There are links to the different images and primary source material at the Library of Congress.
   - TheFreeDictionary by Farlex (*www.thefreedictionary.com/*) is an informative site that includes idioms, information, notable births, a word of the day, a spelling bee, and more. One of the extra features is its Today in History section.

2. Launch iWeb, select a theme, and begin a blog. The main difference between a blog and a plain Web site is that a blog is built on an RSS feed. RSS stands for "Rich Site Summary" or "Really Simple Syndication." iWeb takes care of the need to write the XML because it creates the RSS feed to which people subscribe.
3. Students will prepare a blog entry for each day. They should write about one notable thing that they learned or did in class. Students also visit one of the different sites to summarize one historic event that occurred in the past.

   Note: Instead of typing directly into iWeb, students can type in Pages or TextEdit. In collaborative learning, different group members can write each part, transfer to the computer with the iWeb blog, and combine their work.
4. To make the curriculum more relevant, students should relate the historic event with their current learning. For example, if students write about the birth of a famous mathematician, then it's logical to write about what they learned in math that day. If the historic happening is the publishing of a famous book, then their current event could be about their language arts lesson.
5. Students can add images, audio files, or videos to enhance their blog entry.

   Tip: Classes with digital cameras can get in the habit of taking photos of all their activities. By taking photos of their science labs and other activities, students build up a library of images they can use for their blog.
6. If using a .Mac account, click the Publish button. If using another Web site, then navigate to the File menu and select Publish to Folder and upload the folder to that Web site.

Extras:

If students are creating multimedia in the classroom (for example, podcasts, videos, newsletters, songs, and photo essays), they can publish it as part of the blog. Students will be able to create a multimedia journal of their projects. This Web-based digital portfolio can be shared with all the students and families to help strengthen the home-school connection and create a place where learners can review concepts for assessment.

This project can also be created as an iPhoto calendar or a Pages document. An iPhoto calendar limits the page layout options and ability to customize the entries. Text would also be limited by the size of the date box. In all likelihood, students would not be able to add much detail on each date's entry. Images would also be a bit small. However, at the end of the school year, the calendar could be printed as a keepsake for the students.

In Pages, students would be able to create a multimedia document with videos, images, and audio clips. The length of text would be unlimited as well. However, the multimedia would be accessible only to people with Pages. If the Pages document is exported in other formats such as PDF, the video and audio will not play.

21st-Century Classic Radio

Based on the Radio Show lesson plan contributed by Joanna Seymour, technology integration specialist at St. Patrick School; Cedar Falls, Iowa.

Orson Welles's radio dramatization of The War of the Worlds rocked the nation in 1938, leading thousands of listeners to believe Earth was being invaded by extraterrestrials. At the time, a large portion of the nation's news and entertainment came over radio waves. It's no coincidence that the advent of podcasting has resulted in a resurgence of classroom audio projects. By writing and recording an original radio play, students display creativity and communication skills while demonstrating mastery of the curriculum. With GarageBand's easy drag-and-drop interface, students quickly integrate narration, dialogue, jingles, radio sounds, and other sound effects. Digitally recorded plays can be published and distributed to individuals or groups as a podcast, in a CD collection, or on an iPod.

Project Summary

After reading and listening to several radio dramas, student groups write a radio show based on an event or period of history. Students write commercials that are appropriate for the radio age and create sound effects. Designing commercials improves their synthesizing of the important elements of this time period. The radio shows are recorded using GarageBand or an iPod and voice recorder, imported into iTunes, and then shared with the whole class.

Note: This lesson is highly customizable. Radio shows can be used to adapt readers' theater, reenact historical events, or dramatize key moments in a literature series. Students can also "act out" scientific and mathematical discoveries through a radio drama.

Grade Level/Subject

Elementary, middle, and high-school history, social studies, language arts, and performing arts

Lesson Goals

- Conduct research on a historical event or period.
- Demonstrate an understanding of a historical event through the synthesis of that time period and creation of a radio play.
- Use fluent reading skills to record narration and dialogue with accuracy and inflection.

Learning Objectives

After completing this project, students will be able to:

Academic

- Write and edit a script for a radio play.
- Create commercials for products related to a historical period for the play.
- Demonstrate understanding of a historic event through summarizing.

Technical

- Use a word-processing application to write, revise, and edit their written work.
- Use GarageBand or an iPod and voice recorder to record sound effects.
- Use GarageBand to combine narration, music, and sound effects.
- Use iTunes to organize and enjoy their radio shows.

What You'll Need

This is the recommended hardware and software:

- Macintosh computers with built-in microphones (any iMac, eMac, or laptop)
- iLife tools (GarageBand and iTunes)
- Additional iLife tools (iPhoto and iWeb)
- Pages, TextEdit, or other word processor

  Note: Pages has a template for a screenplay that would be helpful in creating a realistic script for this project.
- USB or other external microphone
- iPods with voice recorders (for mobile recording)

  Note: Before purchasing a third-party iPod voice recorder, check the specifications to ensure that your iPod model is supported. Currently, the iPod Classic, iPod nano, and all 5G iPods can be used with any of the new voice recorders by Belkin, Griffin, and XtremeMac. For more information, see your iPod User's Guide.
- Blank CDs or DVDs for burning copies of projects

Deciding on the Final Product

- Create a compilation CD. By organizing all the radio shows in a single iTunes playlist, the students can burn the collection to a CD. They can also create their own CD labels and covers as an art assignment. The covers and labels can have the same theme as their radio show to continue the project. Commemorative CDs of projects make a great fundraiser that can benefit technology purchases.
- Create audio and enhanced podcasts. All of their audio files can be posted to the school or classroom Web site for download. If the classroom is using a .Mac account, a podcast page in iWeb can be created quickly and easily. Images from iPhoto can be integrated to add a visual element as an enhanced podcast. Once posted to a Web site, the podcasts can be downloaded and transferred onto an iPod for individual learning or review. Having a podcast page also facilitates communication outside the classroom for peer-to-peer teaching.

Outcome-Based Assessment

Student Role

- Students design their strategies for the project, including the following:
  - Organize the tasks to complete the project.
  - Find appropriate music and sound effects in GarageBand.
  - Record any additional sound effects in GarageBand or on iPods.
  - Import their iPod recordings to iTunes.
  - Create the radio show in GarageBand, and combine the sound effects, music, narration, and dialogue.
  - Publish and distribute the radio shows uploading to the Web, transferring to iPods, or through burning CDs.
- With the teacher's guidance and software or Web resources, the students create a rubric to assess the outcomes.

Teacher Role

- Determine the criteria for evaluation of students' work throughout the process, and explain to students how you will assess the various parts of their project, including the following:
  - QuickWrite journals for reflection
  - Steps to the writing process for the radio show script
  - Process of recording the show in GarageBand
  - The effective use of sound effects and music to enhance the recording
  - Accuracy of historical events represented in the radio show
  - Ability of the students to work collaboratively in their group
- Establish and explain your criteria for evaluating students' technical skills, including the following:
  - Audio clarity of their recordings
  - Audio levels of the final product (for example, the music and sound effects don't overpower dialogue)
  - The ability to share their product in iTunes, the Web, or the iPod
- Identify how you will evaluate students' ability to reach their intended outcomes as judged by the final product.

I. Getting Started

Teacher Planning

- Teachers should be familiar with some examples of classic radio shows. Several Web resources are available:
  - Teacher on Wheels Radio Plays, *www.nald.ca/province/nfld/tow/towplays/playcont.htm*
  - National Radio Hall of Fame Museum, *www.radiohof.org*
  - The Museum of Television and Radio, *www.mtr.org/index.htm*
  - The Radio Adventures of Dr. Floyd, *http://doctorfloyd.com*
  - Radio Days, *www.otr.com/index.shtml*
  - Library of American Broadcasting Soundbites, *www.lip.umd.edu/LAB/AUDIO/soundbites.html*
  - The BBC's How to Write a Radio Play, *www.bbc.co.uk/worldservice/arts/features/howtowrite/radio.shtml*
- Teachers should be familiar with the basic functionality of GarageBand. Although the teacher doesn't have to know everything about the application, understanding the navigation and features of GarageBand are important. Specifically, the teacher should know how to create a podcast episode (Figure Radio 1); browse and add jingles, stingers, and sound effects; and record vocals (Figure Radio 2).

Radio 1

Radio 2

- Teachers should be familiar with how to use the voice recorder attachment for the iPod and how to import the audio into iTunes. Within iTunes, they should know how to create playlists and burn a CD.
- Determine the amount of time to be given for the project, and set some suggested time limits to achieve specific milestones. For example, how much time should be given for writing, editing, and revising the script? When should students be expected to finish recording their radio show?

Preparing Students

- Time should be given for students to experience some of the technology that will be used as well. This would include the following:
  - An opportunity for students to experiment with GarageBand and its recording functions. Students should pay special attention to determining the proper distance and volume needed for optimized recording with built-in or external microphones.

  Tip: In general, 6 inches from the microphone is a good distance for audio pick-up.

  - Students should also be familiar with how to add loops and combine sound effects, iTunes recordings, and jingles in GarageBand. It is important to give students time to search the different radio sounds, stingers, and sound effects so that they have a general knowledge of the types of sounds that are included.
  - If iPods are used, students should know how to record with the third-party voice recorder, transfer to iTunes, and organize the voice memos.
- The students will be put into collaborative learning groups. It's a good idea to train multiple students to be the technology expert for each piece of equipment. However, it is not necessary to train all the students on each piece of equipment. If two people per group understand how to record using GarageBand or the iPod, then they can troubleshoot with one another. Also, if one is absent, another is prepared to use the equipment, and the students are still empowered to be the expert in one aspect of the technology.

II. Making Connections

Introducing the Project

- Have students read and listen to some samples of classic radio plays. Students should create a visual organizer that details the parts and characteristics of radio plays in comparison to other types of drama. They can write these thoughts in their QuickWrite journal as part of the project folder.

Connecting the Known Information to New Learning

- Discuss some of their findings.
  - How do radio shows capture imagination?
  - What are some elements that are always present in a radio drama? For example, answers could be sound effects and inflection in speaking.
  - What are some devices that radio dramas utilize to increase tension and excitement? For example, answers could include mood music and the use of cliffhangers.
- Discuss why radio dramas aren't as popular anymore.
  - Why don't we listen to radio dramas nowadays?
  - Why don't we listen to radio in general as much?
  - Attention should be placed on the fact that radio was the main form of mass-media entertainment in the home for decades, so radio shows were often the focal point of family time. Today, radio entertainment must compete with television, rental movies, Internet-based media, and video games (just to name a few things).

- Play the podcast "The Radio Adventures of Dr. Floyd" to students. Discuss how this is in the style of a classic radio show, but it is created with 21st-century computer-based recording equipment. Make special note that it's engaging entertainment and also includes historical information.

III. Planning the Project (Preproduction)

Project Folder

Students begin by creating a project folder to keep track of their research, information, tasks, timelines, and goals. Some of the items that might be included in the project folder are a QuickWrite journal, checklist, brainstorming notes, and production notes.

QuickWrite Journal

Students keep a journal to record thoughts, assess their progress, and set goals toward the completion of the project. It's an informal way for students to be task-oriented and aware of their responsibilities. Students can also use the journal at the end of the project for reflections and reactions when listening to all the audio created. The QuickWrite journal doesn't need to be created on paper. A blog could serve the same purpose. This would also facilitate assessment through a digital portfolio.

Because this lesson centers on recording audio, students can also record their journal entries orally via iPod or GarageBand. This would be beneficial for younger students and ELL students who generally have more highly developed speaking skills than reading and writing skills.

Student Grouping

Students should be divided into collaborative work groups of three to five students to complete this project. Each student should be given a specific role. For example, students could have the following roles: the fact expert, the head writer, the audio editor (in GarageBand), and the foley (sound-effects person). This enables all students to lead one aspect of the project and contribute to others.

IV. Creating the Project (Production)

Tip: If possible, have extra iPods, voice recorders, and digital cameras, just in case a piece of equipment doesn't function properly in class.

Writing the Script

- Each group chooses a historical event or period of history that's being studied. For example, a group can select a historical event such as the Boston Tea Party or an entire period such as the westward expansion. The teacher can also assign a topic for each group to do. They should conduct research on the topic and then use Pages, TextEdit, or another word-processing application to write and edit a script for a 5-to-10-minute radio play (the length will be dependent on age level).
- Students research and write commercials that are appropriate for the radio age. They can work on creating a commercial that is also appropriate for their subject. What type of product would work with their historical era? For example, if it's a radio drama about the Boston Tea Party, maybe they will create a commercial about coffee.

Creating Sound Effects

- Students should make a list of different sound effects that they need for their radio show. If there are any special sound effects that are not found in GarageBand, then they should record it with an iPod.
- If they have external microphones, then they can record the sound effects straight to GarageBand.

Note: One benefit of recording a sound effect straight to GarageBand is that students can save it as a loop to share with others and use in future projects.

- If they use an iPod to record the sound effects, then they need to transfer the recorded sound effects into iTunes so that they will be able to use them in GarageBand.

Recording the Radio Show

- When the script is complete and students have had time to practice, they can record their show in GarageBand. The following are some tips for recording a show in GarageBand:
  - Students should use a different track for each voice so that quieter and louder voices can be modified to play at the same level.

  - Groups should be encouraged to re-record parts that aren't clear.
  - If an audio interface with multiple microphones is used, then students can level audio and record all parts at the same time. This helps develop fluency and inflection of words.
- When vocals are complete, the students should begin adding sound effects and music. They can use the included jingles or create their own tunes. Emphasis should be on adding music and sound effects that are appropriate for their show.

V. Refining the Project (Postproduction)

Editing the Radio Show

- When all vocals have been recorded, mood music has been added, and sound effects have been included, groups can begin editing their radio show. The following are some aspects to focus on:
  - Deleting any unnecessary pauses in dialogue.
  - Adjusting all vocal audio levels so that the students' voices have approximately the same output. If there are sections that are meant to be softer or louder for artistic purposes, then that is fine.
  - Decreasing volume of all jingles and music beds so that they don't overpower any vocals.

Note: GarageBand features a ducking feature that will automatically decrease volume levels for music or sound effects when vocals are played. The tracks with the yellow triangle cause ones with a blue triangle to decrease in volume automatically.

Exporting the Radio Show

- When the radio shows are complete, they can be exported to iTunes. Each radio show can be transferred to one computer so that they can be included in a single playlist.
- With all the audio files in one playlist, a CD compilation of all shows can be burned or transferred to an iPod.

VI. Publishing the Project

Presentation

The radio dramas can be burned to CD and distributed to classmates, families, and other schools. All the finished audio files can be sent back to the iPods during synchronization for anytime, anywhere learning. The shows can also be used as podcasts and placed on the class podcast page.

Additional Activities and Extensions

- The teacher can apply to have the work presented at a School Night at the Apple Store. Students get an opportunity to share their work and what they learned. The School Night at the Apple Store program is a great way to showcase student work and what students are capable of when creating with digital media. For more information, visit www.apple.com/education/schoolnight. If this option is used, it is best to add images to the radio shows so that they are more visually appealing as a presentation. Within GarageBand, an image can be placed in the podcast track to create an enhanced podcast.
- All the radio shows can be published as a classroom podcast. Each group can take turns posting their audio and writing an entry about their radio show's topic. If the class has a .Mac account, iWeb helps them easily post their work as a podcast because it features one-click publishing and will create the RSS feed page.
- Students can take digital photos of key moments in their radio show to create an enhanced podcast. These versions of the radio shows with some visuals can be exported to iTunes and shared via CD, iPod, or podcast page.
- The compilation of all the radio shows can be sold as a commemorative CD. The money that is raised can be used to purchase more technology equipment. Double-check your school bylaws and educational code. Some schools and districts require a partnership with the parent-teacher organization to have a fundraiser like this.

VII. Reflection, Assessment, & Differentiation

Reflection

- Students can add a final entry to their QuickWrite journals that wraps up their thoughts for this project.
- While listening to the other group's radio shows, students can also write their reactions and thoughts to those creations.
- Invite discussion, comments, and journal entries related to this project:
  - What did you learn about the benefits of music and inflection in a radio show for visualizing a story?
  - What were your successes and failures?
  - How can you use what you learned to improve your writing skills in other academic areas?
  - In what ways can vocabulary choice benefit radio shows?
  - What did you learn about working with others?
  - How do you feel about your product and why?
- Students complete the rubrics, justifying their achievements, possibly focusing on the following criteria:
  - *Content choice*: How well did the radio show you recorded represent the era you were studying?
  - *The group work*: How well did the group members communicate and work collaboratively?
  - *Further learning*: How well did your radio show, and the work of others, entertain and engage you to learn more?

Customizing the Lesson for All Learners

All age groups can be taught to create radio shows for any academic area:

- For younger students, the teacher can have the whole class write the radio show together, or they can utilize an already-created readers' theater script. They work in small groups on different parts of the process. Some students work to create sound effects. Other students work to record the radio show. A different group creates or finds jingles that help convey the mood. This will help transfer the knowledge in smaller steps.
- English-language learners should be placed in a group with fluent English speakers. They can help create the sound effects and import other jingles or stingers to the radio show. If there is a group of ELL students who speak the same language, they can create a radio show in their home language on the topic.
- More advanced learners would be expected to take this lesson further. They would be expected to create a library of sound effects that they can save as loops for future use. They would also be expected to include more key vocabulary to their radio show script.

Persuasive Products

Based on the Ad Campaign lesson plan contributed by Elaine Wrenn, technology coordinator, and Marcie Vogel, language arts teacher, at Echo Horizon School; Culver City, California.

21st-century learning skills emphasize several traits including creativity, communication, collaboration, and visual literacy. Understanding how the media can manipulate buyers is an essential skill for dealing with the different products that are being promoted. In this project, students apply what they have learned about persuasive writing and use their media literacy to create a 30-to-60-second commercial on a new product or service that, at a first glance, probably wouldn't have much of an audience. Students will use iMovie to create their project.

Project Summary

As part of a unit on persuasive writing and media literacy, students explore different methods used by advertisers to persuade customers to buy their products or services. They develop a prototype of their own product or service and create a commercial to sell it. The twist to this lesson is that students will deal with products that, at a first glance, would not have any market (like skunk-odor deodorant). Students use Pages, TextEdit or another word-processing program to write a letter to possible investors.

Grade Level/Subject

Upper-elementary, middle-school, and high-school language arts and performing arts

High-school economics

Lesson Goals

- Explain various persuasive techniques used by advertisers to sell products.
- Achieve a deeper understanding of media literacy and techniques that advertisers use to persuade consumers.
- Create a 30-to-60-second commercial to sell their product or service.

Learning Objectives

After completing this project, students will be able to:

Academic

- Analyze professional persuasive techniques to evaluate the truth of claims about products and services.
- Create a product or service that doesn't seem to be enticing in any way, and develop a possible market for it.
- Write persuasive text for an advertisement to convince investors to give them money to manufacture their new product.

Technical

- Use iMovie to create and edit a 30-to-60-second commercial to promote their product.
- Use Pages, TextEdit, or another word processor to write and format a letter to investors.

What You'll Need

This is the recommended hardware and software:

- Macintosh computers
- Video camera
- Props and costumes appropriate for their product
- Tripod and microphones (optional)
- iLife tools (iMovie)
- Additional iLife tools (GarageBand, iDVD, and iWeb for extension activities)
- Pages, TextEdit, or other word processor
- DVDs for compiling and archiving the commercials

Deciding on the Final Product

- iMovie can export and compress in several different formats. Just within iMovie, students can export their movie for a variety of purposes that include video podcasting, DVDs, iWeb, e-mail, and streaming video. Deciding on the compression truly depends on the intended audience. A single project could be exported in a variety of formats to increase access for the audience. The following options present specific purposes and rationale for using them.
- DVD projects are best used when the class or school wants to distribute a hard copy to multiple students, staff, or parents. DVDs created in iDVD have professional-looking menus and are an easy way to compile multiple videos. For many schools, DVDs are the perfect commemorative fundraiser and are used to raise money for technology equipment or other school programs.
- Students can use video podcasts for anytime, anywhere learning. Video podcasts are convenient because they can be watched on a computer or loaded onto an iPod. Once students, parents, or anyone subscribes to the RSS feed, they never need to visit that Web site again. Every time iTunes is launched, it will search the Internet and download the latest episodes of all the podcasts that have been subscribed to. Video podcasts are a great way to send information for reteaching key concepts, strengthening the home-school connection, or communicating with a global audience.
- The ability to send a video directly to YouTube is one of the new export options in iMovie. YouTube is the most-watched video-streaming site on the Internet, and it's one of the fastest-growing forms of digital media distribution. Although any computer user can enjoy a podcast, certain podcasts (enhanced podcasts) still require a free download of iTunes or the QuickTime Player (included on every Mac). YouTube is universal. There is no other software needed to view a YouTube video. Exporting student movies to YouTube helps develop the global audience more quickly than any other form of digital media. However, one drawback to YouTube is that educational institutions often block access to it.

Outcome-Based Assessment

Student Role

- Students design their strategies for the project, including the following:
  - Organize the tasks to the project.
  - Decide on a product or service that most people would never buy or use.
  - Use the writing process to create the text for their investment letter and commercial.
  - Work collaboratively to discuss the persuasiveness of their project.
- With the teacher's guidance and software or Web resources, the students create a rubric to assess the outcomes.

Teacher Role

- Determine the criteria for evaluation of students' work throughout the process, and explain to students how you will assess the various parts of their project, including the following:
  - The thoughts and reflections in their QuickWrite journal
  - The use of the writing process for the dialogue in the commercials and text in the investment letter
  - Appropriate props and costumes for their commercial
  - Ability of the students to work collaboratively in their group
  - Clarity of script and letter, and use of writing conventions
  - Persuasive techniques in both the commercial and investment letter
- Establish and explain your criteria for evaluating students' technical skills, including the following:
  - Use of the video camera (are shots stable and exposed correctly?)
  - Creation of the video to promote their product or service (were titles, credits, video editing, and transitions used appropriately?)
  - Formatting of the persuasive letter to investors
- Identify how you will evaluate students' ability to reach their intended outcomes, as judged by the final product.

I. Getting Started

Teacher Planning

- Teachers should be familiar with some examples of Web-based resources regarding advertising and media literacy. Some sites include the following:
  - Media Awareness Network Common Advertising Strategies, *www.media-awareness.ca/english/resources/educational/handouts/advertising_marketing/common_ad_strats.cfm*
  - Evaluating Bias in Advertising WebQuest, *www.glencoe.com/sec/science/webquest/content/evalbias.shtml*
  - Ad Cracker, a site with interactive tools and samples to create advertising and marketing campaigns, *www.adcracker.com*
  - Merchants of Cool, a Frontline episode that focuses on marketing to teens, *www.pbs.org/wgbh/pages/frontline/shows/cool*
- Teachers should be familiar with the basic functionality of iMovie. Although the teacher doesn't have to know everything about the application, understanding its navigation and features is important. Specifically, the teacher should know how to import footage, trim video clips, insert transitions, and add titles and credits.
- Teachers should understand how students can use storyboards to visualize and plan their commercials.

  Note: Pages has a template for storyboards. Students can import images to represent each shot they will use in the commercial. They can type the dialogue or action that will go with each shot in a scene.
- Determine the amount of time to be given the project, and set some suggested time limits to achieve specific milestones in the creation process. For example, how much time should be given for writing, editing, and revising the letters and scripts? When should students be expected to complete all props and storyboards for their commercial? How much time is needed to shoot and edit the video?

Preparing Students

- Time should be given for students to experience some of the technology that will be used as well. This would include the following:
  - An opportunity for students to use a video camera

- Time to use iMovie to import footage, edit clips, insert transitions, and add titles and credits
- Time to use Pages, TextEdit, or another word processor to type, format, and print a letter

- Have students watch a variety of commercials in preparation for this unit.

II. Making Connections

Introducing the Project

- Share examples of various commercials and infomercials with students. Compare and contrast the similarities and differences between these two forms of persuasion, and discuss the effectiveness of each. Stress the idea of "show, don't tell." Commercials with stories and funny situations often show why a product is useful. However, infomercials typically employ bad actors that tell you why a specific product should be purchased.
- Discuss popular techniques used by advertisers to influence people to believe that they need the product or service. Refer to the print and Internet resources for examples and further explanation.
- Discuss some familiar commercials and the audiences the advertisers are trying to reach. For example, what problem does a product like Pampers diapers solve? Who might use hair restoration medicine?

Connecting the Known Information to New Learning

- Discuss some of the different persuasive techniques, including the following:
  - *Bandwagon*: Everyone else is doing it and so should you.
  - *Testimonial*: A well-known person or expert says that they use a product.
  - *Fear*: There will be terrible consequences if you don't buy the product.
  - *Image*: Using the product will make you more attractive, wealthy, or respected.
  - *Slice of life*: Someone tells a narrative story to demonstrate why the product is desirable.
  - *Slogans*: The commercial uses catchy tunes or sayings that stick in people's heads.
  - *Glittering generalities*: New! Improved!
  - *Logo*: An eye-catching visual image identifies the company or product.
- Discuss some of the products that students purchase. Discuss why the commercials for those products are popular.
  - What makes this commercial appealing to you? Why does it make you want to purchase the product?
  - What would you do to get more people to purchase the product?
- Brainstorm some unusual products that have somehow been created. Possible examples include Flowbee and Robo Cut vacuum hair trimmers, the Clapper, and Spray On Hair Color. Who would purchase these items?

III. Planning the Project (Preproduction)

Project Folder

Students begin by creating a project folder to keep track of their information, tasks, timelines, and goals. Some of the items that might be included in the project folder are a QuickWrite journal, checklist, brainstorming ideas, script, storyboards, and production notes.

QuickWrite Journal

Students keep a journal of their project and use it to record thoughts, assess their progress, and set goals toward the completion of the project. It's an informal way for the student to be task-oriented and aware of their responsibilities.

Students can also use the journal at the end of the project for reflections and reactions when viewing all the commercials created. The QuickWrite journal doesn't need to be created on paper. A blog or wiki could serve the same purpose. This would also facilitate assessment through a digital portfolio or posting to a classroom Web site.

Student Grouping

Students should work in collaborative groups of four to six students. This number helps facilitate the distribution of tasks without leaving anyone out. Groups of more than six will often have students who have nothing to do.

IV. Creating the Project (Production)

Creating the Product or Service

- Students decide on a product or service that, upon a first consideration, nobody would be interested in. Some possible products and services include the following:
  - Dandruff-covered wigs
  - Fish-flavored chewing gum
  - Skunk-odor deodorant
  - Wheel-less skateboards
  - Scented socks
  - Edible crayons
  - A pizza-laundromat
  - A music-pet store
  - A cleaning service for fake plants
- Students should take some time to brainstorm ideas about their product or service. The following are among the factors to consider:
  - Why would anybody purchase the product or service for which they are creating a commercial?
  - Who are the likely consumers they are trying to reach?
  - How can they make their product or service as attractive as possible?
  - What are some key words to use to persuade and develop their target audience?

Writing the Investment Letter and Script

- Students follow the writing process to craft a persuasive letter to investors. Among the key points to highlight are the following:
  - There's a segment of the population with a problem (for example, many students are bullied every year but don't fight back because they follow the path of nonviolence).
  - You have a product or service that will solve that problem (Skunk-Odor Deodorant will repel any bully without causing any real harm).
  - Include specific information on how the product or service will be marketed (print advertising and fun commercials with stories will be created to show people fighting off bullies without really fighting).
- Students follow the writing process to create a script for their commercial. The following are elements to include:
  - A storyline to show the problem and solve it with the product or service.
  - Dialogue (optional) of people conversing in this situation.

Note: Avoid telling the audience about the product like an infomercial. Allow the situation to show why this product or service is essential.

Creating the Commercial

- Draw a storyboard to depict the action in the video. Students can use stick figures to draw the storyboard panels. They should also write the dialogue or action notes by each panel.

  Note: Each panel of the storyboard should represent a different shot in the action. Multiple shots make up a scene in the video.

- Students should be required to rehearse their commercial so they feel more comfortable speaking and moving in front of the camera.
- Students create props, costumes, and backgrounds for their commercial. They should pay special attention to the prop they use if they have a product.
- Using the storyboards and scripts, students shoot their video footage. If there is enough time, students should try to record more than one take for each shot.
- When all the video footage has been shot, students import the clips into iMovie where they will be part of the Event Library.

V. Refining the Project (Postproduction)

Editing the Video

- To use a clip in their video, students select the event, highlight the segment, and drag it to the project area. They continue adding video clips until their commercial is complete.

- Students should insert transitions and add titles and credits as needed.

  Note: Transitions are generally used to show a change in location or time. The majority of scenes have no transitions between shots.

- Students can add narration with a product shot at the end of the video if they want. The Photos Browser gives students access to all the images in iPhoto.

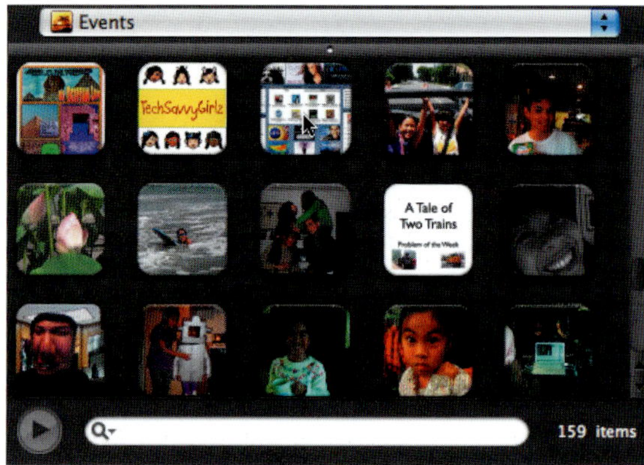

To use one, they drag it to the appropriate spot in their project. To add narration, students click on the Voiceover button and follow the instructions to record their voices.

- Prior to exporting the video, students should watch their entire commercial.

VI. Publishing the Project

Presentation

Students should export their movie in an appropriate format and present them to the rest of the class. During the screening process, students should take a moment to evaluate the persuasiveness of the commercial. If the videos are repurposed for podcasting, then they can be uploaded to a .Mac or other server with iWeb. Alternatively, the videos can be posted on a podcast hosting site or uploaded to YouTube.

Additional Activities and Extensions

- Students can compare and contrast TV commercials with radio ads. How must advertising change when there are no visuals? They can continue their project by creating radio ads for their product or service.
- A DVD can be created with all the videos if they are exported as high-quality QuickTime movies (large size). With iDVD, all the projects can be compiled to create a DVD collection of the commercials. The collection of movies can be shown at an Apple Store during a School Night event. For more information on the School Night at the Apple Store program, visit www.apple.com/education/schoolnight.
- Students can present their vidcos and letters to the principal or parent-teacher organization to evaluate which one is the most persuasive.

VII. Reflection, Assessment, & Differentiation

Reflection

- Students can add a final entry to their QuickWrite journal that wraps up their thoughts for this project.
- While viewing the other group's commercials, students can also write their reactions and thoughts to those creations.
- Invite discussion, comments, and journal entries related to this project:
  - What did you learn about the different techniques used in creating advertising?
  - What were your successes and failures?
  - How can you use what you learned to improve your persuasive writing skills in other academic areas?
  - How will this experience change your viewing of commercials and other advertising?
  - What did you learn about working with others?
  - How do you feel about your product and why?
- Students complete the rubrics, justifying their achievements, possibly focusing on the following criteria:
  - *Content choice*: How well did the commercial represent your product or service?
  - *Group work*: How well did the group members communicate and work collaboratively?
  - *Further learning*: What would you change about your commercial or product to sell it to a different audience?

Customizing the Lesson for All Learners

- For younger students, the teacher can assign a product or service for which the students will create a commercial. Students can work in larger groups to segment the work further.
- English-language learners should be placed in a group with fluent English speakers. They can help create props and other material for their commercial.

"Rapping" Up the Curriculum

Based on the Ancient Egyptian Raps lesson plan contributed by Ted Lai, coordinator of Educational Technology & Media Services at Fullerton School District.

Music is an engaging and effective way to help students learn. Schoolhouse Rock and other educational songs have enhanced learning for years. By using a familiar musical style, such as rap or hip-hop, the curriculum comes to life and becomes more meaningful to the students. Through the process of writing, practicing, and recording their song, students master curricular standards by creating an educational rap to conclude a unit of study. Additionally, students gain experience with communication, creativity, and collaboration.

Project Summary

At the end of a unit of study in history, the students imagine themselves as rap stars from that era. They create a poem about their feelings or experiences as a member of that society and express it through singing it to a beat in GarageBand. This rap is created through the simple process of laying down a beat track, recording vocals, and decorating the audio with vinyl scratching and other instruments.

Grade Level/Subject

Elementary, middle, or high-school social studies/history, language arts, and performing arts

Lesson Goals

- Students will explore how poetry and music in rap form can help creatively express what they know about a topic.
- Students utilize popular music to relate to their studies.

Learning Objectives

After completing this project, students will be able to:

Academic

- Summarize some meaningful part of ancient Egypt (or other curricular area) through music.
- Create and perform an educational rap.
- Understand that rap is a form of poetry set to a regular beat.
- Reinforce syllabication and creative rhyming in poetry.

Technical

- Use GarageBand to add vocal tracks (real instruments).
- Record their voices on a vocal track and manipulate it.
- Add beats, instruments, and vinyl-scratching loops to their rap.
- Export a GarageBand composition to iTunes and create a rap playlist.

What You'll Need

This is the recommended hardware and software:

- Macintosh computers
- Over-the-ear headphones (one or more per group as needed)
- USB or other external microphones (optional but recommended)
- Headphone splitters (optional)
- iLife tools (GarageBand and iTunes)
- Additional iLife tools (iPhoto, iMovie, iDVD, and iWeb for extension activities)
- Blank CDs for creating compilations

- GarageBand Jam Pack: Remix Tools (optional but recommended)
- A legal image library to gather digital images for a variety of possible extensions to this activity (optional)

Deciding on the Final Product

- Create a CD compilation. All the audio created in this project can be compiled in a single iTunes playlist as a listening station. A playlist also helps the teacher and students burn a CD compilation of all the educational raps or hip-hop songs created. Relevant cover art can also be produced.
- Create music videos. Students can find relevant images (from legal sources) and create music videos. This would also showcase the integration of the iLife applications such as iPhoto, iMovie, and iTunes. Students can use iMovie to compile the music videos. iDVD can be used to create a compilation DVD of all the videos.
- Create a podcast site. The songs that have been created can be posted without adaptation to create an audio podcast. Enhanced podcasts can be created with GarageBand and its included Media Browser. Students would bring in some of their relevant digital images. If music videos were created with iMovie, then they can be exported as video podcasts. The class would need a site, such as the school server, to post their podcast, or the teacher can sign up for a free account at a podcast host such as SwitchPod at http://switchpod.com. One of the simplest ways to create a podcast site would be to use a .Mac account and iWeb. This member of the iLife suite can be used to create very simple podcast pages without worrying about the XML coding, and it offers one-click publishing.

Outcome-Based Assessment

Student Role

- Students design their strategies for the project, including the following:
  - Brainstorm the vocabulary that is integral to their topic.
  - Select words that can rhyme in their poem.
  - Write their poem that will become a rap.
  - Sing their poem to a beat.
  - Add sound effects and musical riffs to enhance the rap.
- With the teacher's guidance and software or Web resources, the students create a rubric to assess the outcomes.

Teacher Role

- Determine the criteria for evaluation of students' work throughout the process, and explain to students how you will assess the various parts of their project, including the following:
  - QuickWrite journals for reflection
  - The writing process (brainstorming, writing, and revising their poem)
  - The interpretation of the poem into rap or hip-hop
- Establish and explain your criteria for evaluating students' technical skills, including the following:
  - Clarity of their recording
  - Appropriateness of loops and instruments to enhance their song
  - Editing of empty spaces so that lyrics are in tempo
- Identify how you will evaluate students' ability to reach their own intended outcomes as judged by their final product.

I. Getting Started

Teacher Planning

- Teachers should become familiar with some appropriate hip-hop or rap examples that can be shared with students. Teachers should also understand the strong link between poetry, rap, and hip-hop. There are many excellent resources for learning about poetry, rap, and hip-hop for kids. Among them are the following:
  - Edu-Basics site, *www.edubasics.com/*
  - ReMix Project site, *http://web.mac.com/tntnzing/iWeb/ReMix_Ed/*
  - The Health Raps site, *www.aetn.org/healthraps/*
  - The Education World page on poetry, *www.educationworld.com/a_sites/sites013.shtml*
  - Songs for Teaching, *www.songsforteaching.com/*
- Teachers should be familiar with GarageBand. It's not necessary for the teacher to understand all the details of GarageBand; however, it is important for the teacher to be able to navigate the basic interface and work with recording and adding loops. If an external microphone is used, the teacher should understand how to plug it in to the computer and select it as an input in the GarageBand preferences if it isn't recognized automatically.
- Determine the amount of time to be given for the project, and set some suggested time limits to achieve specific milestones in the creation process. For example, when should the poem be completed? How much time should be given for rehearsing the rap? What amount of time is needed for recording?
- Decide the length of the poem to create. For example, a typical fifth-grade group should be able to create a sixteen-line poem broken into four equal stanzas. Exemplary projects would include more than sixteen lines of focused, curriculum-based lyrics. Each stanza should emphasize the content.

Preparing Students

- Listen to some educational rap and hip-hop songs. To aid in their music appreciation and understanding, the teacher can have students count 1–2–3–4 with the song or tap to the beat so that they understand that each measure of music contains four beats and the lyrics are sung to a specific tempo and rhythm. Jump-rope rhymes are also a good way to teach the rhythm of lyrics.
- Give an introductory demonstration of the GarageBand interface, how to add loops, and how to record vocals. Special attention should be placed on the fact that loops and recorded lyrics can be edited and shifted so that they match the beat better. If an external microphone is used, the teacher should also allow for some time to experiment with connecting it to the computer.

  Tip: In the Control menu, there is a selection called Count In. With this feature activated, students will have four beats counted before they need to begin recording. It's a worthwhile tool that helps students hear the beat before beginning to sing.

II. Making Connections

Introducing the Project

- Discuss the similarities and differences between poetry and forms of music such as rap and hip-hop. Essentially, rap and hip-hop are poems sung to music and a beat.
- Explore a few examples of rhyming poetry and rap or hip-hop lyrics. Lead students in a discussion comparing and contrasting these two forms of expression. One possible area to focus on is the rhyming. Where are rhymes usually seen or heard? If there's a variety of poems and raps, the students should understand that a four-line stanza often has rhyming at the end of the third and fourth lines, but it's sometimes present on the second and fourth lines. Another area to focus on is syllabication. Few songs have drastically different syllabication on each line.

- Discuss how songs often tell a story or describe life for a specific person or group of people during an era in history. How are the songs organized? For example, song stanzas or verses are often organized into subtopics like paragraphs are.

Connecting the Known Information to New Learning

- As a class, brainstorm some of the different topics that the students think a rapper might sing about if he/she lived in the period of history they were studying. What are some of the thoughts and feelings they might have for those topics? For example, a rapper in ancient Egypt might have sung about the Nile because it gave them life. Discuss how those feelings would influence the song. For example, a song about the Nile would probably be happier than a song about slavery.
- Create a list of possible topics that a rapper in that period might have sung about. For example, in ancient Egypt, a rapper's topics might have included songs about the Pharaohs, pyramids, the Nile, gods and goddesses, or farming.

III. Planning the Project (Preproduction)

Project Folder

Students begin by creating a project folder to keep track of their research, information, tasks, timelines, and goals. Some of the items that might be included in the project folder are a QuickWrite journal, checklist, brainstorming notes, and production notes.

QuickWrite Journal

Students keep a journal of their project and use it to record thoughts, assess their progress, and set goals toward the completion of the project. It's an informal way for the student to be task-oriented and aware of their responsibilities. Students can also use the journal at the end of the project for reflections and reactions when viewing all the audio created. The QuickWrite journal doesn't need to be created on paper. A blog or wiki could serve the same purpose. This would also facilitate assessment through a digital portfolio.

Student Grouping

Students will work in cooperative learning groups. Each group should be approximately four students. This project can be completed with two students, but a group shouldn't be larger than four or there will be some students who do not get involved. Having this number facilitates interaction and communication but also stresses individual accountability.

IV. Creating the Project (Production)

Creating the Poem

- Students decide on the topic their group will write about.
- Students spend time brainstorming what knowledge they have of this topic and the vocabulary associated with it. They can use mind-mapping software such as Omni Group's OmniGraffle or Inspiration's Kidspiration or Inspiration to help them organize their brainstorming. They can also utilize online mind-mapping Web sites like http://thinkature.com or http://bubbl.us.
- As their list of vocabulary develops, students begin sorting the words into categories and creating lists of rhyming words that would make sense in their poem.

- Students write a rough draft of their poem, making sure there is regular syllabication in each line (four to eight syllables per line works well). Their poem should also demonstrate some kind of rhyming pattern.
- Students should read over their poem and revise as necessary, looking for areas of irregular syllabication or any grammatical errors that would interfere with comprehension of their topic.

Rehearsing the Song

- In class, home, or recess, students should be encouraged to meet with their group members to practice singing to a beat.
- After the students have spent some time rehearsing their song, they should be encouraged to revise their song if some sections are awkward to sing.

Recording the Song

- Students gather around their computer and select a beat track to accompany them. Students should utilize headphones so that they do not re-record the beat track or metronome ticks in their vocal track. If more than one student at a time is singing in a single track, then they will need to use a headphone splitter so that both students will be able to hear the beat.
- Each student records a stanza on a different track. This allows the group to level the volume to the same output.
- As students complete their recording, the group should listen to the recordings to determine whether any re-recording is necessary. Specifically, they should listen for clarity of singing and their rhythm.
- If there are any vocal sound effects or call-and-responses echoes, then these should be recorded at this time as well.

V. Refining the Project (Postproduction)

Editing and Fine-Tuning the Recording

- If there are any empty spaces at the beginning or ending of a recorded phrase, it is possible to crop out the blank section so that it's easier to begin the vocals on the first beat of a measure.

  Note: The rap will sound better if each stanza begins at the beginning of a measure. Empty measures between stanzas can be filled by vinyl scratching or other sound effects.

- Work with each track's volume slider so that the volume output on each voice is approximately the same. Special attention should be given to each track's output meter to make sure the volume doesn't go to the red. When the red dots light up, that indicates there will be "clipping," so the vocals will get distorted. Make sure each track's output indicator light does not clip. Students should also check the master track's output as well.

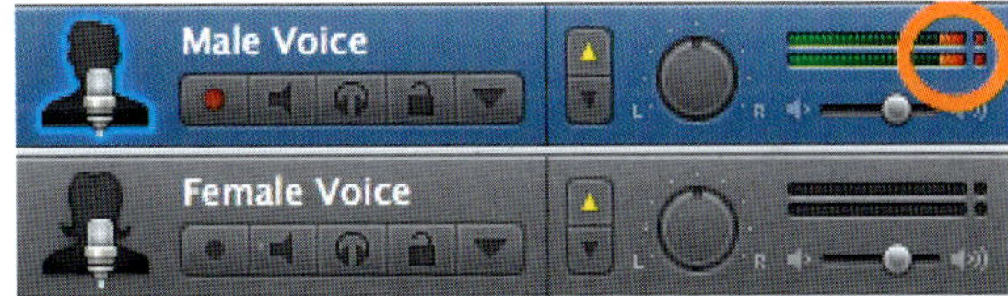

Enhancing the Song

- Sound effects can be added to create a more realistic rap or hip-hop sound. For example, vinyl scratching and simple urban guitar loops can be added to give the song more character.
- Spaces can be added between stanzas to give students more time to insert sound effects. For example, by having a single measure of rest between stanzas, students can import vinyl scratching that won't overpower the vocals.

VI. Publishing the Project

Presentation

Students present their finished songs to the class and discuss what they learned and how it was expressed through song. All songs can be added to an iTunes playlist so that the raps can be burned on a compilation CD.

Additional Activities and Extensions

- Students can create a music video. To create a music video, they gather relevant photos from legal sources and organize them in iPhoto. Because of the iLife suite integration, any image in iPhoto and song in iTunes can be brought into iMovie. In iMovie, they combine the song with images, titles, and effects to create the music video.
- Students can export the finished movies in video podcast format. These video podcasts can be uploaded onto iPods or posted on a podcast page for distribution to parents and the outside community.
- Students can hold a film festival to showcase their work. This can be done at the school independently or as a showcase during a bigger event such as an open house or family fun night.
- The teacher can apply to have the work presented at a School Night at the Apple Store. Students would get an opportunity to share their work and what they learned in a theater setting. The School Night at the Apple Store program is a great way to showcase student work and display what they are capable of creating with digital media. For more information on this program, visit www.apple.com/education/schoolnight.
- If this structure becomes an annual tradition, or if several rap projects are created throughout the year, all old songs can be used as examples for other students. Commemorative CDs can be sold as fundraisers in the school.

VII. Reflection, Assessment, & Differentiation

Reflection

- Students can add a final entry to their QuickWrite journal that wraps up their thoughts for this project.
- While listening to other groups' songs, students can also write their reactions and thoughts to those compositions.
- Invite discussion, comments, and journal entries related to this project:
  - What did you learn about rap, hip-hop, and poetry?
  - How did using music help you master what you were learning?
  - In what way can this help you study in the future?
  - What were your successes and failures?
  - What did you learn about working with others?
  - How do you feel about your product and why?
- Students complete the rubrics, justifying their achievements, possibly focusing on the following criteria:
  - *Content choice*: How well does the finished rap represent the topic your group chose?
  - *Group work*: How well did the group members communicate and work collaboratively?
  - *Further learning*: How well did your rap, and the work of others, entertain and engage you to learn more? In what way can you use music in the future to learn the curriculum?

Customizing the Lesson for All Learners

Any curricular area can be used as the topic of the raps, and any grade level can sing the songs.

- For younger students, the teacher can lead a group writing session to create a rap. All students can rehearse and sing the rap in smaller groups. If there are older grade levels available as "tech buddies," then they can help facilitate the recording and editing process.
- In literature, students can create rap songs about critical moments in the story. To extend that, students can also add lyrics on facts and opinions about the characters' actions.
- In math and science, students can create songs about specific concepts, procedures, or discoveries. They can also rap about word problems, math facts, or lab notes.
- English-language learners can be partnered in groups with fluent English speakers. ELL students can contribute on the music and artwork, and they can write and read any parts that match the level of their language ability. Alternatively, ELL students can rap in their native language.
- Older students and high achievers would be expected to integrate more key vocabulary terms, stanzas, and a possible chorus. The important thing is to level the expectations appropriately to the students in the classroom.

Literary Tableaux

Podcasts, movies, television, and radio didn't always exist. The *tableau vivant*, a French term for "living picture," was a powerful form of entertainment before any of these newer technologies became commonplace. A tableau is more than a photo or painting; it's a snapshot in time that depicts characters frozen in action. Tableaux can represent mundane activities or a key moment in a story. A powerful tableau encourages the viewer to imagine the details of the story influenced the scene.

Project Summary

In this lesson, students consider pivotal scenes in a literary story they're reading for class and create a tableau to represent that moment. Emphasis is put on telling a story with the still image as students utilize props, costumes, and digital photography to bring a literary moment to life. The different images are compiled in iMovie and enhanced with narration and the Ken Burns effect to create a modernized version of the *tableaux vivants* art form.

Grade Level/Subject

Upper-grade elementary, middle-school, or high-school language arts and performing arts (can be modified for primary students as well)

Lesson Goals

- Integrate performing arts through cross-curricular learning to increase visual literacy.
- Communicate important scenes in literature through digital means.

Learning Objectives

After completing this project, students will be able to:

Academic

- Identify pivotal moments in a literature story.
- Analyze significant scenes and represent them as artistic tableaux vivant.

Technical

- Use a digital camera to record images.
- Import, organize, and edit images in iPhoto.
- Create a video in iMovie. Specifically:
  - Integrate images from iPhoto through the Photos Browser.
  - Record narration with the iMovie audio features.
  - Use the Ken Burns effect to add motion and emphasis.

What You'll Need

Here is the recommended hardware and software:

- Macintosh computers
- Digital camera
- TextEdit, Pages, or other word processor for writing the script
- iLife tools (iPhoto and iMovie)
- Other iLife tools (GarageBand, iWeb, and/or iDVD for extension activities)
- Costumes and backdrops appropriate to the literature

Deciding on the Final Product

- iMovie can export and compress in several different formats. Just within iMovie, students can export their movie for a variety of purposes that include video podcasting, DVDs, iWeb, e-mail, and streaming video.

Deciding on the compression truly depends on the intended audience. A single project could be exported in a variety of formats to increase access for the audience. The following three options present specific purposes and rationale for using them.

- DVD projects are best used when the class or school wants to distribute a hard copy to multiple students, staff, or parents. DVDs created in iDVD have professional-looking menus and are an easy way to compile multiple videos. For many schools, DVDs are the perfect commemorative fundraiser and are used to raise money for technology equipment or other school programs.
- Students can use video podcasts for anytime, anywhere learning. Video podcasts are convenient because they can be watched on a computer or loaded onto an iPod. Once students, parents, or anyone subscribes to the RSS feed, they never need to visit that Web site again. Every time iTunes is launched, it will search the Internet and download the latest episodes of all the podcasts to which the user has subscribed. Video podcasts are a great way to send out information for reteaching key concepts, strengthening the home-school connection, or communicating with a global audience.
- The ability to send a video directly to YouTube is one of the new export options in iMovie. YouTube is the most-watched video-streaming site on the Internet, and it's one of the fastest-growing forms of digital media distribution. Although any computer user can enjoy a podcast, certain podcasts (enhanced podcasts) still require a free download of iTunes or the QuickTime Player (included on every Mac). YouTube is universal. There is no other software needed to view a YouTube video. Exporting student movies to YouTube helps develop the global audience more quickly than any other form of digital media. However, one drawback to YouTube is that educational institutions often block access to it.

Outcome-Based Assessment

Student Role

- Students design their strategies for the project, including the following:
  - Organize the individual tasks to the project.
  - Design appropriate backgrounds and costumes to help communicate the scene.
  - Plan the most effective body positioning and facial expressions to represent the selected scene.
  - Take digital photos of the tableaux.
  - Download their digital photos into iPhoto.
  - Import the images into iMovie.
  - Use the writing process to create narration for the tableaux scenes.
  - Work collaboratively to create the video with narration.
- With the teacher's guidance and software or Web resources, the students create a rubric to assess the outcomes.

Teacher Role

- Determine the criteria for evaluation of students' work throughout the process, and explain to students how you will assess the various parts of their project, including the following:
  - QuickWrite journals
  - The number of tableaux that each group should create (although teachers can have student groups create one tableau each, they will develop a better summary of the story with multiple tableaux)
  - Writing process for the narration

- Rationale for scene selection
- Appropriateness of costumes, props, and backgrounds for tableaux
- Ability of the students to work collaboratively in their group

- Establish and explain your criteria for evaluating students' technical skills, including the following:
  - Clarity of the images they take with digital cameras
  - Ability to import images into iPhoto for use in iMovie
  - Effectiveness of images, narration, and Ken Burns effect to represent their story
- Identify how you will evaluate students' ability to reach their intended outcomes as judged by their final product.

I. Getting Started

Teacher Planning

- Teachers should be familiar with the basic functionality of iPhoto and iMovie. Although the teacher doesn't have to know everything about these applications, understanding their navigation and features is important. Specifically, the teacher should know how to import and organize images into iPhoto. They should also know how to use iMovie's Photos Browser, Voiceover feature, and the Ken Burns effect. Because students will be exporting their final video, teachers should know the options in the Share menu.
- Determine the amount of time to be given the project, and set some suggested time limits to achieve specific milestones in the creation process. For example, how much time should be given for writing and editing the tableaux narrations? How much time is needed to create props, costumes, and backgrounds? When should students be expected to take, import, and organize images in iPhoto? How much time is needed to compile the video in iMovie and record narration?
- The teacher might want to assign specific parts of the literature story to each group. For example, have a few groups work on key moments in the beginning of the story, while other groups work on scenes from the middle, and some students develop tableaux for the ending of the story.

Preparing Students

- Time should be given for students to experience some of the technology that will be used as well. This would include the following:
  - An opportunity for students to take digital photos with the camera, import the images into iPhoto, and organize them in an album or event
  - Time to use iMovie so that the students are familiar with how to import images with the Photos Browser, record narration, add titles, and add motion to the images with the Ken Burns effect

II. Making Connections

Introducing the Project

- Discuss the different forms of entertainment we enjoy in our country. Specifically, students should talk about the following:
  - What are some forms of visual entertainment we enjoy? For example, this can include TV, movies, live theater, musicals, and so on.
  - Learn about *tableaux vivants* and see some examples. Some possible sites include the following:
    - The Wikipedia entry on tableau vivant, *http://en.wikipedia.org/wiki/Tableau_vivant*
    - The Kate Matthews collection at the University of Louisville Web site, *http://digital.library.louisville.edu/collections/matthews/*
    - The photography of Jeff Wall. The San Francisco Museum of Modern Art features

some of his work, *www.moma.org/exhibitions/2007/jeffwall/*

    - The 24/7 Media Group has created a series of high-quality, coffee table books with many images that can be considered *tableaux vivants*. Their *Day in the Life* series (titles like *A Day in the Life of Thailand*) and the 24/7 series published with DK contain rich photography that tries to tell a story with each image. After publishing *America 24/7*, DK released an additional book for each of the 50 states. For information, visit *www.247mediagroup.com/index.html* or *www.america24-7.com/gallery/index.shtml*. MSNBC has an article and interactive slideshow talking about the project that included over 25,000 photographers around the country, *www.msnbc.msn.com/id/3729734/*.

  - One possible exercise is to download some of the tableau examples from the Kate Matthews collection, Jeff Wall, or the 24/7 books and display them for students. Have students discuss how these are different from just a photo. What are some of the details they notice about body positioning and facial expressions?
  - The essential concept to understand is that tableaux vivant are like a freeze-frame of action. They differ from most portraits because they tell a story. Like Michelangelo's *Last Supper*, they are a window into a significant moment in a story and tell a little about the characters involved.

Connecting the Known Information to New Learning

- Discuss some of the pivotal scenes in one of the core literature stories that students are reading. When deciding on a scene, students should ask themselves, "What makes this scene an important moment in the story?"
- In small groups, brainstorm how they can represent this moment in the book through a tableau. Specifically, what body positioning, props, and costumes will help tell the story.

III. Planning the Project (Preproduction)

Project Folder

Students begin by creating a project folder to keep track of their research, information, tasks, timelines, and goals. Some of the items that might be included in the project folder are a QuickWrite journal, checklist, brainstorming notes, and production notes.

QuickWrite Journal

Students keep a journal of their project and use it to record thoughts, assess their progress, and set goals toward the completion of the project. It's an informal way for the student to be task-oriented and aware of their responsibilities. Students can also use the journal at the end of the project for reflections and reactions when viewing all the videos created. The QuickWrite journal doesn't need to be created on paper. A blog or wiki could serve the same purpose. This would also facilitate assessment through a digital portfolio.

Student Grouping

Students should work in collaborative learning groups of four students to decide on their essential scenes and design their tableau project. For more involvement, student groups can work in smaller pairings to work on the details of the project (such as costumes, narration, and props). The groups should not be larger than six students or else there will be members who are not as engaged.

IV. Creating the Project (Production)

Recording the Tableaux

- Students should take some time to decide on pivotal scenes in their literature. Among the things to consider are the following:
  - What are some of the important scenes in the story? Select one to three scenes your group will create tableaux for (teachers can decide on how many).
  - What makes each moment in the story pivotal? What action is happening in the scene, and what might be some of the thoughts and emotions that the characters are experiencing?
  - What are some appropriate props, costumes, and backgrounds that would help tell the story of the tableaux you are creating?
- Students practice staging the scene. How many characters are needed? What body positions and facial expressions are appropriate to communicate this scene?
- For each scene tableau, students pose and have someone take a digital photo of that moment.
- Import the images into iPhoto, and organize them into an album or event.

Writing the Narration

- Student groups summarize their tableau by describing the action and events that are happening in the scene.
- Students should emphasize details to really show the viewer why this moment in the book is pivotal.

Creating the Video

- Students launch iMovie and click the Photos Browser button to find their images.
- The groups drag and drop their tableaux images into the project area for the video.

  Note: The default length an image will display is 4 seconds. To change this, click the tiny clock symbol located on the bottom left of the photo thumbnail. This will reveal the window to alter the duration of the image. The maximum time is 60 seconds, but the image can be used multiple times to accommodate lengthier narration. To determine the length the clip duration should be set for, students should practice reading their narration and time themselves.

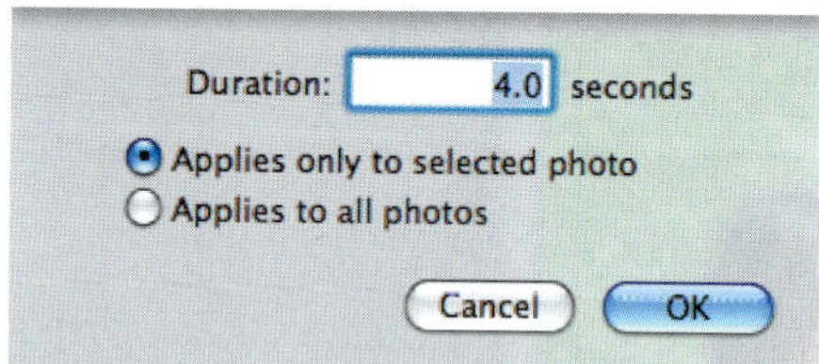

- With the image duration lengthened, click the Voiceover button. Follow the onscreen instructions for recording a voiceover. Speak clearly, and record the narration for that tableau image.

- Continue narrating each tableau scene that the group has created.
- Add titles and credits as needed.

V. Refining the Project (Postproduction)

Enhancing the Video with the Ken Burns Effect

- Specific details in each image can be highlighted through panning and zooming.
- Activate the Ken Burns effect by clicking the Crop button and selecting the clip.

- To add motion to an image, follow these steps:
  1. Select Ken Burns in the Project viewer.
  2. Change the size and/or centering of the green and red rectangles that represent the start and end points of the image clip.
  3. Click Done to save the changes to the clip.

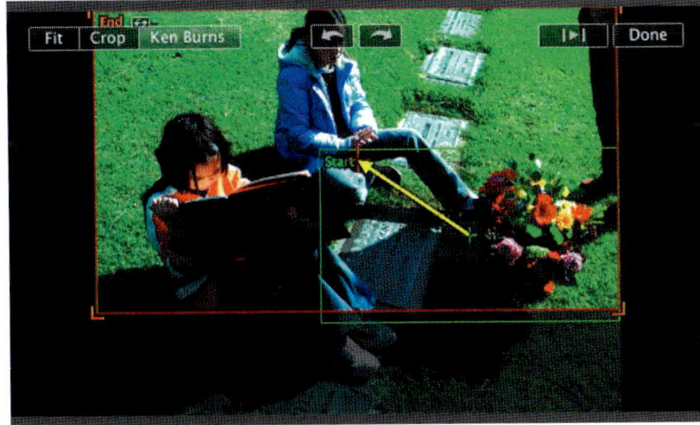

- Additionally, students can add transitions between their clips if they have more than one tableau in their video.

VI. Publishing the Project

Presentation

Students should export their movie in an appropriate format and present them to the rest of the class. If the tableaux videos are used for podcasting, then they can be uploaded to a .Mac or other server with iWeb. Alternatively, the videos can be posted on a podcast hosting site or uploaded to YouTube.

Additional Activities and Extensions

- Students can record the tableau with dialogue instead of just narration. Although the characters in the image will be static, the addition of dialogue will help emphasize the action and importance of the scene. With dialogue, students can practice dramatic voice and inflection.
- A DVD can be created with all the videos if they are exported as high-quality QuickTime movies (large size). With iDVD, all the projects can be combined to create a DVD collection of the literary tableaux. This DVD can be sold as a commemorative fundraiser to bring in extra money for technology or other school projects.
- Students can experiment with lighting to explore how shadows and highlights can enhance or change the dramatic feel of the tableaux.

VII. Reflection, Assessment, & Differentiation

Reflection

- Students can add a final entry to their QuickWrite journal that wraps up their thoughts for this project.
- While looking at other groups' videos, students can write their reactions and thoughts to those creations.

- Invite discussion, comments, and journal entries related to this project:
  - In what ways can visual literacy help us communicate?
  - In what ways could a tableaux vivant be entertaining for people?
  - What were your successes and failures?
  - How might this activity change the way you read stories or take photos?
  - What did you learn about working with others?
  - How do you feel about your product and why?
- Students complete the rubrics, justifying their achievements, possibly focusing on the following criteria:
  - *Content choice*: How well did your tableau represent the action and setting of your pivotal scene?
  - *The group work*: How well did the group members communicate and work collaboratively? In what ways did the group share in the responsibility of creating your project?
  - *Further learning*: What would you change about your tableaux images or video?

Customizing the Lesson for All Learners

- For younger students, the teacher can assign specific moments in the literature to them. The tableaux can be a whole-group brainstorm on appropriate body language, facial expressions, props, costumes, and so on.
- English-language learners should be placed in a group with fluent English speakers. They can help take the photos or pose in the tableaux. English-language learners and students with disabilities can also help with costumes, props, video editing, and planning.
- More advanced learners would be expected to take this lesson further. They could create narration from the different points of view of the characters in the tableau. They can also experiment with lighting or mood music.
- This lesson can also be adapted to other curricular areas. The following are some possibilities:
  - Pivotal moments in history
  - Noteworthy discoveries in science
  - Famous people they are studying

The 14th Colony

Whether we agree or disagree with the practice, colonialism played a huge part in the establishment and development of the United States of America. Although mistakes were made, early colonies faced huge struggles, and land was taken from the Native American inhabitants, the original 13 colonies marked the birth of a great nation. How did the English, Spanish, Dutch, French, and other countries decide on a fitting location for a colony, and how did the settlement's environment affect its economy, clothing, activities, and growth? Students contemplate the formation of this country as they simulate the creation of their own colony.

Project Summary

Students compare and contrast the attributes of the 13 original colonies to determine a location for the next new settlement that could have been established in those days. Working in collaborative learning groups, students create a Web site to showcase their colony. Through research, writing, and multimedia, students communicate why their location for a colony would have been a logical one. The end product is a Web site of information, facts, and images to showcase their new settlement and make the study of colonial America more relevant to our students.

Grade Level/Subject

Upper-elementary and middle-school history-social studies

Lesson Goals

- Analyze the locations of the original 13 colonies.
- Compare and contrast the natural surroundings, basic economics, food, and climate of the 13 colonies.
- Create a Web site to communicate their findings and present their new colony.

Learning Objectives

After completing this project, students will be able to:

Academic

- Compare and contrast the environment of the 13 original colonies by observing a map and researching information on the Internet.
- Synthesize what they know of the original 13 colonies to decide on a location for a new settlement.
- Create a new colony and write a "history" of their settlement.

Technical

- Research information on the Internet.
- Create a Web site in iWeb about your colony. Specifically:
  - A home page introducing your settlement
  - Separate pages for the surrounding environment, food, and climate
  - A blog with a "history" of your colony
  - Images, audio, and video to enhance your Web site (if desired)

What You'll Need

This is the recommended hardware and software:

- Macintosh computers
- Digital camera (optional)
- Safari
- Pages, TextEdit, or other word processor
- iLife tools (iPhoto, iWeb)

- Other iLife tools (GarageBand and iMovie)
- Period costumes for photos (optional)

Deciding on the Final Product

- Publishing the 14th Colony Web site will be much more seamless with a .Mac account, but it can also be loaded on a school or classroom site. Ideally, this is a project that will last for a few weeks as students add more blogs and information to their Web site. The ongoing work helps students immerse themselves in the environment and make colonial America more relevant.
- The Web site itself can be an environment to showcase other student work on colonial America. The blog entries can summarize what students are learning. Alternatively, student can record their blog entries and transform them into audio or enhanced podcasts.

Outcome-Based Assessment

Student Role

- Students design their strategies for the project, including the following:
  - Organizing the tasks to the project
  - Finding appropriate historical images of settlements in colonial America
  - Taking digital photos and importing and organizing them into iPhoto
  - Using the writing process to create the text for their Web site and blogs
  - Working collaboratively to discuss where they should begin a colony and why
- With the teacher's guidance and software or Web resources, the students create a rubric to assess the outcomes.

Teacher Role

- Determine the criteria for evaluation of students' work throughout the process, and explain to students how you will assess the various parts of their project, including the following:
  - QuickWrite journals for reflection or anecdotal thoughts
  - Writing, revising, and editing the text for the Web site and blogs
  - Logic of the area they select for their colony
  - Appropriateness of the food, economy, and activities they might expect to enjoy at their chosen location
  - Ability of the students to work collaboratively in their group
- Establish and explain your criteria for evaluating students' technical skills, including the following:
  - Layout and navigation of the Web site
  - Ability to import images into iPhoto and use them on their Web site
  - Use of blogs to create a daily journal of settlers in colonial America
- Identify how you will evaluate students' ability to reach the intended outcomes as judged by their final product.

I. Getting Started

Teacher Planning

- Teachers should be familiar with the basic functionality of iWeb. Although the teacher doesn't have to know everything about the application, it is important to understand the different features and options in iWeb. Specifically, the teacher should know how to create a welcome page, a blog for updates, and more pages for additional information. Furthermore, the teacher should be familiar with formatting their page with the Media Browser, Inspector window, and Font panel. Because students will be creating blog entries, teachers should also understand the RSS inspector options.

- Teachers should also be familiar with the use of digital cameras and how to import, organize, edit, and use their images in iPhoto. Specifically, teachers should know how to organize images by creating an album or event.
- Determine the amount of time to be given the project, and set some suggested time limits to achieve specific milestones in the creation process. For example, how much time should be given for comparing and contrasting the original 13 colonies to decide on the location for the 14th colony. When should students be expected to finish writing the text describing their site, food, and economy? How much time is needed to integrate blogs and images of their daily life in iWeb?

Preparing Students

- Students need to learn about life in colonial America. Specifically:
  - What the environment around the colony was like (including climate, food, and nearby landmarks)
  - What kinds of businesses and structures were located in the colonies
  - How the colonists survived and made a living economically
- Students can visit specific Web sites with information on lives of colonial Americans. These can include the following:
  - Liberty! The American Revolution by PBS, www.pbs.org/ktca/liberty/perspectives_daily.html
  - America's Story by the Library of Congress, www.americaslibrary.gov/cgi-bin/page.cgi
  - Social Studies for Kids' pages on the 13 colonies, www.socialstudiesforkids.com/articles/ushistory/13colonies1.htm
  - Archiving Early America, www.earlyamerica.com/
  - Memorial Hall Museum Online, www.memorialhall.mass.edu/home.html
- Time should be given for students to experience some of the technology that will be used as well. This would include the following:
  - An opportunity for students to download, import, and organize images from the Internet into iPhoto
  - Time to use iWeb so that the students are familiar with how to create a basic Web site, add additional pages, integrate a blog, and use the Inspector window, Media Browser, and Font panel

II. Making Connections

Introducing the Project

- Examine maps of early settlements like Jamestown, and discuss some of the similarities and differences in the colonies. Specifically, students should talk about the following:
  - What are some of the landforms and environmental reasons colonists selected that specific location? For example, there are rivers near each colony.
  - Why are these similarities notable? For example, proximity to a river ensured an abundance of fresh water for agriculture and consumption.
  - What types of products did they create to sustain their economy?
  - What kinds of foods were they likely to eat?

Connecting the Known Information to New Learning

- Discuss the different problems colonists faced when beginning a settlement.
- Think about some of the issues that people in early America faced. For example, lack of food, hostile Native Americans who felt threatened, and lack of shelter are possible topics.

- Brainstorm the various issues that the students would need to consider if they were starting their own colony. For example, bringing seeds, having tools, and establishing barriers for protection are possible topics.
- Examine maps of different regions on the eastern and southern coasts to find a suitable location for their own colony.

III. Planning the Project (Preproduction)

Project Folder

Students begin by creating a project folder to keep track of their research, information, tasks, timelines, and goals. Some of the items that might be included in the project folder are a QuickWrite journal, checklist, brainstorming notes, and blog entries.

QuickWrite Journal

Students keep a journal of their project and use it to record thoughts, assess their progress, and set goals toward the completion of the project. It's an informal way for the student to be task-oriented and aware of their responsibilities. The journal can also be utilized at the end of the project for reflections and reactions when viewing all the Web sites created. The QuickWrite journal doesn't need to be created on paper. A blog or wiki could serve the same purpose. This would also facilitate assessment through a digital portfolio.

Student Grouping

Students can work in collaborative learning groups of two to four students to decide on a location and design their colony and Web site. For more involvement, working in pairs is beneficial, but groups should not be larger than four students or else there will be members who are not as engaged.

IV. Creating the Project (Production)

Finding a Location and Establishing the 14th Colony

- As students examine the locations of the 13 colonies and decide on their own, they should consider the following:
  - How does climate affect each settlement, and what are the various hardships that each colony encountered because of weather?
  - What types of products were created to sustain the economy of each colony?
  - What are the kinds of foods that could be caught or harvested in your region?
- Students should take time to research the daily lives of people in colonial America as a basis for information in their blog.
- Students should learn about the background history of the different groups who established the original 13 colonies.

Writing About the 14th Colony's Location and Attributes

- Student groups brainstorm and write a plausible history of their colony. Some details should include the following:
  - Reasons why they began their colony (religious persecution, economic opportunities, and so on)
  - Characteristics of the environment around their settlement
  - The name of their colony and where it was derived from
- Although all the information can be fit on a single Web page, students should be encouraged to utilize multiple

pages with images. The possible pages could include the following:

- Welcome page for their colony.
- A Web page on the background and history of the settlement.
- A food page on the sustenance that settlers harvest or hunt.
- An economics page that details the different products that their colony might produce. For example, southern colonies were almost entirely agricultural, but the New England colonies sustained themselves with a combination of fishing and farming industries.

Creating a Blog Journal

- Students create a blog to record the daily lives of the colony inhabitants. Details can possibly include the following:
  - Daily struggles of the colonists
  - The games of that time period
  - Education of the children
  - Friendly encounters with the local people
  - Details on the different buildings that make up the settlement

V. Refining the Project (Postproduction)

Enhancing the Web Site

- Students should make sure all text for Web pages and blog entries are typed in a word processor such as TextEdit or Pages so that a spell checker can be used.
- Appropriate images should be imported into the Web pages and blogs to integrate an element of visual literacy.
- Some blog entries can be recorded in GarageBand to create a podcast for posting on the Web site.

VI. Publishing the Project

Publishing the Web Site

If the classroom has a .Mac account, they can publish to the Web with a single click in iWeb. If the 14th Colony projects are to be posted on a school or classroom Web site, then navigate to the File menu, and select Publish to a Folder. This will place all the pages and accompanying media in a folder that can be uploaded to a server. Once the page has been uploaded, instructions for subscribing to the blog feed can be distributed to the parents so that they get all future updates.

Projects can also be burned on a CD and browsed on the computer without needing to post to the Internet. However, this would mean that all future changes and blog entries would not be included on the CD unless a new one was burned.

Additional Activities and Extensions

- Any blog entry can be recorded in GarageBand to create an audio podcast. Importing appropriate images would transform the recording into an enhanced podcast. Students can add a podcast page to their Web site and drag and drop these files onto the new page. A different RSS feed will be written for the podcasts, but information can be sent home to parents on how to download the free iTunes application and subscribe to the podcast feed.
- Students can plan and create survival videos for colonists. To do this extension, students should think about the essential needs of the colonists. Some possible examples include videos on planting seeds and growing agriculture, rules for playing traditional games from that time period, or fashion for the various seasons. They can create a historical Survivor or Fear Factor episode.

VII. Reflection, Assessment, & Differentiation

Reflection

- Students can add a final entry to their QuickWrite journal that wraps up their thoughts for this project.
- While looking at other groups' Web sites, students can also write their reactions and thoughts to the other colonies.
- Invite discussion, comments, and journal entries related to this project:
  - What did you learn about the difficulties that colonists faced in this country?
  - What were your successes and failures in this project?
  - What are some of the essential elements of creating a successful colony?
  - What did you learn about working with others?
  - How do you feel about the Web site for your colony and why?
- Students complete the rubrics, justifying their achievements, possibly focusing on the following criteria:
  - *Content choice*: How well does your 14th colony embody the essential elements for a successful settlement?
  - *The group work*: How well did the group members communicate and work collaboratively?
  - *Further learning*: In hindsight, what might be some ways you'd change your Web site? If you were sending a colony to a distant planet, what are some things you would look for in a habitable planet? In our world today, what are some reasons people might leave their homes to colonize another planet?

Customizing the Lesson for All Learners

- English-language learners should be placed in a group with fluent English speakers. They can help download images for the site. Alternatively, they could create Web sites in their native language, but they might need further scaffolding to understand the concept of creating the 14th colony.
- More advanced learners would be expected to take this lesson further. They could create travel brochures to attract more settlers to their colony. In Pages, they can use the flyer or brochure template to create appealing print material for their colony. Alternatively, they can create Web pages and use their persuasive writing skills to convince settlers to come to their colony.

Acknowledgments

When I was asked to help write *The Macintosh iLife '06 in the Classroom*, I considered it one of the biggest honors in my life ... something that happens just once in a lifetime. In my mind, it wasn't even a reality until the actual book was printed and shipped. Fast forward to 2008. Here I am finishing my second book with Peachpit Press, and I still can't believe my fortune. To claim that I have this opportunity purely through my own skill would be a lie, so I feel that I should thank the people involved in this project, not to mention the rest of my life, who have influenced my speaking, writing, and thoughts.

This opportunity would never have come to fruition without Peachpit Press. Executive editor Cliff Colby has put his trust in me to help write this book for Peachpit. Kim Wimpsett helped me clean up my writing and focus my ideas ... and I believe that she will be one of my first investors when I open up a pizza-laundromat. Jim Heid has once again written an awe-inspiring, informative book on the iLife suite. It's an honor to have Mr. Heid's amazing tips and tutorials support these lesson ideas and classroom strategies for technology integration.

Thanks to Apple. What more can be said about an organization that creates the Apple Distinguished Educator program to celebrate innovative educators around the world? Apple has changed my life and continues to help me grow as an educator, presenter, and person. Specifically, I'd like to thank Cheryl Lee for her constant support and friendship. I'd also like to acknowledge the ADEs in this program. All of them are amazing in different ways, but I especially want to thank Jeanne Halderson ... collaborator, proofreader, "idea bouncer-offer," and friend.

I'd like to once again thank every student I've taught. It doesn't matter whether Apple, M-Audio, or the National Educational Computing Conference honors me. I owe so much of that to the students. As an educator, I wanted to engage all students with technology so that they would master the curriculum. Judging by the amazing products they created, I think it worked. I especially want to thank the TechSavvyGirlz group (Jamie, Jolene, Janabelle, Julia, Zoe, and Genevieve). They help keep my ideas fresh and relevant while inspiring students and teachers across the country.

Thanks to all the educators around the world. High-stakes testing, negative media attention, and lack of financial support make the job more difficult, but somehow, teachers persevere. The best teachers understand the need to utilize the latest technology to make the curriculum meaningful for all students.

Thank you to my family. My two daughters, Zoe and Genevieve, are brilliant (OK, I'm biased), funny, and definitely tech savvy. My wife, Trang, ADE Class of 2007, has been an inspiration to me. She fully supports what I do, is a great mom, is my biggest cheerleader, and still manages to keep me grounded. Remarkably, she does all this while pursuing her own interests and career. I also want to thank my parents. I may not be a doctor, lawyer, or engineer, but I think they're proud of me ... and for that, I'm grateful.

Lastly, I want to thank all the readers of this book. You're making a difference in the classroom, inspiring students and colleagues. I'm grateful that you're helping support educational technology as well as my daughters' college funds. This "twice-in-a-lifetime" experience is more meaningful because of you.

Engage. Educate. Empower.

—Ted Lai

Biography

Ted Lai is a veteran teacher and educational technology advocate. After two years performing educational school assemblies, he worked as a classroom teacher for eight years. He left the classroom to train educators on strategies and best practices for enhancing teaching and learning with technology. He is currently an educational technology coordinator with the Fullerton School District in Orange County, California. Honored as an Apple Distinguished Educator, a GarageBand Advocate, an M-Audio M-Powered Educator, and one of the "Best of NECC" presenters in both 2006 and 2007, Ted speaks at local, regional, and national conferences about educational uses for podcasting, iPods, video, audio, GarageBand, and the rest of the iLife suite. A self-described "presentaholic," Ted is also the founder of PodPiper Productions and advises the TechSavvyGirlz project. Ted is married to Trang Lai and has two children, Zoe and Genevieve.